HARDPRESS.NET
HOME OF HARD-TO-FIND BOOKS

The Harleian Miscellany
by William Oldys

Address:
HardPress
8345 NW 66TH ST #2561
MIAMI FL 33166-2626
USA
Email: info@hardpress.net

THE

HARLEIAN MISCELLANY;

OR, A

COLLECTION

OF

SCARCE, CURIOUS, AND ENTERTAINING

PAMPHLETS AND TRACTS,

AS WELL IN MANUSCRIPT AS IN PRINT,

FOUND IN THE LATE

EARL OF OXFORD'S LIBRARY,

INTERSPERSED WITH

HISTORICAL, POLITICAL, AND CRITICAL

NOTES.

———

VOL. IV.

LONDON.

PRINTED FOR ROBERT DUTTON, GRACECHURCH-STREET.

1809.

CONTENTS.

VOL. IV.

CONTENTS.

CONTENTS.

POPE JOAN:

A DIALOGUE [1]

BETWEEN

A PROTESTANT AND PAPIST;

Manifestly proving,

THAT A WOMAN, CALLED JOAN, WAS POPE OF ROME;

Against the Surmises and Objections made to the Contrary,

By Robert Bellarmine and Cæsar Baronius, Cardinals: Florimondus Ræmondus, N. D. and other Popish Writers,

Impudently denying the same.

BY ALEXANDER COOKE.

London, printed by John Haviland, for William Garrat; and are to be sold at his shop in Paul's Church-yard, at the sign of the Bull's Head. 1625. Quarto, containing one hundred and forty pages.

To the most Reverend Father in God, Tobias, my Lord Archbishop of York's Grace, Primate and Metropolitan of England.

IT is lamentable to consider how many stars are fallen of late from heaven, how many goddesses on earth have departed from the faith, and given heed unto the spirit of errors and doctrines of slanderers, to wit, the Papists; yet, methinks, it is no matter of wonderment, because we read, that, [2] " If men receive not the love of the truth, that they might be saved, God, in his justice, will give them strong delusions to

---

1 This is the 191st number of the Catalogue of Pamphlets in the Harleian Library.
2]. 2 Thess. ii. 10, 11.

believe lyes, that they may be damned': for few or none of these late apostates, for any thing I can learn, were ever in love with the truth. Among us they were, but they were not of us, as now appears by their departing from us; for, if they had been of us, they would have continued with us; doubtless, they would never have fallen to popery. For, though popery be managed after the most politick manner, yet, in itself, it is a gross religion; and the perfecters thereof as shameless men in avowing manifest untruths, and denying known truths, as ever set pen to paper; all which it is as easy to prove, as to object against them. But my purpose, at this time, is, to lay open their shame in denying known truths; which, though it may be shewed by divers particulars, as, namely, by [1] Parsons's and [2] Bishop's denying that they call their Pope their Lord God; by [3] Bellarmine's denying that any Jesuit had any hand in the powder-treason; by their [4] general denying that Pope Honorius the First was an heretick, and by such like; yet most apparently their impudency appears in denying the report of Pope Joan, which is proved by a cloud of witnesses, in this discourse (which I make bold to present unto your Grace) for they are driven to feign, to forge, to cog, to play the fools, and, in plain English, to lye all manner of lyes for the covering of their shame in this. Onuphrius, Harding, Saunders, Cope, Genebrard, Bellarmine, Bernartius, Florimondus, Papyrius Masso, Baronius, Parsons, and divers others, who have joined hand in hand, with purpose to carry this cause away by a strong hand, are so intangled in it, that it is with them, as with birds in the lime-twigs, which stick the faster in, by how much they flutter the more to get out. Which if your Grace, upon perusing at your best leisure, shall find true, my humble desire is, that you will give me leave to publish it under your Grace's name; partly, that, by it, the simpler sort (for I write not for the learned) may have a taste, by this, of the honesty, or rather dishonesty, of Papists, in handling of points in controversy; and, partly, that it may be a testimony of that reverent respect, which I acknowledge due to such church-governors, as your Grace is, who give atendance unto reading, which the [5] apostle willed Timothy to do, and, after the example of the ancient bishops, preach often, drawing on others, not by words only, but by example also, to performance of like exercises. Hereafter, if it please God, that health and means of books serve, I shall light on some more profitable argument. In the mean while, I pray God strengthen your Grace's hands to the finishing of the Lord's work, in the province wherein you sit, as one of the seven angels in the seven churches mentioned in the Revelation; that, by your Grace's means, the epha, wherein popish wickedness sitteth, may be lifted up between the earth and the heaven, and carried out of the north into the land of Sinar, and set there upon his own place.

Your Grace's at Commandment,

ALEXANDER COOKE.

1 N. D. In his Warnword to Sir Francis Hastings's Watchword, Encounter I. cap. 2.
2 In his Reproof of Dr. Abbot's Defence of Mr. Perkins's Preface to the Reader, p. 10.
3 Apologia ad lib. Jacob Mag. Britan. Regis, cap. xv. p. 208.
4 Bellarm. Paron. Pighius, &c.   5] 1 Tim. iv. 13.

To the Popish, or Catholick Reader.

PAPIST, or Catholick, chuse whether name thou hast a mind to (for, though I know, that, of late years, thou art proud of both, even of the name [1]papist, as well as of the name [2]catholick, yet I envy thee neither; only I would have thee remember, that that firebrand of hell, Hildebrand, commonly called Gregory the Seventh, [3]was the first man who challenged it, as his sole right, to be called Papa, that is Pope, whence thou art called papist; and that divers are of opinion, as [4]Hugo de Victore noteth, that, in some sense, the devil might be called a catholick.) I offer unto thee here a discourse touching Pope Joan, (if thou darest read it, for fear of falling into thy Pope's curse) whose popedom I will make good unto thee, not by the testimonies of Pantaleon, and Functius, and Sleidan, and Illyricus, and Constantius Phrygio, and John Bale, and Robert Barnes, because thou [5]hast condemned their persons, and their books too, to hell; but by the testimonies of thy brethren, the sons of thy own mother, because as [6]one saith, *firmum est genus probationis, quod etiam ab adversario sumitur, ut veritas etiam ab inimicis veritatis probetur:* ' That is a strong proof, which is wrung out of the adversary, when the enemies of truth are driven to bear witness unto the truth.' And, as [7]another, *Amici contra amicum, & inimici pro inimico, invincible testimonium est:* which sounds, as I conceive it, thus: ' The testimony of a papist against a papist, and the testimony of a papist for a protestant, is without exception.' The reason why I have framed it in way of dialogue, was, that I might meet more fully with all the cavils, which thy proctors use in pleading of this case; and that it might be better understood of common readers, who are sooner gulled with continued discourses. If I have spoken truly, I would have thee bear witness with me unto the truth; if otherwise, I am content thou strike me: for, though I hold thy pa-pism, in so me respect, to be worse than atheism, agreeably to a speech fathered upon Epiphanius, χεῖρον ἡ κακοπιεία τῆς ἀπιστίας, heresy is worse than infidelity, and, by consequent, thyself a dangerous neighbour to dwell by; because, as one of thy own [8]doctors writes, *certè periculosius est cum hæreticis, quam cum samaritanis quam cum gentilibus, aut Mahumetanis agere:* ' It is, questionless, more dangerous to dwell by an heretick, than to dwell by a Samaritan, by an Heathen, by a Turk:' yet I am not so far out of love with thee, but I can be content to learn of thee, as [9]St. Augustine did of Tyconius the heretick, if thou canst teach me. Yea, I profess, that, though it may be gathered out of [10]Campian, thy champion and Tyburn-martyr, that thou believest one heaven cannot hold

1 Baron. Annot. in Martyrol. Rom. Octob. 16. b.   Lorinus in Act. Apost. cap. xx. vers. 30. Anastasius Cochelet. Palæstrita Honoris D. Hallensis pro Lipsio. cap. i. pag. 5.
2 Bellarm. Lib. iv. de Ecclesia, cap. 4.   Rhem. Annot. in Act. xi. 26.   3 Baron. Annot. in Martyrol. Rom. Jan. 10. c.   4 Annot. in 1 ad Cor. xiii.   5 In indice Lib. prohibit.   6 Novatian. de Trinitate, cap. 18. num. 86. inter Opera Tertulliani.
7 Vives de Instrumento Probabilitatis.   8 Maldonat in Johan. iv. 9.   9 Lib. ii. Retract. cap. 18.   10 Ratio. 10.
A 2

thee and such as are of my opinion; though [1]Costerus wish strangely,
That he may be damned both body and soul, if any of us be saved;
yet that hath not estranged me so far from thee, but that I wish thee
well, even eyes to see the truth, and ingenuity to acknowledge it.

———

Protestant.

WELL met, and welcome home, Sir. What new book have you
brought us down from London this mart?

Pap. Oh, I have an excellent book, which discourseth at large
about Pope Joan, whose popedom you cast in the catholicks teeth so
often.

Prot. What language is it in, I pray you? French, or Latin, or
English, and who made it?

Pap. It was [2]first written in French, but I have it in Latin. The
author of it is one Florimondus Ræmondus.

Prot. Florimondus Ræmondus! What is he, that I never heard of
him before? Is he, and his book, of any credit?

Pap. He himself is reputed [3]a very famous man for life and learning;
so that at this present, he is one of the French King's council at Bourdeaux, and, as for his book, it is of wonderful esteem.

Prot. With whom I pray you?

Pap. Even with Cardinal Baronius; for [4]he holds it the worthiest
discourse that ever was made of that argument: he professeth, that
he could have found in his heart to have inserted it into his annals,
but that it is somewhat too large; for by it, as the Cardinal further
[5]noteth, he hath so confounded all the pack of hereticks, who heretofore upbraided the catholicks with it, that now they are ashamed of
that which they have said.

Prot. But hath any man else the like opinion of it?

Pap. Yea, marry, Possevin is of the same mind; for Possevin [6]saith,
that he hath killed the hereticks outright; that, since the publishing
of that book, the hereticks are silenced, they dare talk no more of a
Pope Joan.

Prot. And who else I pray you?

Pap. Lipsius, for he writ to his friend, that 'Ita plene omnia exe-
quutus est, ut nobis nihil reliqui fit præter credere & assentiri.' Florimondus had handled the matter so fully, that there remained nothing
for any man to do, but to believe, and to say Amen to that which he
had done.

Prot. This is much: but have you read it?

Pap. Read it! Yea I have read it again and again: besides, I have

1 Fleri nequit, ut Lutheranus moriens salvetur, gehennam evadat, ex æternis ignibus eripiatur.
Si mentior, damner ipse cum Lucifero, saith Costerus. Resp. ad Refutationem Lucæ Osiandr.
Proposit. 8. pag. ult.   2 An. 1602. Possevin. in errat. & fraternis. 1. 10. quæ haben-
tur ad finem To. iii Apparat. fac.   3 Vir, cum primis illustris ac pius, & doctrina in-
signis, Baronius Annal. Tom. x. ad An. 853. Numb 6c.   4 Præ cæteris commendan-
dus, f ma nobilis Florimundus: Baronius loco citato.   5 Sic confecit monstrum istud,
ut novatores p. dent, qare scripserunt vel somniasse. ibid.   6 Prorsus confodit Hæreticos
qui Commentum illud sparserunt in vulgus, ut amplius ea de fabula hiscere non audeant In
Apperatu sac. verbo, Florimondus. See Gretser, Tom. ii. defens. Bellar. Lib. iii. Cap. 24. Col. 987.

compared it with that which is written of the same argument, by Buchingerus, in Germany, by Charanza, in Spain, by Onuphrius, and Bellarmine, and Baronius, in Italy; by Turrian, and Bernartius, in Belgia; by Pontacus, in Aquitania, by Genebrard, and Papyrius Massonus, in France; by Saunders, by Cope, by Harding, by Father Parsons, and others of our own country.

Prot. And what say you now, after the reading of all these, to the story of Pope Joan? Tell me in good earnest, and dissemble not.

Pap. I say, the very truth is, that the whole story of Pope Joan is [1] a fable, a [2] fond and vain fable, a [3] mere fable, an [4] heretical fable, a [5] ridiculous fiction, and so [6] known to the learneder sort of protestants among you; but that you will not leave to delude the world with it, for lack of other matter. Yea [7], I say further, there are so many improbabilities and moral impossibilities in this tale, as no man, of any mean judgment, discretion, or common-sense, will give credit thereto, but will easily see the vanity thereof; and, in a word, [8] I say, he was a knave that devised it, and he is a fool that believeth it.

Prot. Now this is excellent in good truth, I see there is mettle in you: But what reason have you on your side, that you are so peremptory? Did it run for courant, without controulment, till within these forty years, or thereabout, to wit, till the year 1566, that Onuphrius, the friar, began to boggle at it? Was not Onuphrius the first that ever, by reason, sought to discredit the report of it? And yet doth not even [9] he confess, that many men of worth, as well as of ordinary sort, believed it for a truth? Is it not to be found in Marianus Scotus, in Sigebert, in Gotefridus Viterbiensis, in Johannes de Parisiis, in Martinus Polonus, in Petrarch, in Boccace, in Ranulfus Cestrensis, in Johannes Lucidus, in Alphonsus de Carthagena, in Theodoricus de Niem, in Chalchondylas, in Wernerus Rolenink, in Platina, in Palmerius, in Nauclerus, in Sabellidus, in Trithemius, in Volaterran, in Bergomensis, in Schedel, in Laziardus, in Fulgosus, in Textor, in an epistle written by the universities of Paris, Oxford, and Prague, to all at Rome; in Mantuan, in Crantius, in Charanza, and a [10] number more of your own faction, and of your own friends? of which some were Grecians, some Italians, some Spaniards, some French, some Germans, some Polonians, some Scots, some English, and yet never a one of them a Lutheran. Yea, do we not find it in some of your stories set down in pictures? And is not so much to be gathered by that image of her's, which is set up amongst the rest of the images of the Popes, in the renowned church of Siena in Italy, and is to be seen there at this day; which the Bishop of that place would not suffer to be defaced, at the last repairing of that church, though your Jesuits

1 Onuph. Annot. in Plat. in vita Joh. viii.   2 Harding inh is answer to Juel's apology.
3 N. D. Part. ii. C. 5. Num. xxi. p. 391. of the 3 Convers.
4 Idem Num. xxvi. p. 403.   5 Ibid.   6 Idem Num. xxi. p. 391.
7 Idem Num xxxvi. p. 403.
8 Impudentissime ficta, stultissime credita. Bernartius de utilitate legendæ Hist. Lib. ii. p. 105. in marg.   9 Multos & magni nominis viros historiam hanc suscipere, eam quoque vulgo veram existimari. Loco supra citato.
10 Barthol. Cass. ii. part. Catal. gloriæ mundi, nona Consideratio. Job. Turrecremat. in Summa, Lib. iv. Part. 2. Cap. 20. Carolus Molinæus. Comment. in Parisiens. Consuetud. Tit. 1. No. 26. Cælius Rhodigin. Antiquarum Lect. Lib. viii. Cap. 1.

did earnestly request him to deface it? Was there not made of old,
for fear of such like after-claps, a stool of easement, on which they
were set at their creation, for proof of their humanity? was there
not a marble image set up, as a monument thereof, in that place
where she miscarried, to wit, in one of the chiefest streets in Rome?
Which monument was to be seen likewise within these few years, even in
Pius the fifth's time.   And is it not written by men among yourselves,
That your popes, when they go in procession, refuse to go through
that street, in detestation of that fact, and go further about? how say
you, is it not even thus?

Pap.   It is written, I confess, that our popes, in detestation of that
fact, when they go in procession to the Lateran church, refuse to go
through that street, but they who write so mistake the matter.   For
the true reason why they turn out of that street, which is the nearer
way, is, for that that street is *angusta et anfractuosa*, a narrow street,
and such a one as winds this way, and that way, and in that respect,
unfit for so great a train, as ordinarily accompanies the Pope, to pass
orderly through; as [1] Onuphrius, and [2] Bellarmine, and [3] Florimondus
have observed.

Prot.   Say you so? Why, but if it be true, which Philippus
Bergomensis hath storied, this observation is false; for, *Eo omisso,* [4] saith
he, speaking of the Pope's turning out of that place of the street,
wherein dame Joan was delivered, ' Declinat ad diverticula, vicosque
& sic, loco detestabili postergato, reintrantes, iter perficiunt quod
coeperunt;' that is, leaving that way, they turn into by-lanes, and by
streets; and as soon as they are beyond that detestable place, they turn
into their high-way again, and so go on in their procession.   For if,
upon their leaving that street, they enter into by-lanes and by-streets,
and as soon as they are past that ominous place, turn in again; the
reason why they leave that street cannot be, for that it is narrow and
winding in and out.   For no question, but those by lanes are as narrow;
and by their turning out, and returning into the same way again, they
wind as often in and out, as if they went along through the same street,
though it were very crooked.   But howsoever, shift it among you:
for it sufficeth me, that you cannot deny, but that which I told you
concerning this point, is written by men of your own religion; especially
seeing [5] Platina, who knew Rome well enough, and was desirous to
cover the Popes nakedness herein, as much as he could with any
honesty, confesseth, that this is probable enough.   What have you to
say to the rest of my speech?

Pap.   Much.   For whereas you say Onuphrius was the first who by
reason sought to discredit the report of it; that is not so.   Johannes
de Columna, a good writer of chronicles, long before Onuphrius, hath
likewise utterly rejected the vanity of this fable, as [6] Doctor Harding
noteth.

Prot.   Johannes de Columna's history is extant in Latin in the
university library at Oxford; and in French, in New College library.

---

1 Loco supra citato
3 Fabula Joannæ, cap. 21. p. 184.
5 De Vitis Pont. in vita Joh. viii.

2 Lib. iii. de Rom. Pont. cap. 24.
4 In Supplement Chron. ad An. 858.
6 Confutat. of the Apology, Part iv. Fol. 166.

But there is not one word, good, or bad, for, or against Pope Joan in it. If he rejected it, he rejected it by silence.

Pap. But [1] Johannes Aventinus rejected it in plain words: And he wrote a good many years before Onuphrius.

Prot. Johannes Aventinus (I grant) rejects it as a fable in one word, but he gives no reason of his rejecting of it. Besides, [2] Bellarmine casts him off as a writer of small credit; and [3] Baronius brands him, not merely for a scabbed sheep, but for an heretical scabby beast, destitute both of honesty and learning; and divers of your popes have [4] cried down this history, as unworthy of reading; wherefore I see no reason, that his reasonless rejecting of it doth any way prejudice the truth of it. What have you else to say?

Pap. First I would know, Who told you there was such a marble image in one of the streets at Rome?

Prot. [5] Theodoricus de Niem, who was secretary to one of your popes, told me that; for ' Adhuc vetus statua marmorea illic posita figurativè monstrat hoc factum,' saith Theodoricus de Niem; that is, Unto this day an old marble image erected in that place sheweth the matter under a figure.

Pap. Indeed [6] I cannot deny but that in former ages many have said so, and, to confess a truth, I myself have read as much in Antonius, archbishop of Florence, and in Peter Mexia. But verily that image resembled no such thing. For neither was it like a woman lying in child-bed, nor was the boy, which was engraven by her, like a child in the swadling-clouts, but like one of some years.

Prot. This your exception is to no purpose; for that age was a learnless and a witless age. And therefore, perhaps, had no more skill in engraving, carving, and painting, than [7] they had (of whom we read in an epistle of Sir Thomas More's unto Erasmus) who pictured an hare and a grayhound so like, that no man could know the one from the other, till he, full wisely, writ under, This is the dog,—This is the hare; as they of whom Appian writes, making mention of some, [8] who were driven to set either under, or above their pictures, ' Hoc est bos, illud equus, hic arbor,' that men might know what kind of creature it was that they had painted. Questionless [9] Æneas Silvius, pointing to a better time than that of Pope Joan's, condemns the painters and carvers thereof, for notorious bunglers, saying thus, ' Si ducentorum, trecentorumve annorum, aut sculpturas intueberis, aut picturas; invenies non hominum, sed monstrorum portentorumque facies;' that is, If thou observe the engraven or painted images, which were made two or three-hundred years ago, thou shalt find, that they are faced more like monsters, and hobgoblins, than men. Now if they were such, what marvel, though intending to engrave a woman travelling, or rather newly delivered of a child, they did it but untowardly? But what I pray you doth that image represent, if it represent not Pope Joan?

1 Annalium Boiorum, Lib iv.   2 Joh. Aventinus author parum probatæ fidei.
saith Bell. Append ad Lib. de sum. pont. Cap. 10.   3 Infectam hæresis scabie
bestiam, pietate & doctrina omnino desertam. Baron. Annal To. x. ad 996. Num. 54.
4 In Indicibus Lib. prohibitorum.   5 Lib. de Privilegiis & Juribus Imperii.
6 Florimond. Lib. citato, cap. 21. num. 2.   7 Inter opera Mori impressa Basil.
1563. Pag. 441.   8 Ælian. de varia hist. Lib. x.   9 Epist. 120.

Pap. ¹ Cardinal Bellarmine seems to like of their opinion, who guess that some heathenish priest, who was about to offer sacrifice, and had his man before him, is denoted thereby. But I am rather of ² Florimondus's mind, who thinks it was an idol, even an image of some of the gods of the heathen.

Prot. If it had represented a sacrificing priest, and his man, the man should have been engraved behind, and not before his master. For the servant followeth his master, ³ as the young man, that bare Jonathan's armour, followed Jonathan ; wherefore you have reason to leave Bellarmine in this. But why do you incline to Florimondus ; doth he give you any reason for this opinion ; or alledgeth any author of his opinion ?

Pap. Yes ⁴ he professeth that he followeth Onuphrius therein, who was a most diligent antiquary.

Prot. But he lyes in that. For Onuphrius speaks not one word good or bad of this marble image. He passeth it over in silence, as though no man had ever spoken of it.

Pap, I marvel if that be so. But yet I rest persuaded upon Florimondus's next reason, that that image resembled not Pope Joan. For if the engraver had purposed to express such a matter, and to continue thereby the memory thereof to the world's end, he would have set some ⁵ inscription over it ; for so do all men who erect monuments for remembrances.

Prot. That is not so, for we read in ⁶ Eusebius, that the ⁷ woman who was cured by our Saviour Christ of her issue of blood, &c. erected, after the custom of the heathen, an image of him no doubt for remembrance sake. But we read of no inscription written upon it. In the book of ⁸ Joshua we read, that the Israelites were commanded to lay twelve stones upon an heap, as a memorial unto their children for ever : And yet it is plain by the circumstances, they set nothing thereon in writing. When you paint St. Peter, you paint him with keys in his hand, and set no inscription over his head, nor under his feet, as ⁹ Baronius confesseth. Wherefore, for any thing I yet hear, it is most probable that it was set up for a monument of Pope Joan.

Pap. Enjoy your conceit. But ¹⁰ I can tell you one thing : That image is now removed out of that place. For Sixtus Quintus, that great builder and mender of high-ways, when he made that street straight wherein that image was, was forced to remove that image.

Prot. Belike, that image would have been some blemish unto the street, if it had remained ; and that made him move it.

Pap. Yea marry would it.

Prot. Now well fare his heart that was so careful to rid the streets of such a combersome monument. But who told you that Sixtus Quintus removed it upon that occasion ?

---

1 Lib. iii. de Rom. Pont. Cap. 24.   2 Cap. citat. num. 6.
3] 1 Sam. xiv. 12. 13.   4 Cum Onuphrio Panvino antiquitatis perscrutatore
diligentissimo vetus aliquod idolum existimavi. Florim. Ibid.
5 Inscriptionem præfixisset. pag. 188   6 Lib. vii. Hist. Cap. 14.   7 Matt. ix. 21.
8 Cap. iv. 7. 8.   9 Obervat. in Annal. tom. 1. ad an. 57. apud Possevin. in apparat.
sac. verbo, Cæsar Baron.   10 Sixtus Quintus hunc vicum rectiorem duci curavit, quæ
factum est ut imago illa sublata sit. Florim. Cap. 21 Pag. 189.

Prot.   [1] Florimondus.

Pap.   Was it he?   Then know him for a lyar, whilst you live; for it was Pius Quintus, and not Sixtus Quintus, who removed it.

Prot.   And Pious Quintus removed it, and cast it into Tiber, not for that it disgraced the street; but *ut memoriam historiæ illius aboleret;* that he might extinguish the memory of that shameful act.   And this is witnessed not only by some travellers, who were at that time in Rome; but by [2] Elias Hassenmuller, one (once) of your fiery order of Jesuits.   Your Florimondus will not deserve (I fear) half the commendation you have given him.

Pap.   I doubt not but he will acquit himself like a man, of whatsoever you can say against him.   But whence had you that of the stool of easement, I pray you, for [3] in Bellarmine I read, that, ' de sede ad explorandum sexum nulla usquam ' mentio :'   Of a stool of easement, to try the Pope's sex, there is no where any mention; and in [4] Onuphrius, That it is but a mere toy, and an idle conceit of idle people.

Prot.   That of the stool of easement, is recorded by Philippus Bergomensis, [5] a man of great worth in his time, as Trithemius witnesseth.   For upon mention made of Pope Joan's story, ' Ad evitandos similes errores statutum fuit,' [6] saith he, ' ne quis de cætero in B. Petri collocaretur sede, priusquam per perforatam sedem futuri Pontificis genitalia ab ultimo Diacono Cardinale attrectarentur.'   That is, for avoiding like error in future times, it was decreed, that no man should be held for pope, till the youngest cardinal deacon had found by trial, while he set upon a stool of easement, that he was a man.   And it is likewise testified by [7] LaonicusChalchondylas.   For upon relation of that story, he goes on thus: ' Quapropter ne decipiantur iterum, sed rem cognoscant, neque ambigant; pontificis creati virilia tangunt, & qui tangit, acclamat: Mas nobis Dominus est,' that is, Lest they should be deceived again, they make proof by feeling; and he that feeleth makes it known by crying out: We have a man Pope.   And by Friar Robert[8]: For, ' duxit me spiritus ad Lateranense Palatium, & posuit me in porticu ante sedes Porphyrii ubi dicitur probari Papa an sit homo.'   My good spirit (saith he) led me unto the palace of Lateran, and set me in the gallery before the chairs of Porphyry, wherein they say the Pope is tried whether he be a man or no man.   And you may find as much in a later papist, who, within these few years, writ a book of the harmony of Romish magistrates, and in it this.

Pap.   You say true indeed.   For I now remember [9] Florimondus confesseth so much, yet he reproveth the author for writing so.   But let us go on; for I long to hear of whom you heard that such a chair was to be seen, in the Pope's palace, within these few years.

1 Loco citato.   2 Historia Jesuitici Ordinis, Cap. 10. de Jesuitarum Patre & Matre.
3 Lib. iii. de Rom. Pont. Cap. 24·   4 Fabulosum, & ab imperito vulgo fictum.
Annotat in Plat. in vit. Joh. viii.   5 Nobiliter doctus, historiographus celeberrimus
Trith. de Scrip. Eccles verbo, Jacobus Bergomensis.   6 In Supplement. Chron. ad
An. 858.   7 De Rebus Turcicis, Lib. vi. Pag. 98.   8 Lib. Visionum
impressus Paris 1513. Cap. 3. Fol. 25.   9 Cap. 18, p. 150. In ridiculorum authorum
grege annumerandus est.

Prot. I heard that of [1] Sabellicus. For, writing of the same matter, ' Spectatur adhuc in Pontificia domo marmorea sella (saith he). circa medium inanis, qua novus Pontifex continuò ab eius creatione recedit, ut sedentis genitalia ab ultimo diacono attrectentur; that is, There is to be seen at this day, in the Pope's palace, a chair of marble, wherein the new pope presently upon his election is set down, that, as he sits, the lowest deacon may make trial of his humanity by touching. And you may find as much in William Brewin, who lived in the year 1470; for, in [2] Capella Salvatoris, saith he, ' Sunt duæ vel plures cathedræ de lapide marmoreo & cubio, cum foraminibus in iis sculptis, super quas cathedras, ut audivi ibidem, est probatio Papæ, utrum sit masculus, annon;' that is, In the chapel of our Saviour, there are two or three marble chairs with holes in them, wherein, as I heard there, they make proof whether the Pope be a man or no.

Pap. [3] Florimondus acknowledgeth, there is yet such a chair, wherein the Pope sits after his election. But that he sits therein, to such an end as you speak, that he utterly denies.

Prot. And what is his reason?

Pap. [4] Because he sits therein not in a corner, but in the great church of St. John Lateran, whither all the world, almost, comes to see him; where he is attended by the whole college of cardinals, and whereat there are many ambassadors of kings and princes; for a closer place were fitter for such a purpose. They might more conveniently have made trial of his humanity in the conclave where he was chosen.

Prot. And so they did, it seems; for, presently upon their electing of him, before they proclaimed him pope, they set him in a chair in their conclave, as you may read in the book of holy ceremonies, dedicated to Leo the Tenth. Whereby you may see how idly [5] Bellarmine talks, who, taking upon him to clear the point, never speaks of his sitting in the chair in the conclave, but only of his sitting in certain other chairs at St. John Lateran's, as though he had been chaired only in publick, and not in private; and that he himself had said sufficiently to the point in question, by proving, that in publick there was no such conclusion tried with the Pope; whereas the conclusion was tried in secret. But can you tell me what the end is, why the pope sits in such a chair in publick?

Pap. Marry to the end that thereby he may be put in mind, that he is not God, but man; inasmuch as he stands in need of a close-stool as well as others; for so saith [6] Florimondus.

Prot. I promise you, and he had need be put in mind thereof. For, though [7] some papist shamefully deny it, therere have been popish clawbacks, [8] who in plain words, have termed the Pope, as [9] St. Thomas termed Christ, their Lord and God; and there are

1 Æneid 9. Lib. i.　　　　2 Wilhelmus Brewin in codice manuscripto de 7. Ecclesiis
principalibus urbis Roma.　　　　3 Cap. xx. p. 176.　　　　4 Ibid p. 181.
　　　5 Lib. iii. de Rom. Pont. Cap. 24.　　　　6 Cap. xx. p. 177 and 118.
7 N. D. in his Warn-word to Sir Francis Hastings's Encounter I. Cap. ii. Fol. 30.
8 Cap. Cum Inter. extrav. Joh. xxii. Impress. Paris. 1513, & Lugduni, 1555.
9 Joh. xx. 28.

still[1] who give him such titles as are due to God, and ascribe like power to him and God.   But methinks they should not need to have set him in such a chair to such a purpose; for his own necessity would have driven him to set himself thereon ordinarily every day; and his chamber-pot would have served to put him in mind of his humanity sufficiently.   For Antigonus the Elder knew by that, that he was man and not God, as[2] Plutarch writeth: Besides, methinks they should not have intended such a mystery by such a ceremony, because they set him therein before he was in his *Pontificalibus;* for, till he be mitered, till he be crowned, till he have received the keys, whereby is denoted his power to bind and loose; and a rod, whereby is denoted his power to punish the obstinate; methinks there should be no great fear of forgetting himself.   For, till such ceremonies are performed, he is not in his ruff.   Again, had it not been better, think you, if they had aimed at any such mark, to have caused a boy to come every morning unto the Pope's chamber-door (after the example of[3] Philip, King of Macedonia) who should have whooped him out of his bed, and bid him remember, that he was mortal?

Pap.   If you like not Florimondus's conjecture touching that ceremony, what say you to[4] Bellarmine's, which is: That he is set on such a stool, to signify how he is raised from base estate to supreme honour?

Prot.   I say Bellarmine's conjecture is as improbable and fond as Florimondus's.   For your Popes, since Pope Joan's days, have been chosen, for the most part, out of the number of your cardinals.   And your cardinal's estate is not so base, as that he, who is advanced from that unto the papacy, can be truly said to be taken in any sort from off a close-stool.   For they are generally princes[5] fellows.   Yea some of them, you cannot but know, have not been ashamed to prefix their own names before their own king's, using these words; I and my King: wherefore, unless you can render me some better reason, why your Popes are set on such a seat, I shall remain persuaded, that, in former times, it was for proof of their humanity, upon the accident aforesaid.

Pap.   Enjoy your opinion for me.   But where read you that there was such an image in the church of Siena, which the Jesuits would have defaced, but that the bishop of the place would not suffer them?

Prot.   That I have heard by many travellers, and read in Master Bell; both in his book of[6] Motives concerning the Romish Religion, and in his[7] Survey of Popery; whereunto never a papist of you all dare answer.

Pap.   Yes we dare, though we do not.   But I can tell you news:[8] That image of Pope Joan, which was set up in the Church of Siena, is cast down by the commandment of Clement the Eighth, by the

1 Plane supremum in terris numen. Stapleton. princip. fidei doctrin. praefat. ad Greg. xiii.
2 Part ii. Moral. Lib. de Iside & Osiride.   3 Stobaeus Serm. 19. ex Æliano.
4 Lib. iii. de Rom. Pont. Cap. 24.   5 Cardinalatus celsitudo ac splendor, dignitati regiæ comparatur. Sixtus v. in constitut. 5 in princip. & sect. Prætereą Joh. Franciscus Leo in Thesauro Fori Ecclesiastici, Part. I. Cap. ii. Num. 1.   6 Lib. 2. Cap. 6. Conclus. iii. p. 80.   7 Part III. Cap. ii. p. 191.   8 Florim. Cap. xxii. p. 194.

means of Cæsar Baronius, at the request of Florimondus. Cæsar Baronius hath certified Florimondus so much by a letter, and, for joy, [1] Florimondus hath published it unto the world.

Prot. What? Is that image cast down too? Florimondus might do well to make request to the present Pope, that those books which write of Pope Joan may be burned; in hope, that the present Pope will as readily burn the books, as Clement the Eighth threw down that image, and Pius Quintus the other. And so, in time to come, when all evidences are embezzled, and all monuments defaced, and made out of the way, it will be a plain case there was never any Pope Joan.

Pap. Oh! this angers you, I perceive. And yet why should you be angry at the throwing down of this? For, suppose it had stood still, is there any sense, that, because of such an image, we should be bound the rather to believe there was such a Pope? [2] I can tell you, if we believe painters and carvers, we may soon mar all; for, in St. Andrew's church at Bourdeaux, one of the excellentest churches in all France, our Saviour Christ is described ascending up to heaven upon the back of a flying eagle, which stands not well with the scripture.

Prot. That is true, if we believe your painters and carvers, we shall soon mar all indeed: For we find the Trinity painted by you, sometimes in the likeness of a man with three faces; sometimes in the likeness of a man with two heads, having a dove between them; both which fashions of painting the Trinity are monstrous, in [3] Bellarmine's opinion. We find our Saviour Christ painted with long hair, as though he had been a Nazarite by vow; which conceit is controuled by [4] scripture. We find him set on a weather-cock upon the top of the temple of Jerusalem, as though that temple had had a spire-steeple like ours [5], which is neither so, nor so. We find the Virgin Mary treading on the serpent's head, which the [6] the scriptures foretold, that Christ himself should do. We find her set out in a gown of wrought gold, whereas, no question, she was meanly appareled, and with a pair of beads in her hand; whereas, of a thousand years after Christ, there were [7] no beads in the world. In like sort we find [8] Moses painted with two horns, [9] John Baptist in a raw camel's skin, [10] John the Evangelist like a beardless boy, when he writ his gospel. Mary Magdalen in a loose gown, [11] St. Jerome in his cardinal's robes, all which is false as God is true. Besides, your painters recommend unto us a saint on horseback, whom they call George; and another saint on foot, as big as a giant, whom they call Christopher; and a she saint, broken upon a wheel, and whom they call Catharine; and a fourth, drawn in pieces with horses, whom they call Hippolytus; whereas, in all antiquity, [12] there is no mention of any such saints; so that you never spoke a truer word in your life, than this, That, if we believe painters and carvers, we shall

1 Page 195.

2 Si ea, quæ ab artificibus manu finguntur, credamus esse vera, interdum veteris & novi Testamenti historiam pervertemus, &c. Florim. p. 195.   3 Lib. ii. de Imag. Cap. 8.
4 For Nazarites must drink no wine, Numb. vi. 3. yet our Saviour did, Mat. xi. 19. and xxvi. 29.   5 Tho. de Truxillo. Ord. Prædic. Domin. 1. Quadrag. conc. 1.   6 Gen. iii.
7 Teste Polydoro Virgil. de Invent. Rerum. Lib. v. Cap. 9.   8 Hieron. ab. Oleastro in Exod. xxxiv. & Aug. Steuchus in Recognit. Vet. Test. ad Hebraicam Verit. in Exod. xxxiv.
9 Jansen. Concord. Evang. Cap. xiii.   10 In novis Bibliis Sixti Quinti, & Clem. viii. yet he writ it ninety; ætatis annum excedens, ut docet Baron. Annal Tom. i. ad An. 99. Num. 2.
11 Scultingius Confessio Hieronymana. Polyd. Virg. de Invent Rerum. Lib. iv. 9.
12 For proof whereof, see D. Rayn. de Rom. Ecclesiæ Idololat. Lib. I. Chap. v. Num. xxi, &c.

soon mar all.   But what, if book-proof concur with painting and carving, may we not then, without fear of marring all, give credit to painters and carvers?   Your [1] Bellarmine is of opinion, that there can be no error in substance, as long as, besides book-proof, there be monuments of stone, or of brass, for the proof of any ancient report.   And, if he speak the words of truth, the truth is with us; for, besides monuments of stone, we have the testimonies of many writers.

Pap.   But not so many as you brag of, I believe; and, besides [2], those you have are but paltry writers.

Prot.   That shall be seen by a more particular view of them: Wherefore, first, what say you to Charanza, the last of them whom I named, who was a divinity-reader among you, and, afterwards [3], Archbishop of Toledo in Spain?   Was he a paltry writer?   or, Hath he not this story, in your opinion?

Pap.   I think he hath it not.   For [4] Florimondus names Charanza among them, who disproved the story of Pope Joan, before he himself fell to disprove it.

Prot.   Doth he so?   Doubtless then, he belyes Charanza; for this is all that [0] Charanza writes of that argument: *Johannes viii, Papa* 105 *sub Petro, sedit An.* 2. *mens.* 1. *dies* 4.   *De hoc ferunt, quod malis artibus pontificatum adeptus est, quoniam, cum esset fæmina, sexum mentitus est; & postea a servo compressa, doloribus circumventa, mortua est.* Which, in English, is thus: John the Eighth, the one hundred and fifth Pope from St. Peter, sat two years, one month, and four days. They report of this person, that he got the papacy by evil means, because he feigned himself to be a man, whereas, in truth, he was a woman; who, being afterwards begot with child by one of her servants, fell in travel and died thereon; and this is not disproving of it, is it trow you?

Pap.   No verily, if he say no more of it; but perhaps he saith more, and you conceal it from me.

Prop.   Not a word, I warrant you, in way of disproving it: Wherefore let us go on, and observe who, and what manner of men, the rest are, who bear witness with us in this case.   What say you to Krantius? Hath he not this story?   or, Is he but a paltry writer?

Pap.   Krantius is commended by [6] Pontanus, for a famous historiographer.   And, seeing he wrote before Luther's days, there is no reason, as [7] Bellarmine notes upon another occasion, that he should be suspected to write any thing for love or hatred.   But hath he this story?

Prot.   Yea; [8] for these are his own words: ' Johannes Anglicus, ex Moguntia mulier, mentita sexum, quum acutissimo ingenio & promptissima lingua doctissimè loqueretur, adeo in se convertit omnium animos, ut pontificatum adipisceretur, uno famulo sexum ejus cognoscente, a quo compressa prægnans efficitur; & fertur peperisse apud Colosseum, An. 2. necdum expleto, in partu moritur:' Which, in

1 Lib. II. de Rom. Pont. Cap. xi.   2 Si hujus commenti authores spectes, nihil
Illis virtus. Florim. cap. xxxi. nu. i.   3 Possevinus Apparat. sacro. verbo, Barth.
Charanza.   4 Cap. xxxi. num. vi.   5 In Sum. Conc. p. 370. Edit. Paris. 1564.
6 Chronograph. lib. ii.   7 Krantius, homo Germanus, & qui ante Lutheranus contentiones scripsit, proinde nec odio nec amore ducebatur lib. ii. de Effectu Sacram. cap. ix.
8 Metrop. lib. ii. edit. Colon. 1574, & Francofurt. 1590.

effect, sounds thus: John English, a woman of Mentz, dissembled her sex, and being of a quick wit and glib tongue, and one that could speak very scholar-like, she so won the hearts of all men, that she got the papacy, no man knowing any other, but that she was a man, save one of her servants, who afterwards got her with child. They say she was delivered near the Colosses, before she had sitten full two years. Thus Krantius.

Pap. And hath Mantuan the same, whom you cited next before Krantius?

Prot. Yea, Mantuan, who is commended by [1] Trithemius for a great divine, an excellent philosopher, and a famous poet, the only man in all Italy in his time: Mantuan, [2] at whom the people pointed, as he went in the streets, and said, This is he; which was wont to be held a matter of extraordinary credit. Mantuan, of whom Picus Mirandula, Pontanus, Beroaldus, Baronius, Possevin, and divers others [3], give honourable testimony. This Mantuan hath this story; for, falling to describe hell, and what manner of persons were in hell:

> ' Hic, ' saith he, pendebat adhuc sexum mentita virilem
> ' Fœmina, cui triplici Phrygiam diademate mitram
> ' Extollebat apex, & Pontificalis adulter.'

Which in effect sounds thus much: Here hanged the woman who went like a man, and came to the popedom. And here hanged he, that committed adultery with her.

Pap. You say right; for I remember now that [5] Florimondus confesseth the tale is in Mantuan. But Mantuan deserves no credit in this; for he writes worse of her than ever any did before him; and feigns [6], very ridiculously, that her horsekeeper, who got her with child, and she were both hanged together.

Prot. Mantuan talks of no horsekeeper of her's, but in general of one, who committed adultery with her; nor of any hanging, save of their hanging in hell, which is likely enough to be true. Your Florimondus can lay his finger upon nothing, but he grimes it. He can comment upon no man's words, but he wrests them. There is not a word in Mantuan more, concerning her, than that which is comprehended in the three verses cited.

Pap. At better leisure, I will examine your words more narrowly.

Prot. Is not this plain?

Pap. What is there in the Epistle of the Universities of Oxford, Paris, and Prague, which makes for you?

Prot. In that Epistle set out by Huldericus Hutten, Anno 1520, we read thus: ' Joh. successor Leonis IV, cœpit circa An. Dom. 854, & sedit an. 2. & mens. 5. fœmina fuit, & in papatu impregnata.' John, who succeeded Leo IV, was chosen Pope about the year 854.

1 De Script. Ecclesiasticis, verbo, Baptista Mantuanus.
Hieron. Carmelita, ad initium Tom. ii. Operum Mantuani. sacro, tom. i. verbo, Baptista.   4 Tom. iii. lib. iii. Alphonsi. fol. 44. edit. Francof. 1573.
5 Cap. 22. num. 5.   6 Stabuli pontificii præfectum cum illa, laqueo in collum inserto suspensum, commentatur Florim. ibid. & cap. 23. num. 6.
2 Philip. Beroaldus,
3 Possevin. in Apparat.

She was a woman, and got with child in her papacy. Is not this plain?

Pap. Yes, but what find you in Ravisius Textor?

Prot. 'Scitum est ex Chronicis, & á majoribus scriptum (saith [*] Ravisius Textor) Johannem Anglicum ab Ephebis sexum virilem simulasse, & tandem fato nescio quo, aut fortuna certè volente, ad Pontificatum pervenisse, in quo annos circiter duos sederit, post Leonem IV, neque prius innotuerit facti veritas, quám, á quodam ex domesticis impregnata, tandem emiserit partum.' That is, It is a thing well known by the Chronicles, and written by our ancestors, that John English, from her youth up, carried herself as though she had been a man, and at length, by I know not what destiny, certainly by very great luck, she became Pope, and sat about two years, after Leo the Fourth, and nobody knew her cousenage, till she was with child by one of her menial servants, and delivered thereof.

Pap. What find you in Fulgosus?

Prot. Marry I find in [2] Fulgosus, [3] who was a noble and learned man, and sometimes Duke of Genoa, that John the Eighth was found out to be a woman.

Pap. And what in Laziardus?

Prot. 'Johannes Anglicus in Cathedra Petri sedit Annis duobus, Mensibus septem, Diebus quatuor, saith [4] Laziardus. Hic, ut fertur, Fœmina fuit, &c.' That is, John English sat in St. Peter's chair two years, seven months, and four days. This, as the report goeth, was a woman, &c.

Pap. And who was the next you cited before this?

Prot. Hartmanuus Schedel, a doctor of physick, yet not ignorant of holy scriptures, a very witty and well spoken man, as [5] Trithemius witnesseth.

Pap. Oh! Schedel, I confess, [6] reports this. [7] But he reports it so coldly, so fearfully, so faintly, that a man may well see he doubted of it. For he confesseth, that he knew not whether it was so or no; and therefore fathers it upon one Martin, I know not whom.

Prot. Fie, that you should say so. Doth he not use the very words without change, which Platina useth in relating the same, whereof we shall have occasion to speak 'ere we part? And against which you can take no exceptions. And doth he not (to imprint the matter deeper into the reader's memory) set her picture down with a child in her arms?

Pap. Yes indeed I cannot deny that. But, to be plain with you, I care not what he saith of it. For, as [8] Florimondus noteth, [9] he was one of the stinking brood of the Hussites, and lived in Nurenberg, what time Nurenburg was infected with Husse's heresy. And therefore, no marvel, if, to curry favour with them, he touched by the way the supposed popedom of Joan the woman.

1 In Officina Tit. Mulieres virilem habitum mentitæ. 2 De Dict. Factisque memorabi-
libus, lib. viii. cap. 3. Tit. de Fœminis quæ doctrina excel. 3 So saith Allen, cap. 5.
of his Defence of the Seminaries; and Possevin. Apparat. sacr. verbo, Baptista Fulgosus.
4 Epitom. Histor. universalis, cap. 9. 5 Lib. de Scriptoribus Ecclesiasticis.
6 In Chron. Ætatum Mundi Ætate 6. 7 Schedel. de hac Johanna Verba facit. sed ita
jejune, ita exiliter, ita incerte, ut de ea re dubitasse videatur. Florim. lib. cit. cap. 4. Num. 3.
8 Loco citato. 9 Ex impura Hussitarum Familia, &c.

B 2

Prot. See how you lavish. This Hartmannus Schedel, born in Nurenberg, was [1] student in Padua, where he was created doctor of physick by the great Mathiolus. And he was so far from Husse's mind, that in the same [2] book he hath one whole chapter intituled, *De Hæresi Hussitarum, & ejus Origine.* That is, Of Husse's Heresy, and of the Original thereof. Wherein he follows Æneas Silvius step by step [3], who speaks spitefully and bitterly against Husse and all his followers. It seems Florimondus, of whom you learned this, is one of some stinking brood of lyars.

Pap. Well, who is next?

Prot. Jacobus Bergomensis, a man well seen in scripture, and an excellent humanist, witty, eloquent, of good conversation, and a most famous historiographer, as [4] Trithemius reports of him. This Jacobus Bergomensis, I say, writes thus of this point: [5] 'Johannes vii. Papa, Natione Anglicus, post Leonem Pontificem Pontifex factus, sedit Ann. 2. mens. 5. Hunc tradunt fuisse fœminam, quæ adolescens admodum, ex Anglia, Athenas cum quodam doctissimo Amasio suo profecta, ibidem, bonarum artium præceptores audiendo, tantum profecit, ut Romam veniens paucos admodum etiam in sacris literis haberet pares. Ea quippe legendo, disputando, docendo, orando, tantam benevolentiam & gratiam sibi comparavit, ut, mortuo Leone prædicto Pontifice, in ejusdem locum, ut multi affirmant, omnium consensu Pontifex crearetur: Verùm postea, à familiari compressa, gravidatur, & Papa existens peperit. Nam ex Vaticano ad Lateranensem Basilicam aliquando ad Litanias profecta, inter Colosseum & S. Clementem, præter spem doloribus circumventa, sine obstetrice aliqua publicè peperit, &, eo loci mortua ibidem, sine ullo honore cum fœtu misera sepulta est. Ad cujus detestandum spurcitiem, & nominis continuandum memoriam, in hodiernum usque summi Pontificis rogationem cum populo & clero sacram agentes, cum locum partus, medio ejus in itinere positum, abominentur, eo omisso, declinant ad diverticula vicosque; & sic, loco detestabili postergato, reintsantes iter perficiunt quod cœperunt. Et ad evitandos similes errores statutum fuit, ne quis de cætero in B. Petri collocaretur sede, priusquam per perforatam sedem futuri pontificis genitalia ab ultimo Diacono Cardinale attrectarentur.' That is, John the Seventh, by country English, was created Pope next after Leo, and sat two years and five months. They say this was a woman, and that she went very young out of England to Athens, with a certain great clerk, who was in love with her; and that there, by hearing of good professors, she profited so much, that, when she came to Rome, she had few like her in divinity. Whereupon, by her reading, disputing, teaching, and praying, she got herself so much favour, that, upon Leo's death, she was chosen Pope into his room (as many men say) by common consent. But see the luck of it; a while after she was got with child by one of her acquaintance, and delivered thereof in the time of her papacy. For, going upon a time from the Vatican to St. John Lateran's in procession, between the Colosses and

1 Ego Hartmannus Schedel. Doctor Patavinus, &c. circa An. 1440. fol. 252. b.
2 Circa An. 1410. fol. 238. a.   3 Historia Bohemica. cap. 35.   4 Lib. de Ecclesiastic. Scriptoribus.   5 Supplement. Chron. Lib. xi. ad An. 851, impres. Venetiis An. 1486.

St. Clement's, 'ere ever she was aware, she fell in travel, and was delivered in the high street, without the help of any midwife. But she died presently, and was buried without any solemnity in the same place, with her little one by her. Now, in hatred of her filthy dealing, and for continuing of the memory of so lewd a part, the popes to this day, when they go in procession, in respect of their dislike of that place of her travel, which was in the midst of her way, forsaking it, do turn into by-lanes and by streets, till they have left that on their backs; and then, returning into the same street again, they go forward with their procession. And, for avoiding of like mischief in time to come, it was decreed that none should be consecrated pope, before the youngest cardinal deacon had tried by touching, whilst the party to be consecrated sat on a close-stool, that he was a man. Thus Bergomensis.

Pap. Is not this be that wrote Supplementum Chronicorum, in the year 1503?

Prot. No, but this is he who wrote Supplementum Chronicorum, in the year 1486, as ' Trithemius witnesseth, and the book itself convinceth. Your ' Florimondus was deceived, who, seeing (perhaps) that it was printed in the year 1503, thought it was written in the year 1503.

Pap. That error is not so great, though an error. But, if it be he that I mean, I say with ' Florimondus, that his reporting of it is an argument of his ignorance, and so let him go.

Prot. So you may cast off all the rest, if you be disposed, and make short work of our conference, for you may say of every one: His reporting of it is an argument of his ignorance. When ' Volaterran, an historiographer of good note, shall be brought in, saying, Johannes vii. Anglicus, quem dissimulato Viri Habitu dicunt Fœminam alioquin doctissimam fuisse, deprehensamque, in Via apud S. Clementem, quando peperit;' that is, John English, the seventh of that name, who (as they say) carried himself like a man, whenas, indeed, she was a notable well learned woman; and discovered so to be by her delivery of a child in the way near to St. Clement's: You may reply, Volaterran's reporting of it is an argument of his ignorance.

Pap. And what if I did so? Yet you shall know anon, that I have a better answer to him, and to the rest. But mean while go on, and tell me what Trithemius saith to the matter.

Prot. Trithemius ' Abbot of St. Martin's monastery in Spanheim, a reverend and an exceeding great learned man, writes ' thus: ' Sancto Leone papa mortuo, eodem Anno, Johannes Anglicus successit 2 Annis, & mensibus 5, quem ferunt quidam Fœminam extitisse, & uni soli familiari cognitam, & ab eo compressam, peperisse in strata publica. Et ob id eum nonnulli inter pontifices ponere noluerunt, quasi indignum facinus abhorrentes. That is, In the same year that Pope Leo died, John English succeeded for two years and five months. Now some say she was a woman, and that she was known so to be

1 Lib. de Scriptoribus Ecclesiasticis.   2 Lib. citato page 37.   3 Ibid.
4 Anthropologia, lib. xxii. page 503. edit. Basil An. 1559.
5 Reverendus & undecunque doctissimus Vir, Paulus Langius in Chron. Citisense ad An. 1515.   6 In Chron. Monasterii Hirsaugiensis.
B 3

but to one only, by whom at length she was begot with child, and delivered thereof in the high-way. And for this cause some would not reckon her among popes, in disliking her villainous fact. Thus Trithemius. With whom in substance agreeth Sabellicus, [1] a man of great reckoning in Venice, yea one of the famousest men in his time for all manner of good learning: Of whose books [2] Pius the Third professed he made as much reckoning as Alexander did of Homer's Iliads. Johannes Anglicus *hujus Nominis* vii. *fit inde Pontifex*, saith [3] Sabellicus. *Fuit is Moguntiaco oriundus.*

Pap. Stay you there, and save a labour. For I confess with [4] Florimondus, that Sabellicus, by relying too much on Platina, hath put it in his history, doing therein very indiscreetly.

Prot. And what think you of Wernerus Rolenink, who is reckoned by [5] Paulus Langius, among the famous scholars of the order of Carthusians, and commended by [6] Trithemius, for a man of good learning, and much devotion [7], whose words are these : ' Iste Johannes Anglicus cognomine, sed natione Moguntinus, circa hæc tempora dicitur fuisse. Et erat Fœmina Habitu vestita virili : Sic in divina Scriptura profecerat, ut par ei non inveniretur, & in papam eligitur. Sed post impregnata, cum publicè in processione pergeret, peperit & moritur. Et hic sextus videtur fuisse papa, qui nomen sanctitatis sine re habuit usque huc. Et similiter sicut alii à Deo plagatus fuit ; nec ponitur in catalogo Pontificum.' That is, this John, by his Sirname English, by his country of Mentz, is reported to have sat as pope about this time. And she was a woman : But went in man's apparel. She profited so well in divinity, that she had no fellow, and so was chosen to be pope. But, after a while being great with child, as she went in publick procession, she was delivered thereof, and died. And this seems to be the sixth pope, which, to this day, was called holy, and proved nought. And, therefore, he was plagued by God, as the rest before him were plagued. Neither is she in the register of popes. How say you ? Did not Wernerus indiscreetly in relating it thus plainly ?

Pap. Yes marry did he. But I wonder not at him, for relating of it, because in the same place (as [8] Florimondus observes) he writes, that, inasmuch as she was a German, no German could ever since be chosen pope. Which is a lye with a latchet. For divers Germans, since that, have been advanced unto the popedom, as Damasus the Second and Victor the Second, with others.

Prot. True: Divers Germans have been popes, since Joan the Woman's popedom ; and, if Wernerus writ the contrary, Wernerus lyed shamefully. But he had no rule of his tongue, who chargeth Wernerus with such a matter. For these are Wernerus's words, which follow presently upon the former : ' Nugantur aliqui, hac de causa nullum Alemannum in papam eligi, quod falsum esse constat.' Some prattle, that for this

1 Sabellicus Vir undecunque doctissimus claret hodie apud Venetos maximo in precio. Trithem. lib. de Script. Ecclesiasticis.   2 Papir. Mason. de Urb. Episc. lib. vi. in Pio iii.
3 Æneid. 9. lib. i.   4 In similem impudentiam incidit Sabellicus, &c. saith Florimondus loco supra citato.   5 In Chron. Citizense, post An. 1493.
6 Lib. de Script. Ecclesiasticis.   7 Fascicul. Temporum, Ætate 6, ad An. 854.
8 Lib. citato, cap. 7, pag 64 & 65.

cause no German may be chosen pope, which is apparently false·
Whereby you may see, that he reproveth that in others, for which he
is injuriously reproved by your Florimondus.   Your Florimondus
may be a man in office, but, if he goes on as he begins, he will hardly
prove himself honest.

Pap.   Good words, I pray you, Sir; Florimondus may be honest
enough, for any thing you say against him.   For he[1] writes, that he
hath two editions of this Wernerus; the one bearing date what[2] year
it was printed, the other without date, but very ancient.   And these
two (as he saith) do differ in reporting the story of Pope Joan, and in
nothing else.   Now it may be, that, though in yours it be as you say,
yet in his it is otherwise.

Prot.   I myself have seen two editions of Wernerus as well as
Florimondus; yea, I have seen four; one[3] printed in the year 1479,
another printed by Nicholas Gotz, of Seltestad. I know not when, for
it carries no date: A third without note, either of the printer, or
of the place where it was printed, or of the time when it was printed.
But, questionless, very ancient: A fourth printed at Frankfort, 1584.
In the three ancient ones, there is not a word different in the narration
of Pope Joan: Nor in the fourth, saving that the words *Nugantur
aliqui*, &c. are in the fourth, and not in the other.   But in none of
them is there any such thing as Florimondus chargeth him with.
But, will you hear what the next man saith to the point in
question? He is Matheus Palmerius, [4] an Italian, and one of the choice
men which were at the council kept by Eugenius the Fourth, against
the council of Basil. ' Pontifex 106. Johannes Anglicus (saith [5] Palmerius) sedit Annis 2, Mensibus 3. Fama est hunc Johannem Fœminam
fuisse, & uni soli familiari cognitam : Qui eam complexus est, &, gravis
facta, peperit Papa existens : Quamobrem eum inter Pontifices non
numerant quidam, ideò nomini numerum non facit.' That is, John
was a woman, yet not known so to be but to one of her familiars,
who lay with her. She was delivered in the time of her papacy :
And, because some reckon her not among the Popes, there are no
more Johns for her, than if she had never been. Thus Palmerius.

Pap.   Be it so. But what saith Platina, I pray you, for your
purpose ?

Prot.   Platina,[6] keeper of the library in the Vatican, a man of
great wit and learning, [7] writes thus : ' Johannes Anglicanus, ex
Moguntiaco oriundus, malis artibus (ut aiunt) pontificatum adeptus
est : mentitus enim sexum, cum fœmina esset, adolescens admodum
Athenas cum amatore docto viro proficiscitur, ibique præceptores
bonarum artium audiendo tantum profecit, ut Romam veniens paucos
admodum etiam in sacris literis pares haberet,   nedum superiores.
Legendo autem, & disputando doctè, & acutè, tantum benevolentiæ
& authoritatis sibi comparavit, ut, mortuo Leone, in ejus locum (ut

---

1 Loco Citato.   2 Viz 1480,   3 By Henry Quentel.
4 Math. Palmerius, Natione Italus——qui in Conc. Florentino (quod Eugenius Papa iv. contra
Basil. Synodum celebravit) inter præclarissimos viros annumeratus fuit. Trithem. Descript.
Eccles.   5 In Chron. ad Ann. 853.   6 Bartholomæus Platina Apostolicus
abbreviator, vir undecunque doctissimus, &c. Trith. de Script Eccles.
7 De Vitis Pontif. in Joh. viii.

Martinus ait) omnium consensu pontifex crearetur: Verùm postea à servo compressa, cum aliquandiu ventrem occultè tulisset, tandem, dum ad Lateranensem Basilicam proficisceretur, inter theatrum (quod Colosseum vocant à Neronis Colosso) & S. Clementem, doloribus circumventa peperit: Eoque loci mortua pontificatus sui Anno 2, mense. 1, diebus 4, sine ullo honore sepelitur.' The meaning of which is, John English, born at Mentz, got the popedom (as men say) by evil means. For he dissembled his sex, being a woman, indeed: And, when she was very young, she went to Athens with a scholar, who was in love with her; where, by hearing good readers of all good learning, she profited so well, that when she came to Rome, she had few fellows, but never a one her better. Now by reading and disputing, learnedly and wittily, she got so much credit, that, upon Leo's death, she was chosen in his room, as Martin writes, by common consent. But, within a while after, she proved with child by one of her servants; and, though she carried all closely for a time, yet, at length, as she went to St. John Lateran's, between the theatre, called the Colosses, and St. Clement's, she fell in travel, and was delivered of a child, and died in the place; which was in the second year, first month, and fourth day of her reign: And she was buried without any solemnity. How like you this?

Pap. So and so. But Bernartius is of opinion, that this was never written by Platina, but was foisted into him. For I have heard, ' saith he, by Antonius Hetweeld, a man of good report, and an alderman of Lovain, that one Engelbertus Boonius, a reverend man, and dean of a great church in Germany, had oftentimes told him, that he had seen many ancient manuscripts of Platina in the Vatican at Rome, and perused them diligently, and yet found never a word in any of them touching Pope Joan.

Prot. That dean had the luck of it, if he light on such ancient manuscripts, as the alderman of Lovain told Bernartius of. But how came the manuscripts in the Vatican to be many and old, seeing printing was in use, and Platina died Anno 1481? And how chanced it, that neither Onuphrius, nor Bellarmine, nor Baronius, who have had as free access into the Vatican library as any, could never light on these manuscripts? How chanced it, that none, since Bernartius, thought good to except in that sort against Platina? Onuphrius, Bellarmine, and Baronius's acknowledgment, that this story is in Platina, persuade me, that either Bernartius belyed the alderman, or the alderman belyed the dean, or the dean made a fool of the alderman: For, questionless, if there had been any such manuscripts, some of them would have found them out, and made it known to the world, ere this. For they are glad of narrower fig-tree leaves to cover their nakedness withal, than such manuscripts, if they were forth-coming: But, perhaps, you have some better answer behind than this.

Pap. I have. For what could you reply, if I answered that

1 Impudens aliquis nebulo interpolavit scripta Platinæ. Audivi ex Antonio Hetweldio, amplissimo laudatissimoque viro, Consulari Lovaniensi, dixisse sibi sæpius Engelbertum Boonium vidisse se Romæ, in Bibliotheca Vaticana, antiquissima Platinæ exemplaria manuscripta, sedulò examinasse, & de Joanne fœmina ne literam quidem reperisse. Bernartius de Utilitate legendæ Hist. lib. ii. p. 111.

which [1] Bellarmine hath upon another occasion, to wit, that Platina wrote not by pubick authority, nor took his history out of the publick registers of the church?

Prot. I could quickly tell you, that both Bellarmine and you speak without book. For, besides that, Platina [2] himself professeth, that he writ by the commandment of Sixtus the Fourth, [3] Onuphrius confesseth, that he followed Damasus, Anastasius, and such historiographers as had written before of the same matter.

Pap. But what say you to [4] Florimondus, whose answer is, That Platina reported it rather to shew his reading, than for that he thought it true?

Prot. What is Florimondus's reason for that?

Pap. Marry, if he had thought it true, saith [5] Florimondus, he would have exaggerated it, and made the worst of it, that thereby he might have revenged himself of the Popes at whom he was angry. For Paul the Second, as all men know, racked him, and deprived him of all his dignities, and justly cast him into prison, and kept him there as long as himself lived.

Prot. That Paul the Second racked Platina, and deprived him of his dignities, and kept him long in prison, is very true: But that he cast him justly into prison, is false. For [6] Trithemius witnesseth, that Paul the Second dealt [7] cruelly therein. Yet, suppose all to be true: Doth it follow in your Florimondus's logick, Paul the Second wronged Platina, *ergo,* Platina hated all Popes? And why not then: Sixtus the Fourth gratified Platina many ways: Sixtus the Fourth set Platina at liberty, and restored him to his dignities: *Ergo,* Platina loved all Popes? If one man's kindness could not work love towards all, it is not likely that one man's unkindness should breed an heart-burning against all: Wherefore, notwithstanding this, we may well think that Platina wrote as he thought: And the rather, for that, in the words following, he professeth, [8] that such a thing might well happen. What say you to Chalcocondylas, the Athenian, whom I named next before Platina, as a witness for us in this controversy?

Pap. I say, Chalcocondylas hath not this tale.

Prot. What, man? Are not [9] these his words? ' Constat mulierem quandam in Pontificatum esse subvectam, quia Sexus ignorabatur. Nam Italiæ occidentales penè omnes barbam radunt. Cum autem illa mulier gravida esset facta, & ad festum sive sacrificium prodiisset, peperit infantem inter sacrificium in conspectu Populi. Quaproper, ne decipiantur iterum, sed rem cognoscant, neque ambigant, Pontificis creati virilia tangunt, & qui tangit, acclamat: Mas nobis Dominus est.' That is, It is well known, that a certain woman was made Pope, by reason they knew not her sex: For all (almost) in the western parts of Italy, shave their beards. Now, when she was great with child, and came abroad to solemnise some day, or to say service, as she was at

1 Tom. ii. de Pœnitentia, lib. iii. cap. 13.   2 Procemio Lib. de Vitis Pontif. in Epistola ad Zistum iv.   3 Annotat. in Plat. in vit. S. Petri Apostoli.   4 Lib. citato, cap. 4. p. 36. 5 Si hæc vera sibi persuasisset, tanquam unguis in ulcere fuisset, & odium, quod in Pontifices conceperat, audacius evomuisset.   6 De Script. Ecclesiasticis, verbo, Bartholomeus Platina.   7 Crudelissimè.   8 Apparet, ea quæ dixi ex his esse, quæ fieri posse creduntur.   9 De Rebus Turcicis, lib. vi. p. 98.

service, she was delivered of a child in the sight of all the people. Wherefore, lest hereafter they should be deceived in like sort, they make trial of his manhood by touching, and he that toucheth proclaimeth, We have a man to our Pope.

Pap. I confess, these words are in Chalcocondylas, translated into Latin. But, I say with [1] Baronius, that, though it be in the Latin, yet that was by Clauserus the translator's bad dealing, who foisted it in. It was not written in the Greek by Chalcocondylas.

Prot. How proves Baronius that?

Pap. Nay, he meddles not with proving of it, but refers you over to Florimondus for it. For Florimondus hath excellently well, as Baronius [2] saith, discovered Clauserus's cousenage therein.

Prot. How, I pray you? For I know you have Florimondus at your finger's end.

Pap. Why, [3] Florimondus compared Clauserus's translation into Latin, with a Frenchman's translation of the same into French; and, by that, he saw this tale was not in Chalcocondylas, for he found nothing of it in the Frenchman's translation.

Prot. And is this Florimondus's reason, so much commended by Baronius, whereby he discovers Clauserus's cousenage? Now the vicar of S. Fools be ghostly father to them both : For why might not the Frenchman as well leave it out, as Clauserus put it in?

Pap. Oh, a faithful translator, as [4] Florimondus notes, durst not have left it out, if he had found it in the Greek.

Prot. Nor put it in, if he had not found it in the Greek : Durst he? And why may not we hold Clauserus as faithful an interpreter, as the Frenchman? Yea, why may not we hold him more faithful, seeing the Frenchman was a Papist? For [5] Papists hold it lawful, in translating, to omit offensive matter: And so doth no Protestant. The truth is, Clauserus shewed himself an honest man in translating it: And the Frenchman shewed himself a popish companion in concealing it: Which appears by the Greek, printed at Colen, *Anno* 1615, wherein it is, and by Gretser's confession, ' Fac sunt qui velint, ea quæ leguntur, Lib. vi. Hist. Laonici, non ab authore, sed ab interprete Clausero esse.' Going on thus, ' ægre credo. Nam, in Bibliotheca Bavarica Monachii, tres extant Historiæ hujus Manuscripti Codices, & unus ibidem in Bibliotheca Academiæ Ingolstadiensis, in quibus omnibus hoc de Joh. Papa fœmina fabulamentum legitur : Nec credibile est interpretem ipsos etiam Græcos Codices vitiare potuisse.' There are who hold opinion, [6] saith he, that, that which is read of Pope Joan, in the sixth book of Chalcocondylas, was never written by the author, but chopped in by Clauserus the translator; which I can hardly believe. For there are three MSS. of Chalcocondylas, in one library in Bavaria, and another in the library of the university of Ingolstadt; in all which, this tale of

1 Annal. Tom. x. ad Ann. 853, num. 66. Quamvis, apud Chalcocondylam Latinè redditum, ejusmodi fabulare petitur esse descripta, non tamen ab ipso authore positum scias, sed ab impostore Clausero fraudulenter appositum.   2 Ibid. Imposturam egregiè detexit Florimondus.
3 Florim. fabula Joannæ, cap. 6. num. 2.   4 Florim. Fab. Joannæ, cap. 6. num. 2. Fidus interpres prætermittere non ausus fuisset, si in Græco exemplari exaratum invenisset.
5 Gretser, lib. ii. de Jure, &c. prohibendi lib. malos, cap. 10.
6 Tom. ii. Defens. Bellar, lib. iii. cap. 26. col. 906.

Pope Joan is to be read: And it is not credible, that Clauserus, the translator, did or could corrupt all these Greek copies.

Pap. Well, if this answer please you not, know further, that it matters not what Chalcocondylas writes of this matter. For, in rendering the reason why she could not so well be known to be a woman, he writes, That in the western parts of Italy, all, almost, shave their beards; wherein he was grossly deceived, as [1] Florimondus observes. And, if in that, why not in the other?

Prot. He was not deceived in that of shaving: For, by the Pope's canons, the Italian priests, yea, all the priests of the western church, are to be shaven: ' Hic Papa (Anicetus) clericos comam & barbam radere in signum clericatus jussit,' [2] saith Pontacus. That is, Pope Anicetus commanded the clergy to shave both their heads and their beards, in token that they were of the clergy. And ' Occidentalis Ecclesiæ Clerum, ab ipsis Ecclesiæ Christianæ primordiis, barbam radendi morem tenuisse, [3] asserit Gregorius VII.' Pope Gregory VII. avoucheth, that, from the apostles days, the western clergy did shave their beards. To whom [4] Durandus, who lived about the year 1280, subscribeth; for he acknowledgeth, that before, and in his time, they were shaved, proving the lawfulness of it out of Ezekiel, and shewing the mysteries that are imported by it. Yea, [5] Johannes Pierius Valerianus, as you shall hear hereafter, witnesseth the same, imputing your error, in electing Pope Joan, to the ordinary shaving of beards; because, by that means, a man could hardly know a man from a woman. Will not Florimondus leave lying? What think you of Theodoricus de Niem, one of your Popes secretaries; is it doubtful whether I wrong him in calling him to be a witness in this case?

Pap. I think you wrong him. For [6] Florimondus reckons him among them who would readily have taken up such a tale against the Popes, if he had heard of it, and yet did not.

Prot. Florimondus is like himself, to say no worse, for these are [7] Theodoricus's own words: ' Johannes vocatus de Anglia, & fuit mulier de Moguntia nata, quæ studuit Athenis sub virili habitu, & in tantum profecit in artibus ipsis, quòd tandem veniens Romam, & per biennium in eadem schola artes ipsas liberales legit, & adeò sufficiens fuit, quòd etiam majores & nobiliores urbis ejus lectiones frequenter audierint. Ea postea in Papam concorditer eligitur á Romanis, & Papatum biennio & amplius tenuit; sed tunc, divitiis, ocio, & deliciis vacans, non potuit continere sicut prius fecit, dum ardenter in paupertate posita literarum studio insistebat, unde, dum quadam die in rogationibus cum clero Romano, sicut tunc moris erat, in solenni processione incederet, Papalibus ornata divitiis & ornamentis, edidit filium suum primogenitum, ex quodam ejus cubiculario conceptum, prope templum Pacis in urbe, ut adhuc vetus statua marmorea illic posita figurativè demonstrat. Unde summi Pontifices, dum ad Lateranensem de Basilica Principis Apostolorum, & è contrà vadunt, illud rectum iter

---

1 In eo quod de barba radenda asserit turpiter lapsus est. Flor. cap. 6. num. 1.
2 Chronograph. lib. ii.   3 Greg. vii. lib. viii. Regist. Epist. 10. ut refert Salmeron,
Disput. 18. in 1 Cor. xi. p. 167. & Baron. Annal. tom. i. ad ann. 58. num. 142.
4 Rational. divin. Offic. lib. ii. de Ministris, &c.   5 Pro sacerdotum barbis.
6 Cap. v. num. 5 & 6.   7 Lib. de Privilegiis & Juribus Imperii.

non faciunt, imò per alios vicos, per indirectum transeunt, illud aliquantulum prolongando.' That is, John, called English, was a woman born at Mentz, and she studied at Athens, going in man's apparel, where she profited so well in the arts, that coming to Rome, she read there the liberal sciences, and was held so sufficient a reader, that many of the better sort became her ordinary hearers. Afterwards with one consent she was chosen Pope, and lived in it two years and upward. But betaking herself, more than before, to her idleness and pleasure, she could not live continently as she did in her poor estate, when she plied her book diligently; whereupon one day, as she went with the clergy and people of Rome, according to the custom of that time, in solemn procession, being attired in papal manner, she was delivered of her first begotten son, begotten by one of her chamber, near the temple of Peace, which stands in the city; as is evident by an old marble image, which stands there to this day, to denote so much in a figure. And hereupon it is, that when the Popes go from the Vatican to St. John Lateran's, and back again, they go not the direct way thither, but by other streets further about, and so make their journey longer. Thus Theodoricus de Niem.

Pap. I do not remember any particular answer unto this man's testimony. Wherefore go on, and let me hear what the rest say. Yet if you will, for brevity sake, you may pass over the testimonies of Petrarch, and Boccace, and Lucidus, and of our countryman Higden, and some such others, because [1] Florimondus acknowledgeth that they speak to it.

Prot. Content. What think you of John of Paris, [2] who lived about the year 1280, and read publickly with great commendation, in the university of Paris, both divinity and humanity; believed not he this story?

Pap. I cannot tell. What say you?

Prot. I think he did. For shewing how sometimes a man may lawfully dispute and take exception against the Pope, in respect of his person, he [3] notes, that such a person may be chosen as is not capable; ' ut si esset fœmina, vel hæreticus, sicut fuerunt aliqui, qui ob hoc non enumerantur in Catalogo Paparum.' As for example, saith he, if he prove a woman, or an heretick, as some have done, who in that respect are not reckoned in the Catalogue of Popes.

Pap. It seems by his words, I cannot deny, that he alludes to such a matter. But did you not alledge Gotefridus Viterbiensis, for proof of the same? I pray you let me hear him speak, for [4] Dr. Harding reckons him among them who say nothing of her.

Prot. True, Dr. Harding doth so. But so doth no man else of his side, to my remembrance: Which is a great probability that Harding belyes him. But not to stand upon probabilities, the history itself puts the matter out of doubt; for between Leo the Fourth and Benedict the Third, we [5] read thus, not in the margent, nor in any other letter, but the current of the text, and same letter, *Papissa Joanna non numeratur.*

1 Cap. 3 & 4.   2 Trithem. de Script. Eccles. verbo, Joh. Paris. & Possevinus in Apparat.
sac. verbo, Joh. Paris.   3 De Potestate Regia & Papali, cap. 25.   4 Answer to
Bishop Jewel's Apology.   5 Gotefrid. Viterb. Chron. part. xx. in Catalogo Rom. Pont.

That is, Joan, the she Pope, is not registered. Whereby it is manifest that he knew of her, though he said little of her.

Pap. When lived this Gotefridus; and what manner of man was he?

Prot. He lived, as [1] Trithemius witnesseth, in the year 1185, and was a priest well seen in the holy scripture, and not ignorant of human knowledge; so that you have little cause to except against him either as a late writer, or a rash writer. But shall we at length hear what evidence Martinus Polonus affords us in this case?

Pap. With all my heart; for there are [2] divers who hold opinion that that which is in Polonus, touching Pope Joan, is cogged into him by Heroldus, who first printed him, or some such like fellow.

Prot. Do they say so? And can they shew me any book, written or printed, wherein it is not in [3] Polonus, thus?'Post hunc leonem Johannes Anglus, natione Moguntinus, sedit an. 2. mens. 5. diebus 4. Hic, ut asseritur, fœmina fuit, & quum in puellari ætate à quodam suo amasio in habitu virili Athenas ducta fuit, in diversis scientiis ita profecit, ut nullus sibi par inveniretur: adeò ut post Romæ [4] trivium legens, magnos magistros, & discipulos & auditores haberet. Et, quum in urbe, & vita & scientia, magnæ opinionis esset, in papam concorditer eligitur. Sed in papatu per familiarem suum imprægnatur: verùm tempus partus ignorans, quum de sancto Petro in Lateranum tenderet, angustiata inter Colosseum & S. Clementis ecclesiam peperit, & postea mortua ibidem (ut dicitur) sepulta fuit. Et, propterea quòd dominus papa semper eandem viam obliquat, creditur omninò à quibusdam, quòd ad detestationem facti hoc faciat. Nec ideo ponitur in catalogo sanctorum pontificum, tam propter mulieris sexum, quàm propter deformitatem facti.' Which in effect, sounds thus in English: After this Leo, John English, by her country of Mentz, sat two years, five months, and four days. This Pope, as they say, was a woman, and being carried in her youth in man's apparel to Athens, by one who was in love with her, she profited so much in divers kinds of learning, that she had no fellow; insomuch that coming to Rome, and reading there grammar, logick, and rhetorick, she had of the greatest rabbins there many auditors and scholars. And being much esteemed of in that city, both for her life and learning, with one voice she was chosen Pope. Now in the time of her papacy, she was got with child by some of her familiars; and not knowing she was so near her reckoning, as she went from St. Peter's to St. John Lateran, between the Coloss, and St. Clement's church, she was delivered of a child; but died thereon, and was there, as they say, buried. And, because the lord the Pope doth always shun that way, it is thought by some, that he doth it in dislike of the accident. And she is not numbered among the popes; partly because of her sex, partly because of the filthiness of her fact. Can they, I say, shew me any book written or printed, wherein it is not in Polonus thus? Doth not Onuphrius, and Bellarmine, and Bernartius, and Ba-

---

1 De Script. Eccles. verbo, Gotefridus Viterb. Gotefridus was Imperialis aulæ Capellanus, & Notarius. Possevin. Apparat. sac. verb. Gotefrid. Viterb.   2 Verius dixerim, hæc omnia ex Heroldi Officina manasse, &c. Florim. cap. 2. num. 5.   3 Polonus in Chron. ad An. 855.   4 Gra. loquitur Dia. vera docet, Re. verba collocat. Mu. canit. Ar. numerat. Ge. ponderat. As. colit astra. The three first make Trivium. The four latter Quadrivium.

ronius, and N. D. with many others of your side, who shew more wit than honesty in pleading this case, confess that Polonus writ this; and that this is to be found in Polonus? Doth not [1] Antoninus, who lived long before Heroldus, cite it as it is in Polonus at this day?

Pap. Yes, the most do. But some, as I told you before, suspect the worst, and namely [2] Dr. Bristow; for he reports that, many years ago, a Protestant, who was counted a great historian, brought out the same Martinus, in a fair written hand, to shew him this story. And behold, she was not in the text, but in the margent, in another hand. Whereupon, when he saw that, now I perceive, quoth he, that this author also faileth you.

Prot. What Protestant was that, who had Martinus in so fair a written hand? Can you tell me his name, or the place where he abode, that I may inquire further, for satisfying myself in the truth of this matter?

Pap. Nay, I know no more than I have told you. For the doctor names no particular circumstance. But I make no question of the truth of it. For I presume that such a doctor would not lye.

Prot. Oh, no. A popish priest lye! that is not credible, no more than it is credible, that [3] a priest of the order of Aaron would deceive. But you know what a long story that [4] doctor tells, of one Margaret Jessop, who was cured of her lameness by the sacrament of miracle, that was kept at St. Gudilac's church at Brussels; and how he amplifies every point, and sets it out with all the circumstances, as though it were as true as the gospel; whereas [5] the senate of Brussels, by way of proclamation within a few years after, did discover all to be but a pack of knavery. And therefore you must pardon me, if notwithstanding I give him not the lye, yet I believe him not in this, considering it is an old said saw: ' Qui versatur in generalibus, versatur dolose:' He that speaks only in generality, means falsely.

Pap. Well, be it that Polonus writ this, yet know you that as [6] Bellarmine and [7] N. D. note, he was a very simple man; and that his manner of writing was vain, and nothing like to be true in [8] Dr. Harding's judgment. Yea know, that he was only famous for tales, for that is [9] Bernartius's censure of him.

Prot. See the rashness of our latter generation of papists. Polonus was an [10] archbishop, and the Pope's penitentiary. [11] He was learned in the holy scriptures, and not ignorant of secular learning; he was one whom [12] Platina relied on much, for matters of history, and thought worthy the commendation of great learning, and singular good life. He was the man, whom the author of Fasciculus Temporum, and Jacobus Bergomensis, two good historiographers, professed that they followed especially. And yet, with our present papists, he is but a simple man, &c. Are you not ashamed of this exception?

1 Summa Hist. Part. ii. Tit. xvi. cap. 1. sect. 7. cap. 10. Demand 45. pag. 371.
venit. non decipiet nos. 1. Mac. vii. 76. in Vulg.
5 Meterran. Hist. Belg. Lib. x.
7] 3. Convers. part ii. cap. 5. num. 29. pag. 399.
Challenge.
homo. Lib. ii. de Utilitate legend. Hist. pag. 113.
nitentiarius Papæ. Possevin. Apparat. sacer. verbo, Martinus Polonus.
11 Trithem. de Script; Eccles. verbo, Martinus-singularisque vitæ. Plat in vita Victor. iii.

2 In his reply to Dr. Fulke.
3 Dixerunt: Homo sacerdos de semine Aaron
4 Motive 5.
6 Lib. iii. de Rom. Pont. cap. 24.
8 Answer to Bishop Jewel's
9 Martinus Polonus, fabulis tantum celebris, cætera obscurus
10 Archiep. Cosentinus, & Pœ-
12 Vir magnæ doctrinæ

Pap. No.   For I will prove his simplicity by many arguments.

Prot. And how, I pray you ?

Pap. Why, first by this, [1] that he would needs persuade us that Pompilius, who was Numa's father, succeeded next to Romulus.   For this is a mere tale, and yet he writes it as a truth.

Prot. Away, away. ' Post Romulum regnavit Numa Pompilius, [2] saith Polonus.   That is, Numa Pompilius reigned next after Romulus ; but not Pompilius who was Numa's father.

Pap. [3] Secondly, he would persuade us, that Numa, of a tribune of the people, was made a King, which is another tale.

Prot. He would not, for he [4] writes plainly, that tribunes were ordained sixteen years after the reign of the Roman Kings, when the people complained of the hard measure that they received at the hands of the consuls and of the senate.   He knew no such officers in the time of the kings.

Pap. [5] Thirdly, he would persuade us, that the church, which is now called Sancta Maria Rotunda, and in old time Pantheon, built by one Agrippa, was before that the house of one Cybele, supposed to be the mother of the gods, which is a toy, and a conceit of an idle head.

Prot. This is false too.   For [6] he saith only, that Pantheon was built by Agrippa at Cybele's motion, who was the mother of the gods, which is confirmed for true by many others ; he saith not, that it was first Cybele's, and afterwards turned to the honour of all the gods.

Pap. [7] Fourthly, he would make us believe, that that famous theatre, made by Titus, was the Temple of the Sun ; which is mere foolery.

Prot. No, no, *Ante Colosseum fuit templum Solis*, saith [8] Polonus : before the Coloss there was a Temple of the Sun.   But, that Titus's theatre was that temple, Polonus saith not.

Pap. [9] Yes, he saith, that the Temple of Peace, commonly called the Everlasting Temple, fell the same night that Christ was born ; whereas it is plain by all ancient histories, that it was not built till Vespasian's days, a good many years after Christ was born.

Prot. The ancient histories witness, that Vespasian built a Temple of Peace : but that does not argue, there was no Temple of Peace before.   Some write, that Romulus built a Temple of Peace.   And [10] Clemens Alexandrinus writes, that Numa built a Temple of Peace. But it concerns not Polonus's credit, whether there was any or none ; for he saith not, that the Temple of Peace fell the same night that Christ was born.   He only [11] saith, that the golden image which Romulus set up in his palace, avowing, that it should not fall down, till a virgin was delivered of a child, fell down in the night wherein Christ was born ; though, if he had said the other, the matter had not been

1 Bernart. Lib. citato, pag. 113.   Florim. cap. 2. num. 6.   2 Lib. de quatuor majeribus Reguis & Rom. urbis exordio. cap. de Rectoribus & Regimine urbis, pag. 10.
3 Bernart. & Florim. locis citatis.   4 Supputat. post exactos Reges ad Christum usque. cap. de binis Coss. pag. 12.   5 Bernart. & Florim. locis citatis.
6 In Chron. in Domitian. pag. 38.   7 Bernart. & Florim. locis citatis.
8 Lib. de 4. majoribus Reguis, & cap. de Templis Idoloram, p. 8.   9 Bernart. & Florim. locis citatis.   10 Stromat. Lib. v.   11 In Chron. ad Annum Christi 1

great. For he was neither the first, nor the last; [1] many of good note, both before, and since, have written as much; namely, [2] Petrus Damianus, [3] Petrus de Natalibus, [4] Jacobus de Voragine, and the author of that first sermon upon Christ's nativity, which is extant among the sermons ascribed to [5] Bernard. If you have no better arguments to prove his simplicity, you may soon prove yourself a malicious slanderer.

Pap. My arguments are good against him, as you shall hear more fully anon. But for the present tell me, what Marianus Scotus hath that makes for you. For I cannot think it is true, that Marianus' Scotus hath this story.

Prot. You jest, I am sure. For do we not read thus in [6] him? *Leo Papa obiit kalend. Augusti. Huic successit Joanna mulier, an. 2. mens. 5. dies. 4.* that is, Leo the Pope died in the kalends of August. After him succeeded Joan the woman, who sat two years, five months, and four days. And, which I would have you note by the way, this Marianus' [7] was born in the year 1028. and [8] lived in great credit in his life-time, and when he died was held a saint; and at this day is reputed, by your [9] Baronius, *Nobilis Chronographus,* a worthy chronologer.

Pap. [10] I do not deny but that you may read so in some printed copies. But I deny, there is any such thing to be read in the more ancient hand-written originals, found in Flanders, and other places.

Prot. Do you not deny but that we may read so in some printed copies? Verily you might have yielded unto me, that I may read so in all printed copies, for you are not able to produce any printed copy (except it be of yesterday's printing) wherein it is not. But you deny it to be in the more ancient hand-written originals found in Flanders, and other places. And upon what ground, I pray, deny you that? For [11] Baronius, your cardinal historiographer, confesseth, that that ancient hand-written original, which the first printed copy followed, hath the story. And it is so ordinary with you papists to bely hand-written originals, that he, who knows you, cannot in wisdom believe any of you upon your bare words.

Pap. I have good ground of that which I deny, I would you should well know. But first, I challenge you to make proof that we papists, as you call us, belye any hand-written originals, for methinks you therein charge us deeply.

Prot. The proof of that is plain. For, first, one of your bishops, even [12] Bishop Lindan, to make good his own conceit of the right reading of the text, John xxi. 22. (about which you know there hath been hot contention) which he maintained to be this: If so I will he remain

---

1 Tabella de collapso Romæ Pacis Templo, tempore Christi ortus, multiplicium haud vulgarium fuit scriptorum authoritate firmata. Baron. Annal. Tom. x. ad Ann. 853. Num. 61.
2 Hom. quæ legitur apud Lips. Tom. vii. & Satur. tom. vi.   3 In Catal. Sanct.
lib. ii. cap. 1.   4 Ser. e de Die Nativit. Dom.   5 Fol. 297. Edit.
Paris. 1617.   6 Marian. Scotus in Chron. ætate 6. ad An. 854.
7 So he himself writeth in Chron. ad Ann. 1028.   8 Ab omnibus honore habatur, & non sine opinione sanctitatis sepelitur. Trithemius de Script. Eccles. verb. Marianus.
Joh. Major. de Gestis Scotorum. Lib. iii. cap. 5.   9 Annal. Tom. i. ad Ann. 34. Num. 140.   10 N. D. Lib. citate, Num. 27. p. 397.   11 In scripto Codice ex quo prodiit prima Editio ita legitur. Baron. Annal. tom. x. ad Ann. 853. Num. 59.
12 De Opt. Gen. Interpret. lib. ii. cap. 6.

till I come, what is that to thee? Alledged for proof thereof the testimony of an ancient hand-written original kept at Aix in Germany; whereas, in truth, it is not so read in that copy, but according to the Greek : if I will that he remain till I come, what is that to thee? As [1] Franciscus Lucas, a man of your own coat, witnesseth.   Again, the same Bishop Lindan [2] protested, that he saw an ancient hand-written original of the Psalms in Hebrew, found in England; whereby it was apparent, that the Hebrew Bible is defective at this day in some points.   Yet the same [3] Lucas, who came to the sight of the same copy, assures us, that that Psalter makes rather to the contrary.   In like manner [4] Onuphrius, your friar above-named, alledged certain hand-written originals of Maximus, a monk, by which it is manifest, as he saith, that Honorius the First condemned the Monothelites: yet Turrian, the Jesuit, who had access to the self-same manuscripts, confesseth (as [5] Andradius relateth) that Maximus makes no mention of Honorius condemning them.   And whereas your great Goliah of Gath, [6] Bellarmine I mean, to prove that Honorius's name was thrust by fraud into the sixth general council among the Monothelites, affirmeth, that Anastasius (which was then in written hand only) did testify so much; now, that Anastasius [7] is printed, we see Bellarmine's fraud.   For Anastasius testifieth no such thing.   [8] Anastasius himself reckons Honorius for a Monothelite.   In this controversy about Dame Joan, divers of your [9] proctors plead, as out of the hand-written originals of the same Anastasius, that, upon Leo the Fourth's death, the see was void but fifteen days, and then Benedict was chosen.   Yet our printed Anastasius makes it evident, they belyed the hand-written Anastasius; for, in the printed, there is not a word of the number of days between Leo's death, and Benedict's election.   Lastly, whereas your grand historiographer, Baronius, was informed by letters, from such as yourself, that Zoticus was shot through with darts, and so martyred; and he, who certified him thereof, assured him, that he sent a true copy out of the hand-written original acts of Zoticus, whereupon Baronius put it in print : [10] Baronius was glad to retract it since; because (though he light upon the same acts) he could find no such thing in them.   How say you? Do not these particulars prove, that many of you are excellent at facing matters out, under pretence of hand-written originals, which, when they come to viewing, make nothing for you?

Pap. If all be true you say, it will prove, I grant, some bad dealing in some few persons among us.   But you shall never be able to prove as much by me; for I will prove whatsoever I say.

Prot. Go to then; make you proof unto me that this story is not in the more ancient hand-written originals of Marianus Scotus; and, if you do so, I will yield.

1 Notat. in Joh. xxi. 22.   2 Lib. citato, cap. 3, & 5.   3 Notat. in Psal. xiii.   4 Annot. in Platin. in Honorio i.   5 Defens. Fidei Trident. Lib. ii.   6 Lib. iv. de Rom. Pont. cap. 11.   7 Moguntiæ, ann. 1601.   8 In Leone ii.   9 Onuph. Bell. Bernart. locis supr. cit. & Florim. cap. 14. num. 1. & Sanders de visibili Monarch. lib. vii. pag. 612.
10 Quod arundinibus percussum martyrium consummasse Zoticum diximus, emendamus. Hæud enim fidelem nacti sumus testem, qui ea se ex Actis ejus descripsisse, per literas ad me datas, testatus est.   Accepi post hæc Acta Martyria, & nihil tale in illis reperi In Martyrologium Rom. Jan. 10. L.

Pap. Will you so ? Then I argue thus : [1] if this story had been in the most ancient hand-written originals of Marianus Scotus, they, who writ since his time, would have alledged him for proof of it. But no man, till now of late, alledged him for proof of it. Wherefore this was not in the most ancient hand-written originals of Marianus Scotus.

Prot. I deny the consequence of your proposition, viz. they who writ since Marianus's time, would have alledged him for proof of it, if so be it had been written in the most ancient hand-written originals. For, First, till of late, there was no controversy about it, which made men less careful to avouch their authors for it. Secondly, Marianus's chronicle, till printing came to some perfection, was rare, it seems, and hard to come by. For [2] Polonus, reckoning up the books out of which he took his story, names not Marianus among them. No more doth [3] Onuphrius, where he reckons up the authors whom Platina followed. Onuphrius, I say, doth not reckon Marianus among them. Jacobus Bergomensis and Wernerus Rolenink, in their prefaces to their histories, wherein they shew whom they followed, pass by Marianus as a man unknown to them. And so do others. But, for making of this matter plain, tell me, have you not heard, [4] that Anastasius the Second, one of your popes, would have restored Acatius, the bishop of Constantinople, who stood excommunicated by some of your pope's predecessors, but that God prevented your pope, and struck him with a fearful death ?

Pap. Yes, I have heard so much. But [5] I take it to be as vain a fable as this of Pope Joan.

Prot. Yet you cannot deny but that it is recorded for true, by [6] Anastasius Bibliothecarius, by [7] Rhegino, by [8] Marianus Scotus, by [9] Sigebert, by [10] Luitprandus, by [11] Albo Floriacensis, by [12] Gratian, by [13] Polonus, by [14] Platina, by [15] Volaterran, by [16] Jacobus Bergomensis, by [17] Wernerus Rolenink, by [18] Trithemius, by [19] Charanza, by [21] Johannes de Turrecremata, and [17] by others.

Pap. No, indeed, I cannot deny that, for all these, I know, report it as true.

Prot. Yea, and that in their most ancient hand-written originals : Do they not, for aught you have seen or heard to the contrary ?

Pap. Good. But what of all this ?

Prot. You shall see anon. In the mean time tell me only, whether they, who writ since Rhegino and Marianus's time, alledge Rhegino, or Marianus, for the author of it?

Pap. [18] Bergomensis, Rolenink, Trithemius, Turrecremate, [18] and such like, alledge Gratian for the author of it. But I do not remember that any historiographer alledgeth Rhegino, or Marianus Scotus, for it.

Prot. If this, touching Anastasius the Second, may be in the most ancient hand-written originals of Rhegino and Marianus Scotus,

1 Si ita sit ut ipsi fingunt, qui post Marianum de Joanna scripserunt, nonne ipsum Marianum in sua sententiae patrocinium ascivissent, & suam hac arce opinionem munivissent. Florim. cap. 2. num. 4. 2 Praefat. in Chron. 3 Annot. in Plat. in vit. B. Petri. 4 Anastasius Papa voluit occulte revocare Achatium Constantinop. Episc. damnatum, quare divino nutu percussus est. 5 Bell. Lib. iv. de Rom. Pont. cap. 10. & Append. ad lib. de summo Pont. & Pighius Eccles. Hierarch. lib. iv. cap. 8.
6 De Vit. Pontif. in Anastas. II. 7 Chron. lib. i. ad ann. 414.
8 Aetate 6. ad ann. 499. 9 In Chron. ad ann. 491. 10 De Vit. Pont. in Anastas. II. 11 De Vit. Pont. in vita Anastas. II.
12 Dist. 16. c. Anastasius. 13 In Chron. ad ann. 498. 14 De Vit. Pont. in Anastas. II. 15 Lib. xxii. 16 Supplem. Chron. ad ann. 495.
17 Fascic. Temp. ad ann. 484. 18 De Script. Eccl. verbo, Anastas. 19 Summa Conc. 20 Summa de Eccl. lib. ii. cap. 103. 21 Nauclerus, Antoninus, locis infra cit. 22 Locis supra citatis. 23 Nauclerus, vol. ii. Chronogr. general. 17. 24 Antoninus, part II. Hist. Tit. 11. cap. 1. Sect. viii.

though they, who have written since their times, alledge them not for authors of it; why may not the other, touching Pope Joan, be in the most ancient hand-written originals of Marianus Scotus, though they, who writ since his time, alledge him not for the author of it? Have you not another argument?

Pap. Yes, for [20] Bellarmine writes, that he who set forth Krantius's Metropolis at Colen, in the year 1574, doth witness, *in antiquissimis exemplaribus Mariani Scoti non haberi Joannem fœminam*, That in the ancient copies of Marianus Scotus there is no mention of Joan the woman.

Prot. And what was he that set forth Krantius, can you tell me that? Doth Bellarmine, or [21] N. D. (who twangs on the same string with Bellarmine) name him?

Pap. No, but what is that to the purpose? He, whosoever he was, witnesseth so much. And is not that enough?

Pap. No, believe me; no reason that a nameless sir should be credited against all printed copies, especially if it be true, which [22] Bellarmine saith, in another case: *author sine nomine, est sine authoritate;* a man without a name is without credit [23]; and, *canon à concilio, cujus ne nomen quidem extet, facilè contemni potest.* A canon out of a council, whose name is not known, may very well be scorned. But would you know why Bellarmine and N. D. did not name him? Questionless, not for that they know not what his name was; but because he was but a base fellow, a printer, a poor batchelor of the law; a man of small esteem in the world; for he is named, in the first page of the book, *Gerwinus Calenius Lippiensis*, and his whole stile is no greater, than *Legum Licentiatus.* And what was such a fellow, to carry away such a matter as this, upon his bare word? But, which is more to be marked, this fellow barely saith, without any proof in the world, that the manuscripts of Marianus Scotus, which are extant, discover the falshood of them who put this story into the printed Marianus; implying, that all manuscripts, not the ancient only, want it. Which neither Bellarmine, nor N. D. durst, or dare avouch, the contrary being confessed directly by Baronius, and may out of themselves be gathered by consequence. Besides, he saith as much for clearing of Sigebert, as Marianus Scotus, for [24] these are his very words: ' quæ hic author de Johanne fœmina refert, in odium Romanorum pontificum conficta fuisse ab illis, quos ipse deceptus sequitur, ut alios omittamus quos Onuphrius in Platinam scribens recenset, tesantur Marianus Scotus & Sigebertus, quorum quæ supersunt M S. exemplaria, fraudem illorum detegunt qui eorum impressis voluminibus id inseverunt.' That this, which the author thereof reports touching Pope Joan, is but counterfeit stuff, devised to make the Pope odious; to say nothing of such proofs as Onuphrius gives in his annotations upon Platina, Marianus Scotus and Sigebert do testify; whose manuscripts, remaining on record, discover their falshood, who have chopped this tale into their printed volumes. And yet neither Bellarmine, nor N. D. durst alledge him to prove that Sigebert is corrupted.

1 Lib. iii. de Rom. Pon. cap. 24.   2 Lib. citato, num. 27. pag. 397.
3 Lib. iv. de Rom. Pont. cap. 13.   4 Lib. i. de Matrimonio, cap. 17.
5 Annot. in Lib. ii. Krantii Metrop.

Pap. Peradventure they durst have alledged him to that purpose also, though they did not; for, doubtless, there is no such story in Sigebert.

Prot. Why? But all the printed copies do convince you of shameless lying, in so saying. For thus [1] they read: 'Johannes papa Anglicus. Fama est hunc Johannem fœminam fuisse & uni soli familiari cognitam qui eam complexus est, & gravis facta peperit papa existens. Quare eam inter pontifices non numerant quidam, ideo nomini numerum non facit.' John the English pope. The report is, that this John was a woman, and that one only, who used to lie with her, knew so much; and that at length, even in the time of her papacy, she was delivered of a child. Whereupon it is that some reckon her not among the popes, and that there is not one Pope John the more in number for her. What say you, is it not even thus?

Pap. I confess the printed copies make for you in this also. But, in the ancient, true, and approved copies of Sigebert in writing, this, which you talk of, is not: *aliquis impudens nebulo interpolavit scripta ejus.* Some paltry fellow hath been tampering with his writings, as [2] Bernartius notes. Marry whether it was Geffrey the monk, or one Robert, who continued the story of Sigebert for some years, I know not; but between them it is as [3] Onuphrius supposeth. And I am sure Sigebert never writ it. [4] *Cui rei adserendæ fidus & adpositus mihi testis est Gilbertus Genebrardus,* which is witnessed very fully by Genebrard.

Prot. The [5] canonists, when popes alledge popes for proof, do note, that it is *familiaris probatio.* Meaning such belike, as that in the proverb, Ask my fellow, if I be a thief. And so, methinks, is this of yours, which is fetched from your fellow Genebrard. But what saith Genebrard for your purpose?

Pap. [6] Genebrard saith, there be many manuscripts of Sigebert, wherein this is not.

Prot. Yea, but that is the question. And how doth Genebrard prove it? Names he any place where they are, or any person who hath seen them?

Pap. No not he, but [7] N. D. doth, for in the monastery of Gemble, in Flanders, there is extant, saith N. D. the original of Sigebert, which wants this story.

Prot. What! the original of Sigebert? Who told N. D. that the original of Sigebert was in that monastery? Or was he there, and saw it with his own eyes?

Pap. N. D. saith nought of that. But you may have further proof thereof out of [8] Bellarmine; for he writes that Molanus, a doctor of Lovain, saw the copy.

Prot. But Bellarmine saith not, that Molanus judged it to be the original of Sigebert; which yet N. D. avoucheth as confidently, as if he had held the candle, while Sigebert wrote it. Neither doth Bellar-

---

1 Sigebert. Gemblacensis in Chronico ad an, 854. Printed at Paris, 1513.   2 Lib. supra citato, pag. 110.   3 Annot. in Plat. in Vit. Joh. viii.   4 Bernartius loco citato.   5] 9 q. 3. patet. in Glossa Joh. Andrew. Familiaris est hæc Probatio quum Papa alium Papam adducit in testem.   6 Lib. iv. Chronolog. ad ann. 855.   7 Lib. citato Num. 27, page 397.   8 Lib. iv. de Rom. Pont. cap. 24.

mine tell us, to whom Molanus told this; or in what book he writ this. So that yet there is no just proof brought, that so much as one copy wants it, much less that it is foisted into such copies as have it.

Pap. Is there not? Hearken then to Florimondus, [1] who writes, that one Protasius, the credit of the order of Franciscans, swore to him that he saw such a book in that monastery; and that, reading it all over, he found no word touching such a pope.

Prot. This would have moved me somewhat to believe, that the copy in that monastery wants this, if Florimondus had sworn for the satisfying of his reader, touching the truth of his report; as he urged the Franciscan to swear to him for the justifying of that, which he told. But Florimondus delivers it barely of his word. And I have found him oft false of his tongue. Wherefore I cannot trust him. [2] Florimondus would make us believe, that Michael the emperor's letter sent to Pope Nicholas, wherein the emperor objecteth whatsoever might sound to the disgrace of the Roman see, is extant to this day: Yet [3] Baronius testifieth, that they are not extant. He writes, that the Pope burnt them. Yea, Florimondus himself in another [4] chapter (forgetting the proverb, *Mendacem esse memorem oportet*) confesseth, that they are lost. Yet be it so, that the copy which is in that monastery wants this: Unless Florimondus can prove that it is the original, or truly copied out of the original, he speakes not to the point, as I shall shew by and by.

Pap. Yea but he proves that it is the very original itself. For there (as [5] he saith) Sigebert lived, there he wrote this book with his own hand, there he left it at his death as a monument of his love. There it is shewed by the monks to such as come thither, for a rare and ancient monument.

Prot. Sigebert lived not there, when he writ that book. He writ both that, and many others, in the monastery of St. Vincentius, within the city of Metensis. Which I speak not of my own head, as Florimondus doth, but out of [6] Trithemius. For in Trithemius you may read so.

Pap. Yet you cannot disprove Florimondus, in that which he saith of his dying there; and bequeathing of that book by his will, to that monastery for a legacy.

Prot. No indeed. But neither can he prove his own saying. Now you know that *Actori, non Reo, incumbit Probatio:* The plaintiff, and not the defendant, must bring in his proof. That which is nakedly affirmed, is sufficiently answered, when it is barely denied. *Si dicere, probare est; pari Ratione, inficiari, refutare est:* As you may read in [7] Bellarmine.

Pap. Why, but the monks of that house do shew it to all comers as Sigebert's own.

1 Protasius Franciscani Ordinis decus, ad stringendam fidem prius jerejurando devinctus, mihi obtestatus est, &c. Florim. cap. 5. Num. 5.
2 Cap. 27. Num. 6 Extat adhuc Michaelis ad Nicolaum Epistola, &c.
3 Annal. Tom. x. ad. an. 863. Num. 75. Non extat ipsæ blasphemæ Michaelis Imperatoris Literæ, traditæ sunt Igni.   4 Chap. 10. num. 4.   5 Florimond. cap. citat. num. 5.
6 Sigebertus, cum in Cœnobio S Vincentii Metensi ad instruendos pueros esset positus, scripsit Historiarum Lib. Trithem. de Script. Ecclesiasticis, Verbo, Sigebertus.
7 Lib. iii. de Rom. Pont. cap. 29.

Prot. That I believe. For I have [1] read of a monk, who gave out, that he had brought from the east some of the sound of the bells, which hung in Solomon's Temple [2]: And that he could shew, among other relicks, some of the hairs which fell from the Seraphical angel, when he came to imprint the five wounds of Christ in St. Francis's body. And I have [3] read of others, who shew the pilgrims that go to Jerusalem a three-cornered stone, and bear them in hand that it is the very stone whereof [4] David spoke, saying, ' The stone, which the builders refused, is the head of the corner.'

Pap. Tush, those monks do but cozen folks.

Prot. No more do the monks of Gemble, in my opinion ; though, it may be, they are rather cozened, than cozeners. For many a Papist persuades himself he hath that, which indeed he hath not. As for example : Many papists are persuaded they have that Sindon, wherein Christ's body was lapped, when it was interred, wherein (as they say) is to be seen to this day the picture of Christ ; whereas indeed ([5] by some of their own men's confessions) they have but one made after that fashion. Again, many are persuaded, they have one of those nails, wherewithal Christ was nailed on the cross : [6] Whereas they have but one fashioned after that nail ; or at most, some nail wherewithal some martyr of Christ was tormented. And in like manner are they themselves deceived in their conceit of other relicks. But that, which makes me most suspicious of your monks of Gemble, is this : I have read, that among many other goodly relicks, which are shewed at Rome by the Pope's commandment, there is a bible shewed, which they say was written by St. Jerom himself, even with his own hands ; and yet one of your own profession professeth freely, that he, perusing it thoroughly, found it was written by the commandment of one King Robert, and by a bungling scrivener : ' Illum ego diligentius inspectum comperi scriptum esse jussu Regis (ut opinor) Roberti, Chirographo Hominis imperiti,' saith [7] Valla. Now I suppose, if we had access to Gemble in Flanders, perhaps we might find as much for discovering of their falshood, in that which they report of the original of Sigebert; as your fellow found for the discovering of the others falshood, who gave out, that the Bible which they shewed was of St. Jerom's writing.

Pap. Suppose it be not the original of Sigebert which is at Gemble; yet you will not deny (I hope) but that it is some ancient copy, which they esteem so much of.

Prot. Be it so. But will you thereupon conclude, that the author never writ it? I presume you are not so ignorant, but you know, that words, sentences, and memorable accidents have, sometimes by negligence, sometimes by wilfulness, been left out of copies? As for example, the words (No not the son of man, Mark xiii. 32. Whereon your [8] Jesuits, as upon a chief foundation, built their doctrine of Æquivocation) were wanting in many Greek copies, as [9] St. Ambrose testifieth ; and yet both you and we do hold opinion, that they were set

---

1 Vergerius Annotat. in Catalogum Hæret. Romæ conflatum, An. 1559 Fol. 17.   12 Ibid.
3 Bellonius Observat. lib. ii. cap. 83.   4 Psalm. cxviii. 22.
5 Gretzer. lib. i. de Cruce, cap. 65. page 240.   6 Idem lib. i. cap. 20. page 50.
7 De Donatione Constantini.   8 Apology in defence of ecclesiastical subordination) England, cap. 12. fol. 200.   9 Lib. v. de Fide, cap. 7.

down by the author in the first copy. In like sort, the story touching Christ's sweating agony, and the angel's comforting him, Luke xxii. 43, 44. was not to be found in many copies, as [1] Hilary and [2] Jerome witness, Which came to pass, not for that it was never written by St. Luke, but (as [3] Bellarmine in part, and [4] Sixtus Senensis more fully notes) for that some simple catholicks, fearing it made for the Arians, rased it out of their books. So the story of the adulterous woman, in John the viii, was [5] wanting in many manuscripts both Greek and Latin, and namely in a manuscript of [6] Eusebius; yet that doth nothing prejudice the truth of our printed copies at this day, in which it is; no not in the opinion of you that are papists. For as [7] Bellarmine proveth out of Austin, this history was blotted out of many books, by the enemies of God's truth. In much like sort (it seemeth) that the words of Ælfricus, which make against transubstantiation, were cut out of a fragment of an epistle of his in the library of Worcester, as [8] M. Fox proveth evidently. And as this story of Pope Joan is cut out of a very fair [9] manuscript of Ranulfus Cestrensis, which is to be seen [10] at this day in the library of New College in Oxford.

Pap. Is this story torn (indeed) out of Ranulfus Cestrensis in New College in Oxford? Who, think you, was so mad?

Pap. Why, who but a Papist? For do not [11] they give direction, that *quæ famæ proximorum, & præsertim Ecclesiasticorum, & Principum detrahunt, corrigentur atque expurgentur?* That such things should be altered or put out, which tend to the discredit of the clergy? And doth not this touch at the quick their ecclesiastical state? Doth not Possevine advise, that the [12] note in John Nevison the lawyer, which mentioneth Pope Joan, should be rased out? *Dele* ([13] saith he) *quia Johannes hæc Fæmina chimæra est, & impostura calumniatorum:* Blot it out, or rend it out, quoth Possevine, for it is but a fiction, and a forgery.

Pap. You are too suspicious of papists. But, if these answers whereon I have hitherto insisted, please you not, let it be as you would have it, that all these historians writ so. [14] Yet I deny, that any credit is herein to be given unto them, because they report it but by hearsay, with *ut asseritur.*

Prot. That is false, For Marianus Scotus reports it simply without *ut asseritur,* as before I shewed. And Laonicus Chalcocondylas reports it as a certain truth, saying Constat, &c. So do Ravisius Textor and [15] others.

Pap. That, which you say of Marianus Scotus, is true, if we were to be judged by the printed copy, which Heroldus set out. But I

1 De Trinitat. lib. x.　　2 Lib. ii. contra Pelag.　　3 Lib. i. de Verbo Dei. cap. 16.　　4 Bibl. sanctæ lib. i.　　5 Jansen. Concord. Evang. cap. 76.
5 Euseb. lib. iii. hist. cap. 39. teste Bellar. lib. i. de. Verbo Dei. cap. 16.
7 Ibid.　　8 Acts and monuments, Allegations against the six articles, page 1304. edit. 1570　　9 Lib. v.　　10. An. 1606.
11 Index lib. prohib. per Clementem VIII. De Correctione lib.
12 Joh. Nevisanus Sylva Nuptialis. p. 319.　　13 In apparat. sacro, Verbo, Joh. Nevisanus.　　14 Onuph. Annot. in Platin. in Vit. Joh. VIII. per ut aiunt, & tradant, eam refert.　　15 Barthol. Cassanæus 2. Part. Catalogi Gloriæ Mundi, mea Consideratio. Turrecremat Sum. de Eccles. part. ii. lib. iv. cap. 20. Cælius Rhodiginus antiquarum lectionum, lib. viii. cap. 1.

C 4

can assure you, that Heroldus unconscionably corrupted this place, and many others. For it is thus [1] written in the written copy, after which the first edition was printed. *Johannes qui, ut asseritur, fuit Mulier*. John, who, as the report goes, was a woman.

Prot. So your [2] Cardinal Baronius would make us believe (I grant) but he brings no other proof thereof than *teste meipso*. Which, however it may go for proof among princes, yet is no proof among scholars. And for my part, without proof, I believe nothing, whosoever he be that speaks it, especially if he be a Papist. For as [3] Sigismund the emperor said of Julian the cardinal legate at the council of Basil, when one commended him highly to him: 'Tamen Romanus est;' yea but he is a Roman; so I may say of any papist, reporting things unknown: Yea, but he is a Papist. Yet be it so, as Baronius saith it is. Why may it not be true, though it be delivered with *ut asseritur*?

Pap. Why? [4] Because lyes are commonly so soothed.

Prot. Indeed many lyes pass in such general terms. As for example: Men say, [5] saith your legend, that St. Patrick drove with his staff all the venomous beasts out of Ireland; and that he obtained of the Lord, that no Irishman should abide the coming of Antichrist. The former of which [6] Harpsfield Cope confesseth to be a lye; and so I think all the generation of your papists think of the latter. Else, why do none of your great master alledge it to clear your pope from being Antichrist? Men say, saith Nangiacus as [7] Genebrard reporteth, that Kentishmen have tails like brute beasts, because their ancestors mocked Austin the monk, when he came to preach unto them. Now that this is a lye well worthy of a whetstone, yourself (I hope) will acknowledge. Yet truth now and then is so delivered. When Boniface the martyr was demanded on a time, whether it was lawful, at the administration of the lords supper, to use a wooden chalice? It is said he answered thus, saith [8] Duaren: *Olim aurei Sacerdotes ligneis vasis, nunc lignei aureis utuntur*. In old time, golden priests used wooden chalices, now wooden priests use golden chalices. Mark (fertur) it is said, saith Duaren, yet [9] no question but he answered so. In like manner, it is written, that [10] Pius the Second was wont to say, marriage was upon just reason forbidden priests, but now upon better reason to be restored to priests. Of which his saying there is made no question, as may appear by this, that a [11] Jesuit replieth only to it, that it was recanted by him, and denieth not that it was spoken of him. That Alexander the Third trampled the emperor Frederick under his feet, and commanded one to say that which is in the [12] Psalms, Thou shalt walk upon the Lion and Asp, the young Lion and the Dragon shalt thou tread under thy feet:

---

1 Leo Papa obiit Kal Aug. Huic successit Johanna Mulier An. 2 Mens. 5. Dieb. 4. Hæc in Codice impresso Heroldi Opera qui mala fide Locum hunc cum aliis multis corrupit. Nam in scripto Codice, ex quo prodiit prima Editio, ita legitur: Johannes, qui, ut asseritur, fuit Mulier.

2 Annal. Tom, x. ad An. 853. num. 60.   3 Rerum memorabilium Paraleipomen. Hist. Abbat. Virpergens. annexa, p. 393.

5 A golden Legend in the life of St. Patrick.   4 Harding Loco supra citato.   6 Dial. lib. iii. cap. 28.

7 Chronol. lib. iii. ad. an. Christ. 595.   8 De sacris eccle. Benefic. ac Minist. lib. ii. cap. 4.   9 Alciat. Parerga Juris lib. vii cap. 24. & de consecrat. Dist. 1. c. Vasa.

10 Pius II. dixisse fertur Sacerdotibus magna ratione sublatas esse nuptias, majori restituendas, videri. Platina in Vita Pii II. Fulgos. de dict. &c. lib. vii. cap. 2.

11 Pisanus de continentia. cap. 12.   12 Psalm. xci. 13.

Is [1] recorded by some with, *ut fertur*, and yet [2] they have little to say for themselves, who call the truth thereof in question. That merry cardinal, who seeing, after the death of Clement the Fourth, that his fellow cardinals called still for the assistance of the Holy Ghost, and yet could not agree upon the election of a new Pope, [3] cried out: *Domini, discooperiamus tectum cameræ hujus, quia Spiritus Sanctus nequit ad nos per tot tecta ingredi.* My good masters, I pray you let us untile the roof of this room: For I fear the holy Ghost cannot get to us through so many slates, is merrily [4] reported upon election of Gregory to have made these verses:

> *Papatus munus tulit Archidiaconus unus,*
> *Quem patrem patrum fecit discordia fratrum.*

Yet who doubts but he made them? [5] Nicholas Clemangis, Archdeacon of Bayonne in France, doth write upon hearsay, that, when Balthasar, commonly known by the name of John the Twenty-third, held a council at Rome, and caused, as the manner is, before the first session, a mass to be said for the assistance of the Holy Ghost; presently, upon the council's setting themselves down, and Balthasar's advancing himself into his chair of state, a dreadful owl (which is ordinarily thought to presage some evil) comes out of her hole, crying after her evil-favoured fashion, and flying to the middle balk of the church, staring just in Balthasar's face, to the great astonishment of Balthasar himself, and all the whole council, so that he was glad to break off for that time. Yea, he writes, that at the next session she appeared again, staring in the Pope's face, as before, and could not be scared away with flinging of sticks, or with whooping, till one felled her with a stick, and so killed her. Yet no man hath cause to doubt of the story, for he had it of a trusty man, and a faithful friend of his, who assured him, of his credit, that it was true. That [6] St. Cyril intreated the Pope, he might say the Moravians their service in a known language; and that, when there was some sticking at the motion, a voice was heard, as it were, from heaven, saying, *Omnis spiritus laudet Dominum, & omnis lingua confiteatur ei;* Let every thing that hath breath praise the Lord, and let every tongue confess his holy name: Upon hearing whereof, the Pope granted St. Cyril his suit, is but reported with, ferunt. And yet, though [7] Cossurus, in that respect, make some question of the truth of it, [8] Ledesma and [9] Bellarmine receive it for true: That the worst Christians, in Italy, are the Romans; that, of the Romans, the priests are the most wicked; and, of the priests, the lewdest are made cardinals; and of the cardinals, the baddest chosen to be pope; it is [10] written, but with asseritur. Yet,

---

1 Decret. de sac. Eccl. Minist. lib. i. cap. 2.   2 See Tortura Torti. p. 262. and the B. of Lincoln's book against a nameles Catholick, page 282.
3 Onuph. Annot. in Plat. in Vit. Greg. X.   4 Onuph. ibid.
5 Disput. super mater.   Conc. Generalis, quæ habetur in Fasciculo Rerum expetend. impress. Colon. 1535. fol. 201. b. Et in Bibl. sanct. Patrum Bygmæ, Tom. viii. edit. Paris. 1576.
6 Æneas Sylvius Hist. Bohemica, cap. xiii.   7 In Enchirid. Controv. cap. xix. de Precibus Latine recitandis.   8 De divin. Script. quavis lingua non legend. cap. xxxii.   9 Lib. II. de Verbo Dei, cap xvi.   10 Sir Edward Sandys, in his Relation of the Religion used in the West, p. 91.

to them that are skilled in histories, and have observed the course of the world at Rome, there are not many things more certain. 'In Bavaria palam ferunt, Jesuitas dolium in Collegium subvexisse, è cujus fundo effracto meretrix in publicas plateas prolapsa sit,' saith [1] Hassen Muller. They say openly, in Bavaria, that the Jesuits caused a tub to be carried unto their college, which breaking by the way, a wench dropped out of the one end of it, in the midst of the street. And why may not this be true, though it go but by report? The Papists believe, as true, far more incredible reports than this, which concern protestants. But to conclude this point, Doth not [2] Harpsfield Cope avouch, That, if men reject stories, upon this quirk, that they are related with *ferunt & dicitur*, they will soon mar all? You had best devise a better answer than this, for fear you be one of them who mar all.

Pap. Take you no care for that: Yet, in way of further answer to Polonus, who is taken, as [3] N. D. writes, to have been the first relator of this fable, [4] I say, there are so many incongruities, simplicities, absurdities, varieties, and contrarieties in his very narration of it, as it discovereth the whole matter to be a mere fable, and fiction indeed, and him a very simple man: *Post Leonem sedit Johannes Anglus, natione Margantinus.* After Leo the Third, sat John English, by nation a Margantine; but were this country of Margantia is, no man can tell.

Prot. N. D. whose words you use, doth Martinus Polonus open wrong, in reporting this of him. For, first, he saith not, that she sat after Leo the Third, but Leo the Fifth. Secondly, he calls her not Margantine, but Maguntine, which is witnessed by [5] Onuphrius himself, who cites his words to his best advantage, that he might have the rather whereat to cavil. If any blind book have Margantine, it is but the scrivener's fault, such as is committed once and again in that book of N. D. whence this sweet cavil is taken, [6] where, for Magdeburgians, we read Magdebugians; for in Polonus there is an *r* too much, and in N. D. there is an *r* too few. Now, where Maguntia is, every man can tell, to wit, in Germany.

Pap. [7] Yea, but it followeth in Polonus: *Quæ alibi legitur fuisse Benedictus iii.* which otherwise is read to be Benedict the Third. So as this man seemeth to confound him with Benedict the Third, and consequently ascribeth to him the same time of his reign, that is assigned to Benedict, to wit, two years and five months; and yet, presently after, he saith, that Benedictus was a Roman, son to Prateolus, &c.

Prot. The substance of this your answer is false, and feigned of N. D. his own head; for in Polonus there are no such words, as *Quæ alibi legitur fuisse Benedictus 3.* neither ascribeth he to her the same time of reign that is assigned to Benedict; for he ascribes to Benedict two years and five months, whereas he ascribes to Pope Joan two years, five months, and four days; or, as some [8] of you say, but two years, one

1 Historia Jesuitici Ordinis, cap. vi.   2 Cope. Dialog. III. cap. xi. p. 355.
3 Num: xxvii. p. 397.   4 N. D. p. 399, and 400.
5 Annot. in Plat. in vit. Joh. viii.   6 Page 396.   7 N. D. page 400.
8 Onuph. loco citato.

month, and four days. **N. D.** might, with as great reason, charge Anastasius to confound Leo the Second, and Benedict the Second, his next successor, because he [1] ascribeth to Leo the Second the same time of his reign, within five days, which he ascribes to Benedict the Second. Questionless, [2] Polonus ascribes to Clemens, nine years, two months, and ten days; and so he doth to his next successor, Anacletus, without difference, yet he confounds them not. Polonus ascribes to Celestinus the First, eight years, and nine days; and so he doth to Sixtus the Third, his next successor, and yet confounds them not.

Pap. [3] Why, but what a foolish speech is it of Polonus, when he saith, John, an Englishman, by nation of Maguntia; for Maguntia is in Germany, as you told me before. And how could she, being an English woman, be of Maguntia?

Prot. You run counter; she was no Englishwoman, neither doth Polonus say she was: She was Joan English, as [4] N. D. truly translated Johannes Anglus in Polonus, but not Joan, or John of England; English was her sirname, as [5] Fasciculus Temporum observed; but England was not her country, her country was Maguntia, that is, Mentz. There are many who carry the name of Scot, French, Gascoigne, Westphaling, Holland, Welch, which were not born in those countries, but in several shires in England. Guitmundus, who wrote against Perengarius, was [6] Norman by name, but not by his country, saith [7] Possevine. *Defuncto Stephano successit Romanus nomine, natione Hispanus.* After the death of Pope Stephen, one Romanus by name, though by birth a Spaniard, succeeded, saith Antoninus.

Pap. [8] Such writers, as lived the very time wherein this matter is pretended to have fallen out, that is to [9] say, with Leo the Fourth, and Benedict the Third, from the year 847 to 858, write nothing hereof at all. *Ergo*, there was no such matter.

Prot. Who are these writers, I pray you, of whom you speak?

Pap. The [10] first, and chiefest, is Rabanus Maurus, abbot of the monastery of Fulda, wherein this Pope Joan of yours, they say, lost her maidenhead. Rabanus Maurus writes nothing of her.

Prot. Nor of any other particular Pope, doth he? Rabanus [11] wrote commentaries upon the whole scripture, and some other treatises, but he wrote no history: Though, if he had, yet could he not have written of this Pope Joan, for her knavery was not discovered till after the year 855, in [12] which Rabanus died. Rabanus lived not to hear of her delivery of a child, as she went in progress.

Pap. Rabanus died in the year 856, and not in the year 855, as [13] Baronius notes. Trithemius, who noted out the year 855 for the year of his death, was deceived, and so are you.

Prot. Whether Trithemius was deceived in assigning the year 855 for the year of Rabanus's death; I mean not to stand arguing with

1 Anastas. de vit. Pont. in Leo. ii. & Benedict ii.　2 Chron. ad An. Christ. 94 & 103.
3 Oouph. Hard. & Bellar. locis supra citatis.　4 Num. xxx. Page 400.　5 See before.
6 Guitmundus Normannus cognomento, non natione.　7 Apparat. sac. verbo Guitmundus. Sum. Hist. Part. II. Tit. xvi. cap. 1. sect. 14.　8 Florim. cap. x. num. 1.
9 Hoc est ab. Ann. 847. ad Ann. 858.　10 Florim. loco citato.
11 Trithem. de Script. Eccl. verbo, Rabanus.　12 Trithem. ibid.
13 Annal. Tom. x. ad An. 856. Num. xxvi. Possevin. Apparat. sac. verbo, Rabanus.

you, because it is all one to my purpose, though he died in the year
856; for Pope Joan was not discovered till after the year 856; and
therefore, since he died in that year, by Baronius's and your own confession, he could not write of her.

Pap. 'Strabus, whose fellow monk bereaved her of her maidenhead,
as the tale goes: Strabus, I say, writes nothing of her.

Prot. Strabus writes nothing of his fellow monks, who, by the
instigation of the devil, wearied Rabanus of his abbotship, through their
continual grumbling against him, for giving himself more to the study
of divinity, than to pleading about their worldly business. Yet we
read thereof, in [2]Trithemius and in [3]others: Wherefore it doth not
follow, Strabus wrote not of Pope Joan: *Ergo,* there was no Pope
Joan; especially if it be considered that Strabus wrote no history, but
glosses upon the bible, and lived not till Pope Joan's days, but died
about the year 840: For how could he write of that which fell out
after his death? Who is your next man?

Pap. 'Haimo, who writ a book of virtue and vice, writes nothing
of her.

Prot. No marvel, for he died in the year 834, at least twenty
years before she was Pope. If Haimo had written of her, his writing
had been as strange, as her delivery of a child.

Pap. How prove you that Haimo died in the year 834? For, by [5]
Baronius, it should seem he died in the year 853.

Prot. Though Haimo had died in the year 853, it helps you not
in this case; for, till after that time, this Joan was not made Pope:
But, that Haimo died in the year 834, it is witnessed by [6]Trithemius,
and acknowledged by [7]Sixtus Senensis, and by Possevine. Wherefore
go on.

Pap. Anastasius Bibliothecarius, [8]a man of great reputation, that
lived in both these popes times, and [9]was secretary to them both, and
was present at both their elections, and wrote the particulars thereof,
writes nothing of her; but sheweth, among other points, that Leo the
Fourth died the sixteenth day before the kalends of August, and that
all the clergy of Rome gathered together, and, with one consent, did
chuse Benedict the Third, &c.

Prot. Where read you that Anastasius was secretary to both these
Popes? Or that he was present at their elections? [10]Platina, writing of
an accident which fell out in the year 884, notes that Anastasius, at
that time, was a man of good account in Rome; but neither he, nor
any man else, notes that he was secretary to Leo the Fourth, and
Benedict the Third, or that he was present at their elections.[11] Bellarmine
himself durst say no more, but that he was present at the election of
many popes, who either lived before, or after this woman-pope. He
durst not say, that he was at the election of these, as you say. Again,

1 Florim. loco citato.　　　2 De Script Eccles. verbo, Rabanus.　　　3 Sixt. Senensis
Bibl. sanctæ, lib. iv. verbo, Rabanus, & in Possevin. Apparat. sac. verbo, Rabanus.
4 Florim. page 84.　　　5 Annal. tom. x. ad an. 853. num. 71.
6 De Script. Eccl. verbo, Haimo.　　　7 Bibl. sanct. lib. iv. verbo, Haimo. Apparat. sacr.
tom. ii. verb. Haim.　　　8 N. D. Part II. cap. v. p. 392.　　　9 Florim. p. 84.
10 In vita Joh. viii. num. cx. Anastasius a Joh. viz. viii. Præfectus est Bibliothecæ S. Rom.
Ecclesiæ, Baron. Annal. to. ix. ad. an. 787. num. ix.　　　11 Lib. III. de Rom. Pont. cap. xxiv.

who told you that Leo died the sixteenth day before the kalends of August? Anastasius [1] writes, that Leo the Fourth *Papa obdormivit in Domino 16 Calend. August.* but that is but the fifteenth day before the kalends of August, and not the sixteenth. Thirdly, whereas, to win credit to this your author, you commend him as a man of great reputation; it is worth the noting, which is noted [2] by one of your own friends, that, in the age wherein he lived, *Doctissimi censebantur, qui vel solam Grammaticam callerent;* they were counted great clerks, who were skilled so much as in the grammar [3]. That, in this chronicle of Anastasius, the phrase is harsh, rude, and barbarous; that many things are avowed therein, which are far from true; that, therein, there are many errors in the account of time, and some things wherein he crosseth himself; which censure, for the main point, is approved by many of your own mother's children; for many papists, in many particulars, condemn it; as for example, [4] this man of great reputation reckons Anicetus before Pius, and Anterius before Pontianus, whereas, your [5] chroniclers reckon Pius before Anicetus, and Pontianus before Anterus. [6] This man of great reputation records, that Marcellinus, one of your popes, was brought to offer incense unto idols, and that he did so; whereas your [7] Baronius inclines rather unto the contrary. This man of great reputation [8] records, that the priests of Rome, by the advice of Liberius, chose Felix, a priest, to be a bishop, instead of Liberius; whereas [9] your chroniclers, of greatest esteem, maintain, that Felix was chosen priest by hereticks only, and not by consent of Liberius. This man of great reputation [10] records, that Liberius subscribed to the Arian heresy, which neither [11] Pighius nor [12] Onuphrius can abide to hear of. This man of great reputation [13] records, that Anastasius, the second pope of that name, communicated with Photinus the heretick, who was all one with Acacius the Eutychian; and that he purposed with himself to restore Acacius, who was deposed by his predecessors, but could not effect it, because God struck him with sudden death; all which is false and fabulous in [14] Bellarmine's opinion. This man of great reputation [15] records, that, after Marcellinus, the bishoprick of Rome lay void, seven years, six months, and five and twenty days; whereas, by [16] Baronius, it lay void but twenty-five days in all. This man of great reputation [17] records, that the cross of Christ was found in Eusebius the Pope's days, about the year 310; whereas, by [18] Baronius, it was not found till the year 316. This man of great reputation [19] reckons Honorius the First among the hereticks called Monothelites; whereas the [20] most of your side, and, by name, Bellarmine, [21] would gladly clear Honorius from this imputation. This

1 In vita Leo nis iv. page 293.   2 Joh. Albinus Typographus Mogunt. Præf. ad unicum Lectorem, quæ præfigitur Anastasio. Qui sciret tantum grammaticam isto seculo rudi, doctissimus habebatur. Baron. Annal. tom. ix. ad ann. 802. num. xii.   3 Albinus loco citato.   4 Anastas. de Vit. Pontif. in vita Aniceti. &c.   5 Platina de Vitis Pontif in vita Aniceti. & Onuph. in Chron. Rom. Pontif.   6 In vita Marcel.   7 Annal. tom. ii. ad ann. 302. num. 95, 96, &c.   8 In vita Liberii.   9 Baron. tom. iii. ad an. 355. num. 57.   10 In vita Liberii.   11 Pigh. Hierar. Eccles. lib. iv. cap. viii.   12 Anno in Plat. in vit. Fel. cap. ii.   13 In vit. Anast. ii.   14 Lib. iv. de Rom. Pont. cap. x. & Append. ad lib. de summo Pont. cap. xiv.   15 In vita Marcellini cessavit episcop. ann. 7. m. 6, dieb. 25.   16 Annal. tom. ii. ad ann. 304. num. 25 and 26.   17 In vit. Euseb.   18 Annal. tom. iii. ad ann. 326. num. 41.   19 In vit. Hon. i.   20 Onuph. Annotat. in Plat. in vita Honorii. i. &c.   21 Lib. iv. de Rom. pont. cap. xi.

man [1] tells us, that Alexander the First sat but eight years, and a few odd months; whereas [2] Baronius tells us, that he sat ten years, and odd months. This man [3] giveth to Pius nineteen years, four months, and three days; whereas [4] Baronius gives him but ten years. This man [5] makes Soter sit nine years, and upward; whereas, by [6] Baronius, he sat not full four years. This man [7] saith, that Anterus sat twelve years, one month, and twelve days; whereas [8] Baronius saith, he sat not a whole month. This man [9] alloweth Dennis but two years, and a little more; whereas, [10] Baronius allows him eleven years, and more. This man [11] writes, that Stephen the Fifth sat seven years, and seven months; whereas, by [12] Baronius's reckoning, he sat but seven months, and two or three odd days. And so, in many other things, this man of great reputation alloweth of that, whereof you allow not, and disalloweth that which you allow: And therefore what reason have you to press us with his authority in this controversy?

Pap. Great reason; for, though he missed sometimes the truth, yet he aimed always at it; and, though he was unkindly dealt withal by some of the popes, yet he was not carried away with malice, and moved thereby, as many are, to write an untruth.

Prot. What? Was Anastasius, the man of great reputation, unkindly dealt withal by some of the popes? Who told you that tale?

Pap. I had it of [13] Florimondus; and I think he was induced to say so, because we read, in Leo the Fourth's time, one Anastasius was degraded by Pope Leo and a council of sixty-seven bishops.

Prot. That Anastasius, who was degraded by Leo the Fourth and the council, was he, as [14] Platina sheweth who stood up antipope against Benedict the Third; it was not this Anastasius; which you may learn of him who made the index alphabetical for the more ready finding out of the most memorable points in Anastasius's Chronicle; for he [15] distinguisheth Anastasius Bibliothecarius from Anastasius degraded by Leo, and set up in opposition against Benedict the Third. But, let Anastasius be of as great reputation, as you are disposed to have him of: How soon after Leo's death, doth Anastasius report, that the clergy chose Benedict the Third? Can you tell me that?

Pap. Yea; the see was void, after Leo the Fourth, just fifteen days, and no more; and then not Joan, but Benedict the Third was chosen.

Prot. Who told you so?

Pap. Marry, [16] Onuphrius, [17] Bellarmine, [18] Bernartius, [19] Florimondus, and [20] Papyrius Massonus; for they say, that these are Anastasius's own words: 'Sanctissimus Leo Papa IV. obdormivit in Domino, 16. Calend. Aug. sepultus ad Sanctum Petrum; & cessavit Episcopatus dies 15. Quo mortuo, mox omnis Clerus Romanæ sedis, universi proceres, cunctusque populus ac senatus congregati sunt, &c, uno conamine Benedictum Pontificem promulgârunt.' That is, The most holy Pope, Leo the Fourth, died in the Lord, the sixteenth of the

1 In vit. Alex. i.   2 Baron. Annal. tom. ii. ad an. 132. num. 1.   3 In vit. Pii. i.
4 Baron. tom. ii. ad ann. 167. num. 1.   5 In vit. Soteris.   6 Baron. tom. ii. ad ann. 179. num. 51.   7 In vita Anteri.   8 Baron. tom. ii. ad ann. 238. num. 1.
9 In vita Dionysii.   10 Tom. ii. ad an. 272. num. 21.   11 In vita Stephani v.
12 Annal. tom. ix. ad ann. 887. num. 1.   13 Florim. cap. xiv. num. 1.
14 De Vitis Pont. in vit. Bened. III.   15 In Indice, littera, a verbo, Anastasius.
16 Annot. in Plat. in vit. Johan. viii.   17 Lib. iii. de Rom. Pont. cap. 24.
18 De Utilitate Legend. Hist.   19 Cap. xiv. pag. 123.   20 De Urbis Episc. in Benedict. III.

calends of August, and was buried at St. Peter's; and the bishoprick was void fifteen days. Now, presently upon his death, the whole Roman clergy, with all the nobles, and commons, and officers of the city, met, and, as one man, agreed that Benedict should be pope.

Prot. They all lye falsely, for the wordes (*Et cessavit Episcopatus dies* 15.) are not to be found, as before I told you, in Anastasius; so that whatsoever they build upon this circumstance, as the most of their building is, is built upon a false foundation, and therefore cannot stand: Yet, besides, I would have you know, that Anastasius purposely passed over in silence divers things which touched the Popes; for, ' Multa de Sergio desiderari videntur apud Anastasium,' [1] saith Baronius: Anastasius wants many things touching Sergius. Again, ' Johannis VIII. res gestæ desiderantur apud Anastasium, fortasis prætermissæ ob odiosam Photii restitutionem,' saith ' the same [2] Baronius.' The acts of John the Eighth are wanting in Anastasius, perhaps, because he was loth to record that odious restoring of Photius.

[3]Anastasius forbears to speak of Luitprandus's sacking of St. Peter's church, which is without the walls of Rome; and so doth Paulus Diaconus too; not for that he was ignorant of the fact, since he lived in the same time, but for that he was loth, by telling truth, to discredit Luitprandus: Besides, under Benedicite be it spoken, I fear Anastasius, when he was printed, passed ill fingers; I fear something was put out of him, which was in his manuscript.

Pap. What presumptions have you of it?

Prot. Great: For I read in Platina, and in Volaterran, that Bibliothecarius (by whom they mean Anastasius, who lived three hundred years before Sigebert) made mention, in his history, That Adrian the First first gave power to Charles the Great to confirm the election of the Bishop of Rome, and to nominate other bishops within his dominions; and yet I find not this in the printed Anastasius. Now I think it more probable, that some put this out of Anastasius, when he came to the press, which was Anno 1602, than that Platina and Volaterran should belye his manuscript.

Pap. Methinks, Anastasius should not have written any such thing; for Baronius and Binnius do confidently affirm, that no man writ so before Sigbert, who lived *ad Annum* 1112.

Prot. Tut, they both lye therein grosly; for Gregory the Sixth, who lived and died anno 1047, a good many years before Sigebert, in an oration, which he made to his cardinals upon his death-bed, testified as much in effect, as Sigebert: For, ' Laudatus est olim prædecessor noster Hadrianus prædicandæ memoriæ, quod investituras ecclesiarum concessit Carolo Magno, ita ut nullus electus consecraretur ab Epis-

1 Annal. Tom. x. ad Ann. 947. num 6.   2 Ibid. ad Annum 882. num 6.
3 Multa prætermissa ab Anastasio inveniuntur, & inter alia depredatio Bafilicæ S. Petri, quæ in Vaticanis collibus extra urbis mœnia posita erat Bason. Annal. Tom. ix. ad Ann. 739. num. 6. Plurima de eodem Rege (viz. Luitprando) P. Diaconus prætermisisse convincitur; sed haud tanto viro notam inureret, &c. Baron. Annal. tom. ix. ad Ann. 744. num. 22. In Vita Paschal. I. Anthropol. 22. lib. Annal. Tom. ix. ad Ann. 774. Not. in Vitam Hadriani, Tom. iii. Conc. pag. 252. Apud Antonioum, Num. Hist. Part. II. tit. 16. cap. i. sect. 19.

sopo, nisi prius à rege baculo & annulo insigniretur,' saith he. But let us leave Anastasius, and come unto the next, who, living in those days, passeth over Pope Joan in silence.

Pap. [1] Ado, Bishop of Vienna, who lived at the same time, hath not a word of this your Pope Joan.

Prot. Ado lived not at the same time, nor near the same time, if either [2] Gesner, or [3] Possevinus, or [4] Laurentius de la Barre, or [4] Angelus Rocca may be credited : For he, as they say, wrote a brief chronicle, from the beginning of the world to his own time, to wit, to the year 1353 ; wherefore it is not much material, whether he miss her, or mention her. Say on.

Pap. [5] Theophanes Freculphus wrote, in these days, an history, from the beginning of the world to his own time; and yet he writes nothing of her.

Prot. If Freculphus had written an history of that length, yet there was little reason why he should have mentioned her ; for we [7] read not, that he lived above the year 840: But, indeed, his history goes not so far; he writ only to the year of Christ 550, as [8] Bodin observeth ; or to the year 560, as [9] Pontacus noteth ; or, at furthest, to the year 600. For, having spoken a few words of Gregory the Great, and Boniface, who succeeded him, he ends presently his story. Who is your next man ?

Pap. [10] Aimonius, a monk of St. Germains, and a famous French writer, speaks nothing of her.

Prot. Aimonius, or Ammonius, or Annonius, (for he is diversely named) your famous French writer, drew out his story, by [11] your own men's confession, but to the year 898, or at furthest to [12] 844, which fell nine or ten years short (at least) of Pope Joan's time; and therefore, methinks, you should not look, that he should write of her.

Pap. [13] Audomarus, the Parisian, omits her also, in his history.

Prot. Where might a man see Audomarus, I pray you ? [14] Canus tells of a bishop, in his country, which was wont to cite authors, that never were : Now I wish you be not of kindred to him in this ; for I find no mention of any such historiographer in Trithemius, or in Gesner, or in Possevinus. Neither doth Bellarmine, nor Baronius cite any such, in their disputes about this matter. When you can tell me certain news of such a writer, you shall have a more certain answer : In the mean time proceed.

Pap. Nay, stay a little ; for, though neither Bellarmine, nor Baronius, mention Ademarus (for so is his right name, and not Audomarus, as it is erroneously printed) where they speak of this matter,

1 Bellarm. lib. iii. de Rom. Pont. cap. 24. N. D. num. 24. p. 393. & alii.
2 In Bibliotheca, verbo, Ado. 3 Apparatus sacer, verbo, Ado.
4 In Hist. vet Patrum, edit. Paris. 1583, ad initium, Chron. Adonis.
5 In Biblioth. Vatican. impress. Romæ, anno 1591. Tit. Authores, quorum in opere citantur nomina. 6 Florini. pag. 84. 7 Freculphus floruit anno 830, & quod excurrit. Possevin. Apparat. sac. verbo, Freculphus.
8 In method. Hist. Freculph. Historicos ab Orbe condito ad annum Christi 560. Cron. digerit.
9 Chron, lib. ii. pag. 110. 10 Onuphrii Annotat. in Plat. in Vita Johan.
VIII. Harding. loco in initio citato. Florim. p. 84. 11 Annonius usque ad annum 898. Historiam texuit, saith Vasq. de Adorat. lib. II. cap. ix. disp. 7.
12 Gesner. Chron. lib. iv. ad annum 844 13 N. D. num. 24. p. 392.
14 Episcopus quidam nostras eos Authores citavit interdum, quos nulla unquam habuit ætas. Canus, Loc. Com. lib. xi cap. 6. fol. 327.

yet Ademarus is mentioned by Genebrard and Onuphrius, where they treat of this matter, as B. C. observed well, in his [1] Doleful Knell of Thoma Bell, where he taxeth Sutcliffe for captious quarrelling with father Parsons (as he calls him) for citing Ademarus, calling him a counterfeit.

Prot. B. C. is a fit patron for father Parsons, but an unfit match to deal with Dean Sutcliffe: Dean Sutcliffe, no doubt, scorns him ; and good cause why. for who, but a fool, would appeal to one of his own fellows, for trial of his truth? Are not Genebrard and Onuphrius as like to cite a counterfeit author, as Parsons?

Pap. [2] Lupus Servatus saith nothing of her.

Prot. Why, what occasion had he to speak of her, since he writ no books of history? Besides, ' Lupus Servatus migravit ad dominum, Anno 851,' saith [3] Trithemius: That is, Lupus Servatus died in the year 851. So that, though, as a prophet, he might have foretold of her delivery, yet, as an historian, he could not have reported her delivery.

Pap. Yea ; but Lupus, abbot of Ferrara, in an [4] epistle of his to Benedict the Third, calls Leo Benedict's predecessor ; and thereby sheweth, as [5] Baronius gathereth, that there was no such pope, as Pope Joan, between Benedict and Leo.

Prot. What? Doth Baronius gather such a conclusion of such premises? Verily he gathereth where no man streweth ; for, I pray you, doth this follow? John the Ninth, speaking of Stephen the Sixth, [6] calls him his predecessor ; ergo, there was no pope between John the Ninth and Stephen the Sixth? If not, as indeed it doth not (for there were two popes who came between them, the one called [7] Romanus, the other [8] Theodorus) then neither will it follow, that, because Leo is called Benedict's predecessor, therefore there was no such Pope, as Pope Joan, between Benedict and Leo. ' Interdum Rom. Pon- tifices non solum eos, qui proximi Episcopi fuere, sed plerosque dis- junctissimos, illo nomine (praedecessoris) complectuntur.' The Popes of Rome, by the name of Predecessor, do sometimes understand, not such as were popes immediately before them, but such as lived very long before them, saith [9] Massonus.

Pap. [10] Yea, but this Lupus, in divers of his epistles, doth complain of the miserable estate of the church in his time. And therefore, if any such horrible matter as this of Pope Joan had fallen out, [11] doubtless, he would have spoken of it, and mourned pitifully for it.

Prot. Doubtless, Baronius, if you give any credit to him, will make a fool of you. For doth not [12] he mention divers of his com- plaining epistles, sent to great personages ; wherein yet he complains of nothing, but that courtiers robbed his corban, I mean his monastery.

1 Pag. 296 & 297   4 Florim. pag. 84..   3 In Chron. Monasterii Hirsaugiensis,
ad Ann. 851.   4 Epistola 103, quæ habetur apud Baron. Annal. Tom. x. ad
Annum 856. num. 8. & Florim. cap. 14. num. 4.   5 Annal. Tom. x. ad Annum 855.
num. 6y.   6 Baron. Tom. x. ad Annum 900. num. 8.   7 Idem. ad Annum
901. num. 1.   8 Idem, ibid.   9 De Urbis Episc. lib. v. in Cælest. III. fol. 212.
10 Baron. Tom. x. ad Ann. 853. num. 69.   11 Certè, fi quod tam nefandum scelus
accidisset, dicere minimè omisisset, sed implacabili luctu vir zelo plenus planxisset.
12 Tom. x. ad Ann. 846. num. 10.   12, 13, 14, 15, 17.

[1] That he wanted an ambling nag to ride to Rome on. [2] That he wanted Tully de Oratore, Quintilian, and Donate upon Terence. And [3] that there was not such licentiousness in France (among the laity) that the people neither feared God nor the Devil. Of faults among the clergy, Lupus complains not at all.

Pap. [4] Luitprandus, who writ an history, speaks nothing of her.

Prot. What history of Luitprandus do you mean? that which is intitled De Vitis Pontificum, that is, Of the Popes Lives; which was printed the [5] other year at Mentz with Anastasius; or his history of such accidents as fell out through Europe.

Pap. I mean the latter; for I see the former, though it carry the name of Luitprandus, [6] cast off by the printer, as none of his.

Prot. Now then you are a wise man, to tell me that Luitprandus mentions not Pope Joan. For ‘ Luitprandus, Ticinensis Diaconus, historiam per Europam gestorum libris 6. ab an. 858. ad 30. usque Othonis magni ferè continuat,’ [7] saith Genebrard; that is, Luitprandus, deacon of such a church in Italy, continues his history of accidents which fell out in Europe, from the year 858, to the thirtieth year (almost) of Otho the Great. By which you may see that he began his history after Pope Joan's time: And therefore had no cause to speak of her.

Pap. [8] Lambertus Schafnaburgensis hath not a word of her.

Prot. To this I answer, First, that he lived not in the same time with her; he lived Anno 1077. Secondly, I say that this Lambertus did but touch by the way all ages, from the beginning of the world to the year of Christ 1040, as [9] Pontacus truly observed; though he discoursed at large of the thirty-seven years that followed. Thirdly, this Lambertus, doth not so much as name Stephen the fourth, or Paschalis, or Eugenius, or Valentinus, or Gregory the Fourth, or Sergius the Second, or Leo the Fourth, or Benedict the Third, or Nicholas, or Adrian the Second; and therefore what marvel, if he speak not of this Pope Joan?

Pap. [10] Otho Frisingensis, who lived about the year 1150, makes no mention of this story.

Prot. But he doth. For John the Seventh ([11] saith he) was a woman.

Pap. [12] They who lived within a few years after her, and writ at length of all other accidents, write nothing of her; and that is another presumption, it is but a fable which is reported of her.

Prot. Who are they you mean?

Pap. The first is [13] Johannes Diaconus, who, in the year 870, writ of the Popes lives.

1 Ad Ann. 855. Num. 14.   2 Ad Ann. 856. num. 10.   3 Ad Ann. 856. num. 20.
4 N. D. pag. 392. Florim. pag. 84.   5 Anno 1602.   6 Job. Albinus Præfat. ad
Lectorem.   7 Chron. lib. iv. ad Ann. 955.   8 N. D. and Florim. locis citatis.
9 Lib. ii. Chron.   10 Florim. pag. 85. Onuph. in Plat. in. Vita Joh. VIII.
11 Lib. vii cap. 35. Rerum in Orbe. gestarum. Impress. Argentorati, Ann. 1515.
12 Qui pauló post illius statem floruerunt, nihil de ea scripserunt, &c. Florim. cap. 10.
pag. 84.   13 Florim. loco citato.

Prot. That Johannes Diaconus writ St. Gregory the Great's life,[1] I grant; and,[2] as some say, Clement's; but that he writ of any more popes, I utterly deny. You have a pretty gift in alledging writings that never were, but say on.

Pap. [3] Milo Monachus, who lived Anno 871, saith nothing of her.

Prot. Milo Monachus, I believe, saith nothing of her, nor any other Pope; for he writ no history. They, who commend him,[4] do commend him for a rhetorician, and for a poet, and for a musician, but not for an historiographer.

Pap. [5] Passeratius Rabertus, who lived in the year 881, saith nothing of her.

Prot. This Passeratius is, surely, some author of your own devising. For no man can tell any news of him. But, perhaps, you would say Paschasius Ratbertus, for[6] such a one lived about the time you speak of. Yet this writ no history. This writ neither at length, nor in brief, any of the Popes lives.

Pap. Yea, but[7] Rhegino, who lived in the year 910, and comprehendeth briefly all the choice matters which fell out in the time of this supposed Pope Joan, writes nothing of her.

Prot. Rhegino writes nothing of John the Second, nor of Boniface the Fourth, nor of Deusdedit, nor of Boniface the Fifth. He writes not a word of Sergius the Second, nor of Leo the Fourth, nor of Benedict the Third, and therefore no marvel, though he write nothing of this Joan the woman Pope.

Pap. [8] Why, but the greatest enemies that ever the Popes had, who lived in, and after those times, and were ready to cast in the Popes teeth whatsoever they knew, or knew not, to the end they might disgrace them, yet never objected this of Pope Joan. Which confirms me much in my opinion, that this is but a tale, devised long after by some crafty-headed hereticks.

Prot. Who are these, I pray you?

Pap. [9] John Bishop of Ravenna is one of them, Methodius Illyricus another, and Michael Palæologus, the Emperor of Constantinople, a third.

Prot. How know you, that these never objected Pope Joan's lewdness to the disgrace of the Roman Papacy? Have you read all that they writ, and all that they spoke?

Pap. Nay, their writings are not extant,[10] I confess. But a man may know how they slandered the Popes by the answers of many godly men, made in defence of the Popes. For as we catholicks at this day are forced to make mention of your objections, when we undertake to answer your books: so in those days the catholicks were driven to

1 For so I read in Trithem. de Script. Ecclesiast. verbo, Joh. Diac.
2 Possevin. in Apparat. sac. verbo, Joh. Diaconus.   3 Florim. loco citato.
4 Trithem. lib. citato. verbo, Milo. Sigevert. ad ann. 879.   5 Florim. loco citato.
6 Trithem. lib. citato. Possevin. Appar. sac. verbo, Paschasius.   7 Florim. loco citato.
8 Cum omnes scribendi principes, quorum alii hæretici, alii schismatici, alii anathemate separati———quæcunque odium suggessit, in pontifices ex omni vitæ præteritæ causa collecta probra turpiter evomuerint———nihil autem de Joanne Pontificatu dixerunt: Existimaudum est quæcunque de ea postea divulgata sunt, posteriorum hæreticorum fraude fuisse excogitata. Florim. cap. 10. num. 5 & 6.   9 Florim. num. 4.   10 Florim. ib.

make mention of the slanders which they refuted. Now, in their refutation of slanders, there is no such thing as this of Pope Joan.

Prot. Why, peradventure, they knew that in this they were slandered with a matter of truth ; and therefore they held it best to pass it over in silence. Questionless, your fellows at this day do so often. When Beza objected this very matter in the assembly of Poissy, before the Cardinal of Lorrain, and the Sorbonists of Paris, who answered him? Do not your [*] own men confess, that no man said a word to him? When the Hussites (as you call them) objected the same at the council of Constance, [2] was not silence their answer? We read in a [3] book lately set forth, intitled, Synodus Parisiensis, that [4] St. Ambrose asked, ' Qua ratione, quáve authoritate, imagines Angelorum vel aliorum Sanctorum adorandæ sint, cùm ipsi sancti angeli vel sancti homines vivos se adorari noluerunt ?' What reason, or what warrant men had to worship the images of men and angels, seeing the angels themselves, and holy men alive, refused to be worshipped? Now the two great cardinals, [5] Bellarmine and [6] Baronius, snarl at this book, seeking by all means to disgrace it. [7] Bellarmine expresly professeth the confuting of it : and [8] Baronius sets the most of it down in his annals, even word for word, making glosses here and there upon it, in way of answer to it. But both of them pass slily by the words of St. Ambrose. If we had not had the book itself, we should never have known, by their answers, of such an argument of St. Ambrose's making against images. In like manner these [9] two champions undertake to answer such arguments as are made to justify the report of Gregory's delivering Trajan out of hell. Yet there is one argument made by their [10] opposites, which they never touch : and that is this : That, in St. Gregory's church at Rome, the sum of that story is engraved in an ancient stone. Upon which argument the Jesuit Salmeron [11] stands much. If their opposites writings were not extant, by their answers, we had never heard of such an objection. Wherefore, if you would persuade me that these eager enemies objected not this against the Pope, you must bring better proof than this, that you find no foot-stepping of it in the answers made unto them. But go on with your argument. What other enemies silence persuades you that this story is a fable?

Pap. [12] Hincmarus Archbishop of Rheims, Theodorus de Niem, Waltramus Bishop of Norinberg, Benno the Cardinal, bitter enemies unto the Pope, pass this over in silence. And this is a great argument to me, there was no such thing.

Prot. That Hincmarus Archbishop of Rheims should have lived at enmity with your popes, it is not for your popes credit it should be known ; for he was singularly well learned, very wise, and very honest,

1 Johannes Sanmartinus in fabulam Joannæ Pseudopontif. Romanæ à corrupto historiarum albo erasam é Flor. &c. and Florim. cap. 6. pag. 58.   2 Silentio satisfecerunt catholici doctores, &c. Florim. cap. 6. num. 6.   3 Synodus Parisiensis, ann. Christ. 824. Francofurti impress. apud Hæredes Wechel. 1596. pag. 145.   4 In Epist. Pauli ad Rom.
5 Append. ad lib. de Cultu Imag.   6 Annal. Tom. ix. ad ann. 825. num. 1.
7 Loco citato, in initio.   8 Num. 5, &c.   9 Bellar. lib. ii. de Purg. cap. 8.
Baron. Annal. Tom. viii. ad ann. 604. pag. 182. &c.   10 Alphons. Salmeron. in 1 Cor. xv. Disput. 27.   11 Cujus rei extat insigne Romæ monumentum lapidi antiquissimo inscriptum in æde sacra ipsius Gregorii————quod ego propriis oculi hausi, &c. Salmeron loco citato, pag. 239 & 240.   12 Florim. cap. 10. pag. 87.

as [1] Trithemius witnesseth; insomuch that your great cardinal [2] Baronius, when he hath occasion to cite him, intitles him, [3] Saint Hincmarus; wherein his epitomiser [4] follows him.

Pap. Well: [5] what say you to Theodoricus de Niem?

Prot. I say (which before I proved) that he mentions the story.

Pap. And what say you to Waltram, bishop of Norinberg?

Prot. I say, there are few of his works extant; and, in [6] those which are extant, he shews no gall against the popes; only he proves that the Emperor hath right to the investiture of bishops.

Pap. [7] Why, but do you not think that Benno, the cardinal, who spoke so much evil of Gregory the Seventh, and other popes, would have noted this, if he had known of it?

Prot. No. Benno (no doubt) knew much foul matter by many other popes, which he did not touch. There are many shameful things reported in other stories by many of your popes, which Benno hath not in his story. But do you think in good earnest, that Benno the Cardinal was the author of that book which goes under his name, and is intitled *Vita & Gesta Hildebrandi?*

Pap. Nay, indeed I do not. I rather think it was made by some Lutheran, and falsly fathered on Benno. And of that mind is [8] Bellarmine in part, and [9] Florimondus wholly.

Prot. So was not Orthuinus Gratius, who set it out at Colen, in the year 1535. For he, though as hot a papist as any of the crew, held it for Benno's own, and [10] professed that he rather believed him than Platina, and Stella, and Sabellicus. But see you not by the way your own folly, in that you conclude there was no Pope Joan, because the writer of that story makes no mention of any such Joan? I hope (if he were a Lutheran that made it) he knew there was a common fame of such a matter: and therefore, if he had been disposed to have disgorged himself of all that lay on his stomach, he would have cast up that with the rest. But go forward.

Pap. [11] Rupertus, the English bishop, who, because he was excommunicated by the Pope, devised and raked together all manner of lyes against the Pope, did not for all that object this.

Prot. [12] Rupertus, the English bishop, whom you mean, was the man commonly called Grosthead. [13] A great philosopher, excellently well seen both in Greek and Latin, a reader of divinity in the schools, a famous preacher in the pulpit, a man of holy life and conversation; even so holy, that, in the opinion of the whole clergy of France and England, there was not such another among the prelates of that time; though it pleased your Pope Innocentius the Fourth, to call him old

1 Vir in divinis Scripturis singulariter doctus——sapientia & honestate morum conspicuus. Trithem. de Script. Eccles. verbo, Hincmarus.   2 Tom. ix. ad ann. 760. Nub. 3. 3 S. Hincmarus.   4 Joh. Gabri. Bisciola Epit. Baron. ad ann. 760. 5 Florim. pag. 87.   6 De Investitura Episcoporum, printed at Basil, anno 1566. 7 Florim. cap. 10. num. 5 & 6.   8 Lib. iv. de Rom. cap. 13.   9 Florim. pag. 88. 10 Malo magis huic Benoni Cardinali quàm Platinæ, &c. credere. Epist. ad Lector. fol. 39. in Fascic. Rerum expetend. & fugiend.   11 Florim. pag. 88 & 89. Rupertus Episc. Angl.——quæcunque potuit excogitare convicia est ementitus.
12 Magnus habetur Philosophus Latinis & Græcis ad plenum eruditus, lector in Theologia scholis, prædicator in populo, &c. Matth. Paris. Hist. Angl. in Hen. III, pag 1162. See the English Martyrology, made by a Popish Priest, Octob. 9. Printed ann. 1608. 13 Quis est iste senex delirus, surdus, & absurdus, saith Innocent IV. Matth. Paris, ib.

fool, surd and absurd companion, and to threaten he would make him a by-word and an astonishment unto the world. And, to say truth this man had many bickerings with the Pope, insomuch that in one letter [1] he signified unto him, that by his writs with (*non obstante*) he brought upon the world a Noah's flood of mischiefs, whereby the purity of the church was defiled, and the quietness of the commonwealth hindered. That, by his reservations, commendams, provisions of benefices for persons who sought to fleece, and not to feed the flock of God, he committed such a sin, so contrary to the doctrine of the apostles and the evangelists; so hateful, so detestable, so abominable to Christ Jesus, as never sin was, but the sin of Lucifer; nor never shall be, but the sin of Antichrist, whom the Lord shall destroy with the breath of his mouth at his coming. He signified unto him, that no man could, with a good conscience, obey any such mandates as he sent, though they came from the highest order of angels. For they tended not to edification, but to the utter undoing of the church. Are these the lyes, by reporting whereof he sought to revenge himself upon your Pope? Alas! the [2] College of Cardinals confessed before the Pope, that they could not blame him for writing thus, for he said nought but truth.

Pap. [3] Another Englishman, Mathew Paris by name, made a hotch-potch of all the villainies he could remember, and yet he hath not this.

Prot. Mathew Paris, indeed, tells many foul tales of the Popes and the Papists. As for example: [4] He reports how *Satanas, & omne contubernium inferorum.* That is, The devil of hell, and all his hellish crew, writ letters gratulatory to the whole rabblement of the popish clergy, acknowledging their kindness, in that, following their pleasures, and giving over preaching, they suffered more souls to go to hell than ever went before.

[5] He reports how Gregory the Seventh set the whole church on a hurry, by deposing married priests from their priesthood, and forbidding the laity to hear their service; because he had no precedent for such his proceeding, and because, as some thought, it was an unadvised part, contrary to the opinion of the ancient fathers, who wrote that the sacraments of the church, by the invisible working of the spirit, have like effect, whether they be administered by good or bad men, &c.

[6] He reports, how a cardinal legate, at a council held in London, inveighing against priests Lemans, was taken the same night after in bed with a whore.

[7] He reports how Germanus, archbishop of Constantinople, signified unto the cardinals of Rome, that the Grecians stumbled much at this, that the cardinals desired to be accounted his disciples, who said: silver and gold I have none, and yet were wholly set upon gathering of silver and gold.

1 Apud Matth. Paris, pag. 1161. cardinals, Matth. Paris, pag. 1162. omne injuriarum genus conflavit. Florim. Conquest. ann. 1072. pag 10. 1125. pag. 93. 7 In Hen. III. pag. 617.

2 Ut vera fateamur, vera sunt quæ dicit, said the 3 Impuro ore alter Anglus nomine Matth Paris. 4 Hist. Angl. in Guil. cap. 10. pag. 89. 5 Ibid. ann. 1074. 6 In Hen. I. ad ann.

[1] He reports, how the Pope enjoined by one mandate to the bishops of Canterbury, Lincoln, and Salisbury, that they should provide for three hundred Romans, in benefices next vacant, and they should give no benefice, till they had provided for so many competently.

[2] He reports, how Hugh, the cardinal, bragged, when Innocentius departed from Lyons, that whereas there were four stews at his coming thither, he had left them but one. Marry that reached from one end of the town to the other.

[3] He reports, how the Franciscans and Minorites, by commandment of the Pope, appointed all sorts of people, young and old, men and women, base and noble, weak and strong, sound and sick, to go for the recovery of the Holy Land. And yet the next day, yea sometimes the same hour, for money, they dismissed them again.

[4] He reports how Pope Innocentius IV. stirred up the Christian people of Brabant and Flanders, to war against Conradus the Emperor, promising them, for their labour, forgiveness of all their sins. Yea, he promised such warriors not only forgiveness of sins for their own use, but forgiveness of sins for their parents also. The fathers and mothers of such as warred against Conradus, had all their sins forgiven them, as well as the warriors themselves.

These and many such like tales he tells by the Pope, which the truth itself forced him to do. But he meddles not with any thing which was done by any pope, within one thousand years after Christ. And therefore no marvel, though he spoke nothing of Pope Joan.

Pap. [5] John, of Calabria, a man famously known for a railer against the popes, spoke nothing of this.

Prot. John, of Calabria [6] told our King Richard the First, that Anticrist was as then born in Rome, and that he should be made pope. [7] John, of Calabria, was generally reputed a prophet, and a man of great learning. Yet John, of Calabria, was so far from railing against your popes, that (if [8] Bellarmine say true) he spoke very honourably of them. And therefore his silence, in this case, doth not help you.

Pap. [9] Yea, but Dantes, the Italian poet, would surely have touched this story, if he had heard any inkling of it.

Prot. Why so? Dantes found fault only with six of your popes, viz. with Anastasius II, Nicholas III, Boniface VIII, Clement V, John XXII, and Celestine V, as [10] Bellarmine notes. Whereby it is plain, that he never purposed to rave up all the filth which he found written of your popes. Questionless, he might well have heard of this, for [11] he lived after Martinus Polonus, and in Martinus's days the report of this was common. Have you any more to say?

Pap. [12] Yea. And not only the Latin writers, but even the Greek historiographers, Zonaras, Cedrenus, Curopalatas, and others, that wrote before Martinus- Polonus, of matters concerning the Latin

1 In Hen. III. pag. 712 ad ann. 1240.   2 In Hen. III. ad ann. 1251. pag. 1089.
3 In Hen. III. ad ann. 1249. pag. 1017. & 539. & 757.   4 In Hen. III. pag. 1100. ad
ann. 1251.   5 Florim. cap. 10. pag. 89.   6 Roger Hoved. Annal. pars
posterior in Rich. I. pag. 588.   7 Possevin. Apparat. sacer. verb. Cyrillus Carmelita.
8 Append. ad Lib. de Summo Pon. cap. 11.   9 Florim. Loco citato.
10 Append. ad Lib. de Summ. Pont. cap. 14.   11 Polon. Dante Antiquor. Bell. ibid.
12 N. D. pag. 393.

church in those days, and were no friends to the same, and would have been content with such an advantage against it, write nothing thereof at all.   Which is an evident proof there was no such matter.

Prot.   What! an evident proof?

Pap.   'Yea, an evident proof, which you may perceive by Sutcliffe's answer to father Parsons (as he calls him) ; for he never, I warrant you, so much as once names these Greek historiographers, but suppresseth that cunningly, or rather maliciously, because he could frame no colourable answer unto it.

Prot.   Dr. Sutcliffe never intended to trouble himself, or his reader, with laying open Parson's foolery in every particular.   Otherwise, assure yourself, he would not have passed by this.   For it is a matter of no great cunning to shape this argument its answer.   For tell me, had not you once a pope called Mark, who sat, as divers of your own ² histories note, two years, eight months, and twenty days? And had you not another pope called Marcellus, ² who sat above five years ?

Pap.   We had. But what of that ?

Prot.   Your ⁴ Pontacus, and ⁵ Genebrard confess that all the Greek writers, in a manner, omit to speak of the former: and ⁶ that all the Greek writers, without exception, omit to speak of the latter. Now if you, notwithstanding their passing by of those, be yet persuaded that these were popes, why may you not rest persuaded that there was a Pope Joan, though they do pass by her, and write not one word of her? I hope you believe many things whereof they write nothing.   We read in your ⁷ legend, yea in your ⁸ mass books, that Heraclius the Emperor, when he would have entered in by the gate, by which our Saviour went to his passion, clad like a king, with the cross on his shoulders ; that he was miraculously hindered, and could not get thorough, till he had cast off his princely attire, and put off his hose and his shoes.   Do not you believe this? I am sure you do.   Yet ⁹ Gretser acknowledgeth, that the Grecians, such as Cedrenus and Zonaras, write nothing of this, professing that he likes it never a wit the worse for their silence.   For they, as he further notes, omitted many other matters of truth, whereof no man doubts.   But how know you, that no Grecian ever writ of such an accident ? It seems that they did ; because Chalcocondylas, a Grecian, of later years, hath writ thereof, as before I have shewed you.   And ¹⁰ Barlaam the Greek monk alludes thereto.   For, from whence could they have it, but from the Grecians his ancestors? You must bring more evident proof than this is, or else you will never persuade any man of sense and reason, that the story of Pope Joan, which is commended to us by so great a cloud of witnesses, is fabulous.

Pap.   ¹¹ Why, but Hermannus Contractus, and Conradus Abbas Urspergensis, and others more, write nothing of this Joan of yours.

---

1 B. C. in his doleful knell of Thomas Bell. book ii. page 296.   2 Plat. de Vita
Pont. in Vita Mar.   Flores Hist. ad ann. 341.   3 Plat. in Vita Marcell. r. Onuph. in
Chron. ad ann. 304.   4 Lib. ii. Chronogr.   5 Chronol. Lib. iii.
6 Pontac. & Geneb. Locis citatis.   7 Aurea Legend, Exaltation of the Holy Cross.
8 Breviar. Rom. in Officio Exaltat. S. Crucis.   9 Lib. i. de Cruce, cap. 57. pag. 170.
10 De Papæ Principatu, cap 14.   11 N. D. Pag. 362.

Prot, And what of that? Will you conclude thereupon, that there was never any such woman pope? Tell me in good earnest, do arguments, taken from authority of a few men, hold negatively? Is it a good argument, St. Paul, St. Luke, and Seneca, do not say that Peter was at Rome: *ergo,* Peter was not at Rome? Bellarmine denies this argument. Respondeo, saith [1] Bellarmine: ' Nihil concludi ex argumentis ab authoritate negativè. Non enim sequitur, Lucas, Paulus, & Seneca non dicunt petrum fuisse Romæ, igitur non fuit Petrus Romæ. Non enim isti tres omnia dicere debuerunt; & plus creditur tribus testibus affirmantibus, quam mille nihil dicentibus; modo isti non negent, quod alii affirmant;' that is, I answer, negative arguments are nought worth. For it follows not, that St. Peter was never at Rome, because St. Luke, St. Paul, and Seneca, do not report that he was at Rome. For these three were not bound to report all that was true. Besides, three witnesses, speaking to a cause, deserve more credit than a thousand who stand mute, not denying that which is witnessed by the three. And in another place, Certe, saith [2] Bellarmine, ' Magis credi debet tribus testibus affirmantibus, quam infinitis nihil dicentibus;' that is, verily a man should rather believe three witnesses speaking to a cause, than infinite, who neither speak *pro* nor *con.* Again, tell me whether Dennis, bishop of Athens, was not afterwards bishop of Paris; though Ado, bishop of Triers, in Germany, and Suidas, a Greek writer, make no mention of that his second bishoprick? Your Lipomanus resolves upon Metaphrastes, and one Michael Syngelus's word, that Dennis was bishop of Paris, though Ado and Suidas speak not of it. Their passing it over in silence doth not prejudice Metaphrastes and Syngelus's report, who say he was bishop of Paris, in [3] Lipomanus's opinion. And why then, though these and many more say nothing of Pope Joan, might there not be such a pope, since as many, and as learned as they, do reckon her among the popes; [4] Salmeron, one of your prime Jesuits, notes, that when one historian reports a matter, and another passeth it by, the latter's silence doth not prejudice the truth of the other historian's relation: ' Ea lex apud historiographos observatur (saith he) ut quando unus ex duobus historicis aliquid affirmat, quod alius supprimit, non deroget affirmanti qui tacet.

Pap. [5] Yea, but there are in the Pope's library six or seven tables of popes, wherein there is no mention of her.

Prot. And what of that? Your pope's library is compared by [6] Baronius to a Draw-net, which gathers together good and bad. Your Pope's library hath in it books of all sorts, approved, disproved; profitable, unprofitable. [7] It hath counterfeit and forbidden books, as well as books of better reckoning. They are simple people (as we read in [7] Baronius) who believe reports the rather, for that they are

1 Lib. ii. de Rom. Pont. cap. 8. vide Lib. ii. de Indulg. cap. 20.   2 Lib. i. de Extrema Unctione, cap. 6.   3 Tom. i. de Sanct. Hist. Præfat. in Martyrium S. Dionysii per Metaphrasten.   4 Prolegom. vi. in Evang.   5 Onuph. & Harding loco supra citatis.   6 Omnia copiosa Bibliotheca (in particular he means the Vatican) refert similitudinem sagenæ missæ in mare, ex omni genere piscium congregantis, bonos & malos contheens, libros probatos & improbatos, utiles & inutiles simul amplexans, saith Baron. Annal. tom. viii. ad ann. 604. num. 50.   7 Rom. Biblioth. habet libros tam suppositos, tum improbatæ lectionis. Cope, Dialog. 4. cap. 19. pag. 567.   8 Loco supra citato.

to be found in books which are in the Pope's library.   Yet, suppose
these seven tables be of the best note, will you yield thus much to
me, that he who is numbered in these seven tables, or at least in as
many, as authentical as these, as a pope, was a pope?

Pap.   No, not I.   For I know that Leo the Eighth is numbered as
a pope in [1] many tables, and in [2] some of those seven, if not in them
all.   And yet I am of [3] Baronius's mind, that Leo the Eighth was an
intruder and an usurper; and that he was not worthy to be called a
pope.   But why asked you of me this question?

Prot.   If this be no good argument, Leo the Eighth is numbered
among the popes in seven tables that are in the Pope's library, or in
seven as authentical as these in the Pope's librarary, *ergo*, Leo the
Eighth was a pope: what reason have you to think yours good, which
is this in effect: Joan, the woman-pope, is not numbered among the
popes in seven tables, which are in the Pope's library: *ergo*, there was
no such Joan, a woman-pope? If seven tables, speaking out for a pope,
do not convince the being of such a pope, why should their silence
convince the not being of a pope? Might they not as well leave out
one who had been pope, as put in one who never was pope?

Pap.   But why should they have left her out?

Prot.   Partly for her sex's sake, because she was a woman; and
partly in regard of the filthiness of her fact; for so your stories note.
And this need not seem strange to you, if you would but observe that
other popes, upon other occasions, have been passed by, by divers, as
no popes.   As for example: Felix the Second was a pope and martyr,
as Bellarmine [4] teacheth.   For, ' Felicem II. ut papam & martyrem
ecclesia catholica veneratur,' saith Bellarmine.   And he sat in the
popedom one year, four months, and two days, as we read in [5] Platina.   Yet, by [6] Genebrard's confession, Marcellinus omits to speak of
him in his chronicle, because he was suspected of heresy.   And, for
the same cause, or some such like cause, [7] St. Austin and [8] Optatus
mention him not among the popes, in their memorial of popes.   Nor
yet Bristow, in his table of popes, which is printed with his wise demands.   In like manner, that one Cyriacus was pope, it is acknowledged by [9] divers.   Yet it is rare to find him in any catalogue of
popes.   For, as a [10] great papist writeth, ' Iste Cyriacus in catalogo paparum non annumeratur, quia credebant ipsum non propter devotio-
nem, sed propter oblectamentum virginum dimisisse episcopatum.'
Cyriacus is not in the register of popes, because it was thought he left
the popedom, not for devotion, but for the love that he bare to certain
wenches.   Or, if you like it better, that Cyriacus is not in the register of popes, ' Hoc ex indignatione cleri accidit, pro eo quod in ordi-
ne dignitatis suæ usque ad finem permanere noluisset.'   It came to

1 Bristow's. printed with his Demands.   2 Onuph. Annot. in Plat. in Vitam Alex-
andri III.   3 Non dignus qui Pontifex numeretur, sed intrusus & occupator potius
nominandus.   Annalium, Tom, x. ad ann. 964.   4 Lib. iv. de Rom. Pont. cap. 9.
5 In Vit. Felicis II.   6 Chron. Lib. iii. ad ann. 368.   7 Epist. 165.
8 Lib. ii.   9 Golden Legend, in the Life of Ursula.   Polon. ad ann. 238.   Suppl.
Chron. ad ann. 285.   Ranulf. Cistrens. in Polychron. Lib. iv. cap. 20. Petrus de Natalibus in.
Catal. Sanct. Lib. ix. cap. 87.   10 Joh. de Parisiis de Potestate regia & papali, pag. 217.
cap. 5.   In Sext. Lib. i. cap. 7. de Renunciatione, in Glossa.

pass by this means, that the clergy were angry at him, for that he would not continue pope till his death. For so, some of you say, blessed Bernard told holy Elisabeth, when she desired to know the reason thereof. Damasus the Second hath his place in [1] many popish chronicles in the throng of popes; yet there are [2] many on the other side who let him go for one that is naught, and never number him. And in much like sort they [3] deal with others.

Pap. [4] If Pope Joan were omitted for the filthiness of her fact, why was that close-stool reserved, and that monument of her's, whereof you told me before, set up in one of the high streets in Rome? For the stool and the image were as like to continue the memory of her, as any record in writing. To be plain with you, I do not see how you can rid your hands of contradiction in this point.

Prot. Well enough. For may not some be of one opinion, some of another? May not some think good to continue the memory of that, which others, for shame of the world, would have forgotten? [5] Did not some of your fellow-papists in France deny, that John Chastell was taught by the Jesuits to murther Henry the Fourth of France, because they were loth to make the Jesuits odious? And yet did not others help to erect a pillar of stone near to the king's palace, whereby so much was notified? If any man should affirm, that the same man, who omitted Pope Joan for the filthiness of her fact, erected such a monument of her in the streets, and prescribed such a stool to be kept for such a purpose, I know not how he could deliver himself from contradiction. But, speaking of divers men, his speech hangeth well enough together; there is no shew of contradiction in it. For further proof whereof, it is worthy your consideration, that, when Paul the Third, moved with the Spirit of God, (as [6] Harding saith) and desirous to reform the church, gave charge to his best learned, wisest, most godly and zealous men that he knew, four cardinals, three bishops, and two others, to enquire and search out what abuses and disorders were in the church, and especially in the court of Rome; which they did, offering up unto him a libel, containing the sum of all their proceedings. Some thought their labours worthy of registering; others thought them fitter to be burnt, which appears by this, that the libel is printed in Crab's edition of the council, *anno* 1551, and yet put into the *Index librorum prohibitorum*, by Paul the Fourth (one of those four cardinals who exhibited it to Paul the Third) and left out of Dominicus Nicolinus's edition of the councils at Venice, Auspiciis Sixti Quinti, in the year 1585; and out of Severinus Binnius's edition at Colen, 1606.

Pap. [7] Yea, but give me leave I pray you. If Pope Joan were omitted for the filthiness of her fact, yet should there have been mention made of the vacancy of the see, for that time she was pope, or else there will be a manifest error in chronology.

1 Plat. in Vita Damasi II. Polonus in Chron. circa ann. 1040.   2 Consent nonnulli hunc inter Pontifices nequaquam numerandum esse, saith Plat. loco citato.
3 Felix IV. teste Massæo de Urbis Episcop. Lib. ii. in Vita Johan I. pag. 85.
4 Florim. cap. 22. pag. 190.   5 See Le Franc's Discourse, printed anno 1602.
6 In his rejoinder to M. Jewel about the Mass, pag. 177.   7 Bellarm. Lib. iii. De Rom. Pont. Cap. 34.

Prot. A manifest error in chronology? A foul absurdity, indeed, to miss two years in reckoning! But, I trow, there are fouler than this, however the matter will be salved; for Onuphrius and Bristow reckon two hundred and thirty popes to Gregory the Thirteenth, and [1] Genebrard two hundred and thirty-four, whereas, by Platina's account, there should be two hundred and thirty-five, for he reckons, to Paul the Second, with whom he ends, two hundred and twenty Popes; after whom, to Gregory the Thirteenth, every man reckons fifteen; which makes up the number of two hundred and thirty-five: yet Vesteganus, in his table printed at Antwerp, 1590, numbers no more than two hundred and thirty-one. Again, do not [2] some of your chronologies record, that Euaristus sat thirteen years? Whereas [3] others say he sat but nine years. Do not [4] some of them say, that Dennis sat eleven years? [5] Others that he sat but two years? And do not these differences, and such as these are, whereof we have spoken before in part, argue manifest errors in your chronologies? If no further inconveniencies follow, upon Pope Joan's omission, than a manifest error in chronology for that space she lived, we may well enough believe, that some omitted her, not for that she was not, but that they were ashamed of her; for two years and odd months break no square in your chronologies, any more than an inch with a bungling carpenter.

Pap. [6] Yea, but no-body, within four hundred years after, mentions her popedom; [7] and, is it possible, that all writers should so conspire together, that the truth thereof could never be certainly known, till four hundred years after?

Prot. You lavish, when you talk of four hundred years after; for I have proved unto you already, by the books that are yet extant, that it was known sooner. But, suppose we had no writer, who lived within four hundred years of Pope Joan, to produce for proof, Will you, in that respect, deny the story; do not you papists commend unto us may stories, as true, for which you can bring us no proof out of any writer who lived within four hundred years after? [8] You tell us of an image of Christ, which was made by Nicodemus, who came to our Saviour by night, for fear of the Jews; and of it you report wonderful things. But you are not able to name the man (shall I say, within four hundred years of Nicodemus? nay, not within six hundred years of Nicodemus) who writeth any such thing. Again, [9] you tell us, that St. Luke drew certain pictures of the Virgin Mary: but [10] Theodorus Lector is the ancientest man, that your friends alledge for proof of this; and he lived, at least, five hundred years after. Thirdly, [11] you write, that our Saviour Christ, wiping his face with an handkerchief, imprinted his image therein, and sent it to Agbarus for a token: but you can name no author for this, but [12] Evagrius, who [13] lived six hundred years after Christ. Fourthly, [14] the most of

1 So doth Massonus de Urbis Episcopis.   2 Anastas. in Vita Euaristi.
3 Baron. Annal. Tom. ii. ad ann. 121. num. 1.   4 Idem, Tom. ii. ad ann. 272. num. 27.
5 Anastas. in Vita Dionysii.   6 Florim. cap. i. pag. 6.   7 B. C. in his Doleful
Knell of Thomas Bell, pag. 295 and 296.   8 Bellarm. Lib. ii. de imag. cap. 10.
9 Idem. loco citato, & Gretser. de Cruce, lib. ii. cap. 1.   10 Lib. 4 Collectaneorum.
11 Bellarm. loco citato, & Baron. Annal. tom. i. ad ann. Christi 31. num. 61.
12 Lib. iv. cap 26.   13 See Baron. Annal. tom. viii. ad ann. 594. num. 30.
14 Bellarm. lib. i. de Clericis, cap. 9. Pamelii Annotat. in Cypr. 'Epist. lii. num. 29. Cararias, de Potestate Rom. Pont. lib. i. cap. 18. Pet. de Natal. in Catal. Sanct. lib. viii. cap. 53.

you hold it for a certain truth, that Adrian the Pope was content, that Charles the Great should nominate the bishop of Rome, and other bishops of his dominions; and yet there are, among yourselves, who write, that there can be no proof made thereof, out of any writer who lived within four hundred years of Charles the Great's time.

That the Virgin Mary made that coat of our Saviour's, which was without seam, our [1] Rhemists teach; and [2] others of you add to that, that, as our Saviour grew in height and in breadth, so the coat on his back grew : do you think, that there is an author within four hundred years after our Saviour's time, that taught so ?

[3] Turrian reports, and [4] Gretser after him, That the apostles made this canon, in a council which they kept at Antioch : ' Ne decipiantur fideles ob idola, sed pingant ex opposito divinam humanamque manufactam impermixtam effigiem Die veri, ad Salvatoris Domini nostri Jesu Christi, ipsiusque servorum, contra idola & Judæos; neque errent in idolis, neque similes sint Judæis.' That is, Let not the faithful people be deceived by idols, but let them, on the contrary part, make the image of our Saviour Christ, both God and man, and the images of his servants; and let them not be deceived by idols, nor shew themselves like unto the Jews. But I do not believe, that this can be proved to be a canon of that council, by any writer within four hundred years of that time. Your [5] rabbins alledge [6] two councils, the one kept, as they say, in the year 303, the other in the year 324 ; both sounding much to the Pope's praise, and advancing of his authority; but, for any thing I read, the most learned among you can bring no proof, within four hundred years after, that any such councils were then kept. Nicholas the First, who lived in the year 860, is the first whom [7] Bellarmine names for that purpose.

Pap. [8] Why, what say you to our ancient English histories written in the Latin tongue ? To wit, William of Malmsbury, Henry Huntington, Roger Hoveden, Florentius Vigorniensis, and Matthew of Westminster : For I have one argument, of no small moment, [9] as it seemeth to me, taken from them, for the overthrowing of the fable of Pope Joan.

Prot. When lived these writers, from whence you draw your argument ?

Pap. The [10] first four lived five hundred years ago, and the latest of them three hundred years.

Prot. Fie, five hundred years ago! [11] William of Malmsbury continues his story to the year 1143 ; and [12] Henry Huntington his story till the reign of Henry the Second, which was 1154; and [13] Roger Hoveden continues his story to the year 1201 ; which argues, that the first four lived not five hundred years ago. But, What is your argument out of them ?

1 Annot. in Joh. xix. 23. in Marg.　　2 Rudolphus de Vita Jesu, Part. II. cap. 63. p. 221. Col. 2.　　3 Turrian. Lib. I. contra Magdeburg. cap. xxv.　　4 Gretser, Lib. II. de Cruce, cap. i. tom. i.　　5 Bellarm. Lib. II. de Rom. Pont. cap. xxvi. Baron. Annal. tom. x. ad annum 963. num. 35.　　6 Concilium Romanum & Synuessanum. 7 Loco supra citato.　　8 N. D. Num. 25. pag. 395.　　9 B. C. student in divinity, in his Doleful Knell of Thom. Bell, printed 1607, lib. ii. pag. 297, commends this for a very excellent argument.　　10 N. D. num. 25.　　11 Scripsit Historiarum Libros ad an. 1142, saith Possevin. Apparat. sac. Verbo, Guliel. Malms. but by the book itself (fol. 108) it is plain he continued it to the year 1143.　　12 Vide Histor. Lib. viii. in Fine.　　13 Fol. 464, b.

Pap. No one of them all makes mention of this pope.

Prot. Oh, Is that your argument? Why, I say to that, That our English histories might omit her upon like reason, as others of other countries omitted her, for her sex's sake, and for the filthiness of the fact. And do not you think this probable?

Pap. No, by no means: ' For our English writers, above others, should have mentioned her, if any such had been.

Prot. And why, I pray you?

Pap. * Because King Alfred, living in Rome when Leo the Fourth died, and Benedict III. was chosen, must needs have known also Pope Joan, if any such had entered, and lived two years and a half between them.

Prot. How know you, that King Alfred lived in Rome when Pope Leo died, and Benedict was chosen?

Pap. * Because we read, that his father delivered him into the hands of Pope Leo the Fourth, to be instructed and brought up by him; and that the Pope received him with great kindness, and detained him there with him.

Prot. That Alfred's father sent him to be anointed King, and that the Pope anointed him at his father's motion, we read * indeed; but that his father delivered him to Leo to be instructed and brought up by him, we read not in Malmsbury, nor Huntington, nor Hoveden, nor Florentius; nor yet that the Pope detained him there with him: But, perhaps you can prove he staid at Rome, though it be not recorded that Leo detained him with him; now, therefore, let me hear your argument.

Pap. * That Alfred lived in Rome some number of years, seemeth evident: First, for that he returned more learned, and otherwise better qualified, than any Saxon King had been before him.

Prot. This argument is framed out of your fingers ends, and not out of the stories; for the * stories mention two journies which Alfred took to Rome; the former, when he was five years old, in the year 853, in which he was accompanied with the nobility: The second, when he was six years old, in the year 854, in which he went in his father's company, who staid in Rome a year. Now, though I find it not set down in particular, that he returned with his father, yet it is very likely by the circumstances; for the ⁷ stories note, That he was always brought up in the King's court: And it is without all doubt, whensoever he returned, that he returned not better learned, nor better qualified; for, at twelve years old, and upward, he knew not a letter in the book; which the * stories with great grief report. What is your next argument?

Pap. * That Alfred lived in Rome some number of years, seemeth evident, for that we find no mention of his acts in England until the

---

1 N. D. p. 394.   2 N. D. p. 395.   3 N. D. p. 394.   4 Roger Hoveden,
Annal. Pars prior. pag. 232. edit. Lond. and Florentius, in Chron ad ann. 853.
5 N. D. p. 395.   6 Hoveden. & Florentius locis citatis.   7 In Regio Curto
semper inseparabiliter nutriebatur, saith Florent. lib. citato, p. 308, & Joh. Asser Episcop.
Shyreburnensis in Hist. Alfredi, pag. 7, which history was printed at London, 1574, with Thomas
Walsingham.   8 Usque ad 12. ætatis annum, proh dolor, illiteratus permansit. Asser. &
Florent. loc. cit.   9 N. D. p. 395.

reign of his third brother, Athelred, in the year 871, at the famous battle of Reading in Berkshire, fought against the Danes.

Prot. Alfred was but twenty-two years old in the year 871, and therefore no marvel, though, being in England, we read nothing of his acts. Yet, not to speak of his hawking and hunting in England, in his younger years, [1] whereof the stories speak much, we [2] read of his marriage three years before the battle of Reading, and of his going to aid the King of Mercia the same year; so that this proceeds on a false ground, as doth the former: Wherefore, unless you have better arguments to disprove the story of Pope Joan, you may prove yourself a fool, but never it a fable.

Pap. I am able to prove it a fable; [3] for our foresaid writers do not only not make any mention of Pope Joan, that came between Leo the Fourth and Benedict the Third, but do expresly exclude the same, by placing the one immediately after the other, and assigning them their distinct number of years beforementioned, to wit, eight years and three months to Leo, and two years and six months, immediately following, to Benedict the Third.

Prot. Who is your first witness of the truth of this?

Pap. [4] Malmsbury in Fastis Reg. & Episcop. Angl. 847 & 855.

Prot. Where might a man see that book of Malmsbury's? for I never read nor heard before of any such book made by him. True it is, that, in the end of Malmsbury, Huntington, Hoveden, Ethelwerdus, and Ingulphus, [5] which are all printed in one volume, there is such a treatise; but that was made by Sir Henry Savile, who set them out: It was not made by Malmsbury; you may as well say, that Malmsbury made the ' Index rerum & verborum,' which follows after it. But who is your next witness?

Pap. [6] Florentius in his Chronicle.

Prot. Doth Florentius, in his Chronicle, give eight years and three months to Leo? Now, for shame of the world, leave lying. Florentius notes, that Leo began his papacy 853, and Benedict the Third, 858; whereby, it is apparent, that, in Florentius's opinion, Leo sat but five years; so is it apparent, that, in his opinion, Benedict sat five years; for Benedict, according to Florentius's reckoning, began 858, and Nicholas, his next successor, began 863. Now, from 858 to 863, there cannot be fewer than five years; so that, in prosecuting this argument, which is of your own devising, you have scarce spoken one true word.

Pap. [7] I pray you tell me how they called this Joan, when she read publickly in the schools at Rome.

Prot. They call her John. How else?

Pap. What; John? And was she called John after her election to to the popedom too?

Prop. Yea, Why not?

Pap. [8] That is not likely; for Sergius, a few years before, had

---

1 Matth. Westm. Flores Hist. ad an. 871. fol. 245.   2 Matth. Westm. lib. citato, ad an. 868. fol. 230.   3 N.D. p. 396.   4 N.D. p. 396. in Marg.   5 At Frankfort, anno 1601.
6 N.D. pag. 396. in margine.   7 Florim. cap. xxx. num. 4.   8 Florim. ibid.

brought in a laudable custom, that the pope elect should not step out of the conclave, before he had changed his proper name.

Prot.   Indeed there are [1] who say, that, because Sergius had a filthy name before his election, to wit, the name of Swine's-snout, he changed it after his election.

Pap.   [2] Yea, but they who say so, are greatly deceived; for Swine's-snout was not his proper name, but the sirname of a noble family, whereof he was descended.

Prot.   So are they greatly deceived, who say that he changed his proper name; for, ' ex paterno nomine a principio Sergius est appellatus;' from his birth he was called Sergius, after the name of his father, as [3] Baronius notes.   The first who changed his name was [4] Sergius the Third, and yet not for the filthiness of his name, but in reverence to St. Peter: ' Cum enim ille Petrus vocaretur, indignum putavit se vocari eodem nomine, quo Christus primum ejus sedis pontificem, principem apostolorum, ex Simone Petrum nominaverat.' For, his name being Peter, he thought it was not meet that he should be called by that name, whereby Christ called the first bishop of that see, even the prince of the apostles, whose name he changed from Simon to Peter, as we read in Baronius, in the same place.

Pap.   I never heard this before; but I like it the better, if it be in Baronius, for [5] I cannot say too much good of that man: Marry, I rather thought you would have taken exception against me, in respect that Platina ascribes this custom of the popes, in changing their names, to John the Twelfth, who, being called Octavian, before his papacy, thought that name too warlike for him, after he was made pope, and therefore took the name of John.   Now I could easily have replied unto this; for, besides that Platina speaks amiss in many other points, it is not likely, that John the Twelfth made any conscience by what name he was called, seeing he lived as licentiously, after he was pope, as before.

Prot.   You have your learning at the second hand : Have you not?

Pap.   I have this out of Florimondus, I confess: But what of that ?

Prot.   Your learned masters deceive you, and especially Florimondus; for [6] Platina is one of them who ascribes the original of this papal custom to Sergius the Second; for which he is reproved by Onuphrius. Onuphrius, and not Platina, ascribes the original hereof to John the Twelfth: ' Johannem hunc XII. primum esse inveni qui nomen in pontificatu mutarit,' [7] saith Onuphrius.   ' Nam, cum antea Octavianus vocaretur, gentili nomine omisso, tanquam parum majestati & religioni pontificis idoneo, se Johannem appellavit;' that is, John the Twelfth was the first, as far as I can learn, who changed his name when he was made pope; whereas, before, he was called Octavian, he left that

1 Fascic. Temp. ad ann. 844. Polyd. Virg. de Invent. Rerum. lib. iv. cap. x. Joh. Stella in vit. Pont. in Sergio ii.   2 Florim. ibid.   3 Annal. tom. x. ad an. 844. num. 1.
4 He would have said Sergius the Fourth, as appeareth, Annal. tom. xi. ad an. 1009.
5 Baronii laudandi finem prorsus invenio nullum, Florim. cap. xxii. num. 6.   Non ignoro Platinam, qui saepius, in aliis etiam rebus, lapsus est, hanc consuetudinem Joh. xii. acceptam referre, &c. Florim. cap. xxx. num. 5.   6 De vit. Pont. in vita Sergii. ii.
7 Annot. in Plat. in vitam Sergii. ii. & Joh. xii.

heathenish name, as little beseeming the Pope's majesty and religion, and called himself John.

Pap. Onuphrius must pardon me, though I believe him not in this.

Prot. Yet Onuphrius, in [1] Florimondus's opinion, was a most painful antiquary: But what if Baronius say as much, Will you not believe him for Baronius's sake?

Pap. How can Baronius say so much, if you wronged him not before, when you told me, that he referred this custom of changing names to Sergius the Third? If Sergius the Third begun it, then not John the Twelfth: If John the Twelfth begun it, then not Sergius the Third.

Prot. Look you and Baronius to that; how both tales will hang together; but assure yourself, Baronius saith both: For, notwithstanding the former assertion, coming to speak of John the Twelfth, he useth [2] these words: Hic revera primus inventus qui mutavit sibi nomen, ut qui ex Octaviano vocari voluerit Johannes, pro mutata, non exuta tyrannide. Nam qui dictus est a patre, ob temporale urbis dominium, Octavianus; ob spirituale, nomine Johannes appellari idcirco voluit, vel quod eo nomine ejus patruus Johannes xi. Papa sit appellatus; vel ut in nomine saltem bene posset audire in adulatoris acclamationibus, quibus male usurpatum proferri soleret sacrum illud eloquium (fuit homo missus a Deo, cujus nomen erat Johannes:') that is, This, in truth, is the first who changed his name, who of Octavian would needs be called John; and not for that he meant to leave his tyranny, but for that he resolved to use another kind of tyranny: For he, who was called by his father Octavian, in respect of his temporal authority in the city, would now, in respect of his spiritual, be called John; either for that his uncle, John the Eleventh, was called so, or for that he desired to hear well, at least for his name's sake, whilst, in clawing and fawning acclamations, the people fondly applied unto him that good speech. 'There was a man that was sent from God, whose name was John.' Thus Baronius. Have you not another question to ask?

Pap. [3] Yes. Who was Pope Joan's father?

Prot. What is that to the purpose?

Pap. Much: [4] For the histories expresly set down who was the father of Linus, of Cletus, of Clemens, and of all the rest of the popes: And would they not have done as much for her, if she had been pope?

Prot. It is false, that the histories expressly set down the fathers of all the rest of the popes; for, by the histories, you cannot tell me who was the father of Higinus, or Dennis, or of John the Nineteenth, and that I will prove unto you by the histories; for in [5] them we read, that 'Higini genealogia non invenitur;' No man knows of what parentage Higinus was. And [6] Dionysii generationem invenire non

1 Onuphrius antiquitatis perscrutator diligentissimus, Florim. cap. xxi. num. 6.
2 Tom. x. Annal. ad ann. 955. num. 4.   3 Quisnam hujus Pseudopontificis pater, &c.?
Florim. cap. viii. num. 5.   4 Aliorum quidem Pontificum parentes, ut Lini, Cleti, &
omnium caterorum in Annalibus leguntur. Florim. cap. vii. num. 5.   5 Anastas. de
vit. Pont. in vita Higini, Polon. in Chron. ad ann. 154.   6 Anastas. in vita Dionysii,
Polon. in Chron. ad ann. 257.

potuimus,' we could not find out Dennis the Pope's ancestors. And
' Johan. xix. cognomen & patria ignoratur;' It is unknown of what
sirname, or country, John the Nineteenth was. Again, in the [2] histories, it is expresly written, that Urban the Fourth was begotten, ' ex
patre sutore veteramentario;' that is of a cobler. That [3] John the
Twenty-second was ' filius veteramentarii, resarcitoris videlicet solea-
rum;' that is, the son of a botcher. That [4] Benedict the Eleventh
was ' filius lotricis pauperculæ, the son of a poor laundress. That
[5] Benedict the Twelfth was ' molitoris filius,' the son of a miller. That
[6] Sixtus the Fourth was the son of a mariner. That [7] Adrian the Sixth
was a clothworker's son, or else a brewer's. That [8] Sixtus Quintus was
a base and beggarly fellow's son, even the son, as is said, of a swineherd.
But what the names of these men's fathers were, that is not expresly
written; you may peruse many histories, and find nothing to that
purpose. Your Alexander the Fifth [9] confessed, ' Se nec parentes, nec
fratres, aut aliquem ex agnatis, cognatisve suis unquam vidisse;' That
he never saw either his father or mother, or brother, or any of his
kindred. And can you tell me what was his father's name? [10] Nihil
tam incertum inter historiarum scriptores, quam qui fuerunt parentes
singulorum;' There is nothing more uncertainly set down in histories,
than who were the popes fathers, saith Massonus.

Pap. Well, sir, to be brief with you, I prove it as a fable thus:
[11] Either this Pope Joan was young or old, when she was chosen. If
she were young, that was against the custom to chuse young popes, as
may appear by the great number of popes that lived in that dignity,
above the number of emperors that succeeded often in their youth.
But, if she were old when chosen, then how did she bear a child publickly in procession, as you hereticks affirm? Answer me this: For to
this Sutcliffe saith nothing, in answer to Parsons, as he calls him. And
no marvel, for nothing can with any colour be pretended, as B. C.
assures himself, in his [12] dolefull knell of Thomas Bell.

Prot. I deny the ground of this your reason, to wit, That this Pope
Joan was either young, or old, when she was chosen. For [13] learned
men divide the whole course of man's life, not into youth, and old age,
as you do; but into *pueritiam, pubertatem, adolescentiam, juventutem,
constantem, mediamve, & senectutem.* Now middle age is from thirty-
five to forty-nine, whereof she might have been, and so neither old nor
young: For Leo the Tenth was chosen Pope at thirty-eight years of
age; for he was not forty-six years of age when he died, and yet he sat
as Pope eight years, eight months, and twenty days. And Gregory the
Eleventh, *fuit dum eligebatur in papam forsitan circa 35 annos,* was
about thirty-five years old, as [14] Theodoricus de Niem and [15] Massonus
witness. Again, she might have been chosen young, for any custom

1 Joh. Stella de Vitis Pont. in Joh. xix. ad ann. 999.   2 Onuph. Annot. in Plat. in vita
Urbani iv.   3 Paulus Langius in Chron. Citizen. ad an. 1316.   4 Idem. ad ann. 1303.
5 Papyrius Massonus de Urbis Episcopis. lib. vi. in Benedicto xii.   6 Patre ortus qui
semper nauticam exercuit, Papyr. Mass. lib. cit in Sixto iv.   7 Onuph. Addit. ad Plat.
in vita Adriani vi.   8 Cicarellus in vita Sixti v.   9 Papyr. Masson. de Urb.
Episc. Lib. vi. in Alex. v.   10 De Urbis Episc. lib. ii. in Marcello ii.
11 N. D. num. 35. pag. 402. 403.   12 Lib. ii. pag. 303.   13 De Galeni sententia
universæ vitæ sex sunt omnino ætates. Leonard. Fuchsius Instit. ut. Medicin. lib. i. cap. 5.
14 Nem. Unionis Tract. vi. cap. 39.   15 De Urbis Episcop. lib. vi. in Greg. 21.

you papists have to the contrary.　For Boniface the Ninth, as [1] some write, *erat annorum* 34, *dum eligebatur in papam*, was but thirty-four, when he was chosen Pope : And [2] Innocent the Third was but thirty. Yea, she might have been one of the youths of the parish : For (not to speak of the boy-pope, I mean, Benedict the Ninth, [3] who was chosen Pope about twelve years old :) John the Thirteenth, alias Twelfth, [4] *in juvenili & florida ætate creatur pontifex*, was made Pope when he was in his prime; that is, about the eighteenth year of his age, as [5] Baronius gathereth by circumstances.　But why might not she have been old, since we read, that old women have borne children ? ' Henricus Suevus imperator ex uxore quinquagenaria genuit Fridericum II.' [6] saith Massonus : Henry the Emperor begat Frederick the Second, of his wife, who was fifty years old.　Machutus Episcopus ortus est matre plusquam sexagenaria,' [7] saith Petrus de Natalibus : Bishop Machutus's mother was above threescore years old when she bare him.　' Hic in Palatinatu ante annos aliquot vidi meis oculis, & vocatus interfui partui cujusdam fœminæ, ampliùs annos 56 natæ, quæ binos mares enixa est eodem partu,' [8] saith Franciscus Junius : A few years since, I was intreated to see a woman in this country, above fifty-six years old, who was delivered of two boys at a birth.　N. D. whose steps you follow, hath one good property; for he is always like himself; he is no changeling: He began with lyes, and goeth on with fooleries; yet, in giving the reason why it was not the custom to chuse young popes, he shews himself most a fool.　For the multitude of popes above the emperors came not, by reason of their age, but by other accidents.　In the first three hundred years, while the popes were generally good, they were cut off by martyrdom.　For though it be not true, as [9] Onuphrius notes well, that all the popes, from Saint Peter's time to Sylvester, were martyrs; which yet is confidently avouched by [10] some papists : It is true, I grant, that the most of them were martyrs.　Now in succeeding times, their numbers grew the greater by their poisoning, and evil entreating one of another.　If you peruse diligently the stories of their lives, you shall find, that, of forty popes already dead, and gone to their own place, there was not one that sat a full year : You shall find, that, within the compass of nine years, or little above, [11] there were nine several popes : You shall find, [12] that one man, in thirteen years, poisoned six popes : You shall find, that God in his justice cut them off, for their wicked and abominable lives.

Liberius sat about some six years, [13] saith Cardinal Turrecremata, and then died an evil death : ' Mala morte precibus sanctorum extinctus est.'　He died not for age, but with cursing.

Anastasius the Second sat two years, but God struck him suddenly for his naughtiness, and he died.　Yea, he died, some say, as Arius the arch-heretick died.　For, ' Sunt qui scribunt eum in latrinam effudisse

1 Masson. de Urbis Episc. lib. cit in Bouif. IX. Plat in Bonif. IX.　　2 Masson. lib. III.
de Urb. Episc. in Innocent III.　　3 Glaber. Radulphus. Hist. lib. v. cap. ult. & Masson.
M. iv. in Bened. IX.　　4 Paulus Langius. in Chron Citizens: ad ann. 1389.
5 Annal tom. x. ad ann. 955 num. 3.　　6 De Urbis Episc. lib. v. in Celestin. III.
7 In Catal. Sanct. lib. x. cap. 64.　　8 Annot. Biblicis in Ruth i. edit. ult.
9 Annotat. in Plat. in Vita Higini.　　10 Bristow in his Table of Popes.
11 See Fasciculus Temp. ad ann. 904.　　12 Taste Bennonæ Cardinale in vita
Hildebrand.　　13 Summ. de Eccles. lib. iv. part i. cap. 9.

intestina, dum necessitati naturæ obtemperat,' saith [1] Platina, and [2] Johannes Stella the Venetian.

Clemens the Second kept the popedom but nine months, not for that he was old when he was chosen, but because he was poisoned, as [3] we read in your own writers.

Damasus the Second, [4] who had a hand in poisoning this Clemens, kept the papacy but twenty-three days, not for that he died of age, but by the just judgment of God, that he might be an example to others, as [5] Platina notes, who climb to that dignity by bribery, and unlawful means, to which they should ascend by virtue.

Benedict the Sixth reigned but a year and an half, and then died, either of strangling, or famine, in close prison, as we read in the same Platina, [6] yea in [7] Baronius.

Victor the Third kept the papacy but one year and four months, and died of poison, say [8] Platina, [9] Genebrard, [10] Charanza, and [11] Polonus.

[12] Pius the Third died within a month, not without suspicion of venom.

John the Thirteenth, alias the Twelfth, [13] while he was committing adultery, was slain : Whether [14] thrust through by some, who took him in the act, or [15] stricken by the devil, historians agree not. But your [16] cardinal takes that as more likely, which is more dreadful. For, because, saith he, the life of Pope John was detestable, and marvellous offensive to the Christian people, therefore Christ himself gave out the sentence of condemnation against him. For, while he was abusing a certain man's wife, the devil struck him suddenly into the temple of his head, and so he died without repentance.

Boniface the Seventh sat but seven months, and a few odd days, and then the beast died, saith [17] Krantius.

Marcellus the Second lived but twenty-two days in the popedom; not for that he was full of years when he died, for he was but fifty-five years old, but for that he was poisoned. And, which is strange, it is [18] observed, that he was poisoned, because some thought he would prove an honest pope.

That Sixtus Quintus, after the sixth year of his reign, was fetched away by the devil, by whose help he came to that place; [19] Sir Francis Breton, a monk of the order of the Celestines, protested, that a prior of Saint Bennet's order assured him at Rome. And, [20] they say, your jesuits report as much under-hand in Italy. But, to end this point in a word, [21] your own men tell us in plain terms, that many popes were

1 Plat. in Vita Anastasii II.   2 De Vit. Pont. ad ann 496.   3 Genebrard. Chronol. lib. iv. ad aun. 1046. Æneas Sylvius, in Decad. Blond. Epit. lib. iii.
4 Platina in Vita Clem II.   5 In Vita Damas. II. Supplement. Chron. lib. xii. ad ann. 1042. Joh. Stella, de Vita Pont. ad ann. 1040 in Damaso II.   6 in Vita Bened. VI.
7 Annal. tom. x. ad ann. 974. num. 1.   8 In Vita Victor III.   9 Chron lib. iv. ad ann. 1087.   10 In Summ Conc.   11 In Chron ad ann. 1096.   12 Plat. in vita Pii III.   13 Kran. Metrop. lib. v. cap 1.   14 Plat. in vita Joh. XIII. Blond. Decad. ii. lib. iii.   15 Luitprand. Tichnens. lib vi. cap. xi Sigebert in Chron. ad ann. 903. Trith. in Chron. Monast. Hirsaug.   16 Turrecrema. Summ. de Eccles. lib. ii. cap. 103. & lib. iv. cap. ix. part 1. and so doth Walthramus Episc Naumburgens. Tract. de Investitura Episc.   17 Metrop. lib. v. cap. t.   18 Obiit Die 22, non sine veneni suspicione, quòd nimium rectus quibusdam videretur. Geneb. Chron. lib iv ad ann. 1555.
19 In his Declaration made at Vendosmr, Jan. 28. anno 1601.   20 Relation of the Western Church by Sir Ed. Sands.   21 Pontifices tanquam monstra quædam à media

of short continuance, because God saw they proved monsters, and shamed the true religion: [1] God, in his justice, would not suffer them to live. And so this argument of years hath its answer.

Pap. Yea, but it is a most unlikely thing, that the whole Roman clergy would chuse a pope without a beard, especially a stranger.

Prot. And why might not the Roman clergy, as well as the clergy of Constantinople, [2] whom you upbraid with such a fact, do such a deed; especially if all your clergy in those days, as some of you write, were shaven? For men by shaving may make themselves look like women, and women by often shaving may make themselves look like men. Certainly a [3] learned man among yourselves imputes the error of Joan the woman's choice to this, that your clergy were then shaven. For, by the means of shaving, saith he, the people were so disguised, that men and women were scarce known asunder. And by this it happened that a woman was chosen Pope of Rome, to the perpetual rebuke of that same holy order. The same reason is given also by [4] Chalcocondylas. And by it is another of your arguments answered, which by [5] N. D. is touched in these words : how did they not discern her to be a woman or an eunuch, seeing she had no beard in her old age ? For, it being ordinary, that the clergy should be shaven, why should they dislike her the more for want of a beard ?

Pap. [6] Yea, but was there none, that either by countenance, or voice, or other actions of her, could discern the fraud ?

Prot. Look you to that. But this is sure, if your stories be true, that divers women have lived longer among men, in men's apparel unknown, than Dame Joan lived in the Popedom. For Marina, [7] they say, lived all her life among monks, and no-body knew but she was a monk. [8] Euphrosina lived thirty-six years amongst monks, and was reputed for a monk. So did [9] Eugenia, Pelagia, and Margareta, and no man suspected them of fraud.

Pap. [10] Yea, but how happened it her own lovers had not discovered her, or her incontinent life ?

Prot. That her lovers did not discover her, it is no wonder. For partners in mischief are good in concealments. As for her incontinent life, that discovered her at length: God, according to his [11] promise, bringing forth the shadow of death to light, that is, making known her secret naughtiness.

Pap. [12] Yea, but how could she pas through priesthood, and other ecclesiastical orders; how by so many under-offices and degrees as they must, before they come to be popes, without descrying ? [13] For, nine hundred years from St. Peter, no man was chosen pope that was

brevi Deus sustulit. Platina in vita Christophori. Paucorum labes sinceris maculam, & univers. Eccles. infamiam ingerit. Et in mea opinione ideo frequentius moriuntur Pontifices, ne totam corrumpant Ecclesiam. Joh. Salisb. de Nugis Curialium, lib. vi. cap. 24.
1 N. D. Num. 35. pag. 403.   2 N. D. Num. 28. pag. 396. Bell. lib. iii. de Rom.
Pont. cap. 24.   3 Johan. Pierius Valerianus pro Sacerdotum Barbis, Fol. 21. ad Cardinal. Medicen, printed at Lond. in ædib. Tho. Berthelet. anno 1533.   4 Lib. vi. de Rebus Turcicis.   5 N. D. Mum. 35. pag. 403.   6 Onuph. Annot. in Plat. in Vita Joh. VIII. Florim. cap. 23. pag. 197.   7 Ravis. Textor in Officina. Tit. Mulieres habitum virilem mentita.   8 Ibid. & Pet. de Natal. in Catal. Sanct. lib. iii. cap. 113.   9 Vita. Patrum, lib. i. Pet. de Natal. lib. ii. cap. 3. Pet. de Natal. in Catal. Sanct. lib. ix. cap. 36 & 37.   10 N. D. Pag. 402.   11 Job xii. 22.
12 Onuph. Loco citato. N. D. Pag. 402.   13 Onuph. ibid.

E 3

not brought up in the Roman church, and passed through priesthood, and other ecclesiastical orders.

Prot. That is not so. For [1] Dionysius was made pope of a monk; and [2] Valentinus in the time of his deaconship, before he was priested. And so was [3] Benedict the Fifth too. And as for [4] Leo the Eighth, he was chosen, being but a layman : *per Othonem I. homo laicus Leo intrusus est,* saith Baronius. Your own [5] Genebrard did note, that this note of Onuphrius was worth nothing ; yea, that it was false, as many of his notes are.

Pap. [6] Yea, but Polonus and others say, that this Joan brought forth a child, as she went in procession. Now it is not credible, that a woman, who had gone so many months with child, would then especially go abroad, when there was most fear she might be discovered.

Prot. This is like the rest: for the time of child-birth is uncertain. For, though women go usually ten months, yet sometimes they come sooner, at nine or eight, yea at seven months, as [7] physicians have observed. Honester women than Pope Joan have fallen in travel upon the high way, before ever they were aware, that they were so near their reckoning, as Theophylact observeth ; for, ‘ Novit mulier quòd pariet, quando verò, non novit,’ saith [8] he : ‘ Nam non paucæ 8. mense pepererunt etiam in itinere, nihil præscientes;’ that is, A woman knows she shall be delivered, but the time she knows not ; for divers have been delivered in their eighth month, as they have been in their journies, never dreaming of any such thing. What is your next exception ?

Pap. [9] They say she was buried without any solemnities in the world. And how is that credible, seeing it is a barbarous and savage part, to deprive them of the order of solemn burial, which have borne the greatest offices?

Prot. Is it -o ? Do we not read in scripture, that God in his justice doth use to serve the greatest princes so, who dishonour him ? Do we not read, [10] that Jehoiachim, King of Judah, was to be buried as an ass is buried, &c. Yea, do we not read in some of your own stories, that some of your popes have had as small solemnities ? ‘ Bonifacius VII. post mortem Joh. XV. sedit menses 4, repentina morte interiit, & in tantum eum òdio habuerunt sui, ut post mortem cæderent eum, & lanceis vulnerarent, atque per pedes traherent nudato corpore usque ad campum qui est ante caballum Constantini ; ibi projecere eum atque dimiserunt,’ saith [11] Baronius. Boniface the Seventh, who sat after John the Fifteenth, four months, died a sudden death, and he was so hateful to his own followers, that, after his death, they beat him, and ran him into the body with lances, and dragged him by the feet, all naked, till they came to the field which is near the place where Con-

1 Plat. in Vita Dionysii.   2 Idem in Vita Valentini.   3 Idem in Vita Bened. V.   4 Geneb. Chron. lib. iv. ad ann. 963. annal. tom. x. ad ann. 999. num. 2.
5 Chronol. lib iv. ad ann. 398.   6 Bell. lib. iii. de Rom. Pont. cap. 24.
7 Levinus Lemnius de occultis Naturæ Miraculis, lib. 4 cap. 22 & 23.   8 Comment. in 1 Thess. v.   9 Florim. cap. 23. num. 6.   10 Jer. xxii. 18, 19.   11 Annal. tom. x. ad ann. 985. è veteri Pontif. Vaticano Codice.

stantine's horse stands; there they threw him from them, and there they left him.

Pap. [1] Yea, but it was never heard of before, nor never in use among Christians, to bury a man in the high ways.

Prot. No? Is it not written, that [2] Deborah, Rebecca's nurse, was buried under an oak; and that [3] Rachel, Jacob's wife, a far honester woman than Pope Joan, was buried in the way to Ephrath; though, if it had not, yet Pope Joan was but right served to be buried so; for it was never heard of before, nor never in use among Christians, that a pope should be delivered of a child. The extraordinariness of the case deserved extraordinary exemplary usage. Your friend Papyrius Massonus, [4] much commended by your Cardinal [5] Baronius, [6] holds opinion, that, if there had been any such pope, the Romans could have done no less, in equity, than to have hanged her up in chains after her death: [7] because he finds not that she was shamefully enough hanged after her death, he denies the story.

Pap. Papyrius Massonus is a worthy man indeed: ' Ut ventus fumum, evanescere totam in auras fabulam fecit;' He hath disproved this tale thoroughly [8] in Baronius's judgment. But yet I think with Florimondus, they should have allowed her christian burial; they should have made her a tomb; they should have written epitaphs on her.

Prot. What? Epitaphs on such a whore? That had been a jest indeed. Yet perhaps some mad-cap did so. And how prove you the contrary?

Pap. If she had had a tomb made for her, and epitaphs on her, they would have been forth-coming. For as [9] Florimondus writes, ' Sepulchrorum nunquam intermoritur memoria,' Tombstones continue for ever.

Prot. Indeed I have [10] read, that by law it was provided, than no men should deface tombstones. And I have [11] read also, that to this day, hard by Troy, ' Videre licet magna marmorea sepulchra operis antiqui ex uno lapide, instar cistæ, excavata, quorum opercula adhuc integra sunt;' A man may see many marble sepulchres, wrought after the old fashion, cut hollow like a chest, out of stone, the covers whereof are still whole. But I do not read, that men can shew, which was Priamus's grave, which Hector's, &c. Yet, but for evil fingers, I could have told you where Pope Joan's tomb was. Till Pius Quintus cast it into Tybur, it was to be seen in Rome.

Pap. They say further, that she died instantly. But, though the pains of women be great at such times, yet it comes by throes; they have some intermission; their pain is not like to a sudden apoplexy, on which they die instantly.

Prot. Men do not die instantly who are taken with an apoplexy; they may live long after, and be cured thereof, as [12] physicians say.

1 Florim. cap. 23. 2 Gen. xxxv. 8. 3 Ibid. ver. 19. 4 Papyr.
Masso. vir præstans ingenio & pietate. 5 Tom. x. annal. ad ann. 853. Num. 62.
6 De Urb. Episc. lib. iii. in Bened. III. 7 Ultimo supplicio affecisseut.
8 Loco citato. 9 Loco citato. 10 Polyd, Virg. de Invent. Rerum. lib. vi. cap. 10.
11 Bellos. lib. ii. Observat. cap. 6. 12 Felix Platerus Archiater Basil. Pract. cap. 1.
peg. 46, edit. Basil. 1608.

Your Florimondus herein is out of his element. Neither did she die instantly, though it seems suddenly : for she was delivered of a boy before her death.

Pap. Was she delivered of the boy wherewithal she went; and what was then the cause of her death ? Florimondus accounts this as one of the absurdities which follow on this tale : ' Imo, ut aiunt,' [1] saith he, ' masculum pepererat, quid igitur mortem repentinam attulit?' If a woman be once delivered of the fruit of her womb, there is no danger of death in his opinion.

Prot. Commend me to him, if ever you see him. And ask the woodcock, if he have not known women die in child-bed, as well as in child-birth. [2] Rachel was delivered of her son Benjamin, and yet died shortly. [3] Phinehas's wife was delivered of her son Ichabod, and yet died presently after. And, if they died so, why not Pope Joan ? I pray you, let me hear what exceptions some wiser men take against this story ; for I am weary of Florimondus's fopperies.

Pap. ' How is she said to have gone from the palace of St. Peter to St. John Lateran, whereas the pope lay not then in the Vatican, but at St. John Lateran itself?

Prot. How prove you that the pope lay not then in the Vatican?

Pap. [5] Platina witnesseth, that the pope lay not in the Vatican till Boniface the Ninth's days, to wit, till the year 1350.

Prot. Boniface the Ninth lived in the year 1390, not 1350, wherefore in that circumstance you fail; and so you do in fathering such a fancy upon Platina. For [6] Platina reports only, that the Vatican was repaired by Boniface the Ninth. He saith not, it was first inhabited by Boniface the Ninth; though, if he had, yet the pope might well have gone to see the Lateran, for he had other houses to solace himself and his courtiers in besides the Lateran. He dwelt not always in that; for [7] Gregory the Fourth made two goodly houses, even out of the ground, for the pope's use, as your Anastasius testifieth. And Leo the Third (as we read in the same [8] Anastasius) made another goodly house, near to St. Peter's church, which stands in the Vatican, [9] wherein Leo the Fourth gave entertainment to Ludovick the Emperor. But besides, the stories do not report, she went from St. Peter's palace to the palace of the Lateran; but from St. Peter's church to the Lateran church. For she was delivered, as they went in procession. Now she might go from St. Peter's church to the Lateran church, and yet dwell in the palace of the Lateran. For popes began not always their processions at the next church to them. [10] Leo the Third appointed to go in procession three several days before Ascension-day. And he began the first day at one of [11] St. Mary's churches, and ended at St. Saviour's church. The second day he began at St. Sabina, the martyr's church, and ended at St. Paul's. The third day he began at St. Cross's church in Jerusalem, and ended at St. Lawrence's without the walls. So that this question of yours is answered. Let me know if you have any more to say.

1 Pag. 205.　　2 Gen. xxxv. 17, 18.　　3] 1 Sam. iv. 20, 21.　　4 N. D. of
3 Convers. part II. cap. 5. num. 36. Florim. pag. 202. Bell. lib. iii. de Rom. Pont. cap. 24.
5 Florim. loco citato.　　6 In vita Bonif. IX.　　7 De Vit. Pont. in Vita Greg. IV.
8 In Vita Leon.　　9 Idem in Leone IV.　　10 Platina in Vita Leon. III. &c.
Anastas. de Vit. Pont. in Leon. III.　　11 Ecclesia Dei Genetricis ad praesepe.

Pap. You shall; and, First I will prove it a fable out of their own mouths that report it.

Prot. That is a piece of cunning in good earnest. But how I pray you?

Pap. Marry, even as St. [2] Mark, the evangelist, proved the Jews lyars, by the inconvenience of their testimonies?

Prot. What mean you by the inconvenience of their testimonies?

Pap. Their disagreeing one with another.

Prot. But so did not St. Mark. For those false witnesses, whose testimony (as he notes) was inconvenient, agreed well enough in their tale. [3] They only failed in this, that the matter which they witnessed against him was not capital, though it had been true. For to promise the re-edifying of a church, in three days, is neither felony nor treason. And in this respect St. Mark observes, that their testimony was inconvenient, meaning to condemn him to death. But what great disagreement have you observed among the relaters of this tale?

Pap. [4] Infinite. Insomuch that a man may well think God hath taken a-new the same course with these, which he took of old with them who occasioned him to say : [5] " Come, let us confound their language, that one of them know not what another saith.

Prot. That is much, I long to hear the particulars.

Pap. So you shall by and by. But, First, I pray you, tell me by the way, [6] why Marianus, the first broacher of this tale, gave her such a new-fangled and new-devised name as Joan? Why took he that name which in former ages was proper to men only, and by changing a letter made it a woman's name? Florimondus cannot teach the reason of this.

Prot. Florimondus is a proper 'squire, and you are a wise man to demand such a question. Read the scriptures, and you shall find, that the name of Joan is no new devised name, nor proper to men only. For [7] they mention one Joan, the wife of Chuza. Or, if, for fear of proving an heretick, you dare not read the scriptures, [8] read your legends and festivals, and in them you shall find that your sea saint, Nicholas's mother, was called Joan. If some should hear you demand such a question, they would think the fool rid you. Wherefore, no more of this, if you respect your credit ; fall to shew me the manifold disagreement which you promised.

Pap. I will. [9] And, First, observe with me the confusion that is among them, touching her name before her papacy. Some say, she was called Agnes, some Gilbert, some Isabel, some Margaret, some Tutta or Jutta, others Dorothy.

Prot. Who calls her, I pray you, either Dorothy, or Jutta, or Tutta?

1 Baron. Annal. tom. x. ad ann. 853. num. 67.   2 Mark xiv. 59.
3 Testes quidam inter se recte conveniebant, cum eadem uterque verba, & eodem sensu recitaret.
——Sed quamvis affirmarent Christum dixisse: ego dissolvam,' &c. non judicabant pontifices
propterea Christam ad mortem condemnari. Maldonat, in Mat. xvi. 61.
4 Baron. Annal. tom. x. ad ann. 853. num. 67.   5 Gen. xi.   6 Marianus
eam Johannem novo adinvento & innovato vocabulo appellavit. Quorsum verb nomen, quod
antea solis masculis imponebatur, sola litera mutata, ad mulierem detorsit? Florim. cap. 7. num.1.
   Luke viii. 3. and xxiv. 10.   8 Golden Legend and English Festival, in the Life of
St. Nicholas. and Pet. de Natal. in Catal. Sanct lib. i. cap. 53.   9 Audi quanta inter
eos confusio in conflicta feminae nomine, &c. Baron. Annal. tom. x. ad ann. 853. num. 67. and
Florim. cap. 4. Num. 5. & cap. 7. Num. 4.

Who ever called her Margaret, or Isabel? Yea, who of the ancient sort of writers called her Gilbert, or Agnes? In some of later time I find some difference, one calling her Gilbert, and another Agnes. But, of all those whom I brought in, to give in evidence against her, there is not past one or two, who, either before, or after her papacy, gives her any other name than Joan. And, for aught I know, there is no man, either old or young, who ever christened her Dorothy, or Jutta, or Isabel, or Margaret. Know you any that have done so?

Pap. No; for I find no authors cited for proof of this, neither by Florimondus, nor by Baronius. And I can say no more than I find in them. But what say you to the next difference? ¹ Do not some of your witnesses feign her John the Seventh, some John the Eighth, some John the Ninth?

Prot. Who feigns her to be John the Ninth? Not a man that I know. If you bring not some author for the proof of this point, you must give me leave to think you speak over.

Pap. Over or short, I follow in this Baronius, and N. D. For some, saith Baronius, call her John the Seventh, some John the Eighth, some John the Ninth. Some, saith N. D. do feign her to be John the Eighth, some the Ninth.

Prot. Baronius and N. D. are as like to speak over as you, for they are papists; wherefore I neither believe them nor you, further than I see reason. And herein neither they nor you shew reason. For none of you cite so much as one author, good or bad, for it. ² Besides, your Florimondus confesseth, that we are only troubled about this, whether we should call her John the Seventh, or John the Eighth; he chargeth us not with naming her John the Ninth.

Pap. Well, let that be your difference, that you know not whether to call her John the Seventh, or John the Eighth.

Prot. That difference is not so great. For the like may be shewed in other Popes, which yet you yourself confess were Popes. But who stiles her either John the Seventh, or John the Eighth? Verily, neither Marianus Scotus, nor Sigebert, nor Gotefridus Viterbensis, nor Polonus, nor Platina, nor Palmerius, nor Trithemius's Fasciculus Temporum, nor Krantius, nor Alphonsus è Carthagena, nor Textor, call her either John the Seventh, or John the Eighth, but simply John or Joan. For it seems they were of ³ Onuphrius's mind in this, that ʻ numeri notam habere non debuit sacri ordinis non capax;' that, seeing she was not capable of priesthood, she should not go for one in the number of Johns.

Pap. Yes, by your leave, Platina stiles her John the Eighth, and the next the Ninth; for which he is reproved by ⁴ Onuphrius, and that upon the reason which you mentioned. For these are Onuphrius's words: ʻ Johannes VIII. non IX. est, ut à Platina describitur: nam, etsi Johannes fœmina papa, quam profitetur, fuisset, non tamen numeri notam habere debuisset sacri ordinis non capax:' That is, John questionless is the Eighth, and not the Ninth, as Platina accounts him;

1 Alii eam vocant Joh. vii. alii. viii. alii vero ix. saith Baronius, loco citato. Some do feign him to be John the Eighth, some the Ninth; said N. D. pag. 401.
2 Hoc unum eorum animos torquet, utrum Joh. vii. aut Joh. viii. nomen sibi usurparit. Florim, cap. v. num. 5.　　3 Annot. in Plat. in vita Joh. IX.　　4 Loco citato.

for, though John the woman, whom he talks of, had been pope, yet, seeing she was not capable of priesthood, she should not go for one in the number of Johns.

Prot. Platina stiles her not John the Eighth, Onuphrius, or somebody else, hath abused both Platina and you: For proof whereof, I appeal to Platina, printed in the year 1481 [1], which was the year wherein Platina died; and to the next edition, Anno. 1485. For, speaking of John the woman, in those ancient editions, he sets no numeral note upon her head, but begins his story thus: ' Johannes Anglicus, ex Moguntiaco oriundus, &c.' John English, born at Mentz. Neither stiles he the next the Ninth, but the Eighth. For, coming to that Pope's life, ' Johannes VIII. ' patria Romanus, &c.' saith he: John the Eighth, by his country a Roman, &c. For further proof of which latter point, I appeal to the [2] later editions, whereunto Onuphrius's annotations are annexed. For, though we read thus in them, ' Johannes Nonus, patria ' Romanus, &c.' John the Ninth, by his country a Roman, &c. yet, that that reading is false, and the ancient reading true, it appears by that which is written of the next Pope's life, to wit, Martin the Second, even in those later editions; for [3] Platina, shewing how Martin lived in the time of Charles the Third, adds presently, ' Quem ab Johanne VIII. coronam accepisse scripsimus :' That is, Who was crowned by John the Eighth, as we have written. Now Charles the Third was crowned by John, next before Martin, according to [4] Platina: Wherefore the next before Martin was John the Eighth, in Platina's account, and not John the Ninth, as Onuphrius, or somebody else would make us believe. Which oversight, or fraud of Onuphrius, was not so great, but, by this means, he is forced to alter Platina's numeral note, set to all the Johns that follow, to call him John the Tenth, whom Platina calls John the Ninth; to call him the Eleventh, whom Platina calls the Tenth; to call him the Thirteenth, when Platina calls the Twelfth; and so unto the last, Baldesar Cossa, who was in the number of Johns, according to the ancient editions, the Twenty-third, and not the Twenty-fourth, as he is numbered in the editions with Onuphrius's notes. But say on: What other disagreement have you observed among the reporters of this story?

Pap. ' Some say, she began her papacy in the year 853 ; some, in the year 854 ; some, in the year 857 ; some, in 858 ; some, in 904 ; some, in 653 ; some, in 686.

Prot. Why name you not the authors that write this ? For, to this day, I never read, or heard of any, who placed her either about the year 653, or 686, or 904 ; all the above named historiographers mention her within the compass of five years : till you bring forth your proof, there is great reason to suspect your truth.

1 Platina moritur Romæ, anno 1481.   Trith de Script. Ecclesiast. verbo, Bartholomæus.
2 Such as that of Cologne, anno 1574.   3 De Vitis Pont. in Vita Martini II.
4 In Vita ejusdem Joannis.
5 Alii ponunt hoc anno 853 ; alii, anno sequente; alii, 857 ; octavo, alii ; quidam 904. præter eos qui ponunt eum post Martinum I. anno 853. Alii post Johannem V. Anno 686. Baron. loco citato, & Florim. c. vii. num. 4.

Pap. [1] Peradventure you will suspect my truth, if I tell you, that some say, she succeeded Leo the Fourth ; some, Leo the Fifth ; some, Benedict the Third ; some, Martin the Fifth ; some, John the Fifth.

Prot. I shall indeed ; for I read, in [2] Bellarmine, that ' Omnes, qui istum Johannem admittunt, dicunt eum sedisse post Leonem IV. & ante Benedictum III.' All, who acknowledge such a woman pope, place her after Leo the Fourth, and before Benedict the Third.

Pap. Yea, but you have little reason to believe Bellarmine therein ; for [3] Polonus writes, that she succeeded Leo the Fifth ; and so doth [4] Sigebert too.

Prot. That Leo, whom Sigebert placeth next before Joan the woman, is numbered the Fifth, it is some error in the print, for [5] he names but three popes of that name before that Leo ; wherefore, when Sigebert is corrected, you have no colour of exception from him : No more have you from Polonus ; for, though, according to his account, Leo, before this woman-pope, be Leo the Fifth, yet he is the same man, whom others call Leo the Fourth. Polonus reckons one Leo, as Pope, in the year 698, whom others reckon not at all ; which is the cause of the difference between him and others, in the account of Leo's that follow ; but, in the persons, all agree. What is the next disagreement ?

Pap. [6] Some say, she sat Pope one year, one month, and four days ; some two years, two months, and four days ; some, two years and a half ; some, but two years full. [7] Very many say, she sat one year, five months, and three days ; and they are no small number, who say, she sat but barely four months.

Prot. If this be true, Bellarmine was far wide ; for [8] he writes, that ' Omnes, qui istum Johannem admittunt, dicunt eum vixisse in pontificatu duobus annis & quinque mensibus.' All, that acknowledge that woman Pope, say, she sat as pope two years and five months. He knew none (no more than I) that gave her so little time as four months. He knew no such difference herein, as you talk of ; yet, among the later writers, I confess, there is some difference of some few months ; but Marianus and Polonus, which are two of the principal, agree upon the point ; they write uniformly, that she sat two years, five months, and four days ; And Platina is not far short of that sum, for, by his reckoning, she sat two years, one month, and four days. But, suppose the differences in these circumstances were great and many, What is that to discredit the substance of the story ? We find great difference among them who have written of Pope Lucius ; for [9] some say, he was a Roman ; [10] some, a Tuscan ; some say, he was the son of Lucinus ; [11] some, of Porphyry ; [12] some say, he was chosen

1 Florimondus, loco citato.   2 Lib. III. de Rom. Pont. cap. xxiv.   3 In Chron. ad Annum 855, collat. cum anno 847.   4 In Chron. ad annum 847, collat. cum anno 854.   5 Sigebert names Leo I. ad annum 448. Leo II. ad annum 664. Leo III. ad annum 795 ; and the next is that Leo, who sat ad Annum 847.   6 Alii eum sedisse tradunt anno uno, & mense uno, & diebus quatuor. Alii annis duobus, totidemque mensibus, & diebus quatuor. Alii duobus annis cum dimidio ; duobus tantum annis alii ; alii vero quatuor tantum menses. Baron. loco citato. Florim: cap. vii. num 4.   7 This is in Florimondus, and not in Baronius.   8 Lib. III. de Rom. Pont. Cap. xxiv.   9 Platina, de Vita Pont. in Vita Lucii. I. Onuph. in Chron. Rom. Pont. ad annum 253.   10 Anastasius in Vita Lucii.   11 Idem ibid.   12 Plat. & Onuph. loco citato.

pope in the year 253; [1] some, in the year 254; [2] some in the year 255; [3] some, in the year 259; [4] some, in the year 275. [5] Some say, he sat pope three years, three months, and three days; [6] some, three years and five months; [7] some, three years, seven months, and six days; [8] some, but one year, three months, and thirteen days; [9] some, but eight months, and no longer; and yet there is no man denies that Lucius was pope.

Again, do we not read, that Sergius the Third began his reign in the year 905, as [10] some say? As [11] others, in the year 907? As a [12] third sort, in the year 908? Do not [13] some also write, that he succeeded Benedict the Fourth? [14] Others, that he succeeded Formosus? [15] Others, Christopher? And is not there difference also about the time of his continuance in the Popedom? While [16] some say, he sat seven years, three months, and sixteen days; [17] some, three years only; yet, who ever denied, that there was such a Pope?

We [18] read, that Formosus's carcase was taken up out of his grave by one of his successors, and brought into judgment before a council of Bishops; and that it was spoiled of its papal robes, and clad with a layman's garment! That he was indicted, arraigned, and condemned. But, among them that report this, there is great disagreement; for [19] some say, it was taken up by Sergius the Third, of whom I spoke even now; some say, it was taken up by [20] Stephen the Sixth, whom some call Stephen the Seventh; [21] some say, it had two fingers cut off; [22] some, three: [23] Some say, the head was chopped off; [24] some seem to deny that: [25] Some say, the trunk of the body was cast into Tybur; [26] others say, it was allowed layman's burial. I pray you now, dare you deny the truth of this story, by reason of these differences?

Pap. Why not? doth not [27] Onuphrius upon that reason deny it, saying: 'Quæ de Formosi cadavere ex sepultura a successoribus eruto dicuntur, procul dubio fabulæ magis quam vero similia sunt, quod illorum qui de ea re scripserunt diversitate & repugnantia facile liquet:' That is, the speeches which go touching the digging up of Formosus's body out of his grave, by some of his successors, are questionless fabulous, not true: Which is apparent by the disagreements and disconveniences, which are to be found among them, that write of it.

Prot. Now see you then the disagreement and disconveniences that

1 Matth. Westm. Flores Hist. ad annum 254.   2 Marian. Scot. & Polon. in Chron.
ad annum 255.   3 Abbas Ursperg. ad annum 259.   4 Compilatio in Chron.
ad annum 257.   5 Polon. & Matth. Westm. locis citatis.   6 Marian. Scotus,
loco citato.   7 Albo Florencensis, de Vitis Pont. in Lucio.   8 Onuph. loco
citato.   9 Euseb. lib. VII. Hist. cap. ii. & Abbas Urspergensis, loco citato; &
Hermannus Contractus, cir. a annum 260.   10 Math. Westm. Flores Hist, ad
annum 905.   11 Polon. in Chron. ad annum 907.   12 Baron. Annal. Tom. x.
ad an. 907. num. 2.   13 Herman. Contract. circa an. 907.   14 Luitprandus,
teste Baron. ad an. 908. num. 2.   15 Baron. ibid.   16 Polon ad ann. 907.
17 Baron. Tom. x. Annal. ad ann. 910. num. 1.   18 Baron Annal. Tom. x. ad
annum 907. num. 2.   19 Luitprand. lib. 1 cap. viii. & Abbas Urspergensis, in Chron. ad
annum 897.   20 Platina in Vita Steph. VI.   21 Weruerus Rolenink in Fascic.
Temp. ad annum 904.   22 Luitprandus, loco citato.   23 Abbas Urspergensis, loco
citato.   24 Luitprandus & alii.   25 Papyrius Massonus, lib. III. de
Urbis Episcopis, in Bonifacio VI.   26 Platina in Vita Steph. VI.   27 Annot. in Plat.
in Vita Formosi.

are among you Papists. For, though [1] Baronius confess, [2] it was such a villainous prank, as was never played before; though he confess, [3] it may seem incredible, by reason of the barbarousness of it; yet he grants it true, and avows that they err fouly, who deny that such things befel Formosus; who hold the reports for fables. Notwithstanding the manifold difference in some circumstances, he durst not cast it off as Onuphrius doth. Neither could he indeed upon Onuphrius's reason. For [4] Bellarmine saith true in this, though he miss the truth often, that *sæpissime accidit ut constet de re, & non constet de modo, vel alia circumstantia.* It oftentimes falls out, that men are sure such a thing is done, when yet, they are not sure of the manner how it was done, or of some other such like circumstance. The difference among writers, about a circumstance, doth not weaken any man's argument touching the substance. If it do, to give one instance more, blot out, for shame, St. Ursula and her fellows holiday, out of your [5] kalendar; and all the prayers, which you make to them, in your primmers, portesses, and breviaries. For there was never greater disagreement among the relators of any story, than among the relators of that. Some [6] say, that Ursula was the King of Scotland's daughter; but [7] others say, she was the King of Cornwall's daughter. [8] Some say, her father was called Maurus; but others say, he was called [9] Dionethus, or [10] Dionotus, or [11] Dionocus, or [12] Deonotus; for so diversly do they christen him. And, which concerns the husband, to whom she should have been married, [13] some write, that he was king of England: [14] Others, that he was King of Little Britain. And [15] one calls him Ætherius, another [16] Holofernes, [17] a third Conanus. Now in her company, as some say, there were only eleven-thousand ladies and gentlewomen, virgins; but, as [18] others say, there were sixty-thousand country maidens over and above those eleven-thousand of better rank. Besides, [19] there were divers bishops and lords of the temporalty who accompanied them. Yea, Cyriacus the Pope of Rome, like a good fellow, left his papacy, and followed these pilgrims, say [20] some, though others deny it. For [21] some say, that they went in pilgrimage to Rome, though [22] others hold not that probable. [23] Some say they were martyred on the sea coast: [24] Some before the gates of Cologne. And [25] some say, that all this fell out in the year 238: Some, in [26] Maximus's time: [27] Some, in the year 453. Last of all, [28] some

1 Iütenitatum hactenus scelus. 2 Præ sui immanitate omnibus incredibile. Annal. Tom. x: ad an. 897. num. 3. 3 Erroris conviacuntur qui ista de Formoso negant, & conficta putant. 4 Lib. ii. de Rom. Pont. cap. 5. 5 Octob. 21. 6 Pet. de Natal. in Catal. Sanct. lib. ix. c. 87. 7 Galfridus Monumetens. Hist Brit. Lib. v. cap. 15, 16. 8 Petrus de Natal. Loc. cit. 9 Herman. Flien. in Vita S. Ursula, Octob. 21. 10 Ponticus Virunius Hist. Brit. lib. v. 11 Baron. Annot in Martyrol. Rom. Octob. 21. b. 12 Incertus Author apud Surium, Tom. v. de Vitis Sanct. Octob. 2. 13 Pet. de Natal. Loc. cit. 14 Baron. Loc. cit. 15 Elisabetha Abbatissa Schonaugiæ, in princip. Revelationum. 16 Frater T. in Revelat. scriptis an. 1185. ut refert Flien. Loc. cit. 17 Flien. Loc. cit. 18 Ponticus Virunius & Galfridus Loc cit. 19 Pet. de Natal. Loc cit. 20 Vide supr. p. 65. 21 Harigerus Abbas Lobiensis in Catalog. Episc. Tongrensium in Metropol. 22 Flien. Annot. in vitam Ursulæ. 23 Martyr. Rom. and Baron. Annot. in Martyr. Octob. 21. 24 Flien. Loco cit. 25 Author Chron. Colon. Fol. 68. & Harig. Abbas Loco cit. &c. 26 Baron. in Martyr. Oct. 21. 27 Sigebert. in Chron. ad Ann. 853. 28 Lindan. apud Baron. Annot. in Martyr. Oct. 21.

say, that, if any be buried in St. Ursula's church, though they be infants newly baptized, the ground will cast them up again : Whereas [1] others say, that that is a tale of a tub.

Pap. I know not what to reply to this. But learneder catholicks will answer you, I hope. And, in the mean time, I will go on : [2] By the reporters of this story she was carried first to Athens. Now there was no Athens standing at that time.

Prot. Yes, that there was. For [3] Paulus Æmilius writes, that Gotefridus was made Duke of Athens, and prince of Achaia, about the year 1220. And [4] afterwards, that certain pirates, invading the country of Græcia, slew the Duke of Athens, who was of the house of Brennus, and took the city. In like manner, we read in [5] Matthew Paris, that Johannes de Basingstocke, Archdeacon of [6] Legria, who died in the year 1252, studied at Athens, and that he learned of the learned Grecians many matters unknown to men of the West Church ; especially of one Constantia, the daughter of the Archbishop of Athens. Besides, [7] Æneas Sylvius, who lived since that, doth justify, that, in his time, Athens was not quite razed, but carried the shew of a pretty town. For *Civitas Atheniensis* (quoth he) *quondam nobilissima fuit, &c. eadem nostro tempore parvi oppidi speciem gerit.* The noble city of Athens, at this time, carries but the shew of a little village. Wherefore, neither doth this your exception prejudice the truth of this story. Your next had need be better.

Pap. By the reporters of this story she was not only carried to Athens, but to Athens, for learning. Now, it is a plain case, as [8] Bellarmine writes, that there were no schools at that time, neither in Athens, nor in any place of Græcia.

Prot. What? No schools in any place of Græcia, at that time? Notes Bellarmine that? And that as a plain case? And doth he prove it too?

Pap. Yea, [9] he proves it by divers writers. And first by [10] Synesius who lived a little after Basil and Nazianzen's time. For Synesius writes unto his brother, that Athens retained only the bare name of an university.

Prot. And doth that import (think you) that, in Synesius's opinion, there was no university at Athens? I, for my part, do rather think the contrary : I think Synesius meant, thereby, that Athens was an university, though nothing so flourishing as formerly. Questionless, when [11] Bernard writ, that Peter Abailard had nothing of a monk, saving the name and the cowl, his meaning was, not, that Peter was no Monk, but rather, that he was a monk, though a sorry monk. And I am the rather persuaded, to understand Synesius's words so, because Athens, in St. Basil's time, about some forty years before Synesius, [12] was held

---

1 Flien. Loc. citat. Fabulam anilem esse didici. Vit. Joh. VIII. and Hard. Answer to B. Jewel's apology.
5 In Hen III. ad ann. 1252. p. 1112.
experientissimus.   7 Cosmog. de Europe cap. 11.
nego Athenas, neque usquam alibi in Græcia, fuisse ulla Gymnasia Literarum, lib 1II. de Rom. Pontif. cap. 24.   9 Loco citato.
scribit Athenis nihil fuisse nisi nomen Academiæ.
de Monacho præter Nomen & Habitum. Bern. Epist. 193.
Id. ad an. 364. num. 25, 26.

2 Onuph. Annot. in Platin. in
3 Lib. viii.   6 Lib. vi.
6 Johan. de Legria vir in. Trivio et Quadrivio
8 Constat eo tempore
10 In Epist. ult. ad fratrem suum Synesius
11 Petrus Abailardus nihil habens
12 Baron. Annal. Tom.

the mother of learning: and, in regard thereof, termed Golden Athens by [1] Gregory Nazianzen. For who can think, in so few years, learning should quite be quenched; and that so famous an university should, in so short time, be utterly decayed? But let us suppose, there was no university at Athens in Synesius's time. What is that to prove, that there was no university at Athens in Pope Joan's time, which was four-hundred years after? That university might get life again in so many years. And indeed it did so; for, a hundred years after Synesius's time, Boethius went to study at Athens, as [2] Baronius confesseth; nothing further, that the study of philosophy was revived there in those days. And, as we read in Hector Boetius, John Scotus, who lived about the year 850, *complures Annos Athenis Græcis Literis insudavit*, studied Greek at Athens many years.

Pap. Why, but that there were no schools in any part of Græcia in Pope Joan's days, it is proved by [3] Bellarmine out of [4] Cedrenus and Zonaras. For they record, that, in the sole reign of Michael the emperor, which fell to be about the year 856, Bardus Cæsar restored learning: ' Cum usque ad illud tempus per Annos plurimos ita fuissent extincta omnia studia sapientiæ in Græcia, ut ne vestigium quidem ullum extaret.

Prot. Bellarmine wrongs Cedrenus and Zonaras, in bringing them in, to witness such a point. For they say no more, but that learning was not regarded, of a long time before Bardus Cæsar. They say not, it was quite extinct, [5] but almost extinct. Burdus Cæsar added life unto it, [6] by setting up schools for every one of the liberal sciences, and appointing publick professors, and giving them stipends out of the Exchequer, as Cedrenus and Zonaras write; but he raised it not up simply, to life. For, if it had been stark dead, how could he, upon such a sudden, have gotten professors to furnish his schools? Again, do we not read in the same Zonaras, that, at the same time, whereof Bellarmine speaks, there was a [7] matchless philosopher at Constantinople, and many skilful mathematicians, who were his scholars? And do we not read in [8] Cedrenus, that this philosopher was called Leo, and that he [9] was brought up in learning at Constantinople, though afterwards he learned rhetorick, philosophy, arithmetick, and the other liberal sciences, in the Isle of Antro? And doth not this argue, that Cedrenus and Zonaras do not report, that there was no learning in any place of Græcia? Thirdly, Is it not well known, that, [10] about the year 680, there was kept a general council at Constantinople, whereat there were many bishops of Greece, and among the rest the [11] Bishop of Athens? Is it not well known that there was kept another council at Nice, an hundred years after, viz. [12] about the year 780: At which, there were [13] more bishops of Greece, than at

1 In Monodia in Basilii Magni vitam.   2 Annal. Tom. vi. ad an. 510. num. 2.
3 Loco citato.   4 In Vit. Michael. & Theod. imperat.   5 Philosophia
neglecta jacebat ac propè omnino extincta erat, ut ne scintilla quidem ejus appareret.
6 Cuique Disciplinæ Scholas constituit, & Doctores designavit, & singulis publica stipendia
decrevit.   7 In Philosophicis Rationibus incomparabilem. &c.   8 Loco
supra citato.   9 Literis & Poetis Leo (u ipse fer-bat) initiatus fuit Byzantii.
Rhetoricam, Philosophiam. Arithmeticam, & reliquas Scientias in Antro insula didicit.
10 Bellar. lib. i. de Conc. cap. 5.   11. Conc. Constantinop. 6. act. 17
12 Bellar. lib. i. de conc. cap. 5.   13 350. teste Bellar ibid.

the former? Is it not well known, there was a third council holden at Constantinople, which did exceed in number either of the former two, [1] about the year 870? And, how is it credible so many councils, consisting of many bishops should be kept in Greece, and yet Greece utterly without learning? Wellfare N. D. in comparison of Bellarmine herein, for N. D. durst not, it seemeth, say, with Bellarmine, that, about Pope Joan's time, there was no school in any place of Græcia. He was ashamed to run with his master to such excess of lying. He left him, in this.

Pap. True. But that Athens, at that time, had no school in it at all, nor many years before, [2] N. D. is as confident, as his master Bellarmine; and that circumstance is that which gauls you most; wherefore tell me, what more can you say to it?

Prot. Nay, first tell me how N. D. proves that; for I shall esteem of his position, as I find his proof to be.

Pap. His position is evident, [3] he saith, by Cedrenus and Zonaras, in the places already cited.

Prot. He lyes falsly, Cedrenus and Zonaras make as much for Bellarmine's opinion, as for his; for they speak of the decay of learning through Greece generally, and not in Athens particularly; yet, as you have heard, they make nothing for Bellarmine. N. D. might as well have cast off Bellarmine's witnesses, as Bellarmine's opinion, for insufficient. Have you any more exceptions?

Pap. [4] Yea; for these tale-tellers report, that she came to Rome, and there professed learning openly, and had great doctors to her scholars: But this is a notorious untruth, for there was no learning openly professed at Rome, in those days, as the stories declare.

Prot. The [5] stories declare, that Ina, one of our Saxon Kings, did build a school in Rome, a little before Pope Joan's days, viz. in the year 727; and that, to this end, that the Kings of England, and their children, the bishops, the priests, and the rest of the clergy, might 'repair thither, to be instructed in the catholick faith, and afterwards return home; which school flourished in [6] King Offa's time, viz. 795, and continued, at least, till Alfred's time; for we read, that Marinus, the Pope, who sat in the year 883, freed it from all payments, at [7] Alfred's motion. Now is it likely, that such a school was built, and maintaned for such a purpose, where no learning was publickly professed? Moreover, we read of many other schools kept in the same city, in Stephen the Sixth's time, which was about the year 885; for all the schools in Rome concurred in a joyful manner, bringing Stephen the Sixth to the palace of Lateran, saith [8] one of your popish chroniclers, and Stephen was sorry, with all his heart, he had not wherewith to gratify the schools. And is it to be thought, that all these schools were masterless, that they had no professors, nor readers?

---

1 Bellar. Loco citato.   2 Num. xxxii. pag. 46.   3 ibid.   4 Onuph.
& Harding, Locis supra citatis.   5 Math Weston. Flores. Hist. ad. an. 727.   6 idem
ad an. 795.   7 Idem ad an. 883.   8 Omnes sanctæ Romæ Ecclesiæ scholæ
conjunctæ eundem (Stephan. VI.) ad Lateranense perduxerunt palatium ———gravi mœrore
affectus est, quia quod erogaret clero & scholis non haberet.   Anastas. in Vita Steph. VI.

Pap. [1] If there had been ever such a Joan Pope, which some had forborne to speak of, for reverence to that see; the difference which is found among historians, in numbering of such popes as were called by the name of John, should have risen at that time, and by reason of that occasion; but the difference among historians, about the number of John Popes, arose not from that time, and about that occasion; it arose in Pope John the Twelfth's time, about the year 955; Ergo, there was never such a Joan Pope. Now answer me this argument, if you can, for this is held [2] a doughty one.

Prot. Is it so? Well, hearken then what I answer to it: I say, first, there is no reason, that historians should have differed in their account of Johns from her time, though some, for reverence of that see, forbore to speak of her; so they, who spoke of her, were not to set any numeral note upon her head, as [3] before I shewed you out of Onuphrius. They were not to reckon one John the more for her; neither, indeed, did any historian, before Platina, reckon her in the number of Johns, though they called her by the name of John.

Pap. Yes, Platina set a numeral note upon her head, and called her John the Seventh, and so did many since his time.

Prot. Many, since his time, have called her so, I grant, being moved thereto, as I suppose, by this, that they saw her so called in Platina; but Platina hath been corrupted by some of your generation, as [4] before I noted; for he neither called her John the Seventh, nor John the Eighth. But, secondly, I say, your minor is false; for the difference, which is about the number of Johns, arose not from John the Twelfth, but from this woman, Joan; for, since Platina's time, some called her John the Seventh, some John the Eighth, and so disagreed in the total sum.

Pap. [5] Nay, herein you are out; for, that their disagreement began in John the Twelfth's days, Lambertus, who lived in those days, witnesseth, and your century writers do confess.

Prot. Doth Lambertus witness that? Fie that you should say so, for he hath not one word sounding that way, no more have the century writers.

Pap. Yes, but they have; for they [6] write, that, whenas John the Twelfth was deposed by the cardinals, and Leo the Eighth placed in his room, John the Twelfth got the Popedom again, and kept it four months; which some historians not observing, made two popes of one.

Prot. The century writers do not write this. Your Florimondus and Bernartius, from whence you have this stuff, are shameless fellows to report this by them. They say, indeed, that there is great difference in writers about Pope John the Twelfth; meaning, by John the Twelfth, not him, but into whose room Leo the Eighth was chosen, of whom you talk at random, but another John, who was son to Sergius, commonly called John the Eleventh; But that historians began to differ in their account, by reason of that difference, they say

1 Florim. cap. vii. page 62. Bernart. Lib ii. page 127.   2 Otherem hanc de Joanae confictam fabulam hoc uno dicto damnarunt. Florim. ibid.   3 Page 70.   4 Page 72.
5 Florm. loco supra citato.   6 Cent. x. cap. 10. as Florim. and Bernart. say.

not.   Yea, it is plain, they impute the difference, among the historians, to this, [1] that some called Joan, John the Seventh; some, John the Eighth; wherefore you must cast about for a new argument, for this will not serve your turn.

Pap.   I have arguments good store; whereof the first shall be taken from the time wherein, they say, she sat as Pope; and [2] I will deal especially with Marianus Scotus, the first reporter of this matter; for, if he be confounded, all the rest must rest confounded.

Prot.   Well, fall to your work, and be as good as your word.

Pap.   [3] If Leo the Fourth lived to the year 855, then Marianus Scotus lyed falsely, in reporting that this Joan was called pope in the year 853: for, by his confession, she succeeded Leo the Fourth; but Leo the Fourth lived to the year 855: Ergo, Marianus Scotus lyed falsely, in reporting that this Joan was chosen Pope in the year 853.

Prot.   What is that to the main chance, that Marianus Scotus mistook the year of her entering into the popedom? In histories, a year or two break no square: But how prove you, that Marianus reports, that this Pope Joan was chosen in the year 853?

Pap.   [4] By his own words, for thus he writes: ' Anno octingentesimo quinquagesimo tertio Leo Papa obiit Kalend. Augusti. Huic successit Joanna mulier annis duobus, mensibus quinque, diebus quatuor.' In the year 853, Leo, the Pope, died on the kalends of August, and Joan, the woman, succeeded after him, for the space of two years, five months, and four days.

Prot.   These are not Marianus's words; for he sets not down the year precisely, but in numeral figures, by the side of the text. [5] And it is plain, by conference of years, that he meant to note out the 855th, for her entrance, and not the 853d; for Benedict the Third, who succeeded her, entered not, by his account, till the year 857.   Now, if she had entered 855, she had been pope four years, or thereabouts; for between 853 and 857, there run four years; whereas, in plain words, he notes that she was pope but two years, five months, and four days.   Secondly, it is plain, by Marianus Scotus, that Sergius the Second began his popedom in the year 844, and sat three years.   It is plain, that Leo the Fourth, next successor to Sergius, began his in the year 847, and sat eight years. Now put these odd sums, four, three, and eight, to 840, and they will make 855.   So that whosoever succeeded Leo the Fourth, must begin in the year 855, and that was Joan the woman, in Marianus's opinion.

Pap.   Why, but right over-against these figures, 853, these words are set: ' Leo Papa obiit Kal. Aug.'   Leo, the Pope, died on the kalends of August.   And doth not that argue, that, in Marianus's opinion, Leo died that year?

1 Joh. vii. ut Sabellicus vult, aut viii. ut Platina, vocatus est. cent. ix. cap. 10.
2 Baron. Annal. Tom. x. ad an. 853. num. 64.   3 Baron. ibid.   4 Baron. ibid.
5 See Marianus's Chronicle, and the case will appear to be plain.

Prot. No, no more than the words following. ' huic successit Joanna mulier, &c.' which are set just over-against these figures 854, do argue, that she began her Popedom the next year after ; or that Leo the Fourth began his popedom in the year 852, because, right over-against that number, his entrance upon Sergius's death is mentioned. Is not your next argument better ?

Pap. [1] The people of Rome, about that time, were evil affected towards the Pope ; and so was the greater part of all Italy : For that Charles had subdued them, and given them to the Pope. Now, if such an accident as this had fallen out, it might have given them just cause to have fallen from the Pope again : For they might have pretended, that they would not be subject to a womanish and a whorish government. But we read of no such thing. Ergo.

Prot. Charles rescued Italy out of the hands of the Lombards, with the great good liking both of the Romans, and the rest of Italy. But he never turned them over to live under the Pope's government. All his life he kept them in obedience to himself, and by will bequeathed the whole country to his youngest son Pipin, as [2] Baronius sheweth out of the French histories. Ergo, this argument is naught : Let me have a new one.

Pap. [3] The Popes, about the time of this your supposed pope Joan, did take up roundly both kings and emperors for their adulteries. Which is a plain argument, there was no Pope Joan in that see, guilty of any such crime.

Prot. What kings and emperors were these, whom the Popes took up so roundly for their adulteries?

Pap. Lodovicus, the Emperor, was one : For Gregory the Fifth turned him into a monastery for his adultery with one Judith, that there he might, a-part, do penance for his sin.

Prot. Gregory [4] the Fifth lived almost one-hundred and fifty years after Pope Joan ; and besides, there was no emperor called Ludovick in his time. Perhaps Florimondus would have said Gregory the Fourth, for he lived not long before Pope Joan's time, and in his days there was one Ludowick an emperor.

Pap. Indeed, it may be so, for the numeral figure might soon be mistaken. For Gregory the Fourth, a man may easily set down Gregory the Fifth : And what say you to it?

Prot. I say, Florimondus is a palterer. For Ludowick, who lived in Gregory the Fourth's time, was never noted for an adulterer, with any Judith, nor with any woman else. Judith, his wife, was suspected of that sin with others, and thereupon was veiled, and thrust into a monastery by some of the princes of the empire. And Ludowick himself, upon other pretences, was, for a time, deprived of the empire. But Gregory the Fourth had no hand, either in her veiling, or in his deprivation, as you may see by [5] Baronius. Besides,

1 Florim. cap. 14. Num. 6.   2 Annal. Tom. ix. ad ann. 806. num. 19.   3 Flor. cap. 27. num. 2.,   4 Greg. v. Ludovicum imperatorem adulterii cum Juditha quadam perpetrati reum———cujusdam cœnobii claustris addixit. Florim. ibid.   5 Annal. Tom. ix. ad nan. 833 & 854.

this fell out before Pope Joan's time; and, therefore, doth not hinder, but that there was such a Joan.   Methinks you should be drawn dry, you talk so idly.

Pap. [1] If there had been such a Pope Joan, some historian would have writ either good or bad of her.   But we read nothing of her in any history.

Prot. Do we read nothing of her in any history? Whence have we this of her aspiring to the Popedom, and of her lewd behaviour in the time of her Popedom? Have I not proved it unto you out of the histories?

Pap. Yea, but my meaning is, [2] that we read nothing in any history of her reforming the church; of her determining of causes and questions, usually proposed by bishops to them that are popes, of any intercourse or affairs, that she had with king or emperor.

Prot. No more do we read in any historian, of any such act done by Anastasius the Third, who sat as pope two years, and upward. Anastasius the Third, as [3] Platina witnesseth, did nothing worthy of remembrance.   We read nothing of any great acts done by Leo the Seventh.   He sat three years and six months; yet he did as [4] little as Anastasius, for any thing we read; he neither reformed the church, nor resolved any bishop his doubts, nor intermeddled with any princes.

Pap. [5] Oh, but that age, wherein you feign this Joan lived, was an age wherein fell out great variety of matter, both in the east and in the west.   In it many princes and emperors of great worth reigned. In it many men of great learning lived: And therefore, if there had been any such monster then, we could not but have heard of it on all sides.

Prot. So we have, as before I proved.   But what great variety of matter fell there out in that age more than ordinary?

Pap. [6] In that age, there was old holding and drawing between the eastern and western churches about images.   Many councils were kept by both sides, and many evil words passed on all hands.

Prot. Go, go, I am ashamed of you, and of Florimondus your master.   All stories testify, that the difference between the eastern and western churches, about images, began in the former ages; and that, though they continued some few years after the year 800, yet there was no talk of that matter for divers years before Pope Joan's days: Yet I am willing to hear you speak on.   Wherefore tell me what sort of learned men that age brought out?

Pap. Great store, but it were too long to reckon them.

Prot. It may be so: Yet you must know that they went for learned men in that age, [7] who were but bare grammarians.   And therefore, were they never so many, Pope Joan's acts might pass unwritten.

---

1 Flor. cap. 25. nom 3. 2 Flor. ibid. 3 Ab Anastasio nil memoria dignum gestum est. Plat in Vita Anastasii III. 4 Leo VII nil dignum memoria gessit. Plat in Vita Leonis VII. 5 Flor. Loco suprà citato. 6 Flor. ibid.
7 Qui sciret tantùm grammaticam isto seculo rudi, doctissimus habebatur. Baronius Annal. Tom. ix. ad ann. 892. num. 12.

Pap.   ¹ Yea, but I would gladly know of you, what dukes, what princes, what kings, what emperors, this Joan inaugurated and crowned : What ambasssadors she entertained, what honours she bestowed upon any persons.

Prot.   Indeed, you pose me now ; especially in that which concerns the inaugurating and crowning of dukes, and princes, and kings, and emperors.   For I remember none inaugurated or crowned by her.

Pap.   I thought so.   And therefore you do well to confess it. I trust at length you will also confess that there was no Pope Joan.

Prot.   Why, I pray you ? did every Pope inaugurate and crown either dukes, or princes, or kings, or emperors ?

Pap.   Nay, I say not so,   But in that age the emperors themselves had such a reverend opinion of the Roman Popes, that they would not take upon them to reign, except they gave them their consent, and crowned them.

Prot.   How prove you that ?

Pap.   ² By this, that Adrian the First baptized the two sons of Charles the Great, and after that anointed them kings.

Prot.   This proves not your purpose ; for this fell out in the year 781, as ³ Baronius notes, and not in that age wherein Pope Joan lived. But do you think that every Pope in that age inaugurated some dukes, or princes, or kings, or emperors ? I would gladly know of you, what duke, or prince, or king, or emperor, was inaugurated, or crowned by Pope Eugenius the Second, who sat in the year 824 ; or by Pope Valentinus, who sat in the year 827 ; or by Pope Gregory the Fourth, who succeeded Valentinus ; or by Pope Sergius the Second, who sat in the year 844 ; or by Pope Leo the Fourth, who sat in the year 847.   I am sure, never a one of these crowned any emperor. And I remember not, that any one of these anointed any duke, or king, save Leo the Fourth, who anointed Alfred, the youngest son of Ethelwulfus, King of England.   Which furthered him nothing to the attaining of the kingdom ; for, till the death of his three elder brethren, for all the Pope's anointing him, he lived like a subject, he lived not like a king.   Wherefore, to put you in mind of the main point, though Pope Joan inaugurated, or crowned, no such persons as you speak of, yet you cannot conclude thereupon : *Ergo,* there was no Pope Joan.

Pap.   ⁴ But if she bestowed no honours upon any persons ; if she made no bishops ; if she gave no bishopricks, it is more than probable there was never any such.

Prot.   Oh, but we read, that ' contulit sacros ordines, promovit episcopos, ministravit sacramenta, cæteraque Romanorum Pontificum exercuit munera :' She gave orders ; she made bishops ; she administered the sacraments, and she performed all other offices belonging unto the papacy.

Pap.   Where read you that? I warrant you, you had it out of Bale ; of whom I wish you to see, at your leisure, what ⁴ Florimondus's censure is.

---

1 Flor. cap. cit. num. 6.   2 Flor. ibid.   3 Annal. tom. ix. ad ann. 789. &c.
4 Florim. loco citato.   5 Florim. cap. 8. num. 1 & 2.

Prot. . John Bale for aught I know, is a far honester man than Florimondus. And, to tell you truth, if Florimondus rail upon him, I shall have the better opinion of him. For as [1] Tertullian persuaded himself, that whosoever knew Nero, would easily believe Christianity were good, because it was disliked by Nero: So I persuade myself, that whosoever knows Florimondus, he will the rather be well persuaded of John Bale, because he is reviled by Florimondus. But yet I would have you know, I read not this in Bale only, but in [2] Cornelius Agrippa; a man much commended by [3] Leo X. and in a [4] book of his solemnly privileged by Charles V.

Pap. Well, sir, since these reasons prevail not with you, I will come a step or two nearer to you. And first, to prove your story a fabulous fiction, I argue thus: [5] If the report of Pope Joan be not a fiction, then Nicholas, the first pope of that name, who at the time of her election was a cardinal, gave her a voice, and so consented to her election. But it is not credible that Nicholas gave her a voice, and consented to her election, *ergo.*

Prot. First, I deny that Nicholas was a cardinal at the time of Pope Joan's election. For he was made [6] subdeacon by Sergius II. and [7] deacon by Leo IV. In which order he continued [8] till the death of Benedict III. who sat after Joan. Secondly, I deny we are bound to believe that he gave Pope Joan his voice, though we should grant he was a cardinal. For it was never required, that all the cardinals should give consent to any pope's election. But principally I deny your minor proposition, viz. that it is not credible Nicholas gave her his voice, and consented to her election. And how can you prove it?

Pap. [9] If Nicholas had given her a voice, and consented to her election, then could he not honestly have reproved Photius patriarch of Constantinople, for that he suffered himself of a meer lay-man to be made a patriarch. [10] Neither could he justly have reproved Michael the Emperor, for that he gave his consent to Photius's ordination and election. But, no doubt, he reproved them both honestly and justly. *Ergo,* he never gave Pope Joan his voice, he never consented to her election.

Prot. Why might not he, without note of dishonesty, reprove Photius and the Emperor for their dealing, though he himself had a hand in Pope Joan's election?

Pap. Because he should have been guilty of the same fault, if not of a greater; for a woman, you know, is not capable of holy orders.

Prot. Oh is that it? As though there were not a main difference between Nicholas's fact, to suppose he did it, and the fact of Photius

1 Qui scit illam, intelligere potest, non nisi grande aliquod bonum à Nerone damnatum. Tertull. Apologet. cap. 5. Euseb. Hist. Eccles. lib. ii. cap. 24. 2 De Vanitate Scientiarum, cap. 64. de Sectis Monasticis. 3 Lib. i. Epistol. Epist. 58. te magnopere commendamus. &c. saith Leo the Tenth. 4 Lib. de Vanitate Scientiarum, is mentioned in the emperor's privilege. 5 Si ea fabula vera fuisset, ut Romae hoc tempore sederit foemina, cui in electione ipse Nicolaus tunc Cardinalis suffragium oportuerit contulisse, qua fronte Photium redarguere potuisset (quod saepissimè facit) eo nomine quod cum esset laicus ordinari se episcoporum poscens esset, &c. Baron. Annal. tom. x. ad. ann. 858. num. 70. 6 Anastas. Biblioth. in vita Nicolai I. 7 Ibid. 8 Ibid. 9 Baron. loco supra citato.
10 Imperatorem ipsum acerrima reprehensione perstringit, quod id agere praesumpsisset. Baron. Ibid.

and the Emperor. Photius and the Emperor did that wittingly and willingly, which Nicholas reproves in them. Nicholas chose a woman pope unwittingly. It was with Nicholas, in all likelihood, at the election of Pope Joan, as it was with the [1] two hundred of Jerusalem, who were called by Absalom to Hebron; of whom the scriptures witness, that they went in their simplicity, knowing nothing. Now ignorance, invincible ignorance, such as this was, excuseth, though not from all fault, yet from so great fault. Wherefore you must come nearer me yet, if you mean to drive me from my opinion.

Pap. Have at you then, and that with a [2] golden argument, [3] such as can never be answered, and this is it: ' About one hundred and seventy years after this devised election of Pope Joan, to wit, upon the year of Christ 1020, the church and patriarch of Constantinople being in some contention with Rome, Pope Leo IX. wrote a long letter to Michael the patriarch of Constantinople, reprehending certain abuses of that church, and, among others, that they were said to have promoted eunuchs to priesthood, and thereby also a greater inconvenience fallen out, which was, that a woman was crept to be patriarch. [4] Now, no doubt, Leo would never have durst to write thus, if the patriarch might have returned the matter back upon him again, and said: This was but a slanderous report, falsly raised against the church of Constantinople, but that a woman indeed had been promoted in the Roman church.

Prot. Is this your golden and unanswerable argument? Truly, I am sorry for you, that you have no more skill in an argument; for you presume in this, that Leo would never object that against Constantinople, whereof Rome itself might be convinced; and make that the ground of your conclusion. Now that is a slabby ground, as may appear by this, that it is ordinary with you papists to object that against others, whereof yourselves stand most guilty. It is ordinary with you papists to call your enemies whores first. Do not you complain with open mouths of us ministers, for want of continency; and yet is it not well known, that your priests and monks, [6] like fed horses, have neighed after their neighbours wives; and your nuns have opened their feet (to [7] use the prophet's phrase, when he speaketh of such-like skirts) to every one that passed by, and have multiplied their whoredoms?

' Taceo de fornicationibus & adulteriis, à quibus qui alieni sunt, probro cæteris ac ludibrio esse solent, spadonesq: aut sodomitæ appellantur;' saith [8] Nicholas Clemangis, speaking of your priests.

I say nought of your priests fornications and adulteries, from which crimes, if any man be free, he is made a laughing-stock to the rest, and either called an eunuch or a sodomite.

' Laici usque adeò persuasum habent nullos cœlibes esse, ut in plerisq; parochiis non aliter velint presbyterum tolerare, nisi concubinam

1] 2 Sam. xv. 11.   2 O Locus Epist. opportunus & auro contra non carus, & quo facile
protelam omnia adversariorum tela, &c. Bernart. lib. citato. pag. 109.   3 Ratio ineluctabilis, saith Genebrard. Chron. lib. iv. Maximi ponderis arg. saith Flor. cap. 25. pag 209.
    4 Leo IX. Epist. ad Michaelem Epitc. Constantinop. cap. 23.   5 N. D. lib. citat.
num. 29, pag. 398.   6 Jer. v. 8.   7 Ezech. xvi. 25.   9 De Præsulibus
Simoniacis: In Bibliotheca santorum Patrum, printed at Paris, 1576, pag. 655.

habeat ; quo vel sic suis sit consultum uxoribus ; quæ ne sic quidem usquequaque sunt extra periculum,' saith the [1] same man.

The lay people are so conceited of the incontinence of all priests, that willingly they would not have a parish priest, unless he have a whore of his own, that so they might keep their own wives.   And yet, for all that, they are scarce sure of their own by that course.

'Fornicantur complures Monialium cum suis prælatis, ac monachis, & conversis, & in monasteriis plures parturiunt filios & filias, quos ab iisdem prælatis, monachis, & conversis fornicariè, seu ex incestuoso coitu conceperunt,' saith [2] Theodoricus de Niem, secretary to Pope Urban VI. going on thus, 'Et quod miserandum est, nonnullæ ex hujusmodi monialibus aliquos fœtus earum mortificant, & infantes in lucem editos trucidant, &c.

Many nuns commit fornication with bishops, and monks, and converts, and are delivered of sons and daughters within their monasteries, which were got by those persons, fornicator like, if not incestuously. And, which is most pitiful, very many of these nuns kill, with suberdisauces, the fruit in their wombs ; many kill them after they be born.

· 'Quid (obsecro) aliud sunt hoc tempore puellarum monasteria, nisi quædam veneris execranda porstibula, & lascivorum, & impudicorum juvenum ad libidines explendas receptacula ; ut idem sit hodie puellam velare, quod & publicè ad scortandum exponere; saith [3] Clemangis above-named.

What are nunneries, I pray you, now, save cursed stews, and places or meeting of wanton and shameless youths to satisfy their lusts in? So that now it is all one, to make a wench a nun, and to make her a whore.

'Johannes Cremensis, one of your Romish cardinals, held a council at London, in the year 1125, wherein he inveighed bitterly against such priests as kept concubines, 'dicens summum scelus esse à latere meretricis ad corpus Christi conficiendum surgere,' saying, it was a damnable sin for a priest to arise from a whore to go to say mass ; yet he himself loved a whore with all his heart.   For, as we read in our[4] English stories, 'Ipse cum eadem die corpus Christi confecisset, cum meretrice post vesperam interceptus est;' he himself was taken with a whore the same night after he had said mass.   And, as it seems, he was taken in the manner; for the historiographers note, 'Res notissima negari non potuit;' The matter was so plain, it could not be denied.

Again, do you not condemn us of ignorance [6] reporting by us, that we are afraid to reason with common catholicks ; and that, when we do reason, the common sort of catholicks are able to answer all our arguments, and to say also more for us, than we can say for ourselves ; as though ye were the people only, and wisdom must die with you.   And yet are not we able to prove out of your own mouths, that your priests and monks were generally like the [7] sixscore thousand Ninevites, who

1 Ibid.   2 Nemoris Unionis, Tract. vi. cap. 34.   3 De corrupto Ecclesiæ Statu.
4 Henricus Huntingdon, Hist. lib. vii. ad ann. Christi 1125. Roger Hoveden Annal. para prior
in Hen 1. ann. 1126. Matth. Paris in Hen. 1. ad ann. 1125. pag. 93. Matth. Westm. Flores. Hist.
ad ann. 1125.   5 Huntingdon, Hoveden, Matth. Paris locis citat.   6 Bristow,
Motive 31.   7 Jonas iv. 11.

had not so much wit as to discern between their right hand and the left?

'Videas admitti ad sacerdotium cæterosque sacros ordines homines idiotas & illiteratos, vix morosè ac syllabatim absque ullo intellectu legere scientes, qui *Latinum & Arabicum* æqualiter norunt: saith [1] Clemangis, speaking of the ignorance of your clergy.

Thou mayest see ignorant and unlettered persons advanced to priesthood, and the other holy orders; which cannot read without stuttering and stammering, who have as great skill in the Arabian tongue, as in the Latin. And in [2] another place:

'Quotusquisque hodie est ad pontificale culmen evectus, qui sacras, vel perfunctoriè, literas legerit, audierit, didicerit, imò qui sacrum codicem nisi tegumento tenus unquam attigerit?

How many are now a-days preferred to bishopricks, who, not so much as cursorily, have either read, or heard, or learned the holy scriptures? Yea, who have not so much as touched the Bible, except it were on the outside of the covering?

'Hoc seculo episcopatus & sacerdotia indoctissimis hominibus & à religione alienis deferri solent.—Hodiè episcopi nostri (paucis exceptis) sacrarum literarum scientia cæteris ex populo longè inferiores sunt, saith [3] Duaren.'

In this age, bishopricks and parsonages are bestowed on most unlearned and irreligious men.—At this day, our bishops (except a few) are more unlearned than the common people.

'Pudeat Italiæ sacerdotes, quos ne semel quidem legisse constat novam legem; apud Thaboritas, vix mulierculam invenias, quæ de novo & veteri Testamento respondere nescit,' saith [4] Æneas Sylvius.

Fie upon the priests of Italy, who never read over the New Testament: 'A man can hardly find a woman among the Thaborites, who cannot answer roundly to any thing out of the Old and New Testament.

'Ecclesiarum regimina minus dignis, Romæ videlicet, committuntur, qui ad mulos magis quàm homines pascendos & regendos essent idonei.

The government of the churches, even at Rome, is committed to unworthy persons, who are fitter to look to the keeping of mules than men.

Thirdly, Do not you upbraid us with baseness and vileness: accounting no better of our most reverend bishops, than uncircumcised Philistines, which, as [6] you say, were taken out of the rascality of the whole realm? [7] Do not you give out, that a great part of our clergy resteth in butchers, cooks, catchpoles, coblers, dyers, and dawbers; felons, carrying their mark in their hand, instead of a shaven crown; fishermen, gunners, harpers, inn-keepers, merchants, and mariners; net-makers, potters, apothecaries, and porters of Billingsgate; pinners, pedlars, ruffling ruffians, sadlers, shearmen, and shepherds; tanners,

1 De Præsulibus Simoniacis, in Biblioth. Sanct. part edit. Paris. 1576.   2 De corrupto Ecclesiæ Statu.   3 De sac. Eccles. Minist. & Benefic. lib. 1. cap. 11.   4 Comment. de Dict. & Fact. Alfonsi Regis, lib. 4. Apotheg. 17.   5 Gravamen VII. Nationis Germanicæ, quod habetur in Fasciculo Rerum expetendarum, impress. Colon. 1535. fol. 169. b.   6 Allen's Answer to the Book of English Justice, cap. 3. page 44.   7 Staplet. in the fourth book of the Counterblast. fol. 481. and S. R. in his Answer to Bell's Downfall of Popery, cap. 8. art. 7. num. 4. page 301.

tilers, tinkers, trumpeters, weavers, wherrimen, &c.? Do not[1] you report, that so many bankrupts, and infamous and villainous wretches, are admitted to it, that none, almost, except he be driven thereto by beggary, will enter into it? As though ye only were the sons of nobles, and we the children of fools, and the children of villains, which were more vile than the earth: and yet are we not able to prove against you, that you have made Levites, even bishops and priests, of the blind and the lame, of the flatnosed, broken-footed, and broken-handed, of the crooked-backed and blear-eyed, of the scurvy and scabbed, of the lowest of the people, tag and rag.

' Si quis desidiosus est, si quis a labore abhorrens, si quis in ocio luxuriari volens, ad sacerdotium convolat; quo adepto, statim se ceteris sacerdotibus voluptatum sectatoribus adjungit, qui magis secundum Epicurum, quam secundum Christum viventes, & cauponulas seduli frequentantes, potando, commessando, pransitando, convivando, cum tesseris, & pilo ludendo tempora tota consumunt: crapulati vero & inebriati pugnant, clamant, tumultuantur, nomen dei & sanctorum suorum pollutissimis labiis execrantur, sicque tandem compositum, ex meretricum suarum complexibus ad divinum altare veniunt;' saith[2] Clemangis, speaking of your worthies.

If there be any lazy fellow, any that cannot away with work, any that would wallow in pleasures, he is hasty to be priested. And, when he is made one, and hath gotten a benefice, he consorts with his neighbour priests, who are altogether given to pleasures; and then both he, and they, live, not like Christians, but like Epicures; drinking, eating, feasting, and revelling, till the cow come home, as the saying is; playing at tables, and at stool-ball; and, when they are well crammed and tippled, then they fall by the ears together, whooping, and yelling, and swearing damnably, by God and all the saints in heaven. And, after all matters be somewhat pacified, then, arising out of their whores laps, they go to the mass.

' Asciscuntur nunc (saith[3] Platina) non modò servi & vulgo concepti, ac nati, verumatiam flagitiosi omnes ex flagitioso quoque geniti.'

Now-a-days not only servants, and they which are begotten and born under hedges, are admitted to be of the clergy, but every vile fellow, and every vile fellow's brat.

' Ex aulicis perditissimis & quod omni aetate fuit post christianorum memoriam inauditum, ex militibus deploratissimis, iisque sanguinariis ——Dei loco ad ecclesiae collocantur, imo repentè intruduntur, gubernacula,' saith[4] Lindan. ' Quid quod puerulis & adolescentulis creduntur haec tractanda?'

Wretched courtiers, forlorn and bloody soldiers, a thing never heard of before among Christians, are all upon a sudden thrust in upon the church to manage it in God's stead, yea boys and youngsters are made bishops and prelates in the church.

' Bibones, scortatores, aleatores, & qui haec vitia, vultu, cultu, incessu, totoque habitu prae se ferunt; passim (ad sacerdotium) admit-

---

1 Philopater ad edictum reginae Angliae, num. 192, sect. 3. page 180, alias Stapl. for he is the author, teste Possevino in Apparat. sac. tom. i. verbo Angli.   2 De corrupto ecclesiae statu.   3 In vita Soximi.   4 Panoplia lib. iv. cap. 77. page 404.

tunt.' Erasm. schol. in epistolam Hieron. de veste sacerdotali ad Fabiolam.

Doth not [1] Bellarmine charge us with that fault, whereof you yourselves stand condemned; to wit, with making a woman a pope, from which all the world, save foul-mouthed papists, will questionless acquit us? Doth not [2] Parsons avow, railing, and foul scurrility, to be proper unto us, and to our ancestors only; as though he and his were answerable to Moses in mildness, and of so temperate carriage, that butter would not melt in their mouths, when yet the contrary appeareth by their own books.

The general consent of all, that ever have thoroughly conversed with Parsons, is this, saith [3] Watson the quodlibetting priest, that he is of a furious, passionate, hot, cholerick, exorbitant working humour, busy-headed, and full of ambition, envy, pride, rancour, malice, and revenge: whereunto may be added, that he is a most diabolical, unnatural, and barbarous, butchery fellow, unworthy the name, nay cursed be the hour, wherein he had the name of a priest, nay of a religious person, nay of a temporal lay-man jesuit, nay of a catholick, nay of a Christian, nay of a creature, but of a beast, or a devil; a violater of all laws, a contemner of all authority, a stain of humanity, an imposthume of all corruption, a corrupter of all honesty, and a monopoly of all mischief. And is not this railing? Now, if this be thus, to return to the main point, why may we not think the church of Rome to be faulty in electing Pope Joan, though Leo reproved the church of Constantinople with the same?

Pap. [4] Yea, but how could Leo have answered the patriarch of Constantinople, if the patriarch might have replied truly upon him, that Rome was guilty of such an oversight?

Prot. Leo might have answered the patriarch's reply, as Ahab, who charged Elias with troubling of Israel, answered Elias, (when [5] he replied: I have not troubled Israel, but thou and thy father's house;) to wit, with silence. For otherwise I know not how he could have answered him honestly. No more than I know how other of your popes can answer other replies (in other cases) which may be made upon them. [6] Agatho, one of your popes, avoucheth, that the Roman church never swerved from the tradition of the apostles; that she never gave ear to novelties; that the pope's predecessors had ever boldly strengthened their brethren, according to Christ's commandment unto Peter. For proof thereof, he appeals to all the world. In like manner, Nicholas, another of your popes, speaking of his fellow popes, [7] braves it out, that never one of them was so much as suspected to have held an error. Now if a man should have replied upon them, as any man might have replied truly, that Victor was suspected to have held, that Christ was a pure man, and not God, which is witnessed by [8] Eusebius: that Zepherinus was suspected of Montanism, which is testified by [9] Tertullian: that Marcellinus sacrificed to idols, which is

1 Jam reipsa Calvinistia in Angliæ, mulier est summus pontifex. De notis Ecclesiæ, ib. iv. cap. 11.   2 In the Defence of the Censure, pag. 13.   3 Quodlibet of religion and state, pege 236.   4 N. D. Loco supra citato.   5] 1 Kings xviii. 17, 18.
6 In epistola 1. ad imperatorem.   7 Nichol. 1. epist. ad Michaelem.
8 Euseb. Hist. Eccl. lib. v. cap. 28.   9 Tertul. lib. contra Praxeam.

witnessed by [1] Damasus, and acknowledged by [2] Bellarmine though denied in some sort [3] by Baronius : that Liberius subscribed to the Arian heresy, which is reported by [4] Damasus, by [5] Athanasius, by [6] Jerom, and by [7] Sozomen : that Felix, as [8] some say, was an Arian, or at least, as [9] others say, communicated with the Arians: that Honorius the First was a Monothelite, and for that condemned by name in the [10] sixth and [11] seventh general councils : how could Agatho and Nicholas have answered this reply, think you?

We read that Tarasius, the patriarch of Constantinople, charged your Pope Adrian the First, with the crime of Simony. And do you therefore think that he himself was free from Simony? Or, rather, do you not know that he himself was grievously suspected of simony.

Pap. Yes, I [12] know, that, though Tarasius was an holy man in his life, and approved so to be by miracles wrought after his death, [13] yet he was very greatly suspected of simony : wherefore, I rather think, that you never read he charged Pope Adrian with that fault.

Prot. The epistle which Tarasius wrote to Adrian, wherein he reproved him for that, is extant in print, so that you yourself may read it also, if you will.

Pap. I remember [14] Baronius talks of such an epistle. But he suspects that Balsamon, who first published it, did counterfeit it, to discredit the Roman see. And, indeed, Balsamon loved not Rome.

Prot. [15] Gentian Hervet, who translated the epistle into Latin, was nothing suspicious of it. No more was [16] Bignæus, who put it into his library of holy fathers : nor, Possevine, who mentions it in his *Apparatus sacer.* I see it goeth hard with you, when you are driven to plead, that the evidence I bring is forged. I thought that shift had been proper to us protestants, for [17] you often upbraid us with it ; but now I see it is common to us with you. But why is Baronius suspicious of it?

Pap. Because it was first set out by Balsamon, who loved not Rome.

Prot. Baronius saith, therein, untruly. For proof whereof, I will use no other witness but himself ; his own mouth shall condemn him. For [18] he himself confesseth, that. ' Tarasii epistola ad Adrianum pontificem de simoniaca hæresi profliganda, ab Anastasio ad finem septimæ synodi posita legitur, necnon apud Theodorum Balsamonem in appendice ad Nomocanonem Photii.' That is, that Tharasius's epistle unto Adrian the Pope, treating of the rooting up of the sin of simony, is to be read in the end of the seventh general council, where it was put by Anastasius : and, withal, in Theodorus Balsamon, in his appendix unto Photius's Nomocanon. For, if Anastasius placed

1 In Pontificali in Vita Marcel. tom. ii. ad ann. 302. num. 101, 102. Epist. ad solitariam Vitam agentes.   2 Lib. iv, de Rom. Pont. cap. 8.   3 Annal. 4 Lib. citato in Vita Liberii.   5 In 6 De Script. Ecclesiasticis. Verb. Fortunatianus. 7 Hist. lib. iv. c. 15.   8 Hieron. de Script. Ecclesiast. Verbo Acacius. 9 Sozomen. lib. iv. cap. 10.   10 Act. 16, 17, 18.   11 Act. 7. in Definit. Synodi.   12 See Baronius Annal. tom. ix. ad ann. 806. num. 1 & 2. 13 Baron. Annal. tom. ix. ad ann. 787. Num. 58 and 59.   14 Loco proximè citato. Certè quidem qui eam primus edidit. Theod. Balsamo in suspicionem addicitur imposturæ. 15 Possevin. in Apparat, sac verbo Tarasius.   16 Nor Papyrus Masson. de Urbis Epis. cap. lib. iii. in Adriano. fol. 131. b.   17 Rhem. Annot. in Act. Apost. xvii. 34. 18 Annal. tom. ix. ad ann. 787. num. 4

it at the end of the seventh general council, then was not Balsamon
the first that published it. For Anastasius lived about three hundred
years before Balsamon. For Anastasius lived about the year 860, and
Balsamon lived about the year 1180.

Pap. You speak probably: ' but methinks, though men at that
time had been so far bewitched and distracted of their five wits, as
they could not have known a man from a woman, yet God himself,
who appointed and ordained the seat of Peter, whereof he would the
whole church to be directed, should never have departed so far from
his merciful providence, as to suffer the same to be polluted by a woman, which is not of capacity for holy orders.

Prot. And why, I pray you, might not God as well suffer that
church to be polluted by a woman, as by so many monstrous men,
of whom your own historians write very shamefully? Why might she
not sit there, as well as Sabinian, that base and miserable companion,
' Qui formidabili morte, & culpabili vita, notatus est?' Who is taxed
by your [2] writers, for his vile life and fearful death? Why might not
she sit there as well as [3] Stephen the Sixth, who, as [4] I told you before,
took up the carcass of Formosus, his predecessor, out of the grave,
brought it into judgment before a council of bishops, spoiled it of his
papal robes, clad it with a layman's garment, indicted it, arraigned it,
condemned it, cut off three fingers of it, and cast it into the stream
of Tyber; depriving all them of their orders whom he had ordained,
re-ordaining them again? Why might not she sit there as well as Boniface the Seventh, [5] who robbed Saint Peter's church, and fled for a
time to Constantinople; who, afterwards, by simony, and murdering
two popes, made himself pope; who, in mischief, outstripped the most
notorious robbers and slayers by the high-ways, that ever were; which,
in cruelty, went before bloody Sylla and Cataline, and such as
sought the ruin of their country, [6] as your own Baronius confesseth;
and who, at length, died like a beast? Why might not she sit there, as
well as Sylvester the Second, that famous conjurer, who gave himself,
both body and soul, to the devil, that he might get the popedom, and
died thereafter? Why might not she sit there?

Pap. Nay, stay a little. They say it is a sin to belye the devil.
Now, [7] I persuade myself, that you belye Pope Sylvester; for I [8]
read, that he was reputed a notable man, both for his life and learning.

Prot. How notable he was let Platina speak, who [9] writes, that
' ambitione & diabolica dominandi cupiditate impulsus, largitione pri-
mò quidem archiepiscopatum Rhemensem, inde Ravennatem adeptus,
pontificatum postremò majore conatu, adjuvante diabolo, consecutus
est, hac tamen lege, ut post mortem totus illius esset, cujus fraudibus
tantam dignitatem adeptus erat:' That is, Sylvester the Second, being devilishly ambitious, got first, by bribery, the archbishoprick of

1 Onuph. Annot. in Platinam, in Vita Joh. VIII. Harding, in his Answer to Juel's Apology-
2 Fascicul. Temporum, ad ann. 614.   3 Some say it was Sergius : the
reason of which diversity, see in Dr. Reynold's Conf. ch. 7. Divis. 1. p. 282. edit. 1586. in Marg.
4 Pap. 91.   5 Platina in Vita Bonifacii VII.   6 Bonifacius VII. annume-
randus inter famosos latrones & potentissimos grassatores atque patriæ proditores, Syllas & Ca-
tilinas hortamque studied, quot omnes superavit sacrilegus iste turpissima nece duorum Pontificum, Annal. tom. x. ad ann. 985. num. 1.   7 Florim. chp. 24.   8 Jodocus
Coccius in Catechism. Cathol. lib. vii. Art. 15.   9 Platina de Vitis Pont. in Sylvest. II.

Rheims, then of Ravenna, and after that, by the devil's help, the bishoprick of Rome; yet, upon this condition, that, when he died, he should be wholly his, by whose means he attained to such dignity. Have you not cause to believe, that this fellow was notable for life and learning? But, perhaps, Platina is singular in this. No, [1] Sigebert confesseth, that Sylvester was thought to have got the popedom [2] ill-favouredly; and that he was [3] suspected of negromancy; and, that some said, the devil brought him to his end. The same, in effect, is reported by [4] Benno Cardinalis, by [5] Martinus Polonus, by [6] Johannes Stella, a Venetian, by [7] Philippus Bergomensis, by [8] Ranulphus Cestrensis, by [9] Matthæus Westmonasteriensis, by [10] Fasciculus Temporum, by [11] Charanza, and by Æneas Sylvius: for, ' Non nos fugit Sylvestrum Secundum diabolica fraude Romanum pontificatum ascendisse,' saith Æneas: we are not ignorant that Sylvester the Second got the papacy by devilish subtlety.

Pap.   Tut, all this is to no purpose; [12] Pope Sylvester was learned in the mathematicks; and such was the ignorance of that age, that thereupon they held him for a conjurer.

Prot.   Indeed, [13] William of Malmsbury having related the same story in substance, with the above-named writers, supposeth that some might reply so, saying, ' Sed hæc vulgata, ficta crederet aliquis.' But some men, peradventure, will say, this is but a made tale, ' Eo quod solet populus literatorum famam lædere, dicens illum loqui cum dæmone, quem in aliquo viderint excellentem opere :' Because the common people are wont to say, that scholars, who are singular in any thing, do use a familiar : yet, he concludes, that he believes it for true.   For, ' Mihi verò fidem facit de istius sacrilegio inaudita mortis excogitatio,' [14] saith he, ' I am verily persuaded, Sylvester was such a villian, because of the strangeness of his death.   For, ' Cur se moriens excarnificaret ipse sui corporis horrendus lanista, nisi novi sceleris conscius esset ?' For why should the butcherly fellow have torn his own flesh, as he did, but that he was guilty of some strange sin? Do not you think there is reason in this question? Doubtless, your Onuphrius was afraid to answer it.   And, therefore, in his notes upon Platina, where he labours to clear Sylvester of the imputation of a conjurer, [16] he takes day with his reader, to clear him from so fearful a death.

Pap.   [17] Yea, but Sylvester II. is commended by Sergius IV. a very holy pope, who lived within five years after him; wherefore it is not [18] credible that he died such a shameful death.

Prot.   Say you so? Doth not [19] Baronius confess, that though Stephen VI. was a wicked fellow ; and that as he entered into the popedom like a thief and a murtherer ; so he died like a thief ; yet [20] Ser-

[1] In Chron. ad ann. 998.   2 Non per ostium intrasse creditur.   [3] A quibusdam negromantiæ arguitur.   4 De Vit. & Gest. Hildebrandi,   5 In Chron ad ann. 1007.   6 De Vit. Pont in Silvest. II. ad ann. 995.   7 Supplem. Chron. ad ann. 997.   8 In Polychron. lib. vi. cap. 14.   9 Flores Hist. ann. 998.   10 Ad ann. 1008.
11 In Summa Conc.   12 Comment. de Gest. Conc. Basil. lib. i.
13 Bell. lib. iv de Rom. Pont. Cap. 14. Onuph. ann in Plat. in Vit. Sylvest. M.   14 Lib. ii. de Gestis Rogum Angl. cap. 10. fol. 36.   15 Loco citato.   16 De morte ejus sive Diaboli percussione famam alibi commodius convellam Onuph. Loco supra citato.
17 Bell. lib. iv. de Rom. Pont. cap. 12. Baron. Annal. tom. x. ad ann. 999. num. 7.   18 Facinorosus homo, quique ut fur & latro ingressus est in ovile ovium, laqueo vitam adeo infami exitu, vindice Deo, clausit. tom. x. Annal. ad ann. 909. num. 5.   19 Baronius, ibid.
20 Ad ann. 904. num. 4.

gius III, who succeeded within eight years after him, commended
him; yea John IX, his next successor, who in that age was a singular honest pope, commended him, as a man of blessed memory.
Upon which later confession he makes this observation: Hic consi-
dera lector, quanta solerent successores pontifices quantulumcunq;
reprehensibiles prædecessores reverentia persequi, ut Johannes Stephanum suum prædecessorem tum sedis invasione, tum etiam sessione,
in omnibus planè execrandis facinoribus detestabilem, piæ tamen
recordationis Stephanum appellet.' The effect of which Latin is,
That it is worthy the observation, that the live popes spoke reverently
of the dead popes, were they never so naughty. Wherefore to go on,
Why might not Pope Joan sit there as well as Benedict IX, [1] that ugly
monster, as [2] Platina calls him, [3] who got the room when he was but
twelve years old, [4] who, when he was cast out for his unworthiness, got
it again by a strong hand within a few days after; and, for fear that he
could not keep it long, sold it to another for money, who after his
death [5] appeared partly like an ass, and partly like a bear, confessing
that he carried such a shape, because he lived like a beast in his life-
time? Why might not she sit as well in St. Peter's chair, as Boniface VIII.
who ([6]when he should upon an Ash-Wednesday, as the Popish manner
is, have laid ashes upon an archbishop's head, and religiously told him,
that he was but ashes, and should return to ashes;) cast them in the
archbishop's face and eyes, maliciously telling him, that he was a
Gibelline, and that he should die with the Gibellines; of whom
Celestinus his predecessor, a man famous [7] they say for miracles, [8] prophesied: That, as he entered like a fox, so he should reign like a lion,
and die like a dog, which fell out accordingly?

Why might not she sit there as well as Gregory VII. commonly
known by the name of Hildebrand, [9] who set both the church and
commonwealth on fire; [10] who hired a bad fellow to tumble down great
stones from the battlements of a church upon the emperor's head, to
squeese him in pieces whilst he was at his prayers; [11] who cast the
sacrament into the fire; who ordinarily [12] carried about him a conjuring
book; who shrewdly bebumbed his predecessor Alexander; who
wrested the scriptures to cover his lewdness; [13] who at his death
confessed, that the devil set him on work, to provoke God to wrath
against the world.

Why might not she sit there as well as John XXIII. [14] who was fitter
for the camp, than for the church; for profane things, than for the

1 Teterrimum monstrum.   2 In vita Greg. VI.   3 Rodolphus Glaber. qui tunc
vivebat. Hist. lib. v. cap. ult. Papyrius Massonius de Urb. Episcop. in Benedicto IX.
4 Platina in Benedict. IX. Sigonius de Regno Italiæ, lib. viii. ad ann. 1042.   5 Caput &
cauda erant Asinina, ut reliquum corpus sicut Ursus. Fascic. Temp ad ann. 1034. Plat. in
vita Bened. IX. Polonus in Chron. ad ann. 1044.   6 Petrus Crinitus. lib. viii. de honesta
disciplina, cap. 13. ut legimus in Fasciculo Rerum expetendarum. &c. fol. 44.
7 Celestinus vir sanctissimus, & tam late Pontificatum quàm etiam post miraculis plurimis
illustris. Bell. Appendix ad Lib. de Summ. Pont. cap. 14 & 24.   8 Celestinus V prophe-
tavit in hunc modum, ut fertar, Ascendisti ut Vulpos, regnabis ut Leo, morieris ut Canis. Et
ita sane contigit. Tho. Walsing. in Edu. 1. & Polychron. lib. vii. cap. 40.   9 Hildebrand
Ecclesiasticum subvertit ordinem Christiani imperii, perturbavit regnum, &c. Conventus episcoporum 50. apud Brixian, teste Abbate Uraspergensi in Chron. ad ann. 1080.
10 Benno Cardinalis, lib. supra citato.   11 Ibid.   12 Ibid.   13 Florentinus
Vigorniensis in Chron. pag. 641. Matth. Paris in Guil. Conquest. ann. 1086.
14 Onuph. Append. in Plat. in vita Joh. XXIV.

service of God; as knowing no faith, no religion at all; [1] who taught
again and again, and maintained it before many of good place, that
there was no life after this, but that it was with men as with beasts.
Who, in a word, [2] lived so scandalously, that commonly he was called
by them who knew him, a plain devil incarnate.   Why might not she
sit there as well as John XII, [3] who made deacons in a stable, who
made a boy of ten years old a bishop, who made the Lateran a plain
stews, who drank to the devil; who, when he was at dice, made his
prayers unto Jupiter and Venus, and to such idolatrous gods of the
heathen :   Who at length, was slain even by the devil himself, while he
was committing adultery, as [4] before I noted.   If you cannot deny,
but God hath suffered these, and many as evil as any of these, except
the last, to occupy St. Peter's room, you may well wonder with
[5] Antoninus, at the story of Pope Joan, and say, Oh the depth of the
wisdom of God, how incredible be his judgments, &c.   Buy you have
no cause in this respect to deny it, you have no cause to cast it off as a
fable.   But give me leave to ask you a question.   How should this
tale of Pope Joan's arise, if there was not such a pope?   Was there ever
such a smoke and no fire; such a report and no probability ?

Pap.   No indeed. [6] Great lyes arise always out of some truth.
And so did this.   For John XII, to confess a truth, was a wenching
fellow ; and, among other wenches which he kept, there was one called
Joan, who was all in all with him, and ruled the roast.   Now the
people, perceiving what hand she had over him, termed her pope, and
despised him.   Whereupon the church's enemies took occasion to
slander the church, as though the church had, indeed, had a woman-
pope.

Prot.   This is one of Florimondus's reasons, is it not ?

Pap.   Yes. [7] He mentions this, and likes indifferently well of it.
But he mentions it as out of Onuphrius.   Wherefore take you it
rather as Onuphrius's answer to your question, than as Florimondus's
answer.

Prot.   Content; provided that you tell me, how Onuphrius proves
that John XII. had such a masterful whore called Joan.

Pap.   [8] Onuphrius proves that out of Luitprandus Ticinensis, a
writer of that age.   For he witnesseth (as Onuphrius saith, and
Florimondus believes, that John the Twelfth had three famous whores,
of whom the fairest, and therefore the best beloved, was called Joan.

Prop.   Luitprandus, [9] in the place cited by Onuphrius, witnesseth,
that John the Twelfth kept one famous whore, whom he called Raynera,
whom he made governor of many cities, and on whom he bestowed
many golden crosses and chalices belonging to St. Peter.   In like
manner he witnesseth, that he kept another called Stephana, and that
he lay with married wives, with widows, and with maids, who came to
visit the apostolical churches.   And withal he witnesseth, that he kept
a third called Anna (who was a widow) and her niece; making the

1 Conc. Constant. sess. 11. art. penult.   2 Ibid. Art. 6, &c.   3 Luitprand. Hist.
per Europam gestarum, lib. vi. cap. 7, 8, and 10.   4 Pag. 97.   5 Part ii. tit. 16.
cap. 1. sect. 7.   6 Omnia insignia mendacia ab aliqua veritate originem habent. Onuph.
Annot. in Plat. in vit. Joanne.   Fucis quædam inest veri species. Florim. cap. 29, num. 2.
7 Loco citato, num. 5.   8 Loco supra citato.   9 Lib. vi. cap. 6, 7.

palace of Lateran no better than a baudy-house. But he no where
names any Joan, on whom that worthy head of your church, John the
Twelfth, doated; Onuphrius, I suppose, mistook Joanna, for Anna:
And Florimondus justified the proverb, A fool believeth every thing.
Have you not another answer to second this?

Pap.   Yes, I have two or three besides this.

Prot.   That is well.   And what is the first of them, I pray you?

Pap.   This John the Ninth was made bishop of Bononia, and
afterwards archbishop of Ravenna, and at last Pope of Rome, by the
means of one Theodora, a famous whore, who swayed all matters at
Rome in those days.   Now the people, perceiving that this Theodora
could turn this John which way she would, and lead him whither she
list, they held him worthier the name of a woman than of a man, and,
therefore, called him Joan, and not John.   Whereupon arose the story
of a Joan pope.

Prot.   And who, I pray you, is the father of this answer?

Pap.   [1] Johannes Aventinus, who, by reason he was a German born,
knew best, no doubt, the original of this fable, as [2] Florimondus
sheweth.

Prot.   Then Florimondus believes this too.

Pap.   He thinks it very probable.

Prot.   But so did not his countryman Genebrard.   For, [3] Aventinus
Lib. iv. Annalium Fabellam esse asserit, à Theodora nobili scorto
ortam, [3] saith Genebrard: ' Ego vero è recentioribus adulatoribus in
Romanæ sedis odium, &c.'   That is, Aventinus holdeth that this tale
arose, by reason of a noble whore called Theodora.   But I think, some
latter clawbacks (of the emperors) devised it, to discredit the papal
seat.   Thus Genebrard.   And is not Genebrard's No as good as
Florimondus's Yea?   Especially since Genebrard [4] spent upon his
chronicles ten whole years: Whereas [5] Florimondus, by reason of his
clients, can spare no time for such studies?

Pap.   Genebrard was a worthy man, I [6] know.   But I respect no
man's person, wherefore give me a reason, why you dislike this conceit
of Aventinus, approved by Florimondus.

Prot.   I will.   Yet first I would have you know, that though I
grant, that John, who was first bishop of Bononia, then of Ravenna,
and lastly, of Rome, came to those bishopricks by the means of
Theodora, a famous whore: In respect whereof, your [7] cardinal
historiographer makes question, whether he was a pope or no; and
terms him [8] *Pseudopontifex & Antipapa*, a false Pope and Antipope:
[9] sometimes, *intrusor & detentor injustus apostolicæ sedis;* an intruder
and an usurper of the apostolical chair; yet I deny that this was
John the Ninth, for he was John the Tenth.   John the Ninth came by
good means to the papacy, as your [10] cardinal saith.   [11] He carried
himself honestly in it, and died naturally; but so did not this. [12] This

1 Annal. lib. iv.   2 Page 236.   3 Genebrard. Chron. lib. iv. ad ann. 855.
4 Diuturno 10 annorum studio. Geneb. Præfat Chronograph. ad Pontacum.
5 Fabula Joannæ cap. 31. pag 253. num. 6.   6 Possevin. Apparat. sacr. verbo Gilbertus
Genebrardus.   7 Annal. tom. x. ad an. 925. num. 11. si ipse Pontifex est dicendus.
8 Ad an. 912. num. 12.   9 Ad an. 928. num. 2.   10 Annal. tom. x. ad an. 901.
num. 1.   11 Idem ad ann. 905. num. 1, 2.   12 Frodeard. Hist. Rhemens. lib. iv.
cap. 19.

confirmed a child under five years old in the archbishoprick of Rheims: At which fact, [1] Baronius stands aghast.   [2] Then this, *Turpior nullus, cujus sicut ingressus in cathedram Petri infamissimus, ita et exitus nefandissimus.*   There was never a filthier fellow than this.   This entered with infamy, and died fearfully.   [3] This was stifled with a pillow, by the procurement of one as famous for whoredom, as Theodora who preferred him.

Pap.   This, of whom Florimondus speaks, was stifled with a pillow by Theodora's own daughter.   But it seems you wrong her in her good name.   For she caused him to be stifled, because she could not brook his filthy kind of life, with her mother, as [4] Florimondus notes.

Prot.   Florimondus will never be good.   The daughter disliked not her mother's and the Pope's course of life at all.   She herself [5] played the whore with Sergius, one of your Popes, and had by him John the Eleventh.   [6] She married her husband's brother, and lived with him in incest.   The only cause, why she procured him to be stifled, was her envy to one Peter, the Pope's brother, as [7] Baronius proveth out of Luitprandus.

Pap.   But in good earnest, Was not this John, John the Ninth? Florimondus [8], again and again, calls him John the Ninth.   And, methinks, he should not mistake him so often.

Prot.   In earnest, this was not John the Ninth.   Florimondus was deceived.

Pap.   Why, but Benedict the Fourth succeeded John the Ninth, Did he not?

Prot.   Yes, that is true.   But Benedict the Fourth succeeded not this John, John the Eleventh, as [9] Luitprandus writes; or rather Leo the Sixth, as [10] others write, succeeded this John.

Pap.   Florimondus [11] writes, that Benedict the Fourth succeeded this John; and observes withal a knack of knavery in those, who report this story, in that they fathered this tale upon a John, whom a Benedict succeeded.

Prot.   Observe you then a knack of foolery, or knavery, or rather foolish knavery in Florimondus; for I tell you, once again, that Benedict the Fourth succeeded not this John; [12] all histories are against it.   But suppose he was John the Ninth, if his loose carriage of himself with Theodora gave occasion of the report of a woman-pope, Why was it not recorded, as happening in his time, but above forty years before his time?   John the Ninth was made Pope in the year 901, yet this story is recorded as happening about the year 854.

Pap.   [13] That came to pass by the subtlety of the reporters; for, about the year 800, the Empress, who, in a manner, ruled all the world, was called Theodora.   Now these trifling tale-tellers, hearing of

1 Ista nova, turpia, detestanda, solo auditu horrenda atque pudenda. ann. tom. x. ad ann. 925. num. 9.   2 Ibid. num. 11.   3 Idem ad an. 928. num. 2.   4 Cap. 29. num. 3. 3 Luitprand lib. ii. cap. 13. agnoscente Baron. Annal. tom. x ad an. 908. num. 5. 6 Baron. ad an. 933. num. 11.   7 Ad an. 928.   8 Cap. 29, pag. 235, 236, cap. 30, pag. 240, 241.   9 Lib. iii. cap. 12.   10 Leo Ostiens. lib. i. cap. 57. in fine Baron. Annal. tom. x. ad an. 928, pag. 702.   11 Cap. xxx. pag 242.   12 Baron. Annal. tom. x. ad an. 901. num. 1.   13 Flor. cap. xxx. num. 1.

a Pope Joan in Theodora's time, chopped it into the time of Thedora
the Empress, who lived about thirty years before the harlot Theodora.

Prot. This would rather argue simplicity than subtlety in the
reporters; for, *cui bono*, whether it happened in the one, or in the other
Theodora's time; but it carries no colour of truth with it, for Theodora,
the Empress, never carried any sway in Rome at all. At Constantinople, for a while, in the time of her son's minority, she could do
something; [1] but, in Pope Joan's time, she was turned out of office at
Constantinople; she was deposed from her regency, and thrust into a
monastery, where she was kept till her death. What is one of your
other answers?

Pap. My third answer to your main question is, that, perhaps,
this tale arose from John the Eighth; for John the Eighth dealt not
like a man in the case of Photius, patriarch of Constantinople, but
sheepishly, and like a woman? for John the Eighth received Photius
into communion, who was excommunicated by his predecessors. John
the Eighth suffered himself to be overcome by half a man; whereupon,
in reproach, he was called ' Non papa, sed papissa;' and upon that
reproachful speech, came this tale of a woman-pope.

Prot. Who devised us this answer, I pray you?

Pap. This is [2] Baronius's answer.

Prot. Baronius's answer! Is that possible? Is not Baronius one of
them who holds, that the rumour of the church of Constantinople's
oversight, in suffering a woman to creep in to be a patriarch, occasioned this tale against Rome?

Pap. Yes, marry is he; for having set down Pope Leo's words
touching that rumour: ' Quæ ita erant fama vulgata de ecclesia Con-
stantinopolitana, conversa in Romanam ecclesiam a schismaticis eam
odio prosequentibus, & calumniis proscindentibus, quis non intelligat?'
[3] saith Baronius, that is, Who seeth not, that what was reported of
Constantinople, the same was turned, by schismaticks, as spoken
against Rome?

Prot. And with what honesty can he say both? [4] N. D. who holds
this latter opinion, professeth, that it seemeth most certain, that, in
Pope Leo's time, viz. 1020, there was not so much as any rumour or
mention of any woman-pope that ever had been in the Roman church.
So doth Baronius himself; for verily, [5] saith he, if there had been but
some flying tale of any such accident at Rome, in former days, Pope
Leo should first have cleared it, before he had charged the church
of Constantinople with the like. Was there not so much as a flying
report of a woman-pope before Leo the Ninth's time, in Baronius's
opinion? How then did John the Eighth occasion such a report, who
lived an 140 years before Leo? But let Baronius go with this escape.
What reason have you to think, that the rumour of Constantinople
might occasion this tale against Rome?

1 Baron. Annal. tom. x. ad an. 855. num. 51.   2 Annal. tom. x. ad an. 879. num. 5.
3 Annal. tom. x. ad an. 853. num. 58.   4 Cap. v. num. 29. page 399.
5 Certe si vel levissimus ramusculus per calumniam de his sparsus esset, utique is ab eo
fuisset antea diluendus, quam ut fama perlatum facinus ejusdem generis objecisset. Annal.
tom. x. ad an. 853, num. 66.

Pap. [1] Good reason; for every man knows that Constantinople was called New Rome, and Rome simply. Now a man might easily be deceived, in supposing that to be done in Rome, in Italy, which was reported to be done in Rome, but in Rome, in Græcia.

Prot. That Constantinople was called New Rome, [2] I easily yield unto you; but that it was, at any time, called simply Rome, that your Florimondus is not able to make good ; that is his own fancy, and, in delivering it, he bewrays his own folly : ' Constantinopolis nunquam absolutè dicebatur Roma, sed cum addito, ut est hodie, Nova Roma.' Constantinople was never simply called Rome, but with an addition, as we call at this day, New Rome, saith Gretser. Yet, to suppose it true, why did not the relators of it set it down as happening in Leo's time, but 240 years before, if so be it was occasioned by the report that went of Constantinople in Leo's days ? If it had thence begun, it should have been registered as then happening.

Pap. Well, suppose it were true, what gain you by it ; or what is the church prejudiced by her ? If Pope Joan had been, she had not prejudiced the church, [3] saith N. D.

Prot. But she had ; for, if she was pope, then it will follow thereon necessarily, that the church, according to your learning, once hopped headless : for the [4] church, in your learning, is defined to be a company of Christian men, professing one faith under one head, to wit, the pope; but she, however she carried the name of pope, was no pope, [5] for a woman is not capable of holy orders ; a woman cannot play the pope. Ergo, all the time of Pope Joan, the church hopped headless.

Pap. Indeed, the only inconveniency of such a case is, [6] as N. D. confesseth, that the church should lack a true head for the time. But that is not so great a matter, for so she doth, when any pope dieth, till another be chosen.

Prot. What is that you say ? Doth the church hop headless, when one pope dieth, till another be chosen ? Now, alas! what a pitiful case is the church in then ? Since Christ's time, [7] there have been above two hundred and forty popes; and therefore, by your saying, the church hath been headless above two hundred and forty times. Yea, and sometimes, between the death of one pope, and the chusing of another, there have passed many days, many months, some years. As for example: [8] after Cletus, the bishoprick of Rome was void twenty days ; [9] after Clemens, twenty-two ; after Alexander the First, [10] twenty-five; [11] after Pelagius the First, three months and odd days ; [12] after Pelagius the Second, six months and odd days ; [13] after John the Third, ten months and odd days ; [14] after Sabinian, eleven months and odd days; [15] after Honorius the First, one year and more; [16] after Clemens

1 Florim. Cap. xxv. Num. 8.   2 Constantinop. novam Romam jam inde a Constantini tempore Græci vocabant. Papyr. Masson. lib. ii. de Urbis Episc. in Simplicio. tom. ii. Defen- Bell. lib. ii. cap. 31. col. 812.   3 Part. II. of three Conversions, cap. v. page 389.
4 Bellar. Lib. iii. de Ecclesia, cap. 2.   5 Rhem. Annot. in 1 Cor. xiv. v. 34.
6 Loco. supr. cit.   7 Cicarollus Addit. ad Platinam & Onuph.   8 Anastasius de Vitis Pont. in Eletus.   9 Idem in Clemente.   10 Or 35. Idem in Alex. I.
11 Idem in Pelagio I.   12 Idem in Pelagio II.   13 Idem in Joh. III.
14 Idem in Sabiniano, lib. ii.   15 Idem in Honorio I.   16 Pontacus Chronogr.

the Fourth, two years and more ; [1] after Marcellinus, seven years and more ; after Nicholas the First, [2] as some say, eight years and more ; and after Felix, sometimes the Duke of Savoy, St. Peter's chair stood empty ten years, [3] saith Bodin. Whereupon will follow, that the church hath often, and long together, been headless ; but that is not so great a matter, you say :—Is it not ? Whence, I pray you, should the church have her wit, when she is bereaved of her head ? The saying is, great head, little wit ; but, without question, no head, no wit. When the church is headless, she is witless, and, by consequence, helpless ; and therefore, I take it, you have good cause to beware that you grant nothing, whereon it may be concluded, that your church was once headless.

Pap. [5] But did not St. Austin hold opinion, upon supposition of a like case, that the church of Christ should not be prejudiced ? Did not he, having recited up the popes of Rome from Christ to his days, make this demand, What, if any Judas, or traytor, had entered among these, or been chosen by error of men ? And answereth presently, ' Nihil præjudicaret ecclesiæ, & innocentibus Christianis.'

Prot. Yes ; but, considering the body of your doctrine, you may not answer so, nor think so : for you hold, that your pope is head of the church, and that it is necessary unto salvation to acknowledge him the head ; but so did not St. Austin. You hold, that, in a true church, one bishop must lawfully succeed another, or all is dashed ; but so did not St. Austin : for he puts the case, that some traytor *subrepsisset*, that is, had come in unorderly into the bishop of Rome's seat ; and yet resolves, that that was not prejudicial to God's church. Conform yourselves in these two points, of the pope's headship and succession, to St. Austin's judgment ; and then you may better say, in this case of Pope Joan, that which Austin said in the case proposed, that she had not prejudiced the church of Christ.

Pap. We make more reckoning of St. Austin than you do ; but I will not stand wrangling upon his meaning now [6] because, whatsoever inconvenience can be imagined in this case, is more against you than us : for your church admitteth for lawful and supreme head thereof, either man or woman, which our church doth not.

Prot. Our church admitteth neither man nor woman for lawful and supreme head of the catholick church, as yours doth. Our church teacheth, that Christ only is the head thereof. Our church admitteth neither man nor woman for lawful and supreme head of a particular church ; for our church acknowledgeth the king supreme governor only, not supreme head ; and so she [7] stiled Queen Elisabeth in her time. Though, if we give our princes more, yet the inconveniencies against us are not like the inconveniencies against you, because the next in blood is to succeed with us ; the greatest simonist, who can make his faction strongest, is to succeed with you.

---

1 Anastas. Lib. citat. in Marcellino, & Polonus in Codice Manuscripto, & Pontanus Chronogr. Lib. ii.   2 Teste Platina in Vit. Nichol. i.   3 De Repub. Lib. vi. num. 718.   4 N. D. Part ii. cap. 5. num. 19.   5 Austin. Epist. 165, ad Literas cujusdam Donatistæ.   6 N. D. Loco supra citato.   7 The Oath of Supremacy. 1 Elis.

Pap. What other inconvenience follows upon this accident, to suppose it true?

Prot. If it be true there was such a pope, your church must be discarded as no true church; for thus I argue, [1] That it is no true church, which cannot give, in plain authentical writing, the lawful, orderly, intire, without any breach, and sound notorious succession of bishops. But your church, if Joan was Pope, cannot give, in plain authentical writing, the lawful, orderly, intire, without any breach, and sound notorious succession of bishops; for, by reason of her, Benedict the Third could not orderly succeed Leo the Fourth; she put in a caveat, or rather, was, of herself, a bar to his succession; by her a breach was made in the rank of your popes; she, no fool, but a whore, marred your play.

Pap. No, no; for all that you can rightly gather upon her popedom is, That the Pope's seat stood empty of a lawful pastor for the space of two years, and a few odd months. Now so it did often, by reason of the differences among the electors, as you yourself shewed. And yet no man durst say, nor could truly say, that succession failed, as [2] Baronius writes.

Prot. As Baronius notes? If Baronius may be judge, there is nothing that can mar your succession, neither vacancy, nor entrance in by the window. Whether the chair be empty, or full, by irreption, or by usurpation, it is all one to Baronius. Baronius will not give over his plea of succession. For, though he, not without grief [3], confesseth, that many ugly monsters have sat in St. Peter's chair; though [4] he confesseth, that many apostates, rather than apostolical persons, have occupied that room; though [5] he confesseth, that there have been many popes, which came irregularly to the papacy, and served for no other purpose than cyphers in arithmetick, to make up the number; yet he holdeth their succession sound. Though [6] Baronius writes, that Boniface the Sixth, who got possession of St. Peter's chair, and kept it fifteen days, was a wicked fellow, and not worthy to be reckoned among popes, inasmuch as he was condemned by a council held at Rome. Though he [7] writes, that Stephen the Seventh, [8] such another as Boniface the Sixth, or rather worse, played at thrust-out-rotten with Boniface the Sixth, and kept the papacy five years; though [9] he writes, that Pope Christopher shuffled Leo the Fifth out, and by violence installed himself, and kept it seven months; and that Sergius, at the seven months end, shuffled Christopher out, shearing him a monk, and keeping it to himself, as some say, seven years; as [10] Baronius himself saith, three

1 Bristow, Motive 22.   2 Nihil praeterea ex ea ter miseri novatores lucri capiunt, nisi ut dici possit duobus illis annis & mensibus sedem Pontificiam legitimo vacuam fuisse pastore——quod & alias accidit, ut majori temporis spacio sedes Pontificia, dilata per discordias eligentium, electione vacarit: nec tamen successionem desisse, quis unquam ausus est dicere, quod nec dici potuit. Sed tantum esse dilatam, nullo vero modo sublatam. Baron. Annal. tom. x. ad ann. 853. num. 63.   3 Quot proh pudor! proh dolor! in eandem sedem visu horrenda intrusa sunt monstra, &c. tom. x. ad ann. 900, num. 3.   4 Non apostolici, sed apostatici, tom. x. ad ann. 908, num. 4.   5 Qui non sunt nisi ad consignanda tantum tempora in Catalogo Rom. Pontificum scripti, tom. x. ann. 912, num. 8.   6 Homo nefarius, jam antea bis gradu depositus, &c. non numerandus inter Pontifices, utpote qui damnatus fuit in Rom. Synod. tom. x. ad ann. 897. num. 1.   7 Tom. x. ad ann. 897, num. 1.   8 Apostolicae sedis invasor, & fur & latro ——indignus nomine Rom. Pontif. ibid. ann. 900. num. 6.   9 Tom. x. ad ann. 906, num. 1, ibid.   10 Ad ann. 910, num. 1.

years; yet all this shuffling, in Baronius's opinion, doth nothing stain succession: Yea, though he cannot deny that Boniface the Seventh, who sat as Pope one year and one month, was a [1] wicked varlet, a plain tyrant, a savage beast, an usurper, one that had no good property of a pope: Though he cannot deny, but that Leo the Eighth, who was a schismatick, and an intruder, and an antipope, [2] in his opinion, kept the place almost two years. Though he cannot deny, but that John the Twelfth, [3] who was but like a pope in a play, kept it nine years; and [4] John the Eleventh, the bastardly brat of Sergius above named, who came to it by evil means, and managed it accordingly, kept it six years; and [5] John the Tenth, as false a lad as any of his fellows, who entered by fraud, and ruled with violence, kept it fifteen years; yet this lessens nothing the credit of his succession. I warrant you, Baronius was of Genebrard's opinion, who, though he granted that fifty popes together came in unlawfully, and governed as madly, would not yet let his hold of succession go.

Pap. Iis there any further inconvenience which may light upon us, if this story be true?

Prot. Yes; for if it be granted there was such a pope, the popish priests among you may well doubt of the lawfulness of their mission; and you lay-papists of the sufficiency of the absolutions, which they give you upon your ear confessions, and of the truth of the real presence, and transubstantiation. For, [6] unless the popish priests be priested by a lawful bishop, their priesthood is not worth a rush; [7] unless you lay-papists be absolved by a lawful priest, your absolution is nought worth; and, [8] unless the words of consecration be uttered by a lawful priest, intent upon his business, there follows no substantial change in the creatures of bread and wine. Now how can your priests be assured, that they were priested by lawful bishops; and how can you lay-papists be assured that you are absolved by lawful priests; or that your masses are said by lawful priests; seeing we read (as [9] before I shewed) that Pope Joan gave orders, Pope Joan made deacons, and priests, and bishops, and abbots? For it may be well enough, that the priests of this present age are descended from those who were ordained by her; especially seeing we no where read, that they were degraded by succeeding popes, who had their ordination from her. Her successors dealt not with her shavelings, as Pope John the Twelfth did with Leo the Eighth's shavelings. [10] John the Twelfth degraded them all, and compelled every of them to give him up a paper, wherein it was thus written: *Episcopus weus* (meaning Leo the Eighth)

1 Scelestissmus vir. ad ann. 974. num. 1. nefandissimus parricida, truculentus praedo, qui ne pilum habuisse dici potest Romani Pontificis, ad ann. 985. num. 1.   2 Tom. x. ad ann. 931. num. 38. Ostensus fuit tanquam in scena mimus pontificem agens, tom. x. ad ann. 955. num. 4.   3 Tom. x. ad ann. 931. num. 1-   4 Invasor & detentor injustus Apostolicae sedis ad ann. 928. num. 1.   5 Chronolog. lib. iv. Seculo. 10. ad ann. 904.
6 In Episcopis de jure divino residet ista potestas creandi sacerdotes. Tolet. Summa Casuum Conscient. Lib. i. cap. 1.   7 Anathema sit qui dixerit non solos sacerdotes esse Ministros absolutionis. Conc. Trid. Sess. 14. Can. 10.   8 Semper in Ecclesia pro indubitate habitum est, ita necessarium esse ordinationem sacerdotalem ad Eucharistiam conficiendam, ut sine ea nullomodo confici possit. Bell. lib. iv. de Euchar. cap. 16.   9 Pag. 84.
10 Sigebert. in Chron. ad ann. 963. Baron. Annal. tom. x. ad ann. 962. num. 9. Joh. de Turrecrem. Sum. de Eccles. lib. ii. cap. 103.

nihil sibi habuit, nihil mihi dedit ; had nought for himself, and gave me nought; but so did not Benedict the Third with her's.   Unless you say, that *communis error facit jus,* as [1] lawyers said in the case of Barbarius Philippus, I know not what you can reply with probability to this; and yet that will not serve your turn, for, though it may be so in matters of the commonwealth, in matters of the church it cannot be so.   For an error in the beginning, in matters touching the church, proves often an heresy in conclusion.   In matters of the church, prescription adds no credit to actions of evil beginning.

1 ff De Officio Prætoris.

THE

BATHS OF BATH:

OR,

A NECESSARY COMPENDIOUS TREATISE CONCERNING THE NATURE, USE, AND EFFICACY OF

THOSE FAMOUS HOT WATERS;

Published for the Benefit of all such as yearly, for their Health, resort to those Baths. With an Advertisement of the great utility that cometh to Man's Body, by the taking of Physick in the Spring, inferred upon a Question moved, concerning the Frequency of Sickness, and Death of People, more in that Season than in any other.

Whereunto is also annexed a Censure, concerning

THE WATER OF ST. VINCENT'S ROCKS,

NEAR BRISTOL,

Which begins to grow in great Request and Use against the Stone.

By THO. VENNER, *Doctor of Physick, in Bath.*

London, printed by Felix Kyngston, in 1628- Quarto, containing twenty-six pages.

———

Serenissimæ Principi Mariæ, Angliæ, Scotiæ, Franciæ, & Hiberniæ, Reginæ,
Hoc de Thermis Bathoniensibus opusculum humillime dedicat & consecrat

THO. VENERUS, *Med. Dr.*

TO THE READER.

Good Reader, seeing, in the few years that I have exercised physick at the Baths, the yearly concourse, in the spring and fall, of people of all sorts, and from all parts of this kingdom, to those famous waters; and the little benefit that many, after great expence and trouble, receive thereby; I was induced to publish this ensuing treatise, wherein I have very briefly shewed the nature and efficacy of those waters; touched the causes that many find not comfort, but oftentimes rather hurt, that resort to them; with such advertisements concerning the use of the said waters, which, if they be rightly observed, I am persuaded, few will hereafter complain that they have been at the Baths in vain, and so the waters regain that esteem which, in respect of their singular vertues, they are worthy of. But here you must take from me this one advertisement, which is, That sickness is a symptom of sin; and therefore first, *pœnitentiam agendo* *, before your departure from home, make peace betwixt God and your conscience, and then repair to the Baths, *quæ te faustum ducat, atque sanum reducat, qui solus id potest. Vale†.*

BATH, so called from the baths in it, is a little well-compacted city ‡, and beautified with fair and goodly buildings for receipt of strangers. Although the site thereof, by reason of the vicinity of hills, seem not pleasant, being almost invironed with them; yet, for goodness of air, nearness of a sweet and delectable river, and fertility of soil, it is pleasant and happy enough; but for the hot waters that boil up, even in the midst thereof, it is more delectable and happier than any other of the kingdom.

There are in it four publick baths, so fairly built, and fitted with such conveniency for bathing, as the like, I suppose, is not elsewhere to be found; besides a little bath for lepers, called The Lepers-bath.

They all have the original of their heat from one matter, namely, sulphur, burning in the cavities of the earth, thorough which the waters flowing, receive their heat. They partake of no other mineral that I can find; what may lie hid *in visceribus terræ* §, I know not; of this I am sure, that such diseases, as cannot receive cure elsewhere, here do.

These baths, as they differ in their heat, so in their operations and effects. The King's Bath is the hottest, and it is, for beauty, largeness, and efficacy of heat, a kingly bath indeed, being so hot as can be well suffered. This bath is of so strong a heating, opening, resolving, attracting, and exiccating faculty, and therefore only convenient for cold and moist bodies, and for cold and moist diseases.

Next to the King's Bath, for efficacy of heat, is the Hot Bath, and the difference in their heat is so little, that it is scarcely to be discerned. This bath is good for the same infirmities that the King's Bath is, and, for the effects which it worketh, I cannot find it to be inferior unto it. They are two excellent baths for cold and moist diseases, and for very cold and moist bodies.

The Queen's Bath is a member of the King's Bath, a well only going between them, with a passage therein, to go from one to the other. This bath is not altogether so hot as that, and therefore the use of it is convenient for them that cannot well endure the heat of the King's Bath,

* By repentance. † Where may that God, who is only able to cure thee, lead thee safe, and bring thee home again in good health. Farewell.
‡ See the letter of observations by Tho. Guidott, M. B. in 1074.
§ In the bowels of the earth.

The Cross Bath is for heat the mildest, being very temperately warm. It is a dainty bath for young, weak, and tender bodies, that cannot endure the heat of the hotter baths, or for whom the hotter baths may not be convenient. It is an excellent bath for temperate bodies, by way of preservation, because such the hotter baths may soon distemper, and occasion hurt; neither is this bath good only for such as are of a temperate state and constitution of body, by way of preservation; but for them, and others also, by way of curation, in some cases, where the hotter baths are not fit to be used. This bath, by reason of the mildness of its heat, is of a notable, mollifying, and relaxing faculty; good, therefore, in contractions of any member, in obstructions of the breast, spleen, liver, and kidnies; and effectual also for aches, when it is in its prime and vigour of heat, especially for such, whose temper, or habit of body, shall prohibit the use of the hotter baths. This bath attains not to its perfection of heat, till the weather grow to be constantly hot, and when the other baths, by reason of the fervour thereof, cannot be used, but by such, whose diseases and state of body are intensively cold.

I cannot, in regard of the diversity of bodies, insist upon every particular in the use of these baths; wherefore I will only, for your better instruction and direction herein, give you some special advertisements, and thereupon leave you to some learned physician, that can accordingly guide you in the use of them.

These famous hot waters are of singular force, not only against diseases gotten by cold, or proceeding from a cold and moist cause, but also bring, in time of health, exceeding comfort and profit to all cold, moist, and corpulent bodies; for they open the pores, resolve, attenuate, digest, consume, and draw forth superfluities, and withal strongly heal and dry the whole habit of the body.

They are of excellent efficacy against all diseases of the head and sinews, proceeding from a cold and moist cause, as rheums, palsies, epilepsies, lethargies, apoplexies, cramps, deafness, forgetfulness, trembling, or weakness of any member, aches, and swellings of the joints, &c.

They also greatly profit windy and hydropick bodies, the pain and swelling of any part of the body, so that it proceed not from an hot cause; the sluggish and lumpish heaviness of the body, numbness of any member, pain in the loins, the gout, especially the sciatica; cold tumours of the milt and liver, and the yellow jaundice in a body plethorick or phlegmatick.

They are also very profitable for them that have their lungs annoyed with much moisture; and, to make slender such bodies as are too gross, there is nothing more effectual, than the often use of these waters. Wherefore let those that fear obesity, that is, would not wax gross, be careful to come often to our baths; for by the use of them, according as the learned physician shall direct, they may not only preserve their health, but also keep their bodies from being unseemingly corpulent.

They are also singularly profitable to women; for they help them of barrenness, and of all diseases and imperfections of the matrix, proceeding from a cold and moist cause. They also cure all diseases of the skin, as scabs, itch, old sores, &c. all which to be true, we daily find with admiration, to the exceeding great comfort of many, who, with deplored diseases, and most miserable bodies, resort to these baths, and are there, by the help of wholesome physick, and vertue of the baths, through the blessing of Almighty God, recovered to their former health.

But baths naturally hot (as these our baths are) to bodies naturally hot and dry, are generally hurtful ; and so much the more, as the body is drier, and the bath hotter, because it distempereth and consumeth the very habit of the body, and maketh it carrion-like lean.

Wherefore, seeing, that these our baths are not indifferently agreeable to every constitution and state of body, I do advise, that not any one go into them rashly, or upon a preposterous judgment ; but that he be first advised by some faithful, judicious, and expert physician, and to him expose the state of his body, whereby he may understand, whether or no it may be expedient for him to attempt the same. And whereas there are in Bath divers baths, as I have shewed, and they differing in their heat, and accordingly in their effects, he must also from the learned physician be directed in which to bathe ; neither must he only understand which bath to use, as most convenient for his state of body, but also when and how often to use the same, and how long to abide therein at a time. Besides this, he must take special care not to go into the bath without fit preparation (which is a gross error of many) but must be first purged, as his state of body shall require ; and be also directed in other things how to order himself, before he go into the bath, while he is in the bath, and after that he is come out of the bath, and when he leaveth the bath ; and must also with his bathings and sweatings use such physick-helps, as may work with the baths, according as his disease and present state of body shall require; not relying wholly upon the use of the water for his cure, as many ignorantly, and some basely do, to save their purse. The neglect of all these, or of some of them, either through ignorance or voluntary wilfulness, is the cause, that some, that take great pains to come to the baths, are not by them healed of their infirmities, but oftentimes never return to their homes again; or, if they do, it is most commonly with new diseases, and the old worse than ever they were; whereas those of a generous and religious understanding, using the true helps of physick with the baths, are of their diseases perfectly cured.

Here I may not omit a special reason, why many receive little benefit by the baths, but oftentimes much hurt; and that is, because they take not the aid and directions of a physician present, in the use of the bath ; but bring their physic and directions with them from some physicians in the country where they abode ; perhaps, one that well understands not their state of body, much less the nature and true use of the baths. But, admit that they have their directions from an understanding physician, yet I must tell them, that many accidents fall out oftentimes in bathing, that require the help of a present physician.

Another special reason why many find little good by the baths, is, because they make not such a stay at them, as, in regard of their infirmities, or state of body, is meet ; for some go away before the bath (in regard of the density of body) hath wrought any manner of effect at all on them ; others even then when the bath begins to shew its force and efficacy on their bodies; and some too soon upon much benefit received, by means whereof they easily incur a relapse. Wherefore my counsel herein unto you is this, that you limit not your stay at the baths, before you depart from your homes, but in that be advised and ruled by your physician, when you are at the baths, according as he shall find to be meet for your infirmities and state of body; and think not to receive in four, five, or six weeks an absolute cure for an infirmity, which, perhaps, you have borne two or three years, notwithstanding all the helps and means you have used for the same in your own country. Wherefore let your abode at the baths be, as it shall be requisite for your state of body, and limit not the time, no, not to a spring, or to a fall ; for it may be needful for you to reside there the whole year, it may be more; for, otherwise, by your untimely departure, you may lose the good that you have gotten by the bath, before the time come that you shall think to be fit for the use of the baths again.

But here I know you will object against me, saying, Is it good to make use of your baths in the summer and winter ? Are not those times by all learned and judicious physicians prohibited for bathing in hot baths ? Whereupon grew the custom of frequenting them in the temperate seasons of the year, namely, in the spring and fall?

Whereunto I answer, and first, that bathing in our baths in summer, taking the cool of morning for it, if the season shall be hot and summer-like, brings much more benefit to the body, the disease being of a cold nature, and proceeding from a cold and moist cause (for so you must conceive me) than in the spring or fall, when oftentimes the coldness and variableness of the air takes away the benefit of your bathing; for cold or vaporous air entering into your body after bathing, the pores being open, doth not only very greatly annoy the spirits, and principal parts, occasion wind and tortures in the bowels, but also induce oftentimes irrecoverable effects to the sinews and joints. But if seasons, that are constantly warm, be best for bathing in our baths, and cold times hurtful, why should any reside at them in winter ? I answer, that it is good for them that are in the way of cure, by reason of their former bathings, and that the waters are in their nature as effectually hot in the winter, as in any other time of the year, only the superficies, or upper part of the bath, is cooled by the winds. But in the winter there are some calm days, in which the diseased body, lying nearer to the baths, may well and safely bathe, without any offence or danger in taking of cold after ; for he may keep himself in a warm chamber, having nothing else to do, or take care for, but for his health.

And here I cannot but reprehend the error of most people, that, at the end of May, depart from our baths, and after that month, I know not out of what prejudicate opinion, altogether refrain to come to them till the fall : perhaps, they do this, supposing that, after the spring, till the fall come again, the baths lose their virtue. I must tell them, if this be their conceit, that they are in a great error ;for the waters lose not their vertue at any time, only the disposition of the

ambient air may make them less fit to be used at one time, than at
another. But I would have you to know, as I have afore-shewed, that
our baths may as profitably be used in summer, as in the spring, and
most commonly with far better success in the whole month of June,
than in any of the former months ; and that, in regard of the constant
temperature of this month, and the variable disposition of the months
preceding. I am persuaded, that this untimely going from the baths,
at the very approach of summer, hurts many, and overthrows the good
they have received by them. Wherefore, my advertisement herein is
this, that they, who resort to the baths for prevention of sickness, or
such hereditary diseases, as they fear will befal them, depart from the
baths about the end of the spring: but such as go to them for diseases
already fixed, abide there the whole summer, and longer too, if there
shall be occasion.

And admit, that after the month of June the weather be too fervently
hot to bathe in the hotter baths ; yet the cross bath, which for heat is
the mildest, being, as I have said, in its nature temperately hot, attains
not to its efficacy and perfection, till the weather be constantly warm,
which, for the most part, happens not till towards the end of May, or
the beginning of June. The use of which bath is of excellent efficacy,
not only in the month of June, but after also, yea, all the summer,
according as the state of the body and disposition of the season shall
permit; wherein I leave you to the counsel and direction of some
learned physician resident at the baths.

And now also I must advertise such, as in the declining, or fall of
the year, which we call the Autumn, shall, for the health of their
bodies, repair to our baths, that they defer not their coming till the
middle of September, or after, as many ignorantly do; but that
they rather be there shortly after the middle of August, that they may
have time sufficient for bathing, before the air grow to be too cold, as
commonly it is in October, especially towards the end thereof. But,
perhaps, some, out of an ignorant timorousness, will object, That to
come to the baths before the Dog-days are gone, or too soon upon them,
is hurtful. Herein they are more scrupulous than judicious : But, to
yield them some satisfaction, I answer: Besides the alteration of
seasons from their ancient temperature, in this decrepit age of the
world, that, though the middle part of the day, in the latter part of
August, shall be hot, yet the mornings and evenings, which are the
times for bathing, begin then to be cold, and decline to a temperature;
and the heat of the day, growing up on the bathing, is that which we
specially respect for the health of our patients, for whom we approve
the use of the baths. Wherefore, such as, for the health of their
bodies, repair to our baths, shall, if they be there in the latter part of
August, receive a double commodity: For, first, they shall have the
whole month of September, very convenient for bathing, and physick
also, as shall be occasion ; yea, and part of October, as the disposition
of the season shall permit: Next, sufficient time for their return to
their homes, before the air grow too cold, or the weather distempered ;
for to take cold betwixt the bathings, or to expose the body to travel, in
foul and intemperate weather, upon the use of the bath, induceth, the

pores being open, besides feverish distemperatures and ventosities,
oftentimes very great and dolorous affects of the brain, breast, sinews,
and joints.

I may not let pass, how certain accidents now and then befal some
in their bathing, as, weakness and subversion of the stomach, faintness,
and sometimes swoonings; and these the physician must take special
care to prevent, which may be occasioned by means of the sulphurous
vapours of the bath; yet I must tell you, that these, or the like
accidents our baths do seldom occasion, especially the Cross Bath, but
in them that are weak by nature, that are subject to swooning, or go
into them preposterously, without fit preparation and direction. And
the reason is, because, our baths being large, and having no sulphur in
them, nor in the cavities near adjoining, the vapours are the less
noisome, not so gross and adusted; and therefore not quickly offensive,
but to them that are very weak by nature, or, as I have said, go into
them without fit preparation, or make longer stay in them, than is
meet.

And here I cannot but lay open baths Technology, with such as, for
the health of their bodies, resort to those baths; wherein I am sure to
gain little thanks. But I pass not for it, my purpose being to discharge
a good conscience, and to do my country good. The thing, therefore,
that I would have you to take notice of, is, how the people of that
place, that keep houses of receipt, and their agents, for such they have
in every corner of the streets, and also before you come to the gates,
press upon you, importuning you to take your lodging at such and
such an house, near to such and such a bath, extolling the baths near
which they dwell, above the rest, respecting altogether their own gain,
not your good or welfare. And, when they have gotten you into their
houses, they will be ready to fit you with a physician, perhaps an
empirick *, or upstart apothecary, magnifying him for the best physician
in the town, that will not cross them in removing you to another bath,
though the bath, near which you are placed, be altogether contrary to
your infirmities and state of body, or, at least, not so convenient as
some other. And this is also a special reason, why many, oftentimes,
receive rather hurt, than good, by the use of the baths.

My counsel, therefore, to the learned physicians shall be this: That
they so tender the good of their patients, and their own worth and
reputation, as that, for base gain, they subject not themselves to these
kind of people, in hope to get patients by their means: And to the
patients, that they fall not by any means into the hands of empiricks,
who, by their ill qualified physick, will spoil their bodies, and, by
reason of their pragmatical nature, persuade and put them to unnecessary and preposterous courses, which cannot but produce disaster-
ous effects.

But, seeing that no calling is more disgraced, than by the men of the
same calling, I wish all professors of physick to carry themselves

* Bath being a place, in regard of the baths, that many resort unto for cure of infirmities,
that cannot receive help elsewhere; it were to be wished, that empiricks, and all others, whatsoever they be, being not graduates in the faculty of physick, were utterly prohibited to practise
in the city, or near to the confines thereof, idque sub pœna gravissima.

worthy of their calling, to be faithful and honest in their courses, not to insinuate with any, or, after the manner of our Bath-guides, press upon them to be retained. If an empirick or mountebank seek about for work, I blame them not; let them deceive those that will be deceived; but, for such as are graduated in the noble faculty of physick to do so, it is fiddler-like; a note, if not of some unworthiness in them, I am sure, of a base mind. Let those, therefore, that are physicians indeed, strive to maintain the reputation of their art, and not, by a base insinuating carriage, or mountebank-like tricks, to get a note and repute, vilify their own worth, or disgrace so noble a faculty.

But to draw to an end: When you shall, for your health, repair to the baths, be cautious, and suffer not yourself to be taken up by such as will press upon you; but rest yourself at your inn, and be well advised by a physician that knows the nature and use of the baths, and can well judge of your infirmities and state of body, what bath shall be fitting for your use, and then take up your lodging accordingly: Which course, if it were observed, and the physician carefully and learnedly perform his part, I am persuaded, that many more, than now do, would, for their infirmities, find remedy at the baths, to the great honour of the place; and that scarcely any would depart thence, but much eased and bettered in their state of body.

Thus much I thought fitting to advise and publish concerning the nature and use of our baths; and the rather, that such as preposterously use them, as the greater part, I suppose, do, that resort unto them, may not erroneously detract from the admirable vertues of them. For unto us it doth yearly appear, by the miraculous effects they work, of what excellent efficacy they are, if they be rightly and judiciously used. And seeing that, in the true use of them, there are many things to be considered, I do therefore again advise all such, as are respective of their health, that they enterprise not the use of them without the counsel and direction of some honest and learned physician resident at the baths: Which if they do, the *incommodum* may be *majus commodo.* And so I conclude this treatise.

An Advertisement of the great Utility that cometh to Man's Body by the taking of Physick in the Spring, inferred upon the ensuing Question.

The Spring being the most reviving, flourishing, and temperate Season of the Year, whence is it, that Sicknesses are more frequent in the same, and people sooner die therein, than in any other Season?

THERE may be two reasons yielded for the same; the one taken from the winter preceding, which, by reason of its moisture, filleth the body with crude and excremental humours; and, by its coldness thickening and compacting the same, quieteth them from fluxion; but the heat of the spring approaching, and working on those humours, rarefieth and dissolveth them; which thereupon fluctuating, and putrefying in the body, are the cause of sickness, unless they are expelled by the force of nature, or timely help of physick.

The other reason may be taken from the inconstancy of the spring itself, which sometimes is cold, sometimes hot, sometimes moist, and sometimes dry; which sudden alterations cannot but produce feverish distemperatures, and other infirmities, according to the disposition of the matter congested in the body the winter preceding. From whence it may be concluded, that the sicknesses and deaths of people, which happen more frequently in the spring, than in any other seasons of the year, are not so much to be attributed to the spring, as to the winter, which hath filled the body with superfluities, and prepared it for sickness.

Wherefore, whosoever will be so provident, as, by the timely help of physick, to free his body, as his state and constitution shall require, of the superfluities congested in it, by means of the winter going before, he shall be sure to be far more lively, healthy, and free from sickness in the spring, than any other season of the year, so as he err not over-much in other things. And this purging of the body, and purifying of the blood in the spring, will not only preserve from sicknesses that commonly reign in the spring, but also be a means to keep the body in a perfect integrity the whole year after: And, therefore, I commend the taking of physick in the spring, to all generous people, to them that lead a genial sedentary kind of life, especially to such as are subject to obstructions, or any yearly disease.

You may here demand of me, What time of the spring is fittest for physick, by way of precaution? I answer, That for them that are wont to be affected with sickness in the spring, and whose humours are too cholerick and thin, and consequently subject to fluxion, it is best to take physick at the very beginning thereof; but, for others, about the middle, or after; especially, if the precedent time shall be cold, and not spring-like.

You may also here demand of me, Whether it be not as necessary to take physick in the autumn, which we commonly call the Fall, as in the spring? Whereunto in regard of a generality, I must answer, No: Because the summer prepareth not the body for sickness, filling it with superfluities, as doth the winter; yet, for some bodies it is, as for them that naturally abound with crude and phlegmatick humours, that are subject to obstructions, to cold winterly diseases, or any melancholick affects, as necessary to take physick by way of prevention in the fall, as in the spring; and that, for avoiding the superfluities before the winter, for opening the obstructions, and freeing the body of superfluous melancholy, which then, by reason of the season, increaseth. And the fittest time for the doing thereof, for such as are subject to melancholy, and autumnal diseases, is soon after the beginning of the fall; but, for others, towards the middle thereof.

But, here, I must advertise you, that you expose not your body to the unlearned empirick, that can neither find out the peccant humours, nor parts affected; but to such as are learned in that art, that can well judge of your state of body, and accordingly prescribe you remedies, as your constitution and affected parts shall require. Many men

think, yea, some of a generous note, wherein they bewray their carelesness, if not their stupidity too, that, whilst they are in health, they
may, for prevention, take physick from any one, it matters not from
whom it be, nor what physick it be, so it work with them. I must tell
you, that may overthrow their bodies hereby, and that there is no less
art and judgment required for preserving the body in health, than for
curing of it, being sick; if they did but know how the four humours
are or ought to be proportioned in their bodies, for enjoying, according
to their constitutions, a sound and healthy state, they would, I am
persuaded, be more cautious, than to commit themselves into the hands
of the unlearned, who, by their inconsiderate courses, take humours
from them at an adventure, as well those which are not offensive, as
those which are, to the utter subversion of the œconomy of the body:
Whereof though, perhaps, in regard of their strengths, they are not by
and by sensible, which is that which only cloaketh the errors of
empiricks, and, as a vail, masketh many men's eyes and understanding
herein: Yet they will, as I have in divers observed to their peril, by
little and little incur a relapsed state of body.

It is strange to see the ignorance of most people, how backward they
are to give to the learned professors of physick their due, ready to lay
scandals upon them; but forward to magnify empiricks, their physick,
their honesty, their care, willing to excuse and pass over their gross slips
and absurdities. *O mira hominum stupiditas!* But proceeds this altogether out of ignorance? I suppose, no: For doubtless, many seek
unto them, and magnify their physick, because it is cheap: But such
are fools and gulls, indeed, for they wrong, and even poison their bodies
with gross and ill-qualified physick, to save their purse.

But, to answer the reasons, or rather the words which they produce
and alledge in the favour and behalf of empiricks: To what purpose is
the working of that physick which respecteth not the peccant humours,
nor parts affected, but to the overthrow of the body? What is a supposed honesty in a physician without learning, but a snare, wherein the
ignorant do voluntarily entrap themselves? I say, supposed: For I
cannot think that man to be honest, that usurps a calling, which, with
a good conscience, he is not able to discharge. Or, to what purpose is
the care that empiricks take about their preposterous and ill-composed
medicines, but to the utter ruin of the patient's body? As it too un-
luckily happened of late to a gentleman of good worth and note, who,
taking physick, by way of prevention, of a pill-boasting surgeon, in a
short space, by his ill-qualified and preposterous physick, incurred an
incurable and mortal lapse of his stomach and liver, being in his constant age, and perfect strength of body. Vain, therefore, and very
absurd, is that conceit, which many have in favour of empiricks, viz.
If they do no good, they will do no harm. Admit, that sometimes, by
their trivial petty medicines, they do no harm; yet, nevertheless for
that, I must tell you, that they do much harm; for the sick body relying upon their skill, and they being not able to direct and execute such
courses as shall be fitting and effectual to impugn the disease, while
there is time fitting for the same, the sickness gets the mastery; and
then, perhaps, when their strengths are too much weakened, and the

disease become incurable, they seek help of the learned physician.
So basely verily are most of our people affected to their health, that,
until some practical minister, parish-clerk, apothecary, surgeon, or the
like, have done their utmost hurt, they seek not to the physician.

And here, to vindicate our art from calumny, I cannot but tax
the most sort of people, that being affected with any great or difficult
disease, which, by reason of the nature thereof, or contumacy of the
peccant humours, will have such progress, as that it cannot, in a
short time, by the medicines and best endeavours of the learned
physician, how forceable soever, be evicted, will reject their physician,
and betake themselves, which is an absurdity, *super omnem absurditatem,*
to some ignorant, sottish empirick, and every good wives medicine, to
their great hurt and, oftentimes, overthrow. But, if it happen, that
they recover thereupon, they lay an imputation upon the physician,
and grace their empirick with the cure; whereas, in very deed, the
matter of their disease was wholly, or, at least, the greatest part thereof,
eradicated by such fit and powerful remedies, as the learned physician
had formerly administered unto them: Whereupon, the residue of the
cure was effected by the force of nature, not by the weak endeavours
of the empirick, or trivial medicines of any other whatsoever.

I have, on purpose, enlarged this advertisement, and do leave it for
a memorial and caveat to all posterity, especially to the gentlemen of
this our age, who, for the most part of them, very greatly wrong their
judgment and understanding, in taking physick of the unlearned; and,
wherein they do not only wrong themselves, but also give occasion of
hurt unto others: For the meaner sort of people, following their
example, do the like; whereby it comes to pass, that, in all likelihood,
more untimely perish (which I believe to be true, in the western parts
of this kingdom) under the hands of empiricks, than die otherwise.
Such as will not take notice hereof, *in Empiricorum manus incidant.*
And if any *Asinus Cumanus,* or *Terræ filius,* shall object, that divers
recover under the hands of empiricks; I answer, in a word, that the
recovery is not to be attributed to their physick, but to the strength
of nature, that bears up, both against the disease, and their preposterous
courses.

---

*A Censure concerning the Water of St. Vincent's Rock near Bristol¹,
which begins to grow in great Request and Use against the Stone.*

THIS water of St. Vincent's Rock is a very pure, clear, crystalline
substance, answering to those crystalline diamonds, and transparent
stones, that are plentifully found in those clifts. It is no less commendable for smell and taste, than delectable for colour and substance, and,
for its temperature, excels any other of this kingdom, being almost of a
mean between heat and cold: I say almost, because it is a little more
inclined to cold, than to heat, which maketh it the more effectual for
allaying the burning heat of the bowels; and yet, by reason of its good
temperature, not quickly offensive to the stomach, if it be not lapsed
by cold.

¹ Urbs pulchra, & Emporium celebre.

But, before I deliver my censure and opinion concerning the nature and use of this water, it is fitting that I declare unto you the matter from whence it receives its medicinal faculties, and that is (for I have twice made probation thereof) from sulphur and nitre, and from both, but in a small measure: For the water, at its issuing forth, carrieth with it an obscure heat, being scarcely lukewarm; and the reason thereof is, because the heat of the water and strength of the sulphurous vapours are qualified and abated in the passages thorough the earth; or else it is, because this water issueth but from a small vein of sulphur. And the note that it hath but little nitre in it, besides the probation thereof, is, because it can hardly, or not at all, in the taste be discerned, but by a curious and skilful palate for the purpose. I suppose that this water partakes of other good minerals. But I leave that for a farther search, or to such as shall hereafter live more conveniently for that purpose, than I do. But, whatsoever minerals shall lie hid in the passages of this water, it is sufficient, that it partakes of two so good as sulphur and nitre, and that in such a mixture, as it makes it to be of an excellent temper, and medicinal faculty, in potable uses for divers cases, as shall be hereafter shewed. It were to be wished, that the water issued forth in a more convenient place, as well for access unto it, as for conserving the heat thereof.

This water is frequented for no other use, but for the drinking of it against the stone: It hath also other excellent faculties; but, I suppose (such is the vanity of our time) that the fame thereof will not long hold, but will in a short time have an end, as some other waters, of good force and efficacy against sundry infirmities, in divers places of this kingdom have had, and that by reason of the absurd and preposterous use of it: For, upon notice and experience, that this water hath done some good against the stone, people of all sorts repair unto it, as well such as have not the stone, as those that have, or stand in fear thereof, and abundantly glut and fill themselves therewith, till they vomit and strout again, scarcely one of fifty, I dare say, having the opinion of a judicious physician for the taking of the same, or preparing their bodies for it as is meet; which cannot but bring a disgrace to the water: For admit, that a few chance to receive benefit thereby, some will not, but many much hurt. Neither can the water be good for all bodies that are troubled with the stone, or subject thereunto: And, therefore, I would have you to know, that the ill and preposterous use thereof will weaken the stomach, subvert the liver, annoy the head and breast, occasion cramps, pain in the joints, breed crudities, rheums, coughs, cachexies, the dropsy itself, and consumption.

But I will proceed to shew you the faculties and true use of the water. It notably cooleth the inflammations of all the inward parts, and yet, as I have said, not quickly offending the stomach, as other waters do; and is, withal, of a gentle mundifying faculty. It is, therefore, very effectual, against the burning heat of the stomach, inflammations of the liver and reins, and adustion of the humours, being taken with fine sugar in this proportion, as, half an ounce of sugar, or thereabouts, to a pint of the water. In such as have had hot

H 3

livers, red pimpling faces, and adusted humours, I have caused a tincture of roses and violets to be taken therewith, and that with singular success. It may be given with other good convenient adjuncts, which will not only make it the more grateful to the stomach, but also more effectual for the cases aforesaid, which I leave to the physician to find out, and direct, as shall be best fitting for his patient's body. In inflammation and siccity of the intestines, it is good to give with this water syrup or *Mel. Viol. Sol.* In inflammation of the kidneys, with obstruction also in them, I have given it to such as had withal hot livers, with *Crystallo Minerali*, with wished effect: for the distemper of the kidnies was not only quickly allayed therewith, but also, abundance of sand, and other drossy matter, stopping in them, purged forth.

That this water is good against the stone, strangury, and purulent ulcers of the kidnies, and bladder, it is evident, by reason of its mundifying and cleansing faculty, to be taken with sugar, as aforesaid, or with some good and effectual adjunct, for the speedier carriage of it to the affected places, &c. which, by reason of the diversity of bodies, I cannot here describe, but must leave you, therein, to the advice and counsel, not of a vulgar, but of some learned, judicious, expert physician; and that with this caution, if you be not sure of the accurate judgment and skill of your physician, that you take the water only with sugar, without any other mixture with it. This water is also good in the ulcerations of the intestines, with this proviso, that it be taken with some convenient adjunct, as *Mel Rosat.* &c. to occasion the passage thereof through the belly, diverting it from the veins.

As concerning the use of this water, and first, for inward inflammations: The time of the year best for taking thereof, by way of cure or prevention, is, in the months of April, May, and June, and that in the morning fasting, the body being first prepared thereunto, that is, gently purged, according as the constitution thereof shall require; but, in case of necessity, it may be taken at any other time, respect being had to the season, age, and present state of the body. As for the quantity that is to be taken every morning, and how long to be continued, in that, because of the diversity of bodies, I must leave you to the discretion and judgment of your physician.

As for the taking of this water against the stone, ten rules are to be observed in the use thereof.

The first is, the preparation of the body, that is, that it be exquisitely purged, before you attempt the use thereof; for, the passages being cleared, and the ill matter diverted by stool, the water will the more freely, and with greater force, penetrate unto the reins.

The second is, that it be taken in the morning fasting, the excrements of the belly being first deposed, and that at divers draughts, allowing betwixt every draught or two draughts, taken the one after the other, the space of a quarter of an hour, or somewhat more, till you have taken the whole portion of water, that is intended to be taken each morning, walking and stirring gently your body between every taking;

for that will cause the water to be the sooner distributed through your body,' refraining to go abroad in the air, between, and upon the takings thereof, if the weather shall be any thing cold ; for cold will hinder the distribution of the water.

The third is, the quantity of the water that is to be taken every morning, which must be directed by your physician, that knows your age and state of body.

The fourth is, how many mornings together it is to be taken, as eight or ten more or less, according to the ability of the stomach, strength and state of body, wherein you must likewise be directed by your physician.

The fifth thing to be observed in the taking of the water is, to take it, as near as you can, in the same temper of heat as it issueth forth, or else so hot as you shall be well able to drink it ; and herein every one may gratify his own stomach. But seeing that the place is unfit for the taking of it, and that the water seems, by reason of the rawishness of the place, to be colder at its issuing forth, than it is otherwise ; for, being taken into a stone jug, it warmeth the same; I advise that the water be taken into stone jugs, or other convenient bottles, and the jugs or bottles to be immediately stopped, to keep in the vapours, and so the water to be taken, while it reserveth its heat ; but, if the water should wax cold before you take it, you may heat the jug in a kettle of hot water, till it shall be so hot as you shall like to take it, keeping the jug close stopped all the while ; and so you may do such mornings, when you cannot have the water, it being all overcovered by that Severn, that floweth to the city. If you demand of me, whether the water loseth any thing of its virtue, being so kept ? I must answer you, that it is like by that it looseth somewhat of its sulphurous, but not any thing of its nitrous quality, and therefore it may be well reserved, and used in manner as aforesaid.

The sixth is the time of the year, that is best for the taking of this water, and that in a season that is not cold or rainy ; but hot, or inclining thereunto, as from the beginning of May, to the middle of September ; but after that, in regard of the alterations of the air, and winter approaching, this water is not good to be taken, because it will weaken the stomach and liver, annoy the breast, breed crudities, coughs, &c. as I have already shewed.

The seventh is the diet, that is to be observed all the time of the taking of the water, which is, that it must be but slender, and that of meats of good juice, and easy digestion ; the dinner not to be taken, till the greater part of the water be avoided, and the supper must be always less than the dinner, that the stomach may be the next morning empty for receiving of the water again.

The eighth is, that the body be purged immediately after the taking of the water, that is, when an end is made of taking it, for avoiding some relicks thereof, which perhaps may abide in the body after the use of it, which the physician must be careful to do with a fit medicine. Afterwards a moderation in diet, and all other things, is to be observed.

The ninth is, that it be not given to children that are subject to the

R 4

stone, under twelve years of age, unless they shall be naturally of a
very hot constitution, and that, to them in quantities proportionable to
their age. Neither is it to be admitted to them, that are entered
within the limits of old age, because it will abbreviate their life, *calorem
innatum extinguendo* [1].

The tenth and last thing to be considered in the use of this water,
is, that it be not given to such, as, by reason of the smalness and
streightness of the veins, cannot extreat and pass it away by urine,
though the infirmities of the stone, stranguries, &c. may otherwise
require the use thereof. Neither is it to be given to such, as have
cold stomachs, weak livers, feeble brains, and subject unto rheums ;
in a word, not to phlegmatick, not to any that abound with crudities,
or have a cold and moist habit of body : for in all such it will soon
infringe the natural heat, breed rheums, annoy the breast, occasion
cramps, and divers other infirmities, as I have afore shewed.

The same observations must be kept in taking of this water against
the strangury and ulcerations of the bladder and kidnies, as is directed
in taking thereof, against the stone. In which affects it is good to
give therewith some lubrifying, cleansing extract, or the like. And
here note, that, if the water in all the aforesaid cases be given, with a
fit and convenient adjunct, it will not only be the more effectual, and
sooner conveighed to the affected parts, but less quantities also may
serve to be taken ; and then the stomach will not be so overpressed
and charged therewith, as it is in the common manner of taking it.
But, if it be at any time fit to overcharge and press the stomach therewith,
it is in cases of the strangury and purulent ulcers of the bladder and
kidnies.

I may not omit to give you notice, that divers symptoms or perillous
accidents may happen oftentimes in the use of this water, which, because
they cannot be well rectified or prevented without the presence of a
physician, I here omit to nominate or treat of, and instead thereof,
as also for divers reasons afore nominated, do advise you not to adventure
the drinking thereof, without the advice and presence of a judicious
physician ; which if you do, you may haply, instead of the good you
expect thereby, receive much hurt. As for outward uses, this water
may sometimes asswage the itch, mundify and pallitate old sores ; but
no matter of moment is to be expected from it this way. And thus
much concerning the nature and use of this water, whose vertues will
be better known, if people make a right and good use thereof.

1 By extinguishing the innate heat.

The following letter, though it did not appear for many years after, it has been deemed
advisable to be annexed to the preceding essay, being on the same interesting subject.
                                                                    EDITOR.

A LETTER

CONCERNING SOME

OBSERVATIONS LATELY MADE AT BATH.

Written to his much honoured Friend,

SIR E. G. KNIGHT AND BARONET, M. D. IN LONDON.

BY THOMAS GUIDOTT, M. B.

Facilius ducimur, quam trahimur. Senec.

London, printed in 1674. Quarto, containing twenty pages.

Honoured Sir,

I KNOW you (as well as other ingenious and inquisitive persons) are somewhat concerned, and desirous to understand what success my late enquiries have had into one of the grand mysteries of nature, I mean the baths of this city; considering especially that you were pleased the last summer to afford me the honour of your company and particular acquaintance, and to express a more than ordinary desire of my proceeding in this thing. Concerning which I must tell you, that as I have not been wanting, either to pains or pay, in my proceedings hitherto; so I have had the good hap (which hath been my encouragement) to meet with many considerable discoveries. And though the main body of the matter, collected touching this affair, be not yet ripe for the lancet, but will require a longer time to digest; yet some observations I shall now communicate, which will give a little satisfaction to an earnest desire, and make, in some measure, appear that we have been lame and defective hitherto, in a rational account and true understanding of the nature of these waters.

It hath been indeed the ill fortune of these baths (which, I may truly say, are as good if not better than any baths in the world) to lie a long time in obscurity, and not so much as to be mentioned among the baths of Europe, by any foreign writer, till about the year 1570, when that excellent person, Sir Edward Carne, sent ambassador by Queen Elisabeth, to Pope Julius the Third, and Paul the Fourth, made some relation of them to that famous writer, Andreas Baccius, then at Rome; and writing his elaborate book de Thermis, into which he hath inserted them, upon his relation, Lib. iv. Cap. 13, though somewhat improperly, among sulphurous baths.

About the same time also one John Jones, an honest Cambro-Briton, frequenting the baths for practice, composed a little treatise of them, which he calls Baths Aid, in which are some things not contemptible, though in a plain country dress, and which might satisfy and gratify the appetite of those times, which fed more heartily and healthily too then, upon parson's fare, good beef and bag-pudding, then we do now upon kickshaws and haut-gousts; yet nothing of the true nature is there discovered, only, as almost in all former writers of baths, chiefly catholick, a strong stanch of sulphur, and a great ado about a subterreanean fire, a fit resemblance of hell, at least of purgatory. Our countryman Doctor William Turner, I confess, was more particularly concerned to give a better account, than I find is done in his discourse of English, German, and Italian baths. But whether want of opportunity, or any other impediment was in cause, I know not; but I find that, at this stay, they stood till the famous doctor Jorden took pen in hand, about the year 1630. To whom I thought fit to make some additions, at my first entrance on this place, some five years since; and although that learned and candid physician had chiefly, and more especially, an intent to enlarge the knowledge of our baths in Somersetshire, as he declares to my Lord Cottington, in his dedicatory epistle; and hath performed more than any man before him; yet what was first in intention, was last in execution, and how small a part of that treatise is spent upon this subject, how short he is in some material points, and what objections may be framed against his opinion, I may some time or other, with due respect, more largely treat of, and for the present shall here, with good Shem and Japhet, cast a garment over the nakedness of this my father.

What hath been done since (except in some particular pieces of other tracts, to the authors of which the baths are also indebted for their kindness and good will) is not worth the mentioning. The old saying is true, ' Little dogs must piss,' and what is writ upon an ale-bench claims the greater affinity to the pipe and the candle; especially if the best wine at the feast (which is usually kept till last) be but a silly story of Tom Coriat, and an old Taunton ballad new vamped (the creature's parts lying that way) abusing the dead ghosts of Ludhudibras and Bladud, with a Nonsensico-Pragmatical, Anticruzado-orientado-Rhodomontado-Untruth Le Grand, which we, westerly moderns, call a grote lye, into the bargain. A pretty artifice in rhetorick, to cry a thing up, and besmear, and shed plentifully on the founder ordure, both human and belluine.

> Rode, Caper, vitem, tamen hic, cum stabis ad aras,
> In tua quod fundi cornua possit, erit.

> Goat, bark the vine; yet juice enough will rise
> To drench thy head, when made a sacrifice.

I have industirously omitted Doctor Johnson, Doctor Venner, and some others, in regard it would be improper here to write more historically, which I resolve to do, if my leisure permit, on another occasion. I shall therefore now let you know not so much, what hath been done by others, as what further discoveries have been made by my endeavours, assisted by the careful pains of Mr. Henry Moor, an expect apothecary and chymist of this city.

And here at first I cannot but take notice, how that opinion hath so much prevailed as to be accounted orthodox, and not only received by tradition as certain, but printed as such, that the body of the waters is so jejune and empty, as to afford little or nothing at all whereby to make a discovery of its nature; and that what impregnates the baths is not substantially, materially, or corporally there, but potentially, vertually, and formally, or, to use the author's own words, δυνάμει μᾶλλον ἢ ἐνεργεία, with much more canting after this manner in a small discourse in Latin, written by an itinerant exotick [1]; whenas a slight operation will soon evince it, though white and transparent of itself, being taken immediately from the pump, to contain a considerable quantity of a dusky, gritty, and saline matter, with many transparent particles intermixed with it, to the proportion (as near as I can calculate, sometimes more and sometimes less) of two drams to a gallon of the water. And this I can ascertain, having had several ounces of it done in earth, iron, bell-metal, and glass, and have at this time tree or four ounces by me, untouched, beside what I have made use of in other experiments.

But the thing I shall more peculiarly insist on, at present, is, that by God's blessing, on my industrious search, I suppose I have lighted on the main constituents of the vertues of the bath, in which alone resides what benefit can be expected from the use of these waters, and lodgeth in a saline substance, in a very small proportion to the body of the waters; so that, as they are now, not much more than forty grains are contained in a gallon, insomuch that this little soul, as I may so term it, is almost lost in so gigantick a body, and cannot animate it with that vigour and activity, as may be rationally expected, were a greater quantity of the salt contained in a less proportion of the water. The remainder, which is not saline, being, as I judge, two parts in three of the bulk of the contents, is partly whitish, gritty, and of a lapideous nature, concreting, of itself, into a stony consistence not easily dissolvible; partly more light and dirty, resembling clay, or marle, and discovers itself by an apparent separation from the saline and gritty part mentioned before.

Now the chief vertue of the bath, as I conceive, consisting in the salts, which appear, by undeniable experiments, to be nitrous, and I believe vitrioline (bitumen and sulphur being not primarily, as these salts, but secondarily concerned, which, consisting of unctuous particles, cannot be supposed capable of mixing with the body of the waters, and therefore no way observable in the contents) and no small proportion of other things blended with it; the best way to make it most

1 Car. Claramont. de Aer. Aq. & Loc. T. A. p. 32.

serviceable I conceived to be, to free it from those incumbrances and allays it hath from the other ingredients, and prepare it as exactly as may be performed by art, for the benefit of those especially, who are willing to drink the waters with greater success in a lesser quantity; which they may now do, and have more of the vertue of the waters, in a quart, three pints, or a pottle, than they formerly had in two or three gallons, did they drink as much; which will be, besides other conveniences, a great relief to the stomach, which certainly must be relaxed, and the tone of it injured by that vast quantity of water, which is usually taken diluting its ferment overmuch, and distending its membranes beyond all the bounds of a reasonable capacity.

Besides, what is separated only by an artificial extraction, will better unite again, and mix with the waters, as much more familiar, than the extraneous salts of sal prunella, cream of tartar, &c. which are usually dissolved and drank with the waters; so that a great part of the operation may be ascribed to that; and the waters, being, as we say, between two stools, that of itself, and the dissolvent in it, have not attained to that degree of reputation as they have deserved, and may be procured with much more advantage, if nothing but the same be spent upon the same, a way of improvement altogether equally beneficial to the fluids and solids, to the wet as the dry.

Again, whereas it is a custom here, as in all other places of the like nature, when persons are not willing, or have not conveniences to come to the fountain-head, to send for the waters to the places of their residence, not thinking it much material whether Mahomet go to the mountain, or the mountain come to him, whereby the vertue of the waters is much impaired, though stopped and sealed up with never so much care; this defect may be supplied by the addition of a quantity of the same ingredients, which may repair the loss that hath been sustained by evaporation in the carriage, or any other way of damage, and restore it again, as near as may be, to its pristine vertue, and genuine advantage. Not to mention that, if need require, and the poorer sort cannot procure or pay the freight for the waters, they may take a shorter course, by mixing the salt, which they may have at reasonable rates, with spring water, brought to a proportionable degree of heat at home, and expect more advantage, for aught I know, than those that drink the waters themselves at so great a distance; and I have therefore ordered convenient doses of the salt to be prepared and kept, by Mr. William Child, alderman, and Mr. Henry Moore, two apothecaries in Bath, to whom any one may resort, that shall have occasion.

And, because I am now fallen on this subject, I shall crave leave to remind you of what you well enough understand already, that not only *Dulcius*, but *Utilius, ex ipso Fonte, &c.* and waters, especially impregnated with volatile spirits, such as most acid are, and peculiarly vitrioline, to avoid the inconvenience and expence, not so much of money as vertue, in the carriage, must be drunk on the place where they are, which, in some kind resembling children, that must live by sucking, if once removed from their mother, or nurse, by degrees dwindle away, and at last die.

It is observable in these waters, that with four grains of gall injected into a pint glass of water, or the water poured on it, it immediately turns of a purple colour, which in short time after, as the water cools, abates much of its vividity, and becomes more faint; if the waters be suffered to cool, and be quite cool before the galls are injected, no alteration happens upon a much greater proportion of galls superadded; and what is more remarkable, if the water, which is permitted to cool, be recruited by the fire, and the same trial reiterated, it offers no greater satisfaction in change of colour, than the second experiment. Consonant to what Andreas Baccius, a veteran and experienced soldier in this militia, hath formerly observed, who in his second book de Thermis, cap. x. pag. 69, hath these words, *Nulla Balnei Aqua, eodem cum successu, ac laude, bibitur, longe exportata, quod ad fontem proprium ; maxima enim pars, ex ipso fonte haustæ ac delatæ, amittunt omnem virtutem, multæ non servantur per hyemem : dilutæ pluviis, & quæ utcunque servantur delatæ a propriis fonticulis, fieri non potest, quin amittunt, cum calore suo minerali, vivificos illos spiritus, in quibus omnis juramenti vis consistit, quæ semel amissa, nullo postea extrinseco calore restituitur. Quod est valde notandum.*

I have been the more particular in this, in regard it is a very useful and practical discovery, and may procure more real advantage to mankind, than the vain and unattainable attempts of the philosophers stone, making glass malleable, and the quadrature of a circle.

Some other observations I shall also mention, of no less magnitude, and more contracted circumference, as the dying of the bath-guides skins, the bathers linnen, and the stones in the bottom of the bath, of a yellow colour, and the eating out of the iron rings of bath, the iron bars of the windows about the bath, and any iron infused in it; insomuch as I have now by me a gad of iron, by accident taken up among the stones of the King's bath, so much eaten out, and digested by the ostrich stomach of these waters, that, the sweetness extracted what remains resembles very much a honey-comb, a deep perforation in many places being attempted, and the whole gad itself reduced very much like a sponge.

The first, viz. the tincture, I have discovered to arrive from an ochre, with which the bath abounds, and hath afforded me a considerable quantity, so that now I have near a pound by me, and, with an infusion of that in warm water, tinge stones as exactly of the Bath colour, that they are not discernible one from another. It is further observable, that, the nearer the place of ebullition, where the springs arise, the deeper and finer is the yellow colour; so that in some places, about the cross in the King's bath, and at the head of the great spring, at the south-west corner thereof, it is almost made a natural paint, being laboured together by the working of the springs, and a continual succession of new matter coming on, free from those impurities it contracts in other places, which makes it distinguishable into two or three sorts, according to its mixture with, or freedom from, more adulterating matter. The clouts also and woollen rags, which the guides use to stop the gout withal, besides the walls, slip-doors and posts, when the bath is kept in a considerable time, as in the winter-season it useth to be, are all very much tinged with this yellow substance; and if at any time they chance to lie unwashed, or not thrown away, they send out so ungrateful a scent, that a man had rather smell to a carnation, rose, violet, or a pomander, than be within the wind of so unwelcome a smell, it being the greatest policy to get the weathergage in this encounter. The same thing I have experienced in vessels at home, where, after it had stood some time, in a common infusion of warm water, I have the same reverence for that as pictures, and do aver it to be true, *E longinquo reverentia major*.

One thing more is to be noted before I leave this particular, that, although so much of this yellow matter is continually bred, with which the neighbouring ground is sufficiently replenished, as I have found by digging in some places not far distant, yet nothing of that colour is discovered in the contents; a probable argument it either evaporates, to which I am more inclined, in regard I find it much more copious where the steam of the bath meets with any resistance; or else perhaps, which is less probable, turns colour by the fire in evaporation that way; less probable, I say, because, for further satisfaction, I have decocted the ochre more than once, and find it rather gets than loses in its colour.

The greenish colour ariseth from another cause.

The eating out of the iron, I conceive, must proceed from something corrosive, and, till any one can assure me it is something else, I shall judge it to be vitriol; and that it may appear not to be caused by the bare steam, as rust is bred upon pot-hooks and cotterels (as some imagine) besides the difficulty to conceive how the steam should operate under water, as in the case of the gad beforementioned, I made a lixivium of the contents of the water, and in it infused iron, but a very small time, and found it to do the same as in the bath itself, considering the time of infusion; and the very knives, and spatules, I put in to stir some residence in the bottom, were, almost as soon as dry, crusted over and defended with a rusty coat.

I have other arguments, I suppose, will contribute something more to the confirmation of this opinion; as, that, with the help of the sand of the bath with water, and galls, I make good writing ink, which, in a short time, comes to be very legible; but the infusion of the contents in common water, or the lixivium thereof, with an addition of an inconsiderable proportion of the decoction of galls, makes it tolerably legible, on the first commixture, only the first, viz. that made with sand, casting an eye of decayed red from a mixture of ochre contained in the same. Neither is it altogether to be slighted, that the water itself hath been heretofore used by the best writing-masters for the making ink, who, observing by their experience, that ink made with Bathwater, and the other usual ingredients, had a better colour, and was more lasting than any other, preferred this water before any other for this use, as I have been informed by some credible persons. Also having not long since occasion to pour warm water on the contents of the bath, in order to the making a lixivium, some of the water happened, by an accident, to fall upon a Basil-skin I sometimes use, and immediately turned the red into black, more than the breadth of an ordinary hand, with as much facility as any curriers liquors; allum I know will do the like, but I find no necessity to assert, that, had it any thing to do here, must make the water much tougher, whiter, and sourer, than I find it to be. To which I may add, that many judicious persons, my patients, and some intelligent and eminent physicians also have assured me, that they have perfectly discerned by the taste a mixture of vitriol, and that I need not doubt but that was one principal ingredient. It is also not very inconsiderable, that the Bath-water alone will coagulate milk, though not after the usual way of making a posset; for, after the milk and water are put together, it must boil pretty smartly, else the curd will not rise. I may likewise subjoin as a further probability, that, on the relenting of the salt extracted into an oil *per deliquium*, there is a very sharp stiptick and vitrioline taste perceived in the gross *deliquium*, as also in the clear oil, and the salt itself; not to mention its shooting into glebes, of which I have some small assurances by some trials I have made, not yet sufficiently satisfactory; and therefore I dismiss this part for the present, with the greatest probability, till a further inquiry shall make me positive.

But, as to nitre, there can be no question made about that I suppose; for besides the quick acrimonious cooling, and the nauseous taste, most apparently discoverable both in the infused contents, the salt and the oil (the latter of which, viz. the nauseous taste, I take more particular notice of, in regard it is most predominant, and assigned by Fallopius to nitre, and the waters impregnated with it, which, he says, sometimes do *subvertere stomachum, & facere nauseam, de Therm. Aq- & Met. cap.* 9. besides, I say, these probable conjectures) what will set it beyond all contradiction, is that it hath the true characteristick of nitre, and shoots its needles, as long and firm, to the quantity I have, as any I have seen in the shops, of which I have now lately shot above twenty *stiriæ*, some near an inch in length, which I keep in a glass ready by me, to give any one satisfaction that desires to see it, besides what I have parted with to some friends abroad.

I the rather mention this, in regard it hath been my good hap to bring this to perfection and autoptical demonstration, which hath been in vain attempted by some industrious persons; not that I am in the least willing to arrogate to myself, or derogate from them, more than what is fitting, but to confirm this truth, that there are some *mollia tempora fandi*; some opportunities, when nature will give willing audience, without much ceremony or ado, confessing more by fair persuasions, than racks and torments, and greater importunity. And that we ought to be very cautious how to affirm a thing not to be, upon the failure of a single, or some repeated experiments.

In fine, lest I should too much exceed the bounds of a letter, what concerns the cause of the heat of the waters, I say little of here, only tell you that when I shall come to discourse of that subject, of which I intend, God willing, a large disquisition in another language, I believe I shall find myself obliged not so much to depend on a subterranean fire, as to expect greater satisfaction from another hypothesis.

Many more experiments I have made upon the sand, scum, and mud of the bath, with some observations drawn from the *natura loci*, or ground hereabouts; but, I fear, I have been too tedious already, and therefore, without further ceremony, shall release you out of this purgatory, with the subscription of,

Sir, your most faithful and much obliged servant

THO. GUIDOTT.

For Lord Falkland's History of Edward II. See Vol. I. p. 90.

CONSIDERATIONS

TOUCHING A WAR WITH SPAIN.

Written by

THE RIGHT HONOURABLE, FRANCIS, LORD VERULAM,

VISCOUNT OF ST. ALBANS.

Imprinted 1629. Quarto, containing forty eight pages.

YOUR Majesty hath an imperial name: It was a Charles that brought the empire first into France; a Charles that brought it first into Spain: Why should not Great-Britain have its turn? But to lay aside all that might seem to have a shew of fumes and fancies, and to speak solids: A war with Spain, if the King shall enter into it, is a mighty work; it requireth strong materials and active motions; he, that saith not so, is zealous, but not according to knowledge: But, nevertheless, Spain is no such giant; and he that thinketh Spain to be some great over-match for this estate, assisted as it is and may be, is no good mint-man, but takes greatness of kingdoms, according to their bulk and currency, and not after their intrinsick value.

Although therefore I had wholly sequestered my thoughts from civil affairs, yet, because it is a new case, and concerneth my country infinitely, I obtained of myself to set down, out of long continued experience in business of state, and much conversation in books of policy and history, what I thought pertinent to this business, and, in all humbleness, to present it to your Majesty; hoping, that at least you will discern the strength of my affection, through the weakness of my abilities: For the Spaniards have a good proverb, *Desnariosi empre con la calentura.* There is no heat of affection, but is joined with some idleness of brain.

To war are required a just quarrel, sufficient forces and provisions, and a prudent choice of the designs. So then I will, First, justify the quarrel. Secondly, balance the forces. And, Lastly, propound variety of designs for choice: For that were not fit for a writing of this nature, neither is it a subject within the level of my judgment, I being in effect, a stranger to the present occurrents.

Wars, I speak not of ambitious predatory wars, are suits of appeals to the tribunal of God's justice, when there are no superiors on earth to determine the cause, and they are as civil pleas, either plaints or defences.

There are therefore three just grounds of war with Spain; one upon plaint, two upon defence; Solomon saith, A cord of three is not easily broken, but especially when every one of the lines will hold by itself: They are these: The recovery of the Palatinate, and a just fear of the subversion of our church and religion: For, in the handling of these two last grounds of war, I shall make it plain, that wars preventive, upon just fears, are true defensives, as well as upon actual invasions. And again, that wars defensive for religion, I speak not of rebellions, are most just, though offensive wars for religion are seldom to be approved or never, except they have some mixture of civil titles. But all that I shall say, in this whole argument, will be but like bottoms of thread close wound up, which, with a good needle, perhaps may be flourished into large works.

For the asserting of the justice of the quarrel, for the recovery of the Palatinate, I shall not go so high as to discuss the right of the war of Bohemia, which, if it be freed from doubt on our part, then there is no colour nor shadow why the Palatinate should be retained, the ravishing whereof was a mere excursion of the first wrong, and a super-injustice. But I do not take myself to be so perfect in the customs, records, transactions, and privileges of that kingdom of Bohemia, as to be fit to handle that part; and I will not offer at that I cannot master. Yet this I will say in passage positively and resolutely, That it is impossible and repugnant in itself, that an elective monarchy should be so free and absolute as an hereditary, no more than it is possible for a father to have so full power and interest in an adoptive son, as in a natural, ' Quia naturalis obligatio fortior civili.' And again, that received maxim is almost unshaken and infallible, ' Nil magis naturæ consentaneum est quam ut eisdem modis res dissolvantur quibus constituuntur:' So that, if part of the people or estate be somewhat in the election, you cannot make them nulloes or cyphers in the prorivation or translation; and, if it be said, that this is a dangerous opinion for the Pope, Emperor, and all elective kings; it is true, it is a dangerous opinion, and ought to be a dangerous opinion to such personal popes, emperors, or elective kings, as shall transcend their limits, and become tyrannical.

But it is a safe and sound opinion for their sees, empires, and kingdoms, and for themselves also, if they be wise: ' Plenitudo potestatis est plenitudo tempestatis;' but the chief cause why I do not search into this point, is, because I need it not. And, in handling the right of a war, I am not willing to intermix matters doubtful, with that which is out of doubt: For as, in capital causes, wherein but one man's life is in question, *in favorem vitæ*, the evidence ought to be clear, so much more in the judgment of a war, which is capital to thousands. I suppose therefore the worst, that the offensive war upon Bohemia hath been unjust, and then make the case, which is no sooner made than resolved; if it be made, not enwrapped, but plainly and perspicuously, it is this in these: An offensive war is made, which is unjust to the aggressor; the prosecution and race of the war carrieth the defendant to assail and invade the ancient and indubitate patrimony of the first aggressor, which is now turned defendant. Shall he sit down, and not put himself in defence, or, if he be disposed, shall he not make a war for the recovery? No man is so poor of judgment, as will affirm it. The castle of Cadmus was taken, and the city of Thebes itself invested by Plebidas, the Lacedemonian, insidiously and in violation of league: The process of this action drew on a resurprise of the castle by the Thebeans, a recovery of the town, and a current of the war, even unto the walls of Sparta: I demand, Was the defence of the city of Sparta, and the expulsion of the Thebeans, out of the ancient Laconian territories, unjust? The starving of that part of the duchy of Milan, which lieth upon the river of Adda, by the Venetians, upon contract with the French, was an ambitious and unjust purchase. This wheel, set on going, did pour a war upon the Venetians, with such a tempest, as Padua and Trivigi were taken from them, and all their dominions upon the continent of Italy abandoned, and they confined within the salt waters: Will any man say, that the memorable recovery and defence of Padua, when the gentlemen of Venice, unused to the wars, out of the love of their country, became brave and martial the first day; and so likewise the redemption of Trivigi, and the rest of their dominions, was matter of scruple, whether just or no, because it had force from a quarrel ill begun. The wars of the Duke of Urbine, nephew to Pope Julius the Second, when he made himself head of the Spanish mutineers, was as unjust as unjust might be, a support of desperate rebels, and invasion of St. Peter's patrimony, and what you will. The race of this war fell upon the loss of Urbine itself, which was the Duke's undoubted right, yet in this case not penitentiary, though he had enjoined him never so strait penance to expiate his first offence, and would have counselled him to have given over the pursuit of his right for Urbine; which after he obtained prosperously, and hath transmitted to his family, yet until this day.

Nothing more unjust than the invasion of the Spanish Armada in eighty-eight upon our seas, for our land was holy land to them, they might not touch it; shall I say therefore, that the defence of Lisbon or Cales afterwards was unjust? There be thousands of examples, ' Utor in re non dubia exemplis non necessariis.' The reasons are plain, wars are vindict, revenges reparations; but revenges are not infinite, but according to the measure of the first wrong or damage. And therefore, when a voluntary offensive war, by the design or fortune of the war, is turned into a necessary defensive, the scene of the tragedy is changed, and it is a new act to begin: For, though the particular actions of wars are complicate in fact, yet they are separate and distinct in right, like to cross suits in civil pleas, which are sometimes both just; but this is so clear, as needeth not further to be insisted upon. And yet, if, in things so clear, it were fit to speak of more or less clear, in our present cause, it is the more clear on our part, because the possession of Bohemia is settled with the Emperor; for, though it be true, that *Non datur compensatio injuriarum;* yet were there somewhat more colour to detain the Palatinate, as in the nature of a recovery in value or compensation, if Bohemia had been lost, or were still the stage of the war. Of this therefore I speak no more. As for the title of proscription or forfeiture, wherein the Emperor, upon the matter, hath been judge and party, and hath justified himself: God forbid, but that it should well endure an appeal to a war; for, certainly, the court of heaven, I take it, is as well a chancery to save and debar forfeitures, as a court of common law to decide rights, and there would be work enough in Germany, Italy, and other parts, if imperial forfeitures should go for good titles.

Thus much for the first ground of war with Spain, being in the nature of a plaint for the recovery of the Palatinate, omitting that here, which might be the seed of a larger discourse, and is verified by a number of examples; which is, That whatsoever is gained by an abusive treaty, ought to be restored *in integrum.* As we see the daily experience of this in civil pleas, for the images of great things are best seen contracted into small glasses; we see, I say, that all pretorian courts, if any of the parties be entertained, or laid asleep, under pretence of an arbitrement or accord, and that the other party, during that time, doth cautelously get the start and advantage at common law, though it be to judgment and execution, yet the pretorian court will set back all things *in statu quo prius,* no respect being had to such eviction, or dispossession. Lastly, Let there be no mistaking, as if, when I speak of a war for the recovery of the Palatinate, I meant, that it must be *in linea recta* upon that place; for look in *Jus Feciale,* and all examples, and it will be found to be without scruple, that, after a legation *ad res repetendas,* and a refusal, and a denunciation or indiction of a war, the war is no more confined to the place of the quarrel, but is left at large, and to choice (as to the particular conducing designs) as opportunities and advantages shall invite.

To proceed therefore to the second ground of a war with Spain: We have set it down to be a just fear of the subversion of our civil estate; so then the war is not for the Palatinate only, but for England, Scotland, Ireland, our king, our prince, our nation, all that we have. Wherein two things are to be proved; the one, That a just fear, without an actual invasion or offence, is a sufficient ground of a war, and in the nature of a true defensive; the other, That we have, towards Spain, cause of just fear; I say, *just* fear; for, as the civilians do well define, that the legal fear is ' justus metus, qui cadit in constantem virum,' in private cases; so there is ' justus metus, qui cadit in constantem senatum in causa publica,' not out of umbrages, light jealousness, apprehensions afar off, but out of clear foresight of imminent danger.

Concerning the former proposition, it is good to hear what time saith.

Thucydides, in his inducement to his story of the great war of Peloponnesus, sets down in plain terms, that the true cause of that war was the overgrowing greatness of the Athenians, and the fear that the Lacedemonians stood in thereby; and doth not doubt to call it ' a necessity imposed upon the Lacedemonians of a war;' which are the very words of a mere defensive; adding, that the other causes were but specious and popular : ' Verissimam quidem, sed minime sermone celebratam arbitror extitisse belli causam, Athenienses magnos effectos, & Lacedæmoniis formidolosos, necessitatem illis imposuisse bellandi ; quæ autem propalam ferebantur utrinque, causæ istæ fuerunt, &c.' i. e. The truest cause of this war, though least voiced, I conceive to have been this : that the Athenians, being grown great, to the terror of the Lacedemonians, did impose upon them the necessity of a war; but the causes, that went abroad in speeches, were these, &c.

Sulpitius Galba, consul, when he persuaded the Romans to a preventive war with the latter Philip, King of Macedonia, in regard of the great preparations which Philip had then on foot, and his designs to ruin some of the confederates of the Romans, confidently saith, That they, who took that for an offensive war, understood not the state of the question : ' Ignorare videmini mihi, quirites, non utrum bellum, an pacem habeatis vos consuli ; neque enim liberum id vobis permittet Philippus, qui terra marique ingens bellum molitur ; sed utrum in Macedoniam legiones transportetis, an hostem in Italiam accipiatis:' i. e. You seem to me, you Romans, not to understand, that the consultation before you is not, whether you shall have war or peace ; for Philip will take order you shall be no chusers, who prepareth a mighty war both by land and by sea ; but, whether you shall transport the war into Macedonia, or receive it into Italy.

Antiochus, when he incited Prusias, King of Bithynia, at that time in league with the Romans, to join with him in war against them, setteth before him a just fear of the overspreading greatness of the Romans, comparing it to a fire, that continually took and spread from kingdom to kingdom : ' Venire Romanos ad omnia regna tollenda, ut nullum usquam orbis terrarum, nisi Romanum imperium esset ; Philippum & Nabin expugnatos, se tertium peti, ut quisque proximus ab oppresso sit per omnes velut continens incendium pervasurum :' i. e. That the Romans came to pull down all kingdoms, and to make the state of Rome an universal monarchy; that Philip and Nabis were already ruinated, and now was his turn to be assailed: so that as every state lay next to the other, that was oppressed, so the fire perpetually grazed.   Wherein it is well to be noted, that, towards ambitious states, which are noted to aspire to great monarchies, and to seek upon all occasions to enlarge their dominions, ' crescunt argumenta justi metus ; i. e. All particular fears do grow and multiply out of the contemplation of the general courses and practices of such states; therefore, in deliberations of war against the Turk, it hath been often with great judgment maintained, that Christian princes and states have always a sufficient ground of invasive war against the enemy, not for the cause

of religion, but upon a just fear; forasmuch as it is a fundamental
law in the Turkish empire, that they may, without any other provocation, make war upon Christendom, for the propagation of their
law; so that there lieth upon the Christians a perpetual fear of a war
hanging over their heads from them; and therefore they may at all
times, as they think good, be upon the prevention.

Demosthenes exposeth to scorn wars which are not preventive,
comparing those that make them to country-fellows in a fence-school,
that never ward till the blow be past: ' Ut barbari pugiles dimicare
solent, ita vos bellum geritis cum Philippo? ex his enim is, qui ictus
est, ictui semper inhæret; quod si eum alibi verberes illo manus
transfert, ictum autem propellere aut prospicere neque scit, neque
vult:' i. e. As country fellows use to do, when they play at waisters,
such a kind of war do you, Athenians, make with Philip; for, with
them, he that gets a blow straight falleth to ward, when the blow is
past; and, if you strike him in another place, thither goes his hand
likewise; but to put by, or foresee a blow, they neither have the
skill nor the will.

Clinias the Candian, in Plato, speaks desperately and wildly, as if
there were no such thing as peace between nations, but that every
nation expects but his advantage to war upon another.

But yet, in that excess of speech, there is thus much, that may
have a civil construction; namely, that every state ought to stand
upon its guard, and rather prevent, than be prevented. His words are:
' Quam rem fere vocant pacem, nudum & inane nomen est; reverà
autem omnibus adversus omnes civitates bellum sempiternum perdurat:'
i. e. That, which men for the most part call Peace, is but a naked and
empty name; but the truth is, that there is ever between all states
a secret war. I know well, this speech is the objection, and not the
decision, and that it is afterwards refused; but yet, as I said before,
it bears thus much of truth, That, if that general malignity and
predisposition to war, which he untruly figureth to be in all nations,
be produced and extended to a just fear of being oppressed, then it
is no more a true peace, but a name of peace.

As for the opinion of Iphicrates the Athenian, it demands not so
much towards a war, as a just fear, but rather cometh near the opinion
of Clinias, as if there were ever amongst nations a brooding of a war,
and that there is no sure league, but impuissance to do hurt. For he,
in the treaty of peace with the Lacedemonians, speaketh plain language,
telling them, there could be no true and secure peace, except the
Lacedemonians yielded to those things, which being granted, it
would be no longer in their power to hurt the Athenians, though they
would.

And, to say the truth, if one mark it well, this was in all memory
the main piece of wisdom in strong and prudent councils, to be in
perpetual watch, that the states about them should neither by approach,
nor by increase of dominion, nor by ruining confederates, nor by
blocking of trade, nor by any the like means, have it in their power
to hurt or annoy the states, they serve; and, whensoever any such

cause did but appear, straightway to buy it out with a war, and never to take up peace at credit, and upon interest. It is so memorable, that it is yet fresh, as if it were done yesterday, how that triumvirate of Kings, Henry the Eighth of England, Francis the first of France, and Charles the Fifth, emperor, and King of Spain, were, in their times, so provident, that scarce a palm of ground could be gotten by either of the three, but that the other two would be sure to do their best to set the balance of Europe upright again. And the like diligence was used, in the age before, by that league (wherewith Guicciardini beginneth his story, and maketh it, as it were, the calendar of the good days of Italy) which was contracted between Ferdinando King of Naples, Lorenzo of Medicis, potentate of Florence, and Lodovico Sforza, Duke of Milan, designed chiefly against the growing power of the Venetians, but yet so, that the confederates had a perpetual eye one upon another, that none of them should overtop. To conclude therefore: howsoever some schoolmen (otherwise reverend men, yet fitter to guide penknives than swords) seem precisely to stand upon it, that every offensive war must be *ultio*, a revenge, that presupposeth a precedent assault, or injury; yet neither do they descend to this point, which we now handled, of a just fear, neither are they of authority to judge this question against all the precedents of time; for, certainly, as long as men are men (the sons of the poets allude of Prometheus, not of Epimetheus) and, as long as reason is reason, a just fear will be a just cause of a preventive war; but especially, if it be part of the cause, that there be a nation, that is manifestly detected to aspire to monarchy and new acquists, then other states assuredly cannot be justly accused for not staying for the first blow, or for not accepting Polyphemus's courtesy, to be the last that shall be eaten up.

Nay, I observe further, that, in that passage of Plato, which I cited before, and even in the tenet of that person, that beareth the resolving part, and not the objecting, a just fear is justified for a cause of an invasive war, though the same fear proceed not from the fault of the foreign state to be assailed; for it is there insinuated, that, if a state, out of the distemper of their own body, do fear sedition and intestine troubles to break out amongst themselves, they may discharge their own ill humours upon a foreign war for a cure; and this kind of cure was tendered by Jasper Coligni, admiral of France to Charles the Ninth, the French King, when, by a vive and forcible persuasion, he moved him to make war upon Flanders, for the better extinguishment of the civil wars of France; but neither was that counsel prosperous, neither will I maintain that proposition; for I will never set politicks against ethicks, especially, for that true ethicks are but as a handmaid to divinity and religion: surely St. Thomas, who had the largest heart of the school divines, bendeth chiefly his stile against depraved passions, which reign in making wars, out of St. Augustine, ' Nocendi cupiditas, ulciscendi crudelitas, implacatus & implacabilis animus, feritas rebellandi, libido dominandi, & si quæ sunt similia, hæc sunt quæ in bellis jure culpantur.' And the same St. Thomas, in his own text, defining of the just causes of the war, doth leave it upon very general terms, ' Requiritur ad bellum causa justa, ut scilicet illi qui impugnantur propter aliquam culpam impugnationem mereantur'; for *impugnatio culpæ* is a far more general word, than *ultio injuriæ*.

And thus much for the first proposition of the second ground of a war with Spain, namely, that a just fear is a just cause of a war, and that a preventive war is a true defensive. The second or minor proposition, was this, that this kingdom hath cause of a just fear of overthrow from Spain, wherein it is true, that fears are ever seen in dimmer lights, than facts; and, on that other side, fears use many times to be represented in such an imaginary fashion, as they rather dazzle men's eyes, than open them; and, therefore, I will speak in that manner which the subject requires, that is probably, and moderately, and briefly; neither will I deduce these fears to the present occurrents, but point only at general grounds, leaving the rest to more secret councils.

It is nothing, that the crown of Spain hath enlarged the bounds thereof, within this last six-score years, much more than the Ottomans; I speak not of matches or unions, but of arms, occupations, invasions. Granado, Naples, Milan, Portugal, the East and West-Indies, all these are actual additions to that crown, and in possession; they have a great mind to French Britain, the lower part of Picardy and Piedmont, but they have let fall their bit; they have, at this day, such a hovering possession of the Valtoline, as an hobby hath over a lark, and the Palatinate is in their talons; so nothing is more manifest, than that this nation of Spain runs a race still of empire, when all other states of Christendom stand, in effect, at a stay.

Look then a little further into the titles, whereby they have acquired, and do now hold these new portions of their crown, and you will find them of so many varieties, and such natures, to speak with due respect, as may appear to be easily minted, and such as can hardly, at any time, be wanting; and, therefore, so many new conquests and purchases, so many strokes of the alarum-bell of fear and awaking to other nations, and the facility of the titles, which, hand over head, have served their turn, do ring the peal so much the sharper, and the louder.

Shall we descend from their general disposition, to enlarge their dominions, to their particular dispositions, and eye of appetite, which they have had towards us? they have now sought twice to impatronise themselves, of this kingdom of England, once by marriage with Queen Mary, and, the second time, by conquest, in 1588, when their forces, by sea and land, were not inferior to those they have now; and, at that time, in 1588, the counsel and design of Spain was, by many advertisements, revealed, and laid open, to be, that they found the war, upon the Low-Countries, so churlish and longsome, as they grew then to a resolution, that as long as England stood in state to succour those countries, they should but consume themselves in an endless war; and, therefore, there was no other way, but to assail and depress England, which was a back of steel to the Flemings; and who can warrant, I pray, that the same counsel and design will not return again? So that we are in a strange dilemma of danger; for, if we suffer the

Flemings to be ruined, they are our outwork, and we shall remain naked and dismantled; if we succour them strongly, as is fit, and set them upon their feet, and do not withal weaken Spain, we hazard to change the scene of the war, and to turn it upon Ireland or England, like unto rheums and defluxions, which, if you apply a strong repercussive to the place affected, and do not take away the cause of the disease, will shift and fall straightways to another joint or place. They have also twice invaded Ireland, once under the Pope's banner, when they were defeated by Gray, and after, in their own name, when they were defeated by Mountjoy; so let this suffice for a taste of their disposition towards us. But it will be said, this is an almanack for the old year; since 1588, all hath been well, Spain hath not assailed this kingdom, howsoever, by two several invasions from us, mightily provoked- It is true, but then consider, that, immediately after they were embroiled, for a great time, in the protection of the league of France, whereby they had their hands full; after being brought extreme low, by their vast and continual embracements, they were inforced to be quiet, that they might take breath, and do reparations upon their former wastes; but now, of late, things seem to come on a-pace to their former estate, nay, with far greater disadvantage to us; for now that they have almost continued, and, as it were, arched their dominions from Milan, by the Valtoline and Palatinate, to the Low-countries; we see how they thirst and pant after the utter ruin of those states, having, in contempt almost, the German nation, and doubting little opposition, except it come from England; whereby, we must either suffer the Dutch to be ruined, to our own manifest prejudice, or put it upon the hazard I spoke of before, that Spain will cast at the fairest. Neither is the point of internal danger, which groweth upon us, to be forgotten; this, that the party of the papists in England are become more knotted, both in dependance towards Spains, and amongst themselves, than they have been; wherein again comes to be remembered the cause of 1588; for then also it appeared, by divers secret letters, that the design of Spain was, for some years before the invasion attempted, to prepare a party in this kingdom, to adhere to the foreign at his coming; and they bragged, that they doubted not, but to abuse and lay asleep the Queen and council of England, as to having any fear of the party of papists here; for that they knew, they said, the state would but cast the eye, and look about to see, whether there were any eminent head of that party, under whom it might unite itself; and, finding none worth the thinking on, the state would rest secure, and take no apprehension; whereas they meant, they said, to take course to deal with the people, and particu-larly, by reconcilements and confessions, and secret promises, and cared not for any head of party; and this is the true reason why, after that, the seminaries began to blossom, and to make missions into England, which was about the twenty-third of Queen Elisabeth; at which time, also, was the first suspicion of the Spanish invasion; then, and not before, grew the sharp and severe laws to be made against the papists; and, therefore, the papists may do well to change their thanks; and whereas they thank Spain for their favours, to thank them for their perils and miseries, if they should fall upon them, for that nothing ever made their case so ill, as the doubt of the greatness of Spain: which adding reason of state, and matter of conscience and religion, doth whet the laws against them; and this cause also seemeth, in some sort, to return again at this time, except the clemency of his Majesty and the state do superabound. As for my part, I wish it should, and, that the proceedings towards them may rather tend to security, and providence, and point of state, than to persecution for religion.

But to conclude, these things, briefly touched, may serve as in a subject conjectural, and future, for to represent, how just cause of fear this kingdom may have towards Spain, omitting, as I said before, all present and more secret occurrention.

The third ground of a war with Spain I have set down to be a just fear of the subversion of our church and religion, which needeth little speech; for, if this war be a defensive, as I have proved it to be, no man will doubt, that a defensive war, against a foreigner, for religion is lawful; of an offensive war there is no dispute; and yet, in that instance of the war for the Holy Land and Sepulchre, I do wonder sometimes, that the schoolmen want words to defend that, which St. Bernard wanted words to commend; but I, that, in this little extract of a treatise, do omit things necessary, am not to handle things unnecessary; no man, I say, will doubt, but, if the Pope, or King of Spain, would demand of us to forsake our religion, upon pain of a war, it were as unjust a demand, as the Persians made to the Grecians, of land and water, or the Ammonites to the Israelites, of their right eyes; and we see all the Heathens did still their defensive war *pro aris & focis*, placing their altars before their hearths; so that it is in vain of this to speak further, only this is true, that the fear of the subversion of our religion from Spain is the more just, for that all other catholick princes and states content and contain themselves, to maintain their religion within their own dominions, and meddle not with the subjects of other states; whereas the practice of Spain hath been, both in Charles the Fifth's time, in Germany, and, in the time of the league, in France, by war, and now, with us, by conditions of treaties, to intermeddle with foreign states, and to declare themselves projectors-general of the party of catholicks through the world, as if the crown of Spain had a title of this, that they would plant the Pope's law by arms, as the Ottomans do the law of Mahomet. Thus much concerning the first main point of justifying the quarrel, if the King shall enter into a war; for this that I have said, and all that followeth to be said, is but to shew what he may do. The second main part of that I have propounded to speak of, is the balance or forces between Spain and us; and this also tendeth to no more but what the King may do, for what he may do is of two kinds, what he may do as just, and what he may do as possible; of the one I have already spoken, of the other I am now to speak. I said Spain was no such giant, and yet, if he were a giant, it will be but as it was between David and Goliah, for God is on our side. But to leave all arguments that are supernatural, and to speak in an human and politick sense, I am led to think that Spain is no over-match for England, by that which leadeth all men, that is, experience and reason ; and with experience I will begin, for there all reason beginneth. Is it fortune, shall we think, that in all actions of war, or arms, great and small, which have happened these many years, ever since Spain and England have had any thing to debate one with the other, the English upon all encounters, have perpetually come off with honour, and with the better? It is not fortune sure, she is not so constant: There is somewhat in the nations and natural courage of the people, or some such thing. I will make a brief list of the particulars themselves, in an historical truth, no ways stretched nor made greater by language. This were a fit speech, you will say, for a general, in the head of an army, when they are going to battle ; yes, and it is no less fit speech to be spoken in the head of a council upon a deliberation of an entrance into a war ; neither speak I this to disparage the Spanish nation, whom I take to be of the best soldiers in Europe. But that sorteth to our honour, if we still have had the better hand. In the Year 1578, was that famous Lammas-Day which buried the reputation of Don John of Austria, himself not surviving long after : Don John, being superior in forces, assisted by the prince of Parma, Mondragon, Mansell, and other the best commanders of Spain, confident of victory, charged the army of the states near Rimenant, bravely and furiously at the first, but, after a fight maintained by the space of a whole day, was repulsed, and forced to a retreat, with great slaughter of his men, and the course of his farther enterprizes, wholy arrested ; and this chiefly by the prowess and virtue of the English and Scottish troops, under the conduct of Sir John Norris and Sir Robert Steward, colonels, which troops came to the army but the day before, harrassed with a long and wearisome march. And, as it is left for a memorable circumstance in all stories, the soldiers, being more sensible of a little heat of the sun, than of any cold fear of treaty, cast away their armour and garments from them, and fought in their shirts ; and, as it was generally conceived, had it not been that the count of Bosse was slack in charging the Spaniards upon their retreat, this fight had turned to an absolute defeat ; but it was enough to chastise Don John for his insidious treaty of peace, wherewith he had abused the states at his first coming. And the fortune of the day, besides the testimony of all stories, may be ascribed to the service of the English and Scottish, by comparison of this charge near Rimenant, where the English and Scottish, in great numbers, came in action, with the like charge given by Don John, half a year before at Guyllours, where the success was contrary, there being at that time in the army but a handful of English and Scottish, and put in disarray by the horsemen of their own fellows.

The first dart of war, which was thrown from Spain or Rome upon the realm of Ireland, was in the year 1580 ; for the design of Stuckley blew over into Africk, and the attempt of Sanders and Fitz Morris had a spice of madness. In that year Ireland was invaded by Spanish and Italian forces, under the Pope's banner and the conduct of St. Josepho, to the number of seven-hundred, or better, which landed at Smerwicke in Kerry. A poor number it was to conquer Ireland to the Pope's use, for their design was no less, but, withal, they brought arms for five-thousand men above their own company, intending to arm so many of the rebels of Ireland ; and their purpose was to fortify in some strong place of the wild and desolate country, and that to nestle till greater succours came, they being hastened upon this enterprise upon a special reason of state not proper to the enterprise itself, which was by the invasion of Ireland, and the noise thereof, to trouble the council of England, and to make a certain diversion of certain aids that were then preparing from hence for the Low-Countries. They chose a place where they erected a fort, which they called the Fort del Or, and from thence they bolted like beasts of the forest, sometimes into the woods and fastnesses, and sometimes back again to their den. Soon after, siege was laid to the fort by the Lord Gray, then deputy, with a smaller number than those were within the fort, venturously indeed, but haste was made to attack them before the rebels came in to them. After the siege of four days only, with two or three sallies, with loss on that part, they, that should have made good the fort for some months, till new succours came from Spain, or at least from the rebels of Ireland, yielded up themselves without conditions, at the end of those four days ; and for that there were not in the English army enough to keep every man a prisoner ; and for that also the deputy expected instantly to be assailed by the rebels; and again there was no barque to throw them into, and send them away by sea, they were all put to the sword, with which Queen Elisabeth was afterwards much displeased.

In the year 1582, was that memorable retreat of Ghent, than the which there hath not been an exploit of war more celebrated ; for, in the true judgment of men of war, honourable retreats are no ways inferior to brave charges, as having less of fortune, more of discipline, and as much of valour. There were to the number of three hundred horse, and many thousand foot, English, commanded by Sir John Norris, charged upon an advantage taken by the prince of Parma coming upon them with seven-thousand horses; besides that, the whole army of the Spaniards was ready to march on. Nevertheless, Sir John Norris maintained a retreat without disaray by the space of some miles, part of the way champaign, unto the city of Ghent, with less loss of men than the enemy : The Duke of Anjou, and the Prince of Orange, beholding this noble action from the walls of Ghent, as in a theatre, with great admiration.

In the year 1585, followed the prosperous expedition of Drake and Carlisle into the West-Indies. In which I set aside the taking of St. Jago and St. Domingo in Hispaniola, as surprises rather than encounters. But that of Carthagena, where the Spaniards had warning of our coming, and had put themselves in their full strength, was one of the hottest services and most dangerous assaults hath been known, for the access to the town was only by a neck of land between the sea on the one part, and the harbour-water or minor-sea on the other, fortified clean over a strong rampart barricado, so as upon the ascent of our men they had both great ordnance and small shot that thundered and showered upon them from the rampart in front, and from the gallies that lay at sea in flank; and yet they forced the passage, and won the town, being likewise very well manned. As for the expedition of Sir Francis Drake in the year 1587, for the destroying of the Spanish shipping and provision upon their own coast, as I cannot say that there intervened in that enterprise any sharp fight or encounter, so nevertheless it did straightly discover, either that Spain is very weak at home, or very slow to move, when they suffered a small fleet of English to make an hostile invasion or incursion upon their havens and roads from Cadiz to Cape Sacre, and thence to Cascous, and to fire, sink, and carry away at the least ten-thousand ton of their greater shipping, besides fifty or sixty of their smaller vessels, and that in the sight and under the favour of their forts, and almost under the eye of their great admiral, the best commander of Spain by Sea, the Marquis de Santa Cruce, without ever being disputed with by any fight of importance. I remember Drake, in the vaunting stile of a soldier, would call this enterprise the singeing of the King of Spain's beard. The enterprise of 88, deserveth to be stood upon a little more fully being a miracle of time. There arrived from Spain, in the year 1588, the greatest navy that ever swam upon the seas; for, tho' there have been far greater fleets for number, yet the bulk and building of the ships, with the furniture of great ordnance and provisions, never the like. The design was not to make an invasion only, but an utter conquest of this kingdom. The number of vessels were one-hundred-thirty, whereof galleasses and galleons seventy-two goodly ships, like floating towers or castles, manned with thirty-thousand soldiers and mariners. This navy was the preparation of five whole years at the least; it bare itself also upon divine assistance, for it received special blessing from Pope Sixtus, and was assigned as an apostolical mission for the reducement of this kingdom to the obedience of the see of Rome. And, in further token of this holy warfare, there were, amongst the rest of these ships, twelve called by the names of the twelve apostles. But it was truly conceived that this kingdom of England could never be overwhelmed, except the land-waters came in to the sea-tides: Therefore, was there also in readiness in Flanders a mighty army of land forces, to the number of fifty-thousand veteran soldiers, under the conduct of the Duke of Parma, the best commander, next the French King, the fourth of his time. These were designed to join with forces at sea, there being prepared a number of flat-bottom boats, to transport the land forces, under the wing and protection of the great navy, for they made no other account, but that the navy should be absolutely master of the seas. Against these forces, there were prepared on our part, to the number of near one-hundred ships, not of so great bulk in deed, but of a more nimble motion, and more serviceable, besides a less fleet of thirty ships, for the custody of the narrow seas. There were also in readiness at land two armies, besides other forces, to the number of ten-thousand, dispersed amongst the coast towns, in the southern parts; the two armies were appointed, one of them consisting of twenty-five-thousand horse and foot, for the repulsing of the enemy, at their landing, and the other of thirty-five thousand, for safeguard and attendance about the court, and the Queen's person. There were also other dormant musters of soldiers, throughout all parts of the realm, that were put in readiness, but not drawn together. The two armies were assigned to the leading of two generals, noble persons; but both of them rather courtiers, and assured to the state, than martial men, yet loved and assisted, with subordinate commanders, of great experience and valour.

The fortune of the war made this enterprise, at first, a play at base: The Spanish navy set forth out of the Groyne in May, and was dispersed and driven back by weather: Our navy set forth somewhat later out of Plymouth, and bare up towards the coast of Spain, to have fought with the Spanish navy; and partly upon advertisement, that the Spaniards were gone back, and upon some doubt also, that they might pass by towards the coast of England, while we were seeking them afar off, returned likewise into Plymouth, about the middle of July. At that time, came more constant advertisement, though false, not only to the lord admiral, but to the court, that the Spaniards could not possibly come forwards that year; whereupon our navy was upon the point of disbanding, and many of our men gone a-shore. At that very time, the invincible Armada (for so it was called, in a Spanish ostentation, throughout Europe) was discovered upon the western coast: It was a kind of surprise, for that, as we said, many of our men were gone on land, and our ships ready to depart. Nevertheless, the admiral, with such ships only, as could suddenly be put in readiness, made forth towards them; insomuch as, of one-hundred ships, there came scarce thirty to work. Howbeit, with them, and such as came duly in, we set upon them, and gave them the chace. But the Spaniards, for want of courage, which they called Commission, declined the fight, casting themselves continually into roundels, the strongest ships walling in the rest, and in that manner, they made a flying march, towards Calais. Our men, by the space of five or six days, followed them close, fought with them continually, made great slaughter of their men, took two of their great ships, and gave divers others of their ships their deaths wounds, whereof soon after they sank, and perished, and, in a word, distressed them, almost in the nature of a defeat, we ourselves, in the mean time, receiving little or no hurt. Near Calais the Spaniards anchored, excepting their land forces, which came not. It was afterwards alledged, that the Duke of Parma did artificially delay his coming; but this was but an invention, and pretension, given out by the Spaniards, partly upon a Spanish envy, against the Duke, being an Italian, and his son a competitor to Portugal, but chiefly to save the monstrous scorn and disreputation, which they and their nation received by the success of that enterprise; therefore, their colours and excuses forsooth were, that their general by sea had a limited commission, not to fight, until the land forces were come in to them, and that the Duke of Parma had particular reaches, and ends of his own, under hand, to cross the design. But it was both a strange commission, and a strange obedience to a commission, for men, in the midst of their own blood, and being so furiously assailed, to hold their hands, contrary to the laws of nature and necessity. And as for the Duke of Parma, he was reasonably well tempted to be true to that enterprise, by no less promises, than to be made feudatory, or beneficiary, King of England, under the seignory in chief of the Pope, and the protection of the King of Spain. Besides it appeared, that the Duke of Parma held his place long after in the favour and trust of the King of Spain, by the great employments and services that he performed in France. And again, it is manifest, that the duke did his best to come down, and to put to sea; the truth was, that the Spanish navy, upon these proofs of fight, which they had with the English, finding how much hurt they received, and how little they did, by reason of the activity, and low building of our ships, and skill of our seamen, and being also commanded by a general of small courage and experience, and having lost, at the first, two of their bravest commanders at sea, Petro de Valdez and Michael de Oquenda, durst not put it to a battle at sea, but set up their rest wholly upon the land enterprise. On the other side, the transporting of the land forces failed, in the very foundation; for whereas the council of Spain made full account, that their navy should be master of the sea, and therefore able to guard and protect the vessels of transportation, it fell out to the contrary, that the great navy was distressed, and had enough to do to save itself, and again, that the Hollanders impounded their land forces, with a brave fleet of thirty sail, excellently well appointed; things, I say, being in this case, it came to pass, that the Duke of Parma must have flown, if he would have come into England, for he could get neither barque nor mariner to put to sea; yet, certain it is, that the duke looked still for the coming back of the armada, even at that time, when they were wandering and making their perambulation, upon the northern seas. But to return to the armada, which we left anchored at Calais; from thence, as Sir Walter Raleigh was wont prettily to say, they were suddenly driven away with squibs, for it was no more but a stratagem of fireboats manless, and sent upon them, by the favour of the wind, in the night-time, that did put them in such terror, as they cut their cables, and left their anchors in the sea. After they hovered many days about Graveling, and there again were beaten in a great fight, at which time our second fleet, which kept the narrow seas, was come in, and joined with our main fleet. Thereupon the Spaniards, entering into further terror, and finding also divers of their ships every day to sink, lost all courage, and, instead of coming up into the Thames mouth for London, as their design was, fled on towards the north, to seek their fortunes, being still chaced by the English navy at the heels, until we were fain to give them over, for want of powder. The breath of Scotland the Spaniards could not endure, neither durst they, as invaders, land in Ireland, but only ennobled some of the coasts thereof with shipwrecks, and so going northwards aloof, as long as they had any doubts of being pursued, at last, when they were out of reach, they turned and crossed the ocean to Spain, having lost fourscore of their ships, and the greater part of their men. And this was the end of that sea giant, the invincible armada, which having not so much as fired a cottage of ours at land, nor taken a cockboat of ours at sea, wandered through the wilderness of the northern seas, and according to the curse in the scripture, came out against us one way, and fled before us seven ways, serving only to make good the judgment of an astrologer, long before given, *octogesimus octavus mirabilis annus!* or rather, indeed, to make good, even to the astonishment of all posterity, the wonderful judgments of God, poured down commonly upon vast and proud aspirings.

In the year that followed, 1589, we gave the Spaniards no breath, but turned challengers and invaded the main of Spain; in which enterprise although we failed of our end, which was to settle Don Antonio in the kingdom of Portugal, yet a man shall hardly meet with an action, that doth better reveal the great secret of the power of Spain, which, well sought into, will be found rather to consist in a veteran army, such as, upon several occasions and pretences, they have ever had on foot in one part or other of Christendom, now by the space almost of six-score years, than in the strength of their several dominions and provinces; for what can be more strange or more to the disvaluation of the power of the Spaniards, upon the continent, than that with an army of eleven thousand English land soldiers, and a fleet of twenty-six ships of war, besides some weak vessels for transportation, we should, with the hour-glass of two months, have won one town of importance by Escalida, battered and assaulted another, overthrown great forces in the field, and that, upon the disadvantage of a bridge strongly barricadoed, landed the army in three several places of his kingdom, marched seven days in the heart of his countries, lodged three nights in the suburbs of his principal city, beat his forces into the gates thereof, possessed two of his frontier forts, and, after all this, came off with small loss of men, otherwise than by sickness. And it was verily thought, that, had it not been for four great disfavours of that voyage, that is to say, in the failing of sundry provisions that were promised, especially of cannons for battery, the vain hopes of Don Antonio, concerning the people of his country, to come in to his aid, the disappointment of the fleet, that was directed to come up the river of Lisbon, and lastly, the diseases which spread in the army, by reason of the heat of the season, and of the soldiers misrule in diet, the enterprise had succeeded, and Lisbon had been carried. But howsoever it makes proof to the world, that an invasion of a few English upon Spain may have just hope of victory, or at least of a pass-port to depart safely.

In the year 1591, was that memorable fight of an English ship, called the Revenge, under the command of Sir Richard Greenfield; memorable, I say, beyond credit, and to the height of some heroical fable. And, though it was a defeat, yet it exceeded a victory, being like the act of Sampson, that killed more men at his death than he had done in the time of all his life. This ship, for the space of fifteen hours, sat like a stag amongst hounds at the bay, and was sieged and fought with, in turn, by fifteen great ships of Spain, part of a navy of fifty-five ships in all, the rest, like abettors, looking on afar off. And, amongst the fifteen ships that fought, the great St. Philip was one, a ship of fifteen-hundred tons, prince of the twelve sea apostles, which was right glad, when she was shifted off from the Revenge. This brave ship, the Revenge, being manned only with two hundred soldiers and mariners, whereof eighty lay sick; yet, nevertheless, after a fight maintained, as was said, of fifteen hours, and two ships of the enemy sunk by her side, besides many more torn and battered, and great slaughter of men, never came to be entered, but was taken by composition; the enemies themselves having in admiration the virtue of the commander, and the whole tragedy of that ship.

In the year 1596, was the second invasion that we made upon the main territories of Spain, prosperously atchieved by that worthy and famous Earl, Robert, Earl of Essex, in consort with the noble Earl of Nottingham, that now liveth, then admiral. This journey was with lightning, for, in the space of fourteen hours, the King of Spain's navy was destroyed, and the town of Cadiz taken: the navy was no less than fifty-nine tall ships, besides twenty gallies to attend them; the ships were straightways beaten, and put to flight, with such terror, as the Spaniards were their own executioners, and fired them all with their own hands: the gallies, by the benefit of the shores and shallows, got away; the town was a fair, strong, well-built, and rich city, famous in antiquity, and now most spoken of for this disaster: it was manned with four thousand soldiers on foot, and some four hundred horse; it was sacked and burnt, though great clemency was used towards the inhabitants: but that, which is no less strange than the sudden victory, is the great patience of the Spaniards, who, though we staid upon the place divers days, yet never offered us any play, nor never put us in suit by any action of revenge, or reparation of any times after.

In the year 1600, was the battle of Newport in the Low Countries, where the armies of the archduke, and the states, tried it out by a just battle.

This was the only battle that was fought in those countries these many years, for battles in the French wars have been frequent, but in the wars of Flanders rare, as the nature of a defensive requireth. The forces of both armies were not much unequal, that of the States exceeded somewhat in number, but that again was recompensed in the quality of the soldiers; for those of the Spanish part were of the flower of all their forces. The Archduke was the assailant, and the preventer, and had the fruit of his diligence and celerity, for he charged certain companies of Scotishmen, to the number of eight hundred, sent to make good a passage, and thereby severed from the body of the army, and cut them all in pieces; for they, like a brave infantry, when they could make no honourable retreat, and would take no dishonourable flight, made good the place with their lives. This entrance of the battle did whet the courage of the Spaniards, though it dulled their swords, so as they came proudly on, confidently to defeat the whole army. The encounter of the main battle, which followed, was a just encounter, not hastening to a sudden rout, nor the fortune of the day resting upon a few former ranks, but fought out to the proof by several squadrons, and not without variety of success, *Stat pede pes densusque viro vir.* There fell out an error in the Duke's army, by the overhasty medley of some of their men with the enemies, which hindered the playing of their great ordnance. But the end was, that the Spaniards were utterly defeated, and five thousand of their men, in the fight and in the execution, slain and taken, amongst whom were many of the principal persons of their army. The honour of the day was, both by the enemy, and the Dutch themselves, ascribed much to the English; of whom Sir Francis Vere, in a private commentary, which he wrote of that service, leaveth testified, that of fifteen hundred in number (for they were no more) eight hundred were slain in the field, and, which is almost incredible in a day of victory, of the rest, two only came off unhurt. Amongst the English, Sir Francis Vere himself had the principal honour of the service, unto whom the Prince of Orange, as is said, did transmit the direction of the army for that day; and, in the next place, Sir Horace Vere, his brother, that now liveth, who was the principal in the active part. The service also of Sir Edward Cecil, Sir John Ogle, and divers other brave gentlemen was eminent.

In the year 1601, followed the battle of Kinsale, in Ireland. By this Spanish invasion of Ireland, which was in September that year, a man may guess how long time Spaniards will live in Irish ground, which is a matter of a quarter of a year, or four months, at the most; for they had all the advantages in the world, and no man would have thought, considering the small forces employed against them, that they could have been driven out so soon. They had obtained, without resistance, in the end of September, the town of Kinsale; a small garrison of one hundred and fifty English, leaving the town upon the Spaniards approach, and the townsmen receiving the foreigners as friends. The number of Spaniards, that put themselves into Kinsale, was two thousand men, soldiers of old bands, under the command of Don John de Aquila, a man of good valour. The town was strong of itself, neither wanted there any industry to fortify it on all parts, and make it tenable, according to the skill and discipline of Spanish fortification. At that time the rebels were proud, being encouraged upon former successes; for, though the then deputy, the Lord Mountjoy, and Sir George Carew, president of Munster, had performed divers good services to their prejudice, yet the defeat they had given to the English, at the Black-water, not long before, and the treaty, too much to their honour, with the Earl of Essex, was yet fresh in their memory. The deputy lost no time, but made haste to recover the town, before new succours came, and sat down before it in October, and laid siege to it by the space of three winter months, or more, during which time, some sallies were made by the Spaniards, but they were beaten in with loss. In January came fresh succours from Spain, to the number of two thousand more, under the conduct of Alonzo D'Ocampo; upon the comforts of these succours, Tyrone and O'neale drew up their forces together, to the number of seven thousand, besides the Spanish regiments, and took the field, resolved to rescue the town, and to give the English battle.

So here was the case, an army of English, of some six thousand, wasted and tired with a long winter's siege, inraged in the midst, between an army of a greater number than themselves, fresh, and in vigour, on the one side, and a town, strong in fortification, and strong in men, on the other side; but what was the event? This in few words: That, after the Irish and Spanish forces had come on, and shewed themselves in some bravery, they were content to give the English the honour, as to charge them first; and, when it came to the charge, there appeared no other difference between the valour of the Irish rebels, and the Spaniards, but that the one ran away before they were charged, and the other straight after; and again, the Spaniards, that were in the town, had so good memory of their losses, in their former sallies, as the confidence of an army, which came for their deliverance, could not draw them forth again: To conclude, there succeeded an absolute victory, for the English, with the slaughter of above two thousand of the enemy, the taking of nine ensigns, whereof six Spanish, the taking of the Spanish general, D'Ocampo, prisoner, and this with the loss of so few of the English, as is scarce credible, being (as hath been rather confidently, than credibly reported) but one man, the cornet of Sir Richard Greame, though not a few hurt: There followed, immediately after the defeat, a present yielding up of the town by composition; and not only so, but an avoiding, by express article of treaty accorded, of all other Spanish forces throughout all Ireland, from the places and nests where they had settled themselves in greater strength, as in regard of the natural situation of the places, than that was of Kinsale, which were Castle-haven, Baltimore, and Beer-haven. Indeed they went away with sound of trumpet, for they did nothing but publish and trumpet all the reproaches they could devise against the Irish land and nation; insomuch as D'Aquila said, in open treaty, That, when the devil upon the mount did shew Christ all the kingdoms of the earth, and the glory of them, he did not doubt, but the devil left out Ireland, and kept it for himself.

I cease here, omitting not a few other proofs of the English valour and fortune, in these latter times; as at the suburbs of Paris, at the Raneline, at Drus in Britain, at Ostend, and divers others; partly, because some of them have not been proper encounters between the Spaniards and the English, and partly, because others of them have not been of that greatness, as to have sorted in company with the particulars formerly recited. It is true, that, among all the late adventures, the voyage of Sir Francis Drake, and Sir John Hawkins, into the West-Indies, was unfortunate, but yet, in such sort, as it doth not break, or interrupt our prescription, to have had the better of the Spaniards upon all fights; for the disaster of that journey was caused chiefly by sickness, as well might appear by the deaths of both the generals, Sir Francis Drake and Sir John Hawkins, of the same sickness amongst the rest. The land enterprise of Panama was an ill-measured and immature counsel, for it was grounded upon a false account, that the passages, towards Panama, were no better fortified, than Drake had formerly left them; but yet it sorted not to any fight of importance, but to a retreat, after the English had proved the strength of their first fort, and had notice of the two other forts beyond, by which they were to have marched. It is true, that, in the return of the English fleet, they were set upon by Avellandea, admiral of twenty great Spanish ships, our fleet being but fourteen, full of sick men, deprived of their two generals by sea, and having no pretence, but to journey homewards; and yet the Spaniards did but salute them about the Cape de las Corientes, with no small offer of fight, and came off with loss: Although it was such a new thing for the Spaniards to receive so little hurt, upon dealing with the English, as Avallandea made great brags of it, for no greater matter than the waiting upon the English afar off, from Cape de las Corientes to Cape Antonio, which, nevertheless, in the language of a soldier, and of a Spaniard, he called a Chace.

But, before I proceed further, it is good to meet with an objection, which, if it be not removed, the conclusion of experience, from the time past to the time present, will not be sound and perfect; for it will be said, that, in the former times, whereof we have spoken, Spain was not so mighty, as now it is; England, on the other side, was more aforehand in all matters of power; therefore, let us compare, with indifferency, these disparities of times, and we shall plainly perceive, that they make for the advantage of England at this present time. And, because we will less wander in generalities, we will fix the comparisons to precise times, comparing the states of Spain or England, in the year 1588, with this present year that now runneth. In handling this point, I will not meddle with any personal comparisons of the princes, counsellors, and commanders, by sea or land, that were then, or are now in both kingdoms, Spain and England, but only rest upon real points, for the true balancing of the state of the forces and affairs of both times; and yet these personal comparisons I omit not, but that I could evidently shew, that, even in these personal respects, the balance sways on our side, but because I would say nothing that may favour of the spirit of flattery, or censure of the present government.

First, Therefore, it is certain, that Spain hath not now a foot of ground, in quiet possession, more than it had in 1588. As for the Valtoline and the Palatinate, it is a maxim in state, That all countries of new acquest, till they be settled, are matters rather of burthen, than of strength. On the other side, England hath Scotland united, and Ireland reduced to obedience, and planted, which are mighty augmentations.

Secondly, In 1588, the kingdom of France, able to counterpoise Spain itself, much more in conjunction, was torn with the party of the league which gave law to their king, and depended upon Spain. Now France is united under a valiant young king, generally obeyed, if he will himself King of Navarre, as well as of France, and one that is no ways taken prisoner, though he be tied in a double chain of alliance with Spain.

Thirdly, In 1588, there sat, in the see of Rome, a fiery thundering friar, that would set all at six and seven, or at six and five, if you allude to his name. And, though he would have after turned his teeth upon Spain, yet he was taken order with before it came to that. Now there is ascended to the papacy a personage, that came in by a chaste election, no ways obliged to the party of the Spaniard; a man bred in ambassages and affairs of state, that hath much of the prince, and nothing of the friar; and one, that though he loved the chair of

K 2

the papacy well, yet he loveth the carpet above the chair that is in
Italy, and the liberties thereof well likewise.

Fourthly, in 88, the King of Denmark was a stranger to England,
and rather inclined to Spain; now the King is incorporated to the
blood of England, and engaged in the quarrel of the Palatinate. Then
also Venice, Savoy, and the princes and states of Germany, had but a
dull fear of the greatness of Spain, upon a general apprehension only, of
the spreading and ambitious designs of that nation; now, that fear is
sharpened and pointed by the Spaniards late enterprises in the Valtoline
and the Palatinate, which come nearer them.

Fifthly, and Lastly, the Dutch (which are the Spaniards perpetual
duellists) have now, at this present, five ships to one, and the like proportion in treasure and wealth, to that they had in 88; neither is it
possible (whatsoever is given out) that the coffers of Spain should now
be fuller than they were in 88, for, at that time, Spain had no other
wars save those of the Low Countries, which was grown into an
ordinary; now they have had, coupled with it, the extraordinary of the
Valtoline and the Palatinate; and so I conclude my answer to the
objection raised, touching the difference of times, not entering into
more secret passages of state, but keeping the character of stile whereof
Seneca speaketh, *Plus significat quam loquitur.*

Here I could pass over from matter of experience, were it not that I
hold it necessary to discover a wonderful erroneous observation that
walketh about, and is commonly received contrary to all the true
accounts of time and experience: It is, that the Spaniard, where he
once getteth in, will seldom or never be got out again; but, nothing is
less true than this: Not long since they got footing at Brest, and some
other parts in French Britany, and after quitted them; they had Calais,
Ardes, and Amiens, and rendered them, or were beaten out; they had
since Versailles, and fairly left it; they had the other day the Valtoline,
and now have put it in deposit; what they will do with Ormus, which
the Persian hath taken from them, we shall see; so that, to speak truly
of latter times, they have rather poached and offered at a number of
enterprises, than maintained any constantly, quite contrary to that idle
tradition.

In more ancient times, leaving their purchases in Africk, which they,
after their great Emperor Charles had clasped Germany almost in his
fist, he was forced in the end to go from Ieksparg, and, as if it had
been in a mask by torch-light, to quit every foot in Germany round,
that he had gotten, which I doubt not will be the hereditary issue of
this late purchase of the Palatinate; and so I conclude the ground
that I have to think that Spain will be no over-match to Great-Britain,
if his Majesty shall enter into a war out of experience, and the records
of time.

For grounds of reason, they are many; I will extract the principal,
and open them briefly, and, as it were, in the bud. For situation, I
pass it over, though it be no small point; England, Scotland, Ireland,
and our good confederates, the United Provinces, lie all in a plump
together, not accessible but by sea, or, at least, by passing of great

rivers, which are natural fortifications. As for the dominions of Spain, they are so scattered, as it yieldeth great choice of the ascents of the war, and promiseth slow succours unto such parts as shall be attempted. There be three main parts of military puissance, viz. men, women, and confederates. For men, they are to be considered valour and number; of valour, I speak not; take it from the witnesses that have been produced before; yet the old observation is untrue, That the Spaniards valour lieth in the eye of the looker on, but the English valour lieth about the soldier's heart; a valour of glory, and a valour of natural courage, are two things; but let that pass, and let us speak of number. Spain is a nation thin sown of people, partly by reason of the sterility of the soil, and partly, because their natives are exhausted by so many employments, in such vast territories as they possess, so that it hath been counted a kind of miracle to see ten or twelve thousand native Spaniards in an army; and it is certain (as we have touched it a little before in passage) that the secret of the power of Spain consisteth in a veteran army, compounded of miscellany forces of all nations, which, for many years, they have had on foot upon one occasion or other; and, if there should happen the misfortune of a battle, it would be a long work to draw on supplies. They tell a tale of a Spanish ambassador, that was brought to see the treasure of St. Mark, at Venice, and still he looked down to the ground; and, being asked why he looked down, said, He was looking to see whether their treasure had any root, so that, if it were spent, it would grow again, as his master's had. But, howsoever it be of their treasure, certainly their forces have scarce any root, or at least such a root, as buddeth forth poorly and slowly. It is true they have the Walloons, who are tall soldiers, but that is but a spot of ground; but, on the other side, there is not in the world again such a spring and seminary of brave military people, as in England, Scotland, and Ireland, and the United Provinces; so as, if wars should mow them down never so fast, yet they may be suddenly supplied and come up again.

For money, no doubt, it is the principal part of the greatness of Spain, for by that they maintain their veteran army, and Spain is the only state of Europe, that is a money-grower; but, in this part, of all others, is the most to be considered the ticklish and brittle state of the greatness of Spain. Their greatness consisteth in their treasure, their treasure in their Indies, and their Indies, if it be well weighed, are indeed but an accession to such as are masters by sea, so as this axle-tree, whereupon their greatness turneth, is soon cut in two, by any that shall be stronger than they by sea: Herein, therefore, I refer me to the opinion of all men, enemies, or whomsoever, whether that the maritime forces of Great Britain, and the United Provinces, be not able to beat the Spaniards at sea; for, if that be so, the links of that chain, whereby they hold their greatness, are dissolved. Now, if it be said, that, admit the case of Spain to be such as we have made it, yet we ought to descend into our own case, which we shall find, perhaps, not to be in a state, for treasure, to enter into a war with Spain; to which I answer, I know no such thing, the mint beateth well, and the pulses of the people's heart beat well: But there is another point that taketh away quite this objection; for, whereas wars are generally a cause of poverty or consumption, on the contrary part, the special nature of this war with Spain, if it be made by sea, is like to be a lucrative and a restorative war; so that if we go roundly on at the first, the war in continuance will find itself, and therefore you must make a great difference between Hercules's labours and Jason's voyage by sea for the Golden Fleece.

For the confederates, I will not take upon me the knowledge how the princes, states, and councils in Europe, at this day, stand affected towards Spain, for that trencheth into the secret occurrents of the present time, wherewith, in all this treatise, I have forborne to meddle, but to speak of that which lieth open and in view: I see much matter of quarrel and jealousy, but little of amity and trust towards Spain, almost from all other states: I see France is in competition with them for three noble portions of their monarchy, Navarre, Naples, and Milan, and now freshly in difference with them about the Valtoline. I see once in thirty or forty years cometh a Pope, that casteth his eye upon the kingdom of Naples, to recover it to the church, as it was in the minds of Julius the Second, Paul the Fourth, and Titus the Fifth. As for the great body of Germany, I see they have greater reason to confederate themselves with the Kings of France and Great-Britain, or Denmark, for the liberty of the German nation, and for the expulsion of the Spanish and foreign forces, than they had in the years 1552 and 1553; at which time they contracted a league with Henry the Second, the French King, upon the same articles, against Charles the Fifth, who had impatronised himself of a great part of Germany, through discord of the German princes, which himself had sown and fomented; which league at that time did the deed, and drove out all the Spaniards out of that part of Germany, and reintegrated that nation in their ancient liberty and honour. For the West-Indies, though Spain hath had yet not much actual disturbance there, except it have been from England, yet, nevertheless, I see all princes lay a kind of claim unto them, accounting the title of Spain but as a monopoly of those large countries, wherein they have, in great parts, but an imaginary possession; for Africk, upon the west, the Moors of Valencia expulsed, and their allies, do yet hang as a cloud or storm over Spain; Gabor, on the east, is like an anniversary wind that riseth every year once upon the part of Austria; and Persia hath entered into hostility with Spain, and given them the first blow by taking of Ormus. It is within every man's observation also, that Venice doth think their state almost unfixed, if the Spaniards hold the Valtoline; that Savoy hath learned by fresh experience, that alliance with Spain is no security against the ambition of Spain; and that Bavaria hath likewise been taught, that merits and service do oblige the Spaniards but from day to day; neither do I say for all this, but that Spain may rectify much of this ill blood, by their particular and cunning negociations; but yet there is in the body, and may break out no man knows when, into ill accidents; but, at least, it sheweth plainly that which serveth for our purpose, that Spain is much destitute of assured and confident confederates. And here I will conclude this part, with a speech of a counsellor of state; he said to his master, the King of Spain that now is, upon occasion: ' Sir, I will tell your Majesty thus much for your comfort, your Majesty hath but two enemies, whereof the one is all the world, and the other is your own minister's. And thus I end the second main part I propounded to speak of, which was, the balancing of the forces between the King's Majesty, and the King of Spain, if wars must follow.

For Henry Visc. Falkland's Works, see Vol. I. p. 90, &c.

A

CHRONOLOGICAL CATALOGUE

OR

SHORT REMEMBRANCE

OF THE

PRINCES ELECTORS PALATINE OF THE RHINE,

That have been of the House of Bavaria unto this Day, together with their Succession and Lives.

THE SECOND EDITION.

London : Printed by William Jones, dwelling in Red-Cross-Street, 1631. Duodecimo, containing thirty-eight pages.

Consecrated and dedicated to the most high and peerless Princess, Elisabeth, Princess of Great-Britain, Queene of Bohemia, Duchess of Bavaria, Princess Palatine Electress, &c. By her Majesty's most affectionated and bound in all humble Duty,

W. H.

OTHO THE ELDER.

OTHO, sirnamed the Elder, Earl of Wittelsbach, and governor of the palace of Bavaria, grandfather to Otho the Illustrious, first elector of his house, being descended of Charles the Great, and of the most antient dukes and princes of Bavaria; was a courageous and valiant prince, a cunning and great warrior; was endowed with rare and singular virtues both of body and mind; was employed into Italy and Greece, in divers great ambassages; was fully given to advance the republick; was exceedingly addicted to the military art; he atchieved divers noble exploits in Italy.   Upon which occasion, Henry the Twelfth being deprived and condemned, he, for his singular virtues, was, by the Emperor Frederick the First, created Duke of Bavaria in anno 1180, from the which his predecessors had been dejected, about 231 years before, by Otho the First.   He bought Dachau; annexed to his estate Raning; built the town of Kelham on the Danube, where he was born in a castle of that same name; founded Landshut upon the river Isara.   He died, the 26th of June, anno Christi 1183, while he was yet in controversy with the Bishop of Frissinghen, for some customs of salt, after he had ruled Bavaria three years.   He married Agnes, daughter of Theodorick, tetrarch of Wasserburg, and had these children by her:

> Lewis Prince Palatine of the Rhine.
> Sophia, who was joined in marriage to Herman, Landgrave of Hesse.
> Mechtildis, joined to Rapoto, the second warden of Krainburg.

LEWIS, DUKE OF BAVARIA.

LEWIS, Duke of Bavaria, succeeded Otho.   He was a prince endued with great eloquence, wisdom, piety, and many other virtues; he increased with riches, and beautified much the estate of Bavaria; built many sumptuous works, planted divers new colonies, and built Stroubing, a famous town upon the Danube.   He was a great lover of peace and justice, who never made wars unless he had been forced thereto. Having gone about to repress Albert, Earl of Bogen, who had invaded and spoiled his county, he received a great overthrow by him, and was forced to fly; he warred against the Earls of Artenberg, that had broken the peace, and took from them Wasserburg, and Krainburg Castle: Otho, of Wittelsbach, and Henry Truchses, Baron of Walpurg, being declared rebels to the empire, he spoiled their castles of Wittlesbach and Andeches, and razed them thereafter.   From the Emperor Frederick the Second, he received the county Palatine of the Rhine, and, whilst he went about to take possession of the towns and castles thereof somewhat unwarily, he and his company were taken by the inhabitants of the country, and afterwards released for a great sum of money contributed by the Bavarians.   Thereafter being received of them peaceably, within a short time after, he took his journey; and went into the Holy Land with divers other princes, against the Infidels; from whence, having lost many of his people, and his life being spared to him, he returned with a few that remained.   In the end, while he was walking on the bridge of Kelhaim, he was stabbed with a knife by one Stichius, a fool, that was offended at his jests, and immediately fell down dead among his nobles, the 15th of September, in anno 1231. He was buried in great state and pomp in Sheyrn. He ruled Bavaria, after his father's decease, forty-eight years and more. He married Louisa, daughter of Primeslaus, King of Bohemia, widow of Albert Boggy, a princess of great beauty, and of an high spirit. His children by her were these:

> Otho, Prince Palatine Elector of the Rhine, Duke of Bavaria.
> Lewis, slain by the Emperor Frederick the Second.
> Isabella, married to the Emperor Frederick the Second.
> Anna, married to Rudolph, Duke of Saxony, Angria, and Westphalia.

OTHO THE ILLUSTRIOUS.

OTHO, sirnamed the illustrious, was, in his father's life-time, created both Duke of Bavaria, and Prince Elector Palatine of the Rhine. He made wars against Frederick of Austria, a seditious and unquiet prince; spoiled and burnt a great part of his country, with a great slaughter of the inhabitants; took Sherding, and annexed it to his own estate. Being seduced through the persuasion of Pope Gregory, he conspired with other princes against the Emperor Frederick the Second; wherefore, seeing himself to be in such eminent danger, and accused of disloyalty and high-treason, and fearing the event of the Emperor's displeasure, he turned unto his side again. He joined his forces with the Emperor Courade, his son-in-law, against Conrade of Wasserburg, vanquished him, took from him all his castles and possessions, and chaced him out of the precinct of Bavaria, because he had received and refused to render Albert of Bathaen, a seditious and factious nobleman, and breaker of the peace: Albert, in the end, being taken, he caused his skin to be pulled off him, while he was yet living. He repressed valiantly Albert, bishop of Regensburg, who plotted against the state. He married Agnes, daughter of Henry, the last Palatine Elector of his family, and niece of Henry, sirnamed the Lion, and so was the first Elector Palatine of the House of Bavaria. He died in Landshut, in anno 1269, and was buried in Sheren. He begot these children:

> Lewis the Severe, Duke of Bavaria, and Prince Palatine Elector of the Rhine.
> Henry, Duke of Bavaria, who, after his father's decease, had for his portion and inheritance the country of Nordge, or North Bavaria, and died at Burckhausen, in anno 1290.
> Elisabeth, married to the Emperor Conrade the Fourth, and after his death to Meinhard, Earl of Tyrol Sophia, married to Gebhard of Hirsperg, for his valour and stoutness, shewed against the Bohemians.

LEWIS THE SEVERE.

LEWIS, surnamed the Severe, Duke of Bavaria, Prince Elector Palatine of the Rhine, was born the fifteenth of April 1229. The second year after his father's decease he divided the inheritance with his brother, and had for his part the Palatinate of the Rhine, and Upper Bavaria (whereof the chief towns be Munchen, Wasserburg, and Ingolstadt) together with the government of Regensburg, to wit, Riettenburg, Stephaning, Lengenfield, Rengstauff, and Kalmunt. He was a very virtuous and religious prince, and a great justiciar; he was of a good wit, and adorned with many singular virtues, both of body and mind. He caused to behead his wife Anne, the Duke of Brabant's sister, for suspicion of adultery. He built Furstenfield, to bury her in honourably. About some five years after, he warred against the Marshals of Pappenheim; took, burnt, and rased Wissenburg, a town in Nordge. After other five years, he built the town Fridberg for a defence against the citizens of Augsburg. After the Emperor Lewis's death, the empire having continued without a head, during the space of eighteen years, which was the cause of much sedition, and divers great troubles, both in Italy and Germany, with the consent and approbation of all the princes, had full power and authority given him to choose another emperor in his place. Whereupon he elected Rudolph, Earl of Hasburg, and afterwards married his daughter, and was a constant friend to him all his life time. In the end, being come to Heidelberg, to make peace between Albert and Adolph, both Cæsars at one time; and being taken with a disease, which had swelled his privy members, and, for shame he had thereof, having neglected the remedies too long, he died in the same chamber where he was born, the first of February, in anno 1294, of his age the sixty-fifth, having ruled forty years, and was buried in Furstenfield. He had three wives, the first, Mary, daughter of the Duke of Brabant, and had no children by her. By his second wife, Anne, daughter of Conrade, King of Poland, he had

> Lewis, a frugal and virtuous prince, who died at Norenberg, through the stroke of a lance, that he received of Crato, Earl of Hohenloe, while they were running together.

By Mechtildis, the Emperor's daughter, his last wife, he had

> Rudolph, Prince Elector Palatine of the Rhine, of whom all the Palatine Electors are descended, that have been since.
> Anne, married to Henry, Earl of Catzenelbogen.
> Mechtildis, married to Otho, Duke of Lunenburg.
> Lewis the Fifth, Emperor, of whom are descended all those other princes, that, since that time, have ruled Bavaria, unto this day.

RUDOLPH THE FIRST.

RUDOLPH the First, Prince Elector Palatine of the Rhine, in the beginning, laboured to make peace and agreement between his uncle Albert, of Austria, Emperor, and the Emperor Adolph, his father-in-law. But afterwards began to adhere more closely to Adolph, and suc-coured him in his unfortunate wars against Albert (both of them con-tending for the empire) being kindled with an indignation against his uncle, because he had besieged Alze, a town within his dominions; and, Adolph being slain in the battle, he had much ado to escape with a small number, and save himself in Worms. Having, through the in-tercession of his mother, obtained free pardon and remission from his victorious uncle, for his former offence; notwithstanding, having, within a short while after, become unmindful of the receipt of so great a benefit, was, among others, one that conspired and plotted against him. Wherefore, being besieged again by his uncle, he was forced to demand pardon of him, and withal paid a sum of money to have his towns rendered to him again. Finally, having conceived some hatred and malice against his brother Lewis, for that he was advanced to the Imperial dignity, he was chaced out of his country by him, and fled into England. Where he died, in anno 1319, of his age the forty-fourth. By Mechtild, daughter of the Emperor, Adolph, Earl of Wassaw, he had

> Adolph, Rudolph the Second, and Rupert the First, Pala-tine Electors of the Rhine.

ADOLPH THE SIMPLE.

ADOLPH, sirnamed the Simple, after his father's decease, was, with the rest of his brethren, received in favour by the Emperor Lewis, their uncle; and had the Electoral Palatinate rendered to him, toge-ther with certain towns of Bavaria, and Nordge, or Upper Palatinate. He was a prince void of all ambition, and more given to his private ease and rest, than to take any pains in ordering and ruling the repub-lick. Whereupon he resigned over the electorate to his brother Ru-dolph, about the year 1327. Nevertheless, John, Duke of the Lower Bavaria, being deceased without issue, he went about, among others, to obtain this vacant estate, but was excluded from the same, by the Emperor Lewis, who was a degree nearer to the defunct than he; he died, in anno 1327, and was buried in Shœnau. He married Irmen-gard, daughter of Lewis, Earl of Oentingen, of whom he begot

> Rupert the Second, Palatine Elector, and a daughter that was married to Meinhard, Earl of Artenburg.

RUDOLPH THE SECOND.

RUDOLPH the Second, sirnamed Blind, born at Wolffratzhasen, succeeded his brother, Adolph, in the Electoral Palatinate; but died not long after, about the year 1353. He had by his wife, Anne, daughter of Otho, Duke of Carinthia, one child only, to wit,

Agnes, married to the Emperor, Charles the Fourth, and was crowned with him in Rome.

RUPERT THE FIRST.

RUPERT the First, sirnamed Rufus, was Prince Palatine Elector of the Rhine, after his brother's decease; he founded and erected the University of Heidelberg, in anno 1346. Having joined his forces with Lewis, the Elector of Brandenburg, he fought against a certain cousening miller, that had given himself out for Waldemar, Marquis of Brandenburg; he was by him vanquished and taken prisoner, and was released by the Emperor Charles with much difficulty. He had two wives, the first, Elisabeth of Namur, the second, Beatrix of Bergen, and had no issue by them; he died, in anno 1390, and was buried in Heustat.

RUPERT THE SECOND.

RUPERT the Second, sirnamed Durus, son to Adolph the Simple, succeeded his uncle Rupert in the Palatine Electorate of the Rhine. After the death of the Emperor, Charles the Fourth, having joined his forces with the other dukes of the house of Bavaria, he made war against the Emperor Vinceslaus, for that he detained certain towns and castles of North Bavaria, which his father had taken in pawn for his wife's portion; wherefore, at the commandment of the Emperor, he was pursued in open warfare, by those of Ragensburg, Augsburg, and divers other towns, lying on the Rhine, and, having fought against his enemies near unto Spires, he slew two hundred, took three hundred of them, and compelled the rest to fly into the same city. His country having been spoiled and burnt by some wicked and damnable persons, and having apprehended them, he caused to throw them into an hot furnace, being some forty in number; in the end he gave himself to peace and quietness, and renewed and increased the University of Heidelberg, so far, that it may seem that he was (as it were) the first founder thereof. He was a famous and renowned prince, both in peace and war; he died, in anno 1398, and was buried in

Shonau ; he married Beatrix, daughter of Frederick, King of Sicily, of whom he begot

> Rupert, the Emperor.
> Anne, married to the Duke of Juliers and Bergen.
> Elisabeth married to Procopius, Marquis of Moravia.

RUPERT THE THIRD.

RUPERT the Third, Prince Elector of Palatine of the Rhine, and Duke of Bavaria, was by the princes elected emperor at Bopart, in anno 1406, and sacred by the archbishop at Cologne, after that, Vinceslaus had been deposed from his government. Being very earnestly requested by the pope to make war against John Galeace, Duke of Milan, whose greatness he feared, he went into Italy; where, having fought in the country of Brescia, against the Duke, who was assisted by such as had not as yet made defection from Vinceslaus, he received an overthrow at his hands, and retired back again, not regarding the earnest suit of the Florentines, that intreated for his help, and assistance, taking ship at Venice, and returned into Germany, where he spent the rest of his days in beautifying and adorning of the same. He was severe, of an high spirit and great courage, was expert in warfare, and a great justiciar; being withal much addicted to the advancement of the republick, and conserving of the same in her full integrity and glory. Thus, after he had ruled the empire very commendably nine years and (almost) nine months, he died at Oppenheim, the seventeenth of May, in anno 1410, and was buried at Heidelberg, together with his wife Elisabeth, daughter of Frederick, Burgrave of Noremberg, he had six children by her,

> Rupert, sirnamed Pepin.
> Lewis, Prince Elector Palat. of the Rhine.
> John, Duke of Neuburg.
> Frederick of Amburg.
> Otho, Duke of Newmarckt, in Bavaria, and Monpach on the Neckar.
> Stephen, Duke of Zweibrugken and Obrinca.

LEWIS THE FOURTH.

LEWIS the Fourth, sirnamed Barbatus and Pius, succeeding his father in the electorate, a prince that was famous both in peace and, in war. He was president or moderator of the council of Constance, in anno 1415, warred in the Holy Land, and assisted the order of Teutons, in Prussia, with some troops of soldiers which he brought unto them. He helped likewise the Earl of Vaudemont against those, of Lorrain, by sending unto him a selected company of experimented warriors, who died all in the battle; the Frenchmen, that were on their side, having first begun to fly, and (as it were) betrayed them, in anno 1431. He learned the Greek tongue in his old age; because he had understood that the Emperor Sigismond had found great fault with the barbarous education of unlearned princes. Being very aged, and having waxed blind, he died in anno 1436, and was buried at Heidelberg. He had two wives, the first Blanch, daughter of Henry the Fourth, King of England; the second Mechtild, daughter of Lewis Earl of Piedmont and Savoy, and had by her three sons:

> Lewis, Prince Elector Palat. of the Rhine.
> Frederick, tutor and administrator of the Palatine Electorate.
> Rupert, Archbishop of Cologne.

LEWIS THE FIFTH.

LEWIS the fifth, called the Younger and Virtuous, Prince Elector Palatine of the Rhine, and Duke of Bavaria, being a religious and peaceable prince, a lover of justice, and very mild and affable withal, was much beloved for his singular virtues. He died in anno 1449, and was buried at Heidelberg: he married Margaret, daughter of Amadeus Duke of Savoy, and widow of Lewis, Duke of Anjou, married after his decease to Ulrick, Duke of Wirtemberg, and had, by her,

> Mechtild, married to Lewis, Duke of Wirtemberg.
> Philip, Prince Elector Palatine.

FREDERICK THE FIRST.

FREDERICK the first, sirnamed Victorious, born the first of August, in anno 1425, was at first tutor and administrator to the young Prince Philip, his nephew, and afterwards, by adopting of him to his son, became Prince Elector Palatine; he was a most valiant and courageous prince, most constant and invincible at arms, and fought many dangerous combates; he secured his country from all foreign invasion, and purged the highways of robbers; he was a stout defender of the Imperial dignity and Majesty, against all the subtle and treacherous plots of the popes. He forced Ulrick, Duke of Wirtemberg, to leave off the unlawful suing for his wife's dowry, from Philip, his pupil, which he sought by arms; and afterwards being again invaded by the same prince, that was assisted by Charles, Marquis of Baden and one of his brethren, he vanquished them all in one battle, near unto Heidelberg, and took them prisoners, on the first of July, 1462; whom, after a little while, he set at liberty, for a great sum of money, being content with the honour of so famous a victory. He was never married; he died in anno 1476, of his age the fifty-first.

PHILIP.

PHILIP, born after his father Lewis the Younger's decease, and sirnamed Ingenuous, was prince palatine elector of the Rhine, after the death of Frederick the First; before the wars of Bavaria, he was a most potent, rich, and redoubted prince; but, having refused to make peace, upon very equitable conditions, which the Emperor Maximilian had offered to him, he was by him declared a rebel; and being left by the French-men, that were the cause and instruments of this war, he lost a great part of his dominions, with many of his nobility and others, which were either slain in the battle, poisoned, or executed; he died in Anno 1508, and was buried at Heidelberg. He married Margaret, daughter of Lewis the Rich, Duke of Bavaria, and had twelve children by her, whose names be these:

> Lewis, Prince Elector of Palatine.
> Rupert the Virtuous.
> Frederick, sirnamed Pious, Prince Elector Palatine.
> Philip, Bishop of Freisingen.
> George, Bishop of Spires.
> Henry, Bishop of Utrecht and Worms.
> John, Bishop of Regensburg.
> Wolfgang, Duke of Newmarckt.
> Æmilia, married to George the First, Duke of Stetin and Pomerania,
> Helena, married to Henry, Duke of Meckelburg.
> Elisabeth, married to William the Younger, Landgrave of Hesse, and after his death to Philip the Second, Marquis of Baden.
> The Fourth Daughter was an Abbess.

LEWIS THE SIXTH.

LEWIS the Sixth, Prince Elector Palatine, Duke of Bavaria, &c. was a wise and prudent prince, and a great favourer of learning. Having most prudently pacified many tumults and discords, he was called the Peaceable or Peace-maker. He lived fifty-five years and above, died in Anno 1544, and was buried at Heidelberg; he married Sybilla or Sidonia, Daughter of Albert the Fourth, Duke of Bavaria, but had no issue by her.

FREDERICK the Second, brother to Lewis the Sixth, and sirnamed Pius, Prince Elector Palatine of the Rhine, and Duke of Bavaria, born in December, in Anno 1482, excelling in many high and princely virtues, was much admired and praised of all men. He was so much inclined to pity and devotion, that, in Anno 1546, he abolished and chaced Popery quite out of his dominions, and placed the true and sincere doctrine of Christian * religion in place thereof.   He loved his country and subjects so dearly, that he desired nothing so much as the good and prosperous estate of such as lived under him, and the safety of whole Germany.   He was so much given to peace, that, during those domestick and cruel dissensions that were then, he spared neither cost, charges, labour, nor pains to attain thereto, and thereafter to enjoy the same : Not that he was not skilful and expert in warfare ; seeing that by the states of the empire he was chosen general of the army, when the town of Vienna was besieged by the Turk, and by his nephew most valiantly defended and freed of all danger ; but because he had learned by experience, how blessed and happy a thing peace was.   He was, moreover, a great favourer and cherisher of all sorts of good learning, and learned men.   In such great and weighty affairs of the empire as he meddled with, he proved wary and careful in enterprising, prudent in managing, and fortunate in the event and success.   He died in Anno 1556, of his age the 74th.   He married Dorothy, daughter of Christiern King of Denmark, and had no issue by her.

OTHO HENRY.

OTHO Henry, Prince Elector Palatine, son to Rupert the Virtuous, and nephew to the elector Philip, born in April, in Anno 1502, succeeded his uncle in the Electoral Palatinate, which he had resigned over to him, while he was dying, in Anno 1556 ; and enjoyed the same scarce three years, but died at Heidelberg in Anno 1559, and was buried there also : A prince very commendable in his actions, a stout defender and advancer of true religion, an earnest lover of peace, and withal endued with wisdom and magnanimity.   He married Susanna, one of the house of Bavaria, widow of Casimir, Marquis of Brandenburg, and had no children by her.

FREDERICK THE THIRD.

FREDERICK the Third, son of John Earl of Obrinca, Simmeren and Spanheim, the posterity of Lewis, sirnamed Pious, having here failed, succeeded by right descent to the Palatine Electorate.   He was a peaceable prince, and a singular protector of the muses.   He died in November, in Anno 1576, of his age the 62d.   He married first Mary, daughter of Casimir, Marquis of Brandenburg, in Anno 1537 ; and afterwards Æmilia, daughter of the Earl of Newenar, and widow of Henry of Brederode, in Anno 1569, having no children by her. The first bore unto him these eleven :

> Albert, who died in his infancy.
> Lewis the Seventh, Prince Elector Palatine, &c-
> Elisabeth, married to John Frederick, Duke of Saxony.

: Reformed.

Herman-Lewis, Prince Palatine, who was drowned in the
    river at Bourges in France,
John Casimir, Prince Palatine of the Rhine, &c. Tutor and
    Administrator of the Electorate.
Susanna Dorothy, married to William, Duke of Saxony.
Albert and Charles, who died in their infancy.
Anne-Elisabeth, married to Philip the Second, Landgrave
    of Hesse.
Cunnegunde-Jacob, wife to John Earl of Nassaw, in Dillem-
    berg.
Christopher, Prince Palatine, slain in the Low-Countries.

LEWIS THE SEVENTH.

LEWIS the Seventh, Prince Elector Palatine, Duke of Bavaria,
Earl of Simmeren and Spanheim, born in July, in Anno 1539, was
a very religious prince, of a sincere and unspotted life and conversation.
He brought all the churches of the Palatinate to a most commendable
and good order.   He increased, with great liberality, the revenues of
Heidelberg university, and maintained justice and peace with prudent
dexterity and policy.   He had two wives ; the first, Elisabeth, daughter
of Philip, Landgrave of Hesse, by whom he had many children.   The
other Anne, daughter of the Earl of Emden.   He died, in Anno 1583,
of his age the 44th, and was buried at Heidelberg.   These be the
names of his children :

Anne Mary, married to Charles Prince of Summerland, &c.
Elisabeth, Dorothy, Frederick, and Philip, dead in their
    infancy.
John, Frederick, Lewis, and Christian, dead in their childhood.
Frederick the Fourth, Prince Elector Palatine, Duke of
    Bavaria, &c.
Philip and Dorothy died in their first years.

FREDERICK THE FOURTH.

FREDERICK the Fourth, Prince Elector Palatine, Duke of
Bavaria, &c. born in Anno 1574, after his father's decease, having
lived nine years under the rule and government of John Casimir, his
uncle and tutor, and being, at his death, in Anno 1592, of full age,
succeeded his father in the electorate.   He was a virtuous and religious
prince, favoured learning much, and was very careful in ordering and
settling the estate both of ecclesiastical and civil affairs througout all
his countries.   He founded the town and castle of Manheim between
the mouth of the Neckar and the Rhine, in Anno 1606, where before
stood a mean village and fortress of that name, as a most strong

bulwark, and sure defence, against all the assaults of whatsoever enemies. He died in Anno 1611, and was buried at Heidelberg. He married Louisa Juliana, daughter of William Prince of Orange, who liveth still, and had by her these children :

> Louisa-Juliana, married to John, Prince Palatine of the Rhine, Duke of Zuneiburgh, and Administrator to Catharina Sophia.
>
> Frederick the Fifth, King of Bohemia, Prince Elector Palatine of the Rhine, &c.
>
> Elisabeth-Charlotta, married unto George, Elector of Brandenburg.
>
> Anna-Leonora, dead in her infancy.
>
> Lewis-William, dead within a few days after he was born.
>
> Maurice-Christian, dead in his tender age.
>
> Lewis-Philip, Prince Palatine of the Rhine, who hath allotted to him for his inheritance Lauterberg, &c.

FREDERICK THE FIFTH.

FREDERICK the Fifth, Prince Palatine of the Rhine, Duke of Bavaria, elector and arch-sewer of the sacred Roman empire, and, in vacancy of the same, vicar thereof, and one of the most noble order of the garter, born the sixteenth of August, 1596. After his father's decease, having lived for some little space, under the rule and government of his cousin, John, Prince Palatine of the Rhine, Duke of Zuneiburgh, and administrator, took upon him the government of the Palatinate : A prince (for his age) surpassing far his predecessors, as being adorned with all singular and rare virtues, which are requisite in a true and perfect prince. He beautified the castle of Heidelberg with an huge and strong tower, and divers other reparations ; together with most pleasant, sumptuous, and admirable gardens, walks, waterworks, and other princely ornaments, for the most part cut out of the side of the mountain, where the castle standeth. He continued, with exceeding great cost, the building and fortification of the invincible fort of the town and castle of Manheim, founded by Frederick the Fourth, his father. He pacified the civil dissension of Worms, having sent four-thousand men of war into the city, for that purpose. Being assisted by the other princes of the union, he demolished and razed the new fortifications of the town of Udenheim, standing on the Rhine, which the Bishop of Spires had caused to be built, contrary to the privileges of the country. He was, for the great multitude of his heroical and princely virtues, by the general consent of the Bohemian states, elected King of Bohemia, and was crowned in Prague, the five-and-twentieth of October; and the Lady Elisabeth, his spouse, sole daughter of James, King of Great-Britain, France, and Ireland, &c. the twenty-eighth of that same month, Anno 1619.

He was likewise received and acknowledged for Marquis of Moravia, Duke of Silesia, and Marquis of Lusatia, by all the states of those countries. About a year after, having lost a great battle, which the Emperor and the Duke of Bavaria won, not far from Prague, he was forced to leave Bohemia, and the neighbour-countries that belonged unto him, to his victorious enemy, which, within a few months after the same time, took possession of them all. Not long after these things were past, in the end he lost the Palatinate, with his whole inheritance, which the Emperor Ferdinand took from him unjustly, and gave the same to the Duke of Bavaria, that had helped him in all the wars of Bohemia, and the Palatinate. He lived to the year 1632 in Holland, and from thence went up unto the King of Sweden, hoping, through God's assistance, for to recover his country again; since the which he is departed this life. The names of his children are these:

Prince Frederick-Henry, chosen King of Bohemia, born at Heidelberg, about midnight, the first of January, 1614: He died the seventh of January, 1629, having newly entered into the fifteenth year of his age.

Prince Charles-Lewis, born at Heidelberg, the twenty-second of December, 1617.

Elisabeth, born at Heidelberg, the twenty-sixth of December, 1618.

Rupert, born at Prague, December the seventeenth, 1619.

Maurice, born at Custrin, the sixth of January, 1621.

Louisa-Hollandina, born at the Hague, the twenty-eighth of April, 1622.

Lewis, born at the Hague, the twenty-first of August, 1623; and died in January, 1625.

Edward, born at the Hague, the sixth of October, 1624.

Henrietta, born at the Hague, the seventh of July, 1626.

Philip, born at the Hague, the sixteenth of September, 1627.

Charlotta, born at the Hague, the nineteenth of December, 1628: She died, the twenty-fourth of January, 1631.

Sophia, born at the Hague, the thirteenth of December, 1630.

Henry-Frederick, born at the Hague, February the third, 1631.

God, of his unspeakable mercy, bless, protect, and defend this noble Queen, with her royal progeny *, to the enlarging of his church, to the further ruin of Antichrist, to the comfort of all the godly dispersed through the world.

* God has so far blessed her Royal Progeny, that they now sit upon the throne of Great-Britain; King George the Second being great grandson to Elisabeth, Queen of Bohemia.

AN

HISTORICAL ACCOUNT

OF

THE LIFE AND TRYAL OF NICHOLAS ANTHOINE,

Burnt for Judaism at Geneva, in the Year 1632.

Quarto, containing fifteen pages.

———

NICHOLAS ANTHOINE was born of Popish parents, at Brieu, in Lorrain. His father took a particular care of his education, and sent him to the college of Luxemburg, where he studied five years. From thence he was removed to Pont-à-Mousson, Triers, and Cologne ; where he went on with his studies under the direction of the Jesuits, till he was about twenty years of age. Being returned to his father's, and disliking the church of Rome, he repaired to Metz, and applied himself to M. Ferry, an eminent divine of that city, who instructed him in the Protestant religion, which he heartily embraced. From that time he professed himself a Protestant, and endeavoured to convert his relations to the reformed religion. From Metz, he was sent to Sedan, in order to study divinity ; and from thence to Geneva, where he continued his theological studies. He applied himself particularly to the reading of the Old Testament ; and finding several difficulties in the New, which seemed to him unanswerable, he inwardly embraced the Jewish religion, about five or six years before his tryal. His first doubts were occasioned by his comparing the two genealogies of Jesus Christ, as they are related by St. Matthew and St. Luke ; but when he came to examine the passages of the Old Testament, that are applied to the Messias in the New, he proved so weak as to renounce his Christianity. And, as new notions of religion frequently make a greater impression, than those wherein men have been bred up from their younger years, he grew so zealous for Judaism, that he resolved to make an open profession of it. Accordingly he left Geneva, and returned to Metz, and immediately discovered his opinions to the Jews of that city, and desired to be admitted into their synagogue : But they refused him, for fear of bringing themselves into trouble ; and advised him to go to the Jews of Amsterdam, or Venice. Whereupon he resolved to take a journey to Venice, and earnestly intreated the Jews of that town to circumcise him. But he was again disappointed ; for those Jews refused to comply with his desire, and told him the Senate had forbid them to circumcise any body that was not born a Jew. Anthoine, longing to receive the seal of the Jewish covenant, went quickly to Padua, in hopes that the Jews of that place would be more favourable to him ; but they gave him the same answer. The Jews of that city, and those of Venice, told him, that he might be saved, without making an outward profession of Judaism, provided he remained faithful to God in his heart. This made him resolve to return to Geneva, where he had more acquaintances than any where else. M. Diodati, minister and professor of that city, took him into his house, to be tutor to his children. He pretended to go on with his theological studies, and was for some time teacher of the first class. Afterwards he disputed for the chair of Philosophy, but without any success. All that time he lived outwardly like a true Christian ; for he confessed at his tryal, that he had constantly received the communion ; but, in private he lived, and performed his devotions, like a Jew. At last, being poor, and weary of the condition he was in, and wanting a settlement, he desired a testimonial of the church of Geneva, which was granted him, and went to the Synod of Burgundy, held at Gex, in order to be admitted into the ministry. He was admitted according to custom, promising to follow the doctrine of the Old and New Testament, the discipline and confession of faith of the reformed churches of France, &c. and was appointed minister of the church of Divonne, in the country of Gex.

He had not been long there, when the lord of that place perceived he never mentioned Jesus Christ in his prayers and sermons ; that he took his text only out of the Old Testament, and applied to some other persons all the passages of the Old Testament, which the Christians understand of Jesus Christ. This raised great suspicions against him. When he came to hear of it, he was very much perplexed ; and, being naturally of a melancholy temper, he fell into a fit of madness, in the month of February, 1632, which was looked upon as a manifest judgment of God, because it happened the very next day after he had expounded the second Psalm, without applying it to our Saviour. He grew so distracted, that he moved upon his hands and feet in his chamber, publickly exclaimed against the Christian religion, and particularly in the presence of some ministers of Geneva, who went to see him. He horribly inveighed against the person of Christ, calling him an idol, &c. and saying that the New Testament was a mere fable. He called for a chafing-dish full of burning coals, and told the divines, who were in his chamber, that he would put his hand into the fire to maintain his doctrine, bidding them do the like for their Christ. His madness increased to such a degree, that he ran away in the night from those under whose custody he was, as far as the gates of Geneva, where he was found the next morning half naked, and lying in the dirt ; and, having pulled off his shoes in the name of the true God of Israel, he worshipped him barefooted, prostrated upon the ground, and blaspheming against Christ.

The magistrates of Geneva ordered him to be carried into an hospital, where the physicians took care of him, and he was visited by some divines. His mind was composed by degrees, and then he left off speaking injuriously of Christ, and the Christian religion, but stoutly maintained Judaism. Being thus recovered from his madness, he was committed to jail, where he remained a considerable time before the magistrates took cognisance of that affair; being only visited by several divines, who used their utmost endeavours to make him sensible of the falsity of his doctrine, and the enormity of his conduct, and to bring him over to the Christian religion; but he persisted in his opinions.

M. Ferry,[*] a minister of Metz, who, as I have said before, had converted Antboine to the Protestant religion, hearing of the sad condition, and the great danger he was in, writ a letter about him, the 30th of March, to the ministers and professors of the church and academy of Geneva. It contains several particulars relating to the history of that unhappy man; and therefore, I think it necessary to insert it in this place, and I hope no curious reader will blame me for it. The letter runs thus;

    Gentlemen, and most honoured Brethren,
  ' I beg your pardon for the fault I am going to commit, if you take it to be such: And indeed, I do not pretend to represent any thing to you, but in order to submit it to your censure. I have heard, with an unspeakable grief, what has happened to that poor wretch, who is amongst you; and I beseech you to forgive my freedom in writing to you about it. I do not do it altogether without the request of others. Besides, one must not expect a call to preserve an unfortunate man, who runs himself into destruction; since God and nature, and our ancient acquaintance and friendship, may be a sufficient motive for me to do it. To which I add, that, having been instrumental in bringing him to salvation, I think I have great reason to desire that he may not undo himself, and to endeavour, with your leave, to prevent it. I thank God, since he has thought fit to make him a new example of human frailty, that he has brought him amongst you, that you might prevent his doing mischief, and endeavour to reclaim him. I think, gentlemen, that mildness and patience will be the most proper means to succeed in it. I make no doubt that his illness proceeds from a black and deep melancholy, to which I always perceived he was very much inclined; especially after he had seduced a young man, whom he brought hither from Sedan, in hopes to get something by teaching him philosophy, and then he privately carried him farther, though I had earnestly desired him to send him back, and exhorted the young man to return to Sedan, which was M. Du Moulin's desire, to whom he had been recommended. From that time he could not bear the light in any room of a gentleman's house, where I had placed him, being always uneasy, restless, and silent. Nay, he had much ado to express himself, and it was a hard matter to make him speak, though I earnestly desired him to be more free, and sent for him, and made him dine with me now and then, and took all possible care of him. Which we ascribed to the ill success he had in a Synod of the Isle of France, whither he had been sent with a testimonial, and recommendation of the church and academy of Sedan, notwithstanding which, he did not appear sufficiently qualified for the ministry. After he had enticed away that young man, he writ several letters to me, wherein expressed a great grief for it; and in all of them

* A large account of that eminent divine may be seen in the Historical and Critical Dictionary, lately published in English.

he used many words, which shewed his mind was very much dejected, being above all things sensible of the reproofs he had received for it. So that I thought myself obliged to write to him now and then, to clear his mind of those needless scruples, and of such an unreasonable and dangerous vexation, and to exhort him to apply himself to his study with chearfulness, and a resolution to do better for the time to come. It is therefore highly probable that his melancholy has been heightened by those cloudy thoughts, and likewise by the poverty and want of many things, into which he fell soon after, and whereof he complained to me in his letters, so far as to mention the temptations under which his mind was almost ready to sink. To this I may add the nature of his studies bent upon the Old Testament, on which he writ to me, that he was drawing up a concordance. However, though those things were not the true cause of his illness, you know, gentlemen, that there is a sort of melancholy, in which the physicians acknowledge Ṣ.ṭω ṛì, which is neither a crime nor a divine punishment, but a great misfortune. Certainly, that which he lies under, is very deplorable; but, gentlemen, I think I may say that, though nature is the instrument of God's Providence, yet all accidents ought not to be looked upon as punishments, or signs of a wicked life, nor the madness of that poor wretch as a formal chastisement for his error; there being so many reasons to believe that it proceeds from the disorder of the brain, and from melancholy. His madness seems to be only an exorbitant fit of melancholy, which being allayed by remedies, he appears now in his former state: And, though he errs only in the single point, for which he is prosecuted, there is no reason to infer from it, that he speaks in cold blood, and with a sound mind. For it is the property of that sort of melancholy, to have but one object, leaving the mind free in all other things, as you know better than I. There are some who speak upon any subject with great learning and sedateness, and have but one grain of madness, which they discover only by intervals, to those who hit upon it. I am the more willing to compare that unfortunate man to them, because, in that very thing, wherein he pretends to be wise, he appears most ridiculous; for he says what he would be ashamed of out of his fit, though he were no Christian; since he denies, as I hear, what the very Heathens and Jews acknowledge. And therefore it is not a heresy, but a blasphemy, which proceeds from a mind rather distempered than perverted. His usual frights and horrors are, in my opinion, a certain sign of it; and there is no reason to ascribe them to a divine judgment, and to infer from thence that he is a reprobate. After all, gentlemen, it is certain he imposes upon you, when he tells you that he believed, eight or ten years ago, what he believes now: For, since that time, he has not only given all manner of proofs of his Christianity, but also brought over to the reformed religion his eldest brother, who lives honestly among us; and he has endeavoured to work the same effect upon his father, to whom he has writ many letters, several of which I have opened; wherein he expressed a great zeal, and a wonderful love for Jesus Christ, and the Christian truths, that are taught in our churches. And, in order to bring over his relations to our religion, he writ to them, that he was ready to die for it, if God required it of him. Nay, when he was admitted into the ministry, he acquainted me with it, in a letter from Geneva, dated the twenty-ninth of November; being used to call me, as he did then, his *dear ghostly Father,* whom God had been pleased to make use of, in order to bring him to the knowledge of the true religion: And he desired me to acquaint his relations with it, being fully resolved for the future to lead a better life, and to perform his duty to the utmost of his power. And therefore, gentlemen, and most honoured brethren, I think he ought not to be believed in what he says, during such a disorder of his mind; and I hope, that, if you allow him some time to recover from his phrensy, as I understand you do, he will no longer blaspheme, and God will give you comfort after your labour and patience. To that end, I wish none may have access to him, but such as are familiarly acquainted with him, or for whom he has a particular respect and veneration, and by whom he may be gently used; lest his mind be exasperated by too many visitants, or by an unseasonable, though just severity.

' Gentlemen, give me leave to tell you, that it seems highly necessary, for the edification of the church, that this affair should be managed with great prudence. If you make an example of him, it will, doubtless, prove extremely prejudicial. I intreat you to consider the great scandal it will occasion, far and near, and what might be said against the office and profession of a man converted from Popery, who has learned to judaize among us, in the most famous academies, conversing every day with several pastors. Besides, Judaism being no dangerous sect, it does not seem necessary to prevent the ill consequences of it by a publick punishment; nay, perhaps every body would not approve of it. There are some extraordinary crimes, for which when the guilty person is to be punished, it is not done in publick; and the proceedings are suppressed, to clear the present age from such an infamy, and to leave no marks of it to posterity. However, there is no need of being too hasty in a thing, that may be done as well in time, and when a delay cannot be prejudicial, but rather useful. Servetus had a long time allowed him for his amendment, though he had dogmatised above twenty years in cold blood, and in several places, both by word of mouth, and in written and printed books, about things much more subtle and dangerous; and yet, gentlemen, you know the various discourses, that were occasioned by his execution. I do not say this, because I find fault with it; on the contrary, I think such pernicious errors could not be better suppressed, than by committing the author to the flames. But this man cannot be compared to Servetus, I pray God to give him a better end. And I beseech you, gentlemen and most honoured brethren, not to grow weary in this work of your great charity, wherein he will direct you to use such remedies, as are necessary to reclaim that unfortunate man, and to preserve the church from such an infamy. This is the design of this letter, which I humbly beseech you not to be offended with; otherwise I should be sorry to have writ it, excepting the wishes I have just now made, and my further prayers to God, that he would plentifully bless you and your holy labours, increase your church, and ever keep you under his protection. I beg of you

the continuance of your benevolence, being, with great sincerity,
Gentlemen,

Your most humble, most obedient,
And most affectionate servant,

FERRY.

Metz, March 30, 1632,

M. Mestrezat, a learned divine of the church of Paris, writ two letters to M. Chabrey, his brother-in-law, and minister of Geneva; wherein I find two passages, that deserve likewise to be imparted to the publick. M. Mestrezat thought Anthoine had been a monk. His first letter is dated from Paris, March 12, 1632.

'I am troubled for you (says he, in that letter) about your Antitrinitarian. The writings of our predecessors, *de puniendis Hæreticis*, have not been very edifying, and prove very prejudicial to us, in the countries where the magistrates are our enemies. It is true, the enormity of that man, his blasphemies, his profession of Christianity, and his ministry, aggravate his crime. May God Almighty direct your magistrates in the matter ! If every body had the same thoughts of monks, as I have, none of them should ever be admitted into the holy ministry. I pray God to remove, by the efficacy of his word, the scandal occasioned by that profligate man, and to keep you under his protection.'

The second letter of M. Mestrezat is only dated March 30, 1632, but it was likewise written from Paris. The following passage is to be found in it :

' As to what concerns your Jewish monk, and revolted minister, the most judicious persons in this town wish he may be confined to a perpetual imprisonment, and not be allowed to see any body, but such as are qualified to reclaim him. They are very much afraid of the consequences of a publick execution, lest it should be inferred from it, by our adversaries in these parts, that words spoken against the Pope (the pretended Vicar of Jesus Christ) or against the Host of the Mass, are likewise blasphemies against Christ, and ought to be punished in the same manner ; for they talk in the same strain, and all supreme magistrates are judges of consequences, in their jurisdictions.'

Whilst Nicholas Anthoine was a prisoner, he presented three petitions to the Council. The first is dated March 11, 1632, and begins thus : ' In the name of the great God of Heaven, who is the mighty God of Israel: His holy name be blessed for ever.' Amen. He beseeches the Council to get some papers concerning his faith restored to him, which he had delivered to a divine, who asked for them in their name; that he may revise, correct, and finish them, before any thing be inferred from them. And then he adds : *Enquerez vous de ma vie*, &c. That is, ' Enquire into my life ; I have always endeavoured to live in the fear of God, and to seek and follow the right way to salvation.

God discovers his secret to those who honour him.   What I do is only
to give an account of my faith, to the glory of God, and for the salvation of my soul.   God knows my heart, and is a witness to my integrity and innocence.   Do not draw innocent blood upon your heads, nor
upon your families, and your city; and God, in whose hands we all
are, will bless you, if you love his holy ways.   I beseech him with all
my soul to bless you, and to touch your hearts, that you may be moved
with pity and compassion towards me, the poor and afflicted servant of
the Lord, &c.'

Anthoine presented his second petition the next day, March 12;
which I shall insert at length.

In the name of the Lord, the God of Israel.

Magnificent and most Honoured Lords,
    ' What I am going to represent to you is not with an intent to avoid
death.   According to God, I do not deserve it; for I fear him, I love
him, and bless him, and will bless and worship his holy, glorious, and
adorable name to my last breath.   Nevertheless, according to your
laws and belief, and what is commonly objected to me, you will think
I justly deserve it.   If God would be pleased to do it, he would shew
his great wonders, by delivering me; not for my sake, who am a poor
and miserable sinner, but to glorify his great and adorable name, and
that all the earth might know, that he is the Almighty God, who reigns
in the world.   I invoke his holy name, and implore his grace and
mercy.   Whosoever puts his trust in the Lord shall never be ashamed.
Why should we be afraid of men? God is above all, and nothing comes
to pass without his permission.
    Magnificent and most honoured Lords; Since two things are com-
monly objected to me, 1. That I have strayed from the way to salvation.   2. That, though I were in the right way to salvation, yet, having
such a belief, I should not have embraced the office of minister, nor
come into your city to give you offence; by your leave, I shall endeavour to answer those two points in a few words.
    ' As to the first point, I believe I am in the way to truth and salva-
tion, and shall persevere in it, till I am shewed the contrary by good
reasons taken from the Old Testament.   I worship one only God; I
endeavour to follow the law, to the best of my power; I will fear, love,
and bless the holy name of God to the end of my life.
    ' As to the second point, your Lordships must know, that the people
of Israel refused to admit me among them, and told me that I might
live every where, and among all nations, in the fear of God, without discovering my opinions.   I have endured a thousand hardships in my
way to Venice, and in that city, where I have been, for some time, in a
very miserable condition; and I came away more afflicted still, and
more miserable; nevertheless, I always put my trust in the Lord.   I
could not resolve to live among the Papists, for I had sworn to do it no
more, having a great abhorrence for their idolatry.   Besides, I was
afraid of being charged with inconstancy.   Nay, had I been discovered

among them, they would have been more cruel to me, than your Lordships use to be towards those, who are not accused of any crime, but only prosecuted for religion. I have embraced the ministry, because I thought I was sufficiently qualified for it ; because I was far in years; because I was willing to keep house, and, perhaps, to marry in time; and I had no mind to discover myself at that time. How many are married, and perhaps have quite another belief than yours, and yet will not leave and forsake their children upon such an account! As for what is said, that I have scandalised you and your city by my strange proceedings, it was through a disordered mind ; it is not I ; I do not know who it was : God knows it; and therefore, I think, I deserve to be pardoned in that respect, since it was not I, but a terrible, dreadful, and supernatural power, as the whole town may witness, and no body will be offended at it. Rather than come and surrender myself into your hands, of my own motion, I had rather have fled to the remotest part of the world.

'Magnificent and most honoured Lords; Have a care you do not draw innocent blood upon your heads, and your families, and city, by putting me to death ; for, perhaps, you know not the wonders of God, the mighty God of Israel, and why he has so miraculously transported me into this town. If the beginning of it has been miraculous, perhaps the end will be more miraculous still. I shall never be ashamed, because the Lord is my trust and refuge. Let the holy name of the Lord, the great God of Israel, be for ever blessed and glorified by all men, and in all places.

'Magnificent and most honoured Lords; If you think I deserve to be put to death, and if the Lord God is pleased it should be so, his will be done. If you release me, you will release an innocent soul, which fears the God of heaven. I pray God with all my heart, that he would be pleased to pour his most holy blessings upon you, and to move your hearts, if it be his good will ; being,

Magnificent and most honoured Lords,
Your most humble servant and prisoner,
N. ANTHOINE.

Geneva, March 12, 1632.

On the Eleventh of April, Anthoine was brought to his tryal, and, besides several other things, which I have already mentioned, he declared that he was a Jew, beseeching God to grant him, that he might die for the Jewish religion ; that he believed there had been such a man as Jesus Christ, but he knew not whether he had been crucified ; that he did not believe him to be God, nor the Son of God, nor the Messias, since there is but one God, without any distinction of persons, and the time of the Messias was not come yet ; that he rejected the New Testament, because he found many contradictions in it, and because it did not agree with the Old ; that he got himself admitted into the ministry, because the Jews told him he might outwardly profess any religion, without endangering his salvation, and because he wanted a livelihood ; that, when he took the usual oaths, it was with a mental reservation to what was true and reasonable ; that, being so far engaged, he could not avoid reciting the apostle's creed, and administering the communion; that he never pronounced distinctly the articles of the creed, which concern our Saviour: that he took his texts out of the Psalms, and the Prophet Isaiah; that the next day, after he had preached upon the second Psalm, without applying it to Jesus Christ, he fell into a fit of madness, as he was singing the seventy-fourth Psalm; that he was mad when he came to Geneva, and called Jesus Christ an Idol, &c. that it was true, he had affirmed, that the passages of the Old Testament, quoted in the New, were strained, far-fetched, and wretchedly applied; that he had renounced his Baptism, and continued to do so.

Afterwards they shewed him a paper written with his own hand, but not subscribed by him, which contained these words: ' I acknowledge and confess, that Jesus Christ crucified is the true God, Saviour, and Redeemer of the whole world; and that he is the same with the Father and the Holy Ghost, as to his essence, but distinct, as to his person.' His answer was: That he had been forced to write that confession; and he disowned the doctrine contained in it. Then the famous passage of Josephus, concerning Christ, was alledged against him; to which he made no answer. Being asked, whether he persisted to renounce his Baptism? He said he did. Being exhorted to confess, whether he had frequented the bawdy-houses at Venice, he answered, that he could make no such confession, and prayed God to discover his innocence; adding, that the most beautiful woman in the world would not have tempted him; and then, bending his head, he intreated God to take pity on him, &c. The first Syndic alledged to him several passages of the Old Testament concerning Christ, and then the prisoner was recommitted.

On the sixteenth of April, he was brought again to the bar. His chief answers were: That he had never dogmatised at Geneva; that, when he gave the communion in his church at Divonne, he used these words ' Remember the death of your Saviour;' that he administered Baptism, as other ministers did; that he was in the way to salvation, and fully resolved, with God's assistance, to die for the truth of his doctrine.

Whereupon, the Council condemned him, on the the twentieth of April, to be strangled and burnt, and their sentence was executed on the same day. It imports, that ' Nicholas Anthoine, laying aside all fear of God, was guilty of apostacy and high treason towards God, having opposed the Holy Trinity, denied our Lord and Saviour Jesus Christ, blasphemed against his holy name, renounced his Baptism to embrace Judaism and circumcision, and perjured himself. Which are great and horrid crimes, &c.' The above-mentioned letter of M. Ferry had such an effect upon the ministers of Geneva, that they went in a body to the Council, and intreated the magistrates to put off his execution for some time; but it was to no purpose.

SOME

SMALL AND SIMPLE REASONS,

DELIVERED IN

A HOLLOW-TREE,

IN WALTHAM FOREST,

IN A LECTURE,

ON THE

THIRTY-THIRD OF MARCH LAST.

BY AMINADAB BLOWER,

A DEVOUT BELLOWS-MENDER OF PIMLICO.

Shewing the Causes in general and particular, wherefore they do,
might, would, should or ought, except against and quite refuse the
Liturgy or Book of Common-Prayer.

Printed, Anno Millimo, Quillimo, Trillimo. Quarto, containing eight pages.

M Y dear beloved and zealous brethren and sisters here assembled in
this holy congregation, I am to unfold, unravel, untwist, untye,
unloose, and undo, to your uncapable understandings, some small
reasons, the matter, the causes, the motives, the grounds, the principles,
the maxims, the why's and the wherefores, wherefore and why, we
reject, omit, abandon, contemn, despise, and are and ought to be
withstanders and opposers of the service-book, called by the hard
name of Liturgy, or Common-Prayer, which hath continued in the
church of England eighty-four years.

I have exactly examined and collected some notes and observations
out of the learned Hebrew translated volumes of Rabbi Ananias, Rabbi
Ahitophel, Rabbi Iscariot, Rabbi Simon Magus, Rabbi Demas, and
Rabbi Alexander the coppersmith, and all nor any of their writings
doth in any place so much as mention that book, or any such kind of
service to be used at all by them. I have farther taken pains in
looking over some Chaldean, Persian, Egyptian, Arabian, and
Arminian authors, of which I understood not one word; I also (with
the like diligence and understanding have viewed the Turkish Alchoran,
and there I found not a syllable concerning either liturgy, common-
prayer, or divine service. As for Greek Authors, I must confess I
understand them not, or negatively, for which reason I leave them as

impertinent; and, touching the Latin writers, they are partial in this case, the tongue being Romanian, and the idiom is Babylonish, which seems to me an intricate confusion.

I, having carefully viewed the tomes and tenets of religion, and books of all manner of hieroglyphicks, writings, scrolls, tallies, scores and characters, and finding nothing for the maintaining of that book or liturgy, I looked into the ecclesiastical history, written by one Eusebius, and another fellow they call Socrates, wherein I found many arguments and incitements to move men to such doctrine as is comprised and compiled in the liturgy. After that I searched into the acts and monuments of this kingdom, writen by old Fox, and there I found that the composers of it were bishops and doctors, and great learned school-men of unfeigned integrity, of impregnable constancy, who, with invincible faith, suffered most glorious martyrdom by the papal tyranny, for the writing and maintaining that book, with the true protestant religion contained in it.

Brethren, I must confess, that I was somewhat puzzled in my mind at these things, and I could not be satisfied, till I had consulted with some of our devout brothers. Our brother How, the cobler, was the first I broke my mind to, and we advised to call or summon a synod to be held in my Lord Brook's stable, the Reverend Spencer, the stable groom, being the metropolitan there. At our meeting there was Greene the felt-maker, Barebones the leather-seller, Squire the taylor, with Hoare a weaver, and Davison a bonelace-maker of Messenden, and Paul Hickeson of Wickham taylor, with some four or five bakers dozens of weavers, millers, tinkers, botchers, broom-men, porters, of all trades, many of them bringing notes with them fitting for our pur-pose; which notes they had taken carefully from the instructions of the demi-martyrs and round and sound confessors, St. B. St. P. and St. B. out of which, with our own capacities and ingenuities to boot, we have collected and gathered these sound and infallible objections against the book of common-prayer, or liturgy, as followeth.

For our own parts, my brethren, it is for the reputation and honour of our holy cause and calling to contest, malign, and cavil, where we are not able either to convince by reasons or arguments; therefore I having traced the book from end to end, and yet, upon the matter, to no end for such ends as we would conclude upon, I find nothing in it disagreeing to God's word or agreeing with our doctrine. The first prayer, called the Confession, is quite contrary to our appetites, and profession, for to confess, that ' we have erred and strayed like lost sheep,' is to acknowledge ourselves to be silly horned beasts and cuckolds; our children, by that reckoning, should be lambs, our wives ewes, and we, their innocent husbands, must be rams; and every lay preacher or preaching tradesman would be accounted a bell-wether to the flock or herd.

Neither do we think it fit to make ourselves appear so weak-witted or pusillanimous as to confess, that ' We have left undone those things which we ought to have done, and done those things which we ought not to have done;' for such a confession will lay open our disloyalty, our intrusion, or transgressions, rebellions, and treasons; we shall therein acknowledge ourselves, by omitting of duties, and committing of villainies in church and state, to deserve justly the severity of God, and the King's laws to be our deserved wages : besides, we hold it to be a retractive diminishing of valour, a popish kind of cowardly effeminate submission, which our stout hearts, stiff necks, and stubborn knees will never stoop and bow to, for the old proverb is, Confess and be, &c.

Concerning the second prayer, called the Absolution, for the remission of sins through Christ ; though Christ hath given power and commandment to his lawful ministers, to declare and pronounce in his name, to all true repenting sinners, the absolution and remission of their sins, yet we will not believe it to be available, but esteem it as popish and superstitious.

As for the Lord's Prayer, which the Papists call by the Romish or Latin name of Pater Noster, we must confess it is pithy and short; but, had our advices been at the making of it, it should have been two yards and a half longer, by London measure. Besides, we would like it better, if it were not commanded or enjoined upon us, for our faiths cannot brook to be limited with the compass of any command, decree, edict, law, statute, order, rule, ordinance, government, or authority either of God or the King; besides, in that prayer there is mention made of ' forgiving such as trespass against us,' which our doctrine or natures cannot incline to, for we do never remember a good turn, and very seldom or never forget or forgive an injury. Therefore, for these considerable causes, and many more, we think it requisite to forbear that brief prayer, and zealously to advance the altitude of our spacious cars, to receive the longitude of a three hours repetition, for our fructifying edification.

Thirdly, for the desiring the ' Lord to open our lips, that our mouth might shew forth his praise:' It is known we can do that extempore, by the spirit, and it belongs to our teacher to open his lips and pray; but it is our parts to give spiritual attention, and not to open our lips, but only at the singing of old Robert Wisdom's madrigal, or the like. And, whereas we are commanded to stand at the saying of Gloria Patri, to avoid that ceremony we hold it best not to say it at all.

As for the xcvth Psalm, (or, O come let us sing, &c.) we object against it for two reasons : The one is of falling down, and worshipping, and kneeling : And the other is, we will neither kneel, fall down, or worship, because it is an expression of humility and reverence, which we utterly refuse to give either to God or man. As for the order of reading the first lesson, we could like it better, if it were not so ordered; it were necessary we had freedom to read what, when, and where we list, for order is odious; and, whereas there is appointed a hymn, called by a Latin name, Te Deum laudamus, we do conceive the matter of it to be very good, but that it was composed by a bishop, one Ambrose, of a city and province in Italy called Milan, and that the said Ambrose was not only a bishop, but, for his godly life and holy writings, he was made a saint ; for these causes we leave him and his hymn too, as being too much conformable to edification, decency, order, and obedience.

Likewise the second lesson may be read, but not that which is appointed for the day; for, as is aforesaid, we cannot abide any thing that is appointed or ordered by authority, that, our consciences being at liberty, we may the more freely shew ourselves the lawless sons and daughters of confusion.

And, though it hath been a custom very significant, and as ancient as the primitive times of Christian religion, to repeat the articles of the belief standing, our understanding, notwithstanding, doth withstand that kind of posture, for no other reason, but because the church ordained it, and the law commands it; and truly we do know no sense or reason to stand to any saying of faith, for it is one of our principles, ' that, whatsoever we say, we will stand to nothing.'

Next followeth the Lord's Prayer again (as the protestants call it) and a prayer composed of versicles, wherein the minister and people do (as it were by questions and answers) desire ' God's mercy, and the granting of salvation,' after which they pray, ' O Lord save the King,' which is, by us, wonderfully disliked and omitted; and, when we are to render the cause of it, we shall not want insufficient answers, which we have studiously pondered in the learned colleges of Amsterdam and New-England. Then there followeth, ' Give peace in our time, O Lord,' which we utterly detest; for, if once that prayer be granted, many of us (except the King be more merciful than we deserve) shall be hanged for rebellion and treason, and glad we escape so too; the best, we can look for is the advancing again the protestant religion, and then down go we, with all all our spiritual inspirations, and long-winded repetitions; we shall be silenced (which is a terrible torture) or banished from our zealous sisters; our collections and contributions will be abrogated and annihilated, our puddings and plum-broth will be in the forlorn-hope, and ourselves excluded, extirpated, exiled, excommunicated, as extraordinary, extravagant, unexampled rascals and coxcombs; for these considerations of martial validity, weight, and deep consequence (altogether repugnant and malignant to the holy profession of Brownism and Anabaptism) we will neither have peace (although we dare not fight in war) no peace I will pray for; therefore, good brethren, I pray you no prayer for peace.

And for saying, ' God make our hearts clean within us, and take not thy Holy Spirit from us;' these words are impertinent for us to speak, for we know our hearts to be clear and pure already; and, for the Spirit, it is tied so fast to us, that it cannot be taken from us, or from any that will believe us.

In the Evening Prayer, there is one collect for peace, and another for the enlightening of our darkness; we have already declared our minds, though all the world knows us to be hypocrites; yet we do know, that a godly loyal peace will confound us, therefore we will not hypocritically pray for that which we desire not to have: And for our darkness, though it be palpable to be felt (like the darkness of Ægypt, yea, more dark than ignorance itself) yet we have, by instigation, found light in abundance: Our weights are light, our mothers, wives, sisters, aunts, nieces, daughters, and female servants, are light; our invisible horns are light, our words, deeds, thoughts, consciences, payment of debt, and religion, is light (or of light account); our faith in God, and loyalty to the King, are most translucently light, apparently light, refulgently light, illustrately light, transparently light, internally light, externally light, infernally light, emblazoned, perspicuated, cognominated, propagated, and promulgated, to all the world to be light (lighter than any thing that we call lightness), lighter than vapour, air, smoke, flame, dust, chaff, wind, feather, froth, cork, yeast, fog, puff, blast, a whore, vanity, yea more light than vanity itself.

As concerning *Quicunque vult* (or whosoever will be saved) it is an argument that he, that will be, may be, and he that will not, may chuse whether he will or no; which implies a free-will (a very popish conclusion), also that creed is concluded to be called Catholick, which word we like not.

Next followeth the litany, which is a hard word to us, and sounds in our spacious ears as it were Latin, or the beast's language; we confess there are some few sentences, that may be tolerated; but we ought to remember ourselves, and take heed that we avoid praying against fornication, sedition, conspiracy, false doctrines, heresy, hardness of heart, and contempt of God's word and commandment; for you know, brethren, that these are daily and nightly contemplations, and recreations: Besides, it seems to be a swearing kind of invocation (as) ' By the incarnation, by the nativity and circumcision, baptism, fasting, temptation, agony, bloody sweat, cross, passion, death, burial, resurrection, ascension, and coming of the Holy Ghost,' (all which is most certainly true) but we ought to find out some other by-word, than the word by; for, though by them all true believers are saved, yet that is no warrant or argument we should swear by them.

Then there is praying, that the church may be ruled and governed in the right way; which, if that be granted, what will become of us, that do know ourselves to be none of the true church? therefore that prayer belongs not to us.

Then follow beseechings for blessings to be upon the King, Queen, and royal posterity, and that they may have victory over all their enemies; all the world knows, we are none of their friends, therefore these prayers are Apocrypha to us, neither will we be so simple to pray against ourselves; and the case is plain, that rebellion must be tamed, before the King can be victorious.

Then follows praying for bishops (whom we cannot abide, nor can we shew wherefore) and, amongst the rest, there is a prayer ' for all women labouring with child,' in which prayer many a loose harlot may be comprehended; therefore it had been fitter to have prayed ' for all women labouring with child lawfully begotten,' for, verily, it is sinful to pray for either root, stock, limb, bough, branch, sprig, leaf, fruit, or seed, of the wicked. I like well of the last verse, except one, of the same litany, wherein we pray, ' that the fruits of the earth may be given and preserved to our use,' but with this proviso, that we alone, and none but we, who labour in the holy cause, ' should enjoy them in due time,' or at any time.

Then there are prayers for mercy, for grace, for defence and victory in war, for preservation from plague and pestilence, for bishops again, and curates, for rain, for fair weather, and for relief in dearth and famine ; then there follow eighty-four things, which they call collects, wherein many holy saints are remembered on certain peculiar days; and, though we can justly find nothing but what is agreeable to God's word in the whole liturgy, yet the purity of our singular doctrines doth hold it profane and popish, for we have the spirit to prompt us, insomuch as our grave patriots have lately thought fit to unsaint all the saints, and all the churches and houses of God in London have been, these many months, disrobed of their sanctimonious names, and are all excommunicated out of the weekly diseased bill ; for now the churches are to be called no more St. John's, St. Peter's, but Peter's, Andrew's, James's, John's, George's church or parish, with so many died of such and such diseases, or by such a casualty, or such a rascal hanged himself, for playing a Judas's part against his sovereign.

Next follow the ten commandments, which we neglect to say, because they are of the Old Tesament, and the law was given to the Jews; we that are christians are freed from it by the gospel. Besides, it is said to have two tables, one shewing our duty towards God, the other towards man : Concerning the first of them, we hold ourselves clear from idolatry, swearing, and profanation : For the second, we conceive it not to bind us, either to give honour to the King or magistrates (they being the fathers and protectors of our country, wealth, estates, and all we enjoy under God), nor to our natural parents, if they be not of our faith.

At the communion, there are prayers for the King again, and the Belief, with repeating some portions of scripture, to move men to charity and good works, all which we omit, for only faith is our practice ; and for good works, or charity, we hold it to be unnecessary, and therefore we will neither use or do any : Neither will we receive, lying, standing, sitting, nor kneeling, by any means, nor any way that is commanded by order, in what place or country whatsoever. As for publick or private baptism, we are able to do that ourselves, either in a bason, a river, a brook, a pond, a pool, a ditch, or a puddle ; nor do we hold it fitting, but that we be godfathers and godmothers to our children ourselves, and call them what scripture names we list. Nay, we will church our wives ourselves too. And, as for matrimony, we will save that charge, and take one another's words; for we must take our wives words for our children, and why not for themselves? As for the visitation of the sick, and burial of the dead, they are both fit to be done ; the one is necessary, because the brethren and sisters may meet and salute the feast.

And, as for the burial of the dead, the case is all men's, besides boys, women, and children : But a grave and learned long-standing lecturer did lately find out the right way of burial, for an old man that died in the parish of St. James, near Duke's-place, within Aldgate, at which funeral he preached ; and in his sermon he told the dead man his faults very roundly, and abused the corpse more for ten shillings, than any conformable preacher would have done for twenty ; and when he

came to the laying the body in the ground, he omitted all order and
ceremonies of burial, only thus briefly he said,

> Ashes to ashes, dust to dust,
> Here's the hole, and in thou must.

So there is an end, and an end of my lecture.

A POSTSCRIPT.

It is humbly desired, that the reader do not censure the writer with
any thought, or touch of profanity, for in this foregoing discourse he
hath only decyphered the foolish grounds and tenets which the
teachers of the pestilent sects of schismaticks and separatists do hold
and maintain.

Your's, J. T.

THE

GREAT AND FAMOUS

BATTLE OF LUTZEN,

FOUGHT BETWEEN THE

RENOWNED KING OF SWEDEN AND WALSTEIN.

Wherein were left dead upon the place between five and six thousand
of the Swedish party, and between ten and twelve thousand of the
Imperialists, where the King himself was unfortunately slain, whose
death counterpoised all the other. Pappenheim, Merode, Isolani,
and divers other great commanders were offered up like so many
sacrifices on the Swedish altar, to the memory of their King. Here
is also inserted an abridgement of the King's life, and a relation of
the King of Bohemia's death, faithfully translated out of the French
copy.

Printed 1633. Quarto, containing forty-five pages.

To the Reader.

WE see that, in the greater maps, things are expressed more plainly,
than they can be in the smaller, though they be drawn all by one
skill; So virtue in princes is more perspicuous, than in plebeians; in
the former she is drawn at length, with all her dimensions; in the

M 2

latter she is limned in little, being invisible, unless you approach very near her. And indeed, this is consonant to nature's own wisdom, who suffers the vital spirits in the body to go to the least member, yea to the very finger's end; yet doth she most plentifully bestow them, where she hath the greatest employment for them : So on the vulgar she confers gifts suitable to so low a calling : But, in Princes and Monarchs, she centuples and irradiates her ornaments, because by them she speaks, and gives laws to humanity. Yet is not this rule so general, that it often suffers not an exception : For, as nature distinguisheth between the subject and the prince by sovereignty, so doth she between prince and prince, by virtue and ability. That this is true, this our dear tragical subject will serve for a lively and clear demonstration, whom neither this age, nor any of the former, could parallel, in the management both of the scepter, and the sword. In his whole reign, his prudence at home hath not deserved more admiration than his prowess abroad: For indeed, from his youth upwards, Mars hath been the sphere, wherein he hath moved, into which violated justice first hauled him, and out of which nothing but she appeased, or death could remove him. He was a general before a man, and with a yet unreaped chin mowed down his enemies before him. With many kingdoms, at once, he waged war, from all which he forced conditions, advantageous to him and his. This was not without the amazement of all men, to see a point oppose and conquer so vast a circumference. In his wars I will only observe three things : His way to victory, his behaviour in it, his carriage after it. For the first, he did animate his soldiers rather by fighting, than exhorting; nor did he challenge to himself any advantage above the meanest of them, but honour and command. He knew that it is in empire, as in the body, where the most dangerous diseases flow from the head : Wherefore he worked on their manners by his own, the only firm cement of a general and his army. He well understood that faith and loyalty are not to be expected, where we impose thraldom and servitude ; and therefore at times he would be familiar, as well with the common soldier as the commander. His invention and execution of all military stratagems were ever twins; for in all his conquests he owed as much to his celerity as valour. When his foes were in their tents securely discoursing of him, as a-far off, he, like the wolf, broke into their fable, to their irrecoverable astonishment. They could not withstand the force of his fame, much less that of his arms. One feather more I must add, without which his victories had not been fully plumed, nor could have soared so high, and that was this : He never persuaded any man to an enterprise, in which he would not himself make one. He taught them, as well by hand, as tongue. I may add, that neither antiquity can, nor posterity ever shall produce a prince so patient of all military wants, as of meat, drink, warmth, sleep, &c. all which are necessary to the maintenance of life. In divers sufferings of his, he recalls to my mind the most accomplished of the Romans, Cato, who, leading his troops through the contagious and poisonous desarts, was ever the last of his army that drank, save once, when he began to them all in water taken from a spring suspected to be invenomed.

Thus much of his way to victory, now let us come to his deportment in it. After all his conquests, such a calm immediately ensued, that the passed storm was soon forgotten, and the enemy appeared rather like one suddenly wakened, than frighted. There was not any of his victories that washed not her hands of all cold and innocent blood. He was so severe a justicer, that he often revenged the violating of his merciful decrees even upon the place, and sometimes on men of quality, whom he affected. The laws of retaliation he knew so well, that he gave to all men punctual satisfaction for all offences received from his party, according to the nature of the wrong done. For this cause, his tribunal (like the Roman) stood ever open. All his great atchievements were ever attended by devotion within, and circumspection without. He first praised God, and then provided for man; at once having an eye on his enemies next designs, and his soldiers present necessities. The greatest of his glories, purchased with blood and sweat, could neither change the estate of his mind, or copy of his countenance. The true greatness of his spirit was such, that, in all his actions, he placed ostentation behind, and conscience before him, and sought not the reward of a good deed from fame, but from the deed itself. I conclude this point with this assertion, that honesty had as strict and great a command over him, as necessity over mankind. He was a prince of so great and clear a fame, that envy herself blushed to oppose it, and therefore was forced to assume the mask of religion, under which she might securely display her invectives. Religion, religion, it is thou that shouldest unite, but dost estrange hearts; and makest us seek to take away even those lives that gave us ours. Let a man have in eminency all the cardinal and theological virtues, he of a contrary sect looks on all these through a mist raised by his malice, which makes him either not see them at all, or not as they are. O Jesus, Jesus, in thy best blessed time, gather thy strayed flock into one fold, and let truth and peace kiss each other. This testimony the perfections of this prince drew from me, who was abstemious and continent in every thing, save in the search of glory and virtue.

It now remains, that I say something of the ensuing treatise, in which is contained the last and greatest battle of this king, his deplored death, and other weighty circumstances. The original is French, written by one of the ablest pens of that nation. He begins at the king's coming down into Germany, and extends his story to his death. Of all the modern histories, I dare make it the chorus; for it is written in a stile so attick, and so judicial, that it may well be called the French Tacitus. What hath been before delivered, in other discourses concerning this subject, is to this nought else but a foil. The full and perfect translation of this rare piece I here promise the courteous reader; and, in the mean time, intreat him to wear, as a favour, this branch, by which he may judge the whole body.

DIXI.

THE king, having mustered his troops, and those of Duke Bernard of Saxon Weimar, about Erfurt, the army received command to advance towards Naumburg.

The king came thither in person on St. Martin's Day, and cut in pieces two regiments of Merode, that opposed him by the way. He was no sooner arrived at Naumburg, but he received intelligence, that the enemy's forces lay incamped at Leipsick, and Noerspurg, and stretched thence in length, as far as Weissenfels, and that they were intrenched in a place advantageous. Which proceeding of theirs obliged the king to do the like, at Naumburg, and to seek the means to join his army with the Electoral, which then lay about Torgau, consisting of fifteen thousand men, and reinforced with two thousand horse belonging to the Duke of Lunenburg. He sent divers posts to inform them of his coming, and of the courses were to be taken for their uniting. Walstein and Pappenheim, being lodged between them, had an eye on them both, and made it their only study to hinder their conjunction. On the fourteenth of November, the scouts of the king brought him word, the enemy had sacked and abandoned the city, and castle of Weissenfels, laid plain his trenches, and retired himself towards Lutzen, two German miles from Leipsick. The king, hearing this news, resolved no longer to delay the fight, his courage not permitting him to temporise any further, nor to attend the return of his posts sent to the Elector.

That, which confirmed him in this his resolution, was the assurance of certain prisoners brought him by Relinguen, that Pappenheim was gone to Hall, with six regiments. Wherefore his army had order to march towards the enemy, the fifteenth, three hours before day, and to dare him to a battle. The diligence of the van was such, that it reached the enemy by the second hour after noon, and began the assault. The Imperialists failed not to make head, and a strong resistance. Many charges were given, with advantage, and loss equal, the victory inclining now to this side, then to that, till at length the Swedes gave fire to their small field-pieces, which pierced and broke sundry Imperial companies, and forced them to a retreat. The Swedes became masters of the field, and brought to the king a standard taken from the enemy, with this device, *La Fortune, & l'Aigle Romain*, Fortune, and the Roman Eagle. Hence some drew this prognostick, that the enemy should, before long, part with the one and the other. A thick mist and the night coming upon them, the Swedes were hindered in the pursuit of the enemy, and the victory.

The king remained in the field, and stood in order of battle all night; having no other shelter than his caroach, resolved to follow close his design, and engage the enemy to a general combate. He communicated his intention to the Dukes of Saxon-Weimar, and other remarkable commanders; who passed away that night near his caroach, having nothing over their heads, but the heavenly arch, nor any thing under them, but trusses of straw laid upon the earth. Their field-furniture they left behind, believing they should return to lodge in Naumburg: But the patience of their general made them with ease pass over these inconveniences. Some of the principal officers endeavoured to dissuade the king from giving battle, alledging that the forces of the enemy were great, his seats advantageous ; their own army feeble and wearied with continual marches; and that it was far safer to wait for the arrival of the Saxon, and make so strong an union, as may promise success in the equality of their armies. Their reasons were not received, but crossed by the king with many more solid, derived from the experience of the times past, and the present astonishment of the enemy ; from the courage of his soldiers, and his advantages obtained; from the justice of his arms, from the benediction from above, from the absence of Pappenheim, and the discommodities he should be subject to, in that season now waxing bitter, in case he should suffer the enemy to perfect his trenches, which he had already begun in many places : To which he added his reputation, and how important it was to hasten the combate, saying aloud, ' That he would not suffer Walstein to beard him, without calling him to an account, and letting him see, by proof, that he was not to be faulted, that before this he had not seen him with his sword in his hand; that he desired to make trial of his ability in the field, and ferret him out of his burrows.'

The commanders, perceiving by the language and tone of the king, that his decree to fight was inevitable, and their opposition fruitless, conformed their wills by an humble obedience to his, not without reiterated protestations to subscribe themselves his in their own blood, and seal it with the loss of their lives : Whereat the king rejoiced extremely ; nor could he contain his joy from appearing in his face, but, by his chearful looks, expressed his inward content, and forthwith called for a new sute of chammois, which he presently put on. Then they presented to him his arms, and the Duke Bernard, of Saxon-Weimar, and sundry other princes and officers conjured him, by all things dear and holy, to wear his helmet and cuirass ; but they could not win him to it, he objecting the incumbrance, and laying his hand on the musquet-bullet still remaining in his shoulder, which, to him, made the least weight unsupportable.

The king's design was to begin the combate by the peep of day ; but so thick and dark a mist arose, that it confined the eye to a small distance, and rendered any enterprise not only difficult, but dangerous ; wherefore the king was constrained to expect till the sun had chaced it away, which, till then, had deprived him of all sight of the enemy. The interim, according to his custom, he employed in his devotions, and in making the round of his army, to mark the disposition and countenance of his soldiers, and encourage them to fight manfully. Coming to the quarter of the Swedes and Finlanders, he put them in battle array ; and, with a voice and countenance alike chearful, he thus bespoke them :

' My friends and camerades*, this is the day that invites you to demonstrate what you are ; shew yourselves men of valour, keep your

---

* Camerades is, in English, Chamber-fellows.

M 4

ranks, and fight courageously for yourselves and your king. If this day the bravery of your spirits shine forth, you shall find the heavenly benediction perched on the points of your swords, honour, and a recompence of your valour: On the contrary, if you turn back, and basely and foolishly commit the armed band to the protection of the unarmed foot, you shall find infamy, my disgrace, and your own ruin; and I protest to you, on the word of a king, that not the least piece of you, or of your bones, shall return again into Swedeland.'

This exhortation, delivered in a high and piercing tone, won from the Swedes and Finlanders only these general acclamations: 'That they would approve themselves men of honour; that they had lives only for him, which they were ambitious to preserve in the obtaining of victory and his good graces.'

The Swedes being placed in rank and file, the king embattles the Alman regiments, and thus, in few words, exhorts them:

'My friends, officers, and soldiers, I conjure you, by your love to heaven and me, this day to manifest whose you are: you shall fight not only under me, but with me; my blood and life shall mark you out the way to honour; break not your ranks, but second me with courage: If you perform this, victory is ours with all her glories, you and your posterity shall enjoy it; if you give back, your lives and liberties have one period.'

This speech was answered with an universal shout, and vows reciprocal: 'That they would make it appear they knew the way to victory or to death: That the king should receive all satisfaction in their service, and the enemy should acknowledge he had to do with men of honour.'

Walstein and his principal officers discovered quickly, by his scouts, the resolution of the king, and the countenance of his, and thereupon grounded this resolution, 'That they must needs come to blows.' Walstein was infinitely desirous to avoid the combate; but he was wisely admonished, by some about him, that every step his men made in a retreat would take from their courage, and give it to the enemy, and bring upon his army a panick fear and an utter confusion. He spent that whole night in digging and intrenching, in embattling his army, and planting his artillery in divers places advantageous, the better to sustain the shock of the enemy. Pappenheim was sent for back in post-haste, who was gone to Hall, being very desirous to invest it, not believing that the king would give or accept of battle, before the forces of Saxony were arrived. In the mean time, the utmost endeavours of Walstein were not wanting to hearten his men; and he laid before them honour, reward, their advantages, their forces, the justice of their cause, which God, the Catholick church, the Emperor, and the whole empire justified against the violence and usurpation of a stranger: And all this, and more, he uttered in his litter, which his gout would not permit him to forsake.

This was subject to divers interpretations; some believing, that indeed he felt some symptoms of that sickness very familiar to him ; others maintained this posture to have no good grace on a day of battle, and judged, that Walstein was very willing to preserve himself safe and sound, that he might hereafter serve his master and his party : Others averred he was much indebted to his gout, which did warrant his retreat without his reproach, necessity commanding the stoutest courage to yield to such an enemy.

On the other side, the king being ready at all points, and his army embattled, he would take no refection, because he would be an example to his men, and lose no time. Being placed in the head of Steinsbock's regiment, he thus spoke with a voice audible : ' Now, now is the time, comrades, we must go on undaunted ; let us charge, let us charge in the name of God ; Jesus, Jesus, Jesus, aid me in fighting this day, and favour my right.'

These words were no sooner pronounced, but he gave spurs to his horse, and, with his head inclined, gave a charge to a battalion of twenty-four companies of cuirassiers, which were esteemed the flower of the Imperial army. Two Swedish regiments had order to second him. The artillery of the king was advanced, and five cannon-shot discharged upon the enemy, who answered them with two hundred, which went off with a horrid noise, and lightning, but with small loss to the Swedes, the cannoneers of Walstein not having well taken their aim. But the first shock was fatal to the king, and all the army ; for though the squadrons, led by so brave a chief, with an unheard of resolution, gave on, like thunder, on the enemy, and made him recoil ; yet one shot, from a pistol, gave him new courage, which pierced the king's arm, and broke the bone. When those, next the king, saw him bleed, they were amazed, and cried out ' The king is wounded.' Which words the king heard with much distaste and repining, fearing it would abate the valour of his men ; wherefore, dissembling his grief, with a joyful and undaunted look, he sought to qualify the fear of his soldiers, with these masculine words : ' The hurt is slight, comrades, take courage, let us make use of our odds, and return to the charge.' The commanders that were about him, with hands lifted up, earnestly besought him to retire ; but the apprehension of frighting his men, and his ambition to overcome, prevailed.

The assault being re-begun with vigour and fervour, and the king fighting again in the head of his troops, once more to break those ranks, that were again made up, the loss of blood, and the grief which he felt in the agitation of his body, enfeebled much his spirits and voice, which caused him to whisper these words in the ear of the Duke of Saxon Lavenburgh : ' Convey me hence, for I am dangerously wounded.' He had scarcely ended his speech, and turned head to retire, when a cuirassier, marking this retreat, advanced, upon the gallop, from the battalion of the enemy, and discharged his carabine full in the shoulder of the king, with this insulting speech: ' And art thou there then ? Long it is that I have sought thee.' Some imagined, that it was Pappenheim that gave the blow, by reason he had often vaunted, that an ancient prediction was found amongst the records of his family, that a stranger king should die by the hand of a Pappenheim, with divers scars in his body, and mounted on a white horse. And, for this cause, (having many scars in his face, and divers other parts of his body stitched up) he reflected on himself, and believed the prophecy should be accomplished by his hand. But this needs no other confutation, than the absence of Pappenheim, and the time when the king received his hurt, which was in the very beginning of the assault, before Pappenheim could make one of the adverse party. I may add, that the discretion of this worthy count would not have suffered him to run into an error so uncivil, as to speak so undecently to a prince of that eminency.

When the king had received this mortal wound, which pierced him through and through, he fell from his horse, and gave up the ghost, with nothing but ' My God' in his mouth. He that made this accursed shot was beaten down with a storm of harquebusado's, and sacrificed to the indignation of the Swedes. But, while the groom of the king's chamber, and divers others, lighted to raise the body, the charge began again, more furiously than ever ; the enemy having taken notice of this blow, and concluding that all was now finished, and that he should have Swedes good cheap. This hindered the king's servants from bearing of his body, and summoned every man to regain the stirrup, and withstand the foe; so that the king could not be defended from receiving another pistol-shot in the head, and being twice run through with a sword. The Imperialists fearing him, even after death, and cowardly suspecting his speedy resurrection : The poor groom of his chamber never forsook him, but breathed his last upon his master's carcase, after the receipt of an infinity of wounds.

But neither the king's death, nor the great odds that the enemy had, being strongly intrenched in divers places, could let the Swedes, madded with their inestimable loss, from assaulting the Imperialists with an unspeakable fury ; insomuch that they compelled the battalion of cuirassiers, which made the left wing, to retire into their trenches, whom they dislodged about noon, and gained seven of their cannon, together with many colours and cornets.

Lieutenant-Colonel Relinguen received command to advance, and, with three hundred horse, to charge four regiments of crabbats, commanded by Isolani, which made the right wing of the enemy ; which he performed with so much bravery and courage, that he twice pierced through them, and brought back three standards, leaving behind one of his own. All his officers were wounded, and he himself, in the second onset, had his arm shot through with a pistol-bullet, which forced him to retire. Isolani, General of the Crabbats, lost his life, with a great number of his men. Eighteen of his companies charged some German regiments that guarded the baggage; but they were stoutly opposed, the combate fierce, the assaults reiterated, the earth died crimson, and burdened with carcases ; the Crabbats driven back, though not without some disorder of the German horse, recoiled amongst the carts ; but this disadvantage the enemy could not espy, by reason of a thick cloud which then arose, and gave the Germans opportunity to rank themselves.

The Imperial commanders, Galas, Merode, and Holok, longing to recover their seat, and cannon lost, took selected bands, fired the four corners of Lutzen, to 'blind the Swedes, and keep them from piercing that side to the succour of their friends. This essay was followed by success, the trench forced by the Imperialists, the seven pieces of cannon lost regained, and some Swedish regiments disordered.

The Duke Bernard of Saxon Weimar, seeing the confusion of his men, and being advertised, by Kniphausen, of the king's death, was extremely incensed, and, protesting he had not so base a wish as to survive him, he ran, with his head couched, on the enemy, seconded by the regiments of the Prince of Anhalt and Count Lowenstein. Then the fight became obstinate, on both sides, the charges redoubled, the carcases piled up, the pikes broken, and the difference came to be decided by dint of sword. The eye of man, nor that greater of the world, ever beheld a joust more furious. The Imperialists strove to hold their advantage recovered, and the Swedes to dispossess them of it. The Duke Bernard did wonders that day ; thrice, like lightning, shot he through the forces of the enemy, nor could a wound, received on the left arm, cause him to leave the field, before he had constrained the enemy to abandon the cannon and his post.

The winning of this opened him the way to the conquest of another ; for this valiant prince pressed the Imperialists so hard, that he again disranked them, and compelled them to quit another post, guarded with thirteen cannon. His dexterity in the drilling of his men, in the opening and shutting of his ranks, was such, that they received little or no hurt from the enemy's cannon. The duke, undaunted, pierced through the clouds of smoke, displaced the enemy, and made himself master likewise of this place, and of the cannon, and drove the enemy to a confused retreat. The slaughter was great, and the Swedes, well blooded, made good use of their advantage, and the disorder of their foes, passing over their bellies, killing all that came in their way, and stopping their ears against all motives for quarter.

The duke, possessed of this place, and master of the field, between two and three in the afternoon, thinking there was but one post to force, seated by a windmill, and guarded by three Imperial regiments, endeavoured to remove them, sending, in the mean time, sundry squadrons to chace the fugitives. But then the fight grew more cruel than ever ; for Pappenheim was returned from Hall, and came upon the gallop with certain fresh regiments. His reputation, and his encouragement, gave new spirits to the runaways, and called them to the combate. The duke, having notice of this, quits this place, new-ranks and encourages his men, and gives Pappenheim a meeting in the midway. All the charges past were nothing, in respect of these latter ; Pappenheim employed his utmost cunning and diligence, and shewed himself, in all places, in the head of his troops, to embolden them. On the other side, the Duke Bernard fixed a resolution either to die or overcome : and the Swedes and Finlanders, inraged for the death of their king, fought like lions, and desperately ran upon the enemy. The artillery advanced, and began to thunder, and to enter divers battalions, and to make legs and arms to fly from one place to another. The smaller shot was also so violent, that the squadrons encountered in the palpable darkness, caused by the smoke, without knowledge of their parties.

This furious shock continued two hours, with equal loss to both, victory opening her arms to embrace now one side, then another. Galas, Merode, and Holok were wounded to death, and a cannon-shot cut off Pappenheim by the middle.

His death, and the loss of divers other commanders, staggered the Imperialists, as much as that of the King's incensed the Swedes. Then the enemy (upon the receipt of a new salute from twenty-four cannon, which pierced their thickest troops) began to fly, and the Swedes pressed and pursued them far within night, which favoured the retreat of the fugitives, and hindered the Swedes from ranging further in the chace. Indeed they were so tired, that they had neither breath nor force further to follow them. The Imperialists, giving fire to their camp, and part of their baggage, took some the way of Leipsick, others that of Leutmeritz, towards the frontiers of Bohemia, whither it was thought Walstein was gone, having heard of the loss of the battle, to find a safe place of retreat, and to gather together his dispersed troops.

The Swedes remained in possession of the enemy's camp, and most of his baggage, of one and twenty exquisite cannon, besides inferior ones, and a multitude of standards and cornets. Upon the mustering of their army, they found wanting (over and above the incomparable and irreparable loss of their king) the Major General Isslet, and other colonels, and officers. A Prince of Anhalt, a Count of Nilis, the Colonels Brandestein, Wildenstein, Relinguen, and Winchell, received that day deep and honourable wounds. The Duke Bernard of Weimar also was hurt, to whose valour and conduct the Swedish party (after God) owes the glory of that day, more bloody by far, than that which was fought the year past in the neighbouring fields of Leipsick. The Duke Ernest of Weimar also insinuated himself into the hearts of all men, by his courage and leading that day. The regiments of these two princes, and those of the Prince of Anhalt, of the Count of Lewestein, of Colonel Brandestein, and the two Swedish colonels, sirnamed the Blue, and the Yellow, bore the brunt of that day. The Swedes lost between five and six thousand men, and the enemy between ten and twelve thousand remaining on the place, and two thirds of their army ruined and dispersed, besides the death or mortal wounds of divers of their remarkable commanders, as Galas, Merode, Holok, Piccolomini, Isolani, and divers others. Pappenheim, above all the rest, was bewailed by his party, and not without just cause; his courage, his conduct, his vigilance and experience, having conspired to rank him in the soldiers esteem amongst the bravest generals of these times.

But this glorious victory of the Swedish army suffered an eclipse, by the death of that truly great king, who was the soul of his friends, and the terror and scourge of his enemies. His body could not be found till the next day, when, after a curious search, it was discovered among the dead heaps rifled, and half naked, and so disfigured with blood and dirt, that he could hardly be known. This, at once so doleful and glorious a spectacle of the end of so great a monarch, worked so strongly and effectually on the hearts of his soldiers, that, with tears and lamentations for a loss so irreparable, they made an unanimous vow, upon the place, to revenge his death, and make him revive in the rigorous pursuit of his designs, which he had so often conjured them to continue, especially a little before this battle, when he seemed to presage his end, touching which he discoursed often and seriously with many of his familiars. Amongst other passages, the King marking the multitude of people that flocked about him at his entry into Naumburg, three days before the battle, and hearing their shouts of joy, and this general acclamation, Long live the King, as if now they had nothing to fear, since he was present, he made to the standers-by this short but memorable speech: ' Our affairs answer our desires, but I doubt God will punish me for the folly of the people, who attribute too much to me, and esteem me, as it were, their God, and therefore he will make them shortly see I am but a man. He be my witness, it is a thing distasteful to me. Whatever befall me, I shall receive it as proceeding from his divine will: In this only I rest fully satisfied, that he will not leave this great enterprise of mine imperfect.'

The seventeenth of November, immediately following the day of battle, and the King's death, Duke Bernard of Weimar retired to Weissenfels, to take a general review of his army, and to give rest and breath to his over-wearied troops. By the review of his regiments, it appeared that his army was between fifteen and sixteen thousand strong. The Duke imparted his present estate, and all other necessary particulars, to the court of Saxony, and urged the elector to an uniting of their forces, to the end they might follow close their design, and pursue Walstein to the remotest parts of Austria. After this, all the army, as well Swedish as German, agreed in the election of Duke Bernard for their general, and took a new oath faithfully to serve him, who had deserved so well of the Swedish party by so many benefits, by his vigilancy, his conduct, and the greatness of his fame in war; but, above all, by his resolution and incomparable valour, of which he made so opportune and clear a demonstration on that bloody day of battle. The chancellor Oxesterne, who lay then about Francfort, was sent for in all haste to manage the affairs of the chancery royal, removed to Erfurt; but chiefly, to serve and counsel the desolate and disconsolate queen, environed with griefs and crosses inexpressible, yet but equal to the greatness of her loss. The said chancellor, and the Chevalier Rache, served happily to rectify sundry disorders, and to raise the spirits of such as were dejected; but principally, to stop the flood of tears flowing from the eyes of this most virtuous princess, and to replant in her mind generous and masculine resolutions.

De la Gorde was sent for in post-haste, who was embarked in Swedeland with certain regiments of Swedes and Finlanders, to bring a supply to the camp royal, and reinforce it, the dead king being anchored in this maxim, to make continual levies (notwithstanding the number of his armies) that so he might have men at will to fill up those empty companies, which the sword, mortality, and many other military miseries might unhappily depopulate.

But, notwithstanding the death of this mighty prince, the astonishment and fright of the enemy was such, that he basely forsook divers strong and impregnable places in the electorate of Saxony. Amongst others the city of Leipsick was forsaken, and the castle razed to the ground; Chemnitz was taken, Zwickaw invested and forced, the Duke Bernard following close his good fortune, and making good use of the enemy's amazement. To this he was animated the more, by the fixed decree of the confederate princes, to make all fast, and more and more to knit a firm union with the Swedes, that so both of them jointly might execute and fulfil the intentions and exhortations of the deceased king.

Walstein having notice betimes of his men's infortunity, and the advantage of the Swedes, recovered Leipsick that night, and before day took the way of Leutmeritz, where he recollected his disbanded men, and added to them six fresh regiments that had not been engaged in the battle. After the often sending of his posts to all parts, at length Altringer had order from the Duke of Bavaria to join half his army to that of Walstein.

Notwithstanding the so miserable defeat of the Imperialists, bonfires were made in divers parts of Bavaria, for the death of the king, and *Te Deum* chanted aloud through all the streets of Ingolstadt and Ratisbon. But these vain fires and triumphs served for so many trumpets, to sound forth the praise and glory of the departed king; since, in the enemy's own judgment, his death was thought sufficient to counterpoise the dissipation and slaughter of so puissant an army: And indeed, except this accursed blow, there was no one circumstance that did not oblige the imperial party to a funeral equipage. Nothing was more to be admired than the moderation of the court of Vienna, which expressed no joy in triumph or exultation. They contented themselves with the discharging of a few ordnance, to make the silly people believe they had the better of the day. Some judged this modest behaviour to proceed from sensible losses, suffered in the battle, from the consideration of the Swedish forces, and the difficulty to set on foot again an army of that vastness. Others deemed it to proceed from the dispersed rumour of the Emperor's death, which they thought countervailed that of the King, and cast the imperial court into an irrecoverable dejection.

The failing of the Saxon to appear in the field on the day of battle, when his aid concerned his own honour and the King's good, was attributed to the like sad accident, a rumour being divulged, not only of the duke's death, but the manner of it, to wit, sudden apoplexy: But these false bruits, both of the one and the other, were contradicted, by assured news, that both the princes were living.

That the Saxon was not dead, he gave good proofs, resolving to take occasion by the lock to revenge the ruin of his cities, and depopulation of his country, and to hinder the imperialists from sending into his dominions any more incendiaries.

The continuance of the Emperor's life was favourable to his party; the very name and splendor of majesty being of virtue to animate and retain divers spirits in devotion and obedience to the Austrian line, which else, perhaps, might have followed the chariot of the victorious triumpher.

But, whilst the foolish people spread abroad, either by design, or credulity, the death of these two princes, there came too assured news from Nayence of the King of Bohemia's death. When this unfortunate prince was ready to take a new possession of his country, and the conditions drawn up between him, the King of Sweden, and the governor of Frankendale, he was surprised in Nayence with a contagious disease, presently after his return from Deux-Ponts, where he had visited a prince of his alliance. The care and sufficiency of the physician was so great, that he quickly expelled the pestilent quality, and set him, in all appearance, free from danger; but the great calamities, through which he had passed, had much estranged his constitution from its first purity, and quite altered his colour and complexion. When he thought to quit his tedious bed, and take possession of Frankendale, it unfortunately happened, that the King of Sweden's death came to his ear, which wrought so on his mind and body, that his disease was aggravated, and his death ensued on the twenty-ninth of November. His death was much deplored by those of his blood, by his servants and subjects; yet did their grief receive an allay by his devotion, and his last words full of faith and piety.

The life of this prince was a mere medley, and like a picture with many faces. His entry into the electorate was glorious, his beginning happy, his virtues eminent, and courted he was by the whole empire. His alliance and friends within and without Germany, the consideration of his house, of his dominions, and the great body that depended on his direction, were the cause of his election to the crown of Bohemia; which was fatal to him, and all Germany, which felt the sad accidents that attended this comet, and was forthwith invaded by an universal war in her heart, and all her quarters, which hath never since forsook her, having engaged all the imperial states and provinces, every one whereof to this day carries her marks. And though this prince hath sought all means of reconciliation, hoping that way to quench this wild-fire; yet hath he from time to time found such fatal oppositions, and such an ingrafted malice in the incensed party, that all the motives, propositions, and intercessions of great kings have hitherto been unprofitable; and this good prince hath been constrained to live an exile from his country. At length, when a most pleasing prospect laid at once open to his view the frontiers of his country, and the end of his afflictions, a sudden death deprived him of his sight, and the fruition of so delightful an object.

The calamity of this prince hath given occasion to many licentious tongues and pens to declaim against him, and unjustly to judge of his cause by the sad event. Those, that were of his more inward acquaintance, avow, that he was unfortunate beyond defect, and that the most magnanimous and heroick soul could bear afflictions with no greater moderation and patience, than he did. If many of his virtues have been clouded and obscured by his infelicity, yet there are more which his darker fortune could not hinder from shining forth, and striking envy blind. His great family, his extraction, his allies and confederates, and his princely virtues, methinks, should have contained, within the bounds of honour and truth, certain mercenary, satyrick spirits, who have common places of praises, and invectives, which they draw forth to exalt or depress whom they please, and maintain their looser vein at the cost of princes, and play upon their persons, qualities, and estates, whom the greatness of their births should privilege from such contumelies. We owe honour and respect to princes, of what party soever; whether they be friends, enemies, or neuters: And I thought this short apology due to my so much deplored subject, whom his miseries rendered to some contemptible, though, by others, he was truly honoured, in the midst of his disgraces and afflictions. The King of Sweden gave many brave testimonies of him, being forced oftentimes to give him a stop in the career of honour, lest courage should engage him too far, exhorting him to preserve his life, the good of his country, and the publick cause.

All the comfort of his subjects is contained in that generous unparalleled princess, and in her fair line, and numerous issue, which promiseth them one day an intire liberty, and the re-establishment and subsistence of a house so many ways considerable, as being one of the first, and most ancient of Europe.

The reader, I doubt not, will pardon this digression of the soldier, who held himself obliged to speak for a prince, who had been a long time the common butt of all afflictions and insultations. That which hath made him the more bold, and earnest in his defence, is the near alliance of this prince to mighty monarchs. I shut up all, concerning this point, in this assertion, that all princes have a common interest in the honour of their equals, and should all join to place their crowns and purple above the reach of envy.

The death of these two kings was sufficient to make the Germans approve of the calculation, and prognosticks of their great astrologer Herlicius, who had noted this month of November as fatal to great princes and commanders, and foretold by the aspects, and fiery constellations, the tragical encounters of these two great armies, and the death of such eminent persons, as may well compose the greatest part of the history of our time.

The Swedes were even wedded to sorrow for the death of their King, vowing they would more willingly have suffered the loss of many battles than that of him, if it had lain in their power to dispose of the arrests of heaven, and the fatal laws of the eternal Providence, which, with a diamantine point, marks all things, and gives them a character, which never can be changed, or defaced.

Indeed all the days of this month of November were at strife for superiority in evil, but the sixteenth overcame, to which all stories shall give a brand, in that it gave so strange an alteration to the face of Christendom. The battle fought on that day is ennobled by many memorable accidents, which exalt it above those of former ages. Amongst others, are remarkable the small number of the victors, and the multitude of the vanquished; the violent and furious charges, the durance of the fight, the doubtful event of the combate, when victory (as if she had been the daughter of Janus) had two faces, and looked two ways; the piles of the dead, the loss of eminent commanders, and the different effect which one and the same cause wrought in both parties, the King's death kindling indignation and desire of revenge in the bosom of the Swede; and the death of Pappenheim, and other great commanders, begetting an astonishment in the hearts and looks of the Imperialists. And we may well affirm, that, amongst all the accidents of that saddest of days, this particular hath been most remarkable: that, the Swedes having lost their King in the first shock, this unparalleled mischance served rather to confirm, than shake their courage, and was one of the most apparent causes of the victory.

This also raised as high as heaven the King's renown, that in his fall he crushed in pieces so vast a body; and the hearts of his men were so inflamed with this his disaster, that, after his death, they made the palm and the lawrel to spring out of his blood. Nor was the life of this prince less famous than his death.

His youth was exercised in great affairs, which hardened his body to endure travel, and armed his mind against all sinister accidents, and infused into him a courage, which might easily be provoked, never subdued. The entry of his reign (which was the eleventh of this age, and the seventeenth of his) was thorny and salebrous. At one and the same time, he was confronted by the Danes, the Polonians, and the Muscovites, who on all sides assaulted him: and, though their motives to war were divers, yet all their intentions, like so many lines, met in this center, to ruin the Swede. Sometimes he shewed himself on the frontiers of Denmark, sometimes on those of Muscovy, sometimes again on those of Livonia, and all with that promptness and celerity, that his enemies believed his body to be ubiquitary. And his troubles were increased by the corruption of many of his subjects to a base revolt. But his valour, his dexterity, and the continual travel of his body and mind were such, that he passed through these, and greater impediments without stop, or diminution of his fame. His composition with the Danes and Muscovites was honourable, and to his advantage. The quarrel between him and the Polonian was not about any small petty territory, but the crown and scepter itself, and therefore hardly to be decided.

The prowess and agility of this king were such, that the Polonians saw him in all parts, like another Hannibal, before their gates; and, after many great losses received in Livonia, and Prussia, they took counsel of the pillow, and, to preserve the remainder of those countries unviolated, concluded to come to a treaty, on which attended a truce, which from their souls they wished had been a peace, whereby their repose might be eternised. Our youthful Mars had not a soul so narrow, as to be contented to wear only the lawrel of the North. More wreaths were prepared for him, and a theatre more spacious and glorious. Posterity will hardly believe, that what this prince hath done, was by a man feasible. That the conquest of so many vast provinces, and the ruin of so many armies, was the work only of two years, and a few months. That a puissant empire, formidable in her greatness, in her supports, in her extension, in her armies, in her conquests, and success, fortified with so many garisons, who hath for her bounds the ocean, and the Alps, should, in so short a time, be forced to put on the yoke. A man would think infinite forces were required, to manage well an enterprise of this nature and greatness.

The personal qualities of this prince were admirable. His external bravery consisted in a sweet, yet majestical aspect, in a comely stature, in a piercing eye, in a commanding voice, in an agility, and universal application to all such as might hinder, or further him. But the great guests, that lodged within, were far more illustrious ; a quick spirit, a solid judgment, an incomparable wisdom, an inexpressible courage, an indefatigable nature, and an admirable conduct, which were the happy instruments of all his victories, and the embellishment of this rare piece. I may justly add his incampments, his discipline, his foresight, his direction, and unequalled industry. Nor was his readiness less in the disposition of his affairs, in the government of his men, and his complying with their several humours, which made him as well lord of hearts as provinces and cities. But, above all the rest, his devotion was conspicuous, and his frequent pious exercises, which received no interruption by his most serious employments: and (which draweth near to a miracle) he himself projected and executed all things. It sufficed not him to be only a general, but he would also be a captain, an engineer, a serjeant, a cannoneer, a common soldier, or of any military calling. The most dangerous occurrences dazzled not his judgment, but then was he most venturous, when his valour was most required. He never formed a military project, in the execution whereof he would not himself make one : and (which bred in all amazement) he was never weary, though ever busied, as if action had been his nourishment. I will close up the panegyrick of this worthy with this affirmation, that in him all imaginable brave parts conspired to make him the greatest, and most able captain of Christendom.

There was nothing in him the least way blameable, but his choler, to which the least provocation gave fire ; an humour familiar to fiery spirits chased with continual business, which often falls out cross : but he had a corrective ever ready, which was an overflowing courtesy, and sweetness to him natural, which stopped and repaired the breach his anger had made. For any hasty speech he would give satisfaction, not only to men of eminency, who might justly be offended, but to those also of the meanest condition, born to suffer. In acknowledgment of his nature so apt to take fire at the least distaste, he would often say, ' That he was willing oftentimes to bear with others infirmities, as the flegm of some, and the wine of others, and that therefore reciprocally his choler deserved some support.' And, to say truth, this passion may challenge and win connivance from him, who shall duly consider his working spirit, never weakened, though ever bended ; as also his extraordinary virtues, and his gentlenesss, which, upon occasion, made him familiar with the meanest of his soldiers; so far was he from being puffed up with prosperity, or raising his mind with his fortune.

Some note another oversight in this prince, that he did not better distinguish between the duties of a carabine, and a general, but exposed himself to all dangers, and was too prodigal of a blood so precious. To confess the truth, it is not so much to be wondered at, that he lost his life in this famous battle, as that he parted not with it long before, in so many encounters, where his life ran the same hazard with the basest of his soldiers. And in his defence this may worthily be annexed, that the valour of his men depended on his example, and all his victories had for their original his presence, and forwardness in all battles, which, like a heavenly aspect, sent down influences and irradiations into the spirits of his soldiers, and terror and amazement into those of his enemies.

The soldier hath attempted to draw this prince to the life; and assures himself, that they, who have had the honour to see and serve him in his wars, will confess, that the pourtrait hath some air of his face, if not drawn to the life: and he believes withal, that they, who have felt the puissance of his arms, will be the first to extol and magnify his worth, that thereby they may lessen their own losses, justify their disgraces, and shew to the world, that so powerful an organ was required to operate on them with such success.

Amongst other circumstances, this is the most agreeable and worthy of observation, that this prince hath left his affairs in a state so prosperous and advantageous. The Swedish party is possessed of two thirds of Germany, of the best cities, of most of the rivers from the Vistula to the Danube and the Rhine: it hath also ten armies dispersed through the higher and lower Saxonies, Silesia, Moravia, Bavaria, Franconia, Suabia, Alsatia, and the circle of the Rhine. This party is also backed and countenanced within by the principal forces of the empire, and without by great kings and states, who think themselves interested in the support of it, and prefer sure friends before doubtful and wavering, who will eternally remember the least loss or affront received, and, opportunity serving, be ready to revenge it. To this may be adjoined the experience of the times past, which demonstrates unto us how well, in the Mantuan war, they requited the benefits received from that house at a dead lift; which serves for an infallible argument of their dealings.

It now remains, that the princes and states united continue to make good the advantages bequeathed them, by banishing all jealousies, suppressing of factions, extirpating of schisms and partialities, deciding of all disputes arising from their genealogies, by conferring offices on men not of great descent, but ability; by making use of the times present and past; by quickly seconding their consultation with action, and by a straight conjunction of their councils and forces to seek their own preservation in that of the empire: in any of which, being wanting, neither the care and pains of the deceased king, nor their own armies or advantages, can secure them from being a miserable prey to their enemies, and wretched spectacle to their friends.

The truth is, hitherto the princes and generals united have much abated the pride of the enemy, by deceiving his hopes and apprehensions, and making it evident, by their proceedings, that they were not in vain so long trained up in the king's school, but were still mindful of his instructions and discipline; and that his death did but concenter and redouble their vigour. The Dukes of Weimar tread on Walstein's heels, whom some report to be wounded, others dead, in the forest which lies between Fravestein and Klostergrappe. If he be deceased, he serves as another sacrifice due to the king's tomb. Tubal keeps the greatest part of Silesia and Moravia in obedience; the Prince of Birkenfield shuts up all passages to the Bavarians within the circle of Ingoldstadt and Ratisbon; Horne is master of Alsatia, and hath joined to it the conquest of Schletstadt; Colman and Kentzingon have Senfield, nothing remaining in those parts unconquered, but Fribourg, which they batter, and Brisac, which they play with. Baudisin marcheth through the Archbishoprick of Cologne without resistance, and traverseth his galleries (maugre the Count of Gransfield) from the river of Wesper, even to the gates of Cologne. The troops of Wirtemberg advance towards the Lake of Constance, and are resolved to make good proof of their courage. To be brief, the Swedes shew, that they have no great desire to repass the sea, any more than have the Germans to refall into their wonted slavery.

But, though the King of Sweden hath left his party in an estate prosperous, yet we must needs confess, that the enemy derives from his death great advantages, and that the expence of a little lead hath profited him as much as the gaining of many millions, in that the several heads of the Swedish armies are subject and prone to jealousies and misconceptions; which gives him means and opportunity to preserve what he yet holds, to calm seditions, to recall long-banished peace, and once more to replant her in the empire.

If he make good use of his losses and infortunities, we shall see him forthwith to abandon all counsels tending to blood or violence; to have a care, lest, by the oppression of princes, he make them desperate; to recall his strayed subjects by a general pardon of all their offences, and seek to reign by love, not fear. He will then no more violate peace and the publick faith, under the pretext of conscience, which ought to be persuaded, not forced, as depending on another tribunal than that of men. This way to rest and quiet he is invited also to take, and persist in, because he may now peaceably enjoy all his due rights and titles, the death of the king having cured him of the deadly fear he was in, lest this magnanimous prince should yet soar higher, and aspire to new diadems, and make good his anagram, by changing the name of Gustavus into Augustus.

THE

KING'S MAJESTY'S DECLARATION

TO HIS SUBJECTS,

CONCERNING

LAWFUL SPORTS TO BE USED.

Imprinted at London, by Robert Barker, printer to the King's Most Excellent Majesty; and by the Assigns of John Bill, 1633. Quarto, containing twenty pages.

BY THE KING.

OUR dear father of blessed memory, in his return from Scotland, coming through Lancashire, found that his subjects were debarred from lawful recreations upon Sundays, after evening prayers ended, and upon holidays; and he prudently considered, that, if these times were taken from them, the meaner sort, who labour hard all the week, should have no recreations at all to refresh their spirits. And, after his return, he farther saw, that his loyal subjects, in all other parts of his kingdom, did suffer in the same kind, though, perhaps, not in the same degree; and did, therefore, in his princely wisdom, publish a declaration to all his loving subjects, concerning lawful sports to be used at such times; which was printed and published, by his royal commandment, in the year 1618, in the tenor which hereafter followeth:

BY THE KING.

WHEREAS, upon our return the last year out of Scotland, we did publish our pleasure, touching the recreations of our people in those parts, under our hand; for some causes us thereunto moving, we have thought good to command these our directions, then given in Lancashire, with a few words thereunto added, and most applicable to these parts of our realms, to be published to all our subjects.

Whereas we did justly, in our progress through Lancashire, rebuke some puritans and precise people, and took order, that the like unlawful carriage should not be used by any of them hereafter, in the prohibiting and unlawful punishing of our good people, for using their lawful recreations and honest exercises, upon Sundays and other holi-

N 3

days, after the afternoon sermon or service: we now find, that two sorts of people, wherewith that country is much infected (we mean papists and puritans) have maliciously traduced and calumniated those our just and honourable proceedings; and therefore, lest our reputation might, upon the one side (though innocently) have some aspersion laid upon it, and, upon the other part, our good people in that country be misled, by the mistaking and misinterpretation of our meaning, we have therefore thought good hereby to clear and make our pleasure to be manifested to all our good people in those parts.

It is true, that, at our first entry to this crown and kingdom, we were informed (and that too truly) that our county of Lancashire abounded more in popish recusants, than any county of England, and thus hath still continued since, to our great regret with little amendment; save that now of late, in our last riding through our said county, we find, both by the report of the judges, and of the bishop of that diocese, that there is some amendment now daily beginning; which is no small contentment to us.

The report of this growing amendment amongst them made us the more sorry, when, with our own ears, we heard the general complaint of our people, that they were barred from all lawful recreation and exercise upon the Sunday's afternoon, after the ending of all divine service; which cannot but produce two evils: the one, the hindering of the conversion of many, whom their priests will take occasion hereby to vex, persuading them, that no honest mirth or recreation is lawful, or tolerable, in our religion; which cannot but breed a great discontentment in our peoples's hearts, especially of such as are, peradventure, upon the point of turning. The other inconvenience is, that this prohibition barreth the common and meaner sort of people from using such exercises, as may make their bodies more able for war, when we, or our successors, shall have occasion to use them; and in place thereof, sets up filthy tipplings and drunkenness, and breeds a number of idle and discontented speeches in their alehouses: for, when shall the common people have leave to exercise, if not upon the Sundays and holidays? Seeing they must apply their labour, and win their living in all working days.

Our express pleasure therefore is, that the laws of our kingdom, and canons of our church, be as well observed in that county, as in all other places of this our kingdom; and, on the other part, that no lawful recreation shall be barred to our good people, which shall not tend to the breach of our aforesaid laws, and canons of our church: which to express more particularly, our pleasure is, that the bishop, and all other inferior churchmens, and churchwarden, shall, for their parts, be careful and diligent, both to instruct the ignorant, and convince and reform them that are misled in religion; presenting them that will not conform themselves, but obstinately stand out, to our judges and justices; whom we likewise command to put the law in due execution against them.

Our pleasure likewise is, that the bishop of that diocese take the like straight order with all the puritans and precisians within the same, either constraining them to conform themselves, or to leave the county, according to the laws of our kingdom, and canons of our church;

and so to strike equally, on both hands, against the contemners of our authority, and adversaries of our church. And, as for our good people's lawful recreation, our pleasure likewise is, That, after the end of divine service, our good people be not disturbed, letted, or discouraged from any lawful recreation, such as dancing, either men or women; archery for men, leaping, vaulting, or any other such harmless recreation; nor from having of May-games, Whitson-ales, and morrice-dances; and the setting up of May-poles, and other sports therewith used, so as the same be had in due and convenient time, without impediment or neglect of divine service; and that women shall have leave to carry rushes to the church, for the decoring of it, according to their old custom. But, withal, we do here account still as prohibited all unlawful games to be used upon Sundays only, as bear and bull-baitings, interludes, and, at all times, in the meaner sort of people by law prohibited, bowling.

And likewise we bar, from this benefit and liberty, all such known recusants, either men or women, as will abstain from coming to church or divine service, being therefore unworthy of any lawful recreation after the said service, that will not first come to the church and serve God: prohibiting, in like sort, the said recreations to any that, though conform in religion, are not present in the church, at the service of God, before their going to the said recreations. Our pleasure likewise is, that they, to whom it belongeth in office, shall present, and sharply punish all such as, in abuse of this our liberty, will use these exercises before the ends of all divine services, for that day. And we likewise straightly command, that every person shall resort to his own parish church to hear divine service, and each parish by itself to use the said recreation after divine service; prohibiting likewise any offensive weapons to be carried, or used in the said times of recreations. And our pleasure is, that this our declaration shall be published, by order from the bishop of the diocese, through all the parish churches; and that both our judges of our circuit, and our justices of our peace, be informed thereof.

> Given at our mannor of Greenwich, the four-and-twentieth day of May, in the sixteenth year of our reign of England, France, and Ireland, and, of Scotland, the one-and-fiftieth.

Now, out of a like pious care for the service of God, and for suppressing of any humours that oppose truth, and for the ease, comfort, and recreation of our well-deserving people, we do ratify and publish this our blessed father's declaration; the rather, because of late, in some counties of our kingdom, we find, that, under pretence of taking away abuses, there hath been a general forbidding, not only of ordinary meetings, but of the feasts of the dedication of the churches, commonly called Wakes. Now our express will and pleasure is, that these feasts, with others, shall be observed; and that our justices of the peace, in their several divisions, shall look to it, both that all disorders there may be prevented, or punished, and that all neighbourhood and freedom, with manlike and lawful exercises, be used. And we farther command our justices of assize, in their several circuits, to see, that no man do trouble or molest any of our loyal and dutiful people, in or for their lawful recreations, having first done their duty to God, and continuing in obedience to us and our laws: and of this we command all our judges, justices of the peace, as well within liberties as without, mayors, bailiffs, constables, and other officers, to take notice of, and to see observed, as they tender our displeasure. And we farther will, that publication of this our command be made, by order from the bishops, through all the parish churches of their several dioceses respectively.

Given at our palace of Westminser, the eighteenth day of October, in the ninth year of our reign.

GOD SAVE THE KING.

THE

OLD, OLD, VERY OLD MAN*:

O R,

THE AGE AND LONG LIFE OF

THOMAS PARR,

The Son of John Parr, of Winnington, in the Parish of Alberbury, in the County of Salop, (or Shropshire),

Who was born in the Reign of King Edward the Fourth, in the Year 1483.

He lived one hundred and fifty-two years, nine months, and odd days, and departed this life, at Westminster, the fifteenth of November, 1635, and is now buried in the Abbey at Westminster. His manner of life and conversation in so long a pilgrimage; his marriages, and his bringing up to London, about the end of September last, 1635. Whereunto is added a Postscript, shewing the many remarkable accidents that happened in the life of this Old Man.

WRITTEN BY JOHN TAYLOR.

London: printed for Henry Gosson, at his Shop on London-bridge, near to the Gate, 1635. Quarto, containing thirty-two pages.

To the High and Mighty Prince Charles, by the Grace of God, King of Great Britain, France, and Ireland, Defender of the Faith, &c.

OF subjects, my dread liege, 'tis manifest,
Y'have had the old'st, the greatest, and the least:

* This is the 235th article in the Catalogue of Pamphlets in the Harleian Library.

That, for an old, a great, and little man,
No kingdom, sure, compare with Britain can;
One, for his extraordinary stature,
Guards well your gates, and by instinct of nature,
As he is strong, is loyal, true, and just,
Fit, and most able, for his charge and trust.
The other's small and well composed feature
Deserves the title of a pretty creature:
And doth or may, retain as good a mind
As greater men, and be as well inclin'd:
He may be great in spir't, though small in sight,
Whilst all his best of service is delight.
The old'st your subject was; but, for my use,
I make him here the subject of my muse:
And as his aged person gain'd the grace,
That where his sovereign was, to be in place,
And kiss your royal hand; I humbly crave,
His life's description may acceptance have.
And, as your Majesty hath oft before
Look'd on my poems, pray, read this one more.
                    Your Majesty's
              Most humble subject and servant,
                              JOHN TAYLOR.

The occasion of this Old Man's being brought out of Shropshire to London.

AS it is impossible for the sun to be without light, or fire to have no heat; so is it undeniable that true honour is as inseparably addicted to virtue, as the steel to the loadstone; and, without great violence, neither the one or the other can be sundered. Which manifestly appears in the conveying out of the country of this poor ancient man; a monument, I may say, and almost miracle of nature.

For the Right Honourable Thomas Earl of Arundel and Surrey, Earl Marshal of England, &c. being lately in Shropshire to visit some lands and manors which his Lordship holds in that country, or for some other occasions of importance, which caused his Lordship to be there: the report of this aged man was certified to his honour; who hearing of so remarkable a piece of antiquity, his lordship was pleased to see him, and, in his innate noble and Christian piety, he took him into his charitable tuition and protection: commanding that a litter and two horses (for the more easy carriage of a man so enfeebled and worn with age) be provided for him; also, that a daughter-in-law of his, named Lucy, should likewise attend him, and have a horse for her own riding with him; and, to chear up the old man, and make him merry, there was an antick-faced fellow, called Jack, or John the Fool, with a high and mighty no beard, that had also a horse for his carriage. These all were to be brought out of the country to London by easy

journies, the charges being allowed by his lordship, and likewise one
of his honour's own servants, named Brian Kelley, to ride on horseback
with them, and to attend and defray all manner of reckonings and
expences; all which was done accordingly, as followeth :

Winnington is a hamlet in the parish of Alberbury, near a place called the Welch Pool, eight miles from Shrewsbury, from whence he
was carried to Wim, a town of the earl's aforesaid; and the next day
to Shefnall, a manor-house of his lordship's, where they likewise staid
one night; from Shefnall they came to Woolverhampton, and the next
day to Brimingham, and from thence to Coventry; and, although
Master Kelley had much to do to keep the people off that pressed
upon him in all places where he came, yet at Coventry he was most
oppressed; for they came in such multitudes to see the old man, that
those that defended him were almost quite tired and spent, and the
aged man in danger to have been stifled; and, in a word, the rabble
were so unruly, that Brian was in doubt he should bring his charge no
further, so greedy are the vulgar to hearken to, or gaze after novelties.
The trouble being over, the next day they passed to Daventry, to
Stoney Stratford, to Redburn, and so to London, where he is well
entertained and accommodated with all things, having all the aforesaid
attendants, at the sole charge and cost of his lordship.

One remarkable passage of the old man's policy must not be
omitted or forgotten, which is thus :

His three leases of sixty-three years being expired, he took his last
lease of his landlord, one Master John Porter, for his life, with which
lease he did live more than fifty years, as is further hereafter declared;
but this old man would, for his wife's sake, renew his lease for years,
which his landlord would not consent unto; wherefore old Parr, having been long blind, sitting in his chair by the fire, his wife looked out
of the window, and perceived master Edward Porter, the son of his
landlord, to come towards their house, which she told her husband,
saying, Husband, our young landlord is coming hither : is he so, said
old Parr; I prithee, wife, lay a pin on the ground near my foot, or at
my right toe; which she did; and when young Master Porter, yet
forty years old, was come into the house, after salutations between
them, the old man said, Wife, is not that a pin which lies at my foot ?
Truly, husband, quoth she, it is a pin indeed; so she took up the pin,
and Master Porter was half in amaze that the old man had recovered
his sight again; but it was quickly found to be a witty conceit, thereby
to have them to suppose him to be more lively than he was, because
he hoped to have his lease renewed for his wife's sake, as aforesaid.

He hath had two children by his first wife, a son and a daughter;
the boy's name was John, and lived but ten weeks; the girl was
named Joan, and she lived but three weeks. So that it appears he
did outlive the most part of the people that are living near there,
three times over.

The Life of Thomas Parr.

AN old man's twice a child, the proverb says,
And many old men ne'er saw half his days
Of whom I write; for he at first had life,
When York and Lancaster's domestick strife
In her own blood had factious England drench'd,
Until sweet peace those civil flames had quench'd.
Whenas Fourth Edward's reign to end drew nigh,
John Parr, a man that lived by husbandry,
Begot this Thomas Parr, and born was he
The year of fourteen hundred eighty-three;
And as his father's living, and his trade,
Was plough, and cart, scithe, sickle, bill, and spade,
The harrow, mattock, flail, rake, fork, and goad,
And whip, and how to load, and to unload;
Old Tom hath shew'd himself the son of John,
And from his father's function hath not gone.
    Yet I have read of as mean pedigrees
That have attain'd to noble dignities:
Agathocles, a potter's son, and yet
The kingdom of Sicily he did get.
Great Tamerlane a Scythian shepherd was,
Yet, in his time, all princes did surpass.
First Ptolomy, the King of Egypt's land,
A poor man's son of Alexander's band.
Dioclesian, Emp'ror, was a scriv'ner's son,
And Proba from a gard'ner th' empire won.
Pertinax was a bondman's son, and wan
The empire; so did Valentinian,
Who was the offspring of a rope-maker,
And Maximinus of a mule-driver.
And, if I on the truth do rightly glance,
Hugh Capet was a butcher, King of France.
By this I have digress'd, I have exprest
Promotion comes not from the east or west.
    So much for that, now to my theme again:
This Thomas Parr did live th' expir'd reigns
Of ten great kings and queens, th' eleventh now sways
The scepter, bless'd by th' ancient of all days.
He did survive the Edwards Fourth and Fifth,
And the Third Richard, who made many a shift
To place the crown on his ambitious head;
The Seventh and Eighth brave Henries both are dead,
Sixth Edward, Mary, Philip, Elizabeth,
And bless'd remember'd James—all these by death
Have changed life, and almost 'leven years since
The happy reign of Charles our gracious prince;

Tom Parr did live, as by record appears,
Nine months, one hundred fifty and two years.
Amongst the learn'd, 'tis held in general,
That every seventh year's climacterical,
And dang'rous to man's life, and that may be
Most perilous at th' age of sixty-three,
Which is, nine climactericals ; but this man
Of whom I write (since first his life began)
Did live of climactericals such plenty,
That he did almost outlive two-and-twenty.
For by records, and true certificate,
From Shropshire late, relations do relate,
That he liv'd seventeen years with John his father,
And eighteen with a master, which I gather
To be full thirty-five ; his sire's decease
Left him four years possession of a lease ;
Which past, Lew's Porter, gentleman, did then
For twenty-one years grant his lease agen :
That lease expir'd, the son of Lew's, call'd John,
Let him the like lease, and, that time being gone,
Then Hugh, the son of John (last nam'd before)
For one-and-twenty-years sold one lease more.
And lastly, he hath held from John, Hugh's son,
A lease for's life these fifty years out-run :
And, when old Thomas Parr to earth again
Return'd, the last lease did his own remain.
Thus having shew'd th' extension of his age,
I'll shew some actions of his pilgrimage.
   A tedious time a batchelor he tarry'd,
Full eighty years of age before he marry'd :
His continence to question I'll not call,
Man's frailty's weak, and oft doth slip and fall.
No doubt but he in fourscore years might find
In Salop's county, females fair and kind :
But what have I to do with that ? Let pass.
At th' age aforesaid he first marry'd was
To Jane, John Taylor's daughter ; and 'tis said,
That she (before he had her) was a maid.
With her he liv'd years three times ten and two,
And then she dy'd, as all good wives will do.
She dead, he ten years did a widower stay ;
Then once more ventur'd in the wedlock way :
And, in affection to his first wife Jane,
He took another of that name again,
With whom he late did live; she was a widow
To one nam'd Anthony, and surnam'd Adda :
She was (as by report it doth appear)
Of Gillsel's parish, in Montgom'ryshire,
The daughter of John Lloyd, corruptly Flood,
Of ancient house, and gentle Cambrian blood.

But hold, I had forgot, in's first wife's time,
He frailly, foully, fell into a crime,
Which richer, poorer, older men, and younger,
More base, more noble, weaker men, and stronger,
Have fallen into.
The Cytherean, or the Paphian game,
That thund'ring Jupiter did oft inflame;
Most cruel cut-throat Mars laid by his arms,
And was a slave to love's inchanting charms;
And many a pagan god, and semi-god,
The common road of lustful love hath trod:
For, from the emp'ror to the russet clown,
All states, each sex, from cottage to the crown,
Have, in all ages since the first creation,
Been foil'd, and overthrown with love's temptation:
So was old Thomas, for he chanc'd to spy
A beauty, and love enter'd at his eye,
Whose pow'rful motion drew on sweet consent,
Consent drew action, action drew content;
But, when the period of those joys were past,
Those sweet delights were sowrely sauc'd at last.
The flesh retains what in the bone is bred,
And one colt's tooth was then in old Tom's head:
It may be, he was gull'd as some have been,
And suffer'd punishment for others sin;
For pleasure's like a trap, a gin, or snare,
Or, like a painted harlot, seems most fair;
But, when she goes away, and takes her leave,
No ugly beast so foul a shape can have.
Fair Catherine Milton was this beauty bright,
Fair like an angel, but in weight too light,
Whose fervent features did inflame so far
The ardent fervour of old Thomas Parr,
That, for law's satisfaction, 'twas thought meet,
He should be purg'd, by standing in a sheet,
Which aged, he, one hundred and five year,
In Alberbury's parish church did wear.
Should all, that so offend, such penance do,
Oh, what a price would linnen rise unto?
All would be turn'd to sheets, our shirts and smocks,
Our table-linnen, very porters frocks,
Would hardly 'scape transforming; but all's one,
He suffer'd, and his punishment is done.
    But to proceed, more serious in relation,
He is a wonder, worthy admiration;
He's, in these times, fill'd with iniquity,
No antiquary, but antiquity;
For his longevity's of such extent,
That he's a living mortal monument.

And as high towers, that seem the sky to shoulder,
By eating time, consume away, and moulder,
Until, at last, in piece-meal they do fall,
Till they are buried in their ruins all :
So this old man his limbs their strength have left,
His teeth all gone, but one, his sight bereft,
His sinews shrunk, his blood most chill and cold,
Small solace, imperfections manifold :
Yet did his sp'rits possess his mortal trunk,
Nor were his senses in his ruins shrunk :
But that with hearing quick, and stomach good,
He'd feed well, sleep well, well digest his food.
He would speak heartily, laugh, and be merry,
Drink ale, and now and then a cup of sherry ;
Lov'd company, and understanding talk,
And, on both sides held up, would sometimes walk.
And, though old age his face with wrinkles fill,
He hath been handsome, and was comely still,
Well-fac'd, and, though his beard not oft corrected,
Yet neat it grew, not like a beard neglected ;
From head to heel, his body had all over
A quick-set, thick-set nat'ral hairy cover.
And thus (as my dull weak invention can)
I have anatomiz'd this poor old man.
    Though age be incident to most transgressing,
Yet time, well spent, makes age to be a blessing.
And, if our studies would but deign to look,
And seriously to ponder nature's book,
We there may read, that man, the noblest creature,
By riot and excess, doth murder nature.
This man ne'er fed on dear compounded dishes,
Of metamorphos'd beasts, fruits, fowls, and fishes.
The earth, and air, the boundless ocean,
Were never rak'd nor forag'd for this man ;
Nor ever did physician, to his cost,
Send purging physick through his guts in post :
In all his life-time he was never known,
That, drinking others healths, he lost his own.
The Dutch, the French, the Greek, and Spanish grape
Upon his reason never made a rape ;
For riot is for Troy an anagram,
And riot wasted Troy, with sword and flame ;
And surely that, which will a kingdom spill,
Hath much more power one silly man to kill ;
Whilst sensuality the palate pleases,
The body's fill'd with surfeits and diseases ;
By riot, more than war, men slaughter'd be,
From which confusion, this old man was free.

He once was catch'd in the venereal sin,
And, being punish'd, did experience win ;
That careful fear his conscience so did strike,
He never would again attempt the like.
Which to our understandings may express,
Men's days are shorten'd through lasciviousness :
And that a competent contenting diet
Makes men live long, and soundly sleep in quiet.
Mistake me not, I speak not to debar
Good fare of all sorts, for all creatures are
Made for man's use, and may by man be us'd
Not by voracious gluttony abus'd.
For he that dares to scandal or deprave
Good housekeeping ; Oh ! hang up such a knave :
Rather commend, what is not to be found,
Than injure that, which makes the world renown'd.
Bounty hath got a spice of lethargy,
And liberal noble hospitality
Lies in consumption, almost pin'd to death,
And charity benumb'd, ne'er out of breath.
May England's few good housekeepers be blest,
With endless glory, and eternal rest ;
And may their goods, lands, and their happy seed,
With heav'n's best blessings, multiply and breed.
'Tis madness to build high, with stone and lime,
Great houses, that may seem the clouds to clime :
With spacious halls, large galleries, brave rooms,
Fit to receive a King, Peers, 'Squires, and Grooms ;
Amongst which rooms, the devil hath put a witch in,
And made a small tobacco box the kitchin ;
For covetousness the mint of mischief is,
And christian bounty the high-way to bliss.
To wear a farm in shoe-strings edg'd with gold,
And spangled garters worth a copy hold :
A hose and doublet, which a lordship cost ;
A gawdy cloke, three manors price almost :
A beaver, band, and feather for the head,
Priz'd at the church's tythe, the poor man's bread ;
For which the wearers are fear'd, and abhorr'd,
Like Jeroboam's golden calves ador'd.
  This double, treble-aged man, I wot,
Knew and remember'd, when these things were not.
Good wholsome labour was his exercise,
Down with the lamb, and with the lark would rise ;
In mire and toiling sweat he spent the day,
And to his team he whistled time away :
The cock his night-clock, and, till day was done,
His watch, and chief sun-dial, was the sun.
He was of old Pythagoras' opinion,
That green cheese was most wholsome with an onion ;

Coarse meslin bread, and for his daily swig,
Milk, butter milk, and water, whey, and whig:
Sometimes metheglin, and by fortune happy,
He sometimes sip'd a cup of ale most nappy,
Cyder, or perry, when he did repair,
T'a Whitson ale, wake, wedding, or a fair:
Or when in Christmas time he was a guest,
At his good landlord's house amongst the rest:
Else he had little leisure time to waste,
Or, at the alehouse, huff-cap ale to taste;
Nor did he ever hunt a tavern fox,
Ne'er knew a coach, tobacco, or the pox.
His physick was good butter, which the soil
Of Salop yields, more sweet than candy oil;
And garlick he esteem'd above the rate
Of Venice treacle, or best Mithridate.
He entertain'd no gout, no ach he felt,
The air was good, and temp'rate, where he dwelt,
Whilst mavisses, and sweet tongu'd nightingales,
Did chant him roundelays, and madrigals.
Thus living within bounds of nature's laws,
Of his long lasting life may be some cause:
For, though th' Almighty all man's days doth measure,
And doth dispose of life and death at pleasure,
Yet, nature being wrong'd, man's days and date
May be abridg'd, and God may tolerate.
But had the father of this Thomas Parr,
His grandfather, and his great grandfather;
Had their lives threads so long a length been spun,
They by succession might, from sire to son,
Have been unwritten chronicles, and by
Tradition shew time's mutability:
Then Parr might say, he heard his father well
Say, that his grand-sire heard his father tell
The death of famous Edward the Confessor,
Harold, and William conq'ror, his successor;
How his son Robert won Jerusalem,
O'ercame the Saracens, and conquer'd them:
How Rufus reign'd, and's brother Henry next,
And how usurping Stev'n this kingdom vext:
How Maud the Empress, the first Henry's daughter,
To gain her right, fill'd England full of slaughter:
Of Second Henry's Rosamond the Fair,
Of Richard Cœur de Lyon, his brave heir,
King John, and of the foul suspicion
Of Arthur's death, John's elder brother's son.
Of the Third Henry's long reign, sixty years,
The barons wars, the loss of wrangling peers.
How Long-shanks did the Scots and French convince,
Tam'd Wales, and made his hapless son their prince.

How Second Edward was Caernarvon call'd,
Beaten by Scots, and by his Queen enthrall'd.
How the Third Edward fifty years did reign,
And th' honour'd Garter's order did ordain.
Next how the Second Richard liv'd and dy'd,
And how Fourth Henry's faction did divide
The realm with civil, most uncivil, war
'Twixt long contending York and Lancaster.
How the Fifth Henry sway'd, and how his son,
Sixth Henry, a sad pilgrimage did run.
Then of Fourth Edward, and fair Mistress Shore,
King Edward's concubine, Lord Hastings ————.
Then how Fifth Edward, murther'd with a trick
Of the Third Richard, and then how that Dick
Was by Seventh Henry slain at Bosworth Field,
How he and's son, th' Eighth Henry, here did wield
The scepter; how Sixth Edward sway'd,
How Mary rul'd, and how that royal maid
Elisabeth did govern, best of dames,
And, Phœnix-like, expir'd; and how just James,
Another Phœnix from her ashes claims,
The right of Britain's scepter, as his own,
But, changing for a better, left the crown,
Where now 'tis, with King Charles, and may it be
With him, and his most bless'd posterity,
Till time shall end; be they on earth renown'd
And after with eternity be crown'd.
Thus, had Parr had good breeding, without reading,
He from his sire, and grandsire's sire, proceeding,
By word of mouth hath told most famous things,
Done in the reigns of all those queens and kings.
But he in husbandry hath been brought up,
And ne'er did taste the Heliconian cup;
He ne'er knew history, nor in mind did keep
Aught, but the price of corn, hay, kine, or sheep.
Day found him work, and night allow'd him rest,
Nor did affairs of state his brain molest:
His high'st ambition was a tree to lop,
Or at the furthest to a may-pole's top;
His recreation, and his mirth's discourse,
Hath been the piper, and the hobby-horse.
And in this simple sort he did, with pain,
From childhood live to be a child again.
'Tis strange, a man, that was in years so grown,
Should not be rich; but to the world 'tis known,
That he that's born, in any land, or nation,
Under a twelve-pence planet's domination,
By working of that planet's influence,
Shall never live to be worth thirteen pence;

Whereby, altho' his learning did not shew it,
H'was rich enough to be, like me, a poet.
   But, e're I do conclude, I will relate
Of reverend age's honourable state :
Where shall a young man good instructions have
But from the ancient, from experience grave ?
Roboam, son and heir to Solomon,
Rejecting ancient counsel, was undone
Almost ; for ten of the twelve tribes fell
To Jeroboam, King of Israel ;
And all wise princes, and great potentates,
Select and chuse old men as magistrates,
Whose wisdom, and whose reverend aspect,
Knows how and when to punish, or protect.
The patriarchs long lives, before the flood,
Were given them, as 'tis rightly understood,
To store and multiply by procreations,
That people should inhabit and breed nations ;
That th' ancients their posterities might show
The secrets deep of nature, how to know
To scale the sky with learn'd astronomy,
And sound the ocean's deep profundity ;
But, chiefly, how to serve and to obey
God, who did make them out of slime and clay.
Should men live now, as long as they did then,
The earth could not sustain the breed of men.
Each man had many wives ; which bigamy
Was such increase to their posterity,
That one old man might see, before he dy'd,
That his own only offspring had supply'd
And peopled kingdoms.
But now so brittle's the estate of man,
That, in comparison, his life's a span ;
Yet, since the flood, it may be proved plain,
That many did a longer life retain,
Than him I write of ; for Arphaxad liv'd
Four hundred thirty-eight ; Salah surviv'd
Four hundred thirty-three years ; Eber more,
For he liv'd twice two hundred sixty-four.
Two hundred years Terah was alive,
And Abr'ham liv'd one hundred seventy-five.
Before Job's troubles, holy writ relates,
His sons and daughters were at marriage-states ;
And, after his restoring, 'tis most clear,
That he surviv'd one-hundred forty year.
John Buttadeus, if report be true,
Is his name, that is stil'd The Wand'ring Jew :
'Tis said, he saw our Saviour die, and how
He was a man then, and is living now ;

Whereof relations you that will may read ;
But pardon me, 'tis no part of my creed.
Upon a German's age 'tis written thus,
That one Johannes de Temporibus
Was armour-bearer to brave Charlemain ;
And that unto the age he did attain
Of years three hundred sixty-one, and then
Old John of Times return'd to earth again.
And noble Nestor, at the siege of Troy,
Had liv'd three hundred years, both man and boy.
Sir Walter Raleigh, a most learned knight,
Doth of an Irish countess, Desmond, write,
Of sevenscore years of age, he with her spake ;
The Lord St. Alban's doth more mention make,
That she was married in Fourth Edward's reign ;
Thrice shed her teeth, which three times came again.
The Highland Scots and the wild Irish are
Long-liv'd with labour hard and temp'rate fare.
Amongst the barbarous Indians, some live strong
And lusty, near two hundred winters long :
So, as I said before, my verse now says,
By wronging nature men cut off their days.
Therefore, as times are, he, I now write on,
The age of all in Britain hath out-gone :
All those, that were alive when he had birth,
Are turn'd again unto their mother earth :
If any of them live, and do reply,
I will be sorry, and confess I lye.
For, had he been a merchant, then, perhaps,
Storms, thunder-claps, or fear of after-claps,
Sands, rocks, or roving pirates, gusts and storms,
Had made him, long before, the food of worms :
Had he a mercer, or a silkman, been,
And trusted much, in hope great gain to win,
And late and early striv'd to get, or save ;
Or had he been a judge, or magistrate,
Or of great counsel in affairs of state ;
Then days important business, and nights cares,
Had long before interr'd his hoary hairs ;
But, as I writ before, no cares oppress'd him,
Nor ever did affairs of state molest him.
Some may object, That they will not believe
His age to be so much ; for none can give
Account thereof, time being past so far,
And, at his birth, there was no register :
The register was, ninety-seven years since,
Giv'n by th' Eighth Henry, that illustrious prince,
Th' year fifteen hundred forty, wanting twain,
And in the thirtieth year of that king's reign ;

> So old Parr now was almost an old man,
> Near sixty, e're the register began.
> I've writ as much as reason can require,
> How times did pass, how's leases did expire;
> And gentlemen o' th' county did relate
> T' our gracious king, by their certificate,
> His age, and how time with grey hairs hath crown'd him;
> And so I leave him older than I found him.

A POSTSCRIPT.

THE changes of manners, the variations of customs, the mutability of times, the shiftings of fashions, the alterations of religions, the diversities of sects, and the intermixture of accidents, which have happened since the birth of this old Thomas Parr, in this kingdom, although all of them are not to be held worthy of mentioning, yet many of them are worthy to be had in memory:

In the sixth year of his age, and in the second year of the reign of King Henry the Seventh, one Lambert Simnell, the son of a baker, claimed the crown, and was crowned King of Ireland, and proclaimed King of England, in the city of Dublin: This paltry fellow did put the King to much cost and trouble; for he landed with an army at Fawdrey in Lancashire, and, at a place called Stoke, the King met him, and, after a sharp and short battle, overcame and took him, and, pardoning him his life, gave him a turn-broachers place in the kitchen, and afterwards made him one of his falconers, anno 1487.

In the tenth year of his age, and the Eighth of Henry the Seventh, another youngster claimed the Crown, whose name was Perkin Warbeck, as some write, a tinker's son of Tournay; some say his father was a Jew; notwithstanding, he likewise put the King to much charge and trouble, for he was assisted with soldiers from Scotland and France; besides many joined with him in England, till at the last the King took him, and, on his true confession, pardoned him; he, falling again to his old practice, was executed at Tyburn, 1499.

The same year also, a shoemaker's son, dwelling in Bishopsgate-street, likewise claimed the crown, under the name of Edward, Earl of Warwick, the son of George, Duke of Clarence, brother to King Edward the Fourth; but this young shoemaker ended his claim in a halter at Saint Thomas a Waterings; which was a warning for him, not to surpass *Ne Sutor ultra Crepidam.*

Another counterfeit, the son of a miller, claimed the crown, in the second year of Queen Mary's reign, saying that he was King Edward the Sixth; but, the tenth of May, 1552, those royal opinions were whipped out of him for a while, till he fell to his old claim again, and purchased a hanging the thirteenth of March following. So much for impostures and counterfeits.

For religion, he hath known the time of divers sects and changes, as the Romish catholick religion from his birth, till the twenty-fourth year of King Henry the Eighth, the time of fifty years : And then, the twenty-sixth of his reign, the King's understanding being illuminated from above, he cast the Pope's authority out of this Kingdom, 1534, and restored the ancient and primitive religion, which continued under the title of Protestants, till the end of his son King Edward the Sixth's reign, which was near about twenty years; then was a bloody alteration, or return to papistry, for more than five years, all the reign of Queen Mary; since whose death, the protestant religion again was happily restored, continued, and maintained by the defenders of the true, ancient, catholick, and apostolick faith, these sixty-six years and more, under the blessed governments of Queen Elisabeth, King James, and King Charles. All which time, Thomas Parr hath not been troubled in mind for either the building or throwing down of abbies, and religious houses; nor did he ever murmur at the manner of prayers, let them be Latin or English. He held it safest to be of the religion of the King or Queen that were in being: for he knew that he came raw into the world, and accounted it no point of wisdom to be broiled out of it: His name was never questioned for affirming or denying the King's supremacy: He hath known the time when men were so mad as to kneel down and pray before a block, a stock, a stone, a picture, or a relick of a he or a she saint departed ; and he lived in a time when mad men would not bow their knee at the name of Jesus; that are more afraid to see a white surplice, than to wear a white sheet ; that despise the cross, in any thing but money ; that hold Latin to be the language of the beast, and hate it deadly, because the Pope speaks it; that would patch up a religion with untempered mortar, out of their own brains, not grounded upon the true corner-stone; who are furnished with a lazy idle faith ; that hold good works a main point of popery; that hold their religion truest, because it is contrary to all order and discipline, both of church and commonwealth : These are sprung up since old Tom Parr was born.

But he hath outlived many sectaries and hereticks; For, in the thirty-second year of the reign of King Henry the Eighth, 1540, the third of May, three anabaptists were burnt in the high-way, between Southwark and Newington. In the fourth year of King Edward the Sixth, one George of Paris, a Dutchman, was burnt in Smithfield, for being an Arian heretick, 1551; 1583, one John Lewis denied the godhead of Christ, and was burnt at Norwich, in the twenty-sixth year of Elisabeth. Not long before that, there was one Joan Butcher, alias, Joan of Kent, burnt for the like.

In the third year of Queen Elisabeth's reign, one William Geffrey affirmed one Iohn Moore to be Christ; but they were both whipped out of that presumptuous opinion, 1561.

In the seventeenth of Queen Elisabeth, the sect of the family of love began, 1575, but it took no deep root.

In the twenty-first of Queen Elisabeth, one Matthew Hamont was burned at Norwich for denying Christ to be our Saviour.

In the thirty-third of Queen Elisabeth, one William Hacket was hanged for professing himself to be Christ, 1591.

In the ninth year of King James, the eleventh of April, 1611, one Edward Wightman was burned a Litchfield for Arianism.

So much have I written concerning sects and heresies, which have been in this kingdom in his time; now I treat of some other passages.

He had outlived six great plagues. He was born long before we had much use of printing: For it was brought into this kingdom, 1472, and it was long after before it was in use.

He was above eighty years old before any guns were made in England, 1535.

The vintners sold no other sacks, muscadels, malmsies, bastards, Alicants, nor any other wines but white and claret, till the thirty-third year of King Henry the Eighth, 1543, and then was old Parr sixty years of age: All those sweet wines were sold till that time at the apothecaries for no other use, but for medicines.

There was no starch used in England, till a Flanders woman, one Mistress Dinghen Vanden Plasse, brought in the use of starch, 1564: And then was this man near eighty years old.

There were no bands wore till King Henry the Eighth's time; for he was the first king that ever wore a band in England, 1543.

Women's masks, busks, muffs, fans, perriwigs, and bodkins were invented by Italian courtezans, and transported through France into England, in the ninth of Queen Elisabeth.

Tobacco was first brought into England by Sir John Hawkins, 1565, but it was first brought into use by Sir Walter Rawleigh many years after.

He was eighty-one years old before there was any coach in England: For the first, that ever was seen here, was brought out of the Netherlands, by one William Boonen, a Dutchman, who gave a coach to Queen Elisabeth, for she had been seven years a Queen before she had any coach; since when, they have increased, with a mischief, and ruined all the best house-keeping, to the undoing of the watermen, by the multitudes of hackney or hired coaches: But they never swarmed so thick to pester the streets, as they do now, till the year 1605, and then was the gunpowder treason hatched, and at that time did the coaches breed and multiply.

He hath out lived the fashion, at least forty times over and over.

He hath known many changes of scarcity, or dearth, and plenty: But I will speak only of the plenty.

In the year 1499, the fifteenth of Henry the Seventh, wheat was sold for 4s. the quarter, or 6d. the bushel, and bay salt at 4d. and wine at 40 shillings the ton, which is about three farthings the quart.

In the first of Queen Mary, beer was sold for sixpence the barrel, the cask and all, and three great loaves for one penny.

In the year 1557, the fifth of Queen Mary, the penny wheaten loaf was, in weight, fifty six ounces, and in many places people would change a bushel of corn for a pound of candles.

So much shall suffice for the declaring of some changes and alterations that have happened in his time.

Now, for a memorial of his name, I will give a little touch. I will not search for the antiquity of the name of Parr, but I find it to be an honourable name in the twelfth year of King Edward the fourth; the King sent Sir William Parr, Knight, to seise upon the archbishop of York's goods, at a place called the Moor in Hartfordshire, 1472: This Sir William Parr was knight of the right honourable order of the garter.

In the twenty-second of Edward the Fourth, the same Sir William Parr went with an army towards Scotland, with Richard Duke of Gloucester.

In the year 1543, the thirty fifth year of King Henry the Eighth, July 22, the King was married to Lady Catharine Parr; and, the 24th of December following, the Queen's brother, William Lord Parr, was created Earl of Essex, and Sir William Parr, their uncle, was made Lord Parr of Horton, and chamberlain to the Queen; and the first of King Edward the Sixth, William Parr, Earl of Essex, was created Marquis of Northampton; and in the fourth year of King Edward's reign, 1550, the said marquis was made lord great chamberlain of England, and on the last of April, 1552, he, amongst other lords, mustered one-hundred brave well appointed horsemen of his own charge before King Edward, in the park at Greenwich, his cognisance or crest being the Maidenhead; in the first of Queen Mary, he took part with the lady Jane against the Queen, for which he was taken and committed to the Tower, July 26, and, contrary to expectation, released again shortly after, March 24.

Also, the first Queen Elisabeth, William Parr, Marquis of Northampton, sat, in Westminster Hall, lord high steward, upon a tryal of William Lord Wentworth, who came off most honourably acquitted, April 22.

After the death of King Henry the Eighth, Queen Catharine Parr was married to Sir Thomas Seymor, Lord high admiral, and she died, the second of September, 1548.

And thus I lay down the pen, leaving it to whomsoever can, or will, make more of this old man, than I have done.

A BRIEF RELATION

OF

CERTAIN SPECIAL AND MOST MATERIAL PASSAGES

AND

SPEECHES IN THE STAR-CHAMBER;

Occasioned and delivered, June the fourteenth, 1637, at the censure
of those three worthy Gentlemen,

DR. BASTWICKE, MR. BURTON, AND MR. PRYNNE,

As it hath been truly and faithfully gathered from their own mouths, by
one present at the said censure.

Printed in the Year 1638.   Quarto, containing twenty-eight Pages.   See number
fifty-two in the catalogue.

BETWEEN eight and nine o'clock in the morning, the fourteenth of
June, the lords being set in their places in the said court of Star-
chamber, and casting their eyes upon the prisoners, then at the bar,
Sir John Finch, chief justice of the Common Pleas, began to speak
after this manner.

I had thought Mr. Prynne had had no ears, but methinks he hath ears,
which caused many of the lords to take the stricter view of him ; and,
for their better satisfaction, the usher of the court was commanded to
turn up his hair, and shew his ears ; upon the sight whereof the lords
were displeased they had been formerly no more cut off, and cast out
some disgraceful words of him.

To which Mr. Prynne replied, My Lords, there is never a one of
your honours, but would be sorry to have your ears as mine are.

The Lord Keeper replied again, In good faith he is somewhat saucy.

I hope, said Mr. Prynne, your honours will not be offended, I pray
God give you ears to hear.

The business of the day, said the Lord Keeper, is to proceed on the
prisoners at the bar.

Mr. Prynne then humbly desired the court to give him leave to
make a motion or two ; which being granted, he moves,

First, That their honours would be pleased to accept of a cross bill
against the prelates, signed with their own hands, being that which
stands with the justice of the court, which he humbly craved, and so
tendered it.

Lord Keeper. As for your cross bill, it is not the business of the day; hereafter if the court should see just cause, and that it savours not of libelling, we may accept of it; for my part I have not seen it, but have heard somewhat of it.

Mr. Prynne. I hope your honours will not refuse it, being it is on his Majesty's behalf; we are his Majesty's subjects, and therefore require the justice of the court.

Lord Keeper. But this is not the business of the day.

Mr. Prynne. Why then, my Lords, I have a second motion, which I humbly pray your honours to grant, which is, That your lordships will be pleased to dismiss the prelates, here now sitting, from having any voice in the censure of this cause, being generally known to be adversaries, as being no way agreeable with equity or reason, that they, who are our adversaries, should be our judges; therefore we humbly crave they may be expunged out of the court.

Lord Keeper. In good faith, it is a sweet motion: Is it not? Herein you are become libellous; and, if you should thus libel all the Lords and reverend judges, as you do the most reverend prelates, by this your plea, you would have none to pass sentence upon you for your libelling, because they are parties.

Mr. Prynne. Under correction, my lord, this doth not hold; your honour need not put that for a certainty which is an uncertainty; we have nothing to say to any of your honours, but only to the prelates.

Lord Keeper. Well, proceed to the business of the day: Read the information.

Which was read, being very large, and these five books annexed thereunto, viz. A book of Dr. Bastwicke's written in Latin.

The second, a little book entitled, News from Ipswich. The third, intitled, A Divine Tragedy, recording God's fearful judgments on Sabbath-breakers. The fourth, Mr. Burton's book, intitled, An Apology of an Appeal to the King's most excellent Majesty, with two Sermons for God and the King, preached on the fifth of November last. The fifth and last, Dr. Bastwicke's Litany.

The King's council, being five, took each of them a several book, and descanted there, at the bar, upon them, according to their pleasure.

Mr. Attorney began first with Dr. Bastwicke's Latin book, picking out here, and there, particular conclusions, that best served for his own ends, as did all the other council, out of the former other books, to the great abuse of the authors; as themselves there immediately complained, intreating them to read the foregoing grounds, upon which the said conclusions depended, without which they could not understand the true meaning of them.

Next unto the attorney, Serjeant Whitfeild falls upon the reverend Mr. Burton's book, who vented much bitterness against that unreproveable book, as all that read it, with an honest and orthodox heart, may clearly perceive, swearing, in good faith, my lords, there is never a page in this book, but deserves a heavier and deeper censure than this court can lay upon him.

Next followed A. B. who in like manner descanted upon the News from Ipswich, charging it to be full of pernicious lyes, and especially vindicating the honour of Matthew Wren, Bishop of Norwich, as being a learned, pious, and reverend father of the church.

In the fourth place follows the King's sollicitor, Mr. Littleton, who acts his part upon the Divine Tragedy; to which part of it, concerning God's judgments on sabbath-breakers, he had little to say, but only put it off with a scoff, saying, That they sat in the seat of God, who judged those accidents, which fell out upon persons suddenly strucken, to be the Judgment of God for sabbath-breaking, or words to the like effect; but enlarged himself upon that passage, which reflected upon that late reverend, as he termed him, and learned professor of the law, and his Majesty's faithful servant, Mr. William Noy, his Majesty's late attorney, who, as he said, was most shamefully abused by a slander laid upon him; which was, that it should be reported, that Gods judgment fell upon him for so eagerly prosecuting that innocent person Mr. Prynne; which judgment was this, that he, laughing at Mr. Prynne, while he was suffering upon the pillory, was struck with an issue of blood in his privy part, which, by all the art of man, could never be stopped unto the day of his death, which was soon after : But the truth of this, my lords, saith he, you shall find to be as probable as the rest; for we have here three or four gentlemen, of good credit and rank, to testify, upon oath, that he had that issue long before; and thereupon made a shew, as if he would call for them in before the lords, to witness the truth thereof, with these particular words, Make room for the gentlemen to come in there, but no one witness was seen to appear; which was pretty delusion, and worth all your observations that read it; and so concluded, as the rest, that this book also deserved a heavy and deep censure.

Lastly, follows Mr. Herbert, whose descant was upon Dr. Bastwicke's Litany, picking out one or two passages therein; and so drawing thence his conclusion, that, jointly with the rest, it deserved a heavy censure.

The King's council having all spoken what they could, the Lord Keeper said to the prisoners at the bar;

You hear, gentlemen, wherewith you are charged; and now, lest you should say, you cannot have liberty to speak for your selves, the court gives you leave to speak what you can, with these conditions :

First, Thet you speak within the bounds of modesty.

Secondly, That your speeches be not libellous.

Prisoners. They all three answered, They hoped so to order their speech as to be free from any immodest or libellous speaking.

Lord Keeper. Then speak in God's name, and shew cause why the court should not proceed in censure, as taking the cause *pro confesso*, against you.

Mr. Prynne. My honourable good lords, such a day of the month, there came a *Subpœna* from your honours, to enter my appearance in this court; which being entered, I took forth a copy of the information; which being taken, I was to draw my answer; which I endeavoured to do, but, being shut up close prisoner, I was deserted of all means, by which I should have done it ; for I was no 'sooner served with the *Subpœna*, but I was shortly after shut up close prisoner, with suspension of pen, ink, and paper ; which close imprisonment did eat up such a deal of my time, that I was hindered the bringing in of my answer: You did assign me council, it is true; but they neglected to come to me, and I could not come to them, being under lock and key : Then, upon motion in court, ye gave me liberty to go to them ; but then, presently after that motion, I know not for what cause, nor upon whose command, I was shut up again ; and then I could not compel my council to come to me ; and my time was short, and I had neither pen, nor ink, nor servant to do any thing for me ; for my servant was then also close prisoner, under a pursuivants hands : This was to put impossibilities upon me. Then, upon a second motion for pen and ink, which was granted me, I drew up some instructions, and, in a fortnight's time, sent forty sheets to my council ; suddenly after, I drew up forty sheets more, and sent to them : My Lord, I did nothing, but by the advice of my council, by whom I was ruled in the drawing up of all my answer, and paid him twice for drawing it; and some of my council would have set their hands to it. Here is my answer, I tender it upon my oath, which your lordships cannot deny with the justice of the court.

Lord Keeper. We can give you a precedent, that this court hath proceeded, and undertaken a cause, *pro confesso,* for not putting in an answer in six days ; you have had a great deal of favour shewed, in affording you longer time ; and therefore the court is free from all calumny, or aspersion, for rejecting your answer, not signed with the council's hands.

Mr. Prynne. But, one word or two, my Lords, I desire your honours to bear me ; I put a case in law, that is often pleaded before your Lordships : One man is bound to bring in two witnesses; if both, or one of them, fail, that he cannot bring them in, doth the law, my Lords, make it the man's act ? You assigned me two counsellors ; one of them failed, I cannot compel him ; here he is now before you ; let him speak, if I have not used all my endeavours to have had him signed it ; which my other council would have done, if this would have set his hand to it with him ; and to have put in, long since.

Council. My Lord, There was so long time spent, e're I could do any thing, after I was assigned his council, that it was impossible his answer could be drawn up in so short a time, as was allotted; for, after long expectation, seeing he came not to me, I went to him, where I found him shut up close prisoner, so that I could not have access to him ; whereupon I motioned to the lieutenant of the Tower, to have free liberty of speech with him concerning his answer ; which being granted me, I found him very willing and desirous to have it drawn up ; whereupon I did move, in this court, for pen and paper ; which was granted ; The which he no sooner had gotten, but he set himself to draw up instructions, and, in a short time, sent me forty sheets ; and, soon after, I received forty more ; but I found the answer so long, and of such a nature, that I durst not set my hand to it, for fear of giving your honours distaste.

Mr. Prynne. My Lords, I did nothing, but according to the direction of my council; only I spoke mine own words; my answer was drawn up by his consent, it was his own act, and he did approve of it; and, if he will be so base a coward, to do that in private, which he dares not acknowledge in publick, I will not such a sin lie on my conscience, let it rest with him. Here is my answer; which, though it be not signed with their hands, yet here I tender it upon my oath, which you cannot in justice deny.

Lord Keeper. But, Mr. Prynne, the court desires no such long answer: Are you guilty, or not guilty?

Mr. Prynne. My good Lords, I am to answer in a defensive way: Is here any one, that can witness any thing against me? Let him come in. The law of God standeth thus: That a man is not to be condemned, but under the mouth of two or three witnesses. Here is no witness come in against me, my Lord; neither is there, in all the information, one clause, that doth particularly fall on me; but only, in general, there is no book laid to my charge. And, shall I be condemned for a particular act, when no accusation of any particular act can be brought against me? This were most unjust and wicked. Here I tender my answer to the information, upon my oath: My Lord, you did impose impossibilities upon me; I could do no more, than I was able.

Lord Keeper. Well, hold your peace; your answer comes too late: Speak you, Dr. Bastwicke.

Dr. Bastwicke. My honourable Lords, Methinks you look like an assembly of Gods, and sit in the place of God; ye are called the Sons of God: And, since I have compared you to gods, give me leave a little to parallel the one with the other, to see, whether the comparison between God and you doth hold in this noble and righteous cause. This was the carriage of Almighty God, in the cause of Sodom: Before he would pronounce sentence, or execute judgment, he would first come down, and see, whether the crime was altogether according to the cry that was come up. And with whom doth the Lord consult, when he came down? With his servant Abraham; and he gives the reason: " For I know," saith he, " that Abraham will command his children and houshold after him, that they shall keep the way of the Lord, to do justice and judgment." My good Lords, thus stands the case between your honour and us, this day: There is a great cry come up into your ears against us from the King's attorney; why now be you pleased to descend, and see if the crime be according to the cry; and consult, with God, not the prelates (being the adversary-part, and, as it is apparent to all the world, do proudly set themselves against the ways of God, and from whom none can expect justice, or judgment) but with righteous men, that will be impartial on either side, before you proceed to censure; which censure you cannot pass on us, without great injustice, before you hear our answers read. Here is my answer, which I here tender upon my oath. My good Lords, give us leave to speak in our own defence: We are not conscious to ourselves of any thing, we have done, that deserves a censure this day in this honourable court; but that we have ever laboured to maintain the honour, dignity, and prerogative royal of our sovereign Lord the King. Let my Lord the King live for ever! Had I a thousand lives, I should think them all too little to spend for the maintenance of his Majesty's royal prerogative. My good Lords, can you proceed to censure, before you know my cause? I dare undertake, that scarce any one of your lordships have read my books; and, can you then censure me for what you know not, and before I have made my defence? O, my noble Lords, Is this righteous judgment? This were against the law of God and man, to condemn a man before you know his crime. The governor, before whom St. Paul was carried (who was a very heathen) would first hear his cause, before he would pass any censure upon him; and, doth it beseem so noble and christian an assembly to condemn me, before my answer be perused, and my cause known? Men, brethren, and fathers, into what an age are we fallen! I desire your honours to lay aside your censure for this day, and inquire into my cause; hear my answer read; which if you refuse to do, I here profess, I will clothe it in Roman buff, and send it abroad unto the view of all the world, to clear my innocency, and shew your great injustice, in this cause.

Lord Keeper. But this is not the business of the day: Why brought you not in your answer in due time?

Dr. Bastwicke. My Lord, a long time since, I tendered it to your honour, I failed not in any one particular; and, if my council be so base and cowardly, that they dare not sign it, for fear of the prelates, as I can make it appear, therefore have I no answer? My Lord, here is my answer; which, though my council, out of a base spirit, dare not set their hands unto, yet I tender it upon my oath.

Lord Keeper. But, Mr. Doctor, you should have been brief; you tendered it in too large an answer, which, as I heard, is as libellous as your books.

Dr. Bastwicke. No, my Lord, it is not libellous, though large; I have none to answer for me, but myself, and, being left to myself, I must plead my conscience, in answer to every circumstance of the information.

Lord Keeper. What say you, Mr. Doctor? Are you guilty, or not guilty? Answer, yea or no; you needed not to have troubled yourself so much about so large an answer.

Dr. Bastwicke. I know, none of your honours have read my book: And can you, with the justice of the court, condemn me, before you know what is written in my books?

Lord Keeper. What say you to that was read to you even now?

Dr. Bastwicke. My Lord, he, that read it, did so murder the sense of it, that, had I not known what I had written, I could not tell what to have made of it.

Lord Keeper. What say you to the other sentence read to you?

Dr. Bastwicke. That was none of mine; I will not father that, which was none of my own.

Lord Dorset. Did not you send that book, as now it is, to a nobleman's house, together with a letter directed to him?

Dr. Bastwicke. Yes, My Lord, I did so; but, withal, you may see, in my epistle set before the book, I did at first disclaim what was not mine; I sent my book over by a Dutch merchant; who it was, that wrote the addition, I do not know; but my epistle, set to my book, made manifest what was mine, and what was not; and I cannot justly suffer for what was none of mine.

Lord Arundel. My Lord, you hear, by his own speech, the cause is taken *pro confesso.*

Lord Keeper. Yea, you say true, my lord.

Dr. Bastwicke. My noble Lord of Arundel, I know you are a noble prince in Israel, and a great peer of this realm: There are some honourable lords in this court, that have been forced out, as combatants in a single duel. It is between the prelates and us, at this time, as between two that have appointed the field; the one, being a coward, goes to the magistrate, and, by virtue of his authority, disarms the other of his weapons, and gives him a bulrush, and then challenges him to fight. If this be not base cowardice, I know not what belongs to a soldier. This is the case between the prelates and us: They take away our weapons (our answers) by virtue of your authority, by which we should defend ourselves, and yet they bid us fight. My Lord, Doth not this savour of a base, cowardly spirit? I know, my lord, there is a decree gone forth (for my sentence was passed long since) to cut off our ears.

Lord Keeper. Who shall know our censure, before the court pass it? Do you prophesy of yourselves?

Dr. Bastwicke. My Lord, I am able to prove it, and that from the mouth of the prelates own servants, that, in August last, it was decreed, That Dr. Bastwicke should lose his ears. O, my noble Lords, is this righteous judgment? I may say, as the apostle once said, What whip a Roman? I have been a soldier, able to lead an army into the field, to fight valiantly for the honour of their prince: Now I am a physician, able to cure nobles, kings, princes, and emperors: And to curtalise a Roman's ears, like a cur, O, my honourable Lords, is it not too base an act for so noble an assembly, and for so righteous and honourable a cause? The cause, my Lords, is great; it concerns the glory of God, the honour of our king, whose prerogative we labour to maintain, and to set up in a high manner, in which your honours liberties are engaged: And doth not such a cause deserve your lordships consideration, before you proceed to censure? Your honours may be pleased to consider, that, in the last cause, heard and censured in this court, between Sir James Bagge and the Lord Moone, wherein your lordships took a great deal of pains, with a great deal of patience, to hear the bills on both sides, with all the answers and depositions largely laid open before you: Which cause, when you had fully heard, some of your honours, now sitting in the court, said, you could not, in conscience, proceed to censure, till you had taken some time to recollect yourselves. If, in a cause of that nature, you could spend so much time, and afterwards recollect yourselves, before you would pass censure, how much more should it move your honours to take some time in a cause, wherein the glory of God, the prerogative of his Majesty, your honours dignity, and the subjects liberty, is so largely engaged? My good Lords, it may fall out to be any of your lordships cases, to stand as delinquents at this bar, as we now do : It is not unknown to your honours, the next cause, that is to succeed ours, is touching a person that sometimes hath been in greatest power in this court: and, if the mutations and revolutions of persons and times be such, then I do most humbly beseech your honours to look on us, as it may befall yourselves. But, if all this will not prevail with your honours to peruse my books, and hear my answer read, which here I tender, upon the word and oath of a soldier, a gentleman, a scholar, and a physician: I will clothe them, as I said before, in Roman buff, and disperse them throughout the christian world, that future generations may see the innocency of this cause, and your honours unjust proceedings in it; all which I will do, though it cost me my life.

Lord Keeper. Mr. Doctor, I thought you would be angry.

Dr. Bastwicke. No, My Lord, you are mistaken, I am not angry nor passionate; all that I do press is, that you would be pleased to peruse my answer.

Lord Keeper. Well, hold your peace. Mr. Burton, what say you?

Mr. Burton. My good Lords, your honours (it should seem) do determine to censure us, and take our cause *pro confesso,* although we have laboured to give your honours satisfaction in all things: My Lords, What have you to say against my book? I confess I did write it, yet did I not any thing out of intent of commotion or sedition : I delivered nothing, but what my text led me to, being chosen to suit with the day, namely the fifth of November; the words were these, &c.

Lord Keeper. Mr. Burton, I pray stand not naming texts of scripture now, we do not send for you to preach, but to answer to those things which are objected against you.

Mr. Burton. My Lord, I have drawn up my answer to my great pains and charges, which answer was signed with my council's hands, and received into the court according to the rule and order thereof. And I did not think to have been called this day to a censure, but have had a legal proceeding by way of bill and answer.

Lord Keeper. Your answer was impertinent.

Mr. Burton. My answer (after it was entered into the court) was referr'd to the judges, but by what means I do not know, whether it be impertinent, and what cause your lordships had to cast it out, I know not. But, after it was approved of, and received, it was cast out as an impertinent answer.

Lord Finch. The judges did you a good turn to make it impertinent, for it was as libellous as your book, so that your answer deserved a censure alone.

Lord Leeper. What say you, Mr. Burton, are you guilty, or not?

Mr. Burton. My Lord, I desire you not only to peruse my book, here and there, but every passage of it.

Lord Keeper. Mr. Burton, Time is short, are you guilty, or not guilty? What say you to that which was read? doth it become a minister to deliver himself in such a railing and scandalous way?

Mr. Burton. In my judgment, and as I can prove it, it was neither railing nor scandalous; I conceive that a minister hath a larger liberty than always to go in a mild strain: I being the pastor of my people, whom I had in charge, and was to instruct, I supposed it was my duty to inform them of those innovations, that are crept into the church, as likewise of the danger and ill consequence of them: As for my answer, ye blotted out what ye would, and then the rest, which made best for your own ends, you would have to stand; and now for me to tender only what will serve for your own turns, and renounce the rest, were to desert my cause, which before I will do, or desert my conscience, I will rather desert my body, and deliver it up to your lordships to do with it, what you will.

Lord Keeper. This is a place where you should crave mercy and favour, Mr. Burton, and not stand upon such terms as you do.

Mr. Burton. There wherein I have offended through human frailty, I crave of God and man pardon: And I pray God, that, in your sentence, you may so censure us, that you may not sin against the Lord.

Thus the prisoners, desiring to speak a little more for themselves, were commanded to silence. And so the lords proceeded to censure.

The Lord Cettington's Censure.

I Condem these three men to lose their ears in the palace-yard at Westmister; to be fined five thousand pounds a man to his Majesty: And to perpetual imprisonment in three remote places of the kingdom, namely, the Castles of Caernarvon, Cornwall, and Lancaster.

The Lord Finch addeth to this Censure.

MR. Prynne to be stigmatised in the cheeks with two letters (S and L) for a seditious libeller. To which all the lords agreed. And so the Lord Keeper concluded the censure.

THE Execution of the lords censure in the Star-Chamber upon Dr. Bastwicke, Mr. Prynne, and Mr. Burton, in the palace yard at Westminster, the thirtieth day of June last 1637; at the spectation whereof the number of people was so great (the place being very large) that it caused admiration in all that beheld them, who came with tender affections, to behold those three renowned soldiers and servants of Jesus Christ, who came with most undaunted and magnanimous courage thereunto, having their way strewed with sweet herbs from the house out of which they came to the pillory, with all the honour that could be done unto them.

Dr. Bastwicke and Mr. Burton first meeting, they did close one in the other's arms three times, with as much expressions of love as might be, rejoicing that they met at such a place, upon such an occasion, and that God had so highly honoured them, as to call them forth to suffer for his glorious truth.

Then immediately after, Mr. Prynne came, the doctor and he saluting each other, as Mr. Burton and he did before. The doctor, then, went up first on the scaffold, and his wife immediately following came up to him, and, like a loving spouse, saluted each ear with a kiss, and then his mouth; whose tender love, boldness, and chearfulness so wrought upon the people's affections, that they gave a marvellous great shout, for joy to behold it. Her husband desired her not to be, in the least manner, dismayed at his sufferings: And so for a while they parted, she using these words : Farewel, my dearest, be of good comfort, I am nothing dismayed. And then the doctor began to speak these words.

Dr. Bastwicke. There are many that are, this day, spectators of our standing here, as delinquents, though not delinquents, we bless God for it. I am not conscious to myself, wherein I have committed the least trespass (to take this outward shame) either against my God, or my king. And I do the rather speak it, that you, that are now beholders, may take notice, how far innocency will preserve you in such a day as this; for we come here, in the strength of our God, who hath mightily supported us, and filled our hearts with greater comfort than our shame or contempt can be. The first occasion of my trouble was by the prelates, for writing a book against the Pope, and the Pope of Canterbury said I wrote against him, and therefore questioned me; but, if the presses were as open to us, as formerly they have been, we should shatter his kingdom about his ears. But be ye not deterred by their power, neither be affrighted at our sufferings; let none determine to turn from the ways of the Lord, but go on, fight courageously against Gog and Magog. I know there be many here who have set many days a-part for our behalf, let the prelates take notice of it, and they have sent up strong prayers to heaven for us. We feel the strength and benefit of them at this time, I would have you to take notice of it, we have felt the strength and benefit of your prayers all along this cause. In a word, so far I am from base fear, or caring for any thing that they can do, or cast upon me, that, had I as much blood as would swell the Thames, I would shed it every drop in this cause, therefore be not any of you discouraged; be not daunted at their power, ever labouring to preserve innocency, and keep peace within; go on in the strength of your God, and he will never fail you in such a day as this; as I said before, so I say again, had I as many lives as I have hairs on my head, or drops of blood in my veins, I would give them all up for this cause; this plot of sending us to those remote places, was first consulted and agitated by the Jesuits, as I can make it plainly appear. O see what times we are fallen into, that the lords must sit to act the Jesuits plots! For our own parts we owe no malice to the persons of any of the prelates, but would lay our necks under their feet to do them good as they are men ; but against the usurpation of their power, as they are bishops, we do profess enemies till doom's-day.

Mr. Prynne, shaking the doctor by the hand, desired him that he might speak a word or two. With all my heart, said the doctor.

The cause (said Mr. Prynne) of my standing here, is for not bringing in my answer, for which my cause is taken *pro confesso* against me. What endeavours I used for the bringing in thereof, that, God and my own conscience, and my council knows, whose cowardice stands upon record to all ages. For, rather than I will have my cause a leading cause, to deprive the subjects of that liberty which I seek to maintain, I rather expose my person to be a leading example, to bear this punishment: And I beseech you all to take notice of their proceedings in this cause: When I was served with a subpœna into this court, I was shut up close prisoner, that I could have no access to council, nor be admitted pen, ink, or paper, to draw up my answer by my instructions, for which I feed them twice (though to no purpose) yet, when all was done, my answer would not be accepted into the court, though I tendered it upon my oath. I appeal to all the world, if this was a legal or just proceeding. Our accusation is in point of libel, but supposedly, against the prelates; to clear this now, I will give you a little light what the law is in point of libel, of which profession I have sometimes been, and still profess myself to have some knowledge in; you shall find, in case of libel, two statutes: The one in the second of Queen Mary, the other in the seventh of Queen Elisabeth. That in the second of Queen Mary, the extremity and heighth of it runs thus: That, if a libeller doth go so far and so high as to libel against king or queen, by denomination, the height and extremity of the law is, that they lay no greater fine on him than an hundred pounds, with a month's imprisonment, and no corporal punishment, except he does refuse to pay his fine, and then to inflict some punishment instead of that fine at the month's end. Neither was this censure to be passed on him, except it was fully proved by two witnesses, who were to produce a certificate of their good demeanor for the credit of their report, or else confessed by the libeller. You shall find in that statute, 7 Elis. some further addition to the former of 2 Mariæ, and that only in point of fine and punishment, and it must still reach as high as the person of king or queen. Here this statute doth set a fine of two hundred pounds; the other, but one: This sets three months imprisonment, the former but one: So that therein only they differ. But in this they both agree, namely, at the end of his imprisonment to pay his fine, and so to go free without any further question: But, if he refuse to pay his fine, then the court is to inflict some punishment on him correspondent to his fine. Now see the disparity between those times of theirs, and ours. A libeller in Queen Mary's time was fined but an hundred pounds, in Queen Elisabeth's time two hundred: in Queen Mary's days but a month's imprisonment, in Queen Elisabeth's, three months; and not so great a fine, if they libelled not against king or queen. Formerly the greatest fine was but two hundred pounds, though against king or queen; now five thousand pounds, though but against the prelates, and that but supposedly, which cannot be proved : Formerly, but three months imprisonment; now perpetual imprisonment : Then, upon paying the fine, no corporal punishment was to be inflicted ; but now, infamous punishment with the loss of blood, and all other circumstances that may aggravate it. See now what times we are fallen into, when that libelling (if it were so) against prelates only, shall fall higher, than if it touched kings and princes.

That, which I have to speak of next, is this : The prelates find themselves exceedingly aggrieved and vexed against what we have written concerning the usurpation of their calling, where indeed we declare their calling not to be *jure divine*. I make no doubt but there are some intelligencers or abettors within the hearing, whom I would have well to know, and take notice of what I now say : I here in this place make this offer to them, that, if I may be admitted a fair dispute, on fair terms, for my cause, that I will maintain, and do here make the challenge against all the prelates in the king's dominions, and against all the prelates in Christendom, let them take in the Pope and all to help them, that their calling is not *jure divino*. I will speak it again, I make the challenge against all the prelates in the king's dominions, and all Christendom, to maintain, that their calling is not *jure divino*. If I make it not good, let me be hanged up at the hall-gate : Whereupon the people gave a great shout.

The next thing, that I am to speak of, is this : The Prelates find themselves exceedingly grieved and vexed against what I have written in point of law, concerning their writs and process, that the sending forth of writs and process in their own name, is against all law and justice, and doth intrench on his Majesty's prerogative royal, and the subjects liberties. And here now I make a second challenge against all the lawyers in the kingdom, in way of fair dispute, that I will maintain, the prelates sending forth of writs and process, in their own names, to be against all law and justice, and intrencheth on his Majesty's prerogative royal, and subjects liberty. Lest it should be forgotten, I speak it again, I here challenge all the whole society of the law upon a fair dispute to maintain, that the sending forth of writs and process, in the prelates own names, is against all law and justice, and intrencheth on the king's prerogative royal, and the subjects liberty. If I be not able to make it good, let me be put to the tormentingest death they can devise.

We praise the Lord, we fear none but God and the King. Had we respected our liberties, we had not stood here at this time. It was for the general good and liberties of you all, that we have now thus far engaged our own liberties in this cause. For, did you know, how deeply they have intrenched on your liberties in point of Popery, ; if you knew but into what times you are cast, it would make you look about you : And, if you did but see what changes and revolutions of persons, causes, and actions have been made by one man, you would more narrowly look into your privileges, and see how far your liberty did lawfully extend, and so maintain it.

This is the second time that I have been brought to this place ; who hath been the author of it, I think you all well know. For the first time, if I could have had leave given me, I could easily have cleared myself of that which was then laid to my charge : As also I could have done now, if I might have been permitted to speak ; that book for which I suffered formerly, especially for some particular words therein written, which I quoted out of God's word and ancient fathers, for which notwithstanding they passed censure on me ; that same book was twice licensed by publick authority, and the same words I then suffered for, they are again made use of, and applied in the same sense by Heylin, in his book lately printed, and dedicated to the king, and no exceptions taken against them, but are very well taken.

Aye, said Dr. Bastwicke, and there is another book of his licensed, wherein he rails against us three at his pleasure, and against the martyrs that suffered in Queen Mary's days, calling them schismatical hereticks ; and there is another book of Pocklington's licensed ; they be as full of lyes, as dogs be full of fleas ; but, were the presses as open to us, as they are to them, we would pay them, and their great master that upholds them, and charge them with notorious blasphemy.

Said Mr. Prynne, you all, at this present, see, there be no degrees of men exempted from suffering. Here is a reverend divine for the soul, a physician for the body, and a lawyer for the estate . I had thought they would have let alone their own society, and not have meddled with any of them ; and the next, for aught I know, may be a bishop. You see they spare none, of what society or calling soever ; none are exempted that cross their own ends. Gentlemen, look to yourselves, if all the martyrs, that suffered in Queen Mary's days, are accounted and called schismatical hereticks, and factious fellows : What shall we look for ? Yet, so they are called in a book lately come forth under authority ; and such factious fellows are we, for discovering a plot of Popery. Alas ! poor England, what will become of thee, if thou look not the sooner into thy own privileges, and maintainest not thine own lawful liberty ? Christian people, I beseech you all, stand firm, and be zealous for the cause of God, and his true religion, to the shedding of your dearest blood, otherwise you will bring yourselves, and all your posterities, into perpetual bondage and slavery.

Now the executioner being come, to scar him and cut off his ears, Mr. Prynne said these words to him, 'Come, friend, come burn me, cut me, I fear not ; I have learned to fear the fire of hell, and not what man can do unto me. Come, scar me, scar me, I shall 'bear in my body the marks of the Lord Jesus ;' which the bloody executioner performed with extraordinary cruelty, heating his iron twice to burn one cheek ; and cut one of his ears so close, that he cut off a piece of his cheek. At which exquisite torture, he never moved with his body, or so much as changed his countenance, but still looked up, as well as he could, towards heaven, with a smiling countenance, even to the astonishment of all the beholders, and uttering, as soon as the executioner had done, this heavenly sentence : ' The more I am beaten down, the more am I lift up ;' and, returning from the execution in a boat, made, as I hear, these two verses by the way, on the two characters branded on his cheeks :

S. L. STIGMATA LAUDIS.

STIGMATA maxillis bajulans insignia LAUDIS
Exultans remeo, victima grata Deo.

Which one since thus Englished:

S. L. LAUD'S SCARS.

Triumphant I return, my face descries
Laud's scorching scars, God's grateful sacrifice.

Mr. Burton's heavenly and most comfortable speech, which he made at the time of his suffering, both before, and while he stood in the pillory, which was something distant from the other double pillory, wherein Dr. Bastwicke and Mr. Prynne stood..

THE night before his suffering, about eight o'clock, when he first had certain notice thereof, upon occasion of his wife's going to ask the warden, whether her husband should suffer the next day, immediately he felt his spirits to be raised to a far higher pitch of resolution and courage to undergo his sufferings, than formerly he did; so as he intreated the Lord to hold up his spirits at that heighth all the next day, in his sufferings, that he might not flag nor faint, lest any dishonour might come to his Majesty, or the cause; and the Lord heard him: For all the next day, in his suffering, both before and after, his spirits were carried aloft, as it were upon eagle's wings, as himself said, far above all apprehension of shame or pain.

The next morning, being the day of his sufferings, he was brought to Westminster, and, with much chearfulness, being brought into the Palace-yard, unto a chamber that looked into the yard, where he viewed three pillories there set up. Methinks, said he, I see Mount Calvary, where the three crosses, one for Christ, and the other two for the two thieves, were pitched; and, if Christ were numbered among thieves, shall a Christian, for Christ's sake, think much to be numbered among rogues, such as we are condemned to be? Surely, if I be a rogue, I am Christ's rogue, and no man's. And, a little after, looking out at the casement towards the pillory, he said, I see no difference between looking out of this square window and yonder round hole, pointing towards the pillory; he said, It is no matter of difference to an honest man. And, a little after that, looking somewhat wishfully upon his wife, to see how she did take it, she seemed to him to be something sad, to whom he thus spake: Wife, why art thou so sad? To whom she made answer, Sweetheart, I am not sad. No, said he, see thou be not; for I would not have thee to dishonour the day, by shedding one tear, or fetching one sigh; for behold, therefore, thy comfort, my triumphant chariot, on the which I must ride for the honour of my Lord and Master. And never was wedding day so welcome and joyful a day, as this day is; and so much the more, because I have such a noble captain and leader, who hath gone before me with such undauntedness of spirit, that he saith of himself, I gave my back to the smiters, my cheeks to the nippers, they plucked off the

hair; I hid not my face from shame and spitting; for the Lord God
will help me, therefore shall I not be coufounded; therefore have I set
my face like a flint, and I know I shall not be ashamed. At length
being carried towards the pillory, he met Dr. Bastwicke at the foot of
the pillory, where they lovingly saluted and embraced each other; and,
parting a little from him, he returned, such was the ardency of his
affection, and most affectionately embraced him the second time, being
heartily sorry he missed Mr. Prynne, who was not yet come, before he
was gone up to his pillory, which stood alone next the Star-chamber,
and about half a stone's cast from the other double pillory, wherein the
other two stood, so as all their faces looked southward, the bright sun
all the while, for the space of two hours, shining upon them: Being
ready to be put into the pillory, standing upon the scaffold, he espied
Mr. Prynne, new come to the pillory, and Dr. Bastwicke in the pillory,
who then hasted off his band, and called for a handkerchief, saying,
'What, shall I be last, or shall I be ashamed of a pillory for Christ,
who was not ashamed of a cross for me?' Then, being put into the pillory, he said: 'Good people, I am brought hither to be a spectacle to
the world, to angels, and men; and, howsoever I stand here to undergo the punishment of a rogue, yet, except to be a faithful servant to
Christ, and a loyal subject to the king, be the property of a rogue, I
am no rogue; but yet, if to be Christ's faithful servant, and the king's
loyal subject, deserve the punishment of a rogue, I glory in it; and, I
bless my God, my conscience is clear, and is not stained with the guilt
of any such crime, as I have been charged with, though, otherwise, I
confess myself to be a man subject to many frailties and human infirmities. Indeed, that book intitled, 'An Apology of an Appeal,' with
sundry epistles, and two sermons, for God and the king, charged against
me in the information, I have, and do acknowledge, the misprinting excepted, to be mine, and will, by God's grace, never disclaim it, whilst I
have breath within me. After a while, he having a nosegay in his
hand, a bee came and pitched on the nosegay, and began to suck the
flowers very savourly; which he beholding, and well observing, said,
'Do ye not see this poor bee? She hath found out this very place, to
suck sweetness from these flowers; And cannot I suck sweetness in this
very place from Christ?' The bee sucking all this while, and so took
her flight. By and by he took occasion, from the shining of the sun,
to say, 'You see how the sun shines upon us; but that shines as well
upon the evil as the good, upon the just and unjust; but that the sun
of righteousness, Jesus Christ, who hath healing under his wings, shines
upon the souls and consciences of every true believer only, and no cloud
can hide him from us, to make him ashamed of us; no, not of our
most shameful sufferings for his sake; and why should we be ashamed
to suffer for his sake, who hath suffered for us? All our sufferings be
but flea-bitings to that he endured; he endured the cross, and despised
the shame, and is set on the right hand of God. He is a most excellent
pattern for us to look upon, that, treading in his steps, and suffering
with him, we may be glorified with him: And what can we suffer,
wherein he hath not gone before us even in the same kind? Was he not
degraded, when they scornfully put on him a purple robe, a reed in his

hand, a thorny crown upon his head, saluting him with ' Hail, King of the Jews,' and so disrobed him again? Was not he deprived, when they smote the shepherd, and the sheep were scattered? Was not violence offered to his sacred person, when he was buffetted and scourged, his hands and his feet pierced, his head pricked with thorns, his side gored with a spear, &c.? Was not the cross more shameful, yea, and more painful, than a pillory? Was not he stripped of all he had, when he was left stark naked upon the cross, the soldiers dividing his garments, and casting lots upon his vesture? And was not he confined to perpetual close imprisonment, in man's imagination, when his body was laid in a tomb, and the tomb sealed, lest he should break prison, or his disciples steal him away? And yet did he not rise again, and thereby bring deliverance and victory to us all, so as we are more than conquerors through him that loved us? Here then we have an excellent pattern indeed.' And all this he uttered, and whatsoever else he spoke, with marvellous alacrity.

One said unto Mr. Burton, Christ will not be ashamed of you at the last day: he replied, he knew whom he had believed, and that Christ was able to keep that he had committed to him against that day. One asked him how he did; he said Never better, I bless God, who hath accounted me worthy thus to suffer. The keeper, keeping off the people from pressing near the pillory, he said, Let them come, and spare not, that they may learn to suffer. This same keeper, being weary, and sitting him down, asked Mr. Burton if he were well, and bade him be of good comfort; to whom he replied, Are you well? If you be well, I am much more, and full of comfort, I bless God. Some asked him, if the pillory were not uneasy for his neck and shoulders? He answered, How can Christ's yoke be uneasy? This is Christ's yoke, and he bears the heavier end of it, and I the lighter; and, if mine were too heavy, he would bear that too: O, good people, Christ is a good and sweet master, and worth the suffering for! And, if the world did but know his goodness, and had tasted of his sweetness, all would come and be his servants; and, did they but know what a blessed thing it were to bear his yoke, O, who would not bear it? The keeper going about to ease the pillory, by putting a stone or brick-bat between, Mr. Burton said, Trouble not yourself, I am at very good ease, and feel no weariness at all; and espying a young man at the foot of the pillory, and perceiving him to look pale on him, he said, Son, Son, what is the matter you look so pale? I have as much comfort as my heart can hold, and, if I had need of more, I should have it. One asked him, a while after, if he would drink some aqua vitæ; to whom he replied, that he needed it not; for I have, said he, laying his hand upon his breast, the true water of life, which, like a well, doth spring up to eternal life. Pausing a while, he said, with a most chearful and grave countenance, I was never in such a pulpit before, but little do ye know, speaking to them that stood about him, what fruits God is able to produce from this dry tree: They looking stedfastly upon him, he said, Mark my words, and remember them well; I say, little do you know what fruits God is able to produce from this dry tree; I say, remember it well, for this day will never be forgotten; and, through these holes, pointing to the pillory, God can bring light to his church. The keeper going about again to mend the pillory, he said, Do not trouble yourself so much; but, indeed, we are the troublers of the world. By and by, some of them offering him a cup of wine, he thanked them, telling them, he had the wine of consolation within him, and the joys of Christ in possession, which the world could not take away from him, neither could it give them unto him. Then he looked towards the other pillory, and, making a sign with his hand, chearfully called to Dr. Bastwicke and Mr. Prynne, asking them how they did; who answered, Very well. A woman said unto him, Sir, every Christian is not worthy this honour which the Lord hath cast upon you this day. Alas, said he, who is worthy of the least mercy? But it is his gracious favour and free gift, to account us worthy, in the behalf of Christ, to suffer any thing for his sake. Another woman said, There are many hundreds, which, by God's assistance, would willingly suffer, for the cause you suffer for this day; to whom he said, Christ exalts all of us, that are ready to suffer afflictions for his name, with meekness and patience: but Christ's military discipline, in the use of his spiritual warfare in point of suffering, is quite forgotten; and we have, in a manner, lost the power of religion, in not denying ourselves, and following Christ, as well in suffering as in doing. After a while, Mr. Burton, calling to one of his friends for a handkerchief, returned it again, saying, It is hot, but Christ bore the the burthen in the heat of the day: let us always labour to approve ourselves to God in all things, and unto Christ, for therein stands our happiness, come of it what it will in this world.

A Christian friend said to Mr. Burton, The Lord strengthen you. To whom he replied, I thank you, and I bless his name, he strengthens me. For, though I am a poor sinful wretch, yet I bless God for my innocent conscience, in any such crime as is laid against me; and were not my cause good, and my conscience sound, I could not enjoy so much unspeakable comfort in this my suffering, as I do, I bless my God. Mrs. Burton sends commendation to him by a friend: he returned the like to her, saying, commend my love to my wife, and tell her, I am heartily chearful, and bid her remember what I said to her in the morning, namely, that she should not blemish the glory of this day with one tear, or so much as one sigh. She returned answer, that she was glad to hear him so chearful; and that she was more chearful of this day, than of her wedding-day. This answer exceedingly rejoiced his heart, who thereupon blessed God for her, and said of her, She is but a young soldier of Christ's, but she hath already endured many a sharp brunt, but the Lord will strengthen her unto the end; and he, having on a pair of new gloves, shewed them to his friends there about him, saying, My wife yesterday, of her own accord, bought me these wedding gloves, for this is my wedding-day.

Many friends spoke comfortably to Mr. Burton, and he again spoke as comfortably to them, saying, I bless my God that called me forth to suffer this day. One said to him, Sir, by this sermon, your suffering, God may convert many unto him. He answered, God is able to do it indeed. And then he called again to Dr. Bastwicke and Mr. Prynne, asked them how they did ? Who answered as before. Some speaking to him concerning that suffering of shedding his blood: he answered, What is my blood to Christ's blood? Christ's blood is a purging blood, but mine is corrupted and polluted with sin. One friend asked another standing near Mr. Burton, If there should be any thing more done unto him ? Mr. Burton, overhearing him, answered, Why should there not be more done? For what God will have done, must be accomplished. One desiring Mr. Burton to be of good chear: to whom he thus replied : If you knew my chear, you would be glad to be partaker with me ; for I am not alone. neither hath God left me alone in all my sufferings and close imprisonment, since first I was apprehended. The halbertmen standing round about, one of them had an old rusty halbert, the iron whereof was tacked to the staff with an old crooked nail ; which one observing, and saying, What an old rusty halbert is that? Mr. Burton said, This seems to me to be one of those halberts, which accompanied Judas when he went to betray and apprehend his master. The people, observing Mr. Burton's cheartulness and courage in suffering, rejoiced, and blessed God for the same. Mr. Burton said again, I am persuaded that Christ, my advocate, is now pleading my cause at the Father's right-hand, and will judge my cause, though none be found here to plead it, and will bring forth my righteousness as the light at noon-day, and clear my innocency in due time. A friend asking Mr. Burton, if he would have been without this particular suffering ? To whom he said, No, not for a world. Moreover, he said, that his conscience, the discharge of his ministerial duty and function, in admonishing his people to beware of the creeping in of popery and superstition, exhorting them to stick close unto God and the king in duties of obedience, was that which first occasioned his sufferings; and said, As for this truth I have preached, I am ready to seal it with my blood, for this is my crown both here and hereafter. I am jealous of God's honour, and the Lord keep us that we may do nothing that may dishonour him, either in doing or suffering ; God can bring light out of darkness, and glory out of shame : and what shall I say more ? I am like a bottle which is so full of liquor, that it cannot run out freely ; so I am so full of joy, that I am not able to express it.

In conclusion, some told him of the approach of the executioner, and prayed God to strengthen him. He said, I trust he will. Why should I fear to follow my master Christ ? who said, I gave my back to the smiters, and my cheek to the nippers, that plucked off my hair ; I hid not my face from shame and spitting, for the Lord God will help me, therefore shall I not be confounded ; therefore have I set my face like a flint, and I know that I shall not be ashamed.

When the executioner had cut off one ear, which he had cut deep and close to the head, in an extraordinary cruel manner : yet this champion of Christ never once moved or stirred for it, though he had cut the vein, so as the blood ran streaming down upon the scaffold, which divers persons standing about the pillory seeing, dipped their handkerchiefs in, as a thing most precious, the people giving a mournful shout, and crying for the surgeon, whom the crowd and other impediments for a time kept off, so that he could not come to stop the blood; this patient all the while held up his hands, and said, Be content, it is well, blessed be God. The other ear being cut no less deep, he then was freed from the pillory, and came down, where the surgeon, waiting for him, presently applied a remedy for stopping the blood, after a large effusion thereof; yet for all this he fainted not, in the least manner, though through expence of much blood he waxed pale. And one offering him a little wormwood water; he said, it needs not, yet, through importunity, he only tasted of it, and no more, saying, his master Christ was not so well used, for they gave him gall and vinegar, but you give me strong water to refresh me, blessed be God. His head being bound up, two friends led him away to an house provided for him in King's-street, where being set down, and bid to speak little, yet he said after a pause, This is too hot to hold long : now, lest they in the room, or his wife, should mistake, and think he spoke of himself concerning his pain, he said, I speak not this of myself; for that which I have suffered is nothing to that my Saviour suffered for me, who had his hands and feet nailed to the cross: and, lying still a while, he took Mr. Prynne's sufferings much to heart, and asked the people how he did, for, said he, his sufferings have been great. He asked also how Dr. Bastwicke did, with much compassion and grief, that he, being the first that was executed, could not stay to see how they two fared after him. His wife, being brought to him, behaved herself very graciously towards him, saying, Welcome, sweetheart, welcome home. He was often heard to repeat these words : The Lord keep us that we do not dishonour him in any thing. *Amen.*

Thus, Christian Reader, you have heard the relation of such a censure, and the execution thereof, as I dare say, all circumstances laid together, cannot be paralleled in any age of man, throughout the Christian world, and I think I may take in even the world of Pagans and Heathens to it. Which though it be not drawn up in so elegant a strain as it was delivered and deserved, nor all the heavenly words and eloquent speeches recorded, which were uttered by these three worthies of the Lord, both in the presence of the Lords themselves at their censure, and also at the place of execution : yet I earnestly beseech you, in the bowels of Jesus Christ, that you do not in the least manner undervalue the glory and dignity, either of the persons, or the cause, but rather lay the blame upon the rudeness and mean capacity of the composer, who is an unfeigned well-wisher to them both.

THEEVES FALLING OUT,

TRUE MEN COME BY THEIR GOODS;

o r,

THE BEL-MAN WANTED A CLAPPER.

A Peale of new Villainies rung out:

BEING MUSICALL TO ALL

GENTLEMEN, LAWYERS, FARMERS,

And all Sorts of People that come up to the Tearme :

SHEWING,

That the Villanies of lewd Women doe, by many Degrees, excell those of Men.

BY ROBERT GREENE.

Goe not by me, but buy me, and get by me.

London, printed for Henry and Moses Bell, 1637. In black letter. Quarto, containing forty-eight pages.

To all Gentlemen, Merchants, Apprentices, and Country Farmers, Health.

NEWS and green bushes at taverns new set up; every man hath his penny to spend at a pinte in the one, and every man his eare open to receive the sound of the other. It is the language, at first meetings, used in all countries, What news? In court it is the mornings saluta-tion, and noones table-talke; by night it is stale. In citty, it is more common then What doe you lack? And, in the countrey, whistling at plough is not of greater antiquity. Walke in the middle of Pauls, and gentlemens teeth walke not faster at ordinaries, then there a whole day together about enquiry after news.

News, then, being a fish that's caught evry day, and yet a meate for every man's table, I thinke it not amisse to invite all men to a feast of such news, as hath of late, in shoales, come into my net. I will not hold a byrd in a cage to sing strange notes to my selfe, but let her forth to delight others; and albeit, about two or three years past, the ugly faces of divers damned abuses were set naked upon every post, their vizards being flaid off, both by lanthorne and candle-light, and by the Belman of London, yet villany, when it runnes to seed, being of all other graines the most fruitfull and luxuriant, the candle-light was burnt to a snuf, and the belman fast a sleepe, before these mon-sters, which now are hatcht forth, crept out of their dennes.

In Westminster, the Strand, Holborn, and the chiefe places of resort about London, doe they every day build their nests, every houre fiidge, and in tearme time especially flutter they abroad in flocks. You shall know them by their feathers; and, because, for the most part, they flie in payres, a cock and a hen' together, behold a couple newly alighted on the pearch, a he-foyst and a she-foyst: What they chyrp out, their own voyces can best deliver; and therefore listen to them. Suppose you heare the first set out a throat thus. Farewell.

ROBERT GREENE.

A Disputation between a He-foyst and a She-foyst, Stephen and Kate.

Stephen.

FAIRE Kate, well met, what news about your Westminster building, that you look so blithe? Your cherry-cheekes discover your good face, and your brave apparell bewrayes a fat purse: is fortune now a late grown so favorable to foysts, that your husband hath lighted on some large purchase? Or have your smoothe lookes link't in some young novice, to sweat for a favor all the byte in his boung, and to leave himselfe as many crownes, as thou hast good conditions; and then he shall be one of Pierce Pennilesse fraternitie? How is it, sweet wench, goes the world on wheeles, that you tread so daintily on your typ-toes?

Kate. Why, Stephen, are you pleasant or peevish, that you quip with suche briefe girds? Thinke you, a quartern winde will not make a quick sayle? That easy lifts cannot make heavy burthens? That women have not wiles to compasse crownes, as well as men? Yes, and more, for, though they be not so strong in the fists, they be more ripe in their wits; and it is by wit, that I live and will live, in despight of that peevish scholler, that thought with his conny-catching bookes to have cros-bit our trade. Dost thou marvell to see me thus briske? Faire wenches cannot want favors, while the world is full of amorous fooles. Where can such gyrls as my selfe be blemish't with a thredbare coat, as long as country farmers have full purses, and wanton citizens pockets full of pence?

Steph. Truth, if fortune so favour thy husband, that he be neither smoakt nor cloyde; for I am sure, all the bravery comes by nipping, foysting, and lifting.

Kate. In faith, Sir, No: did I get no more by mine own wit, then I reape by his purchase, I might both goe bare and pennilesse the whole yeere; but mine eyes are staules, and my hands lime-twigs (else, were I not worthy the name of a she conny-catcher) Cyrces had never more charmes, Calipso more inchantments, the Syrens more subtile tunes, then I have crafty sleights, to inveigle a cony, and fetch in a country farmer. Stephen, believe me, you men are but fooles, your gettings are uncertain, and yet you still fish for the gallows; though, by some great chance, you light upon a good boung, yet you fast a great while after; whereas we mad wenches have our tenants (for so I call every simple letcher and amorous fox) as well out of tearme, as in tearme, to bring us our rents : alas ! were not my wits and my wanton pranks more profitable then my husbands foysting, we might often goe to bed supperles, instead of surfeiting; and yet, I dare sweare, my husband gets a hundreth pounds a yeere, by boungs.

Steph. Why, Kate, are you grown so stiff, to thinke, that your faire lookes can get as much as our nimble fingers: or, that your sacking can gaine as much as our foysting? No, no, Kate, you are two bowes down the wind; our foyst will get more then twenty the proudest wenches in all London.

Kate. Lie a little farther, and give me some roome; what, Stephen, your tongue is too lavish, all stands upon proofe; and since I have leasure, and no great businesse, as being now when Pauls is shut up, and all purchases and connies in their burrowes, let us to the taverne, and take a roome to our selves, and there, for the price of our suppers, I will prove that women (I meane of our facultie, traffique, or, as base knaves tearme us, strumpets) are more subtile, more dangerous in the common-wealth, and more full of wiles to get crownes, then the cunningest foyst, nip, lift, prigs, or whatsoever that lives at this day

Steph. Content, but who shall be moderator in our controversies, sith, in disputing *pro & contra* betwixt ourselves, it is but your yea, and my nay, and so neither of us will yeeld to others victories.

Kate. Trust me, Stephen, I am so assured of the conquest, offering so the strength of mine own arguments, that, when I have reasoned, I will referre it to your judgement and censure.

Steph. And trust me, as I am an honest man, I will be indifferent.

Kate. O sweare not so deeply, but let me first hear what you can say for your selfe ?

Steph. What, why more, Kate, then can be printed out in a great volume, but briefly this : I neede not describe the lawes of villanie, because the bel-man hath so amply pend them down in the first part of conny-catching, that, though I be one of the faculty, yet I cannot discover more then he hath laid open.

Therefore, first, to the gentleman foyst, I pray you what finer quality ? What art is more excellent, either to try the ripenesse of the wit, or the agility of the hand then that, for he, that will be master of his trade, must passe the proudest juggler alive, the points of Leger de maine ; he must have an eye to spy the boung or purse, and then a heart to dare to attempt it, for this by the way, he that feares the gallows shall never be a good thiefe, while he lives ; he must, as the cat, watch for a mouse, and walke Paules, Westminster, the Exchange, and such common haunted places, and there have a curious eye to the person, whether he be gentleman, citizen, or farmer, and note, either where his boung lies, whether in his hose or pockets, and then dog the party into a prease, where his staule, with heaving and shoving, shall so molest him, that he shall not feele, when we strip him of his boung, although it be never so fast or cunningly couched about him : What poore farmer almost can come to plead his case at the bar, to attend upon his lawyers at the bench, but, looke he never so narrowly to it, we have his purse, wherein somtime, there is fat purchase, twenty or thirty pounds; and, I pray, how long would one of your traffiquers be earning so much with your chamber-work? Besides, in fayres and markets, and in the circuits after judges, what infinite mony is gotten from honest-meaning men, that either busie about their necessary affaires, or carelesly looking to their crownes, light among us that be foysts: Tush, we dissemble in shew, we goe so neate in aparrell, so orderly in outward apperance, some like lawyers clarks, others like servingmen, that attend there about their masters businesse, that we are hardly smoakt, versing upon all men with kinde courtesies and faire words, and yet being so warily watchfull, that a good purse cannot be put up in a faire, but we sigh, if we share it not amongst us. And though the books of conny-catching hath somewhat hindred us, and brought many brave foysts to the halter; yet some of our country farmers, nay of our gentlemen and citizens, are so carelesse in a throng of people, that they shew us the prey, and so draw on a thiefe, and bequeath us their purses, whither we will or no: For, who loves wine so ill, that he will not eate grapes, if they fall into his mouth? And who is so base, that, if he see a pocket fayre before him, will not foyst in, if he may, or, if foysting will not serve, use his knife and nip? For, although there be some foysts, that will not use their knives, yet I hold him not a perfect workman or master of his mistery, that will not cut a purse, as well as foyst a pocket, and hazard any limbe for so sweet a gain as gold: How answere you me this briefe objection, Kate? Can you compare with either our cunning, or get our gains in purchase?

Kate. And have you no stronger arguments, good man, Stephen, to argue your excellency in villany, but this? Then, in faith, put up your pipes, and give me leave to speake: Your chop-logike hath no great subtilty; for simply you reason of foysting, and appropriate that to your selves, to you men I mean, as though there were not women foysts and nips, as neate in that trade as you, of as good an eye, as fine and nimble a hand, and of as resolute a heart: Yes, Stephen, and your good mistresses in that mistery, for we, without like suspicion, can passe in your walkes, under the colour of simplicitie, to Westminster, with a paper in our hand, as if we were distressed women, that had som supplication to put up to the judges, or some bill of information to deliver to our lawyers, when surely we shuffle in for a boung as well as the best of you all, yea, as your selfe, Stephen, though you be called King of Cutpurses; for, though they smoake you, they will hardly mistrust us, and, suppose our stomack stand against it, to foyst, yet, Who can better play the staule or the shadow then we, for in a thrust or throng, if we shove hard, Who is he that will not favour a woman, and, in giving place to us, give you free passage for his purse? Againe, in the market, when every wife hath almost her hand on her boung, and that they cry, Beware the cutpurses and conny-catchers: Then I, as fast as the best, with my hand basket, as mannerly, as if I were to buy great store of butter and egs, for provision of my house, doe exclaime against them, with my hand on my purse, and say, The world is so bad, that a woman cannot walke safely to market, for feare of these villanous cutpurses; when as, the first boung I come to, I either nip or foyst, or else staule another, while he hath strucken, dispatcht, and gone.

Now, I pray you, gentle Sir, wherein are we inferiour to you in foysting? And yet this is nothing to the purpose: For it is one of our most simple shifts. But yet, I pray you, What thinke you, when a farmer, gentleman, or citizen come to the tearme, perhaps he is wary of his purse, and watch him never so warily, yet he will never be brought to the blow, Is it not possible for us to pinch him, ere he passe? He that is most chary of his crownes abroad, and will cry, Aware the conny-catchers, will not be afraid to drink a pinte of wine with a pretty wench, and, perhaps, go to a trugging-house to ferry one out for his purpose; then with what cunning we can feede the simple fopp, with what faire words, sweete kisses, fained sighs, as if, at that instant, we fell in love with him, that we never saw before? If we meet him in the evening in the streete, if the farmer, or other whatsoever, be not so forward as to motion some courtesie to us, we straight insinuate into his company, and claime acquaintance of him, by some meanes or other, and if his mind be set for lust, and the divell drive him on to match himselfe with some dishonest wanton, then let him looke to his purse; for, if he do but kisse me in the streete, Ile have his purse for a farewell, although he never commit any other act at all. I speake not this onely by my selfe, Stephen, for there be a hundred, in London, more cunning then my selfe in conny-catching. But, if he come into a house, then let our trade alone to verse upon him, for first we faine ourselves hungry for the benefit of the house, although our bellies were never so full, and, no doubt, the pander or bawde, she comes forth like a sober matron, and sets store of cates on the table, and then I fall a boord on them; and, though I can eate little, yet I make havock of all, and let him be sure every dish is well sauced, for he shall pay for a pippen pie, that cost in the market four pence, at one of the trugging-houses, eight pence: Tush, What is dainty, if it be not deare bought? And yet, he must come off for crownes besides, and, when I see him draw to his purse, I note the putting up of it well, and, ere we part, the world goes hard, if I foyst him not of all that he hath; and then, suppose the worst that he misse it, am I so simply acquainted, or badly provided, that I have not a friend, which, with a few terrible oathes and countenance set, as if he were the proudest souldado, that ever bare armes in the Low-country warres, will face him out of his money, and make him walke like a woodcocke home-ward by Weeping-crosse, and so by repentance, with all the crownes in his purse. How say you to this, Stephen, Whether are women foysts inferiour to you, in ordinary coozenage, or no?

Steph. Excellently well reasoned, thou hast told me wonders: But wench, though you be wily and strike often, your blowes are not so big as ours.

Kate. Oh, but note the subject of our disputation, and that is this, Which are more subtile and dangerous in the common-wealth, and to that I argue.

Steph. I, and beshrow me, but you reason quaintly; yet, will I proove your wits are not so ripe as ours, nor so ready to reach into the

subtilties of kinde coozenage; and though you appropriate to your
selfe the excellency of conny-catching, and that you doe it with more
art, then we men doe, because of your painted flatteries and sugred
words, that you flourish rethorically, like nets to catch fooles, yet, will,
I manifest, with a merry instance, a feate done by a foyst, that exceeded
any that ever was don by any mad wench in England.

———

*A pleasant Tale of a Country Farmer, that tooke it in scorne to have his
Purse cut or drawne from him, and how a Foyst served him.*

IT was told me of a truth, that not long since, here in London, there
lay a country farmer, with divers of his neighbours, about law matters;
amongst whom, one of them, going to Westminster Hall, was by a foyst
stripped of all the pence in his purse, and, comming home, made great
complaint of his misfortune; some lamented his losse, and others
exclaimed against the cutpurse; but this farmer he laught loudly at the
matter, and sayde such fooles, as could not keepe their purses no surer,
were well served; and, for my part, quoth he, I so much scorne the
cutpurses, that I would thanke him heartily that would take paines to
foyst mine: Well, sayes his neighbour, then you may thanke me, sith
my harmes learne you to beware; but if it be true, that many things
fall out betweene the cup and the lip, you know not what hands
fortune may put in your owne lap: Tush, quoth the farmer, heers
forty pounds in this purse in gold, the proudest cutpurse in England
win it and weare it: Thus he bosted. There stood a a subtile foyst by,
and heard all, smiling to himselfe at the folly of the proud farmer, and
vowed to have his purse, or venture his neck for it; and so went home,
and bewrayed it to a crue of his companions, who tooke it in dudgion,
that they should be put downe by a pesant: But, wheresoever they
met, they held a convocation, and both consulted, and concluded all,
by a generall consent, to bend all their wits to be possessors of this
farmers boung; and, for the execution of this their vow, they haunted
about the inne where he lay, and dogged him into divers places, both
to Westminster-Hall, and other places, and yet could never light upon
it; he was so watchfull, and smoakt them so narrowly, that all their
travell was in vain: At last, one of them fled to a more cunning policie,
and went and learned the mans name, and where he dwelt, and then he
hyed him to the counter, and entred an action against him of trespasse,
dammages two hundreth pounds: When he had thus done, he feed two
serjeants, and carried them downe with him to the mans lodging,
wishing them not to arrest him till he commanded them; well, agreed
they were, and downe to the farmers lodging they came, where were a
crue of foysts, whom he had made privie to the end of his practise,
stood waiting, but he tooke no knowledge at all of them, but walked
up and downe: The farmer came out, and went to Paules; the cutpurse bad stay, and would not yet suffer the officers to meddle with him,
till he came into the west end of Pauls Church-yard, and there he
willed them to doe their office, and they stepping to the farmer arrested

him: The farmer amazed, being amongst his neighbours, asked the serjeant at whose suite he was troubled? At whose suite soever it be, said one of the cutpurses that stood by, you are wronged, honest man, for he hath arrested you here in a place of priviledge, where the sheriffes nor officers have nothing to doe with you, and therefore you are unwise, if you obey him: Tash, sayes another cutpurse, though the man were so simple of himselfe, yet shall he not offer the church so much wrong, as, by yeelding to the mace, to imbolish Pauls libertie, and therefore I will take his part, and with that he drew his sword; another tooke the man and haled him away; the officer he stuck hard to him, and said he was his true prisoner, and cryed clubbes: The prentises arose, and there was a great hurly-burly, for they tooke the officers part, so that the poore farmer was mightily turmoyld amongst them, and almost haled in peeces: Whilest thus the strife was, one of the foysts had taken his purse away, and was gone, and the officer carried the man away to a taverne, for he swore he knew no such man, nor any man that he was indebted to as then. They sat drinking of a quart of wine; the foyst, that had caused him to be arrested, sent a note by a porter to the officer that he should release the farmer, for he had mistaken the man; which note the officer shewed him, and bad him pay his fees and goe his wayes. The poore countryman was content with it, and put his hand in his pocket to feel for his purse, but there was none; which made his heart farre more cold then the arrest did, and with that, fetching a great sigh, he said, Alas, masters, I am undone, my purse in this fray is taken out of my pocket, and ten pounds in gold in it, besides white money. Indeed, said the serjeant, commonly in such brawles, the cutpurses be busie, and I feare the quarrell was made upon purpose by the pickpockets. Well, sayes his neighbour, who shall smile at you now? The other day, when I lost my purse, you laught at me. The farmer brookt all, and sat male-content, and borrowed money of his neighbours to pay the serjeant; and had a learning, I beleeve, ever after, to brave the cutpurse.

How say you to this, Mistresse Kate? Was it not well done? What choise witted wench of your faculty, or she-foyst, hath ever done the like? Tush, Kate, if we begin once to apply our wits, all your inventions are folly towards ours.

Kate. You say good, goodman Stephen, as though your subtilties were sodaine as womens are; come but to the old proverbe, and I put you downe: 'Tis as hard to find a hare without a muse, as a woman without a scuse; and that wit, that can devise a cunning lye, can plot the intent of deep villanies. I grant the fetch of this foyst was pretty, but nothing in respect of that we wantons can compasse; and, therefore, to quit your tale with another, heare what a mad wench of my profession did relate to one of your faculty.

=====

A pleasant Tale how a Whore conny-catcht a Foyst.

THERE came out of the country a foyst, to try his experience here, in Westminster-Hall, and strooke a hand or two, but the divell a snap he would give to our citizen foysts, but wrought warily, and could not be fetcht off by no meanes; and yet it was knowne he had some twenty pounds about him, but he planted it so cunningly in his doublet, that it was sure enough for finding, although the city foysts laid all the plots they could, as well by discovering him to the gaylors, as otherways; yet he was so politicke, that they could not verse upon him by any meanes; which grieved them so, that, one day at dinner, they held a counsaile amongst themselves how to coozen him, but in vaine; till at last a wench, that sate by, undertooke it, so they would sweare to let her have all that he had; they confirmed it solemnly, and she put it in practise thus: She subtily insinuated her selfe into the foysts company, who, seeing her a pretty wench, began, after twice meeting, to waxe familiar with her, and to question about a nights lodging: After a little nice loving and biding, she was content for her supper, and what else he would bestow upon her, for she held it scorne, she said, to set a salary price on her body: The foyst was glad of this, and yet he would not trust her, so that he put no more but ten shillings in his pocket, but he had above twenty pounds quilted in his doublet. Well, to be short, supper time came, and thither comes my gentle foyst, who, making good cheere, was so eager of his game, that he would straight to bed by the leave of his Dame Bawd, who had her fee too, and there he lay till about midnight, where three or four old hacksters, whom she had provided upon purpose, came to the doore and rapt lustily. Who is there? says the bawd, looking out of the window. Marry, say they, such a justice (and named one about the citty that was a mortall enemy to cutpurses) who is now come to search your house for a jesuite, and other suspected persons. Alas, Sir, sayde she, I have none here. Well, quoth they, ope the doore? I will, sayes she: With that she came into the foysts chamber, who heard all this, and was afraid it was some search for him, so that he desired the bawd to helpe him, that he might not be seene. Why then, quoth she, step into the closet. He whipt in hastily, and never remembred his cloaths: She lockt him in safe, and then let in the crue of rake-hels, who, making as though they searcht every chamber, came at last into that where this lemman lay, and asked her what she was: She, as if she had been afraid, desired their worships to be good to her, she was a poore country maid come up to the tearme. And who is that, quoth they, that was in bed with you? None, forsooth, sayes she: No, sayes one, that is a lye; here is the print of two; and besides, wheresoever the foxe is, here is his skinne, for this is his doublet and hose: Then downe she falls upon her knees, and sayes, Indeede it was her husband: Your husband, quoth they, nay, that cannot be, Minion, for why then would you have denyed him at the first? With that, one of them turn'd to the bawd, and did question with her what he was, and where he was? Truely, Sir, sayes she, they came to my house, and said they were man and wife; and, for my part, I knew them for no other, and he, being afraid, is, indeede, to confess the troth, shut up in the closet.   No doubt, if it please your worship, sayes one rake-hell, I warrant you he is some notable cut-purse or pickpocket, that is afraid to shew his face: Come and open the closet, and let us looke on him? Nay, Sir, sayes she, not for to night; I beseech your worship carry no man out of my house, I will give my word he shall be forth-comming to morrow morning.   Your word, Dame Bawd, sayes one, 'tis not worth a straw.   You, huswife, that says you are his wife, you shall goe with us; and for him, that we may be sure he may not start, Ile take his doublet, hose, and cloake, and to-morrow Ile send them to him by one of my men; were there a thousand pounds in them, there shall not be a penny diminisht.   The whore kneeled down on her knees, and fained to cry pittyfully, and desired the justice, which was one of her companions, not to carry her to prison; Yes, huswife, quoth he, your mate and you shall not tarry together in one house, that you may make your tales all one: and, therefore, bring her away; and as for ye, Dame Bawd, see ye lend him no other cloathes, for I will send his in the morning betimes, and come you with him to answere for lodging him.   I will, Sir, sayes she; and so away goes the wench, and her companions, laughing, and left the bawd and the foyst. As soone as the bawd thought good, she unlockt the closet, and curst the time that ever they came in her house: Now, quoth she, here will be a faire adoe, how will you answere for your selfe? I feare me I shall be in danger of the cart.   Well, quoth he, to be short, I would not for 40 pounds come afore the justice.   Marry, no more would I, quoth she; let me shift, if you were conveyed hence, but I have not a rag of mans apparell in the house.   Why, quoth he, seeing it is early morning, lend me a blanket to put about me, and I will scape to a friends house of mine.   Then leave me a pawne, quoth the bawd: Alas, I have none, sayes he, but this ring on my finger: Why, that, quoth she, or tarry while the justice comes.   So he gave it her, tooke the blanket, and went his ways; whether I know not, but to some friends house of his.   Thus was this wily foyst, by the wit of a subtile wench, cunningly stript of all that he had, and turned to grasse to get more fat.

Kate. How say you to this devise, Stephen? Was it not excellent? What thinke you of a womans wit, if it can worke such wonders?

Steph. Marry, I thinke my mother was wiser then all the honest women of the parish besides.

Kate. Why, then belike, she was of my faculty, and a matrone of my profession, nimble of her hands, quick of her tongue, and light of her tayle; I should have put in Sir Reverence, but a foule word is good enough for a filthy knave.

Steph. I am glad you are so pleasant, Kate; you were not so merry when you went to Dunstable: But, indeede, I must needs confesse, that women foysts, if they be carefull in their trades, are, though not so common, yet more dangerous then men foysts; Women have quick wits, as they have short heels, and they can get with pleasure what we

fish for with danger ; but now, giving you the bucklers at this weapon,
let me have a blow at you with another.

Kate. But, before you induce any more arguments, by your leave in
a little by talke. You know, Stephen, that though you can foyst, nip,
prig, lift, curbe, and use the black art, yet you cannot crosbite without
the help of a woman ; which crosbiting, now adayes, is growne to a
marvelous profitable exercise ; for some cowardly knaves that, for feare
of the gallowes, leave nipping and foysting, become crosbites, knowing
there is no danger therein but a little punishment, at the most the pil-
lorie, and that is saved with a little *Vnguentum Aureum*, as for example :
W. C. is now a reformed man ; whatsoever he hath been in his youth,
now in his latter dayes he is growne a corrector of vice ; for, whosoever
he takes suspicious with his wife, I warrant you he sets a sure fine on
his head, though he hath nothing for his money but a bare kisse ; and,
in this art, we poore wenches are your sure props and stay. If you will
not beleeve me, aske poor A.B. in Turnemill Streete : What a saucy
signior there is, whose purblinde eyes can scarcely discerne a lowse from
a flea, and yet he hath such insight into the mistical trade of crosbiting,
that he can furnish his boord with a hundred pounds worth of plate : I
doubt the sand eyde asse will kicke like a westerne pugge, if I rubbe
him on the gall ; but 'tis no matter, if he finde him selfe toucht and
stirre, although he boasts of the chiefe of the cleargies favor, yet Ile so
set his name out, that the boyes at Smithfield Bars shall chalke him on
the back for a crosbite. Tush, you men are foppes in fetching novices
over the coles. Hearken to me, Stephen, Ile tell thee a wonder :
There dwelt here sometimes a good ancient matron, that had a fayre
wench to her daughter, as young and tender as a morrow masse priests
lemman ; her she set up to sale in her youth, and drew on sundry to
be suters to her daughter, some wooers, and some speeders ; yet none
married her, but of her beauty they made profit, and inveagled all, till
they had spent upon her what they had, and then, forsooth, she and her
young pigion turned them out of doors like prodigall children : She was
acquainted with Dutch, French, Italian, and Spaniard, as well as
English, and at last, so often as the pitcher goes to the brooke, that it
comes broken home, my fayre daughter was hit on the master veine,
and gotten with child ; and the mother, to colour this matter, to save
her daughters marriage, begins to weare a cushion under her owne
kirtle, and to faine her selfe with child, but let her daughter passe as
though she aild nothing : When the fortie weekes were come, and my
young mistresse must needes cry out, forsooth, this old B. had gotten
huswives answerable unto her selfe, and so brought her daughter to bed,
and let her goe up and downe the house, and the old crone lay in child-
bed as though she had beene delivered, and said the child was hers,
and so saved her daughters scape. Was not this a witty wonder,
M. Stephen, wrought by an old witch, to have a child in her age, and
make a young whore seeme an honest virgin ? Tush, this is a little to
the purpose, if I should recite all, how many she had coozened under
the pretence of marriage : Well, poore plaine Signior, see, you were
not stiffe enough for her, although it cost you many crownes, and the

losse of your service; Ile say no more, perhaps she will amend her manners. Ah, Stephen, how like you this geare? In crosbiting we put you downe; for, God wot, it is little lookt to in and about London; and yet I will say to thee, many a good citizen is crosbit in the yeere by odde walkers abroade.

Steph. I cannot deny, Kate, but you have set downe strange presidents of womens preiudiciall wits; but yet, though you be crosbytes, foysts, and nips, yet you are not good lifts: which is a great helpe to your faculty, to filch a boult of satten or velvet.

Kate. Stay thee a word, I thought thou hadst spoken of I. P. C. his wife; take heede, they be parlous folkes, and greatly acquainted with keepers and jaylors, therefore, meddle not you with them; for, I heard say, the belman hath sworne in dispight of the Brasil-staffe, to tell such a foule tale of him, in his second part, that it will cost him a dangerous joynt.

Steph. Kate, Kate, let I. P. beware, for, had not an ill fortune falne to the bel-man, he could take little harme.

Kate. Who is that, Stephen, D. W.

Steph. Nay, I will not name him.

Kate. Why then I pray thee, what misfortune befell him?

Steph. Marry Kate, he was strangely washt alate by a French barber, and had all the haire of his face most miraculously shaven off by the sytbe of God's vengeance, in so mueh that some said he had that he had not; but, as hap was, howsoever his haire fell off, it stood him in some stead, when that brawle was alate; for, if he had not cast off his beard, and so beene unknowne, it had cost him some knockes, but it fell out to the best.

Kate. The more hard fortune that he had such ill hap, but hasty journeyes breede dangerous sweates, and the phisicians call it the *Ale Peria*; yet, omitting all this, againe to where you left.

Steph. You have almost brought me out of my matter, but I was talking about the lift, commending what a good quality it was, and how hurtfull it was, seeing we practise it in mercers shops, with haberdashers of small wares, haberdashers of hats and caps, amongst merchant taylors, for hose and doublets, and in such places getting much gaines by lifting, when there is no good purchase abroad by foysting.

Kate. Suppose you are good at the lift, who be more cunning than we women, in that we are more trusted? For they little suspect us, and we have as close conveyance as you men: though you have cloakes, we have skirts of gownes, handbaskets, the crownes of our hats, our plackards, and for a neede, false bags under our smockes, wherein we may convey more closely then you.

Steph. I know not where to touch you, you are so witty in your answers, and have so many starting holes, but let me be pleasant with you a little; What say you to prigging or horse-stealing? I hope you never had experience in that faculty.

Kate. Alas! simple sot, yes, and more shift to shunne the gallowes then you.

Steph. Why, 'tis impossible.

Q 3

Kate. In faith, Sir, no, and for proofe, I will put you downe with a story of a mad, merry, little, dapper, fine wench, who at Spilsby faire had three horses of her own, or another mans, to sell; as she, her husband, and another good fellow, walked them up and downe the faire, the owner came and apprehended them all, and clapt them in prison; the jaylor not keeping them close prisoners, but letting them lye all in a chamber, by her wit she instructed them in a formall tale, that she saved all their lives thus: Being brought the next morrow after their apprehension, before the justices, they examined the men how they came by the horses, and they confest they met her with them, but, where she had them, they knew not; then was my pretty peat brought in, who, being a handsome trull, blusht as if she had beene full of grace; and being demanded where she had the horses, made this answere: May it please your worships, this man my husband, playing the unthrift, as many more have done, was absent from me for a quarter of a yeere, which grieved me not a little, insomuch that, desirous to see him, and having intelligence he would be at Spilsby faire, I went thither, even for pure love of him, on foote, and being within some ten miles off the towne, I waxed passing weary, and rested me often, and grew very faint; at last there came riding by me a servingman, in a blew coat, with three horses, tide at one anothers taile, which he led, as I gest, to sell at the faire; the serving-man, seeing me so tyred, tooke pitty on me, and askt me if I would ride on one of his empty horses, for his owne would not beare double. I thankt him hartily, and at the next hill got up, and rode till we came to a towne within three miles of Spilsby, where the serving man alighted at a house, and bade me ride on a fore, and he would presently overtake me. Well, forward I rode half a mile, and, looking behind me, could see nobody; so being alone, my heart began to rise, and I to thinke on my husband; as I had rid a little further, looking down a lane, I saw two lusty men comming up, as if they were weary, and marking them earnestly, I saw one of them was my husband, which made my heart as light as before it was sad; so staying for them, after a little unkind greeting betwixt us, for I chid him for his unthriftinesse, he asked me where I had the horse; and I told him how courteously the serving-man had used me; why then sayes he, stay for him; nay quoth I, lets ride on, and get you two upon the empty horses, for he will overtake us, ere we come at the town, he rides on a stout, lusty, young gelding; so forward we went, and lookt often behinde us, but our serving-man came not. At last we, comming to Spilsby, alighted and broke our fast, and tyed our horses at the doore, that, if he past by, seeing them, he might call in; after we had broke our fast, thinking he had gone some other way, we went into the horse faire, and there walkt our horses up and downe to meet with the serving-man, not for the entent to sell them. Now may it please your worships, whether he had stoln the horses from this honest man, or no, I know not; but alas simply I brought them to the horse faire, to let him, that delivered me them, have them againe; for I hope your worships do imagine, if I had stole them as it is suspected, I would never have brought them into so publike a place to sell; yet, if law be any way dangerous for the foolish deed, because I know not the serving-man, it is I must bide the punishment, and as guiltles as any here ; and making a low cursie, she ended ; the justice holding up his hand, and wondring at the woman's wit, that had cleerd her husband, and his friend, and saved herself without compasse of the law.   How like you this, Stephen, cannot we wenches prigge well ?

Steph. I thinke, Kate, I shall be faine to give you the bucklars.

Kate Alas, good Stephen, thou art no logitian, thou canst not reason for thy selfe, nor hast no witty argument to draw me to an exigent ; and therefore give me leave at large to reason for this supper.   Remember, the subject of our disputation is the positive question. Whether whores, or theeves, are most prejudiciall to the commonwealth ? Alas, you poore theeves doe only steale and purloyne from men, and the harme you doe is to imbollish mens goods, and bring them to poverty : This is the only end of mens theevery, and the greatest prejudice that growes from robbing and filching : So much doe we by our theft, and more by our lechery ; for, what is the end of whoredom, but consuming of goods and beggery, and, besides, perpetual infamy ? We bring young youthes to ruine and utter destruction.   I pray you, Stephen, whether had a merchants sonne, having wealthy parents, better light upon a whore, then a cutpurse ? The one onely taking his money, the other bringing him to utter confusion, For, if the foyst light upon him, or the conny-catcher, he loseth, at the most, some hundreth pounds ; but, if he fall into the company of a whore, she flatters him, she inveagles him, she bewitcheth him, that he spareth neither goods nor lands to content her, that is onely in love with his coyne.   If he be married, he forsakes his wife, leaves his children, despiseth his friends, onely to satisfie his lust with the love of a base whore, who, when he hath spent all upon her, and he brought to beggery, beateth him out like the prodigall child, and for a finall reward brings him, if to the fairest end, to begge ; if to the second, to the gallowes ; or, at the last and worst, to the pox, or as prejudiciall deseases.   I pray you, Stephen, when any of you come to your confession at Tyborne, what is your last sermon that you make ? That you were brought to that wicked and shamefull end by following of harlots ; for to that end do you steale, to maintaine whores, and to content their badde humours.   Oh Stephen, enter your owne thoughts, and thinke what the faire words of a wanton will do ; what the smiles of a strumpet will drive a man to act ; into what jeopardie a man will thrust himselfe for her that he loves, although for his sweete villany he be brought to a loathsome leprosie.

Tush, Stephen, they say the poxe came from Naples, some from Spaine, some from France ; but, wheresoever it first grew, it is so surely now rooted in England, that, by S. Syth, it may better be called a *Morbus Anglicus,* then *Gallicus ;* and I hope you will grant all these French favours grew from whores : Besides, in my high loving, or rather creeping, I meane, where men and women do rob together, there alwayes the woman is most bloudy ; for she alwayes urgeth unto death ; and, though the men would only satisfie themselves with the parties coyne, yet she endeth her theft in bloud, murdering parties so deepely as she is malicious.   I hope, gentle Stephen, you cannot contradict these reasons, they be so open and manyfestly probable.   For

mine owne part, I hope you do not imagine but I have had some
friends, besides poore George my husband : Alas, he knowes it, and is
content, like an honest, simple suffragan, to be corrivall with a number
of other good companions; and I have made many a good man, I
meane a man that hath a houshold, for the love of me, to goe home and
beate his poore wife, when, for repentance, I mock him for the
money he spent, and he had nothing for his pence, but the wast
beleavings of others beastly labours.

Stephen, Stephen, if concubines could inveagle Solomon, if Dalilah
could betray Sampson, then wonder not if we, more nice in our wickednesse than a thousand Dalilahs, can seduce poore young novices to their
utter destructions.   Search the gayles, there you shall heare complaints
of whores ; looke into the spittle and hospitalls, there you shall see
men diseased of the French marbles giving instruction to others, that
they are said to beware of whores.   Be an auditor, or care witnesse,
of the death of any theefe, and his last testament is, Take heede of
a whore.

I dare scarce speak of Bridewell, because my shoulders tremble at
the name of it, I have so often deserved it ; yet looke but in there,
and you shall heare poore men, with their hands in their pigeon-holes,
crie, Oh, fie upon whores, when Fowler gives them the terrible lash.
Examine beggers that lye lame by the high way, and they say they
came to that misery by whores.   Some threedbare citizens, that from
merchants and other good trades, grow to be base informers and
knights of the post, cry out, when they dyne with Duke Humfery, O
what wickednesse comes from whores! Prentices, that runne from their
masters, cry out upon whores.   Tush, Stephen, what enormities proceed
more in the common-wealth, then from whoredome? But, sith it is
almost supper-time, and mirth is the friend to digestion, I meane a little
to be pleasant.   I pray you, how many bad profits againe growes from
whores ? Bridewell would have very few tenants, the hospitall would want
patients, the surgeons much worke, the apothecaries would have
surphaling water, and potato rootes, lye dead on their hands ; the
painters could not dispatch and make away their virmillion, if tallow-
faced whores used it not for their cheekes ? What should I say more,
Stephen ? The suburbs should have a great misse of us ; and Shoreditch
would complain to dame Anne a Cleare, if we of the sisterhood
should not uphold her jollity.   Who is that, Stephen, comes in to heare
our talke ? Oh, 'tis the boy, Kate, that tells us, supper is ready.   Why
then, Stephen, what say you to me? have not I proved, that, in
foysting and nipping, we excell you ? That there is none so great
inconvenience in the common-wealth, as growes from whores? First,
for the corrupting of youth, infecting of age, and for breeding of
brawles, whereof ensues murther ; insomuch that the ruine of many
men comes from us, and the fall of many youths of good hope,
if they were not seduced by us, do proclaime at Tyborne, that we
be the means of their misery.   You men theeves touch the body and
wealth, but we ruine the soule, and endanger that which is more precious than the worlds treasure ; you make worke only for the
gallowes, we both for the gallowes and the divell, I and for the surgeon

too, that some live like lothsome lazers, and dye with the French marbles; whereupon I conclude, that I have wonne the supper.

Steph. I confesse it, Kate, for thou hast told me such wondrous villanies, as I thought never could have beene in women, I meane of your profession; who are crocodiles when you weep, basilisks when you smile, serpents when you devise, and the divells chiefe brokers to bring the world to destruction: And so, Kate, lets sit downe to our meate, and be merry.

Thus, countrymen, you have heard the disputation betweene these two coozening companions, wherein I have shak't out the notable villanie of whores, although mistress Kate, this good oratress, hath sworn to weare a long Hambrough knife to stab me, and, all the crue have protested my death; and, to prove they meant good earnest, they beleagred me being at supper: There were some fourteene or fifteene of them met, and thought to have made that the fatall night of my overthrow, but that the courteous citizens and apprentices tooke my part, and so two or three of them were carried to the counter, although a gentleman in my company was sore hurt. I cannot deny but they began to waste away about London, and Tyborn hath eaten up many of them; and I will plague them to the extremity, let them doe what they dare with their bil-bow blades, I feare them not: and, to give them their last adue, looke shortly, countrymen, for a pamphlet against them, called, The Creeping Law, of petty theeves, that rob about the suburbs. The Limiting Law, discoursing the orders of such as follow judges in their circuits, and go about from faire to faire. The Juggling Law, wherein I will set out the discorders at nineholes and wrestling, how they are only for the benefit of the cutpurses. The Stripping Law, wherein I will lay open the lewd abuses of sundry gaylors in England. Beside, you shall see there what houses there be about the suburbs and towns end, that are receivers of cutpurses, stolne goods, lifts, and such like. And, lastly, looke for the bedroll catalogue of all the names of the foysts, nips, lifts, and priggers, in and about London; and, although some say I dare not do it, yet I will shortly set it abroch, and whosoever I name or touch, if he think himselfe grieved, I will answer him.

The Conversion of an English Curtezan.

SITH to discover my parentage would double the greife of my living parents, and revive in them the memory of great amisse, and that my untoward fall would be a dishonour to the house from whence I came: Sith to manifest the place of my birth would be a blemish, through my beastly life so badly misled, to the shire where I was borne: Sith to discover my name might be holden a blot in my kindreds brow, to have a sinew in their stocke of so little grace, I will conceale my parents, kin, and country, and shrowd my name with silence, lest envie might taunt others for my wantonnesse. Know therefore, I was

borne about threescore miles from London, of honest and wealthy
parents, who had many children, but I their only daughter, and
therefore the jewell wherein they most delighted, and more, the youngest
of all, and therefore the more favoured; for, being gotten in the
wayning of my parents age, they doted on me above the rest, and so
set their hearts the more on fire.   I was the fairest of all, and yet not
more beautiful then I was witty, insomuch that, being a pretty parrat,
I had such quaint conceits, and wittie words in my mouth, that the
neighbours said, I was too soon wise, to be long old.   Would to God
either the proverbe had beene authenticall, or their sayings prophecies;
then had I, by death in my nonage, buried many blemishes that my
riper yeeres brought me to : For the extreme love of my parents was the
efficient cause of my follies; resembling herein the nature of the ape,
that ever killeth that young one which he loveth most, with embracing
it too fervently. So my father and mother, but she most of all, although
he too much, so cockered me up in my wantonnesse, that my wit grew
to the worst, and I waxed upwards with the ill weedes.   Whatsoever I
did, were it never so bad, might not be found fault withall; my
father would smile at it, and say, 'twas but the trick of a childe, and
my mother allowed of my unhappy parts, alluding to this prophane
and old proverbe, An untoward girle makes a good woman.

But now I find, in sparing the rod, they hated the child; that over
kind fathers make unruly daughters : Had they bent the wand, while
it had been greene, it would have beene pliant; but I, ill growne in
my yeeres, am almost remedilesse.   The hawke, that is most perfect
for the flight, will seldome prove a hagard; and children, that are
vertuously nurtured in youth, will be honestly natured in age : Fie
upon such as say, Yong Saints, old Devils : It is, no doubt, a divellish
and damnable saying; for what is not bent, in the cradle, will hardly
be bowed in the saddle, my selfe am an instance; who, after I grew
to be six yeeres old, was set to schoole, where I profited so much, that
I writ and read exceeding well, plaid upon the virginals, lute, and
citron, and could sing prick-song at the first sight: insomuch as, by
that time I was twelve yeeres old, I was holden for the most faire and
best qualitied young girle in all that country; but, with this,
bewailed of my well-wishers, in that my parents suffered me to be so
wanton.

But they so tenderly affected me, and were so blinded with my
excellent qualities, that they had no insight into my ensuing follies :
For, I growing to be 13 yeeres old, feeling the yoke of liberty to be loose
on mine owne neck, began, with the wanton heyfer, to aime at mine
owne will, and to measure content by the sweetenesse of mine owne
thoughts; insomuch that, pride creeping on, I beganne to pranke
my selfe with the proudest, and to hold it in disdaine, that any in the
parish should exceede me in bravery.   As my apparell was costly, so
I grew to be licentious, and to delight to be lookt on; so that I haunted and frequented all feasts and weddings, and other places of merry
meetings, where, as I was gazed on of many, so I spared no glances to
survey all with a curious eye-lavour; I observed Ouids rule right,

Spectatum veniunt, veniunt spectentur ut ipsæ,

I went to see, and be seene, and deckt myselfe in the highest degree of bravery; holding it a glory, when I was waited on with many eies, to make censure of my birth. Beside, I was an ordinary dancer, and grew in that quality so famous, that I was noted as the chiefest thereat in all the country; yea, and to sooth me up in these follies, my parents tooke a pride in my dancing, which afterward proved my overthrow, and their hearts breaking.

Thus, as an unbridled colt, I carelessely led forth my youth, and wantonly spent the flower of my yeeres, holding such maydens, as were modest, fooles, and such, as were not as wilfully wanton as my selfe, puppies ill brought up, and without manners; growing on in yeeres, as tide nor time tarieth for no man, I began to waxe passion proud, and to think her not worthy to live, that was not a little in love; that, as divers young men beganne to favour me for my beauty, so I beganne to censure of some of them partially, and to delight in the multitude of many wooers, being ready to fall from the tree, before I was com to the perfection of a blossom; which an uncle of mine seeing, who was my mothers brother, as carefull of my welfare, as nie to me in kin, finding fit opportunity to talke with me, gave me this wholsome exhortation:

A Watch Word to wanton Maydens.

COUSIN, I see the fairest hawke hath often times the sickest feathers; that the hottest day hath the most sharpe thunders, the brightest sun, the most sodaine showre, and the youngest virgins, the most dangerous fortunes; I speake as a kinsman, and wish as a friend, the blossome of a maydens youth (such as your selfe) hath attending upon it many frosts to nip it, and many cares to consume it, so that, if it be not carefully look't unto, it will perish before it come to any perfection.

A virgins honour consisteth not only in the gifts of nature, as to be faire and beautifull, though they be favours, that grace maydens much; for, as they be glistring, so they be momentary, ready to be worne with every winters blast, and parched with every summers sunne: There is no face so faire, but the least moale, the slenderest scarre, the smallest brunt of sicknesse, will quickly blemish.

Beauty (cousin) as it flourisheth in youth, so fadeth in age; it is but a folly that feedeth mans eye, a painting that nature lends for a time, and men allow on for a while, insomuch that such, as only aime at your faire lookes, tye but their loves to an apprentiship of beauty, which broken either with cares, misfortune, or yeeres, their destinies are at liberty, and they begin to loath you, and like of others.

For she, that is looked on by many, cannot choose but be hardly spoken of by some; for report hath a blister on her tongue, and maydens actions are narrowly measured. Therefore, would not the ancient Romans suffer their daughters to goe any further, then their mothers lookes guided them. And, therefore, Diana is painted with a tortoise under her feet, meaning, that a mayd should not be a stragler; but, like the snaile, carry her house upon her head, and keep at home at her worke, so to keep her name without blemish, and her vertues from the slander of envy.

Cousin, I speake this generally, which if you apply particularly to your selfe, you shall find in time my words were well said.

I gave him slender thankes, but with such a frumpe, that he perceived how light I made of his counsell; which he perceiving, shak't his head, and, with teares in his eyes, departed. But I, whom wanton desires had drawne in delight, still presuming in my former follies, gave my selfe either to gad abroad, or else at home to reade dissolute pamphlets, which bred in me many ill-affected wishes, so that I gave leave to love and lust to enter into the center of my heart, where they harboured, till they wrought my finall and fatall prejudice.

Thus, leading my life loosly, and being soothed up with the applause of my too kinde and loving parents, I had many of every degree that made love unto me, as well for my beauty, as for the hope of wealth that my father would bestow upon me; sundry sutors I had, and allowed of all, though I particularly granted love to none, yeelding them friendly favours, as being proud I had more wooers, than any mayd in the parish beside: amongst the rest, there was a wealthy farmer, that wished me well, a man of some forty yeeres of age, one too worthy for one of so little worth as my selfe, and him my father and mother, and other friends, would have had me match my selfe with all; but I had the reines of liberty too long in mine own handes, refused him, and would not be ruled by their perswasions; and though my mother with teares intreated me to consider of mine owne estate, and how well I sped, if I wedded with him; yet carelesly I despised her counsell, and flatly made answere, that I would none of him; which, though it pinched my parents at the quick, yet, rather than they would displease me, they left me in mine owne liberty to love: many there were beside him, mens sonnes of no meane worth, that were wooers unto me, but in vaine; either my fortune or destiny drove me to a worse end, for I refused them all, and with the beetle, refusing to light on the sweetest flowres all day, nestled all night in a cowsheard.

It fortuned, that as many sought to win me, so, amongst the rest, there was an old companion, that dwelt with a gentleman hard by, a fellow of smal reputation, and of no living, neither had he any excellent qualities, but thrumming on the gittron; but of pleasant disposition he was, and could gawll out many quaint and ribaldrous jigs and songs, and so was favoured of the foolish sort for his foppery. This shifting companion, sutable to my selfe, in vanity, would oft-times be jesting with me, and I so long dallying with him, that I began deeply (Oh, let me blush at this confession) to fall in love with him, and so construed all his actions, that I consented to mine owne overthrow: For, as smoake will hardly be concealed, so love will not be long smothered, but will bewray her owne secrets; which was manifest in me, who, in my sporting with him, so bewrayed my affection, that he, spying I favoured him, began to strike, when the iron was hot, and to take opportunity by the forehead; and, one day finding me in a merry vaine, beganne to question with me of love; which, although, at the first,

I slenderly denied him, yet, at last, I granted; so that, not only I agreed to plight him my faith, but that night, meeting to have further talke, I lasciviously consented, that he cropt the flowre of my virginity. When thus I was spoyled, by such a base companion, I gave my selfe to content his humour, and to satisfie the sweet of mine owne wanton desire. Oh, here let me breath, and with teares bewaile the beginning of my miseries, and to exclaime against the folly of my parents, who, by too much favouring me in my vanity in my tender youth, laid the first plot of my ensuing repentance. Had they, with due correction, chastised my wantonnesse, and supprest my foolish will, with their grave advice, they had made me more vertuous, and themselves lesse sorrowfull. A fathers frowne is a bridle to the child, and a mothers check is a stay to a stubborne daughter. Oh, had my parents, in overloving me, not hated me, I had not, at this time, cause to complaine.

But, leaving this digression, againe to the loosnesse of mine owne life, who now having lost the glory of my youth, and suffred such a base slave to possesse it, which many men of worth had desired to enjoy; I waxed bold in sinne, and grew shamelesse, in so much he could not desire so much as I did grant him: Whereupon, seeing he durst not reveale it to my father, to demand me in marriage, he resolved to carry me away secretly, and therefore wisht me to provide for my selfe, and to furnish me every way, both with mony and apparell, hoping, as he said, that, after we were departed, and my father saw we were married, and that no meanes was to amend it, he would give his free consent, and use us kindly, and deale with us as liberally, as if we had matcht with his good will. I, that was apt to any ill, agreed to this, and so wrought the matter, that he carried me away into a strange place, and then using me a while, as his wife, when our mony began to wax low, he resolved secretly to go into the country, where my father dwelt, to heare not only how my father tooke my departure, but what hope we had of his ensuing favour; allthough I was loth to be left in a strange place, yet I was willing to heare from my friends, who, no doubt, conceived much heart sorrow for my unhappy fortunes: So that I parted with a few teares, and enjoyned him, to make all the haste he might to returne. He being gone, as the eagles alway resort, where the carrion is; so, my beauty being bruited abroad, and that, at such an inne, lay such a faire young gentle-woman; there resorted thither many brave young gentlemen and cutting companions, that, tickled with lust, aimed at the possession of my favour, and, by sundry meanes, sought to have a sight of me, which I easily granted to all, as a woman that counted it a glory to be wondered at by many mens eyes; insomuch that, comming amongst them, I set their hearts more and more on fire, that there arose divers brawles, who should be most in my company.

Being thus haunted by such a troope of lusty rufflers, I began to find mine owne folly, that had placed my first affection so lowly, and therefore began as deeply to loath him that was departed, as erst I liked him when he was present, vowing in my selfe, though he had the spoile of my virginity, yet never after should he triumph in the possession of my favour; and therefore began I to affect these new come guests, and one above the rest, who was a brave young gentleman, and no lesse addicted unto me, than I devoted unto him; for daily he courted me with amorous sonnets, and curious pend letters, and sent me jewels and all that I might grace him with the name of my servant; I returned him as loving lines at last, and so contented his lusting desire, that secretly, and unknowne to all the rest, I made him sundry nights my bed-fellow, where I so bewitcht him with sweet words, that the man began deeply to dote upon me, insomuch that, selling some portion of land that he had, he put it into ready mony, and providing horse, and all things convenient, carried me secretly away almost as far as the Bath. This was my second choice, and my second shame: thus I went forward in wickednesse, and delighted in change, having left my old love to looke after some other mate more fit for my purpose. How he tooke my departure, when he returned, I little cared, for now I had my content, a gentleman, young, lusty, and endued with good qualities, and one that loved me more tenderly then himselfe. Thus lived this new entertained friend and I together unmarried, yet as man and wife for a while, so lovingly, as was to his content and my credit; but as the tyger, though for a while she hide her clawes, yet, at last, she will reveal her cruelty; and as the *agnus castus* lease, when it lookes most dry, is then most full of moisture; so womens wantonnesse is not qualified by their warines, nor doth their charines for a moneth warrant their chastity for ever, which I proved true; for my supposed husband, being every way a man of worth, could not so covertly hide himselfe in the country, though a stranger, but that he fell in acquaintance with many brave gentlemen, whom he brought home to his lodging, not only to honour them with his liberall courtisie, but also to see me, being proud if any man of worth applauded my beauty: Alas! poore gentleman, too much bewitcht by the wilinesse of a woman, had he deemed mine heart to be an harbor for every new desire, or mine eyes a sutor to every face, he would not have beene so fond as to have brought his companions into my company, but rather would have mewed me up as a hen, to have kept that severall to himselfe by force, which he could not retaine by kindnes; but the honest minded novice little suspected my change, although I, God wot, placed my delight in nothing more then the desire of new choice, which fell out thus. Amongst the rest of the gentlemen that kept him company, there was one that was his most familiar, and he reposed more trust and confidence in him then in all the rest: this gentleman began to be deeply inamored of me, and shewed, by many signes, which I easily perceived; and I, whose care was pliant to every sweet word, and who so allowed of all that were beautifull, affectioned him no lesse; so that love prevailed above friendship, he brake the matter with me, and made not many suites in vaine, before he had obtained his purpose; for he had what he wisht, and I had what contented me.

I will not confesse, that any of the rest had some seldome favours, but this gentleman was my second selfe, and I loved him more, for the time, at the heele, then the other at the heart; so that, though the other youth bare the charges, and was sir pay for all, yet this new

friend was he that was master of my affections ; which kindnesse betwixt
us was so unwisly cloked, that, in short time, it was manifest to all
our familiars, which made my supposed husband to sigh, and others to
smile, but he that was hit with the horne was pincht at the heart ; yet
so extreme was the affection he bare me, that he had rather conceale his griefe, than any way make me discontent, so that he smothered his sorrow with patience, and brookt the injury with silence, till our
loves grew so broad before, that it was a wonder to the world : whereupon, one day at dinner, I being very pleasant with his chosen friend,
and my choise lover, I know not how, but, either by fortune, or it may
be, some set match, there was a gentleman, there present, popt a question in about womens passions, and their mutability in affection; so
that the controversie was defended, *pro & contra*, with arguments,
whether a woman might have a second friend or no ? At last, it was
concluded, that love and lordship brookes no fellowship, and, therefore, none so base minded to beare a rivall.   Hereupon arose a question
about friends that were put in trust, how it was a high point of treason
for one to betray another, especially in love, insomuch that one gentleman at the boord protested, by a solemne oath, that, if any friend of
his, made privy and favoured with the sight of his mistresse whom he
loved, whether it was his wife, or no, should secretly seeke to incroach
into his roome, and offer him that dishonour to partake his love, he
would not use any other revenge, but, at the next greeting, stab him
with his poinado, though he were condemned to death for the action.
All this fitted for the humour of my supposed husband, and struck both
me and my friend into a quandarie ; but I scornfully jested at it, when
as my husband, taking the ball before it came to the ground, began to
make a long discourse, what faithlesse friends they were that would
faile in love, especially, where a resolved trust of the party beloved
was committed unto them ; and, hereupon, to make the matter more
credulous, and to quip my folly, and to taunt the basenesse of my
friends mind, that so he might, with courtesie, both warne us of our
wantonnesse, and reclaime us from ill, he promised to tell a pleasant
story, performed, as he said, not long since in England, and it was
to this effect :

———

*A pleasant Discourse, how a wise Wanton, by her Husbands gentle Warn-
ing, became a modest Matron.*

THERE was a gentleman (to give him his due, an esquire) here in
England, that was married to a young gentlewoman, faire and of modest behavior, vertuous in her lookes, howsoever she was in her
thoughts, and one that every way, with her dutifull endeavour, and
outward appearance of honesty, did breed her husbands content, insomuch that the gentleman so deeply affected her, as he counted all those
houres ill spent, which he past not away in her company, besotting so
himselfe in the beaty of his wife, that his only care was to have her
every way delighted.   Living thus pleasantly together, he had one spe-

ciall friend amongst the rest, whom he so deerely affected, as he un-
folded all his secrets in his bosome; and what passion he had in his mind,
that either joyed him, or perplexed him, he revealed unto his friend,
and directed his actions according to the sequel of his counsells, so
that they were two bodies and one soule. This gentleman, for all the
inward favour shewed him by his faithfull friend, could not so withstand the force of fancy, but he grew enamoured of his friends wife,
whom he courted with many sweete words and faire promises, charmes
that are able to inchant almost the chastest eares, and so subtily
couched his arguments, discovered such love in his eyes, and such sorrow in his lookes, that dispaire seemed to sit in his face, and swore,
that, if she granted not him the end of a lovers sighs, he would present
his heart, as a tragicke sacrifice, to the sight of his cruell mistresse,
The gentlewoman waxed pittifull, as women are kind hearted, and are
loath gentlemen should dye for love, after a few excuses, let him dub
her husband knight of the forked order, and so, to satisfie his humour,
made forfeit of her owne honour. Thus these two lovers continued,
for a great space, in such places as unchast wantons count their felicity, having continually fit opportunity to exercise their wicked purpose, sith the gentleman himselfe did give them free liberty to love,
neither suspecting his wife, nor his friend: at last, as such trayterous
abuses will burst forth, it fell out, that a mayd, who had beene an old
servant in the house, beganne to grow suspicious, that there was too
much familiarity betweene her mistresse and her master's friend, and,
upon this, watcht them divers times so narrowly, that at last she found
them more private, then either agreed with her master's honour, or her
owne honesty, and thereupon revealed it one day unto her master. He,
little credulous of the light behaviour of his wife, blamed the mayd,
and bid her take heed, least she sought to blemish her vertues with
slander, whom he loved more tenderly then his owne life. The mayd
replyed, That she spake not of envy to him, but of meere love she
bare unto him; and the rather, that he might shadow such a fault in
time, and by some meanes prevent it, least, if others should note it as
well as she, his wives good name, and his friends, should be called in
question. At these wise words, spoken by so base a drudge as his
mayd, the gentleman waxed astonished, and listned to her discourse,
wishing her to discover how she knew, or was so privie to that folly of
her mistresse, or by what meanes he might have assured proofe of it.
She told him, that, to her, her owne eyes were witnesses, for she saw
them unlawfully together; and please it you, Sir, quoth she, to faine
your selfe to goe from home, and then in the backhouse to keepe you
secret, I will let you see as much as I have manifested unto you. Upon
this her master agreed, and warned his mayd not so much as to make
it knowne to any of her fellowes. Within a day or two after, the
gentleman said he would goe a hunting; and so rose very early, and,
causing his men to couple up his houndes, left his wife in bed, and
went abroad. As soone as he was gone a mile from the house, he commanded his men to ride afore, and to start the hare, and follow the
chase, and he would come faire and softly after: they, obeying their
master's charge, went their wayes, and he returned by a back way to

his house, and went secretly to the place where his mayd and he had appointed. In the meane time, the mistresse, thinking her husband safe with his houndes, sent for her friend to her bedchamber, by a trusty servant of hers, in whom she assured that he was a secret pander in such affaires; and the gentleman was not slack to come, but, making all the haste he could, came and went into the chamber, asking for the master of the house very familiarly. The old mayd, noting all this, as soone as she knew them together, went and called her master, and carried him up by a secret paire of staires to her mistresse chamber doore, where, peeping in a place that the mayd before had made for the purpose, he saw more then he lookt for, and so much as pincht him at the very heart, causing him to accuse his wife for a strumpet, and his friend for a traytor: yet, for all this, valluing his owne honour more then their dishonesty, thinking, if he should make an uprore, he should but aime at his owne discredite, and cause him selfe to be a laughing game to his enemies, he concealed his sorrow with silence, and, taking the mayd a part, charged her to keepe all secret, whatsoever she had seene, even as she esteemed of her owne life ; for, if she did bewray it to any, he himselfe would, with his sword, make an ende of her dayes; and with that, putting his hand in his sleve, gave the poore mayd six angels to buy her a new gown. The wench, glad of this gift, swore solemnly to tread it under foot, and, sith it pleased him to conceale it, never to reveale it, so long as she lived. Upon this they parted, she to her drudgery, and he to the field to his men, where, after he had kild the hare, he returned home; and, finding his friend in the garden, that in his absence had been grafting hornes in the chimnies, he entertained him with his wonted familiaritie, and shewed no bad countenance to his wife, but dissembled all his thoughts to the full. As soone as dinner was done, and that he was gotten solitary by himselfe, he beganne to determine of revenge, but not, as every man would have done, how to have brought his wife to shame, and her love to confusion ; but he busied his braine, how he might reserve his honour inviolate, reclaime his wife, and keepe his friend. Meditating a long time how he might bring all this to passe, at last a humour fel into his head, how cunningly to compasse all three : and therefore he went and got him certain slips, which are counterfeit peeces of mony, being brasse, and covered over with silver, which the common people call *slips*. Having furnished himselfe with these, he put them in his purse, and at night went to bed, as he was wont to do, yet not using the kind familiarity that he accustomed ; notwithstanding, he abstained not from the use of her body, but knew his wife, as aforetimes; and, every time he committed the act with her, he laid the next morning in the window a slip, where he was sure she might find it; and, so many times as it pleased him to be carnally pleasant with his wife, so many slips he still laid down upon her cushionet. This he used for the space of a fortnight, till at last his wife, finding every day a slip, or sometimes more or lesse, wondred how they came there, and, examining her waiting mayds, none of them could tell her any thing touching them ; whereupon she thought to question with her husband about it ; but being out of remembrance, the next morning, as she lay dallying in bed, it came into hereminde, and she asked her husband, If he laid those slips on her cushionet, that she of late found there, having never seen any before? I marry did I, quoth he, and have laid them there upon speciall reason; and it is this:

Ever since I was married to thee, I have deemed thee honest, and therefore used and honored thee as my wife, parting coequall favours betwixt us, as true lovers; but late finding the contrary, and with these eyes seeing thee play the whore with my friend, in whom I did repose all my trust, I sought not, as many would have done, to have revenged in bloud, but for the safety of mine own honor, which otherwise would have been blemished by thy dishonesty, I have beene silent, and have neither wronged my *quondam* friend, nor abused thee, but still do hold bed with thee; the world shall not suspect any thing, and to quench the desire of lust, I do use thy body, but not so lovingly as I would a wife, but carelessly as I would use the body of a false harlot or strumpet, and therefore, even as a whore, so I give thee hire, which is for every time a slip, a counterfeit coyne, which is good enough for a slippery wanton, that will wrong her husband that loved her so tenderly, and thus will I use thee for the safety of mine owne honor, till I have assured proofe that thou becomest honest; and thus with teares in his eyes, and his heart ready to burst with sighs, he was silent; when his wife, stricken with remorse of conscience, leaping out of her bed in her smocke, humbly confessing all, beged pardon, promising, if he should pardon this offence, which was new begun in her, she would become a new reformed woman, and never after (so much as in thought) give him any occasion of suspition or jealousie; the patient husband, not willing to urge his wife, tooke her at her word, and told her, that when he found her so reclaimed, he would, as afore he had done, use her lovingly, and as his wife, but, till he was so perswaded of her honesty, he would pay her still slips for his pleasure, charging her not to reveale any thing to his friend, or to make it knowne to him, that he was privy to their loves. Thus the debate ended, I guesse, in some kind greeting, and the gentleman went abroad to see his pastures, leaving his wife in bed full of sorrow, and almost renting her heart asunder with sighs. As soon as he walked abroad, the gentleman his friend came to the house, and asked for the good man; the pander, that was privy to all their practises, said, that his master was gone abroad to see his pastures, but his mistresse was in bed; Why then, sayes he, I will goe and raise her up; so comming into the chamber, and kissing her, meaning (as he wont) to have used his accustomed dalliance, she desired him to abstaine, with broken sighs, and her eyes full of tears; he wondering what should make her thus discontent, asking her what was the cause of her sorrow, protesting with a solemne oath, that if any had done her injury, he would revenge it, were it with hazard of his life. She then told him, scarce being able to speake for weeping, that she had a sute to move him in, which, if he granted unto her, she would hold him in love and affection, without change, next her husband for ever; he promised to do whatsoever it were; then, says she, sweare upon a bible, you will do it without exception; with that he tooke a bible, that lay in the window, and swore, that whatsoever she requested him to do, were it to the losse of his life, he would, without exception, performe it.   Then she holding downe her head, and blushing, began thus: I neede not, quoth she, make manifest, how grossely and grievously you and I have both offended God, and wronged the honest gentleman my husband, and your friend; he putting a speciall trust in us both, and assuring such earnest affiance in your unfained friendship, that he even committed me, his wife, his love, his second life, into your bosome; this love have I requited with inconstancy, in playing the harlot; that faith, that he reposed in you, have you returned with treachery, and falshood, in abusing mine honesty, and his honor.   Now, a remorse of conscience toucheth me for my sins, that I heartily repent, and vow ever hereafter to live only to my husband; and therefore my sute is to you that from hence forth you shall never so much as motion any dishonest question unto me, nor seeke any unlawfull pleasure or conversing at my hands; this is my sute, and hereunto I have sworne you, which oath, if you observe as a faithful gentleman, I will conceale from my husband what is past, and rest, in honest sort, your faithfull friend for ever; at this, she burst afresh into teares, and uttered such sighs, that he thought, for very griefe, her heart would have cleaved asunder; the gentleman, astonied at this strange metamorphosis of his mistris, sate a good while in a maze, and at last, taking her by the hand, made this reply: So God helpe me, faire sweeting, I am glad of this motion, and wondrous joyfull that God hath put such honest thoughts into your mind, and hath made you the meanes to reclaim me from my folly: I feele no lesse remorse then you doe in wronging so honest a friend, as your husband, but this is the frailenesse of man; and therefore, to make amends, I protest anew, never hereafter, so much as in thought, to motion you of dishonesty, only I crave you be silent; she promised that, and so they ended, and for that time they parted. At noone the gentleman came home, and cheerefully saluted his wife, and asked if dinner were ready, and sent for his friend, using him wonderfull familiarly, giving him no occasion of mistrust, and so pleasantly they past away the day together: at night when his wife and he went to bed, she told him all what had past between her and his friend, and how she had bound him with an oath, and that he voluntarily of himselfe swore as much, being hartily sorrie, that he had so deeply offended so kind a friend.   The gentleman commended her wit, and found her afterwards a reclaimed woman, she living so honestly, that she never gave him any occasion of mistrust.   Thus the wise gentleman reclaimed, with silence, a wanton wife, and retained an assured friend.

At this pleasant tale all the boord was at a mutiny, and they said, the gentleman did passing wisely that wrought so cunningly, for the safety of his owne honor, but exclaimed against such a friend, as would to his friend offer such villany, all condemning her, that would be so false to so loving a husband.   Thus they did diversly descant, and past away dinner; but this tale wrought little effect in me, for, as one past grace, I delighted in change: But the gentleman that was his familiar, and my paramour, was so touched, that, never after, he would touch me dishonestly, but reclaimed himselfe, abstained from me, and became true to his friend. I wondring, that, according to his wonted custome, he did not seeke my company; he and I being one day in the chamber alone, and he in his dumps, I began to dally with him, and to aske him, Why he was so strange, and used not his accustomed favours to me? He solemnly made answere, That, though he had played the foole, in setling his fancy upon another mans wife, and in wronging his friend, yet his conscience was now touched with remorse, and, ever since he heard the tale afore rehearsed, he had vowed in himselfe, never to do my husband the like wrong againe. My husband, quoth I, he is none of mine, he hath brought me here from my friends, and keepes me here unmarried, and therefore am I as free for you, as for him, and thus began to grow clamorous, because I was debard of my lust. The gentleman, seeing me shamlesse, wisht me to be silent, and sayde, Although you be but his friend, yet he holds you as deare as his wife, and, therefore, I will not abuse him, neither would I wish you to be familiar with any other, seeing you have a friend that loves you so tenderly: Much good counsell he gave me, but all in vaine, for I scorned it, and began to hate him, and resolved both to be rid of him, and my supposed husband; for, falling in with another familiar of my husbands, I so inveagled him, with sweete words, that I caused him to make a peece of mony to steale me away, and so carry me to London; where I had not lived long with him, but he, seeing my light behaviour, left me to the wide world, to shift for my selfe.

I now being brought to London, and left there at random, was not such a house-dove, while my friend stayd with me, but that I had visited some houses in London, that could harbour as honest a woman as my selfe; when as therefore I was left to my selfe, I removed my lodging, and gate me into one of those houses of good hospitallity, whereunto persons resort, commonly called a Trugging-house, or, to be plaine, a Whore-house, where I gave my selfe to entertaine all companions, sitting or standing at the doore like a staule, to allure or draw in wanton passengers, refusing none that would, with his purse, purchase me to be his, to satisfie the disordinate desire of his filthie lust: Now I began not to respect personage, good qualities, or the gracious favour of the man, when I had no respect of person; for the oldest lecher was as welcome as the youngest lover, so he brought meate in his mouth. Thus, to the griefe of my friends, hazard of my soule, and consuming of my body, I spent a yeare or two, in this base or bad kind of life, subject to the whistle of every desperate ruffian; till, on a time, there resorted to our house a clouthier, a proper young man, who, by fortune, comming first to drinke, espying me, asked me, if I would drinke with him; there needed no great entreaty, for, as then, I wanted company, and so clapt me downe by him, and began very pleasantly to welcome him: The man, being of himselfe modest and honest, noted my personage, and juditially reasoned of my strumpet-like behaviour, and inwardly (as after he reported unto me) grieved, that so foule properties were hidden in so good a proportion, and that such rare wit and excellent beauty were blemisht with whoredomes base deformity; in so much that he began to thinke well of me, and to

wish that I were as honest as I was beautifull.   Againe, see how God
wrought for my conversion; since I gave my selfe to my loose kind of
life, I never liked any so well as him, in so much that I began to judge
of every part, and me thought, he was the properest man that ever I
saw: Thus, we sate both amorous of other, I lasciviously, and he
honestly; at last, he questioned with me, What country woman I was,
and why, being so proper a woman, I would beseeme to dwell or lye in
a base alehouse, especially, in one that had a bad name? I warrant
you, I wanted no knavish reply to fit him, for I told him, the house was
as honest as his mothers: Marry, if there were in it a good wench or
two, that would pleasure their friends at a neede, I guessed by his nose,
what porridge he loved, and that he hated none such.   Well, seeing
me in that voyce, he said little, but shooke his heade, paid for the
beere, and went his way, onely taking his leave of me with a kisse,
which, me thought, was the sweetest that ever was given me.   As
soone as he was gone, I began to thinke what a handsome man he was,
and wisht, that he would come and take a nights lodging with me,
sitting in a dumpe to thinke of the quaintnesse of his personage, till
other companions came in, and shaked me out of that melancholly;
but, as soone againe as I was secret to my selfe, he came into my
remembrance.   Passing over this a day or two, this cloathier came
againe to our house, whose sight cheered me up, for that, spying him
out of a casement, I ranne downe the staires, and met him at the doore,
and heartily welcom'd him, and asked him, if he would drink; I come
for that purpose, sayes he, but I will drinke no more below, but in a
chamber: Marry, Sir, quoth I, you shall, and so brought him into the
fairest roome.   In our sitting there together drinking, at last, the
cloathier fell to kissing, and other dalliance, wherein he found me not
coy; at last told me, that he would willingly have his pleasure of me,
but the room was too lightsome, for, of all things in the world, he
could not in such actions away with a light chamber.   I consented
unto him, and brought him into a roome more darke, but still he sayde
it was too light: Then I carried him into a further chamber, where
drawing a curtaine before the window, and closing the curtaines of the
bed, I asked, smiling, if that were close enough? No, sweete love,
sayes he, that curtaine is not broad enough for the window, some
watching eye may espy us, my heart misdoubts, and my credit is my
life; Love, if thou hast a closer roome then this, bring me to it: Why
then, quoth I, follow me, and with that, I brought him into a backe
loft, where stood a little bed, only appointed to lodge suspicious
persons, so darke, that at noone day it was impossible for any man to
see his owne hands: How now, Sir, quoth I, is not this darke enough?
He sitting him downe, on the bedside, fetcht a deepe sigh, and said,
Indifferent, so, so; but there is a glimpse of light in at the tiles, some
body may, by fortune, see it: In faith, no, quoth I, none but God.
God, sayes he, I why, Can God see us here? Good Sir, quoth I, why
I hope you are not so simple, but you know, Gods eyes are so cleere
and penetrating, that they can pierce through walls of brasse: And
alas, quoth he, sweete Love, if God see us, shall we not be more

ashamed to do such a filthy act before him, then before men? I am
sure, thou art not so shamlesse, but thou wouldst blush to have the
meanest commoner in London see thee, in the action of thy filthy lust,
and dost thou not shame more to have God, the maker of all things
see thee, who revengeth sinne with death; he whose eyes are cleerer
then the sunne, who is the searcher of the heart, and holdeth vengeance
in his hands to punish sinners? Oh, let us tremble, that we but once
durst have such a wanton communication, in the hearing of his Divine
Majesty, who pronounceth damnation for such as give themselves over
to adultery. It is not possible, saith the Lord, for any whoremaster,
or lascivious wanton, to enter into the kingdome of God; for such
sinnes, whole cities have sunke, kingdomes have beene destroyed; and,
though God suffer such wicked livers to escape for a while, yet, at
length, he payeth home in this world, with beggry, shame, diseases,
infamy; and in the other life, perpetuall damnation. Weigh but the inconvenience, that growes through thy loose life, thou art hated of all that are
good, despised of the vertuous, and only well thought of, of repro-
bates, rascals, ruffians, and such as the world hates, subject to their lust,
and gaining thy living at the hands of every diseased leacher. O, what
a miserable trade of life is thine, that livest of the vomit of sin, in
hunting after maladies: But suppose, while thou art young, thou art
favoured of thy companions; when thou waxest old, and that thy
beauty is faded, then thou shall be lothed and despised, even of them
that profest most love unto thee: Then, good sister, call to mind the
basenesse of thy life, the hainous outrage of thy sin, that God doth
punish it with the rigour of his justice. Oh, thou art made beautifull,
faire, and well formed; and wilt thou then, by thy filthy lust, make thy
body, which, if thou be honest, is the temple of God, the habitation of
the divell? Consider this, and call to God for mercy, and amend thy
life: Leave this house, and I will become thy faithfull friend in all
honesty, and use thee as mine owne sister. At this, such a remorse of
conscience, such a fearefull terror of my sin strook into my mind, that
I kneeled down at his feet, and with teares besought him, that he would
helpe me out of that misery, for his exhortation had caused in me a
lothing of my wicked life, and I would not only become a reformed
woman, but hold him as deare as my father that gave me life; whereupon, he kist me with teares, and so we went downe together, where we
had further communication, and presently he provided me another
lodging, where I not only used my selfe honestly, but also was so
penitent, every day in teares for my former folly, that he tooke me to his
wife; and how I have lived since, and lothed filthy lust, I referre my
selfe to the Majesty of God, who knoweth the secrets of all hearts.

Thus, country-men, I have publisht the conversion of an English
curtezan, which, if, any way, it be profitable, either to forwarne youth,
or withdraw bad persons to goodnesse, I have the whole end of my
desire; only craving, every father would bring up his children with
carefull nurture, and every young woman respect the honour of her
virginitie.

THE

ANATOMY OF A WOMANS TONGUE

DIVIDED INTO FIVE PARTS:

A MEDICINE, A POISON, A SERPENT, FIRE, AND THUNDER.

Whereunto is added divers new Epigrams nevers before printed. The fifth Edition, with more new Additions.

London, printed for Richard Harper, and are to be sold at his shop, at the Hospital-Gate, 1638. Duodecimo, containing eighteen pages.

━━━━

The Frontispiece, or Meaning of the wooden Picture, in the Title-Page.

This little emblem here doth represent
The bless'd condition of a man content,
Bless'd with a blessing sent him from above,
A quiet wife wholly compact of love;
In middle of the title I have plac'd them,
With hand in hand, my muse so much hath grac'd them.
The smiling sun, that o'er their heads doth shine,
Doth shew true love is heavenly and divine.
Now, at each corner of the title here,
Men discontented in their minds appear.
One sadly sits, his wife is grown so curst,
Her words like poison make him swell and burst.
Another man is by a serpent stung,
What is this serpent but a woman's tongue?
Another from the fire seems to turn,
To shew that women's tongues like fire will burn.
Another sounds his horn, and doth rejoice,
To drown a scolding woman's clamorous voice.
The cloud of thunder o'er his head, you see,
Doth shew what thund'ring tongues in women be.
Horns roar, and thunder rattles from the sky,
Yet women they will strain their voice as high.
Reader, no longer on the title look,
But cast thine eye a little on the book:
Read it quite o'er, and surely thou wilt say,
Thy money is well laid out, not cast away.

To the new-married Man.

YOUNG man, that now hast ventur'd on a wife,
And know'st not the conditions of her life ;
For thou may'st live perhaps with her a year,
Before her qualities to thee appear :
Make much of her on whom thy love is plac'd,
Be sure thou offer not the first distaste : ·
For, if thou dost, thou openest a way,
For discontent to enter in I say ;
If she be kind of nature, mild, and chaste,
Make much of her, for thou a jewel hast ;
If she be quarrelsome, and curs'd of nature,
Why policy will tame the fiercest creature.
Lions and tigers by policy are tamed,
And other creatures, which here are not named.
Some men will beat their wives, but that's the way,
To make them obstinate and go astray ;
Others no means unto their wives allow,
And say, that is the way to make them bow ;
But such as these are knaves and clownish boors,
For that's the way to make them to be whores.
But, if thou seest her strive to wear the breeches,
Then strive to overcome her with kind speeches.
If this will not prevail, why then be sure,
That such a wife as she is quite past cure.
With evil company refuse to go,
For that's enough to make a sheep a shrew.
And to this end that thou shouldst careful be,
Here thou shalt know what I have done for thee.
If that a woman's tongue seem strange unto thee,
I'll shew what good or evil they may do thee.
Into five parts this tongue I will divide,
The first part is the best, as shall be try'd ;
And these be they in order written under,
A Salve, a Poison, a Serpent, Fire, and Thunder:
And first a woman's tongue a salve I'll prove,
If she be one that doth her husband love.

How a Woman's Tongue may be said to be a Medicine.

THERE was a comely, handsome, proper maid,
That lov'd a young man very well 'tis said,
Unknown to him or unto any other,
For she conceal'd it even from her mother;
But she grew love-sick, and so wond'rous ill,
Because poor wench she could not have her will:
Which made her mother call her them to task,
What ail'd her to be sick, she her did ask.
The bashful maid at first would nothing say,
And yet, she being willing to obey,
Her mother's will, thus she to speak began,
And said she was in love with such a man;
If she enjoy'd him not, she was undone,
And made th' unhappiest creature under th' sun.
Her mother did at this begin to chide,
And said she was too young to be a bride:
Nevertheless to the man's friends she went,
To have both his good will, and their consent.
This motion did the young man's mother please,
But yet she said that he had a disease,
That was the cause of all her grief, alas!
But yet she would not tell her what it was.
But, to be short, they married were with speed,
Unto the love sick maid's content indeed.
And, since she found he was a lusty lad,
She wonder'd what disease her husband had:
She found her husband sound in wind and limb,
And no disease or sickness troubled him,
But on a time he went forth sound and well,
And came home very sick, the truth to tell;
For he had been among a drunken crew,
So the new-married wife his sickness knew:
Husband, quoth she, I now do understand
What your disease is, come give me your hand:
Be of good comfort, for I will assure you,
I, under God, will undertake to cure you.
It is a catching sickness and disease,
Which to prevent, I'll tell you, if you please;
My words shall be as physick for your soul,
If I may freely speak without controul:
He gave consent, and thus she did begin,
To tell her husband 'twas a grievous sin:
It will, quoth she, if you do use this thing,
Both soul and body to confusion bring:
And that in time it will impair your health,
Weaken your body, and consume your wealth:

'Twill rob you of your senses and your wit,
And for all goodness make you quite unfit:
O'erthrow your credit ; O let me persuade
You from this vice ; wherefore should it be said
That you, that are of all men held discreet,
Should come home stumbling, reeling in the street ?
When every little boy, to your disgrace,
Will laugh at you, and jeer you to your face.
And which is more, if this I often see,
It will go near to break the heart of me.
Then, if you love me, and me well respect,
Banish that vice, sweet-heart, and now reject
That company that you esteem so dear,
That ne'er will leave you till they leave you bare.
So with such words as these she did prevail,
For she, poor heart, could neither scold nor rail :
And her kind loving words were not in vain,
For he was never after drunk again.
O happy men that do such wives enjoy,
Whose tongues are medicines to cure annoy.

How a Woman's Tongue may be said to be a Poison.

A MAN that had a nimble-tongued wife,
With whom he liv'd a discontented life :
For she would tell all that her husband did,
And from her gossips nothing should be hid.
If he sometimes did come home drunk to bed,
About the town it should be published.
If he a woman do salute or kiss,
Why all the town forsooth must know of this.
This made the poor man weary of his life,
Because he had such an unnat'ral wife.
Upon a time to his neighbour's house he went,
Much vex'd in mind, and wond'rous discontent.
He sits him down, but not a word he spake,
Until his buttons from his doublet brake ;
It seems his heart, poor man, with grief was thrust,
Which made his buttons from his doublet burst.
He swell'd, as if he poisoned had been,
Which caused them to call their neighbours in ;
Which when the people saw, quoth they, the man
Is surely poison'd ; so away they ran,
Some for strong waters, some for sallet oil ;
Which when he saw, he could no less but smile :
Quoth he, 'tis true, it was a woman's tongue,
That hath, like poison, done me so much wrong.

No poison worse than this, for certainly
It made my buttons from my doublet fly.
O women, be not cruel unto men,
Ill words are worse than poison now and then.

How a Woman's Tongue may be said to be a Serpent.

THERE was a man was by a serpent stung,
And asked counsel both of old and young,
What med'cine to apply unto his sore,
Which every day did vex him more and more ;
At last a woman, old, and lame, and blind,
Told him that if that serpent he could find,
Bid him pull out the sting, and not in vain,
For he should mend, and soon be well again.
It is impossible for me, quoth he,
So many serpents in that place there be,
To find the self-same serpent out again,
That puts me now unto such grief and pain.
Another man stood by that had a wife,
That was a shrew, that raised wond'rous strife :
Quoth he, I have a serpent every night,
That lieth in my bosom, and can bite ;
And sure I think the best way it will be,
To cut that sting out that so troubleth me.
And by experience I do know her tongue
To be that sting that does me so much wrong.
So home he goes, and doth her kindly greet,
And takes his wife and binds her hands and feet.
With that the tempest did begin to rise,
She swore that she would claw out both his eyes.
Ay, quoth the man, I'll give you leave to claw,
Your hands being bound, so he his knife did draw :
What will you murder me, you knave, quoth she ?
No, I will only cut thy tongue from thee,
Reply'd the man : When she heard him say so,
My gentlewoman knew not what to do.
But she intreated him to spare her tongue,
And promis'd she would never do him wrong,
But that she would be loving, kind, and mild,
And even as harmless as the new-born child ;
Bid him do what he will, if base he found her ;
So upon this condition he unbound her,
And, having tamed her by policy,
They ever after lived quietly.
Men have enough to do that marry shrews,
Better tame them by policy than blows.

How a Woman's Tongue may be said to be a Fire.

A simple countryman a wife had married,
So good, that he wish'd longer he had tarried.
To plough and cart he used for to go,
But the poor man was troubled with a shrew:
And, being one day vexed in his mind,
He went abroad some comfort for to find.
He overtook two men in discontent,
That had shrews to their wives, to whom he went.
Well overtaken, honest men, quoth he,
Let not my company offensive be,
Nor me reject, 'cause I am something rude,
And do into your company intrude;
For I walk here, only to ease my mind,
Because small comfort I at home can find.
'Tis true, when any storm is on the sea,
Men seek for harbour, 'cause they safe would be;
And, when a storm upon the land doth rise,
He that makes little haste home is unwise.
But when a storm is in the house, O then,
The field and sea are best for such poor men.
Faith, friend, said they, we know your meaning well,
Our cases are alike, the truth to tell:
And here we walk like pilgrims, as you see,
And right glad of your company we be.
Then one of them out of his pocket took
Some notes out of an old decayed book,
And 'cause the rest should not his words despise,
He took some notes from scripture too likewise;
These were the words, as I remember well,
'The tongue is set upon the fire of hell.'
O, quoth the plough-man, if these things be true,
It will be ne'er the worse for me nor you:
For we, that have our hell upon the earth,
Shall have, I hope, our heaven after death.
So home he goes unto his wife with speed,
And, though that he could neither write nor read,
Yet he had learn'd enough to school his wife,
Hoping hereby to make her mend her life;
So in he comes, and with his wife is bold,
Thinking 'twould not be long 'ere she would scold:
Which to prevent, because he did misdoubt her,
He told her that she carried hell about her;
And that one told him, being a scholar great,
That a woman's tongue it is the devil's seat;

And that it is a most pernicious lyar,
A backbiter and a consuming fire.
The woman, hearing this, did hide her face,
It was a certain sign she had some grace.
When he saw this, he kiss'd her lovingly,
And after that they lived quietly:
And some report her eyes in tears she drench'd,
And, with those tears, hell-fire itself was quench'd.

How a Woman's Tongue may be said to be a Thunder.

THERE was a huntsman did a wife enjoy,
Whose tongue did breed him much annoy;
But when she scolded, he his horn would sound,
Purposely her clamorous tongue he'd drown'd.
But, on a time, her voice so high she roars,
She drowns the horn, and the poor huntsman's fears.
Away he goes unto a neighbour's house,
To drink away his grief, and to carouse:
Neighbour, quoth he, pray take it not in scorn,
Resolve me, what is louder than a horn?
Thunder, quoth he is louder, my good friend.
Now heaven, quoth the huntsman, me defend.
From such like thunder as I heard ev'n now,
That drowned my shrill horn, and fear'd me too.
Thunder brings rain, quoth he, O heavens save you,
Take in your clothes, and say, I warning gave you.
Quoth the other man, you know not what you say,
For there hath been no thunder all this day.
Yes, quoth the huntsman, I dare boldly swear,
Such a like thunder I did never hear,
Not in the element, but here below,
Unto my terror, yet unknown to you.
The thunder is in my wife's tongue too common,
No thunder like the thund'ring of a woman.
He takes his leave, and homewards he makes haste,
Hoping, that now the tempest is quite past;
But, all the way he goes, he cries a-main,
Women, take in your sheets, 'tis like to rain;
For, since it thunder'd, 'tis not yet an hour,
And, after thunder, is usually a show'r:
But, when his wife did come to know of this,
Her tongue did never after do amiss;
Nor was she after known to be so bold,
To thunder with her tongue, to rail, or scold.
Thus policy, by wise men, still is used
To tame a shrew, by whom they are abused.

Thus in five parts I do divide the tongue,
And yet no civil woman do I wrong ;
Nor yet uncivil women can deny,
But that, of them, I speak but sparingly ;
For, I protest, I wish so well to all,
That I will never dip my pen in gall.

THE SONG.

TO THE TUNE OF THE OLD BRIDE.

WHEN the world was made, as I understood,
All that was made, God saw it was good ;
Then God made Adam, and gave him life,
And, of his rib, he made him a wife ;
So mild, so wond'rous mild,
Was Adam's sweet wife,
That it was ne'er known
Her tongue raised strife.

But, when the world received a curse,
Then women, like men, grew worse and worse.
Among these weeds, to supply men's wants,
There grew some medicinary plants,
So good, so wond'rous good,
That man may procure
A wife, as a medicine
To heal the impure.

But do not to that woman sue,
That hath a tongue as long as two ;
For, if thou love her wond'rous well,
Her poison'd words will make thee swell :
Such grief, such wond'rous grief,
Thy heart will possess,
That all thy life-time
Thou wilt live in distress.

Nor come not to that woman's house,
That takes delight to drink and carouse ;
For, when she is drunk, she'll prove thy foe,
And thy reputation overthrow :
So false, so wond'rous false,
Her tongue it will be,
And, in the end, prove
A serpent to thee.

If thou hear a woman curse and swear,
To love such a woman I wish thee forbear;
For all the town doth know full well,
Her tongue is set on the fire of hell:
Such flames, such wond'rous flames,
From her tongue will come,
'Twere better that such
A woman were dumb.

If thou see a woman loud and high,
As loud as thunder from the sky,
Then stop thine ears, and go thy way;
It is no boot for thee to stay:
So loud, so wond'rous loud,
Her tongue it will be,
As thou shalt find
Like thunder to thee.

There is a way to tame a shrew,
And this is it, if thou wilt know;
Thy love must teach her, by degrees,
How she the serpent's head may squeese:
So subtle, so wond'rous subtle,
This serpent appears,
That man and wife
He sets by the ears.

Now, if these lines she understand,
And bring herself under command;
If she her duty so well know,
Then take my word, she'll be no shrew:
So good, so wond'rous good,
This woman will be,
In after-times,
A comfort to thee.

———

Epigram I.

THERE was a fellow, that would undergo
To tame the fiercest and cruell'st shrew,
That lived on the earth; and so 'twas try'd;
For, after that, he had one to his bride,
With whom he liv'd in discontent and strife,
That made him almost weary of his life:
She brought him to his night-cap, and, with grief,
He took his bed, refusing all relief.

It chanced on a time, a bull broke loose
Out of a butcher's yard, or slaughter-house,
Stark-mad, and with his horns the ground up-tears,
With twenty mastiff-dogs about his ears.
The woman-conquer'd man, that lay in bed,
Hearing a noise, steps up, like one half dead,
And, opening the casement in great haste,
Looking upon the bull, did take distaste
To see him hal'd with ropes, and tore with dogs,
With hooting boys skipping about like frogs;
Begins to call to them, Ho, hold your hands,
And understand now how the matter stands;
Why hale you so the bull? Let him alone;
'Tis too much odds, so many unto one:
But, if you'll have him tam'd, be rul'd by me,
Give him a wife, and he'll soon tamed be.

Epigram II.

THERE was an ancient batchelor of late,
Could not endure to hear a woman prate;
And, to prevent the mischief of the tongue,
The man did live a batchelor so long:
An old, decayed maid to him did come,
That lack'd a service, feeble, lame, and dumb
Made signs to him, that he would her prefer,
That she might serve this ancient batchelor.
To whom he said, Now welcome, honest Mab;
For, since I cannot brook a prattling drab,
I'll marry thee, though thou be dumb and old,
Because I know thou wilt not prove a scold:
What shall I say? My mind I'll freely break:
The dumb had better luck, than some can speak.

Epigram III.

JOAN, I do hear, that thou art turned scold,
And I am sorry thou art grown so bold,
Since I do know, when thou wast counted civil;
Can man's ill manners make a woman evil?
Then I to wed persuaded will by no man,
Because I will not overthrow a woman.

Epigram IV.

Ques. PEG, what's the reason you so crabbed are?

Ans. Because to live you have no better care.
Why do you to the ale-house follow me?
Because I you at home had rather see.

Why do you scold, when I at home do come?
Would you be drunk, and have me to be dumb?
And why speak you not of it on the morrow?
Because my heart is then too full of sorrow.
Alas, poor heart, 'tis time for me to mend;
Pity to break the heart of such a friend.

Epigram V.

I had a bird, which, with great care and pains,
I taught to sing; my pleasure was my gains:
But, O! I had a parrot at the last,
That, without teaching, learn'd to speak too fast.

Epigram VI.

A scolding woman vex'd her husband so,
That out of doors he discontent did go;
And, as he sadly went along the street,
A discontented man this man did meet,
Weeping and wailing, wringing of his hands:
Of whom the other man of him demands,
What was the cause, that he lamented so?
O friend, quoth he, the cause of this my woe
Is this: my wife is dead, and I am left
Comfortless, and of comfort quite bereft;
As good a creature as e'er liv'd on earth,
This morning did she lose her vital breath.
Was she so good? Quoth he; so is not mine:
I would my wife had then excused thine.

Epigram VII.

TWO men did walk together in the street;
Neighbours they were, and both of them discreet:
Friend, quoth the one, the death of my good wife
Doth grieve me so, I think 'twill end my life.
And truly, quoth the other, Neighbour John,
I may rejoice, that mine is dead and gone;
For, whilst she liv'd, I ne'er liv'd merry day,
And, now she's dead, I may both sport and play,
Follow my work, and never be controul'd:
No grief like his, that's troubled with a scold.

No sooner had he spoke, but two stout dames
Were scolding, and forgot each other's names ;
Whore, slut, and drab, between these two, were common,
The ordinary language of bad women.
He, that was troubled with the scolding wife,
Did run, as he had run ev'n for his life ;
And would not be persuaded otherwise,
But that his wife then from her grave did rise,
And that she follow'd him, and kept a stir,
Because she heard him talk so much of her :
Art come again, quoth he, for to torment me ?
Now I do wonder who the devil sent thee.
O, if the remembrance of a scold do so,
What will the living presence of them do ?

Epigram VIII.

THERE was a woman known to be so bold,
That she was noted for a common scold ;
And on a time, it seems, she wrong'd her betters,
Who sent her unto prison, bound in fetters :
The day of her arraignment being come,
Before grave elders, this then was her doom :
She should be ducked over head and ears,
In a deep pond, before her overseers.
Thrice was she under water, yet not fainted,
Nor yet, for aught that I could see, was daunted ;
For, when with water she was covered,
She clapp'd her hands together o'er her head,
To signify, that then she could not talk,
But then she would be sure her hands should walk :
She had no power, but yet she had a will,
That, if she could, she would have scolded still :
For, after that, when they did her up-hale,
Fiercely against them all then did she rail.
This proves some women void of reasonable wit ;
Which if they had, then would they soon submit.

Epigram IX.

A countryman, being troubled with a shrew,
Sold all his living and to Spain would go :
His wife went with him ; though she were unkind,
None could persuade her for to stay behind.
They shipping took ; and, as they sail'd along,
The billows rose, the wind grew wond'rous strong,
So that there was a mighty tempest then,
Which caus'd the captain to command the men
To cast their greatest burdens over-board ;
The which was done according to his word.

The countryman, observing what they did,
Took up his wife upon his back, unbid,
And went to cast her o'er into the sea,
Crying aloud, This is a happy day,
This is the greatest burden that I have,
'Tis best for me to make the sea her grave :
But she intreated him to spare her life,
And she would prove a kind and loving wife.
And some report, this fear with her so wrought,
That she became good, that before was naught.

Epigram X.

TWO young men for a maid of late did strive,
'Ere either of them knew the way to thrive :
One challenged the other for to fight ;
But this same challenge did him so affright,
That he, on even terms, gave o'er the sute,
Without an arbitrator to dispute ;
And, 'cause that fighting he did so abhor,
He said, she was not worth the fighting for :
Nevertheless, because he lov'd her, though,
At cross and pile he was content to throw.
Now, reader, do not think the wench mistook him,
The wench was cross enough, for she forsook him ;
Upon the other fellow did she smile,
So cross to one, and to the other pile.

Epigram XI.

HARRY was marry'd to a Guildhall wife,
And he that parchment wench did often curse :
Though she, poor wretch, was still, and void of strife,
Yet he burn'd her, and took on ten times worse.
Well, Harry, if this die, shake off thy fetter ;
Marry no more, for seldom comes the better.

Epigram XII.

AN honest man, being troubled with a scold,
Told her, if she continued so bold,
That he would have a case made out of hand,
To keep her tongue in, under his command.
Well, she had need to have a special care,
Lest she, with scolding, wear her tongue threadbare ;
Which if she do, 'twill be so poor and base,
That, sure, her tongue will not be worth a case.

Epigram XIII.

AN honest waterman, that kept a ferry,
Did take delight to see his children merry ;

s 2

And on the tongs sometimes he'd play a fit,
And the poor children would dance after it ;
And always, when his wife did scold, they say,
The good man he upon the tongs would play ;
Methought it was a strange sight to behold
Man play, children dance, and woman scold.

Epigram XIV.

A wretched woman strove to wear the breeches,
And, to her husband, us'd uncivil speeches :
Nay, she was not content ill words to send him,
But she a box o' th' ear at last did lend him :
The man did for her valour praise her much,
Because she gave him such a gentle touch.
Come, faith, quoth he, the first three bits for sixpence,
Here, take this cudgel, try how thou canst fence ;
I hope I am not such a silly elf,
But I am able to defend myself.
Together by the ears, at last, they fell,
And cudgel'd one another very well.
A porter, loaden with neat's tongues, and sowce,
Enquired for the master of the house.
Faith, friend, quoth he, I'll tell you presently,
For we are striving for the mastery :
At length the woman did begin to yield,
The man, with much ado, did win the field.
Porter (quoth he) now speak your mind to me,
For I am master of the house you see.
Sir, quoth the porter, your wife's friends have sent
Neats tongues and sowce to feed upon this Lent.
How tongues, quoth he ? Take them away again,
For an ill tongue hath almost been my bain ;
Go tell my wife's friends, of all meats that be,
The tongue agreeth worst of all with me.
And, as for sowce, I sowcing have enough :
She cannot only scold, but she can cuff.

Epigram XV.

A woman that did love a cup of ale,
Would oft be drunk, and would as often rail,
And scold at every one she met withal,
And being drunk upon a time did fall
Scolding at every one that passed by,
And being drunk the people let her lie ;
At length a certain parrot heard her talk,
And talk'd as fast as she, and cried, Walk, walk,

Ay, quoth the woman, send me now your hand,
And I'll walk home, and yet she could not stand.
Betwixt these two there is a difference,
I fain would know who spoke the better sense.

Epigram XVI.

JOHN BARRET had a parrot for to sell,
And went about where gentlemen did dwell,
To sell his parrot; at the length he met
A friend of his, that inwardly did fret,
For he, it seems, had marry'd with a shrew,
That vex'd his mind wherever he did go.
Quoth Barret, Friend, will you my parrot buy,
Which can both talk and prate most daintily?
No, quoth the man, I thank you, good John Barret:
Faith, I am too much troubled with a parrot;
Yet, in regard you are a friend of mine,
I am content to change my bird for thine.
O, quoth John Barrett, are you grown so wise?
Your bird I fear will claw out both mine eyes.

Epigram XVII.

A fellow, that was troubled with a wife,
With whom he liv'd a discontented life,
Set up a bill, and colour'd it with green:
Within this place, quoth he, is to be seen
A monster like a woman, more uncivil,
In form a woman, but in speech a devil.

Epigram XVIII.

A woman did demand of me of late,
Why I condemn'd her for her idle prate:
Since that her tongue, although a member bad,
Was all the 'fensive weapon that she had;
I cannot tell, how it did her defend,
But I am sure, that it did me offend:
For a sharp-weapon'd woman I will praise her,
For why her tongue is sharper than a razor.

Epigram XIX.

TWO men complained sorely of their wives,
And said they lived very unnat'ral lives.
My wife, quoth one, my very heart will break,
For she is sullen, and she will not speak.

c 3

O, quoth the other, it is a sweet distress,
For of two evils always chuse the less.
Thy wife wants tongue, and mine she hath too much.
Unhappy are those men, whose wives are such.

Epigram XX.

THERE was a woman, a notorious scold,
That used to be so audacious bold,
That, when her husband to the alehouse went,
Would follow him, although small coin he spent;
And she would scold so wond'rous loud and fierce,
It is past my skill the same for to rehearse:
But, when she was rebuk'd, she would reply,
It was her nature to talk hastily.
If it be so, pray tell me, good John Golding,
What difference is 'twixt hasty talk and scolding.

Epigram XXI.

THERE was a certain man a wife did wed,
That was but meanly taught, but better fed,
For always, when he was dispos'd to play,
This woman would be sullen all the day;
Which vexed him, who thought he had great wrong,
Complaining that his wife had ne'er a tongue:
But I think no, for I have heard it told,
That he was bless'd, because she would not scold.
But he did vex her so, that, at the last,
She that had lost her tongue did prate too fast.

———

An Epitaph.

HERE lies my wife in earthly mould,
Who, when she liv'd, did nought but scold.
Peace, wake her not; for now she's still:
She had, but now I have my will.

———

A Dream.

I wander'd forth a while agone,
And went I knew not whither,
But there were beauties many a one
Appeared all together.

A WOMAN'S TONGUE.

In a pleasant field of mirth,
I walked all about;
In the garden of the earth
A spirit found me out.

Jealousy her heart did wound,
She was made the people's wonder;
Like a tempest was her sound,
And her speech like claps of thunder.

Homewards then I went with speed,
Reason good, and why? Because
I perceiv'd that Jove decreed,
Sweet meat should have sowre sauce.
   Vinegar was mix'd with cream,
   But all this was but a dream.

The faithful Shepherd's dying Song.

To the Tune of
' Madam, be covered, why stand you bare?'

COME, shepherds, cast your pipes away,
No time for mirth when grief is near:
If that you please a while to stay,
My sorrow to you I'll declare.
   Unhappy I that plac'd my love,
   On her that did inconstant prove.

As I sat by my flocks of sheep,
Upon a merry holiday,
Although my flocks I safe did keep,
Yet beauty stole my heart away.

A heavenly beauty came to me,
And did salute me with a smile.
From Cupid's snares I lived free,
Until her looks did me beguile.

I wedded her, made her my own,
She was as neighbour to my heart;
My fortunes I have overthrown,
For she from me did quickly start.

Her company I could not have,
Neither by night, nor yet by day.
I was no better than her slave,
For I did work, when she did play.

s 4

Then was I forc'd the sea to cross,
And leave my wedded wife behind ;
But I was happy in my loss,
Because to me she prov'd unkind.

In three years after I was gone,
She chose herself another mate ;
I found her with another man,
And then she said I came too late.

Then I was shipp'd away again,
I was betray'd I know not how,
And landed on the coast of Spain,
And now again return'd to you.

You woods, you hills, you dales, you groves,
You brooks, and every pleasant spring,
You creatures, come, whom nothing moves,
And hear a woful shepherd sing.

For to my fellow shepherd swains,
I oftentimes have made my mone,
But what my mournful words contains
Is rightly understood of none.

O sacred heavens, why do I spend
My just endeavours thus in vain,
Since what the fates do fore-intend,
They never after change again ?

Nor faith, nor love, nor true desert,
Nor all that woful man can do,
Can win him place within her heart,
That finds he was not born thereto.

And so farewel, kind shepherds all,
Adieu, adieu, false shepherdess,
Thou art the cause of this my call,
For thou hast brought me to distress.

He sent his groans up to the skies,
And yielded up his vital breath ;
The shepherds closed up his eyes,
And laid him in his bed of death.

They sung a mournful elegy,
Over his grave, where, as he lay,
All flesh, quoth they, is born to die,
And this shall be his epitaph :
    Lo, here lies he that plac'd his love,
    On her that did inconstant prove.

A Postscript.

SINCE first my book was printed, I do hear,
Some women no good-will to me do bear:
But I must needs confess, that they were such,
Even of the vulgar sort that I did touch.
And such, whose carriage with their breeding shown,
Unto the world their weakness have made known;
Prov'd themselves guilty of the things I writ,
Shewing but little manners, and less wit.
But, since I find my book hath done some good,
I will go forward, though by them withstood:
It hath converted two, and made them civil,
That were almost as bad as is the devil;
They did confess, they did disgrace their marriage,
And wrong their husbands by their evil carriage;
They did confess, that I was in no fault,
By shewing them how poorly they did halt;
They do confess, how they indebted are
For my good will to them and honest care,
Had to their credit and their reputation,
And glad was I of this their recantation:
And glad was I when this I understood,
That I was born to do a woman good.
　　Henceforth I promise, and I do not flatter,
　　To rest their servant in a greater matter.

A SECOND AND MOST EXACT
RELATION

OF

THOSE SAD AND LAMENTABLE ACCIDENTS,

Which happened in and about the Parish Church of Wydecombe, near
the Dartmoors, in Devonshire,

ON SUNDAY THE 21ST OF OCTOBER LAST, 1638.

*Come, behold the works of the Lord, what desolations he hath made in
the earth.*

PSAL. xlvi. 8.

Imprimatur Thomas Wyke, R. P. Episc. Lond. Cap. Domest. Printed at London
by G. M. for R. Harford, and are to be sold at his shop in Queen's-head-alley,
in Paternoster-Row, at the Gilt Bible, 1638. Quarto, containing thirty-seven
pages.

Though this is called properly the second relation of this wonderful accident ; yet
it includes the former verbatim, and adds and explains some passages, either
omitted or left obscure, by way of appendix.
As for the veracity of this relation, I am in no doubt, being so well attested, and
licensed to be printed by the Bishop of London's domestick chaplain ; but I
could wish that these terrors of the Lord would persuade men to be more afraid
of his judgments, and to seek for his mercy and protection, in the times of need,
by a just discharge of their respective duties.

To the Reader.

I here present thee with a second relation of that wonderful accident,
which the printing of the former book hath given occasion of.
Having now received a full and perfect relation, as is possible to be
hoped for, or procured, assuring thee it is not grounded on information taken up at second-hand ; but those persons being now come to
London, who were eye-witnesses herein, and the chiefest discoverers
of the effects of these terrible accidents : Although thou hadst the
truth in part before, yet not the tythe thereof, the full relation
whereof thou shalt find here annexed, following after the former
relation, supplied in all those particulars, wherein there was any
defect before, supposing it better to annex it, than to dissolve and
blend it with the former. What thou hadst not before, shall only be

supplied now, and no more ; and what thou findest not here, take to
be true, as they are expressed there ; and, although it be larger than
our former, yet we desired, in penning thereof, not to trouble thee
with many words, but only the substance of this sad matter, as con-
cisely as we could ; and, though the price be more, yet suspend thy
censure till thou hast perused it, and then, it may be, thou wilt give
him thanks, who hath been at the pains to add this to the former ;
which he would not have done, unless he could tender it upon very
good authority, and testimony of witnesses, more than needful. We
know fame and report vary exceedingly, not knowing wherein to
pitch our belief, for it much increaseth or diminisheth by flying, according to the apprehension and memory, both of the givers out, and
takers up ; but take this on his word, who only wisheth and intend-
eth thy good. Farewell.

---

*A true Relation of those most strange and lamentable Accidents, happen-
ing in the parish church of Wydecomb, in Devonshire, on Sunday the
21st of October, 1638.*

GOD's visible judgments, and terrible remonstrances, which every
morning are brought to light, coming unto our knowledge, should be
our observation and admonition, ' that thereby the inhabitants of the
earth may learn righteousness ;'* for to let them pass by us, as water
runs by our doors, unobserved, argues too much regardlesness of God,
in the way of his judgments †; not to suffer them to sink into our affections, and to prove as so many terrible warning-pieces, which are shot
off from a watch-tower, to give notice of an enemy's approach, to
awaken and affright us, are but a means to harden our hearts against
the Lord, and to awaken his justice to punish us yet more : But 'to
hear and fear,'‡ and to do wickedly no more ; to search our hearts, and
amend our ways, is the best use that can be made of any of God's remarkable terrors manifested among us. When God is angry with us, it
ought to be our wisdom to meet him, and make peace with him : And,
where we see legible characters of his power and wrath, to learn to
spell out his meaning, touching ourselves ; to leave off all busy, malicious, causless, and unchristianly censuring of others, and to turn in
upon ourselves, remembering, *Vel pænitendum, vel pereundum*, ' Except
we repent, we shall likewise perish.'¶ Certain it is, that we do, in vain,
expect immunity from God's judgments, by slighting, or contemning
them, or increasing in our sinnings against him. If Pharaoh, by the
terror of thundering and lightning, was so affrighted, that he saith to
Moses, ' Intreat the Lord, for it is enough, that there be no more
mighty thunderings and hail.'§ And if Caligula, out of the fear of
thunder, would run under his bed to hide himself : How much more
should we Christians learn to fear and tremble before the most mighty

---

* Eph. iii. 5.   † Isa. xxvi. 9, 11.   ‡ Pœna peccorum terror omnium,
Luke xiii. 5.   § Exod. ix. 28.

God, 'whose voice only can shake the mountains, and rend the rocks, and divide the flames of fire' ; rends churches, amazeth, and strikes dead at his pleasure, the sons of men ? As the prophet David saith, ' He doth whatsoever he pleaseth in heaven and earth ; he causeth the vapours to ascend from the ends of the earth, and maketh lightnings for the rain, and bringeth the wind out of the treasures of the earth ; so unsearchable is his wisdom, and his ways past finding out.' Therefore, this should awe and humble our hearts before the Lord, rising up unto more perfection in godliness, doing unto our God more and better service than ever hitherto we have done, reverencing and sanctifying his dreadful name in our hearts : especially when his judgments break in upon men, even in his own house, 'mingling their blood with their sacrifices,' and that, in a most terrible manner, smiting, and wounding, and killing, as, in this ensuing relation, may appear ; which, for the suddenness and strangeness thereof, and, in a manner, miraculous, considering the many circumstances, I believe few ages can parallel, or produce the like. The Lord teach thee to profit thereby, that it may be as a sermon preached to thee from heaven by the Lord himself.

Upon Sunday the twenty-first of October last, in the parish church of Wydecombe, near the Dartmoors, in Devonshire, there fell, in time of divine service, a strange darkness, increasing more and more, so that the people, there assembled, could not see to read in any book ; and suddenly, in a fearful and lamentable manner, a mighty thundering was heard, the rattling whereof did answer much like unto the sound and report of many great cannons, and terrible strange lightning therewith, greatly amazing those that heard and saw it, the darkness increasing yet more, till they could not see one another ; the extraordinary lightning came into the church so flaming, that the whole church was presently filled with fire and smoke, the smell whereof was very loathsome, much like unto the scent of brimstone ; some said, they saw, at first, a great fiery ball come in at the window, and pass through the church, which so affrighted the whole congregation, that the most part of them fell down into their seats, and some upon their knees, some on their faces, and some one upon another, with a great cry of burning and scalding, they all giving up themselves for dead, supposing the last judgment-day was come, and that they had been in the very flames of hell.

The minister of the parish, Master George Lyde, being in the pulpit, or seat where prayers are read, however he might be much astonished hereat, yet, through God's mercy, had no other harm at all in his body ; but, to his much grief and amazement, beheld, afterward, the lamentable accidents : and, although himself was not touched, yet the lightning seized upon his poor wife, fired her ruff, and linnen next to her body, and her clothes, to the burning of many parts of her body, in a very pitiful manner. And one Mistress Ditford, sitting in the pew with the minister's wife, was also much scalded, but the maid and child, sitting at the pew-door, had no harm. Besides, another woman, adventuring to run out of the church, had her clothes set on fire, and was

* Psal. xxix.

not only strangely burnt and scorched, but had her flesh torn about her back almost to the very bones. Another woman had her flesh so torn, and her body so grievously burnt, that she died the same night.

Also one Master Hill, a gentleman of good account in the parish, sitting in his seat by the chancel, had his head suddenly smitten against the wall, through the violence whereof he died that night, no other hurt being found about his body; but his son sitting in the same seat had no harm. There was also one man more, at the same instant, of whom it is particularly related, who was warrener unto Sir Richard Reynolds, his head was cloven, his skull rent into three pieces, and his brains thrown upon the ground whole, and the hair of his head, through the violence of the blow at first given him, did stick fast unto the pillar or wall of the church, and in the place a deep bruise into the wall, as if it were shot against with a cannon-bullet.

Some other persons were then blasted and burnt, and so grievously scalded and wounded, that since that time they have died thereof, and many others not like to recover, notwithstanding all the means, that can be procured, to help them. Some had their clothes burnt, and their bodies had no hurt; and some, on the contrary, had their bodies burnt, and their clothes not touched, and some their stockings and legs burnt and scalded, and their outward buskings not one thread singed. But it pleased God, yet, in the midst of judgment, to remember mercy, sparing some, and not destroying all, yet very many were sorely scalded in divers parts of their bodies; and, as all this hurt was done upon the bodies of men and women, so the hurt also that was then done unto the church was remarkable.

There were some seats, in the body of the church, turned upside down, and yet they which sat in them had little or no hurt; also a boy, sitting on his seat, had his hat on, and near the one half thereof was cut off, and he had no hurt. And one man, going out at the chancel-door, a dog running out before him, was whirled about towards the door, and fell down stark dead; at the sight whereof he stepped back within the door, and God preserved him alive. Also, the church itself was much torn and defaced by the thunder and lightning; and thereby, also, a beam was burst in the midst, and fell down between the minister and clark, and hurt neither; and a weighty great stone, near the foundation of the church, is torn out and removed, and the steeple itself is much rent; and there, where the church was most rent, there was least hurt done to the people, and not any one was hurt either with the wood or stone, but a maid of Manaton, which came thither, that afternoon, to see some friends, whom Master Fryad, the coroner, by circumstances, supposed she was killed with a stone. There were also stones thrown from the tower, and carried about, a great distance from the church, as thick as if a hundred men had been there throwing, and a number of them, of such weight and bigness, that the strongest man cannot lift them. Also, one pinnacle of the tower was torn down, and broke through into the church.

Moreover, the pillar, against which the pulpit standeth, being but newly whited, is now, by this means, turned black and sulphury. Furthermore, one man that stood in the chancel, with his face toward the bellfry, observed, as it were, the rising of dust or lime, in the lower end of the church, which suddenly, as with a puff of wind, was whirled up, and cast into his eyes, so that he could not see in twelve hours after, but now his sight is restored, and he hath no other hurt. The terrible lightning being past, all the people being in wonderful amaze, so that they spake not one word, by and by one Master Ralph Rouse, vintner in the town, stood up, saying these words : 'Neighbours, in the name of God, shall we venture out of the church?' To which, Mr. Lyde answering, said, ' It is best to make an end of prayers, for it were better to die here, than in another place.' But they, looking about them, and seeing the church so terribly rent and torn, durst not proceed in their publick devotions, but went forth of the church.

And as all this was done within the church, and unto the church, so there were other accidents without the church, of which I will give you a touch. There was a bowling-alley near unto the church-yard, which was turned up into pits and heaps, in manner almost as if it had been plowed. At the same time also, at Brickstone, near Plymouth, there fell such store of hail, and such hail-stones, that, for quantity, they were judged to be as big as ordinary turky-eggs ; some of them were of five, some of six, and others of seven ounces weight.

We are also certainly informed, that, at the same time, as near as it can be guessed, there fell out the like accident unto the church at Norton, in Somersetshire, but as yet we hear of no persons hurt therein : Also it is related by a gentleman who travelled in those parts at that time, he being since come to London, that, where he was, the lightning was so terrible, fiery, and flaming, that they thought their houses, at every flash, were set on fire, insomuch that their horses in the stable were so affrighted that they could not rule them.

The Addition to the former Relation.

THIS church of Wydecombe being a large and fair church newly trimmed, there belonging to it a very fair steeple or tower, with great and small pinnacles thereon, it being one of the famousest towers in all those western parts ; and there being gathered a great congregation, to the number, as is verily believed, of at least three hundred persons.

Master Lyde, with many others in the church, did see, presently after the darkness, as it were, a great ball of fire, and most terrible lightning, come in at the window, and therewithal, the roof of the church, in the lower part against the tower, to rend and gape wide open ; whereat he was so much amazed, that he fell down into his seat ; and unspeakable are the mighty secret wonders the Lord wrought immediately, of which, because thou hast the general relation before, I will give thee this, as near as can be discovered, in the order and course thereof, which first began in the tower, and thence into the church ; the power of that vehement and terrible blast struck in at the north side of the tower, tearing through a most strong stone wall into the stairs, which goes up round with stone steps to the top of the leads; and, being gotten in, struck against the other side of the wall, and, finding not way forth there, it rebounded back again, with greater force, to that side next the church, and piercing through, right against the higher window of the church, took the greatest part thereof with it, and likewise some of the stones, and frame of the window, and so struck into the church, coming with a mighty power; it struck against the north-side wall of the church, as if it were with a great cannon-bullet, or somewhat like thereto, and not going through, but exceedingly shaking and battering the wall, it took its course directly up that isle, strait to the pulpit or seat where master Lyde sat; and in the way, thence going up, it took all the lime and sand of the wall, and much grated the stones thereof, and tore off the side desk of the pulpit; and, upon the pulpit, on the side thereof, it was left as black and moist as if it had been newly wiped with ink.

Then it goes strait up in the same isle, and struck off all the hinder part of the warrener's head (the brains fell backward, intire and whole, into the next seat behind him, and two pieces of his skull) and dashed his blood against the wall; the other piece of his skull fell into the seat where he sat, and some of the skin of his head, flesh, and hair was carried into the chancel, and some of his hair, to the quantity of a handful, stuck fast, as with lime and sand newly tempered, upon one of the bars of the timber-work partition between the church and chancel. And one man, who sat next to the warrener in the same seat, was scalded, and all burnt on that side next the warrener, from the very head to the foot, and no hurt at all on the other side. And, in the second seat behind him, was another struck, in a most fearful manner; for he was so burnt and scalded all over his body, from his forehead downward below his knees, insomuch that he was all over like raw flesh round about; and, which is most wonderful, his clothes not once hurt, neither his head nor hair, who, notwithstanding, died not then, but lived in great misery above a week after.

But to go on in our relation. It is supposed, it having been since by divers judiciously viewed, that here the power or force divided itself two ways; one part whereof struck out of the window over their heads, which tore out, and carried away, some great stones out of the wall with the window, and further they could not trace it; but, with the force of the stroke, at going forth, it struck the lime and sand on the wall with many small stones, or grit, so forcibly, that the lime, sand, and grit returned back, like hail-shot, to the other side of the wall where men did sit, and struck into their faces, much disfiguring them, and smote into the wall, and into the timber of the partition, some of which stones could not be picked out till the next day following.

But the other part of the force descended to the bottom of the wall, just before the warrener's seat, and there pierced in, heaving up all the wall in that place, rending and tearing it from the very ground, as high almost as the height of a man; there it broke through into the chancel, and, about the number of eight boys sitting about the rails of the communion table, it took them up from the seats, and threw them all on heaps within the rails, and not one of them hurt; and, one of them having his hat lying upon the rail, it was cut and burnt half way.

Then it went directly over to the other side of the chancel,' and struck master Hill mortally in his head, so that he died that night; but his son, sitting as close by him as one man can sit by another, for the seat would hold but two, had no harm at all, not so much as once sindged. But it struck against the wall so forcibly, that it beat in the wall behind him, as if it had been shot against with a cannon-bullet, as it is expressed in the former relation; but there, not going through, it recoiled back again, coming about the chancel, as it is conceived, and tore out violently one of the great side-stones of the chancel door, against which it smote, cleaving it all to pieces, and there it is supposed it went forth; but some reasons there are to think it did not, for none of the pieces of the side-stone were carried out with it, but fell down within the chancel; besides, the consideration of the mighty strange and secret works thereof in the body of the church, for there it had rent and tore, and flung about marvellously.

The seats, where men and women sat, were rent up, turned upside down, and they that sat in them had no harm; also, many of those pews and seats rent quite from the bottom, as if there had been no seats there, and those that sat in them, when they came to themselves, found that they were thrown out of their own into other seats, three or four seats higher, and yet had no harm. And, moreover, all the wood, timber, and stones were torn all to pieces, and violently thrown, every way, to the very walls of the church round about.

One man sitting upon the church-bier, at the lower end, the bier was struck and torn, and he that sat thereon was thown into one of the pews by the wall-side, a good distance off.

Many also, both men and women, being very much hurt and scalded in divers places of their bodies, and after divers manners, to the number of fifty or sixty, among whom, Mrs. Lyde, the minister's wife, was one, who suffered herein, as it is related in the former. And also Mrs. Ditford, her gown, two waistcoats, and linnen next her body, burnt clean off, and her back also very grievously down to her waist burnt and scalded, and so exceedingly afflicted thereby, she could neither stand nor go without help, being led out of the church. And one ancient woman was so terribly burnt, and her flesh torn, especially her hand, the flesh was so rotten and perished, that her hand is cut off that it might not endanger her arm; and many of those, that were then burnt and scalded, have since died thereof.

And, furthermore, all the roof of the church is terribly torn, and a great part thereof broken into the church by some great stones, that were torn off the tower; and all the other part hangs fearfully, all ragged and torn in divers places, ready to drop down; it tore likewise all the windows, shook and rent the church walls in divers places, but the chancel roof had little or no hurt. Moreover, a beam was burst in sunder, which fell down between the minister and clerk, yet hurt neither. Nor was there, in all this time, any one hurt either with stick or stone, but only one man that had a little bruise on his back; and, as there was least hurt done where the timber and stone fell most, so, on the contrary, where no timber nor stone fell, there was most hurt done. And all this while, after the terrible noise and lightning, not one in the church can remember they either heard or saw any thing, being all deadly astonished.

And, when the lightning was past, the people being still in a maze, not one could speak a word to another; but by and by master Rouse came a little to himself, standing up, and spake as in the former relation; and, speaking to Master Lyde, he also thereupon began to recover himself, and answered as well as he could, trembling, as is expressed before, not knowing of any hurt that was done, either to his wife or any else; but they, looking about them, saw a very thick mist, with smother, smoke, and smell, insomuch that they, nor any there, saw the danger over their heads. But, they two going forth together at the chancel door, they saw a dog whirled up some height from the ground, taken up and let down again three times together, and at last fell down stone dead, all the lightning being past, neither could they see any thing at all near the dog.

Then presently the rest of the people scrabled forth the church as well as they could; the mist and smother went away by degrees, but was not quite gone in half an hour after : And, being come forth, they saw their danger, which before they knew not; for the tower and church were grievously cracked and shattered, and some of the stones on the church and tower torn off, and thrown every way round about, and huge weighty stones split all to pieces, some thrown distant from the church at least an hundred yards. And one great stone, like a massy rock, was carried off the pinnacle all over the east-end of the church, and over the church-yard, and into another close over the hedge; there it grazed, breaking up the ground deeply, and, as it is imagined, it was done by that massy stone, which was carried, at least, ten yards beyond, and there bruised the ground very deep, where it lay immoveable.

And, on the other side of the church, there is a bowling-green, torn up and spoiled with stones as before; amongst many others there fell therein one great broad stone, like a table, and in the fall was broken all to pieces, they being struck edge-ways into the ground, also many great stones were sunk so deep on all sides the church, that some were struck in even with the ground, and some lower. Some stones were thrown over Master Rouse's house an hundred yards from the church, and sunk into the earth not to be seen, but only the hole, where the stone went down ; and Master Rouse's house, on that side next the church, was torn up, the covering carried off, and one of the rafters broke into the house.

Then a while after, before night, they adventured into the church to fetch out the dead bodies, some whereof being brought forth, and laid in the church-yard; there was then present a woman, being till that time much astonished, coming better to herself, upon sight of the dead bodies remembered, that she brought her child to church with her; they then, going in to seek for it, found her child going hand in hand with another little child, being met coming down one of the isles, and had no hurt, nor seemed to be any thing frighted by their countenances ; neither were there any children in the church hurt at all; but the other child's mother was gone home, never remembering she had a child, till it was brought to her.

But as strange a thing as any of these was that, concerning Robert Mead the warrener; he being not missed all this while, immediately, Master Rouse, his dear acquaintance, remembering him, and seeing him not, nor none knowing what was become of him, Master Rouse, stepping to the window, looked into the church where the warrener used to sit, and there saw him sitting in his seat, leaning upon his elbow, his elbow resting upon the desk, before him; he supposed him to be a-sleep, or astonished, not yet come to himself; he, calling to awake him, wondered he made no answer; then his love to him caused him to venture into the church, to jog him awake, or to remember him, and then, to his much grief, he perceived his friend to be a dead man; for all the hinder part of his head was clean cut off, and gone round about his neck, and the forepart not disfigured, as they supposed when they drew near him.

The Lord of the Manor of Wydecombe, hearing of this sad accident, sent his man, David Barry, that night thither, to hear what news, and to see what hurt was done; but, it being dark, he could see nothing that night, but only hear their relations. But on Monday, the day following, they came to take notice, and view the ruins of the church, and what accidents had fallen out; then all this relation was made apparent to him, and, I may safely say, to thousands more of witnesses, that are ready to give testimony to all this relation.

But having seen, and observed, as much as they could about the church, the tower being locked up, what hurt was done there, was as yet unknown: There being then a motion made to open the door to see what hurt, no man was found willing to adventure, much less ascend up therein, all the people being as yet in a terrible fear; the remembrance of their great hurts and dangers being so fresh in their minds; for, some being to be buried in the church that afternoon, as namely, Master Hill and Robert Mead, their graves being close by one another, the minister read the burial to both at once, and when he came to those words, Earth to earth, ashes to ashes, dust to dust, the fall thereof, making a sudden noise upon the coffins, made them all in a great fear run out of the church, tumbling over one another, supposing that the church was falling on their heads.

But the said David resolved to venture himself to discover what he could, and, calling for the key to open the door, it was brought by the sexton, yet they all persuaded him not to venture, for the tower was so crazy, torn, and shattered, that they were all of opinion, it might fall, as they might well judge by the outside; but, he putting in the key to open the door, it would not unlock it, but run quite through: then the sexton, he trying also, could find no lock, and yet the door still fast; then, an iron bar being used to force it off the hinges, it could not be done thereby, till at last he, espying the bolt of the lock shot into the staple, desired them to hold the door up with the bar, that he might put in his arm to put back the lock, and found there all the wood and wards of the lock gone; then, the door being with much ado forced open, the said David was to go up first, and the sexton to follow him, where he found so much rubbish and stone tumbled down, that he could hardly creep up; he having his sword by his side, it troubled him, he put it off, wishing the clark to hold it, while he made way; but, as they ascended, there came down the stairs a most loathsome smell beyond expression, as it were of brimstone, pitch, and sulphur; he notwithstanding adventured higher, but, the sexton's stomach and courage being overcome, partly by his fear, and also by the smell, he returned back in a great fright, complaining he was poisoned.

A multitude of people being there to observe the discovery, come from divers places thereabouts, to see and hear of this spreading ill news, as daily multitudes do resort there for that purpose, they all stood at a distance, waiting what could be found, but they not knowing what was become of him, because the sexton was so frighted, none daring to come near to look after him. But he getting (with great difficulty, and danger of his life at every step) up to the first story, there he viewed it, and found no hurt done; but, getting with greater difficulty up to the bell-room, he tolled all the bells, to see if they were sound or no, then the people much rejoiced, supposing he was well.

Then looking over head he saw all the joyces and timber under the leads carried away, all rent and torn fearfully, except one beam under the middle, which was bowed down, and a great number of stones lying on the leads in a very strange and dangerous manner; but, his heart encouraging him to venture yet higher, he attempted the leads, and, getting up to the door, he saw a great danger, over his head, at the sight whereof his heart began to fail him, for the stones were carried clean away, under the inside next the church, and, on the outside, so shaken that very little upheld them; then espying yet more danger than before, he saw a great stone over his head, as he supposed, ready to drop down upon uim, that he knew not whether to stay or go down, for fear of the falling thereof; then, attempting to throw it down, cried as loud as he possibly could, being at the top, to stand clear, for fear of danger; he catching hold on somewhat over his head, hung by his hands, and with his feet touched the weighty stone, which tumbled down the stairs, never resting till it came to the bottom; then all the people, at the fall thereof, thought he was killed, but he, presently coming down into the bell-room, tolled the bells, again, and thereby removed their fear.

Then coming down lower, in one place in the stairs, close by the place, where the tower was most rent and shaken, there he espied a thing very strange to him, as if it had been a cannon discharged full of powder, and as if a bullet withal struck and shook it, and, finding no way out, recoiled back to another side, and there rent out a great part of the tower, with mighty stones; and, but a little above it, there was a round patch as broad as a bushel, which looked thick, slimy, and black, and black round about it, to which he put his hand, and felt it soft, and, bringing some thereof in his hand from the wall, came down the stairs to the people, and shewed them that strange compound; all much wondered thereat, and were affrighted, not knowing what it might be; it was like slimy powder tempered with water; he smelling thereto, it was so odious even beyond expression, and in a far higher degree of loathsomness, than the scent which was in the church or tower when they first smelt it, it being of the same kind; they supposing that strong smell came from that, which did overcome the sexton's and this searcher's stomach almost.

Yet all this while he found himself reasonable well, though much offended with smells; and, going home with Master Lyde to supper, he lodged at Master Rouse's, and went well to bed, and, an hour after, he felt something come upon him, as he thought, on the outside of his waist and belly, as if it were a cord twisted about him, two men pulling it with great strength, which griped him in that unspeakable manner three or four times, that he thought himself cut in sunder therewith, not having any breath, nor none knowing what to do to him; he could take nothing down, at present to ease him, but by and by, ridding his stomach by vomiting, being in a great and terrible sweat all this while, insomuch that the sheets, wherein he lay, might have been wringed; at last came up such a loathsome vomit, that smelt of the same nature that that did which he brought out of the steeple, and after this, taking some rest, he was very well, in the morning.

All which most sad and lamentable spectacles were done, as it were, in a moment of time.

This is the sum of those dismal accidents and terrible examples happening in the place aforesaid. And the main drift, in the publication of this great judgment, is for thy humiliation and edification, not only to acquaint thee with the great and mighty works of God's power and justice, who in a moment can do mighty things to us, and arm the creatures against us at his own pleasure, but also to move pity and compassion in us towards our brethren who were patients therein, not judging them greater sinners than ourselves; but believing, ' That except we also repent and sin no more, we shall likewise perish,' or worse things befall us. Which relation you can difficultly read without sighs, nor understand without tears. I know it is the fashion of too many to question and talk, and make things of this nature but a nine days wonder: But let us not deceive ourselves any longer, but consider, we have been lookers on a great while, and others have been made our examples, and felt the smart at home and abroad, whilst we have gone free; but we know not how soon our turns and changes may come; these accidents might as well have happened to us, as them; the Lord therefore in much mercy fit us both for the worst of times and the best of ends. I end all with that prayer in our Litany, commending thee, and this, to the blessing of the Almighty.

From lightning and tempest, from plague, pestilence, and famine, from battle and murder, and from sudden death,

Good Lord deliver us.

THE

MARQUIS OF HUNTLEY'S REPLY

TO

CERTAIN NOBLEMEN, GENTLEMEN, AND MINISTERS,

COVENANTERS OF SCOTLAND:

Sent from their Associates, to signify unto him, that it behoved him
either to assist their designs, or to be carried to Prison in the Castle
of Edinburgh, the 20th of April, 1639.

New published, because of a false Copy thereof lately printed without authority,
or his own consent. Quarto, containing four pages.

TO be your prisoner is by much the less displeasing to me, that my
accusation is for nothing else but loyalty ; and that I have been
been brought into this estate by such unfair means, as can never be
made to appear honourable in those who used them.

Whereas you offer liberty, upon condition of my entering into your
covenant, I am not so bad a merchant, as to buy it with the loss of
my conscience, fidelity, and honour: which, in so doing, I should
make account to be wholly perished.

I have already given my faith to my prince, upon whose head this
crown, by all law of nature and nations is justly fallen, and will not
falsify that faith by joining with any in a pretence of religion, which
my own judgment cannot excuse from rebellion ; for it is well known,
that, in the primitive church, no arms were held lawful, being lifted
by subjects against their lawful prince, though the whole frame of
Christianity was then in question.

Whereas you would encourage me to be a partaker with you by your
hopes of supply from France and other foreign nations, together with
your so good intelligence in England, as that no danger will come from
thence, let me tell you, that, in my opinion, the reasons are but vain,
the French being now more strictly tied, than before, to uphold the
authority of our sacred sovereign, by a new-cemented league of marriage, whereby their interest in his Majesty's progeny will over-balance
you, though your cause were better. Other foreigners are merely unable by their own distractions, and the English have been ever strong
enough for us, when only their own king, and not our's did lead them.

For my own part, I am in your power, and resolved not to leave
that foul title of Traitor as an inheritance upon my posterity ; you
may take my head from my shoulders, but not my heart from my
sovereign.

A

QUESTION OF THE COCK,

AND

WHETHER HIS CROWING AFFRIGHTS THE LION?

Being one of those Questions handled in the weekly conferences of
Monsieur Renaudot's Bureau d'Adresses, at Paris.

[Translated into English, Anno 1640, in six Quarto Pages.]

THE first man said thus : the Germans, going to the wars, had reason to take a Cock with them to serve them for a spur and an
example of watchfulness ; whence came a custom to this day used by
the mule-drivers; some of which tie a Cock upon the foremost carriage ;
and others, that will not trouble themselves with him, provide only a
plume of his feathers. Upon the same ground Phidias made a statue
of Minerva, bearing a Cock upon her helmet ; unless you will rather
think his reason to be, because this goddess is as well president of war
as of study; both which have need of much vigilancy. Though this
bird, for other causes, may be well enough said to pertain to her ; as,
for his being so warlike and courageous, as that he will not part with
his desire of vanquishing, though it cost him his life ; and this desire
he prosecutes with such fury, that Cælius Aurelian reports, that a
man fell mad, having only been pecked by a Cock in the heat of his
fighting. For the passion of choler, being a short madness, is able exceedingly to raise the degree of heat in a temper already so extremely
cholerick, that in time the body of a Cock becomes nitrous ; and in
this consideration it is prescribed to sick persons to make them laxative,
and it is the better, if he were first well beaten, and plucked alive, and
then boiled.

And this courage of the Cock moved Artaxerxes, King of Persia,
when a soldier of Caria had slain Prince Cyrus, to grant him leave to
bear a little Cock of gold upon his javelin, as a singular badge of his
great valour. In imitation whereof, all the soldiers of the same province fell to wear the like upon the crests of their helmets ; and were
thence called Alectryons, that is in Latin, Galli, a name afterwards
given to our nation*, and it may be for the like reason.

The Cock is also the hieroglyphick of victory, because he crows when
he hath beaten his adversary ; which gave occasion to the Lacedemonians to sacrifice a Cock, when they had overcome their enemies. He
was also dedicated to Mars ; and the poets feign that he was a young
soldier, and placed for a centinel by this God of war when he went to

* The Author was a Frenchman.

lie with Venus, but feared the return of her husband; but, this watchman sleeping till after sun-rising, Mars and she were taken napping by Vulcan. Mars, being very angry, transformed this sleeper into a Cock for his negligence; whence, say they, it comes to pass, that, well remembering the cause of his transformation, he now gives warning when the sun draws near to our horizon. Which fable is as tolerable as that of the Alcoran, which attributes the crowing of our cocks to one that, as he saith, stands upon the first heaven, and is of so immense a hugeness, that his head toucheth the second; which Cock crows so loud, that he awakens all the Cocks upon the earth, that immediately they fall to provoking one another to do the like; as if there were one and the same instant of cock-crowing all over the face of the whole earth. The Cock was also dedicated to the sun, to the moon, and to the goddesses Latona, Ceres, and Proserpina; which was the cause that the novices, or those that were initiated in their mysteries, must not eat of a Cock. He was also dedicated to Mercury, because vigilancy and early rising is necessary for merchants; and therefore they painted him in the form of a man sitting, having a crest upon his head, with eagles feet, and holding a Cock upon his fist. But particularly he was consecrated to Æsculapius, which made Socrates, at the point of death, to will his friends to sacrifice a cock to him, because his hemlock had wrought well. And Pyrrhus, curing men of the spleen, caused them to offer a white Cock, whereas Pythagoras forbade his followers to meddle with the life or nourishing of any of that colour.

The inhabitants of Calecut sacrifice a Cock to their deity, whom they conceive in the shape of a he-goat; and Acosta, out of Lucian, assures us, that anciently they worshipped a Cock for a God; which, Christianity not suffering, hath put them upon churches, the spires of steeples, and high buildings, calling them weather-cocks, because, as fans, they shew the coast whence the wind comes, unless you rather think they are set up in remembrance of St. Peter's repentance at the second crowing of a Cock.

The cause of his crowing is commonly attributed to his heat, which makes him rejoice at the approach of the sun, as being of his own temper; of which approach he is sooner sensible than others, because he more easily than any other creature receives the impression of the air, as appears by that harsh voice which he sometimes useth in crowing when he hath been newly moistened by the vapours; and, therefore, the countrymen count it an ordinary sign of rain. And forasmuch as the whole species of birds is more hot, dry, and light than the species of four-footed beasts; therefore the Lion, though he be a solar creature, as well as the Cock, yet is so in a lesser degree than he. Whence it comes to pass, that the Cock hath a pre-eminence over the Lion, which he understands not, till the crowing raise in his imagination some species which in him produce terror. Unless you will say, that the spirits of the Cock are communicated to the Lion, by means of his voice; for that is a thing more material, and so more capable to act than the spirits which come out of sore eyes, which nevertheless do infect those that are sound, if they look on them; nay, to speak with the poet, they do bewitch the very lambs.

The Second said, we must reckon this error (of a Cock scaring a Lion by crowing) among divers other vulgar ones, of which oftentimes the chairs and pulpits ring, as if they were certain truths, when, in the tryal, they prove stark false. It may be some tame lion, grown cowardly by the manner of his breeding, hath been seen affrighted by the shrill sound of some Cock crowing suddenly and near to his ears; which will seem not unlikely to them that, in the beginning of March last past, were present at the intended combate in the tennis-court at Rochelle, between such a lion and a bull; at the sight of whom the lion was so afraid, that he bolted through the nets, throwing down the spectators which were there placed in great numbers, as thinking it a place of greater security; and, running thence, he hid himself, and could by no means be made re-enter the lists. Or it may be the novelty of this crowing surprised some lion that never heard it before, as having always lived far from any village or country-house where poultry are bred; and thereupon the lion at this first motion startled.

It is also possible, and most likely too, that the startle of choler, whereinto the lion falls as soon as any thing displeases him, was mistaken by somebody for a sign of fear, whereas it was a token of his indignation. For I see no shew of reason to imagine in this generous beast a true and universal fear of so small a matter as the voice of a Cock, seeing that this likeness of nature, which is attributed to them, should rather produce some sympathy than any aversion; and yet this enmity, if any were, and that as great as between wolves and sheep, ought no more to scare the lion than the bleating of a sheep affrights a wolf. But the wolf devours the sheep, and assimilates it to his own substance, rather for the good-will that he bears himself, than for any ill-will or hatred that he bears towards the sheep. Besides, we ordinarily see cocks and hens in the court-yards of the houses where lions are kept, which never make any shew of astonishment at their crowing. Nay, I remember, I have seen a young lion eat a cock; it is true, he did not crow any more than those of Nibas, a village near to Thessalonica, in Macedonia, where the cocks never crow. But the lion would have been content with tearing the Cock in pieces, and not have eaten him, if there had been such an antipathy between them as some imagine. But this error finds entertainment for the moral's sake, which they infer upon it, to shew us that the most hardy are not exempt from fear, which often-times arises whence it is least looked for. So that to ask, Why the Crowing of a Cock scares Lions, is to seek the causes of a thing that is not.

The Third said, we must not make so little account of the authority of our predecessors, as absolutely to deny what they have averred, the proof of which seems sufficiently tried by the continued experience of so many ages; for to deny a truth, because we know not the reason of it, is to imitate Alexander, who cut the Gordian knot, because he could not unty it. It is better, in the nature of the Cock and his voice, to seek a cause of the fright of the Lion, who being a creature always in a fever, by his excessive cholerick distemper, of which his hair and his violence are tokens; great noise is to him as intolerable as to those that are sick and feverish, especially those in whom a cholerick humour, inflamed, stirs up the head-ach. Besides, there are some kinds of sound, which some persons cannot endure; and yet can give you no reason for it, but are constrained to fly to specifical properties and antipathies; and such we may conceive to be between the Cock's crowing and a Lion's ear, with much more likelihood than that the remora stays vessels under full sail; and a thousand other effects impenetrable by our reason, but assured by our experience.

Lastly, This astonishment that the Cock puts the Lion into, with his crowing, is not very unreasonable: this king of beasts having occasion to wonder, how out of so small a body should issue a voice so strong, and which is heard so far off, whereas himself can make such great slaughters with so little noise. Which amazement of the Lion is so much the greater, if the Cock be white, because this colour helps yet more to dissipate his spirits, which were already scattered by the first motion of his apprehension.

A QUESTION,

WHETHER THERE BE NOTHING NEW?

Being one of those Questions handled in the Weekly Conferences of Monsieur Renaudot's Bureau d'Addresses, at Paris.

Translated into English, Anno 1640. Quarto, containing six pages.

London, printed by R. B. for Jasper Emery, at the Eagle and Child, in St. Paul's Church-yard, near St. Augustine's Gate.

THE desire to learn is natural, and no less pleasing to the mind of man, than his desire of getting; and, indeed, it is one kind of getting: And as men receive more contentment in one new purchase, than in often thinking on all those which they had made before; so our understanding takes a great deal more pleasure in feeding upon new nourishment, than in chewing the cud upon that which it had already; yea, and among those new repasts, if it light upon any which it never tasted before, it receives it, as our palate is wont to do, with so much the more pleasure: For nature is more pleased with the change, than with the continuation of the use of any thing; the reason is, because, seeking the supreme good, and not finding it in any of those things which he hath yet made trial of, she always hopes to find it elsewhere. This sweetness is that which allays the bitterness of learning to children, who are ravished with the pleasure of learning all those histories, and pedantical conceits, which we can so hardly endure when we are grown to more age. It may be, it makes old men so melancholick, because you can hardly tell them any thing that they know not ; and, therefore, men's talk is tedious to them ; whereas ignorant youth admires and takes pleasure in every thing. And we are so delighted with novelty, that there is no beast so ill-favoured, which seems not pretty, when it is young, witness the ass's foal ; nor no plant of so little delight, as that novelty cannot commend it, as we see in the hop, and the primrose. But,

I distinguish novelty into physical, or natural, moral, and artificial. The first of these is in new productions, whether of substances, or accidents, or of diseases, unknown to the ancients. The second of new and unusual actions. The third of inventions.

According to which distinction we may state this question, and that, in my opinion, must be done thus : There are no new substantial productions ; nature having displayed all her forces, almost these six thousand years (according to the true account, and much more, if we believe the Egyptians and Chinese) and having run through all imaginable varieties of species, by the divers combinations of all her matters ; and, also, through all mixtures of qualities, and other accidents ; which makes it impossible to shew any disease, that is new and unknown to the foregoing ages. But, for actions, it is another case ; their number cannot be determined, because they depend upon the liberty of man, which could be no longer liberty, if our will were not free to pass some set number. Much less can inventions be said to be determinate, and reducible to a certain number, because they depend, in their productions, upon the wit of man, which is infinite in its duration, and in its conceptions, which cannot be bounded, no not by that vacuum, which some have imagined on the further side of the heavens. Of which all our inventions are proofs sufficient.

The second said, that this exception is unnecessary, there being nothing at all new in any of those fore-named classes, according to the testimony of him that was best able to judge, as being the wisest, and who had made the most experiments ; I mean Solomon, who boldly pronounces of his own times, that there was not then, nor should ever be, any new thing. How much more then is it true in our time, being so many years after him ? For, to begin with the *Formæ substantiales*, as they call them, there is not one of that sort new, not only in its species, but even in its individual qualities, which, indeed, appear new to our senses, but yet are not so, for all that ; as the shape of a marble statue was in the stone not only in possibility, but also in act, before the graver made it appear to our eyes, by taking away that which was superfluous, and hindered us from seeing it. And if we believe, that we have so good a horse, that his like was never found ; it is not, because it is so, but, because it seems so ; other horses, as good, or better than that, never coming to our hands. Much less likely is it, that new diseases should be produced, as some have believed, imagining that the ancients were not curious enough to describe all those of their times, or their successors diligent enough to examine their writings, to find them there. As for human actions, do we see any now-a-days, that have not been practised in times past, whether good or bad, valiant or cowardly, in counsel or in execution? And that, which they call invention, is, for the most part, nothing but a simple imitation in deeds, or words. Thus, printing and guns, which, we believe, were invented within these two or three hundred years, are found to have been in use, among the Chinese, above twelve hundred years. So saith Terence of speech, *Nihil est jam dictum, quod non dictum sit prius.* Our very thoughts, though they be innumerable, yet, if they were registered, would be all found ancient.

The third said, That nature is so much pleased with diversity, which is nothing else but a kind of novelty, that she hath imprinted a desire of it, in all things here below, and, it may be, in things above also; for they are pleased in their work, and the supreme and universal causes produce us these novelties. Thus, the different periods of the heavens make new aspects, and new influences, not only every year, but also every month, every day, yea, every moment. The moon, every quarter, shews a several sort of face; and particularly, when she sends all her light towards the sun, she is called new. The sun, at his rising, is new, and so he appears incessantly to some country or other in the world; in each of which he makes new seasons, and, amongst the rest, spring, because it is the most pleasant time, is commonly called, in France, *le renouveau,* because it renews all things; the air decking itself with a more chearful light, the trees cloathing themselves with leaves, the earth with greenness, the meadows being enamelled and embroidered with new flowers. The young man, that feels the down upon his chin, acknowledgeth his mossy beard to be new; upon his wedding-day, he is a new married man; it is a pretty new case to his bride, to find herself made a woman; her great belly and lying-in are also novelties to her; the little infant then born is a new fruit; his first sucking is new; his teeth, at first coming, are new. And so are all other conditions of clerkship, and priesthood, and widowhood, and almost infinite others. Yea, many things, that seem not at all to be new, yet are so, as a river seems very ancient, and yet it renews itself every moment; so that the water, that now runs under the bridge, is not that which was there yesterday, but still keeps the same name, though it be, altogether, other indeed. We ourselves are renewed from time to time, by our nourishment's continual restoration of our wasted triple substance. Nor can any man doubt, but that there are new diseases, seeing nothing is written of them in the books of the ancients, nor of the remedies to cure them, and that the various mixtures of the qualities which produce them, may be in a manner innumerable; and that both sorts of pox were unknown to the ancients. But this novelty appears yet better in men's actions, and divers events in them, which are, therefore, particularly called news. Such are the relations of battles, sieges, takings of towns, and other accidents of life; so much the more considerable, by how much they are ordinarily less regarded. It were also too much injustice to go about to deprive all inventors of the honour due to them, maintaining, that they have taught us no new thing. Do not the sectaries and heresiarchs make new religions? Moreover, who will make any question, whether we have not reason to ask, what new things Africa affords now-a-days, it having been so fertile in monsters, which are bodies intirely new, as being produced against the laws of nature. And, when the King calls down money, changeth the price of it, determines its weight, is not this a new ordinance? In short, this is to go about to pervert, not only the signification of words, but also common sense, in maintaining, that there is nothing new; and it had not been amiss, if the regent, who printed such paradoxes in a youthful humour, had never been served with new laid eggs, nor changed his old cloaths, and, if he had complained, answer might have been made, That there is nothing new.

The fourth said, That there are no new substances, and, by consequence, no new substantial forms, but only accidental ones; seeing nothing is made of nothing, or returns to nothing; and, in all the other classes of things, there are no new species, but only new individuals, to which monsters are to be referred. Yea, the mysteries of our salvation were always *in intellectu divino*: Which made our Saviour say, that Abraham had seen him. And, as for arts and inventions, they flourished in one estate, whilst they were unknown in another, where they should appear afterward in their time. And this is the sense, wherein it is true, that There is nothing new.

THE
PREROGATIVE OF PARLIAMENTS
IN ENGLAND*,

Proved in a Dialogue between a Counsellor of State, and a Justice of Peace.

Written by the worthy Knight,
SIR WALTER RALEIGH.

Dedicated to the King's Majesty, and to the House of Parliament now assembled. Preserved to be now happily, in these distracted Times, published, and printed 1640. Quarto, containing seventy-four Pages.

Counsellor.

NOW, Sir, what think you of Mr. St. John's trial in the Star-Chamber? I know that the bruit ran that he was hardly dealt withal, because he was imprisoned in the Tower, seeing his dissuasion from granting a benevolence to the King was warranted by the law.

Justice.   Surely, Sir, it was made manifest at the hearing, that Mr. St. John was rather in love with his own letter; he confessed he had

---

* This is the 287th article in the Catalogue of Pamphlets in the Harleian Library.

seen your lordship's letter, before he wrote his to the Mayor of Marl-borough, and in your lordship's letter there was not a word whereto the statutes, by Mr. St. John alledged, had reference; for those statutes did condemn the gathering of money from the subject, under title of a free gift; whereas a fifth, a sixth, a tenth, &c. was set down, and required. But, my good lord, though divers shires have given to his Majesty, some more, some less, What is this to the King's debt?

Couns. We know it well enough, but we have many other projects.

Just. It is true, my good Lord; but your lordship will find, that when by these you have drawn many pretty sums from the subjects, and those sometimes spent as fast as they are gathered, his Majesty being nothing enabled thereby, when you shall be forced to demand your great aid, the country will excuse itself, in regard of their former payments.

Couns. What mean you by the great aid?

Just. I mean the aid of parliament.

Couns. By parliament I would fain know the man that durst persuade the King unto it; for if it should succeed ill, In what case were he?

Just. You say well for yourself, my Lord, and perchance, you that are lovers of yourselves, under pardon, do follow the advice of the late Duke of Alva, who was ever opposite to all resolution in business of importance; for if the things enterprised succeeded well, the advice never came in question: If ill, whereto great undertakings are commonly subject, he then made his advantage, by remembering his country council: But, my good Lord, these reserved politicians are not the best servants, for he that is bound to adventure his life for his master, is also bound to adventure his advice: 'Keep not back counsel,' saith Ecclesiasticus, ' when it may do good.'

Couns. But, Sir, I speak it not in other respect, than I think it dangerous for the king to assemble the three estates; for thereby have our former kings always lost somewhat of their prerogatives. And, because that you shall not think, that I speak it at random, I will begin with elder times, wherein the first contention began, betwixt the kings of this land, and their subjects in parliament.

Just. Your Lordship shall do me a singular favour.

Couns. You know that the King of England had no formal parliament till about the eighteenth year of Henry the First, for in his seventeenth year, for the marriage of his daughter, the king raised a tax upon every hide of land by the advice of his privy-council alone. But you may remember how the subjects, soon after the establishment of this parliament, began to stand upon terms with the king, and drew from him by strong hand, and the sword, the great charter.

Just. Your Lordship says well, they drew from the king the great charter by the sword, and hereof the parliament cannot be accused, but the Lords.

Couns. You say well, but it was after the establishment of the parliament, and by colour of it, that they had so great daring; for before that time they could not endure to hear of St. Edward's laws, but resisted the confirmation in all they could, although, by those laws, the subjects of this island were no less free than any of all Europe.

Just. My good Lord, the reason is manifest ; for while the Normans, and other of the French that followed the conqueror, made spoil of the English, they would not endure that any thing but the will of the conqueror should stand for law ; but, after a descent or two, when themselves were become English, and found themselves beaten with their own rods, they then began to savour the difference between subjection and slavery, and insist upon the law, *Meum & Tuum* ; and to be able to say unto themselves, *Hoc fac & vives* ; yea, that the conquering English in Ireland did the like, your Lordship knows it better than I.

Couns. I think you guess aright : And to the end the subject may know, that, being a faithful servant to his prince, he might enjoy his own life, and, paying to his prince what belongs to a sovereign, the remainder was his own to dispose ; Henry the First, to content his vassals, gave them the great charter, and the charter of forests.

Just. What reason, then, had King John to deny the confirmation ?

Couns. He did not, but he, on the contrary, confirmed both the charters with additions, and required the Pope, whom he had then made his superior, to strengthen them with a golden bull.

Just. But your honour knows, that it was not long after, that he repented himself.

Couns. It is true, and he had reason so to do, for the barons refused to follow him into France, as they ought to have done ; and to say true, this great charter, upon which you insist so much, was not originally granted regally and freely ; for Henry the First did usurp the kingdom, and therefore, the better to assure himself against Robert, his eldest brother, he flattered his nobility and people, with those charters : Yea, King John that confirmed them had the like respect ; for Arthur, Duke of Bretagne, was the undoubted heir of the crown, upon whom John usurped. And so to conclude, these charters had their original from kings *de facto*, but not *de jure*.

Just. But King John confirmed the charter, after the death of his nephew Arthur, when he was then *Rex de jure* also.

Couns. It is true, for he durst do no other, standing accursed, whereby few or none obeyed him, for his nobility refused to follow him into Scotland ; and he had so grieved the people by pulling down all the park pales before harvest, to the end his deer might spoil the corn ; and by seizing the temporalities of so many bishopricks into his hands, and chiefly for practising the death of the Duke of Bretagne, his nephew, as also having lost Normandy, to the French, so as the hearts of all men were turned from him.

Just. Nay, by your favour, my Lord, King John restored King Edward's laws, after his absolution, and wrote his letters in the fifteenth of his reign, to all sheriffs, countermanding all former oppressions ; yea, this he did, notwithstanding the Lords refused to follow him into France.

Couns. Pardon me, he did not restore King Edward's laws then, nor yet confirmed the charters, but he promised upon hi absolution to do both : But after his return out of France, in his sixteenth year, he denied it, because, without such a promise, he had not obtained restitution, his promise being constrained, and not voluntary.

Just. But what think you? Was he not bound in honour to perform it?

Couns. Certainly no, for it was determined in the case of King Francis the First of France, that all promises by him made, whilst he was in the hands of Charles the Fifth, his enemy, were void, by reason, the judge of honour, which tells us he durst do no other.

Just. But King John was not in prison.

Couns. Yet, for all that, restraint is an imprisonment, yea, fear itself is an imprisonment, and the king was subject to both : I know there is nothing more kingly in a king, than the performance of his word ; but, yet of a word freely and voluntarily given. Neither was the charter of Henry the First so published, that all men might plead it for their advantage ; but a charter was left, in *deposito*, in the hands of the Archbishop of Canterbury, for the time, and so to his successors. Stephen Langton, who was ever a traitor to the king, produced this charter, and shewed it to the barons, thereby encouraging them to make war against the king. Neither was it the old charter simply the barons sought to have confirmed, but they presented unto the king other articles and orders, tending to the alteration of the whole commonwealth ; which when the king refused to sign, the barons presently put themselves into the field, and in rebellious and outrageous fashion, sent the king word, except he confirmed them, they would not desist from making war against him, till he had satisfied them therein. And in conclusion, the king being betrayed of all his nobility, in effect, was forced to grant the charter of *Magna Chartar*, and *Charta de Forestis*, at such time as he was invironed with an army in the meadows of Staynes ; which charters, being procured by force, Pope Innocent afterwards disavowed, and threatened to curse the barons, if they submitted not themselves, as they ought to their Sovereign Lord ; which when the lords refused to obey, the king entertained an army of strangers, for his own defence, wherewith having mastered and beaten the barons, they called in Lewis of France, a most unnatural resolution, to be their king. Neither was *Magna Chartar* a law in the nineteenth of Henry the Third, but simply a charter, which he confirmed in the twenty-first of his reign, and made it a law in the twenty-fifth, according to Littleton's opinion. Thus much for the beginning of the great charter, which had first an obscure birth from usurpation, and was secondly fostered and shewed to the world by rebellion.

Just. I cannot deny but that all your Lordship hath said is true ; but, seeing the charters were afterwards so many times confirmed by parliament and made laws, and that there is nothing in them unequal or prejudicial to the king ; Doth not your honour think it reason they should be observed?

Couns. Yes, and observed they are in all that the state of a king can permit, for no man is destroyed, but by the laws of the land, no man disseized of his inheritance, but by the laws of the land ; imprisoned they are by the prerogative, where the king hath cause to suspect their loyalty; for were it otherwise, the king should never come to the knowledge of any conspiracy or treason, against his person or state, and being imprisoned, yet doth not any man suffer death, but by the law of the land.

Just. But may it please your Lordship, were not Cornwallis, Sharp, and Hoskins imprisoned, there being no suspicion of treason there?

Couns. They were, but it cost them nothing.

Just. And what got the king by it? For in the conclusion, besides the murmer of the people, Cornwallis, Sharp, and Hoskins having greatly overshot themselves, and repented them, a fine of five or six hundred pounds was laid on his Majesty, for their offences, for so much their diet cost his Majesty.

Couns. I know who gave the advice, sure I am that it was none of mine: But thus I say, if you consult your memory, you shall find, that those kings, which did, in their own times, confirm the *Magna Charta*, did not only imprison, but they caused of their nobility, and others, to be slain, without hearing or trial.

Just. My good lord, if you will give me leave to speak freely, I say, that they are not well advised, that persuade the king, not to admit the *Magna Charta*, with the former reservations. For as the king can never lose a farthing by it, as I shall prove anon; so except England were as Naples is, and kept by garisons of another nation, it is impossible for a king of England to greaten and inrich himself by any way so assuredly, as by the love of his people. For by one rebellion the king hath more loss, than by a hundred years observance of *Magna Charta*: For therein have our kings been forced to compound with rogues and rebels, and to pardon them, yea, the state of the king, the monarchy, the nobility have been endangered by them.

Couns. Well, Sir, let that pass, why should not our kings raise money, as the kings of France do, by their letters and edicts only? For, since the time of Lewis the Eleventh, of whom it is said, that he freed the French kings of their wardship, the French kings have seldom assembled the states, for any contribution.

Just. I will tell you why; the strength of England doth consist of the people and yeomanry; the peasants of France have no courage nor arms: In France, every village and borough hath a castle, which the French call *Chasticau Villina*; every good city hath a good cittadel; the king hath the regiments of his guards, and his men at arms always in pay; yea, the nobility of France, in whom, the strength of France consists, do always assist their king in those levies upon their tenants. But, my lord, if you mark it, France was never free, in effect, from civil wars; and lately it was endangered either to be conquered by the Spaniard, or to be cantonised by the rebellious French themselves, since that freedom of wardship. But, my good Lord, to leave this digression, that, wherein I would willingly satisfy your Lordship, is, that the kings of England have never received loss, by parliament, or prejudice.

Couns. No, Sir, you shall find that the subjects in parliament have decreed great things, to the disadvantage and dishonour of our kings in former times.

Just. My good lord, to avoid confusion, I will make a short report of them all, and then your lordship may object where you see cause. And I doubt not but to give your lordship satisfaction.   In the sixth year of Henry the Third, there was no dispute, the house gave the king two shillings of every plough-land within England; and, in the end of the same year, he had escuage paid him, to wit, for every knight's fee, two marks in silver.   In the fifth year of that king, the lords demanded the confirmation of the great charter, which the king's council, for that time present excused, alledging that those privileges were extorted by force, during the king's minority; and yet the king was pleased to send forth his writ to the sheriffs of every county, requiring them to certify, what those liberties were, and how used; and, in exchange of the lords demand, because they pressed him so violently, the king required all the castles and places, which the lords held of his, and had held in the time of his father, with those manors and lordships, which they had heretofore wrested from the crown; which at that time, the king being provided of forces, they durst not deny.   In the fourteenth year, he had the fifteenth penny of all goods given him, upon condition to confirm the great charter: For, by reason of the wars in France, and the loss of Rochelle, he was then forced to consent to the lords, in all they demanded.   In the tenth year of his reign, he fined the city of London, at fifty thousand marks, because they had received Lewis of France.   In the eleventh year, in the parliament at Oxford, he revoked the great charter, being granted when he was under age, and governed by the Earl of Pembroke, and the Bishop of Winchester.   In his eleventh year, the Earls of Cornwall and Chester, Marshal, Edward Earl of Pembroke, Gilbert Earl of Gloucester, Warren, Hereford, Ferrars, and Warwick, and others rebelled against the king, and constrained him to yield unto them in what they demanded for their particular interest; which rebellion being appeased, he sailed into France; and, in his fifteenth year, he had a fifteenth of the temporality and a dism and a half of the spirituality, and withal, escuage of every knight's fee.

Couns. But what say you to the parliament of Westminster, in the sixteenth year of the king: where, notwithstanding the wars of France, and his great charge in repulsing the Welch rebels, he was flatly denied the subsidy demanded?

Just. I confess, my lord, that the house excused themselves, by reason of their poverty, and the lords taking of arms; in the next year, it was manifest that the house was practised against the king: And was it not so, my good lord, think you, in our two last parliaments? for, in the first, even those, whom his Majesty trusted most, betrayed him in the union; and in the second, there were other of the great ones ran counter.   But your lordship spoke of dangers of parliaments; in this, my lord, there was a denial, but there was no danger at all: But to return where I left, what got the lords, by practising the house at that time? I say, that those, that broke this staff upon the king, were overturned with the counterbuff, for he refused all those lands which he had given in his minority; he called all his exacting officers to account; he found them all faulty; he examined the corruption of other magistrates; and, from all these, he drew sufficient money to satisfy his pre-

sent necessity ; whereby he not only spared his people, but highly contented them with an act of so great justice : Yea, Hubert, Earl of Kent,
the chief justice, whom he had most trusted, and most advanced, was
found as false to the king, as any one of the rest ; and, for conclusion,
in the end of that year, at the assembly of the states at Lambeth, the king
had the fortieth part of every man's goods given him freely towards his
debts : for the people, who, the same year, had refused to give the king
any thing, when they saw he had squeesed those sponges of the common-wealth, they willingly yielded to give him satisfaction.

Couns. But, I pray you, what became of this Hubert, whom the king
had favoured above all men, betraying his Majesty, as he did ?

Just. There were many that persuaded the king to put him to death,
but he could not be drawn to consent ; but the king seized upon his
estate, which was great ; yet, in the end, he left him a sufficient portion,
and gave him his life, because he had done great service in former
times : For his Majesty, though he took advantage of his vice, yet he
forgot not to have consideration of his virtue.   And upon this occasion
it was, that the king, betrayed by those whom he most trusted, entertained strangers, and gave them their offices, and the charge of his
castles and strong places in England.

Couns. But the drawing in of those strangers was the cause, that the
Marshal, Earl of Pembroke, moved war against the king.

Just. It is true, my good lord, but he was soon after slain in Ireland,
and his whole masculine race, ten years extinguished, though there
were five sons of them ; and, the marshal being dead, who was the
mover and ringleader of that war, the king pardoned the rest of the
lords that had assisted the marshal.

Couns. What reason had the king so to do ?

Just. Because he was so persuaded, that they loved his person, and
only hated those corrupt counsellors, that then bore the greatest sway
under him, as also, because they were the best men of war he had,
whom, if he destroyed, having war with the French, he had wanted
commanders to have served him.

Couns. But what reason had the lords to take arms ?

Just. Because the king entertained the Poictovins : Were not they
the king's vassals also ? Should the Spaniards rebel, because the Spanish
king trusts to the Neapolitans, Portuguese, Milanese, and other nations,
his vassals ? seeing those, that are governed by the viceroys and deputies, are, in policy, to be well entertained, and to be employed, who
would otherwise devise how to free themselves ; whereas, being trusted
and employed by their prince, they entertained themselves with the
hopes, that others the king's vassals do.   If the king had called in the
Spaniards, or other nations, not his subjects, the nobility of England had
reason of grief.

Couns. But what people did ever serve the King of England more
faithfully than the Gascoignes did, even to the last of the conquest of
that duchy ?

Just. Your lordship says well, and I am of that opinion, that, if it
had pleased the Queen of England, to have drawn some of the chief
of the Irish nobility into England, and, by exchange, to have made

them good freeholders in England, she had saved above two millions of pounds, which were consumed in times of those rebellions.   For what held the Gascoignes firm to the crown of England, of whom the Duke of Espernon married the inheritrix, but his earldom of Kendal in England, whereof the Duke of Espernon, in right of his wife, bears the title to this day?   And, to the same end I take it, hath James, our sovereign Lord, given lands to divers of the nobility of Scotland; and, if I were worthy to advise your lordship, I should think that your lordship should do the King great service, to put him in mind to prohibit all the Scotish nation to alienate and sell away their inheritance here; for, by the selling, they not only give cause to the English to complain, that the treasure of England is transported into Scotland, but his Majesty is, thereby, also frustrated of making both nations one, and of assuring the service and obedience of the Scots in the future.

Couns. You say well; for though those of Scotland, that are advanced and inriched by the King's Majesty, will, no doubt, serve him faithfully; yet, how their heirs and successors, having no inheritance to lose in England, may be seduced, is uncertain.   But let us go on with our parliament.   And what say you to the denial in the twenty-sixth year of his reign, even when the King was invited to come into France by the Earl of March, who had married his mother, and who promised to assist the King in the conquest of many places lost?

Just. It is true, my good lord, that a subsidy was then denied, and the reasons are delivered in English histories; and indeed, the King, not long before, had spent much treasure in aiding the Duke of Bretagne to no purpose, for he drew over the King, but to draw on good conditions for himself, as the Earl of March, his father-in-law, now did; as the English barons did invite Lewis of France, not long before, as, in elder times, all the kings and states had done, and, in late years, the leaguers of France entertained the Spaniards, and the French Protestants and Netherlands, Queen Elisabeth; not with any purpose to greaten those that aid them, but to purchase to themselves an advantageous peace.   But what say the histories to this denial?   They say, with a world of payments there mentioned, that the King had drawn the nobility dry; and, besides that, whereas, not long before, great sums of money were given, and the same appointed to be kept in four castles, and not to be expended, but by the advice of the peers: It was believed that the same treasure was yet unspent.

Couns. Good Sir, you have said enough?   Judge you, whether it were not a dishonour to the King, to be so tied, as not to expend his treasure, but by other men's advice, as it were, by their licence.

Just. Surely, my lord, the King was well advised, to take the money upon any condition, and they were fools that propounded the restraint; for it doth not appear, that the King took any great heed to those overseers; kings are bound by their piety, and by no other obligation.   In Queen Mary's time, when it was thought she was with child, it was propounded in parliament, that the rule of the realm should be given to King Philip, during the minority of the hoped prince or princess; and the King offered his assurance, in great sums of money, to relinquish the government, at such time as the prince or princess should

be of age.   At which motion, when all else were silent in the house
Lord Dacres, who was none of the wisest, asked who shall sue the King's
bond, which ended the dispute :   For what bond is between a king and
his vassals, but the bond of the King's faith ?   But, my good lord, the
King, notwithstanding the denial at that time, was, with gifts from particular persons, and otherwise, supplied for proceeding on his journey,
for that time, into France ; he took with him thirty casks, filled with
silver and coin, which was a great treasure in those days.   And, Lastly,
notwithstanding the first denial, in the King's absence, he had escuage
granted him, to wit, twenty shillings of every knight's fee.

Couns.   What say you then to the twenty-eighth year of that King,
in which, when the King demanded relief, the states would not consent,
except the same order had been taken for the appointing of four overseers for the treasure ?   As also that the lord chief justice and the lord
chancellor should be chosen by the states, with some barons of the
Exchequer, and other officers.

Just.   My good lord, admit the King had yielded their demands,
then whatsoever had been ordained by those magistrates to the dislike
of the commonwealth, the people had been without remedy ; whereas,
while the King made them, they had their appeal, and other remedies.
But those demands vanished, and, in the end, the King had escuage
given him, without any of their conditions.   It is an excellent virtue in
a king to have patience, and to give way to the fury of men's passions.
The whale, when he is struck by the fisherman, grows in that fury that
he cannot be resisted, but will overthrow all the ships and barques that
come in his way ; but, when he hath tumbled a while, he is drawn to
the shore with a twine-thread.

Couns.   What say you then to the parliament in the twenty-ninth
year of that king ?

Just.   I say, that, the commons being unable to pay, the King
relieves himself upon the richer sort ; and so it likewise happened in
the thirty-third year of the King, in which he was relieved chiefly by
the city of London.   But, my good lord, in the parliament in London,
in the thirty-eighth year, he had given him the tenth of all the revenues
of the church for three years, and three marks of every knight's fee
throughout the kingdom, upon his promise and oath for the observing
of *Magna Charta;* but, in the end of the same year, the King being
then in France, he was denied the aids which he required.   What is
this to the danger of a parliament ?   Especially at this time they had
reason to refuse, they had given so great a sum in the beginning of the
same year ; and again, because it was known that the King had but
pretended war with the King of Castile, with whom he had secretly
contracted an alliance, and concluded a marriage between his son
Edward and the lady Eleanor.   These false fires do but fright children;
and it commonly falls out, that, when the cause given is known to be
false, the necessity pretended is thought to be feigned.   Royal dealing
hath evermore royal success ; and, as the King was denied in the
thirty-eighth year, so was he denied in the thirty-ninth year, because
the nobility and the people saw it plainly, that the King was abused by
the Pope, who, as well in despite to Manfred, bastard son to the

Emperor Frederick the Second, as to cousen the King, and to waste him, would needs bestow on the King the kingdom of Sicily; to recover which, the King sent all the treasure he could borrow or scrape to the Pope, and withal gave him letters of credence, for to take up what he could in Italy, the King binding himself for the payment. Now, my good lord, the wisdom of princes is seen in nothing more than in their enterprises. So how unpleasing it was to the state of England to consume the treasure of the land, and in the conquest of Sicily, so far off, and otherwise, for that the English had lost Normandy under their noses, and so many goodly parts of France of their own proper inheritance ? The reason of the denial is as well to be considered as the denial.

Couns. Was not the King also denied a subsidy in the forty-first year of his reign ?

Just. No, my lord, for, although the King required money, as before, for the impossible conquest of Sicily, yet the house offered to give fifty-two thousand marks, which, whether he refused or accepted, is uncertain; and, whilst the King dreamed of Sicily, the Welch invaded and spoiled the borders of England; for, in the parliament of London, when the King urged the house for prosecuting the conquest of Sicily, the lords, utterly disliking the attempt, urged the prosecuting of the Welchmen; which parliament, being prorogued, did assemble at Oxford, and was called the Mad Parliament, which was no other than an assembly of rebels; for the royal assent of the king, which gives life to all laws, formed by the three estates, was not a royal assent, when both the King and the Prince were constrained to yield to the lords. A constrained consent is the consent of a captive, and not of a king; and therefore there was nothing done there either legally or royally. For, if it be not properly a parliament where the subject is not free, certainly it can be none where the King is bound ; for all kingly rule was taken from the King, and twelve peers appointed, and, as some writers have it, twenty-four peers to govern the realm; and therefore the assembly made by Jack Straw, and other rebels, may as well be called a parliament as that of Oxford. *Principis nomen habere, non est esse princeps;* for thereby was the King driven not only to compound all quarrels with the French, but to have means to be revenged on the rebel lords; but he quitted his right to Normandy, Anjou, and Mayne.

Couns. But, Sir, what needed this extremity, seeing the lords require but the confirmation of the former charter, which was not prejudicial to the King to grant ?

Just. Yes, my good lord, but they insulted upon the King, and would not suffer him to enter into his own castles ; they put down the purveyor of the meat for the maintenance of his house, as if the King had been a bankrupt, and gave order, that, without ready money, he should not take up a chicken. And, although there is nothing against the royalty of a king in these charters (the kings of England being kings of freemen and not of slaves,) yet it is so contrary to the nature of a king to be forced even to those things which may be to his advantage, as the King had some reason to seek the dispensation of his oath from the Pope, and to draw in strangers for his own defence; yea, *Jure salvo*

Coronæ nostræ is intended inclusively in all oaths and promises exacted from a sovereign.

Couns.   But you cannot be ignorant how dangerous a thing it is to call in other nations, but for the spoil they make, as also, because they have often held the possession of the best places with which they have been trusted.

Just.   It is true, my good lord, that there is nothing so dangerous for a king as to be constrained and held as prisoner to his vassals; for by that Edward the Second and Richard the Second lost their kingdoms and their lives.   And for calling in of strangers, Was not King Edward the Sixth driven to call in strangers, commonly against the rebels in Norfolk, Cornwall, Oxfordshire, and elsewhere? Have not the kings of Scotland been oftentimes constrained to entertain strangers against the kings of England? And the King of England at this time, had he not been divers times assisted by the kings of Scotland, had been endangered to have been expelled for ever.

Couns.   But yet you know those kings were deposed by parliament.

Just.   Yea, my good lord, being prisoners, being out of possession, and being in their hands that were princes of the blood, and pretenders. It is an old country proverb, That ' might overcomes right:'   A weak title, that wears a strong sword, commonly prevails against a strong title that wears but a weak one; otherwise Philip the Second had never been Duke of Portugal, nor Duke of Milan, nor King of Naples and Sicily.   But, good lord, *Errores non sunt trahendi in exemplum :* I speak of regal, peaceable, and lawful parliaments. The King, at this time, was but a king in name; for Gloucester, Leicester, and Chichester made choice of other nine, to whom the rule of the realm was committed, and the prince was forced to purchase his liberty from the Earl of Leicester, by giving for his ransom the county palatine of Chester. But, my lord, let us judge of those occasions by their events: What became of this proud earl? Was he not soon after slain in Evesham? Was he not left naked in the field, and left a shameful spectacle, his head being cut off from his shoulders, his privy-parts from his body, and laid on each side of his nose? And did not God extinguish his race? After which, in a lawful parliament at Westminster, confirmed in a following parliament of Westminster, were not all the lords that followed Leicester disinherited? And when that fool Gloucester, after the death of Leicester, whom he had formerly forsaken, made himself the head of a second rebellion, and called in strangers, for which, not long before, he had cried out against the King, was not he in the end, after that he had seen the slaughter of so many of the barons, the spoil of their castles and lordships, constrained to submit himself, as all the survivors did, of which they, that sped best, paid their fines and ransoms, the King reserving to his younger son the earldoms of Leicester and Darby.

Couns.   Well, Sir, we have disputed this king to his grave; though it be true, that he outlived all his enemies, and brought them to confusion; yet those examples did not terrify their successors, but the Earl Marshal, and Hereford, threatened King Edward the First with a new war.

Just. They did so; but, after the death of Hereford, the earl marshal repented himself, and, to gain the King's favour, he made him heir of all his lands. But what is this to the parliament? For there was never a king of this land had more given him for the time of his reign, than Edward, the son of Henry the Third, had.

Couns. How doth it appear?

Just. In this sort, my good lord; in this king's third year, he had given him the fifteenth part of all goods. In his sixth year, a twentieth; in his twelfth year, a twentieth; in his fourteenth year he had escuage, to wit, forty shillings of every knight's fee; in his eighteenth year, he had the eleventh part of all moveable goods within the kingdom; in his nineteenth year, the tenth part of all church livings in England, Scotland, and Ireland, for six years, by agreement from the Pope; in his three and twentieth year, he raised a tax upon wool and fells, and, on a day, caused all the religious houses to be searched, and all the treasure in them to be seized and brought to his coffers, excusing himself, by laying the fault upon his treasurer; he had also in the end of the same year, of all goods, of all burgesses, and of the commons, the tenth part; in the twenty-fifth year of the parliament of St. Edmundsbury, he had an eighteenth part of the goods of the burgesses, and of the people in general, the tenth part. He had also the same year, by putting the clergy out of his protection, a fifth part of their goods; and, in the same year, he set a great tax upon wools, to wit, from half a mark to forty shillings upon every sack; whereupon the Earl Marshal and the Earl of Hereford, refusing to attend the King into Flanders, pretended the grievances of the people. But, in the end, the King having pardoned them, and confirmed the great charter, he had the ninth penny of all goods, from the lords and commons; of the clergy, in the south he had the tenth penny, and in the north the fifth penny. In the two and thirtieth year, he had a subsidy freely granted: In the three and thirtieth year he confirmed the great charter of his own royal disposition, and the states, to shew their thankfulness, gave the King, for one year, the sixth part of their goods. And the same year the King used the inquisition, called Traile Baston: By which all justices and other magistrates were grievously fined, that had used extortion, or bribery, or had otherwise misdemeaned themselves, to the great contentation of the people. This commission likewise did enquire of intruders, barrators, and all other the like vermin, whereby the King gathered a great mass of treasure, with a great deal of love. Now, for the whole reign of this king, who governed England thirty-five years, there was not any parliament to prejudice.

Couns. But there was taking of arms by the Earl Marshal and Hereford.

Just. That is true, but why was that? Because the King, notwithstanding all that was given him by parliament, did lay the greatest taxes that ever king did without their consent. But what lost the King by those lords? One of them gave the King all his lands, the other died in disgrace.

Couns. But what say you to the parliament in Edward the Second's time, his successor: Did not the house of parliament banish Pierce Gaveston, whom the King favoured?

Just. But what was this Gaveston, but an esquire of Gascoigne, formerly banished the realm by King Edward the First, for corrupting the Prince Edward, now reigning? And, the whole kingdom fearing and detesting his venomous disposition, they besought his Majesty to cast him off; which the King performed by an act of his own, ard not by act of parliament; yea, Gaveston's own father-in-law, the Earl of Gloucester, was one of the chiefest lords that procured it. And yet, finding the King's affection to follow him so strongly, they all consented to have him recalled. After which, when his credit so increased, that he despised and set at nought all the antient nobility, and not only persuaded the King to all manner of outrages and riots, but withal transported what he listed of the King's treasure, and jewels, the lords urged his banishment the second time; but neither was the first, nor the second banishment forced by act of parliament, but by the forceable lords his enemies. Lastly, He being recalled by the King, the Earl of Lancaster caused his head to be struck off, when those of his party had taken him prisoner. By which presumptuous act, the earl and the rest of his company committed treason and murder; treason, by raising an army without warrant; murder, by taking away the life of the King's subject. After which, Gaveston being dead, the Spencers got possession of the King's favour, though the younger of them was placed about the King by the lords themselves.

Couns. What say you, then, to the parliament, held at London about the sixth year of that king?

Just. I say, that king was not bound to perform the acts of this parliament, because the lords, being too strong for the King, forced his consent; for these be the words of our own history: ' They wrested too much beyond the bounds of reason.'

Couns. What say you to the parliaments of the White Wands, in the three-and-thirtieth year of the King?

Just. I say, the lords, that were so moved, came with an army, and, by strong hand, surprised the King. ' They constrained (saith the story) the rest of the lords, and compelled many of the bishops to consent unto them.' Yea, it saith further, That the King durst not but grant all that they required, to wit, for the banishment of the Spencers. Yea, they were so insolent, that they refused to lodge the Queen, coming through Kent, in the castle of Leeds, and sent her to provide her lodging where she could get it, late in the night? for which, notwithstanding, some, that kept her out, were soon after taken and hanged, and therefore your lordship cannot call this a parliament, for the reasons before alledged. But, my lord, what became of these lawgivers to the King? Even when they were greatest, a knight of the north, called Andrew Herkeley, assembled the forces of the country; overthrew them and their army; slew the Earl of Hereford, and other barons; took their general, Thomas Earl of Lancaster, the King's cousin-german, at that time possessed of five earldoms; the Lords Clifford, Talbot, Mowbray, Maudint, Willington, Warren; Lords Darcy, Withers, Knevil, Leybourne, Bekes, Lovell, Fitzwilliams, Watervild, and divers other barons, knights, and esquires; and, soon after, the Lord Percy and the Lord Warren took the Lord Badlesmere and the Lord Audley, the Lords Teis, Gifford, Tutchet, and many others, that fled from the battle; the most of which passed under the hands of the hangman, for constraining the King under the colour and name of a parliament. By this your good lordship may judge, to whom those tumultuous assemblies, which our histories falsely call parliaments, have been dangerous; the kings in the end ever prevailed, and the lords lost their lives and estates; after which, the Spencers, in their banishment at York, in the fifteenth year of the King, were restored to their honours and estates? and therein the King had a subsidy given him, the sixth penny of goods throughout England, Ireland, and Wales.

Couns. Yet, you see, the Spencers were soon after dissolved.

Just. It is true, my lord, but that is nothing to our subject of Parliament; they may thank their own insolency, for they branded and despised the Queen, whom they ought to have honoured as the King's wife; they were also exceeding greedy, and built themselves upon other men's ruins; they were ambitious, and exceeding malicious; whereupon that came, that, when Chamberlain Spencer was hanged in Hereford, a part of the four and-twentieth Psalm was written over his head: *quid gloriaris in malitia, potens?*

Couns. Well, Sir; you have all this while excused yourself upon the strength and rebellions of the lords; but what say you now to King Edward the Third? In whose time (and during the time of this victorious King, no man durst take arms, or rebel) the three estates did him the greatest affront, that ever king received or endured; therefore I conclude where I began, that these parliaments are dangerous for a king.

Just. To answer your lordship in order: may it please you, first, to call to mind what was given this great King, by his subjects, before the dispute betwixt him and the house happened, which was in his latter days. From his first year to his fifth year, there was nothing given the King by his subjects; in the eighth year, at the parliament at London, a tenth and a fifteenth was granted. In his tenth year, he seized upon the Italians goods here in England to his own use, with all the goods of the monks Cluniacks, and others of the order of the Cistertians. In the eleventh year, he had given him by parliament a notable relief, the one-half of the wools throughout England, and, of the clergy, all their wools; after which, in the end of the year, he had granted, in his parliament at Westminster, forty shillings upon every sack of wool, and, for every thirty wool-fells, forty shillings; for every last of leather as much, and for all other merchandises after the same rate. The King promising, that, this year's gathering ended, he would thenceforth content himself with the old custom, he had, over and above this great aid, the eighth part of all goods of all citizens and burgesses, and others, as of foreign merchants; and, of such as lived not of the gain of breeding of sheep and cattle, the fifteenth of their goods, Nay, my lord, this was not all, though more than ever was granted to any king; for the same parliament bestowed on the King the ninth sheaf of all the corn within the land, the ninth fleece, and the ninth lamb, for two years next following; now, what thinks your lordship of this parliament?

Couns.   I say, they were honest men.

Just.   And I say, the people are as loving to their King now, as ever they were, if they be honestly and wisely dealt withal; and so his Majesty had found them in his last two parliaments, if his Majesty had not been betrayed by those whom he most trusted.

Couns.   But, I pray you, Sir, whom shall a King trust, if he may not trust those whom he hath so greatly advanced?

Just.   I will tell your lordship whom the King may trust.

Couns.   Who are they?

Just.   His own reason, and his own excellent judgment, which have not deceived him in any thing, wherein his Majesty hath been pleased to exercise them. ' Take counsel of thine heart, saith the book of Wisdom, for there is none more faithful unto thee than it.'

Couns.   It is true; but his Majesty found, that those wanted no judgment, whom he trusted; and how could his Majesty divine of their honesties?

Just.   Will you pardon me, if I speak freely? For I speak out of love, which, as Solomon saith, ' covereth all trespasses.' The truth is, that his Majesty would never believe any man that spoke against them, and they knew it well enough; which gave them boldness to do what they did.

Cons.   What was that?

Just.   Even, my good lord, to ruin the King's estate, so far as the estate of so great a king may be ruined by men ambitious and greedy without proportion. It had been a brave increase of revenue, my lord, to have raised five hundred thousand pounds in land of the King's to twenty thousand pounds revenue, and to raise the revenue of wards to twenty thousand pounds more: forty thousand pounds, added to the rest of his Majesty's estate, had so enabled his Majesty, that he could never have wanted; and, my good lord, it had been an honest service to the King, to have added seven thousand pounds in lands of the Lord Cobham's woods and goods, being worth thirty thousand pounds more.

Couns.   I know not the reason why it was not done.

Just.   Neither doth your lordship, perchance, know the reason why the ten thousand pounds, offered by Swinnerton, for a fine of the French wines, was, by the then lord treasurer, conferred on Devonshire and his mistress.

Couns.   What moved the treasurer to reject and cross that raising of the King's lands?

Just.   The reason, my good lord, is manifest; for, had the land been raised, then had the King known, when he had given or exchanged land, what he had given or exchanged.

Couns.   What hurt hath that been to the treasurer? Whose office is truly to inform the King of the value of all that he giveth.

Just.   So he did, when it did not concern himself, nor his particular; for he could never admit any one piece of a good manor to pass in my Lord Aubigne's book of a thousand pounds land, till he himself had bought, and then all the remaining flowers of the crown were culled out. Now, had the treasurer suffered the King's lands to have been raised, how could his lordship have made choice of the old rents, as well in that book of my Lord Aubigne, as in exchange of Theobalds; for which he took Hatfield in it, which the greatest subject, or favourite, Queen Elisabeth had, never durst have named unto her, by way of gift or exchange? Nay, my lord, so many other goodly manors have passed from his Majesty, that the very heart of the kingdom mourneth to remember it, and the eyes of the kingdom shed tears continually at the beholding it; yea, the soul of the kingdom is heavy unto death with the consideration thereof, that so magnanimous a prince should suffer himself to be so abused.

Couns. But, Sir, you know, that Cobham's lands were intailed upon his cousins.

Just. Yea, my lord; but, during the lives and races of George Brooke's children, it had been the King's, that is to say, for ever in effect; but, to wrest the King, and to draw the inheritance upon himself, he persuaded his majesty to relinquish his interest for a petty sum of money; and, that there might be no counterworking, he sent Brooke six thousand pounds to make friends; whereof himself had two thousand pounds back again, Buckhurst and Berwick had the other four thousand pounds, and the treasurer and his heirs the mass of land for ever.

Couns. What then, I pray you, came to the King, by this great confiscation?

Just. My lord, the King's Majesty, by all those goodly possessions, woods, and goods, loseth five hundred pounds by the year, which he giveth in pension to Cobham, to maintain him in prison.

Couns. Certainly, even in conscience, they should have reserved so much of the land in the crown, as to have given Cobham meat and apparel, and not made themselves so great gainers, and the King five hundred pounds *per annum* loser by the bargain: but it is past; ' *Consilium non est eorum, quæ fieri nequeunt.'*

Just. Take the rest of the sentence, my lord: ' *Sed consilium versatur in iis, quæ sunt in nostra potestate.'* It is yet, my good lord, *in potestate Regis* to right himself. But this is not all, my lord; and, I fear, knowing your lordship's love to the King, it would put you into a fever to hear all: I will, therefore, go on with my parliaments.

Couns. I pray do so; and, amongst the rest, I pray you, what think you of the parliament holden at London in the fifteenth year of King Edward the Third?

Just. I say, there was nothing concluded therein to the prejudice of the King: It is true, that, a little before the sitting of the house, the King displaced his chancellor, and his treasurers, and most of all his judges, and officers of the Exchequer, and committed many of them to prison, because they did not supply him with money, being beyond the seas: for the rest, the states assembled besought the King, that the laws of the two charters might be observed, and that the great officers of the crown might be chosen by parliament.

Couns. But what success had these petitions?

Just. The charters were observed, as before, and so they will be ever; and the other petition was rejected, the King being pleased, notwithstanding, that the great officers should take an oath in parliament to do justice. Now for the parliament of Westminster: in the seventeenth year of the King, the King had three marks and a half for every sack of wool transported; and, in his eighteenth, he had a tenth of the clergy, and a fifteenth of the laity, for one year. His Majesty forbore, after this, to charge his subjects with any more payments, until the twenty-ninth of his reign, when there was given the King, by parliament, fifty shillings for every sack of wool transported, for six years; by which grant, the King received a thousand marks a day, a greater matter than a thousand pounds in these days, and a thousand pounds a day amounts to three hundred sixty-five thousand pounds a year, which was one of the greatest presents that ever was given to a king of this land. For, besides the cheapness of all things in that age, the King's soldiers had but three-pence a day wages, a man at arms sixpence, and a knight but two shillings. In the parliament at Wesminster, in the thirty-third year, he had twenty-six shillings and eight-pence for every sack of wool transported; and, in the forty-second year, three disms and three fifteenths. In his forty-fifth year, he had fifty thousand pounds of the laity; and, because the spiritualty disputed it, and did not pay so much, the King changed his chancellor, treasurer, and privy-seal, being bishops, and placed laymen in their room.

Couns. It seems, that, in those days, the Kings were no longer in love with their great chancellors, than when they deserved well of them.

Just. No, my lord, they were not, and that was the reason they were well served; and it was the custom then, and in many ages after, to change the treasurer and the chancellor every three years, and withal, to hear all men's complaints against them.

Couns. But, by this often change, the saying is verified, That there is no inheritance in the favour of kings. ' He that keepeth the fig-tree,' saith Solomon, ' shall eat the fruit thereof;' for reason it is, that the servant live by the master.

Just. My lord, you say well in both; but, had the subject an inheritance in the prince's favour, where the prince had no inheritance in the subject's fidelity, then were kings in a more unhappy state than common persons. For the rest, Solomon meaneth not, that he that keepeth the fig-tree, should surfeit; though he meaneth he should eat, he meaneth not he should break the branches in gathering the figs, or eat the ripe, and leave the rotten for the owner of the tree; for what saith he in the following chapter, he saith, ' That he, that maketh haste to be rich, cannot be innocent.' And, before that, he saith, ' That the end of an inheritance, hastily gotten, cannot be blessed.' Your lordship hath heard of few, or none, great with kings, that have not used their power to oppress, that have not grown insolent and hateful to the people; yea, insolent towards those princes that advanced them.

Couns. Yet you see that princes can change their fancies.

Just. Yea, my lord, when favourites change their faith, when they forget, that, how familiar soever kings make themselves with their vassals, yet they are kings : ' He that provoketh a king to anger,' saith Solomon, ' sinneth against his own soul.' And he further saith, That ' pride goeth before destruction, and a high mind before a fall.' I say, therefore, that in discharging those Lucifers, how dear soever they have been, kings make the world know, that they have more of judgment than of passion ; yea, they thereby offer a satisfactory sacrifice to all their people; too great benefits of subjects to their king, where the mind is blown up with their own deservings, and too great benefits of kings conferred upon their subjects, where the mind is not qualified with a great deal of modesty, are equally dangerous. Of this latter, and insolenter, had King Richard the Second delivered up to justice but three or four, he had still held the love of the people, and thereby his life and estate.

Couns.   Well, I pray you go on with your parliaments.

Just.   The life of this great King Edward draws to an end, so do the parliaments of this time, where, in fifty years reign, he never received any affront ; for, in his forty-ninth year, he had a dism and a fifteen granted him freely.

Couns.   But, Sir, it is an old saying, that all is well that ends well ; judge you, whether, that, in his fiftieth year in the parliament at Westminster, he received not an affront, when the house urged the King to remove and discharge from his presence the Duke of Lancaster, the Lord Latimer, his chamberlain, Sir Richard Sturry, and others, whom the King favoured and trusted. Nay, they pressed the King to thrust a certain lady out of the court, which at that time bore the greatest sway therein.

Just.   I will, with patience, answer your lordship to the full ; and, first, your lordship may remember by that which I even now said, that never king had so many gifts, as this King had from his subjects, and it hath never grieved the subjects of England to give to their king ; but when they knew there was a devouring lady, that had her share in all things that passed, and the Duke of Lancaster was as scraping as she ; that the chancellor did eat up the people as fast as either of them both : it grieved the subjects to feed these cormorants. But, my lord, there are two things by which the kings of England have been pressed, to wit, by their subjects, and by their own necessities. The lords in former times were far stronger, more warlike, and better followed, living in their countries, than now they are. Your lordship may remember in your reading, that there were many earls could bring into the field a thousand barbed horses, and many a baron five or six hundred barbed horses ; whereas, now, very few of them can furnish twenty fit to serve the King. But to say the truth, my lord, the justices of peace in England have opposed the injusticers of war in England; the King's writ runs over all, and the great seal of England, with that of the next constables, will serve the turn to affront the greatest lords in England, that shall move against the King. The force, therefore, by which our kings in former times were troubled, is vanished away : but the necessities remain. The people, therefore, in these latter ages, are no less to be pleased than the peers ; for, as the latter are become less, so, by reason of the training through England, the commons have all the weapons in their hands.

Couns.   And was it not so ever?

Just.   No, my good lord, for the noblemen had in their armories to furnish some of them a thousand, some two thousand, and some three thousand men; whereas, now, there are not many that can arm fifty.

Couns.   Can you blame them ? But I will only answer for myself, between you and me be it spoken, I hold it not safe to maintain so great an armory, or stable ; it might cause me, or any other nobleman, to be suspected, as to the preparing of some innovation.

Just.   Why so, my lord ? Rather to be commended, as preparing against all danger of innovation.

Couns.   It should be so ; but call your observation to account, and you shall find it as I say ; for, indeed, such a jealousy hath been held, ever since the time of the civil wars, over the military greatness of our nobles, as made them have little will to bend their studies that way ; wherefore, let every man provide according as he is rated in the mus-ter-book ; you understand me.

Just.   Very well, my lord, as what might be replied in the perceiving so much ; I have ever, to deal plainly and freely with your lordship, more feared at home popular violence, than all the foreign that can be made, for it can never be in the power of any foreign prince, without a papistical party, either to disorder or endanger his Majesty's estate.

Couns.   By this it seems, it is no less dangerous to leave the power in the people, than in the nobility.

Just.   My good lord, the wisdom of our own age is the foolishness of another ; the time present ought not to be preferred to the policy that was, but the policy that was to the time present.   So that, the power of the no-bility being now withered, and the power of the people in the flower, the care to content them should not be neglected, the way to win them often practised, or, at least, to defend them from oppression.   The motive of all dangers, that ever this monarchy hath undergone, should be carefully heeded, for this maxim hath no postern, *Potestas humana radicatur in voluntatibus hominum.*   And now, my lord, for King Edward ; it is true, he was not subject to force, yet he was subject to necessity, which, because it was violent, he gave way unto it : *Potestas,* saith *Pythagoras, juxta necessitatem habitat.*   And it is true, that, at the request of the house, he discharged and put from him those beforenamed ; which done, he had the greatest gift, but one, that he received in all his days, to wit, from every person, man and woman, above the age of fourteen years, four-pence of old money, which made many millions of groats, worth six-pence of our money.   This he had in general ; besides, he had, of every beneficed priest, twelve-pence : And, of the nobility and gentry, I know not how much, for it is not set down.   Now, my good lord, what lost the King by satisfying the desires of the parliament-house ? For, as soon as he had the money in purse, he recalled the lords, and restored them, and who durst call the King to account, when the assembly were dissolved ? Where the word of a King is, there is power, saith Ecclesiasticus, Who shall say unto him, what doest thou ? saith the same author ; for to every purpose there is a time and judgment ; the King gave way to the time, and his judgment persuaded him to yield to necessity, *Consularius nemo melior est quam tempus.*

Couns. But yet, you see the King was forced to yield to their demands?

Just. Doth your lordship remember the saying of Monsieur de Lange, That he, that hath the profit of the war, hath also the honour of the war, whether it be by battle or retreat; the King, you see, had the profit of the parliament, and therefore the honour also: What other end had the King than to supply his wants? A wise man hath evermore respect unto his ends: And the King also knew, that it was the love that the people bore him, that they urged the removing of those lords; there was no man amongst them, that sought himself in that desire, but they all sought the King, as, by the success, it appeared. My good lord, hath it not been ordinary in England, and in France, to yield to the demands of rebels? Did not King Richard the Second grant pardon to the outrageous rogues and murderers, that followed Jack Straw, and Wat Tiler, after they had murdered his chancellor, his treasurer, chief justice, and others, broke open his exchequer, and committed all manner of outrages and villainies? And why did he do it? But to avoid a greater danger: I say, the Kings have there yielded to those that hated them and their estates, to wit, to pernicious rebels. And yet, without dishonour, shall it be called dishonour for the King to yield to honest desires of his subjects? No, my lord, those, that tell the King those tales, fear their own dishonour, and not the King's; for the honour of the King is supreme, and, being guarded by justice and piety, it cannot receive neither wound nor stain.

Couns. But, Sir, what cause have any, under our king, to fear a parliament?

Just. The same cause that the Earl of Suffolk had in Richard the Second's time, and the treasurer Fartham, with others; for these great officers, being generally hated for abusing both the King and the subject, at the request of the states, were discharged, and others put in their rooms.

Couns. And was not this a dishonour to the King?

Just. Certainly, no; for King Richard knew that his grandfather had done the like, and, though the King was, in his heart, utterly against it, yet had he the profit of his exchange; for Suffolk was fined at twenty-thousand marks, and one-thousand pounds lands.

Couns. Well, Sir, we will speak of those that fear the parliament some other time; but I pray you go on with that, that happened in the troublesome reign of Richard the second who succeeded, the grandfather being dead.

Just. That King, my good lord, was one of the most unfortunate princes that ever England had; he was cruel, extreme prodigal, and wholly carried away with his two minions, Suffolk and the Duke of Ireland, by whose ill advice, and others, he was in danger to have lost his estate, which, in the end, being led by men of the like temper, he miserably lost. But for his subsidies he had given him in his first year, being under age, two tenths and two fifteenths: In which parliament, Alice Pierce, who was removed in King Edward's time, with Lancaster, Latimer, and Sturry, were confiscated and banished. In his second year, at the parliament at Gloucester, the King had a mark upon every sack of wool, and sixpence the pound upon wards. In his third year, at the parliament at Winchester, the commons were spared, and a subsidy given by the better sort; the dukes gave twenty marks, and earls six marks: Bishops and abbots with mitres six marks, every mark three shillings four-pence; and every knight, justice, esquire, sheriff, parson, vicar, and chaplian paid proportionably, according to their estates.

Couns. This, methinks, was no great matter.

Just. It is true, my lord, but a little money went far in those days: I myself once moved it in parliament in the time of Queen Elisabeth, who desired much to spare the common people, and I did it by her commandment; but when we cast up the subsidy books, we found the sum but small, when the thirty pounds men were left out. In the beginning of his fourth year, a tenth with a fifteenth were granted, upon condition, that for one whole year no subsidies should be demanded; but this promise was as suddenly forgotten as made, for, in the end of that year, the great subsidy of poll-money was granted in the parliament at Northampton.

Couns. Yea, but there followed the terrible rebellion of Baker, Straw, and others; Leicester, Wrais, and others.

Just. That was not the fault of the parliament, my lord, it is manifest that the subsidy given was not the cause; for it is plain, that the bondmen of England began it, because they were grievously pressed by their lords in their tenure of villenage, as also for the hatred they bore to the lawyers and attornies; for the story of those times says, that they destroyed the houses and manors of men of law, and such lawyers, as they caught, slew them, and beheaded the lord chief justice; which commotion being once begun, the head money was by other rebels pretended. A fire is often kindled with a little straw, which oftentimes takes hold of greater timber, and consumes the whole building: And that this rebellion was begun by the discontented slaves, whereof there have been many in elder times the like, is manifest by the charter of manumission, which the King granted *in hæc verba, Rich. Dei Gratia, &c. sciatis quod de gratia nostra spirituali manumissimus, &c.* To which, seeing the King was constrained by force of arms, he revoked the letters patents, and made them void, the same revocation being strengthened by the parliament ensuing. In which the King had given him a subsidy upon wools, called a Maletot. In the same fourth year was the lord treasurer discharged of his office, and Hales, Lord of St. John's, chosen in his place. In his fifth year was the treasurer again changed, and the staff given to Segrave, and the lord Chancellor was also changed, and the staff given to the Lord Scroope: Which Lord Scroope was again, in the beginning of his sixth year, turned out; and the King, after that he had for a while kept the seal in his own hand, gave it to the bishop of London, from whom it was soon after taken and bestowed on the Earl of Suffolk, who, they say, had abused the King, and converted the King's treasure to his own use. To this the King condescended; and though, saith Walsingham, he deserved to lose his life and goods, yet he had the favour to go at liberty upon good sureties; and because the King was but young, and that tho relief granted was committed to the trust of the Earl of Arundel, for the furnishing of the King's navy against the French.

Couns. Yet you see it was a dishonour to the King to have his beloved chancellor removed.

Just. Truly, no, for the King had both his fine, one-thousand pound lands, and a subsidy to boot. And though, for the present, it pleased the King to fancy a man all the world hated, the King's passion overcoming his judgment, yet it cannot be called a dishonour, for the King is to believe the general council of the kingdom, and to prefer it before his affection, especially when Suffolk was proved to be false, even to the King; for, were it otherwise, love and affection might be called a frenzy and a madness, for it is the nature of human passions, that the love, bred by fidelity, doth change itself into hatred, when the fidelity is first changed into falsehood.

Couns. But, you see, there were thirteen lords chosen in parliament, to have the oversight of the government under the King.

Just. No, my lord, it was to have the oversight of those officers, which, saith the story, had imbezzled, lewdly wasted, and prodigally spent the King's treasure; for to grant the commission to those lords, or to any six of them, joined with the King's council, was one of the most royal and most profitable things he ever did, if he had been constant to himself. But, my good lord, man is the cause of his own misery; for I will repeat the substance of the commission granted by the King, and confirmed by a parliament, which, whether it had been profitable for the King to have prosecuted, your lordship may judge.

The preamble hath these words:

' Whereas our Sovereign Lord the King perceiveth, by the grievous complaints of the lords and commons of this realm, that the rents, profits, and revenues of this realm, by the singular and insufficient counsel and evil government, as well of some his late great officers, &c. are so much withdrawn, wasted, eloined, given, granted, alienated, destroyed, and evil dispended, that he is so much impoverished and void of treasure and goods, and the substance of the crown so much diminished and destroyed, that his estate may not honourably be sustained as appertaineth: The King, of his free-will, at the request of the lords and commons, hath ordained William Archbishop of Canterbury, and others, with his chancellor, treasurer, keeper of his privy-seal, to survey and examine as well the estate and governance of his house, &c. as of all the rents, and profits, and revenues that to him appertain, and to be due, or ought to appertain and be due, &c. And all manner of gifts, grants, alienations, and confirmations, made by him of lands, tenements, rents, &c. bargained and sold to the prejudice of him and his crown, &c. And of his jewels and goods which were his grandfather's at the time of his death, &c. and where they be become.'

This is, in effect, the substance of the commission, which your lordship may read at large in the book of statutes, this commission being enacted in the tenth year of the King's reign. Now, if such a commission were in these days granted to the faithful men, that have no interest in the sales, gifts, nor purchases, nor in the keeping of the jewels at the Queen's death, nor in the obtaining grants of the King's best lands, I cannot say what may be recovered, and justly recovered; and, what says your lordship, was not this a noble act of the King, if it had been followed to effect?

Couns. I cannot tell whether it were or no; for it gave power to the commissioners to examine all the grants.

Just. Why, my lord, doth the King grant any thing that shames at the examination? Are not the King's grants on record?

Couns. But, by your leave, it is some dishonour to a King, to have his judgment called in question.

Just. That is true, my lord, but in this, or whensoever the like shall be granted in the future, the King's judgment is not examined, but their knavery that abused the King. Nay, by your favour, the contrary is true, that when a king will suffer himself to be eaten up by a company of petty fellows, by himself raised, therein both the judgment and courage is disputed. And, if your lordship will disdain it at your own servants hands, much more ought the great heart of a king to disdain it. And surely, my lord, it is a greater treason, though it undercreep the law, to tear from the crown the ornaments thereof: And it is an infallible maxim, that he, that loves not his Majesty's estate, loves not his person.

Couns. How came it then that the act was not executed?

Just. Because these, against whom it was granted, persuaded the King to the contrary, as the Duke of Ireland, Suffolk, the chief justice Tresilian, and others; yea, that which was lawfully done by the King, and the great council of the kingdom, was, by the mastery which Ireland, Suffolk, and Tresilian had over the King's affections, broken and disavowed. Those that devised to relieve the King not by any private invention, but by a general council, were, by a private and partial assembly, adjudged traitors, and the most honest judges of the land, forced to subscribe to that judgment: Insomuch, that Judge Belknap plainly told the Duke of Ireland, and the Earl of Suffolk, when he was constrained to set to his hand, that he wanted but a rope, that he might therewith receive a reward for his subscription. And in this council of Nottingham was hatched the ruin of those which governed the King, of the judges by them constrained, of the lords that loved the King, and sought a reformation, and of the King himself; for though the King found by all the sheriffs of the shires, that the people would not fight against the lords, whom they thought to be most faithful unto the King; when the citizens of London made the same answer, being at that time able to arm fifty-thousand men, and told the mayor, that they would never fight against the King's friends, and defenders of the realm; when the Lord Ralph Basset, who was near the King, told the King boldly, that he would not adventure to have his head broken for the Duke of Ireland's pleasure; when the

Lord of London told the Earl of Suffolk in the King's presence, that he was not worthy to live, &c. yet would the King, in the defence of the destroyers of his estate, lay ambushes to intrap the lords, when they came upon his faith; yea, when all was pacified, and that the King, by his proclamation, had cleared the lords, and promised to produce Ireland, Suffolk, and the Archbishop of York, Tresilian, and Bramber, to answer at the next parliament: These men confessed, that they durst not appear; and when Suffolk fled to Calais, and the Duke of Ireland to Chester, the King caused an army to be levied in Lancashire, for the safe conduct of the Duke of Ireland to his presence, whenas the duke, being encountered by the lords, ran like a coward from his company, and fled into Holland. After this was holden a parliament, which was called that wrought wonders; in the eleventh year of this king, wherein the forenamed lords, the Duke of Ireland, and the rest, were condemned and confiscated, the chief justice hanged, with many others, the rest of the judges condemned and banished, and a tenth and fifteenth given to the King.

Couns. But, good Sir, the King was first besieged in the Tower of London, and the lords came to the parliament, and no man durst contradict them.

Just. Certainly, in raising an army, they committed treason; and though it did appear, that they all loved the King, for they did him no harm, having him in their power, yet our law doth construe all levying of war without the King's commission, and all force raised to be intended for the death and destruction of the King, not attending the sequel. And it is so judged upon good reason, for every unlawful and ill action is supposed to be accompanied with an ill intent. And besides, those lords used too great cruelty, in procuring the sentence of death against divers of the King's servants, who were bound to follow and obey their master and sovereign lord, in that he commanded.

Couns. It is true, and they were also greatly to blame to cause then so many seconds to be put to death, seeing the principals, Ireland, Suffolk, and York, had escaped them. And what reason had they to seek to inform the state by strong hand? Was not the King's estate as dear to himself, as to them? He that maketh a King know his error mannerly and private, and gives him the best advice, he is discharged before God and his own conscience. The lords might have retired themselves, when they saw they could not prevail, and have left the King to his own ways, who had more to lose than they had.

Just. My lord, the taking of arms cannot be excused in respect of the law; but this might be said for the lords, that the King, being under years, and being wholly governed by their enemies, and the enemies of the kingdom; and because, by those evil men's persuasions, it was advised, how the lords should have been murdered at a feast in London, they were excusable, during the King's minority, to stand upon their guards against their particular enemies. But we will pass it over, and go on with our parliaments that followeth, whereof that of Cambridge in the King's twelfth year was the next; therein the King had given him a tenth and a fifteenth; after which, being twenty years of age, he rechanged, saith H. Knighton, his treasurer, his chancellor,

X 2

the justices of either bench, the clerk of the privy seal, and others, and retook the government into his own hands.   He also took the admiral's place from the Earl of Arundel, and, in his room, he placed the Earl of Huntingdon; in the year following, which was the thirteenth year of the king, in the parliament at Westminster, there was given to the king upon every sack of wool fourteen shillings, and sixpence in the pound upon other merchandise.

Couns. But, by your leave, the king was restrained this parliament, that he might not dispose of, but a third part of the money gathered.

Just. No, my lord, by your favour.   But true it is, that part of the money was, by the king's consent, assigned towards the wars, but yet left in the lord treasurer's hands.   And, my lord, it would be a great ease, and a great saving to his Majesty, our lord and master, if it pleased him to make his assignations, upon some part of his revenues, by which he might have one thousand pounds, upon every ten thousand pounds, and save himself a great deal of clamour: For seeing, of necessity, the navy must be maintained, and that those poor men, as well carpenters, as ship-keepers, must be paid, it were better for his Majesty, to give an assignation to the treasurer of his navy, for the receiving of so much as is called ordinary, than to discontent those poor men, who being made desperate beggars, may perchance be corrupted by them that lie in wait to destroy the king's estate.   And if his Majesty did the like in all other payments, especially, where the necessity of such, as are to receive, cannot possibly give days; his Majesty might then, in a little roll, behold his receipts and expences; he might quiet his heart, when all necessaries were provided for, and then dispose the rest at his pleasure. And, my good lord, how excellently, and easily, might this have been done, if the four hundred thousand pounds had been raised, as aforesaid, upon the king's lands, and wards; I say, that his Majesty's house, his navy, his guards, his pensioners, his ammunition, his ambassadors, and all else of ordinary charges might have been defrayed, and a great sum left for his Majesty's casual expences, and rewards: I will not say, they were not in love with the king's estate, but I say, they were unfortunately born, for the king, that crossed it.

Couns. Well, Sir, I would it had been otherwise.   But for the assignments, there are among us, that will not willingly endure it.   Charity begins with itself, shall we hinder ourselves of fifty thousand pounds, per annum, to save the king twenty? No, Sir, what will become of our new-years gifts, our presents, and gratuities? We can now say to those, that have warrants for money, that there is not a penny in the Exchequer, but the king gives it away unto the Scots, faster than it comes in.

Just. My lord, you say well, at least you say the truth, that such are some of our answers, and hence comes that general murmur to all men, that have money to receive; I say, that there is not a penny given to that nation, be it for service, or otherwise, but it is spread over all the kingdom; yea, they gather notes, and take copies of all the privy seals, and warrants, that his Majesty hath given for the money for the Scots, that they may shew them in parliament.   But of his Majesty's gifts to the English, there is no bruit, though they may be ten times as much as the Scots. And, yet, my good lord, howsoever they be thus answered, that to them sue for money out of the Exchequer, it is due to them for ten, or twelve, or twenty in the hundred abated, according to their qualities that shew, they are always furnished. For conclusion, if it would please God to put into the king's heart, to make their assignations, it would save him many a pound, and gain him many a prayer, and a great deal of love; for it grieveth every honest man's heart, to see the abundance, which even the petty officers in the Exchequer and others gather both from the king and subject, and to see a world of poor men run after the king for their ordinary wages.

Couns. Well, well, did you never hear this old tale, that when there was a great contention about the weather, the seamen complaining of contrary winds, when those of the high countries desired rain, and those of the vallies, sun-shining days, Jupiter sent them word by Mercury, then, when they had all done, the weather should be as it had been; and it shall ever fall out so with them that complain, the course of payments shall be as they have been. What care we, what petty fellows say? Or what care we for your papers? Have not we the king's ears, who dares contest with us? Though we cannot be revenged on such as you are, for telling the truth, yet upon some other pretence, we will clap you up, and you shall sue to us, before you get out. Nay, we will make you confess, that you were deceived in your projects, and eat your own words; learn this of me, Sir, that as a little good fortune is better than a great deal of virtue: so the least authority hath advantage over the greatest wit. Was he not the wisest man that said, 'The battle was not to the strongest, nor yet bread for the wise, nor riches to men of understanding, nor favour to men of knowledge;' but that time and chance came to them all.

Just. It is well for your lordship that it is so. But Queen Elisabeth would set the reason of a mean man, before the authority of the greatest counsellor she had; and, by her patience therein, she raised upon the usual and ordinary customs of London, without any new imposition, above fifty thousand pounds a year; for though the Treasurer Burleigh, and the Earl of Leicester, and Secretary Walsingham, all three pensioners to Customer Smith, did set themselves against a poor waiter, of the custom-house, called Carwarden; and commanded the grooms of the privy-chamber, not to give him access; yet the queen sent for him, and gave him countenance against them all. It would not serve the turn, my lord, with her, when your lordships would tell her, that the disgracing her great officers, by hearing the complaints of busy heads, was a dishonour to herself; but she had always this answer, 'That if a man complain unjustly against a magistrate, it were reason he should be severely punished; if justly, she was Queen of the Small, as well as of the Great, and would hear their complaints.' For, my good lord, a prince, that suffereth himself to be besieged, forsaketh one of the greatest regalities, belonging to a monarchy; to wit, the last appeal, or, as the French call it, *le dernier resort.*

Couns. Well, Sir, this from the matter, I pray you go on.

Just. Then my lord, in the king's fifteenth year, he had a tenth, and a fifteenth granted in the parliament of London. And the same year,

x 3

there was a great council called at Stamford, to which divers men were sent for, of divers counties, besides the nobility, of whom the king took advice,   Whether he should continue the war, or make a final end with the French ?

Couns. What needed the king to take the advice of any, but of his own council, in matter of peace and war?

Just. Yea, my lord, for it is said in the Proverbs, ' Where are many counsellors, there is health.'   And if the king had made the war, by a general consent, the kingdom in general were bound to maintain the war, and they could not then say, when the king required aid, that he undertook a needless war.

Couns. You say well, but I pray you go on.

Just. After the subsidy in the fifteenth year, the king desired to borrow ten thousand pounds of the Londoners, which they refused to lend.

Couns. And was not the king greatly troubled therewith ?

Just. Yea, but the king troubled the Londoners soon after, for the king took the advantage of a riot, made upon the Bishop of Salisbury's men ; sent for the mayor, and other the ablest citizens ; committed the mayor to prison, in the castle of Windsor, and others, to other castles, and made a lord warden of this city, till in the end, what with ten thousand pounds, ready money, and other rich presents, instead of lending ten thousand pounds, it cost them twenty thousand pounds.   Between the fifteenth year and twentieth year, he had two aids given him in the parliaments of Winchester and Westminster ; and this latter was given to furnish the king's journey into Ireland, to establish that estate which was greatly shaken, since the death of the king's grandfather, who received thence, yearly, thirty thousand pounds; and during the king's stay in Ireland, he had a tenth and a fifteenth granted.

Couns. And good reason, for the king had in his army four thousand horse, and thirty thousand foot.

Just. That, by your favour, was the king's error; for great armies do rather devour themselves, than destroy enemies.   Such an army, whereof the fourth part would have conquered all Ireland, was in respect of Ireland, such an army as Xerxes led into Greece.   In his twentieth year, wherein he had a tenth of the clergy, was the great conspiracy of the king's uncle, the Duke of Gloucester, and of Mowbray, Arundel, Nottingham, and Warwick, the Archbishop of Canterbury, and the Abbot of Westminster, and others, who, in the twenty-first year of the king, were all redeemed by parliament.   And what thinks your lordship, was not this assembly of the three estates, for the king's estate, wherein he so prevailed, that he not only overthrew those popular lords, but, besides, the English chronicle saith, the king so wrought and brought things about, that he obtained the power of both houses to be granted to certain persons, to fifteen noblemen and gentlemen, or to seven of them ?

Couns. Sir, whether the king wrought well, or ill, I cannot judge ; but our chronicles say, that many things were done in this parliament, to the displeasure of no small number of people, to wit, for that divers rightful heirs were disinherited of their lands and livings, with which.

wrongful doings, the people were much offended ; so that the king, with those that were about him, and chief in council, came into great infamy and slander.

Just. My good lord, if your lordship will pardon me, I am of opinion, that those parliaments, wherein the kings of this land have satisfied the people, as they have been ever prosperous, so, where the king hath restrained the house, the contrary hath happened ; for the king's atchievements, in this parliament, were the ready preparations to his ruin.

Couns. You mean by the general discontentment that followed, and because the king did not proceed legally with Gloucester and others. Why, Sir, this was not the first time that the kings of England have done things, without the council of the land : yea, contrary to the law.

Just. It is true, my lord, in some particulars, as even at this time the Duke of Gloucester was made away at Calais by a strong hand, without any lawful trial : for he was a man so beloved of the people, and so allied, having the Dukes of Lancaster and York, his brethren, the Duke of Aumarle and the Duke of Hereford his nephews, the great Earls of Arundel and Warwick, with divers others of his part, in the conspiracy, as the king durst not try him, according to the law : for at the trial of Arundel and Warwick, the king was forced to entertain a petty army about him.   And though the duke was greatly lamented, yet, it cannot be denied, but that he was then a traytor to the king : And was it not so, my lord, with the Duke of Guise? Your lordship doth remember the spur-gauled proverb, that ' Necessity hath no law ;' and my good lord, it is the practice of doing wrong, and of general wrongs done, that brings danger, and not where kings are pressed, in this, or that particular, for there is great difference between natural cruelty, and accidental.   And therefore it was Machiavel's advice, that ' All that a king did in that kind, he should do at once, and by his mercies afterwards, make the world know, that his cruelty was not affected.'   And, my lord, take this for a general rule, that the immortal policy of a state cannot admit any law or privilege whatsoever, but in some particular, or other, the same is necessarily broken ; yea, in a *Aristocratia*, or popular estate, which vaunts so much of equality, and common right, more outrage hath been committed, than in any Christian monarchy.

Couns. But whence came this hatred, between the duke and the king his nephew ?

Just. My lord, the duke's constraining the king, when he was young, stuck in the king's heart ; and now the duke's proud speech to the king, when he had surrendered Brest, formerly engaged to the Duke of Bretaigne, kindled again these coals, that were not altogether extinguished, for he used these words : ' Your grace ought to put your body in great pain, to win a strong hold or town, by feats of arms, before you take upon you to sell or deliver any town, gotten by the manhood, and strong hand, and policy of your noble progenitors:'   Whereat, saith the story, the king changed his countenance, &c. and to say truth, it was a proud and masterly speech of the duke ; besides, that inclusively, he taxed him of sloth and cowardice, as if he had never put himself to the adventure of winning such a place. Undutiful words of a subject do often take deeper root, than the memory of ill deeds does: The Duke of Biron found it, when the king had him at advantage. Yea, the late Earl of Essex told Queen Elisabeth, that her conditions were as crooked as her carcass, but it cost him his head ; which his insurrection had not cost him, but for that speech : ' Who will say unto the king,' saith Job, ' thou art wicked.' Certainly, it is the same thing to say unto a lady, thou art crooked, and perchance more, as to say unto a king, he is wicked, and to say, that he is a coward, or to use any other words of disgrace ; it is one and the same error.

Couns. But what say you for Arundel, a brave and valiant man, who had the king's pardon of his contempt, during his minority ?

Just. My good lord, the parliament which, you say, disputes the king's prerogative, did quite contrary, and destroyed the king's charter and pardon formerly given to Arundel. And, my good lord, do you remember, that, at the parliament, that wrought wonders, when these lords compounded that parliament, as the king did this, they were so merciless towards all, that they thought their enemies, as the Earl of Arundel most insolently suffered the queen to kneel unto him, three hours, for the saving of one of her servants ; and that scorn of his *manebat alta mente repostum.* And, to say the truth, it is more barbarous and unpardonable than any act, that ever he did, to permit the wife of his sovereign to kneel to him, being the king's vassal. For, if he had saved the lord's servant freely at her first request, as it is like enough, that the queen would also have saved him, *Miseris succurrens paria obtinebis aliquando :* For your lordship sees, that the Earl of Warwick, who was as far in the treason, as any of the rest, was pardoned. It was also, at this parliament, that the Duke of Hereford accused Mowbray, Duke of Norfolk ; and that the Duke of Hereford, son to the Duke of Lancaster, was banished to the king's confusion, as your lordship well knows.

Couns. I know it well, and God knows, that the king had, then, a silly and weak council about him, that persuaded him to banish a prince of the blood, a most valiant man, and the best beloved of the people in general, of any man living ; especially, considering that the king gave every day, more than other, offence to his subjects. For, besides that he fined the inhabitants, that assisted the lords in his minority, of the seventeen shires, which offence he had long before pardoned ; his blank charters, and letting the realm to farm, to mean persons, by whom he was wholly advised, increased the people's hatred towards the present government.

Just. You say well, my lord, princes of an ill destiny do always follow the worst counsel, or, at least, embrace the best, after opportunity is lost : *Qui consilia non ex suo corde sed alienis viribus colligunt, non animo sed auribus cogitant.* And this was not the least grief of the subjects in general, that those men had the greatest part of the spoil of the commonwealth, which, neither by virtue, valour, or counsel, could add any thing unto it : *Nihil est sordidius, nihil crudelius,* saith Antoninus Pius, *quam remp. ab iis arrodi, qui nihil in eam suo labore conferent.*

Couns. Indeed, the letting to farm the realm was very grievous to the subject.

Just. Will your lordship pardon me, if I tell you that the letting to farm of his Majesty's customs, the greatest revenue of the realm, is not very pleasing.

Couns. And, why, I pray you, Doth not the king thereby raise his profits every third year, and one farmer outbid another to the king's advantage?

Just. It is true, my lord, but it grieves the subject to pay custom to the subject; for what mighty men are those farmers become, and if those farmers get many thousands every year, as the world knows they do, why should they not now, being men of infinite wealth, declare unto the king, upon an oath, what they have gained, and henceforth become the king's collectors of his customs? Did not Queen Elisabeth, who was reputed both a wise and just princess, after she had brought Customer Smith from fourteen thousand pounds a year, to forty-two thousand a year, make him lay down a recompense for that which he had gotten? And, if these farmers do give no recompense, let them yet present the king with the truth of their receivings and profits. But, my lord, for conclusion, after Bolingbrook arriving in England, with a small troop; notwithstanding the king, at his landing out of Ireland, had a sufficient and willing army: Yet he, wanting courage to defend his right, gave leave to all his soldiers to depart, and put himself into his hands that cast him into his grave.

Couns. Yet you see, he was deposed by parliament.

Just. As well may your lordship say, he was knocked in the head by parliament; for your lordship knows, that, if King Richard had ever escaped out of their fingers that deposed him, the next parliament would have made all the deposers traytors and rebels, and that justly. In which parliament, or rather unlawful assembly, there appeared but one honest man, to wit, the Bishop of Carlisle, who scorned his life, and estate, in respect of right and his allegiance, and defended the right of his sovereign Lord, against the king elect and his partakers.

Couns. Well, I pray go on with the parliaments held in the time of his successor Henry the Fourth.

Just. This king had, in his third year, a subsidy, and, in his fifth, a tenth of the clergy, without a parliament: In his sixth year, he had so great a subsidy, that the house required there might be no record thereof left to posterity; for the house gave him twenty shillings of every knight's fee, and of every twenty pounds, land, twentypence, and twelve pence the pound, for goods.

Couns. Yea, in the end of this year, the parliament pressed the King to annex unto the crown all temporal possessions belonging to church-men, within the land; which, at that time, was the third foot of all England. But the bishops made friends, and in the end saved their estates.

Just. By this you see, my lord, that Cromwell was not the first that thought on such a business. And, if King Henry the Eighth had reserved the abbies, and other church lands, which he had given at that time, the revenue of the crown of England had exceeded the revenue of the crown of Spain, with both the Indies; whereas, used as it was, a little inriching the crown, it served but to make a number of petti-foggers, and other gentlemen.

Couns. But what had the king, instead of his great revenue?

Just. He had a fifteenth of the commons, and a tenth, and a half of the clergy; and withal, all pensions granted by King Edward, and King Richard, were made void. It was also moved, that all crown lands formerly given, at least given by King Edward, and King Richard, should be taken back.

Couns. What think you of that, Sir? Would it not have been a dishonour to the king? And would not his successors have done the like, to those that the king had advanced?

Just. I cannot answer your lordship, but by distinguishing, for, where the kings had given land for services, and had not been over-reached in his gifts, there it had been a dishonour to the king to have made void the grants of his predecessors, or his grants; but all those grants of the kings, wherein they were deceived, the very custom and policy of England makes them void at this day.

Couns. How mean you that, for his Majesty hath given a great deal of land among us, since he came into England, and would it stand with the king's honour to take it from us again?

Just. Yea, my lord, very well with the king's honour; if your lord-ship, or any lord else, have, under the name of a hundred pounds land a year, gotten five hundred pounds land, and so after that rate.

Couns. I will never believe, that his Majesty will ever do any such thing.

Just. And I believe, as your lordship doth, but we spoke before, of those that dissuaded the king from calling it a parliament: And your lordship asked me the reason, Why any man should dissuade it, to fear it? To which, this place gives me an opportunity to make your lordship an answer; for though his Majesty will, of himself, never question those grants; yet, when the commons shall make humble petition to the king in parliament, that it will please his Majesty to assist them in his relief, with that which ought to be his own; which, if it will please his Majesty to yield unto, the house will most willingly furnish and supply the rest; With what grace can his Majesty deny that honest suit of theirs, the like having been done in many kings times before? This pro-ceeding, my good lord, may perchance prove all your phrases of the king's honour false English.

Couns. But this cannot concern many, and, for myself, I am sure it concerns me little.

Just. It is true, my lord, and there are not many that dissuade his Majesty from a parliament.

Couns. But they are great ones, a few of which will serve the turn well enough.

Just. But, my lord, be they never so great, as great as giants, yet, if they dissuade the king from his ready and assured way of his subsistence, they must devise how the king may be elsewhere supplied, for they otherwise run into a dangerous fortune.

Couns. Hold you contented, Sir, the king needs no great dissuasion.

Just. My lord, learn of me, that there is none of you all that can pierce the king. It is an essential property of a man truly wise, not to open all the boxes of his bosom, even to those that are nearest and dearest unto him; for, when a man is discovered to the very bottom, he is after the less esteemed. I dare undertake, that, when your lordship hath served the king twice twelve years more, you will find, that his Majesty hath reserved somewhat beyond all your capacities; his Majesty hath great reason to put off the parliament, at his last refuge; and in the mean time to make trial of all your loves to serve him; for his Majesty hath had good experience, how well you can serve yourselves: But when the king finds, that the building of your own fortunes and factions hath been the diligent studies, and the service of his Majesty, but the exercise of your leisures: He may then perchance cast himself upon the general love of his people; of which, I trust, he shall never be deceived, and leave as many of your lordships, as have pilfered from the crown, to their examination.

Couns. Well, Sir, I take no great pleasure in this dispute, go on I pray.

Just. In that king's fifth year, he had also a subsidy, which is got by holding the house together, from Easter to Christmas, and would not suffer them to depart. He had also a subsidy in his ninth year. In his eleventh year, the commons did again press the king to take all the temporalities of the churchmen into his hands, which they proved sufficient to maintain a hundred and fifty earls, fifteen hundred knights, and six thousand four hundred esquires, with a hundred hospitals; but they, not prevailing, gave the king a subsidy.

As for the notorious prince, Henry the Fifth, I find that he had given him, in his second year, three hundred thousand marks, and, after that, two other subsidies; one, in his fifth year, another in his ninth, without any disputes.

In the time of his successor, Henry the Sixth, there were not many subsidies. In his third year, he had a subsidy of a tonnage and poundage. And here, saith John Stow, began those payments, which we call customs, because the payment was continued; whereas, before that time, it was granted, but for a year, two, or three, according to the king's occasions. He had also an aid and gathering of money, in his fourth year; and the like in his tenth year, and, in his thirteenth year, a fifteenth. He had also a fifteenth for the conveying of the queen out of France into England. In the twenty-eighth year of that king, was the act of resumption of all honours, towns, castles, signiories, villages, manors, lands, tenements, rents, reversions, fees, &c. But because the wages of the king's servants were, by the strictness of the act, also restrained, this act of resumption was expounded in the parliament, at Reading, the thirty-first year of the King's reign.

Couns. I perceive that those acts of resumption were ordinary in former times; for King Stephen resumed the lands, which, in former times, he had given to make friends, during the civil wars; and Henry the Second resumed all, without exception, which King Stephen had not resumed; for, though King Stephen took back a great deal, yet he suffered his trustiest servants to enjoy his gift.

Just.   Yes, my lord, and in after times also, for this was not the last, nor shall be the last I hope.   And judge you, my lord, whether the parliaments do not only serve the king, whatsoever is said to the contrary; for as all King Henry the Sixth's gifts and grants were made void by the Duke of York, when he was in possession of the kingdom by parliament; so, in the time of King Henry, when King Edward was beaten out again, the parliament of Westminster made all his acts void, and him and all his followers traytors, and gave the king many of their heads and lands.   The parliaments of England do always serve the king in possession; it served Richard the Second to condemn the popular lords; it served Bollingbroke to depose Richard.   When Edward the Fourth had the scepter, it made them all beggars that had followed Henry the Sixth; and it did the like for Henry, when Edward was driven out.   The parliaments are, as the friendship of this world is, which always followeth prosperity; for King Edward the Fourth, after that he was possessed of the crown, he had, in his thirteenth year, a subsidy freely given him, and, in the year following, he took a benevolence through England; which arbitrary taking from the people served that ambitious traytor, the Duke of Bucks.   After the king's death, it was a plausible argument to persuade the multitude, that they should not permit, saith Sir Thomas Moore, his line to reign any longer upon them.

Couns.   Well, Sir, what say you to the parliament of Richard the Third's time?

Just.   I find but one, and therein he made divers good laws; for King Henry the Seventh, in the beginning of his third year, had, by parliament, an aid granted unto him, towards the relief of the Duke of Bretagne, then assailed by the French king.   And although the king did not enter into the war, but by the advice of the three estates, who did willingly contribute; yet those northern men, which loved Richard the Third, raised rebellion, under colour of the money imposed, and murdered the Earl of Northumberland, whom the king employed in that collection. By which your lordship sees, that it hath not been for taxes and impositions alone, that the ill-disposed have taken arms, but even for those payments which have been appointed by parliament.

Couns.   And what became of these rebels?

Just.   They were fairly hanged, and the money levied notwithstanding.   In the king's first year, he gathered a marvellous great mass of money, by a benevolence, taking pattern, by this kind of levy, from Edward the Fourth; but the king caused it first to be moved in parliament, where it was allowed, because the poorer sort were therein spared.   Yet it is true, that the king used some art; for, in his letters, he declared, that he would measure every man's affections by his gifts. In the thirteenth year, he had also a subsidy, whereupon the Cornish men took arms, as the northern men of the bishoprick of Durham had done in the third year of the king.

Couns.   It is without example, that ever the people have rebelled, for any thing granted by parliament, save in this king's days.

Just.   Your lordship must consider, that he was not over-much beloved ; for he took many advantages, both upon the people and the nobility.

Couns.   And I pray you, What say they now of the new impositions lately laid by the king's majesty ?   Do they say they are justly or unjustly laid ?

Just.   To impose upon all things brought into the kingdom is very antient ; which imposing, when it hath been continued a certian time, is then called customs, because the subjects are accustomed to pay it ; and yet the great tax upon wine is still called impost, because it was imposed after the ordinary rate of payment had lasted many years. But we do, now-a-days, understand those things to be impositions, which are raised by the command of princes, without the advice of the commonwealth ; though, as I take it, much of that, which is now called custom, was, at the first, imposed by prerogative royal.   Now, whether it be time or consent that makes them just, I cannot define ; Were they just, because new, or not justified yet by time, or unjust, because they want a general consent?   Yet is this rule of Aristotle verified, in respect of his Majesty : ' Minus timent homines injustum pati a principe, quem cultorem Dei putant.'   Yea, my lord, they are also the more willingly borne, because, all the world knows, they are no new invention of the king's ; and if those, that advised his Majesty to impose them, had raised his lands, as it was offered them, to twenty thousand pounds more than it was, and his wards to as much as aforesaid, they had done him far more acceptable service.   But they had their own ends, in refusing the one, and accepting the other.   If the land had been raised, they could not have selected the best of it for themselves ; if the impositions had not been laid, some of them could not have their silks, other pieces in farm ; which, indeed, grieved the subject ten times more, than that which his Majesty enjoyeth.   But certainly they made a great advantage, that were the advisers ; for, if any tumult had followed his Majesty, a ready way had been to have delivered them over to the people.

Couns.   But think you, that the king would have delivered them, if any troubles had followed ?

Just.   I know not, my lord, it was Machiavel's counsel to Cæsar Borgia to do it ; and King Henry the Eighth delivered Empson and Dudley ; yea, the same king, when the great Cardinal Wolsey, who governed the king, and all his estate, had, by requiring the sixth part of every man's goods for the king, raised rebellion ; the king, I say, disavowed him absolutely, that, had not the Dukes of Norfolk and Suffolk appeased the people, the cardinal had sung no more mass ; for these are the words of our story : ' The king then came to Westminster, to the cardinal's palace, and assembled there a great council, in which he protested, That his mind was never to ask any thing of his commons, which might sound to the breach of his laws ; wherefore, he then willed them to know, by whose means they were so strictly given forth. Now, my lord, how the cardinal would have shifted himself, by saying, I had the opinion of the judges, had not the rebellion been appeased, I greatly doubt.

Couns. But, good Sir, you blanch my question, and answer me by examples. I ask you, Whether or no, in any such tumult, the people pretending against one or two great officers, the king should deliver them, or defend them?

Just. My good lord, the people have not staid for the king's delivery, neither in England, nor in France. Your lordship knows how the chancellor, treasurer, and chief justice, with many others, at several times, have been used by the rebels; and the marshals, constables, and treasurers in France have been cut in pieces, in Charles the Sixth's time. Now to your lordship's question, I say, that where any man shall give a king perilous advice, as may either cause a rebellion, or draw the people's love from the king; I say, that a king shall be advised to banish him; but if the king do absolutely command his servant to do any thing displeasing to the commonwealth, and to his own peril, there is the king bound in honour to defend him. But, my good lord, for conclusion; there is no man in England that will lay any invention, either grievous, or against law, upon the king's majesty; and, therefore, your lordships must share it amongst you.

Couns. For my part, I had no hand in it, I think Ingram was he that propounded it to the treasurer.

Just. Alas! my good lord, every poor waiter in the Custom-house, or every promoter might have done it, there is no invention in these things. To lay impositions, and sell the king's lands, are poor and common devices. It is true, that Ingram, and his fellows, are odious men, and therefore his Majesty pleased the people greatly to put him from the coffership. It is better for a prince to use such kind of men, than to countenance them; hangmen are necessary in a commonwealth; yet, in the Netherlands, none but a hangman's son will marry a hangman's daughter. Now, my lord, the last gathering which Henry the Seventh made, was in his twentieth year, wherein he had another benevolence, both of the clergy and laity, a part of which, taken of the poorer sort, he ordained, by his testament, that it should be restored. And for King Henry the Eighth, although he was left in a most plentiful estate, yet he wonderfully pressed his people with great payments; for, in the beginning of his time, it was infinite, that he spent in masking and tilting, banqueting, and other vanities, before he was entered into the most consuming expence of the most fond and fruitless war, that ever king undertook. In his fourth year, he had one of the greatest subsidies that ever was granted; for, besides two-fifteenths, and two disms, he used David's law of capitation, or head-money, and had, of every duke, ten marks; of every earl, five pounds; of every lord, four pounds; of every knight, four marks, and every man rated at eight pounds in goods, four marks, and so after the rate; yea, every man, that was valued but at forty shillings, paid twelve pence, and every man and woman, above fifteen years old, four-pence; he had also, in his sixth year, divers subsidies granted him. In his fourteenth, there was a tenth demanded of every man's goods, but it was moderated. In the parliament following, the clergy gave the king the half of their spiritual livings for one year, and, of the laity, there was demanded eight hundred thousand pounds, which could not be levied in England; but it was a marvellous great gift, that the king had given him at that time.   In the king's seventeenth year, was the rebellion before spoken of, wherein the king disavowed the cardinal; in his seventeenth year, he had the tenth and fifteenth given by parliament, which were, before that time, paid to the pope; and, before that time also, the monies that the king borrowed in his fifteenth year, were forgiven him, by parliament, in his seventeenth year.   In his thirty-fifth year, a subsidy was granted of fourpence in the pound, of every man worth, in goods, from twenty shillings to five pounds, from five pounds to ten pounds, and upwards, of every pound two shillings.   And all strangers, denisens, and others, doubled this sum; strangers, not being inhabitants above sixteen years, four-pence a head.   All that had lands, fees, and annuities, from twenty to five, and so double, as they did for goods: and the clergy gave sixpence the pound.   In the thirty-seventh year, a benevolence was taken, not voluntary, but rated by commissioners, which, because one of the aldermen refused to pay, he was sent for a soldier into Scotland. He had also another great subsidy, of six shillings the pound, of the clergy, and two shillings and eight-pence of the goods of the laity, and four shillings the pound upon lands.

In the second year of Edward the Sixth, the parliament gave the King an aid of twelve-pence the pound of goods, of his natural subjects, and two shillings the pound of strangers, and this to continue for three years; and, by the statute of the second and third of Edward the Sixth, it may appear, the same parliament did also give a second aid, as followeth, to wit, of every ewe, kept in several pastures, three-pence; of every wether, kept as aforesaid, two-pence; of every sheep, kept in the common, one-penny.   Observation.   The house gave the king also eight-pence the pound, of every woollen-cloth, made for sale, throughout England, for three years.   In the third and fourth of the King, by reason of the troublesome gathering of the poll-money upon sheep, and the tax upon cloth, this act of subsidy was repealed, and other relief given the king, and, in the King's seventh year, he had a subsidy, and two-fifteenths.

In the first year of Queen Mary, tonnage and poundage were granted; in the second year, a subsidy was given to King Philip, and to the Queen; she had also a third subsidy, *in annis* 4 & 5.

Now, my lord, for the parliaments of the late Queen's (Elisabeth) time, in which there was nothing new, neither head-money, nor sheep-money, nor escuage, nor any of these kinds of payments was required, but only the ordinary subsidies, and those as easily granted as demanded.   I shall not need to trouble your lordship with any of them; neither can I inform your lordship of all the passages and acts which have passed, for they are not extant, nor printed.

Couns. No, it were but time lost to speak of the latter; and, by those that are already remembered, we may judge of the rest; for those of the greatest importance are publick: but, I pray you, deal freely with me; what think you would be done for his Majesty, if he should call a parliament at this time? Or what would be required at his Majesty's hands?

Just. The first thing that would be required, would be the same that was required by the commons in the thirteenth year of Henry the Eighth; to wit, that, if any man of the commons house should speak more largely, than of duty he ought to do, all such offences to be pardoned, and that to be of record.

Couns. So might every companion speak of the king what they list.

Just. No, my lord; the reverence, which a vassal oweth to his sovereign, is always intended for every speech; howsoever, it must import the good of the King, and his estate, and so long it may be easily pardoned, otherwise not: for, in Queen Elisabeth's time, who gave freedom of speech in all parliaments, when Wentworth made those motions, that were but supposed dangerous to the Queen's estate, he was imprisoned in the Tower, notwithstanding the privilege of the house, and there died.

Couns. What say you to the Sicilian Vespers, remembered in the last parliament?

Just. I say, he repented him heartily that used that speech; and, indeed, besides that it was seditious, this example held not: the French in Sicily usurped that kingdom; they kept neither law nor faith; they took away the inheritance of the inhabitants; they took from them their wives, and ravished their daughters, committing all other insolencies that could be imagined. The king's majesty is the natural lord of England; His vassals of Scotland obey the English laws; if they break them, they are punished without respect: yea, his majesty put one of his barons to a shameful death, for being consenting only to the death of a common fencer; and which of these ever did, or durst commit any outrage in England? But, to say the truth, the opinion of packing the last was the cause of the contention and disorder that happened.

Couns. Why, Sir, do you not think it best to compound a parliament of the king's servants and others, that shall in all obey the king's desires?

Just. Certainly no; for it hath never succeeded well, neither on the king's part, nor on the subjects, as by the parliament before-remembered your lordship may gather; for, from such a composition, do arise all jealousies and all contentions. It was practised in elder times, to the great trouble of the kingdom, and to the loss and ruin of many. It was of later time used by King Henry the Eighth, but every way to his disadvantage. When the king leaves himself to his people, they assure themselves, that they are trusted and beloved of their king; and there was never any assembly so barbarous, as not to answer the love and trust of their king. Henry the Sixth, when his estate was in effect utterly overthrown, and utterly impoverished, at the humble request of his treasurer, made the same known to the house: or, otherwise, using the treasurer's own words, ' He humbly desired the king to take his staff, that he might save his wardship.'

Couns. But, you know, they will presently be in hand with those impositions, which the king hath laid by his own royal prerogative.

Just. Perchance not, my lord, but rather with those impositions, that have been by some of your lordships laid upon the king; which did not some of your lordships fear, more than you do the impositions laid upon the subjects, you would never dissuade his Majesty from a parliament; for no man doubted, but that his Majesty was advised to lay those impositions by his council; and, for particular things, on which they were laid, the advice came from petty fellows (though now great ones) belonging to the Custom-house. Now, my lord, what prejudice hath his Majesty, his revenue being kept up, if the impositions, that were laid by the advice of a few, be in parliament laid by the general council of the kingdom, which takes off all grudging and complaint?

Couns. Yea, Sir; but that, which is done by the king, with the advice of his private or privy-council, is done by the king's absolute power.

Just. And by whose power is it done in parliament, but by the king's absolute power? Mistake it not, my lord : the three estates do but advise, as the prime council doth ; which advice, if the king embrace it, becomes the king's own act in the one, and the king's law in the other ; for, without the king's acceptation, both the public and private advices are but as empty egg-shells. And what doth his Majesty lose, if some of those things, which concern the poorer sort, be made free again ; and the revenue kept up upon that which is superfluous? Is it a loss to the king to be beloved of the commons ? If it be revenue, which the king seeks, is it not better to take it of those that laugh, than of those that cry? Yea, if all be content to pay, upon moderation and change of the species, is it not more honourable, and more safe for the king, that the subjects pay by persuasion, than to have them constrained ? If they be contented to whip themselves for the king, were it not better to give them the rod into their own hands, than to commit them to the executioner ? Certainly, it is far more happy for a sovereign prince, that a subject open his purse willingly, than that the same be opened by violence. Besides that, when impositions are laid by parliament, they are gathered by the authority of the law, which, as aforesaid, rejecteth all complaints, and stoppeth every mutinous mouth. It shall ever be my prayer, that the king embrace the counsel of honour and safety ; and let other princes embrace that of force.

Couns. But, good Sir, it is his prerogative, which the king stands upon ; and it is the prerogative of the kings, that the parliaments do all diminish.

Just. If your lordship would pardon me, I would say then, that your lordship's objection against parliaments is ridiculous. In former parliaments, three things have been supposed dishonour of the king: The first, that the subjects have conditioned with the king, when the king hath needed them, to have the great charter confirmed. The second, That the estates have made treasurers, for the necessary and profitable disbursing of those sums by them given, to the end that the kings, to whom they were given, should expend them for their own defence, and for the defence of the commonwealth. The third, That these have pressed the king to discharge some great officers of the crown, and to elect others. As touching the first, my lord, I would fain learn what disadvantage the kings of this land have had by confirming the great charter; the breach of which hath served only men of your lordship's rank to assist their own passions, and to punish and imprison, at their own discretion, the king's poor subjects, concerning their private hatred, with the colour of the king's service; for the king's majesty takes no man's inheritance, as I have said before, nor any man's life, but by the law of the land, according to the charter: neither doth his Majesty imprison any man (matter of practice, which concerns the preservation of his estate, excepted) but by the law of the land, and yet he useth his prerogative, as all the kings of England have ever used it; for the supreme reason causes to practise many things without the advice of the law; as, in insurrections and rebellions, it useth the martial, and not the common law, without any breach of the charter, the intent of the charter considered truly. Neither hath any subject made complaint, or been grieved, in that the kings of this land, for their own safeties, and preservation of their estates, have used their prerogatives, the great ensign, on which there is written *Soli Deo*. And, my good lord, was not Buckingham in England, and Byron in France condemned, their peers uncalled? And, withal, was not Byron utterly (contrary to the customs and privileges of the French) denied an advocate to assist his defence? For, where law's forecast cannot provide remedies for future dangers, princes are forced to assist themselves by their prerogatives. But that, which hath been ever grievous, and the cause of many troubles very dangerous, is, that your lordships, abusing the reasons of state, do punish and imprison the king's subjects at your pleasure. It is you, my lords, that when subjects have sometimes need of the king's prerogative, do then use the strength of the law; and, when they require the law, you afflict them with the prerogative, and tread the great charter, which hath been confirmed by sixteen acts of parliament, under your feet, as a torn parchment, or waste-paper.

Couns. Good Sir, which of us do, in this sort, break the great charter? Perchance you mean, that we have advised the king to lay the new impositions.

Just. No, my lord, there is nothing in the great charter against impositions; and, besides that, necessity doth persuade them: and if necessity do, in somewhat, excuse a private man, *à fortiori*, it may then excuse a prince. Again, the king's majesty hath profit and increase of revenue by the impositions. But there are of your lordships, contrary to the direct letter of the charter, that imprison the king's subjects, and deny them the benefit of the law, to the king's disprofit. And, what do you do otherwise thereby, if the impositions be in any sort grievous, but *renovare dolores*? And, withal, dig out of the dust the long-buried memory of the subjects former intentions, with their kings.

Couns. What mean you by that?

Just. I will tell your lordship, when I dare: in the mean time, it is enough for me, to put your lordship in mind, that all the estates in the world, in the offence of the people, have either had profit or necessity to persuade them to adventure it; of which, if neither be urgent, and yet the subject exceedingly grieved, your lordship may conjecture, that the house will be humble suitors for a redress. And, if it be a maxim in policy to please the people in all things indifferent, and never suffer them to be beaten, but for the king's benefit (for there are no blows forgotten with the smart, but those); then, I say, to make them vassals to vassals, is but to batter down those mastering buildings, erected by King Henry the Seventh, and fortified by his son, by which the people and gentry of England were brought to depend upon the king alone. Yea, my good lord, our late dear sovereign kept them up, and to their advantage, as well repaired as ever prince did. 'Defend me, and spend me,' saith the Irish churl.

Couns. Then you think, that this violent breach of the charter will be the cause of seeking the confirmation of it in the next parliament, which otherwise could never have been moved?

Just. I know not, my good lord, perchance not; for, if the house press the king to grant unto them all that is theirs by the law, they cannot, in justice, refuse the king all that is his by the law. And where will be the issue of such a contention? I dare not divine, but sure I am, that it will tend to the prejudice both of the king and subject.

Couns. If they dispute not their own liberties, why should they then dispute the king's liberties, which we call his prerogative?

Just. Amongst so many and so divers spirits, no man can foretel what may be propounded; but, howsoever, if the matter be not slightly handled on the king's behalf, these disputes will soon dissolve; for the king hath so little need of his prerogative, and so great advantage by the laws, as the fear of impairing the one, to wit, the prerogative, is so impossible; and the burthen of the other, to wit, the law so weighty, as but by a branch of the king's prerogative, namely, of his remission and pardon, the subject is no way able to undergo it. This, my lord, is no matter of flourish that I have said, but it is the truth, and unanswerable.

Couns. But to execute the laws very severely would be very grievous.

Just. Why, my lord, are the laws grievous, which ourselves have required of our kings? And are the prerogatives also, which our kings have reserved to themselves, also grievous? How can such a people then be well pleased? And if your lordship confess that the laws give too much, why does your lordship urge the prerogative that gives more? Nay, I will be bold to say it, that, except the laws were better observed, the prerogative of a religious prince hath manifold less perils, than the letter of the law hath. Now, my lord, for the second and third, to wit, for the appointing of treasurers, and removing of counsellors, our kings have evermore laughed them to scorn that have pressed either of these; and, after the parliament dissolved, took the money of the treasurers of the parliament, and recalled and restored the officers discharged; or else they have been contented, that some such persons should be removed at the request of the whole kingdom, which they themselves, out of their noble natures, would not seem willing to remove.

Couns. Well, Sir, would you, notwithstanding all these arguments, advise his Majesty to call a parliament?

Just. It belongs to your lordships, who enjoy the king's favour, and are chosen for your able wisdom, to advise the king. It were a strange boldness in a poor and private person, to advise kings, attended with so understanding a council. But, belike your lordships have conceived some other way, how money may be gotten otherwise. If any trouble should happen, your lordship knows, that then there were nothing so dangerous for a king, as to be without money: a parliament cannot assemble in haste, but present dangers require hasty remedies. It will be no time then to discontent the subjects, by using any inordinate ways.

Couns. Well, Sir, all this notwithstanding, we dare not advise the king to call a parliament; for, if it should succeed ill, we, that advise, should fall into the king's disgrace. And, if the king be driven into any extremity, we can say to the king, that, because we found it extremely unpleasing to his Majesty to hear of a parliament, we thought it no good manners to make such a motion.

Just. My lord, to the first let me tell you, that there was never any just prince that hath taken any advantage of the success of counsels, which have been founded on reason. To fear that were to fear the loss of the bell, more than the loss of the steeple, and were also the way to beat all men from the studies of the king's service. But for the second, where you say you can excuse yourselves upon the king's own protesting against a parliament; the king, upon better consideration, may encounter that fineness of yours.

Couns. How, I pray you?

Just. Even by declaring himself to be indifferent, by calling your lordships together, and by delivering unto you, that he hears how his loving subjects in general are willing to supply him, if it please him to call a parliament, for that was the common answer to all the sheriffs in England, when the late benevolence was commanded. In which respect, and because you came short in all your projects, and because it is a thing most dangerous for a king to be without treasure, he requires such of you, as either mislike, or rather fear a parliament, to set down your reasons in writing, why you either misliked, or feared it. And such as I wish and desire it, to set down answers to your objections: and so shall the king prevent the calling, or not calling, on his Majesty, as some of your great counsellors have done in many other things, shrinking up their shoulders, and saying, 'The king will have it so.

Couns. Well, Sir, it grows late, and I will bid you farewell, only you shall take well with you this advice of mine: that, in all that you have said against our greatest, those men, in the end, shall be your judges in their own cause; you, that trouble yourself with reformation, are like to be well rewarded; for hereof you may assure yourself, that we will never allow of any invention, how profitable soever, unless it proceed, or seem to proceed, from ourselves.

Just. If then, my lord, we may presume to say, that princes may be unhappy in any thing, certainly they are unhappy in nothing more, than in suffering themselves to be so inclosed. Again, if we may believe Pliny, who tell us, 'That it is an ill sign of prosperity in any kingdom or state, where such, as deserve well, find no other recompence than the contentment of their own consciences;' a far worse sign is it, where the justly accused shall take revenge of the just accuser. But, my good lord, there is this hope remaining, that, seeing he hath been abused by them he trusted most, he will not, for the future dishonour of his judgment, so well informed by his own experience, expose such of his vassals (as have had no other motives to serve him, than simply the love of his person and his estate) to their revenge, who have only been moved by the love of their own fortunes, and their glory.

Couns. But, good Sir, the king hath not been deceived by all?

Just. No, my lord, neither have all been trusted, neither doth the world accuse all, but believe, that there be amongst your lordships very just and worthy men, as well of the nobility, as others, but those, though most honoured in the commonwealth, yet, have they not been most employed : your lordship knows it well enough, that three or four of your lordships have thought your hands strong enough to bear up alone the weightiest affairs in the commonwealth, and strong enough all the land have found them to bear down whom they pleased.

Couns. I understand you : but how shall it appear, that they have only sought themselves?

Just. There needs no perspective glass to discern it ; for neither in the treaties of peace and war, in matters of revenue, and matters of trade, any thing hath happened either of love or judgment. No, my lord, there is not any one action of theirs eminent, great or small, the greatness of themselves only excepted.

Couns. It is all one ; your papers can neither answer nor reply, we can. Besides, you tell the king no news in delivering these complaints, for he knows as much as can be told him.

Just. For the first, my lord, whereas he hath once the reasons of things delivered him, your lordships shall need to be well advised; in their answers, there is no sophistry will serve their turn, where the judge and the understanding are both supreme. For the second, to say that his Majesty knows, and cares not, that, my lord, were but to despair all his faithful subjects. But by your favour, my lord, we see it is contrary; we find now, that there is no such singular power as there hath been ; justice is described with a balance in her hand, holding it even ; and it hangs as even now as ever it did in any king's days ; for singular authority begets but general oppression.

Couns. Howsoever it be, that is nothing to you, that have no interest in the king's favour, nor perchance, in his opinion ; and, concerning such a one, the misliking, or but misconceiving of any one hard word, phrase, or sentence, will give argument to the king, either to condemn, or reject the whole discourse. And, howsoever his Majesty may neglect your informations, you may be sure that others, at whom you point, will not neglect their revenges ; you will therefore confess it, when it is too late, that you are exceeding sorry that you have not followed my advice. Remember Cardinal Wolsey, who lost all men for the king's service, and, when their malice, whom he grieved, had not outlived the king's affection, you know what became of him as well as I.

Just. Yea, my lord, I know it well, that malice hath a longer life, than either love or thankfulness hath, for as we always take more care

Y 3

to put off pain, than to enjoy pleasure; because the one hath no intermission, and with the other we are often satisfied; so it is in the smart of injury and the memory of good turns: wrongs are written in marble; benefits are, sometimes, acknowledged, rarely requited. But, my lord, we shall do the king great wrong, to judge him by common rules, or ordinary examples; for, seeing his Majesty hath greatly inriched and advanced those that have but pretended his service, no man needs to doubt of his goodness, towards those that shall perform any thing worthy reward. Nay, the not taking knowledge of those of his own vassals, that have done him wrong, is more to be lamented, than the relinquishing of those that do him right, is to be suspected. I am, therefore, my good lord, held to my resolution, by these two, besides the former: the first, that God would never have blessed him with so many years, and in so many actions, yea, in all his actions, had he paid his honest servants with evil for good. The second, where your lordship tells me, that I will be sorry for not following your advice, I pray your lordship to believe, that I am no way subject to the common sorrowing of worldly men, this maxim of Plato being true: *dolores omnes ex amore animi erga corpus nascuntur.* But, for my body, my mind values it at nothing.

Couns. What is it then you hope for, or seek?

Just. Neither riches, nor honour, or thanks; but I only seek to satisfy his Majesty (which I would have been glad to have done in matters of more importance) that I have lived, and will die an honest man.

———

The Author's Epitaph, made by himself.

EVEN such is time, which takes in trust
　　Our youth, and joys, and all we have,
And pays us but with age and dust;
　　Which in the dark and silent grave,
When we have wander'd all our ways,
Shut up the story of our days:
And from which earth, and grave, and dust,
The Lord shall raise me up, I trust.

THE

ACCUSATION AND IMPEACHMENT

OF

JOHN LORD FINCH,

BARON OF FORDWICH,

Lord Keeper of the Great Seal of England, by the House of Commons.

Printed Anno Domini 1640. Quarto, containing twelve pages.

———

Imprimis,

THAT the said John Lord Finch, Baron of Fordwich, Lord Keeper, &c. hath traiterously and wickedly endeavoured to subvert the fundamental laws, and established government of the realm of England, and, instead thereof, to introduce an arbitrary tyrannical government against law; which he hath declared by traiterous and wicked words, counsels, opinions, judgments, practices, and actions.

II. That, in pursuance of those his traiterous and wicked purposes, he did, in the third and fourth years of his Majesty's reign, or one of them, being then speaker of the commons house of parliament, contrary to the commands of the house, then assembled and sitting, deny and hinder the reading of some things, which the said house of commons required to be read for the safety of the king and kingdom, and preservation of the religion of this realm; and did forbid all the members of the house to speak; and said, that, if any did offer to speak, he would rise and go away; and said, nothing should be then done in the house; and did offer to rise and go away; and did thereby, and otherwise, as much as in him lay, endeavour to subvert the ancient and undoubted rights and course of parliaments.

III. That he, being of his Majesty's council, at the justice-seat held for the county of Essex, in the month of October, in the tenth year of his now Majesty's reign, at Strafford-Langton, in the same county, being then of his Majesty's council, in that service did practise, by unlawful means, to enlarge the forest of that county many miles beyond the known bounds thereof, as they had been enjoyed near three hundred years, contrary to the law, and to the charter of the liberties of the forest, and other charters, and divers acts of parliament; and, for effecting the same, did unlawfully cause and procure undue returns to be made of jurors, and great numbers of other persons, who were unsworn, to be joined to them of the jury; and threatened and awed the said jurors to give a verdict for the king; and, by unlawful means, did sur-

prise the county, that they might not make defence; and did use several menacing wicked speeches and actions to the jury, and others, for
obtaining his unjust purpose aforesaid; and, after a verdict obtained
for the king in the month of April following (at which time the said
justice-seat was called by adjournment) the said John Lord Finch,
then Lord Chief Justice of his Majesty's Court of Common Pleas, was
one of the judges assistants for them, and continued, by further unlawful
and unjust practices, to maintain and confirm the said verdict; and did
then and there, being assistant to the justice in eyre, advise the refusal
of the traverse offered by the county, and all their evidences, but
only what they should verbally deliver; which was refused accordingly.

IV. That he, about the month of November, 1635, being then Lord
Chief Justice of the Court of Common Pleas, and having taken an oath
for the due administration of justice to his Majesty's liege people according to the laws and statutes of the realm, contrived an opinion in
hæc verba: 'When the good and safety, &c.' and did subscribe his
name to that opinion, and by persuasions, threats, and false suggestions,
did solicit and procure Sir John Bramston, then and now Lord Chief
Justice of England; Sir Humfrey Davenport, knight, Lord Chief Baron
of his Majesty's Court of Exchequer; Sir Richard Hutton, knight, late
one of the justices of his Majesty's Court of Common Pleas; Sir John
Denham, knight, late one of the barons of his Majesty's Court of Exchequer; Sir William Jones, knight, late one of the justices of the said
Court of King's Bench; Sir George Crooke, then and now one of the
judges of the said Court of King's Bench; Sir Thomas Trevor, knight,
then and now one of the barons of the Exchequer; Sir George Vernon,
knight, late one of the justices of the said Court of Common Pleas; Sir
Robert Barkley, knight, then and now one of the justices of the said
Court of King's Bench; Sir Francis Crawley, knight, then and now one
of the justices of the said Court of Common Pleas: Sir Richard
Weston, knight, then and now one of the barons of the said Court of
Exchequer, some or one of them to subscribe with their names the said
opinion presently, and injoined them severally, some or one of them,
secrecy upon their allegiance.

V. That he the   day of   then being Lord Chief
Justice of the said Court of Common Pleas, subscribed an extra-judi-
cial opinion in answer to questions in a letter from his Majesty, in hæc
verba, &c.

And that he contrived the said questions, and procured the said letter
from his Majesty; and, whereas the said Justice Hutton and Justice
Crooke declared to him their opinions to the contrary; yet he required
and pressed them to subscribe, upon his promise that he would let his
Majesty know the truth of their opinions, notwithstanding such sub-
scriptions, which nevertheless he did not make known to his Majesty,
but delivered the same to his Majesty as the opinion of all the
judges.

VI. That he, being Lord Chief Justice of the said Court of Common
Pleas, delivered his opinion in the Exchequer-chamber against Master
Hampden in the case of ship-money; that he the said Master

Hampden upon the matter and substance of the case was chargeable with the money then in question ; a copy of which proceedings the Commons will deliver to your lordships, and did sollicit and threaten the said judges, some or one of them, to deliver their opinions in like manner against Master Hampden ; and, after the said Baron Denham had delivered his opinion for Master Hampden, the said Lord Finch repaired purposely to the said Baron Denham's chamber in Serjeants-Inn, in Fleet-street, and, after the said Master Baron Denham had declared and expressed his opinion, urged him to retract the said opinion ; which he refusing, was threatened by the said Lord Finch, because he refused.

VII. That he, then being Lord Chief Justice of the Court of Common Pleas, declared and published in the Exchequer-chamber, and western circuit where he went judge, that the king's right to ship-money, as aforesaid, was so inherent a right to the crown, as an act of parliament could not take away ; and with divers malicious speeches inveighed against and threatened all such as refused to pay ship-money ; all which opinions, contained in the fourth, fifth, and sixth articles, are against the law of the realm, the subjects right of property, and contrary to former resolutions in parliament, and to the petition of right ; which said resolutions and petition of right were well known to him, and resolved and enacted in parliament when he was speaker of the Commons house of parliament.

VIII. That he, being Lord Chief Justice of the Court of Common Pleas, did take the general practice of that court to his private chamber ; and that he sent warrants into all or many shires of England to several men, as to Francis Giles of the county of Devon, Robert Benson of the county of York, attornies of that court, and to divers others, to release all persons arrested on any outlawry about forty shillings fees, whereas none by law so arrested can be bailed or released, without a *supersedeas* under seal, or reversal.

IX. That he, being Lord Chief Justice of the Court of Common Pleas, upon a pretended suit begun in Michaelmas term in the eleventh year of of his Majesty's reign, although there was no plaint or declaration against him, did notoriously, and contrary to all law and justice, by threats, menaces, and imprisonment, compel Thomas Laurence, an executor, to pay nineteen pounds twelve shillings ; and likewise caused Richard Barnard, being only overseer of the last will of that testator, to be arrested for the payment of the said money, contrary to the advice of the rest of the judges of that court, and against the known and ordinary course of justice, and his said oath and knowledge, and denied his Majesty's subjects the common and ordinary justice of this realm, as to Master Limericke, and others : and, for his private benefit, endamaged and ruined the estates of very many of his Majesty's subjects, contrary to his oath and knowledge.

X. That he, being Lord Keeper of the Great Seal of England, and sworn one of his Majesty's Privy Council, did, by false and malicious slanders, labour to incense his Majesty against parliaments, and did frame and advise the publishing the declaration, after the dissolution of the last parliament.

All which treasons and misdemeanors, above-mentioned, were done and committed by the said John Lord Finch, Baron of Fordwich, Lord Keeper of the great Seal of England ; and thereby he, the said Lord Finch, hath traitorously, and contrary to his allegiance, laboured to lay imputations and scandals upon his Majesty's government, and to alienate the hearts of his Majesty's liege people from his Majesty, and to set a division between them, and to ruin and destroy his Majesty's realm of England ; for which they do impeach him, the said Lord Finch, Baron of Fordwich, Lord Keeper of the great Seal of England, of high treason, against our Sovereign Lord the King, his crown, and dignity, of the misdemeanors above-mentioned. And the said Commons by protestation, saving to themselves the liberty of exhibiting at any time hereafter, any other accusation, or impeachment, against the said Lord Finch, and also of replying to the answer; that the said John, Lord Finch, shall make unto the said articles, or to any of them, and of offering proof of the premisses, or any of their impeachments or accusations that shall be exhibited by them, as the case shall, according to the course of parliaments, require, do pray, that the said John, Lord Finch, Baron of Fordwich, Lord Keeper of the great Seal of England, may be put to answer all, and every the premisses, and such proceedings, examinations, trials, and judgments, as may be upon every of them had, and used, as is agreeable to law and justice.

THE
LORD DIGBY'S SPEECH,

IN THE

HOUSE OF COMMONS,

To the Bill for Triennial Parliaments, January 19, 1640,

Quarto, containing sixteen pages.

Mr. Speaker,

I RISE not now with an intent to speak to the frame and structure of this bill, nor much by way of answer to objections that may be made ; I hope there will be no occasion of that, but that we shall concur all unanimously in what concerneth all so universally.

Only, Sir, by way of preparation, to the end, that we may not be discouraged in this great work by difficulties that may appear in the way of it, I shall deliver unto you my apprehensions in general, of the vast importance and necessity that we should go thorough with it.

The result of my sense is, in short, this : That unless, for the frequent convening of parliaments, there be some such course settled, as may not be eluded ; neither the people can be prosperous and secure, nor the king himself solidly happy. I take this to be the *Unum necessarium.* Let us procure this, and all our other desires will effect themselves, If this bill miscarry, I shall have left me no publick hopes ; and, once passed, I shall be freed of all publick fears.

The essentialness, Sir, of frequent parliaments to the happiness of this kingdom, might be inferred unto you, by the reason of contraries, from the woeful experience which former times have had of the mischievous effects of any long intermission of them.

But, Mr, Speaker, why should we climb higher than the level we are on, or think further than our own horizon, or have recourse for examples in this business to any other promptuary than our own memories ? nay, than the experience almost of the youngest here ?

The reflexion backward on the distractions of former times upon intermission of parliaments, and the consideration forward of the mischiefs likely still to grow from the same cause, if not reformed, doubtless, gave first life and being to those two dormant statutes of Edward the Third, for the yearly holding of parliaments. And shall not the fresh and bleeding experience in the present age of miseries from the same spring, not to be paralleled in any other, obtain an awakening, a resurrection for them ?

The intestine distempers, Sir, of former ages upon the want of parliaments, may appear to have had some other co-operative causes, as sometimes, unsuccessful wars abroad ; sometimes, the absence of the prince ; sometimes, competitions of titles to the crown ; sometimes, perhaps, the vices of the king himself.

But, let us but consider the posture, the aspect of this state, both towards itself, and the rest of the world, the person of our sovereign, and the nature of our sufferings, since the third of his reign ; And there can be no cause colourably inventable, whereunto to attribute them, but the intermission, or, which is worse, the undue frustration of parliaments, by the unlucky use, if not abuse, of prerogative in the dissolving them.

Take into your view, gentlemen, a state in a state of the greatest quiet and security that can be fancied, not only enjoying the calmest peace itself, but, to improve and secure its happy condition, all the rest of the world, at the same time, in tempest, in combustions, in uncomposable wars.

Take into your view, Sir, a king sovereign to three kingdoms, by a concentring of all the royal lines in his person, as undisputably as any mathematical ones in Euclid : A king, firm and knowing in his religion, eminent in virtue : A king that had, in his own time, given all the rights and liberties of his subjects a more clear and ample confirmation, freely and graciously, than any of his predecessors (when the people had them at advantage) extortedly, I mean, in the petition of right.

This is one map of England, Mr. Speaker. A man, Sir, that should present unto you, now, a kingdom, groaning under that supreme law, which *Salus populi periclitata* would enact; the liberty, the property of the subject fundamentally subverted, ravished away by the violence of a pretended necessity; a triple crown shaking with distempers; Men of the best conscience ready to fly into the wilderness for religion: Would not one swear this were the antipodes to the other? And yet, let me tell you, Mr. Speaker, this is a map of England too, and both, at the same time, true.

As it cannot be denied, Mr. Speaker, that since the conquest there hath not been, in this kingdom, a fuller concurrence of all circumstances in the former character, to have made a kingdom happy, than for these twelve years last past; so it is most certain, that there hath not been, in all that deduction of ages, such a conspiracy, if one may so say, of all the elements of mischief in the second character, to bring a flourishing kingdom, if it were possible, to swift ruin and desolation.

I will be bold to say, Mr. Speaker, and I thank God we have so good a king, under whom we may speak boldly of the abuse of his power by ill ministers, without reflexion upon his person.

That an accumulation of all the publick grievances since *Magna Charta*, one upon another, unto that hour in which the petition of right passed into an act of parliament, would not amount to so oppressive, I am sure not to so destructive a height and magnitude to the rights and property of the subject, as one branch of our beslaving since the petition of right.

The branch, I mean, is the judgment concerning ship-money. This being a true representation of England in both aspects:

Let him, Mr. Speaker, that for the unmatched oppression and enthralling of free subjects, in a time of the best king's reign, and in memory of the best laws enacting in favour of subjects liberty, can find a truer cause than the ruptures and intermission of parliaments: Let him, and him alone, be against the settling of this inevitable way for the frequent holding of them.

It is true, Sir, wicked ministers have been the proximate causes of our miseries; but the want of parliaments the primary, the efficient cause.

Ill ministers have made ill times; but that, Sir, hath made ill ministers.

I have read, amongst the laws of the Athenians, a form of recourse in their oaths and vows of greatest and most publick concernment to a threefold deity, *Supplicum Exauditori, Purgatori, Malorum depulsori*.

I doubt not but we, here assembled for the commonwealth in this parliament, shall meet with all these attributes in our sovereign.

I make no question, but he will graciously hear our supplications: purge away our grievances, and expel malefactors; that is, remove ill ministers, and put good in their places.

No less can be expected from his wisdom and goodness.

But, let me tell you, Mr. Speaker, if we partake not of one attribute more in him; if we address not ourselves unto that, I mean *Bonorum Conservatori*, we can have no solid, no durable comfort in all the rest,

Let his Majesty hear our complaints never so compassionately.

Let him purge away our grievances never so efficaciously.

Let him punish and dispel ill ministers never so exemplarily.

Let him make choice of good ones never so exactly.

If there be not a way settled to preserve and keep them good; the mischiefs and they will all grow again, like Sampson's locks, and pull down the house upon our heads: Believe it, Mr. Speaker, they will.

It hath been a maxim amongst the wisest legislators, that whosoever means to settle good laws, must proceed in them, with a sinister opinion of all mankind; and suppose, that whosoever is not wicked, it is for want only of the opportunity. It is that opportunity of being ill, Mr. Speaker, that we must take away, if ever we mean to be happy, which can never be done, but by the frequency of parliaments.

No state can wisely be confident of any publick ministers continuing good, longer than the rod is over him.

Let me appeal to all those that were present in this house at the agitation of the petition of right. And let them tell themselves truly, of whose promotion to the management of affairs do they think the generality would at that time have had better hopes than of Mr. Noy and Sir Thomas Wentworth, both having been at that time, and in that business, as I have heard, most keen and active patriots; and the latter of them, to the eternal aggravation of his infamous treachery to the commonwealth, be it spoken, the first mover, and insister to have this clause added to the petition of right, that, for the comfort and safety of his subjects, his Majesty would be pleased to declare his will and pleasure, that all ministers should serve him according to the laws and statutes of the realm.

And yet, Mr. Speaker, to whom now can all the inundations upon our liberties, under pretence of law, and the late shipwreck at once of all our property, be attributed more than to Noy; and those, and all other mischiefs, whereby this monarchy hath been brought almost to the brink of destruction, so much to any as that grand apostate to the commonwealth, the now Lieutenant of Ireland?

The first, I hope, God hath forgiven in the other world; and the latter must not hope to be pardoned it in this, till he be dispatched to the other.

Let every man but consider those men as once they were.

The excellent law for the security of the subject, enacted immediately before their coming to employment, in the contriving whereof themselves were principal actors.

The goodness and virtue of the king they served, and yet the high and publick oppressions that in his time they have wrought: And surely there is no man but will conclude with me, that as the deficience of parliaments hath been the *causa causarum* of all the mischiefs and distempers of the present times: So the frequency of them is the sole catholick antidote that can preserve and secure the future from the like.

Mr. Speaker, let me yet draw my discourse a little nearer to his Majesty himself, and tell you, that the frequency of parliaments is most essentially necessary to the power, the security, the glory of the king.

There are two ways, Mr. Speaker, of powerful rule, either by fear, or love; but one of happy and safe rule, that is, by love, that *firmissimum Imperium quo obedientes gaudent.*

To which Camillus advised the Romans. Let a prince consider what it is that moves a people principally to affection, and dearness, towards their sovereign, he shall see that there needs no other artifice in it, than to let them enjoy, unmolestedly, what belongs unto them of right: If that have been invaded and violated in any kind, whereby affections are alienated, the next consideration, for a wise prince that would be happy, is how to regain them, to which three things are equally necessary.

Reinstating them in their former liberty.

Revenging them of the authors of those violations;

And, securing them from apprehensions of the like again.

The first, God be thanked, we are in a good way of.

The second, in a warm pursuit of.

But the third, as essential as all the rest, till we be certain of triennial parliaments, at the least, I profess I can have but cold hopes of.

I beseech you, then, gentlemen, since that security for the future is so necessary to that blessed union of affections, and this bill so necessary to that security; let us not be so wanting to ourselves, let us not be so wanting to our sovereign, as to forbear to offer unto him this powerful, this everlasting philter, to charm unto him the hearts of his people, whose virtue can never evaporate.

There is no man, Mr. Speaker, so secure of another's friendship, but will think frequent intercourse and access very requisite to the support, to the confirmation of it: Especially, if ill offices have been done between them; if the raising of jealousies hath been attempted.

There is no friend but would be impatient to be debarred from giving his friend succour and relief in his necessities.

Mr. Speaker, permit me the comparison of great things with little: What friendship, what union, can there be so comfortable, so happy, as between a gracious sovereign and his people? And what greater misfortune can there be to both, than for them to be kept from intercourse, from the means of clearing misunderstandings, from interchange of mutual benefits?

The people of England, Sir, cannot open their ears, their hearts, their mouths, nor their purses, to his Majesty, but in parliament.

We can neither hear him, nor complain, nor acknowledge, nor give, but there.

This bill, Sir, is the sole key that can open the way to a frequency of those reciprocal endearments, which must make and perpetuate the happiness of the king and kingdom.

Let no man object any derogation from the king's prerogative by it. We do but present the bill, it is to be made a law by him; his honour, his power, will be as conspicuous, in commanding at once that a parliament shall assemble every third year, is in commanding a parliament to be called this or that year: There is more of his Majesty in ordaining primary and universal causes, than in the actuating particularly of subordinate effects.

I doubt not but that glorious King Edward the Third, when he made those laws for the yearly calling of a parliament, did it with a right sense of his dignity and honour.

The truth is, Sir, the kings of England are never in their glory, in their splendor, in their majestick sovereignty, but in parliaments.

Where is the power of imposing taxes? where is the power of restoring from incapacities? Where is the legislative authority? marry, in the King, Mr. Speaker. But how? In the King, circled in, fortified and evirtuated by his parliament.

The King, out of parliament, hath a limited, a circumscribed jurisdiction: But, waited on by his parliament, no monarch of the east is so absolute in dispelling grievances.

Mr. Speaker, in chacing ill ministers, we do but dissipate clouds that may gather again; but, in voting this bill, we shall contribute, as much as in us lies, to the perpetuating our sun, our sovereign, in his vestical, in his noon-day lustre.

A

BRIEF DISCOURSE

CONCERNING THE

POWER OF THE PEERS AND COMMONS OF PARLIAMENT,

IN POINT OF JUDICATURE.

Written by a learned Antiquary, at the request of a Peer of this Realm.

Printed in the year 1640.   Quarto, containing twelve pages.

SIR,

TO give you as short an account of your desires, as I can, I must crave leave to lay before you, as a ground, the frame or first model of this state.

When, after the period of the Saxon time, Harold had lifted himself into the royal seat, the great men, to whom but lately he was no more than equal, either in fortune or power, disdaining this act of arrogancy, called in William, then Duke of Normandy, a prince more active than any in these western parts, and renowned for many victories he had fortunately atchieved against the French King, then the most potent monarch in Europe.

This duke led along with him, to this work of glory, many of the younger sons of the best families of Normandy, Picardy, and Flanders, who, as undertakers, accompanied the undertaking of this fortunate man.

The usurper slain, and the crown by war gained, to secure certain to his posterity what he had so suddenly gotten, he shared out his purchase, retaining in each county a portion to support the dignity sovereign, which was stiled, *Demenia Regni*, now the *Ancient Demesnes*; and assigning to others his adventurers, such portions as suited to their quality and expence, retaining to himself dependency of their personal service, except such lands as, in free alms, were the portion of the church : These were stiled *Barones Regis*, the King's immediate freeholders, for the word *Baro* imported then no more.

As the King to these, so these to their followers, subdivided part of their shares into knights fees, and their tenants were called *Barones, Comites*, or the like; for we find, as in the King's writ, in their writs, *Baronibus suis & Francois & Anglois*, the sovereign gifts for the most part extending to whole counties or hundreds, an earl being lord of the one, and a baron of the inferior donations to lords of townships or manors.

As thus the land, so was all course of judicature divided, even from the meanest to the highest portion ; each several had his court of law, preserving still the manner of our ancestors the Saxons, who *jura per pagos reddebant ;* and these are still termed Court-barons, or the Freeholders Court (twelve usually in number) who, with the Thane, or chief lord, were judges.

The hundred was next, where the Hundredus, or Aldermanus, lord of the hundred, with the chief lord of each township within their limits judged ; God's people observed this form, in the publick, *Centuriones & decem judicabant plebem omni tempore.*

The county, or *Generale Placitum*, was the next ; this was so to supply the defect, or remedy the corruption of the inferior ,: *Ubi Curiæ Dominorum probantur defecisse, pertinet ad Vicecomitem Provinciarum.* The judges here were *Comites, Vicecomites, & Barones Comitatus, qui liberas in hoc terras habeant.*

The last and supreme, and proper to our question, was *Generale Placitum apud London, universalis Synodus,* in charters of the *Conqueror ; Capitalis Curia* by *Glanville ; Magnum & Commune Concilium coram Rege & Magnatibus suis.*

In the Rolls of Henry the Third it is not stative, but summoned by proclamation : *Edicitur Generale Placitum apud London,* saith the book of Abingdon ; whither *Episcopi, Duces principes, Satrapæ Rectores, & Causidici ex omni parte confluxerunt ad istam Curiam,* saith Glanville : Causes were referred, *propter aliquam dubitationem, quæ emergit in Comitatu, cum Comitatus nescit dijudicare.* Thus did Ethelwold, Bishop of Winchester, transfer his suit against Leostine, from the county *ad Generale Placitum ;* in the time of King Ethelred, Queen Edgine against Goda, from the county, appealed to King Etheldred at London. *Congregatis principibus & sapientibus Angliæ,* a suit between the Bishops of Winchester and Durham, in the time of St.

Edward: *Coram Episcopis & Principibus Regni, in præsentia Regis ventilata & finita.* In the tenth year of the *Conqueror*, *Episcopi, Comites, & Barones Regni potestate adversis provinciis ad universalem Synodum pro causis audiendis & tractandis convocati,* saith the book of Westminster. And this continued all along, in the succeeding kings reign, until towards the end of Henry the Third.

As this great court or council, consisting of the king and barons, ruled the great affairs of state, and controlled all inferior courts; so there were certain officers, whose transcendent power seemed to be set to bound in the execution of princes wills, as the steward, constable, and marshal, fixed upon families in fee for many ages. They, as tribunes of the people, or Ephori among] the Athenians, grown, by manly courage, fearful to monarchy, fell at the feet and mercy of the King, when the daring Earl of Leicester was slain at Evesham.

This chance, and the dear experience Henry the Third himself had made at the parliament at Oxford, in the fortieth year of his reign, and the memory of the many streights his father was driven unto, especially at Runnymead near Stanes, brought this king wisely to begin what his successor fortunately finished, in lessening the strength and power of his great lords; and this was wrought by searching into the regality they had usurped over their peculiar sovereigns, whereby they were, as the book of St. Albans term them, *Quot Domini tot Tyranni:* And by the weakening that hand of power which they carried in the parliaments, by commanding the service of many knights, citizens, and burgesses to that great council.

Now began the frequent sending of writs to the commons; their assent was not only used in money, charge, and making laws, for, before, all ordinances passed by the King and peers, but their consent in judgments of all natures, whether civil or criminal : In proof whereof I will produce some few succeeding precedents out of record.

When Adamor, that proud prelate of Winchester, the King's half brother, had grieved the state by his daring power, he was exiled by joint sentence of the King, lords, and commons; and this appeareth expresly by the letter sent to Pope Alexander the Fourth, expostulating a revocation of him from banishment, because he was a church-man, and so not subject to any censure ; in this the answer is, *Si Dominus Rex & Regni majores hoc vellent,* meaning his revocation, *Communitas tamen ipsius ingressum in Angliam jam nullatenus sustineret.* The peers subsign this answer with their names, and *Petrus de Mountford,* vice *totius Communitatis,* as speaker or proctor of the commons.

For by that style Sir John Tiptoft, prolocutor, affirmeth under his arms the deed of intail of the crown by King Henry the Fourth, in the eighth year of his reign, for all the commons.

The banishment of the two Spencers, in the fifteenth of Edward the Second, *Prelati Comites & Barones & les autres Peeres de la terre & Communes de Roialme* give consent and sentence to the revocation and reversement of the former sentence; the lords and commons accord, and so it is expressed in the roll.

.. In the first of Edward the Third, when Elisabeth, the widow of Sir John de Burgo, complained in parliament, that Hugh Spencer the younger, Robert Baldock, and William Cliff, his instruments, had, by durance, forced her to make a writing to the King, whereby she was despoiled of all her inheritance ; sentence is given for her in these words, *Pur ceo que avis est al Evesques, Counts, & Barons & autres grandes & a tout Communalte de la terre, que le dit escript est fait contre ley, & tout manere de raison si fuist le dit escript per agard del Parliam. dampue elloques al livre a la dit Elis.*

In An. 4 Edw. III, it appeareth by a letter to the Pope, that, to the sentence given against the Earl of Kent, the commons were parties, as well as the lords and peers; for the King directed their proceedings in these words, *Comitibus, Magnatibus, Baronibus, & aliis de Communitate dicti Regni ad Parliamentum illud congregatis injunximus, ut super his discernerent & judicarent quod rationi & justitiæ conveniret, habere præ oculis solum Deum, qui eum concordi unanimi sententia tanquam reum criminis læsæ majestatis morti adjudicarent ejus sententia, &c.*

When, in the fiftieth year of Edward the Third, the lords had pronounced the sentence against Richard Lions, otherwise than the commons agreed, they appealed to the King, and had redress, and the sentence entered to their desires.

When, in the first year of Richard the second, William Weston and John Jennings were arraigned in parliament, for surrendering certain forts of the King's, the commons were parties to the sentence against them given, as appeareth by a memorandum, annexed to that record. In the first of Henry the Fourth, although the commons refer, by protestation, the pronouncing of the sentence of deposition against King Richard the Second unto the lords, yet are they equally interested in it, as it appeareth by the records ; for there are made proctors or commissioners for the whole parliament, one bishop, one abbot, one earl, one baron, and two knights, Gray and Erpingham, for the commons ; and to infer that, because the lords pronounced the sentence, the point of judgment should be only theirs, were as absurd as to conclude, that no authority was vested in any other commissioner of Oyer and Terminer, than in the person of that man solely, that speaketh the sentence.

In 2 Hen. V, the petition of the commons importeth no less than a right they had to act and assent to all things in parliament, and so it is answered by the King ; and, had not the journal roll of the higher house been left to the sole entry of the clerk of the upper house, either out of a neglect to observe due form, or out of purpose to obscure the commons right, and to flatter the power of those he immediately served, there would have been frequent examples of all times to clear this doubt, and to preserve a just interest to the commonwealth ; and how conveniently it suits with monarchy to maintain this form, lest others of that well-framed body, knit under one head, should swell too great and monstrous, it may be easily thought ; for monarchy again may sooner groan under the weight of an aristocracy, as it once did, than under a democracy, which it never yet either felt or feared.

ANCIENT CUSTOMS

OF

ENGLAND.

——

BEING desirous for my own particular satisfaction to search and enquire after reverenced antiquity, it was my hap to light on an old manuscript, which, altho' in sound is Saxon-like, yet in something it savours of the Danish matters, and of the ancient British laws under the rule and government of the Danes; which writing, writ in the Saxon tongue, I have translated into English word for word, according to the true sense and meaning thereof.

" IT was sometimes in the English laws, that the people and the laws were in reputation; and then were the wisest of the people worship-worthy, each in his degree, Lorle and Chorle, Theyn and Undertheyn. And if a Chorle so thrived, that he had full five hides of his own land, a church and a kitchen, a bell-house and a gate, a seat and several offices in the King's hall; then was he thenceforth the Theyn's right-worthy. And if a Thyen so thrived, that he served the King, and on his message, or journey, rode in his houshold; if !then he had a Theyn that him followed, who to the King's expedition five hide had, and in the King's palace his lord served, and therewith his errand had gone to the King, he might, afterward, with his fore-oath his lord's part play at any need. And if a Theyn so thrived, that he became an earl, then was he right-forth an earl right-worthy. And if a merchant so thrived, that he passed thrice over the wide sea of his own craft, he was thenceforth the Theyn's right-worthy. And if a scholar so thrived through learning, that he had degree, and served Christ, he was thenceforth of dignity and peace so much worthy as thereto belonged, unless he forfeited so, that the use of his dignity might be taken from him."

These ruins of antiquity make shew of a perpetuity of nobility, even from the beginning of this island; but times are changed, and we in them also. For King Edward the Confessor, last of the Saxon blood, coming out of Normandy, bringing in then the title of Baron, the thane from that time began to grow out of use; so at this day men remember not so much as the names of them. And, in process of time, the name of baronage began to be both in dignity and power so magnificent above the rest; as that, in the name of the baronage

* Printed in the year 1641.

of England, all the nobility of the land seemed to be comprehended. As for dukes, they were (as it were) fetched from long exile, and again renewed by King Edward the Third. And marquisses and viscounts were altogether brought in by King Richard the Second, and King Henry the Sixth.

But our kings descended of the Norman blood, together with the crown of the kingdom, granted an hereditary and successory perpetuity unto honourable titles; such, I mean, as are the titles of earldom, and baronies, without any difference of sex at all, which thing I thought good to make manifest, by the examples of the more ancient times.

In the reckoning up whereof, that I may the better acquit and discharge myself, I shall, in the first place, desire the reader to observe three things.

First, Concerning the disposition and inclination of our King in the creating of the nobility.

Secondly, Of the custom of transferring of honours and dignities by families. And,

Thirdly, Of the force of time, and the change and alteration of things.

For why; our kings (who in their kingdoms bred alone the absolute rule and sway) are with us the efficient causes of all political nobility. The titles of named nobility, by our custom, have this natural and common, together with the crown itself, that, the heirs male failing, they devolve unto the women, except in the first charters it be in express words otherwise provided; and yet, so that regard is always to be had of the time, which is every where wont to bear sway in the formality of things.

In this manner (Harold being overcome) William the First, king and conqueror, having obtained the sovereignty, according to his pleasure, bestowed dignities and honours upon his companions and others: some of them so connexed and conjoined unto the fees themselves, that, yet to this day, the possessors thereof may seem to be ennobled even with the possession of the places only: as our bishops at this day, by reason of the baronies joined unto their bishopricks, enjoy the title and pre-eminence of barons in the highest assemblies of the kingdom, in parliament. He gave and granted to others dignities and honours, together with the lands and fees themselves. He gave unto Hugh Lupus, his kinsman (a Norman) the Earldom of Chester: *Ad conquirendum & tenendum sibi & Hæredibus, adeo libere per gladium, sicut ipse Rex tenuit Angliam per Coronam.* To Hanus Rufus (then earl of Bretagne in France) and his heirs, the earldom of Richmond: *Ita libere & honorifice, ut eundem Edwinus Comes antea tenuerat.* And the earldom of Arundel (which Harold possessed) he granted, with a fee, unto Roger of Montgomery. The first two of which honours (the heirs male failing) by women passed unto other families; but the latter earldom, Robert, the son of Roger, being attainted of treason, returned unto King Henry the first, who gave the same in dowry unto Queen Adeliza, his wife. But the succeeding kings, more sparingly, bestowed such dignities, to be holden of them in fee, granting, for the better and more honourable maintenance of their stock and honour, the third part of the pleas of the county (as they term it) which they, in their charters, call *Tertium denarium*, or the third penny; so that he, that received the third penny of any province, was called earl of the same; and so by custom the women, the heirs male failing.

And if any earl or baron, dying without sons, had many women his heirs, howsoever order was taken, either by way of covenant, or partition, concerning the lands and possessions, according to the common laws of the kingdom, yet the dignity and honour (a thing of itself indivisible) was still left to be disposed of, according to the King's pleasure, who, in bestowing thereof, usually respected the prerogative of birth; by which right, King Henry the Third, after the death of John the Scot, dead without issue (other lands and revenues being, by agreement, given to his three sisters) united the earldom of Chester, with the honour thereof, unto the crown. This is manifest in the earldom of Arundel, which (after Robert Bellisme, son to the aforesaid Roger Montgomery, driven out by Henry the First) King Henry the Second bestowed upon William of Albany, Queen Adeliza his mother's husband, and, by a new charter, confirmed it in fee, together with the inheritance, to him and his heirs, with the third pleas of Sussex, whereof he created him earl. But Hugh the Great, nephew of this William the First, being dead without issue, all the earldom was divided among his four sisters, whose dignity and honour, for all that, together with the castle of Arundel, was, by Edward the First, at length, given to Richard Fitz-Alan, (the nephew) son to John Fitz-Alan, and Isabella, the second of the aforesaid sisters.

I will now pass from Henry the Third, to Edward the First, his son, there being for a time great dissension betwixt him and certain of his nobility, viz. Gilbert of Clare, Earl of Hertford and of Gloucester; Humphrey of Bohun, Earl of Hereford and Sussex, and constable of England; and Roger Bigod, Earl of Norfolk, marshal of the kingdom; and that all those noblemen, at length, had lost their earldoms and offices; they, being reconciled to the King, afterward they again, by new charters, received the same in this manner: The first of them to himself and Joan his wife, the same King's daughter, his second wife, for term of both their lives; and to the children to be by both of them begotten (his two daughters by his first wife being excluded,) This Joan (called Joan of Acon) bare unto her husband Gilbert a son, called also Gilbert; but she, the second time, secretly married unto one Radulph, of Mount Hermeri, without the King her father's knowledge, and, in her own right, made the same Radulph earl, so long as she lived; but, she being dead, Gilbert, her son by the aforesaid Gilbert, succeeded again into the earldom, Radulph, his father-in-law, being yet alive. In the same manner he restored to the aforesaid Humphrey of Bohun his earldom and constableship, unto whom he also gave in marriage Elisabeth, another of his daughters, widow to John Earl of Holland; and to the third he restored the earldom of Norfolk, and the office of Marshal, with the yearly increase of a thousand marks, upon condition, if the heirs male of his body to be begotten failed, both should return again to the King. At length this Roger died, without issue, in the 35th year of him the said Edward the First, viz. in the last year of his reign; and King Edward, his son, the second of that name, both by a new creation and charter, gave the earldom, and the marshalship, to Thomas of Brotherton, and his heirs male.

These things I have thus propounded, thereby to shew, how, according to the diverse dispositions of princes, and change of times, it hath, by little and little, varied in the first bestowing of dignities and honours: Of which thing, that new law, and to them of ancient time unknown, made by King Edward the First, seemed afterward to be of no small moment, whereby, he favouring certain private men, more careful of their own sirname, than of their posterity, it was thought good by him to decree to make fees to belong to men only. That law which I would in Latin call *Gentilitium Municipale,* and which the lawyers commonly call, *Jus talliatum,* and *Talliabile,* or the law of cutting off; for that it cutteth off successions before general, and restraineth them to the particular heirs of families, which seemeth to have given an occasion of change in the giving and bestowing of dignities and honours. For, ever since that time, in the creating of any new earl, it is begun to be altered by express words in all charters, provided that it shall be but for term of life only, or descend unto the heirs male alone, the women being quite excluded. And for this I need not examples to prove; for why, the thing itself proveth the same. But the force and efficacy of this law of entail, (or of cutting off) I have thought good, thus, in few words, to declare.

And what I have said concerning earls, the same may be said also of barons, created by charters; but in barons created by rescripts, or writs of summons, yet resting upon most ancient custom, not so.

For in them (one only excepted, sent forth to Henry Bromflet, wherein it was provided him, that same Henry, and his heirs male of his body, lawfully begotten, only to be barons of Vesey) women, the heirs male failing, were not in ancient time forbidden, or imbarred, but that they might be accounted, and by name stiled honourable, with the pre-eminence of the dignity, and calling of barons; and after they had borne a child, according to the ancient favour of our laws, and the custom of the kingdom, graced their husbands also with the same honour, and with the same, by inheritance, ennobled their children, yea without the possessions of those places, from whence the name of such dignities and honours may seem first to have risen. For fees and local possessions, circumscribed by the law, are translated and carried from one family unto another, and usually inrich their lords, and owners, the possessors thereof, but yet of themselves neither being, nor taking away nobility, either dative or native; by example, to manifest these things, were but needless, and of little consequence, for why, all the most ancient baronies, and the more ancient sort of barons, at this day, are, in this point, on my side; and, if any shall object against me in this point, unto him I will oppose either the force of time, or the carelesness and lack of looking unto.

But customs are still like themselves, nor must we detract from the authority of Kings, who although they have such supereminent and undeterminate prerogative, as that they may seem sometimes to have of favour granted some things beside the law, yet it shall not appear they requested to have done, or yet suffered to have been done, any thing contrary to the custom of stocks and families; so sometimes they, not regarding the solemnities of ceremonies, and charters, have only by their becks (that I may so say) suffered dignities and honours to be tranferred, as in Randulph Blundeville, Earl of Chester and of Lincoln, is to be seen, for the earldom of Chester he permitted, after the manner, to descend to John the Scot, his nephew, by Maud, the elder of his sisters: But the Earldom of Lincoln, the King thereunto consenting, he, yet alive, delivered unto Hawisia, another of his sisters, then married to Robert Quincey, by his deed, in the seventh year of Henry the Third.

These things, I say, were of old and ancient time, but at this day not so, for such is the force of time, and change in altering the forms of things, as that, in eating out of the old, bringeth still in new; so unto earls, whom we said in ancient time to have been rewarded with the third penny of the province, whereof they were earls, to maintain their honour and dignity, a certain sum of money is, at this day, yearly paid them out of the exchequer, and they enjoy the titles of such places, as wherein they have no jurisdiction, administration, or profit at all. Barons also, who, as the fathers and senators in ancient times, among the Romans, were chosen by their Sestertia, were in like manner wont to be esteemed and valued by knights fees, for why, he which had, and possessed, thirteen knights fees, and a little more, was to be accounted among the barons, are now more seldom times chosen for their virtue, their great wealth, and large possessions.

Neither is there any let, but that a man may hold, and still retain, the name and title of a barony, the head of which barony (as they term it) he hath afterward sold, or alienated to some other common person.

In brief, our King's Royal Majesty is always, like itself, constant and the same; which having regard to the virtue, stock, wealth, and substance of any man, whereby he may, with his counsel's service, profit the commonwealth, may in every place freely give and bestow dignities and honours, sometimes chusing no more barons than one, out of one and the same family. The custom of the succession of the former and more ancient baron being still kept whole, and not in any hurt, as we see Edward the Sixth wisely to have done in the family of the Willoughby's of Ersby, which brought forth also another barony of Parham; wherefore we acknowledge our kings to be the fountains of political nobility, and unto whom we may, with thanks, refer all the degrees of honours and dignities; wherefore I may not, without cause, seem to rejoice, on the behalf of our nobility of Great-Britain, which hath had always kings themselves authors, patrons, governors, and defenders thereof, that when lands, fees, and possesions, subject to covenants, or agreements, are still tossed and turmoiled with the storms of the judicial courts, and of the common law, it is only unto the Kings themselves beholding, and resteth upon heroical order and institutions, proper and familiar unto itself; so that,

> *Per Titulos numerentur avi, semperque renata*
> *Nobilitate virent, & prolem fata sequantur :*
> *Continuum propriâ servenlia lege tenorem.*

viz.

By titles great men's ancestors are known, the posterity of whom enjoy the same, to their flourishing and everlasting fame.

William the Conqueror, after the death of Harold, having confined the kingdom to himself, laid the foundations of ancient and worthy nobility, which afterwards, by his successors, according to the diverse occurrents, and occasions, by little and little, became at length, in the reign of King Henry the Third, and Edward the First, to appear a godly and stately building, who having vanquished the Welchmen, and contending with the Scots, bordering upon them, for principality and sovereignty, intreating of all things, concerning the common weal, with the three states of the kingdom, which consisteth of the nobility, the clergy, and commonalty, they themselves in their royal majesty, sitting in parliaments, appointed unto every man a pre-eminence, according to the place of his dignity, from whom especially all the nobility of our age may seem to derive the diverse and appointed degrees of dignities and honours.

Now to abreviate much that might have been writ, in the continuance of this discourse, I shall desire to straighten my purpose to some handsome conclusion, by the observation of the degrees and sitting of our English nobility, in the parliament chamber, out of the statute of the 31st of King Henry the Eighth, who, of his princely wisdom, with the full assent of the whole parliament, caused a particular act to be made, for the placing of the nobility, in the upper house of parliament, the effect whereof I have here recited.

That forasmuch as in all great assemblies and congregations of men, having degrees and offices in the commonwealth, it was thought fit and convenient, that order should be taken for the placing and sitting of such persons, as are bound to resort to the same, to the intent that they, knowing their places, might use the same without displeasure; the places of which great offices deserve respect and admiration; and though meerly officiary, and depending on life, and the king's gracious election, without any hereditary title or perfection; yet are they of such high dignity, that all hereditary honour whatsoever, under the degree of royalty, may, at all times, without disparagement, give them place and precedency. The placing of these most noble and great officers both in the Parliament-house, and other assemblies, is after this worthy and distinct order:

That is to say, the lord chancellor, the lord keeper, or lord treasurer, the lord president of the king's privy-council, and the lord privy seal, being of the degree of barons of the parliament, are above to sit on the highest part of the form, on the left side, in the parliament chamber; and above all dukes, except those, which are the king's sons, the king's brothers, his uncles, his nephews, or his brothers or sisters sons; but if any of these four great officers aforesaid shall be under the degree of a baron, then he, or they, to sit on the uppermost part of the sacks, in the midst of the parliament chamber, in such order as is afore shewed.

As touching the other, it was enacted, that the lord great chamberlain, the lord constable, the lord marshal, the lord admiral, the lord steward, and the lord chamberlain of the king's houshold, shall be placed next to the lord privy seal, each of them above all other personages, being of their own estates or degrees; and holding the same precedence, as they are formerly named.

Lastly, the principal secretary, being of the degree of a baron, shall be ranged above all barons (not having any of the former offices also), and this range and precedency to continue to all the great officers in general, which are before named; both in parliament, in the council-chamber, in the star-chamber, at the tryal of peers, and in all other assemblies whatsoever.

This in brief is the effect of the statute, expressing the dignity and place of our most principal and supremest temporal officers, of which the first and chiefest is the lord chancellor, or lord keeper, who is said to be the king's conscience, his mouth, and confirmation, for by him all the rigours of the law are bridled, the king's will in grace consultations revealed, and his gifts and prerogatives confirmed; before him, all the great business of the commonwealth is dispatched, either at council-table, in the star-chamber, or in the chancery, where he hath a principal voice and precedence; and lastly, he hath the keeping of the great seal of the kingdom, in which is expressed a reputation so serious, that all subjects lives and estates are depending on the same.

The next place is the lord high treasurer of England, to whose trust the king's treasure is committed, who is a man of that noble, worthy, sweet, and generous disposition, of important confidence, of noble estimation, excellent in wisdom, and high in estimation, that to his wisdom and excellent judgment, is referred the whole management of the king's intire estate, and the provident regard of the wealth and flourishing prosperity of all the king's subjects: He is the prime officer of judicature between the king and his tenants, and hath dependence on the council-table, the exchequer, and the king's royal house and family.

The next to these is the lord president of the king's most honourable privy-council, and is the chief man, next the king, belonging to the high and honourable assembly, and hath in his power, under the King's Majesty, the management of the privileges of that honourable table.

The next is the lord privy seal, an especial ensign of credit belonging to this kingdom, having custody and charge of the king's lesser seal, which gives testimony of the king's favours and bounty, but also making the way clear and accessible to the great seal, in which consists the strength of his Majesty's confirmations. These first four great officers are civil, and of judicature, as depending on the publick state. After whom follow six other, which are as well military as civil, having the managing of all matters of honour, and warlike proceedings.

The first of which is the lord chamberlain of the kingdom, whose office is of the greatest employment in all publick assemblies, as coronations, parliaments, triumphs, or any solemnity, where the king himself rideth in person: Which office is not officiary, but honorary, depending, by a feudal right, unto the noble house of the Earls of Oxford.

After this is the lord constable of the kingdom, who was the first and principal general, under the king, of all the land forces, and in all occasions of martial affairs, had the principal nomination of officers, and ordering of ammunition for such employment.

Then is the lord marshal of the land, a great and renowned officer, in whom consist the solutions of all differences in honour, and dispensation of all things appertaining to the great or lesser nobility.

Next followeth the office of the lord admiral of the land, who is the king's general and chief commander at sea, and hath care and charge of all his Majesty's royal navy, and the censuring of all marine causes whatsoever.

The next following is the lord steward of the king's houshold, in whose trust and government is reposed the ordering of all the great and noble families, the discussion of all controversies, the placing and removing of officers, and the disposing of all things therein, for his Majesty's renown and dignity.

The last of these great officers is the lord chamberlain of the king's royal houshold, unto whose great trust, faith, and integrity, is committed the guard of the king's royal person; he hath the controul and commandment of all officers, and others, whose dependence is on the king's person; and howsoever some would limit his rule above the sayters, yet it is over the whole court, and in all places wheresoever the king is present; with many other privileges, which at this time cannot be fully recited.

After all these great offices, and officers, I must necessarily add one great officer more, namely, the king's chief and principal secretary of state, who deserves a due respect, by his high and honourable place, in regard he is so intimate and nigh to all affairs of his Majesty, either private or particular.

The Form of the King's Majesty's Writ, to the Peers, to assemble in Parliament.

' CAROLUS, &c. Charissimo consanguineo suo E. Comit. D. salutem. Quia de advisamento & assensu concilii nostri pro quibusdam arduis urgentibus negotiis nos, statum & defensionem regni nostri Angliæ & Ecclesiæ Anglicanæ concernent. quoddam parliamentum nostrum apud civitatem nostram Westmonast. tertio die Novembris prox. futur. teneri ordinavimus, & ibid. vobiscum ac cum prælat. magnatibus & proceribus dict. Regni nostri colloquium habere, tractare, vobis sub fide & ligeanciis, quibus nobis tenemini, firmiter injungend. mandamus, quod considerat. dictorum negotiorum ardui-tate & periculis imminentibus, cessante excusatione quacunque, dict. die & loco personaliter intersitis nobiscum, ac cum prælatis, magnatibus & proceribus prædictis, super dictis negotiis tractatur. vestrumque consilium impensur. & hoc sicut nos & honorem nostrum ac salvationem & defensionem regni & ecclesiæ prædictorum expeditionemque dictorum negotiorum diligitis, nullatenus omittatis. Teste me apud West. decimo octavo die Septembris, anno regni nostri 16.

The Form of the Writ to the Sheriff, &c. for the Election of the Knights and Burgesses to assemble in Parliament.

' REX Vic. N. &c. salut. quia de advisamento & assensu concilii nostri pro quibusdam arduis & urgentibus negotiis nos, statum & defensionem Regni nostri Angliæ & Ecclesiæ Anglicanæ concernent. quoddam parliamentum nostrum apud civitatem nostram West. tertio die Novembris, prox. futur. teneri ordinavimus, & ibid. cum prælatis magnatibus & proceribus dicti Regni nostri colloquium habere & tract.

Tibi præcipimus firmiter injungentes quod facta proclamation. in prox. comitat. tuo post receptionem hujus brev. nostri tenend. die & loco prædict. duos milit. gladiis cinct. magis idoneos & discretos comit. prædict. & de qualib. civitate com. illius duos cives, & de quolibet burgo duos burgenses de discretior. & magis sufficientibus libere & indifferenter per illos 'qui proclam. hujusmodi interfuer. juxta formam statutorum inde edit. & provis. eligi, & nomina eorundem milit. civium & burgensium, sic electorum, in quibusdam indentur. inter te & illos qui hujusmodi electionis interfuerit, inde conficiendum, sive hujusmodi electi præsentes fuerint vel absentes, inseri, eosque ad dict. diem & locum venire fac. Ita quod iidem milites plenam & sufficien-tem potestatem pro se & communitate comit. prædicti, ac dict. cives & burgenses pro se & communitate civitatum & burgorum prædictorum divisim ab ipsis habeant ad faciendum & consentiendum his quæ tunc ibid. de communi consilio dicti regni nostri (favente Deo) contigerint ordinari super negotiis antedictis; ita quod pro defectu potestatis hujusmodi, seu propter improvidam electionem milit. civium, aut burgensium prædictorum, dicta negotia infecto non remaneant quovis modo. Nolumus autem, quod tu nec aliquis alius vic. dicti regni nostri aliqualiter sit electus. Et electionem illam in pleno comitatu factam, distincte & aperte sub sigillo tuo & sigillis eorum qui electioni illi interfuerint nobis in cancellar. nostr. dict. diem & locum certifices indilate, remittens nobis alteram partem indentur. prædictarum præ-sentibus consuet. una cum hoc breve. Teste meipso apud West. 18 die Septembris, Anno Regni nostri 16.

The Prerogative of the High Court of Parliament.

OF all the courts of judicature in England, the court of parliament is the chiefest and greatest council of estate, called and appointed by the King's Majesty; the lords of the upper house, by personal writs of summons; and for the commons house, a general writ is sent to the sheriff of every shire, or county, to call together all such freeholders (which can dispend forty shillings yearly out of their own free lands, at least) for the electing two gentlemen for knights of the shire; the like is directed to the cinque-ports, for choice of their barons; to each city, burrough-town, and university, for choice of two burgesses, for every of them, to represent their several bodies in parliament.

The Time and Place of Meeting.

This honourable assembly's meeting is noticed by the King's Majesty, to all his subjects, by proclamation.

The end of calling this great assembly, is either the disturbance of the church, by heresy or schism, danger of the kingdom, by war offensive or defensive, or for the relief of the subject, disturbed in the courts of justice by ill customs, undue execution of the laws, oppression, &c.

From this high court lies no appeal, the determination thereof being presumed to be the act of every particular subject, who is either present personally, or consenting by his assignee, suffraged by himself.

This honourable assembly consists of two houses, upper and lower. The upper is made up by the lords spiritual and temporal, as archbishops, bishops, dukes, marquisses, earls, viscounts, barons, no member of that house being under the degree of a baron, all which await the writ of summons, without which, no place, no vote there; and none may absent themselves after summons, without special proxy from his Majesty, whence he hath power to depute one of the said members to give his voice for him in absence.

His Majesty, who, by his prerogative royal, hath the sole power, as of calling, so dissolving this honourable assembly, sits on a throne in the upper end of the house; on his right hand the Prince of Wales, on the left, the Duke of York. The greatest officers of the kingdom, as the lord-keeper (who is the speaker or mouth of the house) treasurer, privy seal, &c. have places some on the right, some on the left hand of the throne: The form whereof is recited in the statute of 31, Henry the VIII.

The Manner of giving Voices in the Upper House, is thus.

The lords spiritual and temporal in their parliamentary robes, the youngest bishop reads prayers; those being ended, the clark of the house readeth the bills (being first writ in paper) which being once read, he that pleaseth may speak either for, or against it.

The Manner of the Lower House is in this Sort.

The first day each member is called by his name, every one answering for what place he serveth; that done, they are willed to chuse their speaker, who (though nominated by the King's Majesty) is to be a member of that house; their election being made, he is presented by them to the King sitting in parliament, where after his oration or speech (the lord-keeper approving in behalf of the king) he petitions his Majesty in behalf of the house: First, for their privileges, from all molestations, during the time of sitting. Secondly, that they may enjoy freedom of speech. Thirdly, that they may have power to correct any of their own members that are offenders. Fourthly, to have favourable access to his Majesty upon all occasions, the speaker (in behalf of the house of commons) promising regard and full repect, as befitting loyal and dutiful subjects.

The Use of the Parliament

Consists in abrogating old, or making new laws, reforming all grievances in the commonwealth, whether in religion or in temporal affairs, settling succession to the crown, grants, subsidies, &c. and, in sum, may be called the great physician of the kingdom or republick.

The Speaker's Place in the House of Commons.

The speaker sits in a chair, placed somewhat high to be seen and heard the better of all; the clark of the house sits before him in a lower seat, who reads such bills as are first propounded in their house, or sent down from the lords, for, in that point, each house hath equal authority to propound what they think meet.

All bills be thrice in three several days read, and disputed on, before put to question; and so good order is used in the house, that he, that intends to speak to any bill, stands up bare-headed (for no more than one speaks at a time) speaking to the speaker, not one to another, being against the rule of the house; and he that speaketh is to speak no more that day to the bill he hath spoken to, to avoid spinning needlesly out of time; and their speeches must be free from taunts of their fellow members, that are of contrary opinions.

The speakers office is, when a bill is read, as briefly as he may to declare the effect thereof to the house; and to bills first agreed on by the lords, and sent to the commons for assent, if they do assent, then are they returned, subscribed thus, *Les communs ont assentus:* So likewise, if the lords agree to what is sent to them from the house of commons, they subscribe, *Les seigneurs ont assentus:* If the two houses cannot agree (every bill being thrice read in each house) then sometimes the lords, sometimes the commons, require a meeting of some of each house, whereby information may be had of each others mind, for the preservation of a good correspondency between them, after which meeting, for the most part, (though not always) either part agrees to the bill in question.

The assent or dissent of the upper house, is each man severally by himself, and then for so many as he hath by proxy, they saying only, Content, or Not content, and by the major part, it is agreed to, or dashed. But, in the lower house, no member can give his voice to another by proxy; the major part, being present only, maketh the assent, or dissent. After a bill is twice read there, and engrossed (being disputed on enough, as conceived) the speaker asketh if they will go to question, and if agreed to, holding the bill up in his hand, saith, As many as will have this bill pass concerning such a matter, say, Yea; and those that are against it, No: And if it be a doubt, which cry is bigger, the house is divided, the one part that agrees not to the bill, being bid to sit still; those that do, to go down with the bill, so plurality of voices allows or dashes. But no bill is an act of parliament, ordinance, or edict of law, though both the houses unanimously agree in it, till it hath the royal assent.

Touching the Royal Assent.

When bills are passed by both houses, they ought to have for approbation the royal assent, which usually is deferred till the last day of the sessions, but may be given at any time during the parliament; touching which, it hath been a question much debated, whether the royal assent given to any one bill doth not, *ipso facto*, conclude that present session? The question is of great consequence, for, if thereby the session be at an end, then ought every other bill, although passed both the houses, to be read again three times in either house, and to have the same proceeding as it had at first, as if nothing had been formerly done therein; so must it be done of all other acts of the house: But, the first session of the first parliament of King James, the house being then desirous to have a bill passed forthwith by the royal assent, which should be security to the warden of the fleet, touching the delivery of Sir Thomas Sherly, out of execution (for it was then questionable whether he was subject to an action of escape) did agree that the giving of the royal assent to one bill or more did not dissolve the sessions, without some special declaration of his Majesty's pleasure to that purpose, 18th of April, 1604. And likewise in the Journal Anno 1 & 2. Phil. & Mariæ. 21 Novem. That the King and Queen came on purpose into the parliament house to give their assent to Cardinal Pool's bill, and upon question made it was then resolved by the whole house, that the session was not thereby concluded, but that they might proceed in their business, notwithstanding the royal assent given.

At the giving of the royal assent, it is not requisite the King should be present in person, for by the express word of the statute of 33 Henry the Eighth, cap. 21, the King's royal assent by his letters patents, under his great seal, signed by his hand, and declared and notified in his absence to the lords spiritual and temporal, and to the commons assembled in parliament, is, and ever was of as good strength and force, as if the King had been there in person personally present, and had assented openly and publickly to the same, according to which statute the royal assent was given by commission, Anno 38. H. 8, unto the bill for the attainder of the Duke of Norfolk.

The Manner of giving the Royal Assent.

The royal assent is given in this sort: After some solemnities ended, the clark of the crown readeth the titles of the bills in such order as they are in consequence; as the title of every bill is read, the clark of the parliament pronounceth the royal assent according to his instructions given him by his Majesty in that behalf; if it be a publick bill to which the King assenteth, he answereth, *Le Roy le voet;* if a private bill be allowed by the King, the answer is, *Soit fait come il est desire.* If a publick bill which the King forbeareth to allow, *Le Roy se amsera.* To the subsidy bill, *Le Roy remercie ses loyaulx,* subjects accept benevolence *et ausi le voult.*

To the general pardon.

' Les prelates seigneurs et commons en cest present parliament assemblies, en nom de tours voutre autres subjects, remercient tres humblement vostre Majestie, et preut Dieu vous donere eu suite bene vie et longe.

viz.

The bishops, lords, and commons, in this present parliament assembled, in the name of all your other subjects, do most humbly thank your Majesty, and beg of God to give you a long and happy reign.

THE

COPY OF AN ORDER

AGREED UPON

IN THE HOUSE OF COMMONS,

Upon Friday the Eighteenth of June,

Wherein every Man is rated according to his Estate, for the King's Use.

Printed in the Year MDCXLI.

DUKES, one hundred pounds.
Marquesses, eighty pounds.
Earls, sixty pounds.
Viscounts, fifty pounds.
Lords, forty pounds.

Baronets and Knights of the Bath, thirty pounds.

Knights, twenty pounds.

Esquires, ten pounds.

Gentlemen of one hundred pounds per annum, five pounds.

Recusants of all degrees to double protestants.

Lord Mayor, forty pounds.

Aldermen Knights, twenty pounds.

Citizens fined for Sheriffs, twenty pounds.

Deputy Aldermen, fifteen pounds.

Merchant Strangers, Knights, forty pounds.

Common-council men, five pounds.

Livery-men of the first twelve companies, and those that fined for it, five pounds.

Livery-men of other companies, fifty shillings.

Masters and wardens of those other companies, five pounds.

Every one free of those companies, one pound.

Every Freeman of other companies, ten shillings.

Every Merchant that trades by sea, inhabiting in London, ten pounds.

Every Merchant Stranger that trades within land, five pounds.

Every English Merchant residing in the city of London, and not free, five pounds.

Every English factor that dwells in London, and is not free of the city, forty shillings.

Every stranger protestant, handy-craft trade, and artificer, two shillings.

Every papist stranger and handy-craft, four shillings.

Every widow, a third part, according to her husband's degree.

Every Judge, a Knight, twenty pounds.

Every King's Serjeant, twenty-five pounds.

Every Serjeant at Law, twenty pounds.

Every one of the King's, Queen's, and Prince's Council, twenty pounds.

Every Doctor of Civil Law, and Doctor of Physick, ten pounds.

Every Bishop, sixty pounds.

Every Dean, forty pounds.

Every Canon, twenty pounds.

Every Prebend, twenty pounds.

Every Archdeacon, fifteen pounds.

Every Chancellor and every Commissary, fifteen pounds.

Every Parson or Vicar at one hundred pounds per annum, five pounds.

Every office worth above one hundred pounds per annum, to be referred to a committee, to be rated every man that may spend fifty pounds per annum, thirty shillings.

Every man that may spend twenty pounds per annum, five shillings.

Every person that is above sixteen years of age, and doth not receive alms, and is not formerly rated, shall pay six-pence per pole.

THE

CURATES CONFERENCE;

OR,

A DISCOURSE BETWIXT TWO SCHOLARS;

Both of them relating their hard Condition, and consulting which Way to mend it.

Interpone tuis interdum gaudia curis.

[From a Quarto, containing thirteen pages, printed in the Year 1641.]

———

Master Poorest.

WELL met, good Master Needham.

Master Needham. I am heartily glad to see you here, how have you canvased the course of the world this many a day, good Master Poorest.

Mr. P. Good Sir, take the pains as to walk into St. Paul's church, and we will confer a little before sermon begins.

Mr. N. With all my heart, for I must not so suddenly leave your company, having not enjoyed your society this long time.

Mr. P. Good Sir, tell me, are you resident in Cambridge, in the college still; I make no question but the university, and your merits, have preferred you to some good fellowship, parsonage, or the like good fortune.

Mr. N. Alas! good Master Poorest, this is not an age for to bestow livings and preferments freely; it is now, as it was said long ago: *Si nihil attuleris, ibis, Homere, foras.* I tell you, it is a pity to see, how juniors and dunces take possession of colleges; and scholarships and fellowships are bought and sold, as horses in Smithfield. But I hope you are grown fat in the country, for there is not such corruption there, as there is among the Muses.

Mr. P. I will deal plainly with you. I staid in the University of Oxford, till I was forced to leave it for want of subsistance. I stood for three or four several scholarships, and though I was found upon examination sufficient, yet I do seriously protest, that one time I was prevented by half a buck, and some good wine, that was sent up, to make the fellows merry; and, another time, a great lady's letter prevailed against all ability of parts, and endowments whatsoever; a third time, the warden of the college had a poor kinsman, and so he got the major part of the fellows on his side, for fear, and flattery, that there were no hopes to swim against so great a stream; and so I was forced to retreat into the country, and there turn first an usher, and at last was made curate, under a great prebend, and a double-beneficed rich man, where I found promises beyond performances; for my salary was inferior by much to his cook, or his coachman, nay, his barber had double my stipend; for I was allowed but eight pounds per annum, and get my own victuals, cloaths, and books as I could; and when I told him the means were too little, he said that, if I would not, he could have his cure supplied by another, rather for less than what I had; and so I was yoaked to a small pittance, for the space of twelve years.

Mr. N. Is it possible,that there should be such a concurrence of hard fortunes? It was no otherwise in our * university, when I stood for preferment; for, at first, a lawyer's son had the scholarship, because his father had done some business for the college at common law; and a doctor of physick's son was preferred in my place to a fellowship, because his father had cured the master's wife of a tympany; and so, finding all hopes gone there, I went home to my friends, and, within a while after, I was made a minister, and served a cure.

Mr. P. Where, I pray you, is your charge?

Mr. N. It is in a little poor parish, hard by Pinchback, in Lincolnshire, where the churchwarden is scarce able to give the minister more than a barley bag-pudding to his Sunday's dinner. Where are you placed?

Mr. P. I serve a cure hard by Hungerford, in Wiltshire; where my allowance is so short, that, was it not more for conscience, to be in this my calling, I had rather be a cobler, and sit and mend old shoes.

Mr. N. I protest, I think we curates are worse dealt withal by the rich double beneficed-men, than the children of Israel were by the Ægyptians; for, though they made them work hard, yet they allowed them straw, and other materials, and good victuals; for they longed after the flesh-pots of Ægypt, which proves they had them a long time; but we are forced to work, and yet can get nothing; and yet these should be either fathers or brethren to us, but they were enemies to them; and yet they dealt better with them, than these do with us.

Mr. P. They deal as badly with us, as they do with their flocks, I mean their parishioners; for they starve their souls, and pinch our bodies.

Mr. N. I wonder how these lip-parsons would do, should there be but once a general consent of all the curates to forbear to preach or read prayers but for one three weeks, or a month only, how they would be forced to ride for it, and yet all in vain; for how can one person supply two places at one time, twenty miles distance?

Mr. P. By my consent they should have, for every benefice, a wife; they should have variety of pleasure, as well as of profit; but, withal, I think that course would quickly weary their bodies and purses too.

Mr. N. Wives! oh strange! no, I would not live to see that day, for, if they be so fearfully covetous, having but one, I wonder what they would be, having so many.

* Cambridge.

Mr. P. Oh, Sir, I tell you, they might, by this course, in time stand in no need of curates, nor clarks neither; for, if they could speak as much in the church as at home, they might serve the turn; and they are all masters of art, to gather up the small tithes and Easter-book, as well as the clark.

Mr. N. Nay, now since we are fallen upon it, I will tell you, our parson hath a living in London, as well as here, and his wife is so miserably proud, that both livings will scarce suffice to maintain her; insomuch, that she takes out of the curate's wages, as, half of every funeral sermon, and out of all burials, churchings, weddings, christenings, &c. she hath half duties, to buy lace, pins, gloves, fans, blackbags, sattin petticoats, &c. and towards the maintenance of a puny servitor to go before her; nay, she pays half towards the maintenance of a coach, which she either gets from her husband, or else from the curate, by subtracting his allowance at the quarter-day; and, what is more, she made her curate in London to enter into bond privately to her husband, to leave the place at half a year's warning; or else her husband, the parson of the place, would not have granted him a license for the place.

Mr. P. Oh strange! Is it possible, that this old remainder of popery should be yet upheld by our clergy, to have such Pope Joans to rule the church. I have heard say, there are three places in which a woman never should bear any sway; the buttery, the kitchen, and the church; for women are too covetous by nature to keep a good house; and too foolish to rule a church.

Mr. N. Alas! Master Needham, there is a necessity in this, for I think our parson hath scarce wit enough to do it; and though he had, yet his wife's tongue would put him out of his wits, if he should not let her have her will.

Mr. P. What care I how she punished him, so that she did not intrench upon our liberties; but, alas! she breaks her husband's back, and pinches our bellies.

Mr. N. Such a piece of correction hath our parson too; for I bought one new cloke* in six years, and that money too was given me in legacy by a good parishioner; and she, oh how she envied my felicity, and informed her husband, that I waxed proud; and advised him to get another in my place.

Mr. P. Is it possible! and yet our she-regent is not unlike her; for she frets fearfully to hear that a worthy gentleman, who lives in the parish, loves me so much; it gauls her to the quick, if the parishioners, out of their loves, give me any thing to mend my salary; oh she thinks all is lost that goes beside her hands!

Mr. N. Well, but what does your great parson with all his wealth? Does he keep good hospitality? Or is he charitable to the poor, what's his name? Dr. Proud.

Mr. P. Alas nothing less; he weareth cassocks of damask, and plush, good beavers, and silk stockings: can play well at tables, or gleek, can hunt well, and bowl very skilfully; is deeply experienced in

* Gown.

A a 2

racy canary, and can relish a cup of right claret; and so passeth the time away : what is your great overseer's * name ?

Mr. N. Dr. Harding. What goodness lodgeth in his corpse ?

Mr. P. Little or none, he is worse than yours; for he never comes to visit his parish, but, horse-leech like, he sucks them ; he loves preying better than praying, and forces his parish to humility, by oppressing them; he was a main projector for two shillings and nine-pence in the pound, and looks like a piece of reesed bacon, ever since the plot failed; he is tormented with the yellow jaundice, and a wanton wife, which, like two incarnate devils, will force him to believe a bell before he comes thither.

Mr. N. It is no great matter; it is but just that he, that torments others, should taste the same sauce himself.

Mr. P. I will tell you what his custom is, when he comes amongst us; he neither prays, nor preaches ; the one I think he will not, the other I fear he cannot perform.

Mr. N. Oh strange! how came he then by such livings ?

Mr P. Easily enough, for it is money that makes the parson's horse to go now a-days †, for they may say to parsons, as it hath been of old said of books. *quanti emisti hunc ?*

Mr. N. I will assure you, I am afraid he is discontented at our church government, as well as many other great parsons ; for they force and strictly enjoin their curates to read all divine service, which they never do themselves.

Mr. P. It is a strange world, that they should flourish and flow in wealth for doing nothing, and the poor curates, that do all, can get nothing ; I will tell you truly, he has not given his parish a sermon these three quarters of a year.

Mr. N. I wonder how they can answer the canon, which enjoins them to preach once a month.

Mr. P. Pish, what do you talk to them of the canons; they, who can make new ones, think they may slight the old ones ; their canons are like those laws which caught flies, but could not hold hornets or great bees ; they are the curates, who are set to be cannoniers: these endure the heat of the day, of this once or twice a-day preaching; alas ! they say, as the priests did once to Judas, ' What is that to us ? See you to that.'

Mr. N. You speak truth, and I will maintain it, that our doctor differs not much from the weathercock on the church steeple ; for as it is placed highest, says nothing, is sounding brass, or some such metal, and turns as the wind ; so he rules all the parish, seldom preaches, is void of charity, and turns in his courses every time ? for sometimes he is all for ceremony, sometimes indifferent, sometimes against them ; he hath made a terrible combustion, where and how to place the Lord's table ; it stood in the church, anon it must be advanced into the quire ; then it must be cast and west, and presently after north and south, covered, uncovered, railed, without rails, of this fashion, of that, of this wood, of another ; nay, he himself, who was the first that altered it, hath now, within this month or two, altered his opinion, and placed it again in the body of the church : oh fine weathercock !

* Rector.   † These cert nly were sad days, when the word of God was set to sale.

Mr. P. Oh lamentable! that curates should be shadows to such empty shells; but our great doctor is of another strain; he cares not much, I think, whether there was any table or communion at all, so that he may receive his tithes; it is not so much to him whether it be an altar, or a table, so that he can get the gold that comes from it; he is so taken with covetousness, that, so he may get money, what cares he for either preaching or praying? I tell you, he threatened a poor widow, to put her into the court; because (as he was told) she had thirteen eggs in a nest, and yet gave him but one for tithe.

Mr. N. Well, our master is as full of law, as yours can be of covetousness; he threatened one of his parishioners for sneezing in prayertime, because he hindered his devotion; nay, he made one jaunt it up a foot into the arches* fourscore miles, because he desired to receive the communion in his seat; nay, I protest, that the parishioners, when they hear he is going away, do usually make him some feast, but it is for joy, that they shall be rid of him till next summer.

Mr. P. What is yours a good able scholar?

Mr. N. Yes, he is a scholar good enough, but he preaches Christ out of contention.

Mr. P. That is something yet, but, alas! our parson is as bad as one of Saunderson's doctors; for he was made doctor † in Scotland, when our King was there: I will warrant you, that he knows not whether St. Ambrose was a Greek or a Latin father.

Mr. N. Oh miserable!

Mr. P. Nay, he holds Greek for heathenish, and Hebrew for Jewish languages, and Latin, he says, is the language of Rome, and so holds ignorance best in these; he scarce knows the difference betwixt *annus* ‡ and Annas‖, and betwixt *anus* ** or *anas*††: I have heard him read *opa. tenebr.* for *opera tenebrarum,* because they were cut a little short, and said the printers deserved to be punished for curtailing Latin: I heard him also decline *senex* for an old man, *genitivo senecis* ‖‖, and was confident that he was right too.

Mr. N. Oh! such doctors had need to pray, that popery may come in again, for then it was well when the priest could read Latin, whether it was right or wrong.

Mr. P. And yet he is loaden with no less than a good parsonage, a great vicarage, two prebendships, and another place worth fourscore pounds by the year; it is impossible sure for him to preach, for telling his money.

Mr. N. Any of those places would suffice you, or myself, but, alas! Wishes and Woulders, you know how the proverb runs; these optative moods are meerly poor and beggarly.

Mr. P. I deal plainly with you, I was offered a place in the city of London, but the name of it frightened me; it was at St. Peter's-poor §§, and, I thought, I had enough of poverty already, and so I refused it.

Mr. N. Just so was I offered to serve a cure more north by far than

---

* The Archbishop's court. ‡ Without doing a proper and regular exercise before the university, for his degree. ‡ A year. § The father of Caiaphas the High Priest. ** An old woman. †† A desk or drake. ‖‖ Instead of senis. §§ In Broadstreet.

A a 3

this is, but the name of it startled me, and turned aside all resolution towards it; for it was at a place called Sterveling in Cumberland.

Mr. P. Nay. I will tell you more, Master Needham; I thought to have gone up to London, had not our doctor's curate there, one Master Hand-little, told me plainly, that most curates in London lived upon citizens trenchers; and, were it not that they were pitiful and charitable to them, there was no possibility of subsistance; and that, of late, it went harder with them, than before; for ever since the parsons have so enhanced their revenues, the citizens have mainly withdrawn their purses, so that now the curate must live upon his set pittance, or else starve.

Mr. N. Well, Master Poorest, I do not intend to stay longer in the country, for I will wait here in town upon hopes a while.

Mr. P. Do as you please, but you will find the old proverb true, London lick penny.

Mr. N. I am resolved upon it, though I go to the three-penny ordinary; my reason is, I do hear say, that there are great store of clarks places about London, that are good allowances for scholars, some worth two hundred pounds and upwards per annum; I know some of the parish clarks are worth seven or eight thousand pounds; oh their fees come in sleeping or waking; what think you of the plot?

Mr. P. I marry, such places are worth the while, but how should one catch them?

Mr. N. I will assure you, it is a shame, that such mechanicks should live in such state as they do; many of them are as greedy of funerals, as vultures of dead carcases; and they are most of them in an ill name, for exacting most grossly in their fees; hence it is that some of them rule the whole parish, and parson, and all; you shall see them, upon festival-days, as well cloathed as the chiefest citizens; their fingers as full of rings of gold, as an old ale-wife, that has buried four or five husbands; and their necks set as big with a curious ruff, as any the proudest Dons in Spain; oh what pure rich night-caps they wear, and good beavers! besides all this, they can have their meetings usually in taverns of three or four pounds a sitting, when poor curates must not look into a red lettice, under fear of a general censure.

Mr. P. Oh strange! I think it was well if curates could turn parish clarks; if it be as you say, it is the better course by far.

Mr. N. Come, come, I tell you, we are bound to look out for ourselves, and I know no more safer course than this, for most of the clarks have trades to live upon beside; but I hope their charter will fail, and then others may come into their places.

Mr. P. What say you, Master Needham, how strong are you, will you go and shew me that pretty banqueting-house for curates, I mean the three-penny ordinary, for I can go no higher?

Mr. N. I, I, with all my heart, for I am almost at the same ebb; but let us hope better; things will not always ride in this rack.

Mr. P. Sir, I conceive plainly, that we curates are but as the stalking-horses to the clarks, for they get wealth by our labours,

Mr. N. Are you advised of that? You would say so indeed, should you but see some of their bills, so much for burials, so much for the knell, so much for the grave; for the corpse more, if coffined; more yet, if in such a church-yard; more than that, if in the church; higher yet, if it be in the chancel; beyond all these, if buried with torches, and sermon, and mourning with attendance; but it is put upon the highest strain, if it be a stranger. Besides, for marriages by banes, or by license, for making the certificate; so for churchings, and divers other ways, and nothing to the curate all this while.

Mr. P. Well, I conceive it more than ever I did; but now let us leave off discourse, and fall to our commons. What a pretty modicum I have here? Sure this ordinary-keeper has been some cook or scullion in a college: how dextrously the fellow plays the logician, in dividing the meat? It is an excellent place sure, to learn abstinence by; I promise you, I will visit this house, as my stock holds out. It is just one degree above dining with Duke Humphry, it is as good as a preservative against surfeits.

Mr. N. Oh, good brother, it is as fine a refreshment as may be; I hold it wonderous good, for here a man shall be sure to rise from his meat, as many others use to sit down to it, with a stomach.

Mr. P. I will tell you one thing, which I had almost forgotten, I was offered the other day to go a voyage to the East-Indies, to be preacher in a ship.

Mr. N. Excellent well, oh refuse it *nx*; it is far beyond living a-shore, for ten pounds per annum; I know you will find brave worthy merchants, you cannot want, if you undertake it.

Mr. P. I promise you, I had determined to have gone in one of his Majesty's ships, upon our narrow seas; but, if the voyage be so good, I will away (God willing) next spring.

Mr. N. I will tell you what I intend, if I miss of hopes this way here, to sollicit to be a preacher to a regiment of soldiers, if there be any service this next summer; for we cannot be lower than now we are; I would have given you, Master Poorest, one pint of wine, but *ultra posse non est esse**, as you know.

Mr. P. I am as willing to have done the like to yourself, not having seen you so long since, but my purse denies ability.

Mr. N. I must be gone at one of the clock, to meet with a gentleman of the inns of court; well, good brother, God bless us both, and send us better times, and a happy meeting. Farewel.

---

* Or, no one can go beyond his ability.

A DESCRIPTION

OF THE FAMOUS

KINGDOM OF MACARIA;

Shewing its excellent government, wherein the inhabitants live in great prosperity, health, and happiness; the king obeyed, the nobles honoured, and all good men respected; vice punished, and virtue rewarded. An example to other nations.

In a Dialogue between a Scholar and a Traveller.

[From a Quarto, containing fifteen pages, printed at London for Francis Constable, Anno 1641.]

---

*To the high and honourable Court of Parliament.**

Whereas I am confident, that this honourable court will lay the corner-stone of the world's happiness, before the final recess thereof, I have adventured to cast in my widow's mite into the treasury; not as an instructer, or counsellor, to this honourable assembly, but have delivered my conceptions in a fiction, as a more mannerly way, having for my pattern Sir Thomas Moore, and Sir Francis Bacon, once Lord Chancellor of England; and humbly desire that this honourable assembly will be pleased to make use of any thing therein contained, if it may stand with their pleasures, and to laugh at the rest, as a solace to my mind, being inclined to do good to the publick. So humbly craving leave, that I may take my leave, I rest, this twenty-fifth of October, 1641.

Traveller.

WELL met, Sir, your habit professes scholarship; Are you a graduate?

Scholar. Yes, Sir, I am a Master of Arts.

* This was the parliament which met at Westminster on the third of November, 1640, and having chosen Mr. Lenthall their speaker, fell immediately upon their grievances, as ship-money, innovations in religion, &c. To accuse Mr. Secretary Windebank, of being a great promoter of Popery; to vote Archbishop Laud a traitor, and the author of all the troubles in Scotland; to impeach the Lord Strafford of high treason, and to declare the Lord Keeper Finch to be a traitor. And instead of driving out the Scots, who had invaded England, with a powerful army, and offered to put themselves under the protection of the French king, suffered them to remain in a body, in the North of England, advanced them three hundred thousand pounds, and obliged the king to disband his army, and to leave himself and kingdom to the mercy of those rebels. Hence we may gather the intention of this little treatise, which, composed by way of novel, was designed to intimate a new model of government therein specified, as the properest means to reconcile the destructive breach, that then was beginning to appear between the king and his parliament.

Trav. But, what do you hear in the Exchange? I conceive you trade in knowledge, and here is no place to traffick for it; neither in the book of rates is there any imposition upon such commodities: So that you have no great business either here, or at the custom-house. Come, let us go into the fields; I am a traveller, and can tell you strange news, and much knowledge; and I have brought it over the sea, without paying any custom, though it be worth all the merchandise in the world.

Schol. We scholars love to hear news, and to learn knowledge; I will wait upon you, go whither you will.

Trav. Well, we will go into Moorfields, and take a turn or two; there we shall be out of this noise, and throng of people.

Schol. Agreed; but, as we go, what good news do you hear of the parliament?

Trav. I hear that they are generally bent to make a good reformation; but that they have some stops and hinderances, so that they cannot make such quick dispatch as they would; and if any experience, which I have learned in my long travels, may stand them in stead, I would willingly impart it for the publick good.

Schol. I like that well; I pray you declare some good experience, that I may say that I have gained something by the company of travellers.

Trav. In a kingdom called Macaria, the king and the governors do live in great honour and riches, and the people do live in great plenty, prosperity, health, peace, and happiness, and have not half so much trouble as they have in these European countries.

Schol. That seemeth to me impossible: You travellers must take heed of two things principally in your relations; first, that you say nothing that is generally deemed impossible; secondly, that your relation hath no contradiction in it, or else all men will think that you make use of the traveller's privilege, to wit, ' to lye by authority.'

Trav. If I could change all the minds in England, as easily as, I suppose, I shall change yours, this kingdom would be presently like to it: When you hear the manner of their government, you will deem it to be very possible, and, withal, very easy.

Schol. I pray you, declare the manner of their government, for I think long till I hear it.

Trav. As for brevity in discourse, I shall answer your desire. They have a great council, like to the parliament of England; but it sitteth once a year for a short space, and they hear no complaints against any but ministers of state, judges, and officers; those they trounce soundly, if there be cause: Besides, they have five under councils; to wit

A Council of Husbandry.
A Council of Fishing.
A Council of Trade by Land.
A Council of Trade by Sea.
A Council for new Plantations.

These sit once a year, for a short space, and have power to hear and determine, and to punish malefactors severely, and to reward benefactors honourably, and to make new laws, not repugnant to the laws of the great council, for the whole kingdom, like as court-leets and corporations have, within their own precincts and liberties, in England.

Schol. I pray you, Sir, declare some of the principal laws made by those councils.

Trav. The Council of Husbandy hath ordered, that the twentieth part of every man's goods, that dieth, shall be employed about the improving of lands, and making highways fair, and bridges over rivers; by which means the whole kingdom is become like to a fruitful garden, the highways are paved, and are as fair as the streets of a city; and, as for bridges over rivers, they are so high, that none are ever drowned in their travels.

Also, they have established a law, that, if any man holdeth more land than he is able to improve to the utmost, he shall be admonished, first, of the great hinderance which it doth to the commonwealth; secondly, of the prejudice to himself; and if he do not amend his husbandry, within a year's space, there is a penalty set upon him, which is yearly doubled, till his lands be forfeited, and he banished out of the kingdom, as an enemy to the commonwealth.

In the Council of Fishing, there are laws established, whereby immense riches are yearly drawn out of the ocean.

In the Council of Trade by Land, there are established laws, so that there are not too many tradesmen, nor too few, by enjoying longer or shorter times of apprentiships.

In the Council of Trade by Sea, there is established a law, that all traffick is lawful, which may inrich the kingdom.

In the Council for new Plantations, there is established a law, that every year a certain number shall be sent out, strongly fortified, and provided for at the publick charge, till such times as they may subsist by their own endeavours: And this number is set down by the said council, wherein they take diligent notice of the surplusage of people that may be spared.

Schol. But you spoke of peace to be permanent in that kingdom, how can that be?

Trav. Very easily; for they have a law, that, if any prince shall attempt any invasion, his kingdom shall be a lawful prize: And the inhabitants of this happy country are so numerous, strong, and rich, that they have destroyed some, without any considerable resistance; and the rest take warning.

Schol. But you spoke of health, how can that be procured by a better way, than we have here in England?

Trav. Yes, very easily; for they have an house, or College of Experience, where they deliver out, yearly, such medicines as they find out by experience; and all such as shall be able to demonstrate any experiment, for the health or wealth of men, are honourably rewarded at the publick charge, by which their skill in husbandy, physick, and surgery, is most excellent.

Schol. But this is against physicians.

Trav. In Macaria, the parson of every parish is a good physician, and doth execute both functions; to wit, *cura animarum, & cura corporum* *; and they think it as absurd for a divine to be without the skill of physick, as it is to put new wine into old bottles; and the physicians, being true naturalists, may as well become good divines, as the divines do become good physicians.

Schol. But you spoke of the great facility that these men have in their functions, how can that be?

Trav. Very easily; for the divines, by reason that the society of experiments is liable to an action, if they shall deliver out any false receipt, are not troubled to try conclusions, or experiments, but only to consider of the diversity of natures, complexions, and constitutions, which they are to know, for the cure of souls, as well as of bodies.

Schol. I know divers divines in England that are physicians, and therefore I hold well with this report: and I would that all were such, for they have great estimation with the people, and can rule them at their pleasure.

But how cometh the facility of becoming good divines?

Trav. They are all of approved ability in human learning, before they take in hand that function; and then they have such rules, that they need no considerable study to accomplish all knowledge fit for divines, by reason that there is no diversity of opinions amongst them.

Schol. How can that be?

Trav. Very easily; for they have a law, that, if any divine shall publish a new opinion to the common people, he shall be accounted a disturber of the publick peace, and shall suffer death for it.

Schol. But that is the way to keep them in error perpetually, if they be once in it.

Trav. You are deceived; for, if any one hath conceived a new opinion, he is allowed every year freely to dispute it before the great council; if he overcome his adversaries, or such as are appointed to be opponents, then it is generally received for truth; if he be overcome, then it is declared to be false.

Schol. It seemeth that they are Christians by your relation of the parochial ministers, but whether are they Protestants or Papists?

Trav. Their religion consists not in taking notice of several opinions and sects, but is made up of infallible tenets, which may be proved by invincible arguments, and such as will abide the grand test of extreme dispute; by which means none have power to stir up schisms and heresies; neither are any of their opinions ridiculous to those who are of contrary minds.

Schol. But you spoke of great honour, which the governors have in the kingdom of Macaria.

Trav. They must needs receive great honour of the people, by reason that there is no injustice done, or very seldom, perhaps once in an age.

* The care both of souls and bodies.

Schol. But how come they by their great riches which you speak of?

Trav. It is holden a principal policy in state, to allow to the ministers of state, judges, and chief officers, great revenues; for that, in case they do not their duty, in looking to the kingdom's safety, for conscience-sake, yet they may do it for fear of losing their own great estates.

Schol. But how can the King of Macaria be so rich as you speak of?

Trav. He taketh a strict course that all his crown lands be improved to the utmost, as forests, parks, chaces, &c. by which means his revenues are so great, that he seldom needeth to put impositions upon his subjects, by reason he hath seldom any wars; and, if there be cause, the subjects are as ready to give, as he to demand; for they hold it to be a principal policy in state, to keep the King's coffers full, and so full, that it is an astonishment to all invaders.

Schol. But, how cometh the King's great honour which you speak of?

Trav. Who can but love and honour such a prince, who, in his tender and parental care of the publick good of his loving subjects, useth no pretences for realities, like to some princes, in their acts of state, edicts, and proclamations?

Schol. But you travellers must take heed of contradictions in your relations; you have affirmed, that the governors in Macaria have not half so much trouble, as you have in these European kingdoms, and yet by your report they have a great council, like to our parliament in England, which sits once a year; besides that, they have five under-councils, which sit once a year; then how cometh this facility in government?

Trav. The great council heareth no complaints, but against ministers of state, judges, and chief officers; these, being sure to be trounced once a year, do never, or very seldom, offend: So that their meeting is rather a festivity, than a trouble. And, as for the judges and chief officers, there is no hope that any man can prevail in his suit by bribery, favour, or corrupt dealing; so that they have few causes to be troubled withal.

Schol. I have read over Sir Thomas Moore's Utopia, and my Lord Bacon's New Atalantis, which he called so in imitation of Plato's old one; but none of them giveth me satisfaction, how the kingdom of England may be happy, so much as this discourse, which is brief and pithy, and easy to be effected, if all men be willing.

Trav. You divines have the sway of men's minds, you may as easily persuade them to good as to bad, to truth as well as to falshood.

Schol. Well, in my next sermon I will make it manifest, that those, that are against this honourable design, are, first, enemies to God and goodness; secondly, enemies to the commonwealth; thirdly, enemies to themselves and their posterity.

Trav. And you may put in, that they are enemies to the King and his posterity, and so, consequently, traitors; for he that would not have the King's honour and riches to be advanced, and his kingdom to be permanent to him, and to his heirs, is a traitor, or else I know not what a traitor meaneth.

Schol. Well, I see that the cause is not in God, but in men's fooleries, that the people live in misery in this world; when they may so easily be relieved; I will join my forces with you, and we will try a conclusion, to make ourselves and posterity to be happy.

Trav. Well, what will you do towards the work?

Schol. I have told you before, I will publish it in my next sermon, and I will use means that, in all visitations and meetings of divines, they may be exhorted to do the like.

Trav. This would do the feat, but that the divines in England, having not the skill of physick, are not so highly esteemed, nor bear so great a sway as they do in Macaria.

Schol. Well, what will you do towards the work?

Trav. I will propound a book of husbandry * to the high court of parliament, whereby the kingdom may maintain double the number of people, which it doth now, and in more plenty and prosperity than now they enjoy.

Schol. That is excellent; I cannot conceive, but that, if a kingdom may be improved to maintain twice as many people as it did before, it is as good as the conquest of another kingdom, as great, if not better.

Trav. Nay, it is certainly better; for, when the towns are thin and far distant, and the people scarce and poor, the King cannot raise men and money upon any sudden occasion, without great difficulty.

Schol. Have you a copy of that book of husbandry about you, which is to be propounded to the parliament?

Trav. Yes, here is a copy; peruse it, whilst I go about a little business.———— Well, have you perused my book?

Schol. Yes, Sir, and find that you shew the transmutation of sublunary bodies, in such a manner, that any man may be rich that will be industrious; you shew also, how great cities, which formerly devoured the fatness of the kingdom, may yearly make a considerable retribution without any man's prejudice, and your demonstrations are infallible; this book will certainly be highly accepted by the high court of parliament.

Trav. Yes, I doubt it not, for I have shewed it to divers parliament-men, who have all promised me fair, as soon as a seasonable time cometh for such occasions.

Schol. Were I a parliament-man, I would labour to have this book to be dispatched, the next thing that is done; for, with all my seven liberal arts I cannot discover, how any business can be of more weight than this, wherein the publick good is so greatly furthered; which to further, we are all bound by the law of God and nature.

Trav. If this conference be seriously considered of, it is no laughing-matter; for you hear of the combustions in France, Spain, Germany, and other christian countries; you know that a house

---

* This alludes to Hartlib's book of Husbandry, which was offered with such proposals.

divided against itself cannot stand; this may give the Turk an advantage, so that England may fear to have him a nearer neighbour than they desire. Why should not all the inhabitants of England join, with one consent, to make this country to be like to Macaria, that is numerous in people, rich in treasure and ammunition, that so they may be invincible?

Schol. None but fools or madmen will be against it; you have changed my mind, according to your former prediction, and I will change as many minds as I can, by the ways formerly mentioned, and I pray you, that, for a further means, this conference may be printed.

Trav. Well, it shall be done forthwith.

Schol. But one thing troubleth me, that many divines are of opinion, that no such reformation, as we would have, shall come before the day of judgment.

Trav. Indeed, there are many divines of that opinion; but I can shew an hundred texts of scripture, which do plainly prove, that such a reformation shall come before the day of judgment.

Schol. Yea, I have heard many plain texts of scripture to that purpose; but, when I searched the expositors, I found that they did generally expound them mystically.

Trav. That is true; but worthy St. Jerom, considering that those places of scripture would not bear an allegorical exposition, said thus, *Possumus, sicut & multi, alii omnia hæc spiritualiter exponere, sed vereor, ne hujusmodi expositionem prudentes lectores nequaquam recipiant* [*].

Schol. I am of St. Jerom's mind, and therefore with alacrity let us pursue our good intentions, and be good instrument in this work of reformation.

Trav. There be natural causes also to further it; for the art of printing will so spread knowledge, that the common people, knowing their own rights and liberties, will not be governed by way of oppression; and so, by little and little, all kingdoms will be like Macaria.

Schol. That will be a good change, when as well superiors as inferiors shall be more happy; well, I am imparadised in my mind, in thinking that England may be happy, with such expedition and facility.

Trav. Well, do you know any man that hath any secrets or good experiments? I will give him gold for them, or others as good in exchange; that is all the trade I have driven a long time; those riches are free from customs and impositions, and I have travelled thro' many kingdoms, and paid neither freight nor custom for my wares, though I value them above all the riches in the kingdom.

Schol. I know a gentleman that is greatly addicted to try experiments, but how he hath prospered I am not certain; I will bring you acquainted with him, perhaps you may do one another good.

Trav. Well, I have appointed a meeting at two of the clock this day; I love to discourse with scholars, yet we must part; if you

---

[*] We, as many others, can expound all those things in a spiritual sense; but, I fear, that the prudent reader will, by no means, receive such an exposition.

meet me here the next Monday at the exchange, I will declare to you some more of the laws, customs, and manners of the inhabitants of Macaria.

Schol. I will not fail to meet you for any worldly respect: and, if I should be sick, I would come in a sedan; I never received such satisfaction and contentment by any discourse in my life; I doubt not but we shall obtain our desires, to make England to be like to Macaria; for which our posterity, which are yet unborn, will fare the better; and, though our neighbour countries are pleased to call the English a dull nation, yet the major part are sensible of their own good, and the good of their posterity, and those will sway the rest; so we and our posterity shall be all happy.

NEWS FROM

HELL, ROME, AND THE INNS OF COURT,

WHEREIN IS SET FORTH

THE COPY OF A LETTER WRITTEN FROM

THE DEVIL TO THE POPE.

The true Copy of the Petition delivered to the King at York. The Copy of certain Articles of agreement between the Devil, the Pope, and divers others. The Description of a Feast, sent from the Devil to the Pope, together with a short Advertisement to the high Court of Parliament, with sundry other particulars. Published for the future peace and tranquillity of the inhabitants of Great Britain, by J. M.

Printed in the Year of Grace and Reformation, 1641. Quarto, containing twenty-two pages.

To our dearly beloved son, the most pious and most religious primate of the Roman church, and to all our dearly beloved children the cardinals and lordly bishops in Europe.

Haste, Haste, Post, Haste.

Your intire Prince and God of this World, Lucifer, Prince of Darkness and Superstition, King of Styx and Phlegethon, supreme Lord of Gehenna, Tartaria, Colmakia, Samoyedia, Lappia, Corelia, and

Colmagoria, Prince Abyssus, and sole Commander of Seberia, Altenia, Pechcora, and of all the infernal Furies and their Punies, the Jesuits, Priests, and Seminaries,

Sendeth Greeting.

Most

DEARLY beloved son, and you our dutiful children, whose sanctity we reverence, whose persons we adore, whose wisdoms we admire, at whose policies we wonder, at whose power we muse, and at whose invincible stratagems we stand amazed.

Nor can we, in the first place, but extol, applaud, and most highly commend thee our dear son, for the extraordinary care in the advancement of our kingdom.

And, as next in place, the extraordinary diligent and vigilant care of all our beloved children the lordly bishops, in the advancement of our regal power to the great enlargement of our infernal dominions, by their rare and subtle plots and stratagems.

And in a more special manner we are pleased, through our infernal grace and favour, to extol them for this their present and excellent invention, in sowing discord amongst the English hereticks, as also in provoking the Scotch hereticks to an apparent opposition against their king, yea so far as to an invasion of the territories of England, all which services are most dear and acceptable unto us.

In respect of which services, as also for their fidelity to us, and our kingdom, we have caused our principal secretary of state, *Don Antonio Furioso Diabello*, to make an especial inrolment of their names in our calendar amongst those our dear servants, the plotters of the gunpowder treason, and the most renowned the complotters of the former invasion of England, in the year of Grace 1588, and since the creation of the world 5609; both which services, although their events were no ways answerable to our royal expectation, yet those instruments, that so freely adventured themselves in them, shall be ever renowned in our court infernal, and most acceptable to our person.

And, for the better encouragement of these our trusty and well beloved servants in the speedier advancement of this work, now intended for the utter extirpation of all hereticks, and increase of our regal power, we are pleased by this our royal manual to give unto them assurance of our aid and best assistance, in the most efficacious manner that our princely power can extend unto; and, because our former stratagems, put in execution by our beloved cousin and counsellor the King of Spain, were by him no ways effected according to our princely expectation, we have now therefore imposed our princely command upon our beloved servant the King of France, at the humble suit made unto us, by our children the lordly bishops, and by some of our servant of greatest quality in the realm of England, as also by our servants the Jesuits and Roman catholicks of England, to have a puissant army in readiness, for the invasion of England, at such a time, as those our children and servants shall conceive it most convenient and efficacious.

And further our will and pleasure is, that you our dear son shall still persist to stir up and encourage our children the archbishops, as also thy disciples and our loyal subjects and servants, the jesuits, priests, and seminaries, to this work, that they, with all their might, together with our powerful policies granted unto them, may strive to effect this work with all celerity, that we may once more see our kingdom of superstition re-established, in the monarchy of Great-Britain, and Ireland.

The motives, to be pressed, inducing them to the expeditious effecting of the same are principally their respect to our kingly honour, and, next, their own increase of greatness; for we promise and assure them, by the word of a king infernal, that every of them shall reign as princes under us, not only over the bodies and estates of men, but also over their souls, by and through the many infernal graces by us most freely and benignly conferred on them. And hereby, to make them the more sensible of these our several graces conferred on them, we are pleased therefore here at present to express but some few of them in particular; as, namely, pride, vain-glory, hypocrisy, self-love of themselves, and of this present world, love of will worship, and advancement of idolatry, together with that special gift of covetousness, the only pillar to all the rest of our infernal graces conferred on them.

Thirdly, In respect of the clear passage by us made for them, by setting the hereticks for this long time at variance amongst themselves, by our trusty servants, the lawyers, and advancement of idolatry amongst them; the only means, in our princely wisdom, conceived to be to the breaking of the bond of unity and peace, thereby to provoke the great God of heaven to leave them to themselves, and to our powerful stratagems: We are likewise pleased to take special notice of that service by our children the lordly bishops, in working the dissolution of the assembly of parliament, in May last past, 1640, by which means nothing was effected for the good of hereticks, either concerning their church or commonwealth; so as the success of this design of ours was no way hindered. You are likewise to let them know from us, that the noblemen of England are disheartened, the gentry daunted, the commonalty divided, the number of our servants the Roman Catholicks infinitely increased, and the realm in general greatly oppressed, not only by the sundry monopolies, but also by the invincible oppressing power of our children the lordly bishops, the multitude of our servants, corrupt judges, base-minded lawyers, seditious attornies, and wooden-headed doctors of our civil law, proctors, pro-thonotaries, registers, advocates, sollicitors, and apparators, whom we have caused to swarm, like to the Egyptian locusts, over all the land, for the sowing of discord, and blowing the coals of contention amongst all the inhabitants of the same; they having all of them, long since, received instructions by some of our infernal spirits, sent forth from us to that effect.

You are likewise to let them know, that, out of our princely

respect to them, and their damnable actions, for our honour, we are
pleased to take special notice of that service which they most willingly
endeavoured to effect, for the confusion of all the hereticks inhabiting
England, Scotland, Ireland, and the Netherlands, by the late, conceived,
invincible armada, procured from Spain in the year of our reign 5660,
which, through the providence of the celestial powers then over them,
and the disturbance of Martin Harper Trump, here below, failed of
that success which we, together with them, expected and hoped for, to
our no less sorrow than theirs.

Nor can we but applaud the diligent care taken by our children
and servants of greatest quality in that kingdom, in preventing the
discovery of that invasive plot, by the hereticks, and their small well-
meaning state, through their speedy flight to Dover road, and private
conference there with Don Oquindo, the Generalissimo of Spain, to
that effect : all which was most exquisitely performed, especially
by our Hispaniolized lack-Latin lord, our dearly beloved servant.

And, lastly, Our hope is, that this present plot, set on foot by these
our trusty and well-beloved children and servants, aforenamed, and
by their earnest endeavours, and our assistance, once effected, will
crown all our labours, to our unspeakable terrestrial glory, and their
eternal favours, by us to be conferred on them in our royal palace
of perdition, where we have already imposed our Royal command upon
our trusty and well-beloved cousin and counsellor, Peoter Tretyacove,
chancellor ; Evane Becklemeesheve, our knight Marshal ; Richardo
Slowe, treasurer ; and Don Serborus, grand porter of our said palace,
to give them free admitance into our royal presence.

Thus, no ways doubting of your singular care and diligence, in
fulfilling this our royal will and pleasure hereby expressed, we do
further impose our royal favour and princely respect to be by you
presented unto our trusty and well-beloved cousin and counsellor your
present nuncio in the court of England, as also unto our beloved
children and servants, the bishops, jesuits, priests, and seminaries,
our faithful agents in this invincible plot, and also to all our faithful
subjects and servants, the Roman Catholicks of England.

We are pleased to remain your royal sovereign, and patron of all
your damnable plots and stratagems now in hand.

> Given at our infernal palace of Perdition, this first of
> September, and in the 5661st year of our most
> damnable reign.

POSTSCRIPT.

Since the above-written, we are credibly informed of the intention
of a most scandalous petition, to be delivered by a small number of
heretical lords unto their king at York, which doth not a little touch
our honour, and the discovery of this our present stratagem ; Our,

express will and pleasure is, that there be some speedy course taken for the suppressing of the same, and the authors thereof severely punished, and Pomfret Castle allotted unto them for their abode, until our will and pleasure be further known, and this our design be effected: Of which fail you not, as you tender our royal favour, the success of this our design, and your own safety. Farewel.

Antonio Furioso Diabelo, Principalio Secretario.

Consider this, and mark the substance well,
It seems a letter from the fiend of hell:
Whate'er the form or method seem to be,
Th' intent thereof was quite the contrary.
Had not this rung a knell in some men's ears,
They had ne'er been freed from their slavish fears
Of tyranny, oppression, and the bishops pride;
Judges, and lawyers: a wicked crew, beside,
Of doctors, proctors, that the realm did sway,
Trod under foot God's truth, turn'd night to day:
Strove to confound Great Britain's monarchy,
Justice and truth pervert, advanc'd impiety;
And all, by this Rome's doctrine to prefer,
Obey the Pope, and serve King Lucifer:
That is the cause, why them he doth applaud,
That he thereby, with them, may have the laud,
And honour due, unto his servants all,
That strive, by him, to work Great Britain's fall.

A true Copy of the Petition, which was, by the Lords, presented unto the King at York, September the Twelfth, 1640.

To the King's most Excellent Majesty.

The humble Petition of your Majesty's most loyal Subjects, whose names are hereunder subscribed, in the Behalf of themselves and divers others.

MOST GRACIOUS SOVEREIGN,

THE sense of that duty we owe to God's sacred Majesty, and our nearest affection to the good and welfare of this your realm of England, have moved us, in all humility, to beseech your royal majesty to give us leave to offer to your princely wisdom the apprehension, which we, and others your faithful subjects, have conceived of the great distemper and danger now threatening this church and state, and your royal person, and of the fittest means to remove and prevent the same.   The evils and dangers, whereof your Majesty may be pleased to take notice of, are these : That your Majesty's sacred person is exposed to hazard and danger, in this present expedition against the Scotish army; and that, by occasion of this war, your Majesty's revenues are much wasted, your subjects burdened with cote and conduct-money, billeting of soldiers, and other military charges ; and divers rapines and disorders committed, in several parts of this your realm, by the soldiers raised for that service ; and the whole realm full of fears and discontentments.

The sundry innovations in matters of religion ; the oath of canons lately imposed upon the clergy, and others of your Majesty's subjects ; the great increase of popery, and employing of popish recusants ; and others ill affected unto religion are established in places of power and trust, especially in commanding of men and arms, both in the field, and in sundry other counties of this your realm; which by the laws they are not permitted to have any arms in their own houses.   The great mischief that may fall upon this kingdom, if the intention, which hath been credibly reported, of the bringing in of Irish and foreign forces should take effect; the heavy charge of merchants, to the great discouragement of trade ; the multitude of monopolies, and other patents, whereby the commodities and manufactures of this kingdom are much burdened, to the great and universal grievances of your people, the great grief of your subjects, with the long intermission of parliaments, and the late and former dissolving of such as have been called, without the happy effects, which otherwise they might have produced.   For remedy whereof, and prevention of the danger that may ensue to your royal person and the whole state, they do in all humility and faithfulness beseech your Majesty, That you will be pleased to summon a parliament in some short and convenient time, whereby the causes of those and other great grievances, which your people suffer under, may be taken away, and the authors and counsellors of them may be brought to such legal trial, and condign punishment, as the nature of their offences shall require; and that the present war may be composed, by your Majesty's wisdom, without bloodshed, in such a manner as may conduce to the honour of your Majesty's person and safety, the comfort of your people, and uniting of both the realms against the common enemies of the reformed religion.

And your Majesty's Petitioners shall, &c.

The names of such earls and barons, as subscribed this petition, viz. Earls Bedford, Hertford, Essex, Mulgrave, Warwick, Bullingbroke, Rutland, Lincoln, and Exeter.   Viscounts :   Lord Say and Seal, Mandifield, Brooke, Hertford, North, Willoughby, Saville, Wharton, Lovelace, and Saint John.

Articles of Agreement, made, concluded, and done, this Twenty-eighth of September, in the year of grace 1641, and of the World 5662, by and between the High and Mighty Prince, Lucifer, King of Styx and Phlegethon, the Holy and most Superstitious Primate of the Roman Church, the Cardinals, Bishops, Jesuits, Priests, and Seminaries, of the one Party; and Judge Bribery, Lawyer Corruption, Attorney Contention, Sollicitor Sedition, Justice Connivance, Jailor Oppression, and State Negligence, of the other Party, in Manner and Form following:

I M P R I M I S,

IT is this day mutually agreed, by and between the several parties above named, that there shall be a league offensive and defensive concluded and confirmed by both parties, at or before Holy-rood day next ensuing the date hereof.

Item, That, whereas there hath been lately, by the subtle practices of some parliamentary reformists, a discord and dissension raised between the state ecclesiastick and the state of the inns of court, whereby there hath happened no small prejudice unto the ecclesiastick state; the like whereof is to be doubted may also fall upon the state of the inns of court, and so, consequently, upon the crown and dignity of our Sovereign Lord, King Lucifer: It is, therefore, mutually agreed, that all former controversies and contentions between both parties shall cease, and that all unity, peace, and concord shall be embraced, on either side, according to the expressions in the precedent article, to the honour of our Sovereign Lord King Lucifer, his crown and dignity.

Item, It is agreed, That the said state of the inns of court, and the state ecclesiastick aforesaid, shall jointly and severally use the uttermost of their strength, power, and policy, to resist and suppress all such proceedings of this present parliament, which shall any way tend to the reformation and suppression of oppression, extortion, bribery, contention, and tradition : and that they shall and will, with all their might, power, and policy, endeavour, and strive to broach, advance, and maintain all the said several impieties again, to the honour of our Sovereign Lord King Lucifer, his crown and dignity.

Item, It is agreed by and between our Sovereign Lord King Lucifer, and the whole state ecclesiastick, of the one part, and Judge Bribery, That forthwith, upon the dissolution of this present parliament, he the said Judge Bribery is then again to put in practice the taking of bribes, passing of false judgment, and maintaining his false and corrupt sentences, and decrees, to be things sacred and infallible; oppressing the innocent by close imprisonment, and also favouring all jesuits, priests, and seminaries, if any of them happen by the instruments of justice to be laid hold on; animating and instructing all attornies, sollicitors, and clerks, for and to the sowing of strife and contention amongst the people of the land, to the honour of our Sovereign Lord King Lucifer, his crown and dignity.

Item, It is agreed by and between our Sovereign Lord King Lucifer, and Lawyer Corruption, that he the said Lawyer Corruption shall, notwithstanding any parliamentary reformation, still persist in taking fees, both of plaintiff and defendant, nor shall ever bring any honest cause to its period, until he hath, in fees, devoured the whole substance, both of plaintiff and defendant; neither shall he the said Lawyer Corruption, ever, at any time, give any true and prevalent advice to any his clients, but shall delude and delay them until he hath drained them as aforesaid, to the utter ruin of them, their wives and children, to the honour of our Sovereign Lord King Lucifer, and the propagation of his crown and dignity.

To their own present, rich impiety, and assured successful perdition.

Item, It is agreed and concluded, by and between our Sovereign Lord King Lucifer, and Attorney Contention, that he the said Attorney Contention shall and will, at all times, in all places, and upon all occasions, use his best diligence, to sow debate, strife, variance, and contention amongst the people of the land, without exception of persons; yea, he shall not omit to set the father against the son, and the son against the father; as also one brother against the other, to the utter ruin of their estates, houses, and families; to that end, he shall dispose of himself and all his imps, into all the the quarters and several corners of the kingdom; neither shall there be any market-town, or place of habitation, but he shall seat himself there, to the intent and purpose aforesaid, to the honour of our Sovereign Lord King Lucifer, his crown and dignity, and to the advancement of the said science of iniquity.

Item, It is agreed by and between our Sovereign Lord King Lucifer, and Sollicitor Sedition, that he the said Sollicitor Sedition shall and will, at all times, use his best endeavour to stir up, animate, and encourage all people of what condition, degree, and profession soever, unto suits in the law; and that he the said Sollicitor Sedition shall and will prove faithful unto all lawyers and attornies, and shall and will be slow in the prosecution of any man's cause whatsoever, and spin out the thread thereof to its full length, especially in the courts of equity, by multiplicity of begetting orders, and by not omitting to have this clause inserted into every of his orders, viz. unless cause be shewed to the contrary, at the next court day by the defendant; as also by falsifying of orders through the corrupting of registers, and corrupting of council in an honest cause, by deceiving his clients through false and unjust bills of charges, by bribing the judges of the several courts, and the masters of the Chancery, richly, to the honour of our Sovereign Lord King Lucifer, his crown and dignity, and the eternal damnation of Sollicitor Sedition.

Item, It is agreed and concluded *in perpetuum,* between our Sovereign Lord King Lucifer, and Jailor Oppression, that, whereas, through the rigour of the law, many poor Christian souls are committed unto his keeping and safe custody for sundry causes, and sometimes for no just cause at all, he the said Jailor Oppression shall and will, by himself, his clerks and servants, be void of all mercy and compassion towards them, and shall and will, as much as in him lieth, endeavour to work the utter ruin of the estates and lives of all such as shall be committed to his custody; and, to that end, he the said Jailor Oppression shall, nor will not be slack, in giving bribes, otherwise stiled new-year's gifts, yearly unto all the judges of the courts of justice, for and towards the better encouragement and animation of them, to the commitment of all such to prison as are or shall be brought before them on the least occasion; and that he the said Jailor Oppression shall be ever ready to yield his daily attendance on the judges in their courts, thereby to stir them up to be mindful of him to that effect; and lastly, it is agreed and concluded, that he, the said Jailor Oppression, shall and will, by himself and his servants, set such snares and gins for all those committed to his custody, that they, being once intrapped within his prison-doors, shall never find the way out, during the continuance of their lives, or of their estates, at least, to the honour of our Sovereign Lord King Lucifer, his crown and dignity, and to the eternal perdition of Jailor Oppression.

Item, It is agreed by and between our Sovereign Lord King Lucifer, and Justice Connivance, that he the said Justice Connivance shall not, nor will have any regard or respect to the justness of any poor man's cause, nor shall ever incline his ear to any his just complaints, but shall and will ever connive and bear with the oppressor, defrauder, and deceiver; and that he, the said Justice Connivance, shall and will ever prefer the value of a goose, a pig, a capon, a brace of partridges, a good fat sheep, a boar at Christmas, or a letter from a friend, written in favour of Sir Oppressor, Mr. Defrauder, and Dick Deceiver, far before justice itself, or the justness of any honest man's cause whatsoever; nor that he, the said Justice Connivance, shall ever execute justice in any poor man's cause, but, on the contrary, he shall oppress them, and have his mittimusses ready written by his clerk, Mr. Double Fees, for the speedy commitment of them to prison; neither shall he ever incline his ear to hear their just complaints against the several golden persons of worship aforesaid, to the honour of our Sovereign Lord King Lucifer, his crown and dignity, and the benefit of Jailor Oppression.

Item, It is agreed by and between our Sovereign Lord King Lucifer, and State Negligence, that he, the said State Negligence, shall ever prefer his own peace and present benefit, before the welfare and future prosperity of his king and country; and also, that he, the said State Negligence, shall not, at any time, take notice of the illegal proceedings in any of the courts of justice, nor shall addict himself, or ever endeavour to suppress, nor prevent, by any good or wholsome laws, the practice of tyranny, oppression, injustice, extortion, bribery, contention, idolatry, and the like, but shall and will solely addict himself unto the pastimes of hunting, hawking, gaming, and whoring, and the utter rejection of the present and future benefit and welfare of his native country, to the honour of our Sovereign Lord King Lucifer, the prosperity of his religious vicegerent, and the peace and tranquillity of all his servants the jesuits, priests, seminaries, and Roman Catholicks of England.

In witness of the truth of these presents, and of every particular contained in the same, the parties above-named have hereunto set their hands and seals, the day aforesaid, and in the 5662d year of the reign of our most damnable Sovereign Lord, King Lucifer, &c.

Signed, sealed, and delivered in the presence of us

WILLIAM LAUD, Bishop.
NISI PRIUS CRAULY, Judge.
BRIBING LONG, Justice.
CORRUPT FOUNTAIN, Lawyer.
JUMPING JUMPER, Attorney.
JAMES IN GRAIN, Jailor.
ROBERT KILFART, Sollicitor.
And RUDINE HAPHUDIBRASS CYTINKYCLOPA-
RIUS, Notarius Publicus.

———

Here followeth a brief relation of a great feast, which, from Lucifer Prince of Hell, was, by the hands of Cardinal Pegusious, presented to the view, disposal, and approbation of the Pope of Rome, in the year of Jubilee, 1641.

Pope.
MY Lord Cardinal Pegusious and you, the rest of my holy brethren, I beseech you view these excellent varieties, and variety of excellencies, well dressed and most exquisitely set forth and garnished. But the contents of every dish, I believe, is best known to you my Lord Pegusious, from whom I desire to be satisfied concerning the contents, qualities, and operation of every several dish.

Cardinal. May it please your holiness, these varieties of dishes, which your holiness here thus set forth, were all of them prepared for the only table of our high and mighty monarch, King Lucifer, your holiness's sole patron and protector; a certain number of which dishes his Majesty hath graciously been-pleased to cause them to be presented to your holiness's disposal, and the residue of them only to your holiness's view and approbation, being to be preserved for his Majesty's own peculiar palate.

Pope. I beseech you, my Lord Cardinal, let me have them brought hither before me, in order, according to the appointment of my sovereign, and most munificent patron.

Card. Your Holiness's will and pleasure shall be accomplished; and here, in the first place, may it please your Holiness to take notice, that the first dish, by his Majesty's appointment, to be presented to your Holiness's disposal, is this large Latin charger, containing twenty-two lordly English bishops, stewed with the fire of contention, on the chafing-dish of exasperation, and seasoned with the several spices of man's invention, as with the spice of the mass, priesthood, holy-days, altars, candles, rails, holy-bread, holy-water, holy-ashes, devout prayer for the dead, invocation of saints, offerings at the altars, excommunications, and the strong and operative spice of the high commission. It is also garnished about with the several heretical doctrines of all the new-intitled priests of England ; and this dish his Majesty hath appointed to be disposed of by your Holiness.

Pope. I will surely taste of it; it looks lovely ; oh, admirable ! It is a most *Laud*-able dish of meat: I can find nothing wanting in this dish, but only three grains of the spice of accomplishment, and then it had been devoutly seasoned for my palate ; but, I pray, what is the next dish, my lord ?

Card. The next dish, may it please your Holiness, is a silver charger, comprehending all the contrivers and complotters of the dissension between England and Scotland, of the last Spanish invasion of England, and the practisers with the French, for the subversion of all the hereticks in England, Scotland, and Ireland : it is seasoned with all our jesuitical practices, church-policies, and all our English Roman Catholick treacheries, and garnished with all our English Roman statists: this dish of meat is now almost cold, and therefore at this present unfit for your Holiness's palate ; it only wants the breath of the Earl of Strafford's fiery zeal to heat it, by a laudable blast or two.

Pope. However, I pray let me taste of it. Oh, the lamentation of a sinner ! Pity, pity, yea, a thousand pities is it, that this dish had not been kept hot and seasoned to the proof, that we might have sung most laudably, *te Lucifer Laudamus.* But, my Lord Cardinal, what is the next dish ?

Card. May it please your Holiness, this dish contains a certain number of false and corrupt judges ; it is seasoned with the spice of aged detestable covetousness, bribery, extortion, oppression, injustice, unmercifulness, and with perversion of all the statute-laws, garnished with ship money, forest-money, loan-money, and a multitude of *nisi prius's*; but this dish is, by his Majesty's special order, to be preserved for his own peculiar palate.

Pope. His Majesty's will be done: I shall be ever ready and obedient to all his Majesty's commands, nor will I presume to taste of it, but only pass my judgment on it, that it is a princely dish, fit only for his Majesty's table.

What is the next, I pray, my Lord ?

Card. The next, may it please your Holiness, is a large golden charger, containing a very great number of base-minded, covetous, unjust, extorting, and oppressing lawyers, who value every word, by them uttered at a bar of justice, at a far higher price, than your Holiness doth your bulls, issued forth for remission of sins ; and these caterpillars his Majesty King Lucifer hath brought into such great esteem with all the inhabitants of England, as that no man of quality thinks his house to stand, unless it be supported by one of those vermin pillars, and brood of contention : this dish is seasoned with the spice of extorting fees from one twenty-one shillings piece, to five, to ten, yea, to twenty ; especially by those, who are stiled the judge's favourites; all this is given sometimes but for the speaking of two or three words ; it is likewise seasoned with the taking of fees on both sides, deluding clients, spinning out the thread of an honest cause to its full length, tintil the purse-strings, both of plaintiff and defendant, crack; and then they are tied together, by a commission into the country, where these caterpillars are reverenced and feared like so many gods by all the people: this dish is garnished with some ten-thousand pestiferous pettifogging, seditious, ten-groat attornies; one of whose perfidious bills of charges, in one term, advances itself sometimes unto the sum of five, ten, twenty, yea, thirty pounds; especially, when he finds his client naturally inclined to the conditions of an ass; and, on every of these garnishes, hangs five coney-catching deceitful sollicitors, properly termed lawyers limetwigs, traps, or nets, to catch the poor silly creatures called clients; and this dish his Majesty hath also reserved for his own table.

Pope. It is a princely dish, indeed, and fit only for the peculiar table of so great a monarch, as is our most damnable Sovereign, King Lucifer; the operation and vertue of which dish is able to season a whole kingdom, to be fit meat for his majesty's palate, especially if there be but the operative spice added to it, called, The action of the case.

But what is this dish, my Lord Cardinal?

Card. May it please your Holiness, this dish contains a certain number of base muckworms, stiled doctors of our civil law, chancellors, and officials: this dish is also seasoned with unjust spice of extortion, oppression, fraud, and deceit, and garnished about with a most damnable crew of proctors, notaries, registers, delegates, advocates, sumners, and petty apparitors; these have, for many years, proved notable instruments of strife and vexation unto the inhabitants of England, and, through their deceivable ways, have mightily oppressed the people, being not much inferior unto the precedent of the golden charger.

But to this dish, may it please your holiness, there hath happened this year a very great mischance in the cooking; for, when we thought it should have been most laudably boiled up to its greatest height of catholick operation, there happened a spider to fall into it, through a sudden blast of reformation, which bath made it somewhat dangerous now for your Holiness to taste of; for the lamb, that was most richly seasoned in it, is now, through this sudden and unexpected misfortune, putrefied; and the duck, being a watery fowl, is quite dissolved; and this dish, by his Majesty's special order, is to be left now to your Holiness's disposal.

Pope. I am much bound to his Majesty for his gracious favour to me herein? I shall be very careful, through deliberation, and mature consideration, to study, for the fittest disposal thereof, during the time of my vicegerency here, and then return it again to his Majesty's disposal. But I pray you, my Lord Cardinal, what do these copper vessels contain?

Card. May it please your Holiness, this covered mess is a gallimawfry; or, as the Fleming calls it, a hodgepodge, wherein are sundry meats stewed together; it contains a certain number of beasts, called corrupt masters of the Chancery, and half a dozen corrupt clerks of the Chancery; also one-hundred and fifty of their puny clerks, commonly termed attornies in Chancery; it also contains six new attornies of the court of Requests, and some sixty of their puny clerks : this hodgepodge is seasoned with the spice of bribery, false witnesses, stiled Knights of the post, a spice greatly in request in those courts, especially in the examiners office, and the late Coventry affidavit office ; but his Majesty's special command is, to have this covered mess preserved in its present condition, lest contention should seize amongst the inhabitants of England, and unity and peace take place, which cannot but tend much to his Majesty's detriment, and loss of dominion, in that kingdom ; and, to that end, he hath caused the same to be sealed up, and to be conveyed from Coventry to Manchester by the Golden Finch.

Pope. Good, my Lord Cardinal, I beseech you, let his Majesty's will and pleasure herein be very carefully accomplished, for it concerns much his Majesty's honour and our safety.

But what is this dish, my Lord ?

Card. This, may it please your Holiness, is likewise a hodgepodge, containing meats of sundry sorts and operations ; it contains a certain number of prothonotaries, registers, and clerks of the Star-chamber, Chancery, Court of Requests, King's-bench, Common-pleas, and the Exchequer; this gallimawfry is seasoned with subornation of false witnesses, falsifying of orders and decrees ; it is garnished with the subtle practices of the renter-warden of the Fleet, and his imps, as also with Killvert, Killfart, Killbennet, Killbishop, and the like instruments of lawyers gain ; the operation of this dish chiefly consists in the confusion of men's estates, to extract gold out of all men's purses, to suppress virtue and peace, and to advance iniquity and contention ; to wrong and oppress every man, and to do right to no man.

And this mess is also to be reserved for his Majesty's table.

Pope. Good, my Lord Cardinal, I pray you let me taste of this mess, the operation whereof, by your relation, appears to be admirable. I wish, from my heart, that I might also grow capable of that virtue of extracting gold out of the English nation, as some of my predecessors have done before me. I confess, the study of this art was begun by my physician most laudably ; but alas ! and woe is me, it was marred by a robustious storm of wind out of the North, and quite spoiled by a vehement shower of puritanical rain. And what is this next mess, my Lord ?

Card. May it please your Holiness, this is also a hodgepodge, containing sundry coarse meats, as scriveners, brokers, usurers, jailors, bailiffs, serjeants, informers, perjured churchwardens, justices of the peace, and bumbailiffs; this mess is seasoned with parchment, deceit, extortion, usury, oppression, murdering of Christian souls in prisons, through famine, false information, injustice, neglect, and tyranny; and is garnished with a number of irreligious mayors, sheriffs, foederies, escheaters, clerks of the assize, clerks of the peace, constables, and headboroughs. But this mess is, by his Majesty's order, to be disposed of unto his servants.

Pope. Indeed, my Lord Cardinal, methinks this mess hath a very bitter relish with it, else my mouth is quite out of taste ; I conceive it to be a mess fit only for his Majesty's hell-hounds. But what is this last mess ?

Card. I conceive this mess to be very well known to your Holiness, for it is seasoned with most of those operative spices, that all the meat dressed in your Holiness's kitchen is seasoned with; this mess contains divers justicial birds of Middlesex, as namely, the long, the hearn, the snipe, the hooker, the jay, and the like of them; seasoned with the fees and bribes of all the whores and thieves that live in Westminster, Covent-Garden, Holborn, Grub-Street, Clerkenwell, Rosemary-Lane, Turnbull-Street, Ratcliff, Southwark, Bankside, and Kent-Street; this dish is also garnished with the new year's gifts of the whores, thieves, and cutpurses dwelling in the forenamed several places; but this mess is, by his Majesty, reserved for his own peculiar palate.

Pope. Oh Venerable Bede! Oh holy Garnet! Oh sanctified Faux! Oh reverend Beckett! Oh beloved Ravilliack, Campion, Watson, Parsons, Moreton, Sands, and admired Bellarmine, I call you all to witness this day, whether you, or any of you, have ever, as yet, been capable of such a delicious feast, adorned with so many varieties, beautified with so many several rarities, and seasoned with such delectable spices. *Sancte Benedicte, ora pro nobis.*

And thus, rendering all humble and hearty thanks, with all reverence in all obedience, unto his Majesty, our most damnable prince and protector, Lucifer, King of Styx and Phlegethon, I remain his Majesty's humble servant, and vicegerent, at his Majesty's sole disposal during life,

Papa Romanorum.

Advice and Motives to the Honourable Assembly in Parliament.
E. S. I. E. W. J. S.

THE stake's three crowns, four nations gamesters are;
There's three to one, and yet no man that dare
Take these great odds; The cause is, as they say,
The fourth knows both our stock, and cards we play.
This turns the odds, and makes most gamesters think
We're but in jest, and play our cards, and wink.
The set goes hard, when gamesters think it best,
Tho' three men vie it, the fourth sets his rest.
My masters, you that undertake the game,
Look to 't, your country's safety, and her fame,
Are now at stake; be careful how you cut,
And deal, as known occasions put you to 't.
The cards are strangely shuffl'd, for your parts,
'Tis odds you ever get the ace of hearts:
Yet the five fingers, and some helps beside,
Lie in the pack dispers'd, be those your guide,
That you possess, to tell you what you want,
Lest the mistake of one poor trick should daunt
Your spirits quite, and make you fling away
Your liberty, not to be lost by play.

Detest foul juggling, now 'tis in your powers ;
Let none but square play pass, the game is yours ;
For, here you see, Hell, Rome, and all their train,
Plot to confound all your good laws again.
Then have a care, expel Rome's imps, make sure,
Your laws and liberties may still endure
To future ages ; posterities then may
Have cause to bless your memories for aye.

———

1. LAMENT, lament, you bishops all,
    Each wear his blackest gown ;
Hang up your rochets on the wall,
    Your pride is going down.
2. It needs must grieve each Romish heart,
    To hear this sad relation ;
All canons are not worth a fart,
    Made in the convocation.
3. The bishops holy synod, and
    The priests of Baal, that there
Consented, and concluded all,
    Are now in grievous fear
4. To be depriv'd of priestly style,
    Of coat canonical ;
And quite be banished this isle,
    They fear they must be all.
5. Ah ! poor *Et cætera* is now dead,
    Which grieves the bishops most ;
What they would have immortal made,
    Hath now giv'n up the ghost.
6. Alas ! that new begotten oath,
    Like snow against the sun,
It did begin to melt away,
    When th' parliament begun.
7. All ceremonies are good cheap,
    And I will tell you how :
The tippet, hood, and surplice eke,
    Are good for nothing now.
8. And, which I know more woeful is,
    And most their courage quails,
There was a grievous murther made,
    Amongst their holy rails.
9. Oh ! when this sad and heavy news
    Unto that synod came,
The birds and beasts were in a muse,
    Ass, wren, and duck, and lamb.
10. And then a doleful ditty these
    Did thus lament together,
Alas ! we must all run away,
    When shall we run, and whither ?

11. Shall we, with Windebank, to France,
          Or fly to Holland, where
     The Finch is flown, for us a place,
          Before-hand, to prepare?
12. No, quoth the duck, we'll fly to Rome,
          And there rest without fear
     Of parliament, and then the lamb
          May come up in the rear.
13. And there we'll drink a health to all
          The puritans confusion,
     That have thus strongly wrought our fall
          By parliament conclusion.

    THE judges, and the lawyers all,
Attornies, proctors, clerks,
Sollicitors, and advocates,
Must now stand in their sarks,
And penance do for all their faults;
Their bribes they must restore;
Their cheats and tricks, which they did use,
They practise must no more.
The people long they have beguil'd,
And many a one undone;
God's curse their wealth for this doth melt,
As snow is by the sun.
Their children and posterity
The gallows doth devour;
Themselves have made a league with hell,
To reign still by his power.
God is the God of unity,
Of love and peace alone;
But these men, for deceit and strife,
The like of them there's none.

                              Probatum est.

    Received by me, Fountain of Iniquity, this 22d of September,
1641, by the help of Judge Bribery, and the furtherance of Lawyer
Impiety, of Romanus Treachery, the sum of ten pounds of damnable
simplicity, nine pounds of superstitious ignorance, seven pounds of
idolatrous folly, six pounds of wilful stupidity, and three pounds of
perverseness, to and for the use of Impatience; and, by his appointment, to be delivered unto Genteel Prodigality, to and for the use of
Mistress Inconstancy, daughter and sole heir unto Mistress Leachery,
the grand-child of Mistress Bawdry, dwelling next door unto Mistress
Beggary.

    By the new prison near the whipping thong.
    At no great distance from Mr. Justice Long.

Long hath a long time been a knave,
Receiving bribes from every slave;
Long ever hath a shelter been full sure
For every thief, a cutpurse, and a whore;
Long knows full well his Christmas how to keep,
On cost of whores, those are his only sheep :
His capons, woodcocks, hearns, snipes, and jays,
Providers of good chear on all assays.
Long may he feast his body, fill his purse
By such a crew of hellish imps. God's curse
Assuredly will fall on him and his,
And prove his fatal recompence for this.
Long may he be a knave, of such great fame,
To all whores glory, his own eternal shame.

THE

FORERUNNER OF REVENGE.

BEING TWO PETITIONS:

The one, to the King's most excellent Majesty; the other, to the most honourable Houses of Parliament.

Wherein are expressed divers Actions of the late Earl of Buckingham; especially concerning the Death of King James, and the Marquis of Hamilton, supposed by poison. Also may be observed the Inconveniences befalling a State, where the noble Disposition of the Prince is misled by a Favourite. By George Eglisham, Doctor of Physick, and one of the Physicians to King James of happy Memory, for his Majesty's Person, above ten Years Space.

Quarto, containing Twenty-three Pages, printed at London, in the Year MDCXLII.

To the most potent Monarch, Charles, King of Great-Britain.

SIR,

NO better motive there is for a safe government, than the safe meditation of death (equalling kings with beggars) and the exact justice of God requiring of them, that the good suffering misery in this life should receive joy in the other; and the wicked, flourishing securely in this, might be punished in the other. That which pleaseth lasteth but a moment; what tormenteth is everlasting. Many things we see unrewarded or unpunished in this inferior world, which, in the universal weight of God's justice, must be counterpoised elsewhere.

But wilful and secret murther hath seldom been observed to escape undiscovered or unpunished; even in this life, such a particular and notable revenge perpetually followeth it, to the end that they who are either Atheists or Machiavelists may not trust too much to their wits in doing so horrible injustice. Would to God your Majesty would well consider what I have often said to my master, King James, The greatest policy is honesty; and howsoever any man seem to himself wise in compassing his desires, by tricks, yet, in the end, he will prove a fool: For falshood ever deceiveth her own master, at length, as the devil (author of all falshood) always doth, leaving his adherents desolate, when they have the greatest need of his help; no falshood without injustice, no injustice without falshood, albeit it were in the person of a king.

There is no judge in the world more tied to do justice than a king, whose coronation tieth him unto it by solemn oath, which, if he violate, he is false and perjured.

It is justice that maketh kings, justice that maintains kings, and injustice that brings kings and kingdoms to destruction, to fall into misery, to die like asses in ditches, or a more beastly death, eternal infamy after death, as all historians from time to time do clearly manifest.

What need hath mankind of kings but for justice? Men are not born for them, but they for men; what greater, what more royal occasion in the world, could be offered to your Majesty, to shew your impartial disposition in matters of justice, at the first entry of your reign, than this which I offer in my just complaint against Buckingham, by whom your Majesty suffereth yourself so far to be led, that your best subjects are in doubt whether he is your king, or you his. If your Majesty know and consider how he hath tyrannised over his lord and master, King James, (the worldly creator of his fortunes) how insolent, how ingrate an oppressor, what a murtherer and traitor he hath proved himself towards him, how treacherous to his upholding friends, the Marquis of Hamilton and others, your Majesty may think (giving way to the laws demanded against him) to yield a most glorious field for your Majesty to walk in, and display the banner of your royal virtues.

Your Majesty may perhaps demand, what interest I have therein, what have I to do therewith, that I should stir, all others being quiet? Sir, the quietness or stirring of others expecteth only a beginning from me, whom they know so much obliged to stir, as none can be more, both in respect of knowledge of passages, and in regard of human obligation, and of my independency from the accused, or any other that his power and credit can reach unto; many know not what I know therein, others are little or nothing beholding to the dead; others, albeit they know it as well as I, and are obliged as deep as I, yet dare not complain so safely as I, being out of their reach, who are inseparable from him by his inchantments, and all to obscure myself until the power of just revenge upon him be obtained from God.

What I know sufficient against him, I have set down in my petition against him to the parliament; to which if your Majesty dismiss him, sequestered from your Majesty chiefly in an accusation of treason, you shall do what is just, and deliver yourself and your kingdom from the captivity in which he holdeth them and your Majesty oppressed. How easily I may eclipse myself from his power to do me harm, unless he hath legions of infernal spirits at his command to pursue me, your Majesty may well know, I being *ultra mare* to these dominions, where he ruleth and rageth.

How far I am obliged to complain more than others, I will, in few words, express, that neither your Majesty, nor any man, may think otherwise, but that I have most just reason not to be silent in a wrong so intolerable, the interest of blood, which I have to any of them, of whose death I complain; either by the house of Balgony Lunday or Silverton-Hill, albeit it is easy to be made manifest and sufficient to move me, yet it is not the sole motive of my breach of silence. But the interest of received courtesy, and the heap of infallible tokens of true affection, is more than sufficient to stir me thereto, unless I would prove the most ingrate in the world, and senseless of the greatest injuries that can be done unto myself; for who killed King James, and the Marquis of Hamilton, in that part of the injury, which is done unto me therein, he hath done as much as robbed me of my life, and all my fortunes and friends.

With such constant and loving impressions of me, as are neither to be recovered nor duly valued; for his Majesty, from the third year of my age, did practise honourable tokens of singular favour towards me, daily augmented them in word, in writ, in deed, accompanied them, with gifts, patents, offices, recommendations, both in private and publick, at home and abroad, graced so far, that I could scarce ask any thing, but I could have obtained it.

How much honour he hath done unto me, there needs no witness unto your Majesty, who is sufficient for many; no less is my Lord Marquis of Hamilton's friendship established by mutual obligation of most acceptable offices continued by our ancestors these three generations, engraven in the tender minds and years of the Marquis and me, in the presence of our sovereign King James. For the Marquis's father, who with the right hand on his head, and the left on mine, did offer us (young in years so joined) to kiss his Majesty's hand, recommending me to his Majesty's favour, said, I take God to witness, that this young man's father was the best friend that ever I had, or shall have in this world. Whereupon, the young lord resolved to put trust in me, and I fully to addict myself to him, to deserve of him as much commendations as my father did of his father.

This royal celebration of our friends rooted itself so deep in my mind, that to myself I purposed this remembrance, giving it to my young lord, and to my familiar friends, and set it upon the books of my study. *Semper Hamiltonium, &c.*

> Always the King and Hamilton
> Within thy breast conserve,
> Whatever be thy actions,
> Let princes two deserve.

Neither was it in vain, for both our loves increased with our age, the Marquis promising to engage his life and whole estate for me, if need was, and so share his fortunes with me; and not only promising, but also performing, whenever there was occasion; yea, for my sake offering to hazard his life in combate, whose mind in wishing me well, whose tongue in honouring of me, and whose hands and means in defending me (both absent and present unto the last period of his life) hath ever assisted me.

I should be more tedious than was fit, if I should rehearse every particular favour so manifestly known to the whole court, and to the friends of us both. Who then can justly blame me demanding justice, as well for the slaughter of the Marquis of Hamilton, as of my most gracious sovereign King James, seeing I know whom to accuse? My profession of physick, nor my education to letters, cannot serve to hinder me from undertaking the hardest enterprise that ever any Roman undertook, so far as the law of conscience will give way.

> Why should I stay at the decay,
> Of Hamilton's the hope?
> Why shall I see thy foe so free,
> Unto this joy give scope?
> Rather I pray a doleful day
> Set me in cruel fate:
> Than thy death strange without revenge,
> Or him in safe estate.

> This soul to heaven, hand to the dead I vow;
> No fraudful mind, nor trembling hand, I have:
> If pen it shun, the sword revenge shall follow:
> Soul, pen, and sword, what thing but just do crave?

What affection I bore to the living, the same shall accompany the dead; for, when one (whose truth and sincerity was well known unto me) told me, that it was better for the chiefest of my friends, the Marquis of Hamilton, to be quiet at home in Scotland, than eminent in the court of England; to whom, by the opinion of the wiser sort, his being at court will cost him no less than his life; sith that, I, stretching forth mine arm (apprehending some plots laid against him) answered, If no man dare to revenge his death, I vow to God, this hand of mine shall revenge it: Scarcely any other cause to be found, than the bond of our close friendship, why, in the scroll of noblemen's names, who were to be killed, I should be set down next to the Marquis of Hamilton, and under these words, (viz. The Marquis, and Doctor Eglisham to embalm him) to wit, to the end that no discoverer or revenger should be left; this roll of names, I know not by what destiny, found near to Westminster, about the time of the Duke of Richmond's death, and brought to the Lord Marquis by his cousin, the daughter of the Lord Oldbarro, one of the privy-council of Scotland, did cause no terror in me, until I did see the Marquis poisoned, and remembered, that the rest therein noted were dead, and myself, next pointed at, only surviving. Why stay I any more? The cause requireth no more the pen, but the sword.

I do not write so bold, because I am amongst the duke's enemies; but I have retired myself to his enemies, because I was resolved to write and do earnestly against him, as may very well appear: For, since the Marquis of Hamilton's death, the most noble Marquis de Fiatta, ambassador for the most Christian King of France, and also Buckingham's mother, sent on every side to seek me, inviting me to them. But I did forsake them, knowing certainly the falshood of Buckingham would suffer the ambassador rather to receive an affront, than to be unsatisfied of his blood-thirsty desire of my blood, to silence me with death (for, according to the proverb, The dead cannot bite) if he could have found me. For my Lord Duke of Lenox, who was often crossed by Buckingham, with his brother and the Earl of Southampton, now dead, and one of the roll found of those that were to be murdered, well assured me, that, where Buckingham once misliked, no apology, no submission, no reconciliation, could keep him from doing mischief.

Neither do I write this in this fashion, so freely, for any entertainment here present, which I have not, nor for any future, which I have no ground to look for; seeing Buckingham hath so much misled your Majesty, that he hath caused, not only here, but also in all nations, all British natives to be disgraced and mistrusted; your Majesty's most royal word, which should be inviolable, your hand and seal, which should be infringeable, to be most shamefully violated, and yourself to be most ingrate for your kind usage in Spain; which Buckingham maketh to be requited with injuries in a most base manner; under protestation of friendship, a bloody war being kindled on both sides, whereby he hath buried with King James the glorious name of Peace-making King, who had done much more justly and advisedly, if he had procured peace unto Christendom; whereby small hope I have of obtaining justice on my most just complaint, unto which my dear affection unto my dear friends murdered, and extreme detestation of Buckingham's violent proceedings hath brought me. Your Majesty may find most just causes to accuse him in my petition to the parliament, which shall serve for a touch-stone to your Majesty, and a whet-stone to me and many other Scotchmen; and which, if it be neglected, will make your Majesty to incur a censure amongst all virtuous men in the world, that your Majesty will be loth to hear of, and I am astonished to express at this time.

A serpent lurketh in the grass.

No other way there is to be found to save your honour, but to give way to justice against that traitor, Buckingham, by whom manifest danger approacheth to your Majesty, no otherwise than death approached to King James.

If your Majesty will, therefore, take any course therein, the examination upon oath of all those, that were about the King and the Marquis of Hamilton in their sickness, or at their deaths, or after their deaths, before indifferent judges (no dependants on Buckingham) will serve for sufficient proof of Buckingham's guiltiness. In the mean time, until I see what be the issue of my complaint, without any more speech, I rest

Your Majesty's daily Suppliant,

GEORGE EGLISHAM.

———

To the most honourable the Nobility, Knights, and Burgesses of the Parliament of England.

The humble Petition of George Eglisham, Doctor of Physick, and one of the Physicians to King James of happy Memory, for his Majesty's Person, above the Space of ten Years.

WHEREAS the chief human care of kings, and courts of parliament, is the preservation and protection of the subjects lives, liberties, and estates, from private and publick injuries, to the end that all things may be carried in the equal balance of justice, without which no monarchy, no commonwealth, no society, no family, yea, no man's life or estate can consist, albeit never so little : It cannot be thought unjust to demand of kings and parliaments the censure of wrongs, the consideration whereof was so great in our monarch of happy memory, King James, that he hath often publickly protested, even in the presence of his apparent heir, that, if his own son should commit murder, or any such execrable act of injury, he would not spare him, but would have him die for it, and would have him more severely punished than any other : For, he very well observed, no greater injustice, no injury more intolerable can be done by man to man, than murder. In all other wrongs fortune hath recourse ; the loss of honour, or goods, may be repaired, satisfaction may be made, reconciliation may be procured, so long as the party injured is alive. But, when the party injured is bereft of his life, what can restore it ? What satisfaction can be given him ? Where shall the murderer meet with him, to be reconciled to him, unless he be sent out of this world to follow his spirit, which, by his wickedness, he hath separated from his body ? Therefore, of all injuries, of all the acts of injustice, of all things most to be looked into, murder is the greatest ; and, of all murders, the poisoning, under trust and profession of friendship, is the most heinous ; which, if you suffer to go unpunished, let no man think himself so secure to live amongst you, as amongst the wildest and most furious beasts in the world : For, by vigilancy and industry, means may be had to resist, or evict, the most violent beast that ever nature bred ; but, from false and treacherous hearts, from poisoning murders, what wit or wisdom can defend ?

This concerneth your lordships, every one in particular, as well as myself. They (of whose poisoning your petitioner complaineth) viz.

King James, the Marquis of Hamilton, and others, whose names after shall be expressed, have been the most eminent in the kingdom, and sat on these benches, whereon your honours do now sit. The party, whom your petitioner accuseth, is the Duke of Buckingham, who is so powerful, that, unless the whole body of a parliament lay hold on him, no justice can be had of him. For, what place is there of justice, what office of the crown, what degree of honour in the kingdom, which he hath not sold; And sold in such craft, that he can shake the buyer out of them, and intrude others at his pleasure?

All the judges of the kingdom, all the officers of state, are his bound vassals, or allies, and are afraid to become his out-casts, as it is notorious to all his Majesty's true and loving subjects; yea, so far hath his ambitious practice gone, that what the king would have done, could not be done, if he opposed it; whereof many instances may be given, whensoever they shall be required: Neither are they unknown to this honourable assembly, howsoever the means he useth be, whether lawful or unlawful, whether human or diabolick, so he tortureth the kingdom, that he procureth the calling, breaking, or continuing of the parliament, at his pleasure; placing and displacing the officers of justice, of the council of the king's court, of the courts of justice, to his violent pleasure, and as his ambitious villainy moveth him. What hope, then, can your petitioner have, that his complaint should be heard, or, being heard, should take effect? To obtain justice he may despair; to provoke the duke to send forth a poisoner, or murderer, to dispatch him, and send him after his dead friends already murdered, he may be sure of this to be the event. Let the event be what it will, come whatsoever can come, the loss of his own life your petitioner valueth not, having suffered the loss of the lives of such eminent friends, esteeming his life cannot be better bestowed, than upon the discovery of so heinous murders. Yea, the justness of the cause, the dearness and nearness of his friends murdered, shall prevail so far with him, that he shall unfold unto your honours, and unto the whole world, against the accused, and name him the author of so great murders, George Villers, Duke of Buckingham; which, against any private man, are sufficient for his apprehension and torture. And, to make his complaint not very tedious, he will only, for the present, declare unto your honours the two eminent murders committed by Buckingham, to wit, of the King's Majesty, and of the Lord Marquis of Hamilton; which, for all the subtlety of his poisoning art, could not be so cunningly conveighed, as the murderer thought, but that God hath discovered manifestly the author. And, to observe the order of the time of their death, because the Lord Marquis of Hamilton died first, his death shall be first related, even from the root of his first quarrel with Buckingham, albeit many other jars have proceeded, from time to time, betwixt them.

Concerning the Poisoning of the Lord Marquis of Hamilton.

BUCKINGHAM, once raised from the bottom of fortune's wheel to the top, by what desert, by what right or wrong, no matter it is; (by his carriage the proverb is verified) 'Nothing more proud than basest blood, when it doth rise aloft.' He suffered his ambition to carry himself so far, as to aspire to match his blood with the blood royal both of England and Scotland. And, well knowing, that the marquis of Hamilton was acknowledged by King James to be the prime man in his dominions, who, next to his own line, in his proper season, might claim an hereditary title to his crown of Scotland, by the daughter of King James the Second, and to the crown of England, by Joan of Somerset, wife to King James the First, declared, by an act of parliament, heretrix of England to be in her due rank, never suffered the king to be at rest, but urged him always to send some of his privy-council to solicit the marquis to match his eldest son with Buckingham's niece, making great promises of conditions, which the mean family of the bride could not perform without the king's liberality, to wit, fifty thousand pounds sterling, valuing five hundred thousand florins with the earldom of Orkney, under the title of Duke, and whatsoever the marquis would accept, even to the first duke of Britain.

The glorious title of a duke the marquis refused twice, upon special reasons reserved to himself.

The matter of money was no motive to cause the marquis to match his son so unequal to his degree, seeing Buckingham himself, the chief of her kindred, was but a novice in nobility, his father obscure amongst gentlemen, his mother a serving-woman; and he, being infamous for his frequent consultation with the ring-leader of witches, principally that false Doctor Lambe, publickly condemned for witchcraft; whereby the marquis, knowing that the king was so far bewitched by Buckingham, that, if he refused the match demanded, he should find the king's deadly hatred against him; and seeing that Buckingham's niece was not yet nubile in years, and that, before the marriage should be confirmed, a way might be found out to annul it; unto which he was forced by deceitful importunity: therefore he yielded unto the king's desire of the match: Whereupon, Buckingham and his faction, fearing that delays would bring lets, urged my Lord Marquis to send for his son, upon a Sunday morning betimes, in all haste, from London to Court at Greenwich; where never a word was spoken of marriage, to the young lord, till a little before supper, and the marriage made before the king after supper. And, to make it more authentick, Buckingham caused his niece to be laid in bed with the marquis's son, for a short time, in the king's chamber, and in his Majesty's presence, albeit the bride was yet innubile. Many were astonished at the sudden news thereof, all the marquis's friends fretting thereat, and some writing unto him very scornful letters for the same.

The marquis, having satisfied the king's demands, did what he could to prevent the confirmation of the marriage, and intended to send his son beyond the seas, to travel through France, and so to pass his time abroad, until that means were found out to unty that knot, which Buckingham had urged the King to tie upon his son.

But Buckingham, to countermand the marquis's design, causes the marquis's son, to be sworn gentleman of the prince's bed-chamber, and so to be detained with him within the kingdom, until that the bride was at years ripe for marriage.

The time expired that Buckingham's niece became marriageable; Buckingham sent to the marquis, to desire him to make the marriage to be compleatly confirmed.

The marquis (not willing to hear of any such matter) answered briefly, he scorned the motion.

This answer was reported to Buckingham, who seeing himself like to be frustrated of his ambitious matching of his niece, and perceiving that the lord marquis was able to raise a great faction against him, whether King James did live or die, was mightily incensed against the marquis: at the first encounter with him, did challenge him for speaking disdainfully of him and his house.

The marquis replied, he did not remember any offensive words uttered by himself against Buckingham. Buckingham then proudly said unto him, out of the words of thy mouth I will judge thee; for you have said, you scorn the motion of matching with my house, which I made unto you. The marquis answered, that, if he had said so, it became not the duke to speak unto him in that fashion. So Buckingham threatened to be revenged: The marquis uttered his defiance; and thus the quarrel began, which four or five times was reiterated, and as often reconciled by the Marquis de Fiatta, a little before the Marquis of Hamilton fell sick; wherein it is very evident, that the quarrel hath been very violent, that needed so many reconciliations. The duke's fire of his anger and fury being unextinguishable, as King James did often censure him in his absence, albeit a favourite; that he was wonderful vindicative, whose malice was insensible towards my Lord Marquis of Hamilton, did well shew itself, as shall appear hereafter.

Hardly can any man tell, whether, by the marquis in his sickness, Buckingham was more suspected, than accused, of the poison given, or to be given him; for he would not taste of any thing that was sent to him by any of Buckingham's friends, but he would have some of his servants taste of it before: And for the love that was mutual between him and your petitioner (which he would never suffer to go out of his sight during his sickness) your petitioner cast off all that he took in that time, unto whom his suspicion of Buckingham he expressed by name before sufficient witness, who will testify it upon oath, if there be any course taken therein for the search thereof. All the time of his sickness, he intreated your petitioner not to suffer my lord of Buckingham to come near him; and your petitioner having often sent word, and also sometimes signified himself to Buckingham, that there was no fit opportunity to see the marquis, pretending something to be ministred to him: But, when your petitioner could find no more excuses, he told my lord marquis, that he had put away my lord of Buckingham so often, that he could not keep him away any longer, but that he must needs see him.

Then he, knowing Buckingham's visitation to proceed of dissimulation, requested your petitioner, at last, to find the means to get him away quickly; which your petitioner did, interrupting Buckingham's discourse, and intreating him to suffer my lord marquis to be quiet.

This did evidently shew my lord marquis's disliking and distrusting of Buckingham, whereas he was well pleased with other noblemen's company. All the time of his sickness, the duke and my Lord Denbigh would not suffer his own son to come to him, pretending that he was also sick; which was false for the time that my lord marquis called for him. After this, your petitioner advised his lordship to dispose of his estate, and of his conscience; his sickness was not without danger, which your petitioner, four days before my lord's death, did in such manner perceive, that he had cause to despair of his health, but intreated him to commit all the care of his health to God and his physicians, assuring, howsoever he had gotten wrong abroad, he should get none in the cure of his disease.

At length his lordship burst out in those words to my Lord Denbigh, ' It is a great cruelty in you, that you will not suffer my son to come to me when I am dying, that I may see him, and speak to him before I die.' So they delayed his coming with excuses, until my lord's agony of death was near, to the end that he should not have time to give his son private instructions to shun the marriage of Buckingam's niece, or to signify unto him the suspicion of poison: For they had rather his son should know any thing, than either of these; yet many did suspect his poison before he died : For, two days before his death, two of his servants died with manifest signs and suspicion of poison, the one belonging to the wine-cellar, the other to the kitchen.

The fatal hour being come, that my lord marquis deceased, your petitioner intreated all that were present, to suffer no man to touch his body, until he returned to see it opened. For then he protested earnestly, that, all the time of his sickness, he judged him to be poisoned; but this poison was such, and so far gone, that none could help it: Nevertheless, to have the matter concealed, Buckingham would have him buried that same night in Westminster church, and the ceremonies of his burial to be kept afterwards, saying, that such delicate bodies as his could not be kept.

But his friends, taking hold of the caveat before given by your petitioner, refused so to do, and replied, that they would have him, as became him, to be buried in Scotland, in his own chapel, where all his ancestors have been buried for more than these four-hundred years; and that his body must first be visited by his physicians.

No sooner was he dead, when the force of the poison had overcome the force of his body, but it began to swell in such sort, that his thighs were swoln six times as big as their natural proportion; his belly became as big as the belly of an ox, his arms as the natural quantity of his thighs, his neck as broad as his shoulders, his cheeks over the top of his nose, that his nose could not be seen or distinguished; the skin of his forehead two fingers high swelled, the hair of his beard, eye-brows, and head, so far distant from one another, as if an hundred had been taken out between each one; and when one did touch the hair, it came away with the skin as easily, as if one had pulled hay out of an heap of hay. He was all over, his neck, breast, shoulders, arms, and brows, I say, of divers colours, full of waters, of the same colour, some white, some black, some red, some yellow, some green, some blue, and that as well within his body, as without.

Also, the concavities of his liver green, his stomach, in some places, a little purpurated with a blue clammy water, adhering to the sides of it; his mouth and nose foaming blood mixed with froth mightily, of divers colours, a yard high. Your petitioner, being sent for to visit his body, and his servants all flocking about him, saying, See, see, presently weeping, said, he was poisoned, and that it was not a thing to be suffered.

Moreover, he said, that, albeit his speech might cost him his life, yet, seeing his sorrow had extorted that speech out of him, he would make it manifest, and would have a jury of physicians. Presently, some of my Lord Marquis of Hamilton's friends said, We must send to my lord duke, that he may send his physicians; but your petitioner replied, What have we to do with the duke's physicians? Let us have indifferent men. Captain Hamilton, hearing your petitioner so boldly take exceptions at Buckingham, and judging that he had good reason for what he had spoken, said, ' For all that, let us send to the duke, and signify, that all who have seen the marquis's body, both physicians, chirurgeons, and others, may see that he is poisoned, and that his friends desire more physicians out of the college of London, besides the duke's physicians, to bear witness in what case the marquis's body is in; and then, if the duke's conscience be guilty (said the captain) it will shew itself,' as indeed it did: For the duke, being advertised hereof, sent for his own physicians, and others out of London, whom he caused first to be brought unto him, before they went to see the marquis's body, giving them his directions in these words, viz.

" My Masters, there is a bruit spread abroad, that the Marquis of Hamilton is poisoned; go see, but beware what you speak of poison (which he said in a threatening form of delivery) for every nobleman that dieth must be poisoned."

If his conscience had not been guilty, should not he have commanded the physicians to enquire, by all means possible, and make it known, rather than to suppress the speech of poisoning so worthy a man.

These physicians being come, your petitioner with one hand leading Doctor More to the table, where the marquis's body was laid, and with the other hand thowing off the cloth from the body, said unto him, ook you here upon this spectacle.

At the sight whereof Doctor More, lifting up both his hands, heart, and eyes to the heavens, astonished, said, Jesus bless me, I never saw the like, I cannot distinguish a face upon him; and in like manner all the rest of the doctors, and also the chirurgeons, affirmed, that they never saw the like, albeit that they have travelled and practised through the greatest part of Europe : Only one, that said, My Lord of Southampton was blistered all within the breast, as my lord marquis was. Doctor Leicester, one of Buckingham's creatures, seeing Doctor More and others so amazed at the sight of my lord's body, drew first him aside, and then the others, one after another, and whispered them in the ear to silence them.

Whereupon many went away, without speaking one word ; the others, who remained, acknowledged, that those accidents of the dead body could not be without poison; but they said, they could not know how such a subtle art of poisoning could be brought into England ; your petitioner replied, that money would bring both the art, and the ...st, from the furthest part of the world into England, from whence, since your petitioner's departure, he hath conferred with the skilfullest pest-masters that could be found, who visit the bodies of those that die of the venom of the pest.

They all admire the description of my lord marquis's body, and testify, that never any of the pest have such accidents, but carbuncles, rubons, or spots, no such huge blisters with waters, and such a huge, uniform swelling to such dimensions, above six times the natural proportion. But he hath met with some, who have practised the poisoning of dogs, to try the force of some antidotes, and they have found, that some poisons have made the dogs sick for a fortnight, or more, without any swelling, until they were dead, and then they swelled above measure, and became blistered, with waters of divers colours; and the hair came away with the skin, when it was touched.

The physicians then, who remained, were willing to certify under their hands, that my lord marquis was poisoned. But your petitioner told them, it was not needful, seeing we must needs attend God's leisure to discover the author, the manner being so apparent, and so many hundreds having seen the body to witness it, for the doors were kept open, for every man to behold, and to be witness who would.

The Duke of Buckingham making some counterfeit shew of sorrow to men of great quality, found no other shift to divert the suspicion of the poisoning of the marquis from him, but to lay it upon his master, the King, saying, that the marquis, for his person, spirit, and carriage, was such as he was born worthy to reign ; but the King, his master, hated him to death, because he had a spirit too much for the common-weal; whereby the duke did shew himself no good subject to the King, who made the King's honour to be tyrannical, and the King a blood-thirsty murderer, and a most vile dissembler, having heaped so many honours daily upon the marquis, even to the very last, making him lord high steward of his Majesty's house, and Judge of the very court, whom he had made before viceroy of Scotland, for the time of the parliament of Scotland, Earl of Cambridge, privy-counsellor in England, and knight of the garter, as if he had raised him to all these honours, that the murdering of him might be the less suspected to proceed from him

The King's nature hath always been observed to have been so gracious, and so free-hearted towards every one, that he would never have wished the marquis any harm, unless that Buckingham had put great jealousies and fears into his mind; for, if any other had done it, he would have acquainted his favourite therewith. And then was it Buckingham's duty to remove from the King such sinistrous conceits of the marquis, as the marquis hath often done of Buckingham, upholding him upon all occasions, and keeping the King from giving way to introduce any other favourite: Wherefore Buckingham, in that diversion of the crime from him, hath not only made the King, but also himself, guilty of the marquis's death.

But Buckingham's falshood, and ill intention, was long before rightly discovered, when he did what he could to make the Earl of Nethersdale and my Lord Gordon (both near kinsmen of my lord marquis) so incensed at him, that they had like all three to have killed one another, if it had not been that my lord marquis, by his wisdom, did let them all know how they were abused.

If any dissimulation be greater than Buckingham's, let any man judge: For, when my lord marquis's body, was to be transported from White-hall, to his house at Bishopsgate, Buckingham came out muffled and furred in his coach, giving out, that he was sick for sorrow of my lord marquis's death; but, as soon as he went to his house out of London, before his coming to the King, he triumphed, and domineered with his faction so excessively, as if he had gained some great victory. And, the next day coming to the King, he put on a most lamentable and mournful countenance for the death of my lord marquis. No greater victory could he have gotten to his mind, than to have destroyed that man, who could, and would, have fetched his head off hhis shoulders, if he had outlived King James, to have known his carriage in the poisoning of him in his sicknes; wherefore he thought it most necessary to remove the marquis before-hand.

The same day that my lord marquis died, Buckingham sent my lord marquis's son out of town, keeping him as prisoner, that none could have private conference with him, until his marriage of Buckingham's niece was compleated; but always either my Lord Denbigh, or my Lady Denbigh, or my Lord Duke of Buckingham, or the Duchess of Buckingham, or the Countess of Buckingham was present, that none could let him understand how his father was murdered. Even your petitioner himself, when he went to see him, within a few days after his father's death, was intreated not to speak to him of the poisoning of his father, which he did conceal at his first meeting, because their sorrow was too recent. But he was prevented of a second meeting, neither would Buckingham suffer the young lord to go to Scotland, to see his father's funeral, and to take order with his friends, concerning his father's estate, for fear that their intended marriage should be overthrown.

This captivity of the young lord marquis lasted so long, until that Buckingham caused his Majesty, King Charles, to take the young lord with himself and Buckingham into St. James's Park, discharging all others from following them; and there to persuade and urge the young lord, without any more delay, to accomplish the marriage with Buckingham's niece, which instantly was performed; so that Buckingham trusteth and presumeth, that, albeit the young lord should understand how his father was poisoned by his means, yet, being married to his niece, he would not stir to revenge it, but comport with it.

To all that is observed before, it is worthy to be added, that the bruit went through London, long before the Lord Duke of Richmond's death, or his brother's, or my Lord of Southampton's, or of the marquis, that all the noblemen, that were not of the duke's faction, should be poisoned, and so removed out of his way.

Also a paper was found in King-street, about the time of the Duke of Richmond's death, wherein the names of all those noblemen, who have died since, were expressed; and your petitioner's name also set next to my Lord Marquis of Hamilton's name, with these words: To embalm. him. This paper was brought by my Lord Oldbarro's daughter, cousin-german to the lord marquis: Likewise a mountebank, about that time, was greatly countenanced by the Duke of Buckingham, and by his means procured letters patents, and recommendations from the King, to practise his skill in physick through all England; who coming to London, to sell poison, to kill man or beast within a year, or half a year, or two years, or a month or two, or what time prefixed any man desired, in such sort that they could not be helped nor discovered. Moreover, the Christmas before my lord marquis's death, one of the prince's footmen said, that some of the great ones at court had gotten poison in their belly, but he could not tell who it was.

Here your honours considering the premisses of my Lord Duke of Buckingham's ambitious and most vindicative nature; his frequent quarrels with my lord Marquis, after so many reconciliations; his threatening of the physicians, not to speak of the poison; his triumphing after my lord marquis's death; his detaining of his son almost prisoner, until the marriage was compleat with his niece; the preceding bruit of poisoning Buckingham's adversaries; the paper of their names found, with sufficient intimation of their death, by the conclusion of the word, embalming; the poison-monger, mountebank, graced by Buckingham, may suffice for ground to take him and torture him, if he were a private men: And herein your petitioner most earnestly demandeth justice against that traytor, seeing by act of parliament it is made treason to conspire the death of privy-counsellor. Out of this declaration, interrogateries may be drawn for examination of witnesses; wherein more is discovered to begin withal, than was laid open at the beginning of the discovery of the poisoning of Sir Thomas Overbury.

Concerning the Poisoning of King James of happy Memory, King of Great Britain.

THE Duke of Buckingham, being in Spain, advertised by letter, how that the King began to censure him in his absence freely, and that many spoke boldly to the King against him, and how the King had intelligence from Spain of his unworthy carriage in Spain; and how the marquis of Hamilton (upon the sudden news of the prince's departure) had nobly reprehended the King, for sending the prince with such a young man, without experience, and in such a private and sudden manner, without acquainting the nobility or council therewith; wrote a verry bitter letter to the Marquis of Hamilton, conceived new ambitious courses of his own, and used all the devices he could to disgust the prince's mind off the match with Spain so far intended by the King; made haste home, where, when he came, he so carried himself, that, whatever the King commanded in his bed-chamber, he controlled in the next; yea, received packets to the King from foreign princes, and dispatched answers without acquainting the king therewith, in a long time after. Whereat perceiving the King highly offended, and that the King's mind was beginning to alter towards him, suffering him to be quarrelled and affronted in his Majesty's presence; and observing that the King reserved my Lord of Bristol to be a rod for him, urging daily his dispatch for France, and expecting the Earl of Gondmor, who, as it seemed, was greatly esteemed and wonderfully credited by the King, and would second my Lord of Bristol's accusations against him. He knew also that the King had vowed that, in despite of all the devils in hell, he would bring the Spanish match about again, and that the Marquis of Inicosa had given the King bad impressions of him, by whose articles of accusation, the King himself had examined some of the nobility and privy-council, and found in the examination, that Buckingham had said, after his coming from Spain, that the King was now an old man, it was now time for him to be at rest, and to be confined to some park, to pass the rest of his time in hunting, and the prince to be crowned.

The more the King urged him to be gone to France, the more shifts he made to stay; for he did evidently see, that the King was fully resolved to rid himself of the oppressions wherein he held him.

The king being sick of a certain ague, and that in the spring was of itself never found deadly; the Duke took his opportunity, when all the King's doctors of physick were at dinner, upon the Monday before the King died, without their knowledge or consent, and offered to him a white powder to take, the which he a long time refused; but, overcome with his flattering importunity, at length took it in wine, and immediately became worse and worse, falling into many swoonings and pains, and violent fluxes of the belly, so tormented, that his Majesty cried out aloud of this white powder, 'Would to God I had never taken it, it will cost me my life.'

In like manner also the countess of Buckingham, my Lord of Buckingham's mother, upon the Friday after, the physicians being also absent and at dinner, and not made acquainted with her doings, applied a plaister to the King's heart and breast; whereupon he grew faint, and short-breathed, and in a great agony. Some of the physicians after dinner, returning to see the King, by the offensive smell of the plaister, perceived something to be about him, hurtful to him, and searched what it should be, and found it out, and exclaimed that the King was poisoned. Then Buckingham, entering, commanded the physicians out of the room, caused one of them to be committed prisoner to his own chamber, and another to be removed from court; quarrelled with others of the King's servants in his sick Majesty's own presence so far, that he offered to draw his sword against them in his Majesty's sight. And Buckingham's mother, kneeling down before his Majesty, cried out with a brazen face, ' Justice, Justice, Sir, I demand justice of your Majesty.' His Majesty asked her, for what ? ' For that which their lives are no ways sufficient to satisfy, for saying that my son and I have poisoned your Majesty.' ' Poisoned me ?' said he; with that turning himself, swooned, and she was removed.

The Sunday after his Majesty died, and Buckingham desired the physicians, who attended his Majesty, to sign with their own hands a writ of testimony, that the powder, which he gave him, was a good and safe medicine, which they refused.

Buckingham's creatures did spread abroad a rumour in London, that Buckingham was so sorry for his Majesty's death, that he would have died, that he would have killed himself, if they had not hindered him ; which your petitioner purposely enquired after of them that were near him at that time, who said, that, neither in the time of his Majesty's sickness, nor after his death, he was more moved, than if there had never happened either sickness or death to his Majesty.

One day when his Majesty was in great extremity, he rode post to London, to pursue his sister-in-law, to have her stand in sack-cloath in St. Paul's for adultery. And, another time in his Majesty's agony, he was busy in contriving and concluding a marriage for one of his cousins.

Immediately after his Majesty's death, the physician, who was commanded to his chamber, was set at liberty, with a caveat to hold his peace; the others threatened, if they kept not good tongues in their heads.

But, in the mean time, the King's body and head swelled above measure, his hair, with the skin of his head stuck to the pillow, and his nails became loose upon his fingers and toes.

Your petitioner needeth to say no more to understanding men, only one thing he beseecheth, that taking the traytor, who ought to be taken without any fear of his greatness, the other matters may be examined, and the accessaries with the guilty punished.

THE

SPIRITUAL COURTS EPITOMISED,

IN A

DIALOGUE BETWIXT TWO PROCTORS,

BUSY-BODY AND SCRAPE-ALL,

AND

Their Discourse of the Want of their former Employment.

London, printed in 1641. Quarto, containing six pages, with a wooden cut in the title-page, representing the Bishops-court in great confusion.

Busy-body.

WE are utterly undone, this parliament hath not only rendered us contemptible to the world, but hath deprived us of our practice; the King's advocate hath not got a fee for an *ex officio* business this half year; myself have drawn no articles against one that repeated sermons with his family this twelve-month; my Lord of Canterbury might have spared the making of a table of fees, he needed not to have turned out the register for extortion, unless the issue had been better.

Scrape-all. It is true, Mr. Busy-body, but we do not suffer an eclipse in the high commission only, but in all other courts. Bow-Church, that on a court-day used to be fuller than at a sermon on a Sunday, and the audience court in S. Paul's, where a man could not hear with his own ears; the prerogative, consistory, and archdeacon's, with the dean and chapter's courts, that were wont to be crouded, like money into an usurer's bag, are very quiet and peaceable now; we cannot talk false Latin now, but it will be understood; we cannot get ten pounds in part for the probate of a will, as corpulent Mr. Copper-nose, our brother, the English proctor, could; we cannot put Ponsonby's name to articles, for incontinency, with the privity of the judge, as heretofore we could, and then compound for the penance ourselves, as we have done with the judge before his sentence.

Busy-body. No more can we send our messengers into the country, that pry into people's actions there, as Alderman Abell's spirits would into a butt of unlicensed wine. You know, when many articles were drawn in the name of *me necessarii promotoris officii*, against any that we knew was rich, upon no ground at all, but hope that he would refuse to take his oath, either to accuse or forswear himself, if he did refuse, then we would be paid our fees; Mr. Advocate, for perusing and subscribing the articles, a piece, that is, two fees, when it was all but one labour; myself for drawing them, running up and down, sending my man, and twenty pains more, that, heaven knows, I never took, my fees treble, and the office would be careful enough for their fees; for expedition, for extraordinary attendance, bonds, and twenty things more, they would not want much of twenty times their fees; and then, he remaining obstinate, my lord's grace would deal with him, as he did with others, into prison with him, no redemption. O money causes were pure good ones; a parson would spend more money, by delay, than the benefice is worth. We could not endure alimony, many of them were *in forma pauperis*.

Scrape-all. A pox on them, I had rather the judge would have given sentence against my client, than bestowed a *pauper* on me; I am sure the creature, if he followed not his own business better than I, he would have a cold bargain of it; for my part, I fitted him, but sometimes he would present a George or the like to my man, and, if he looked after it, so; if not, *vale pauper.* I got very well by a wench that has been undone in a dark entry: Sir John would commute her penance into ten pounds, towards the repair of Paul's, and then we would share it. A shop-door could not be open on a holy-day, but the next Sunday the church was saluted with a *corum nobis*; and, if he did not appear, whether he heard of it or no, *dominus eum in scriptis excommunicavit..* Let him appear, when he would, he must render down his contumacy fees, or he remains and is accounted *pro excommunicato*; and when he is restored *Christi fidelium*, he must pay the officers fees; faith, such businesses were pretty toys.

Busy-body. And I have gained well by a poor will, when the estate has not amounted to above forty pounds. I would persuade the executor for confirmation to prove it *per testes,* but first it must be proved in *communi forma,* and by that time some twenty marks or such a sum would redound to me out of the forty; I never cared much for an administration.

Scrape-all. But I did, for I would get more by it, the inventory (which my man should ingross, as if one word were afraid of another) the account, and the *quietus est,* and the gratuity (which I never failed of), than you could by an ordinary will. All Bloomsbury, Coventgarden, Long-acre, and Beech-lane, were as fearful of me, as of a constable, or Justice Long; many a time have I stepped in with them for my fees, and have had all content possible. I should have thought it an ill day in the vacation, if I had not got a piece.

Busy-body. Oh, brother! You would not believe how I delighted in a commission, which I would go into the country withal, and expedite; and, if they would not give me ten pounds for it (which if a country proctor had done, he would not have required above a piece) I would not make many delays for the matter, but have got it taxed by any surrogate (whom I could persuade) to twelve or fourteen pounds; a motion flies down, and an excommunication after it, and so I lived in as much state as Augustus Cæsar. Over your country, commissions would afford good profit.

Scrape-all. Faith, brother, and I have cheated many of my brethren in the country, who used to send me up businesses ready roasted; I would pretend caveats were entered, and detain the business in my hands a week longer than the time, and then make them pay me, as fully for them, as if my man had ingrossed them himself.

Busy-body. O, but I was as good at an appeal as could be, for, when the cause was ready for sentence, if I thought the adverse party would not appeal, if sentence went against him, I would persuade the judge to give sentence against my client, and then I would be sure to appeal, and, when I had appealed, my bill would exceed a taylor's; there would be *pro solicitatione, pro sportulagio, pro privato sigillo,* and *pro* twenty things more, that were never done. A notable merry fellow had a poor cause appealed thrice; and then the adverse party got a commission of review, my client still having sentence; which, when he told, how his enemy had appealed so often, and was yet gone further; says he, I have a proctor that will follow to the devil, if I whip him with a silver lash. And, on my conscience, I should have looked as scurvily upon a poor client, as a beggar does upon a beadle, or a whipping-post: for God's sake, brother, how long is it since these blessings failed?

Scrape-all. Faith, ever since the parliament begun, or rather before. At the visitation at St. Magnus's church, when Doctor Duck was hunted dry-foot into the water, where, had he not dived, the spaniels would have tore him in pieces, they catched hold of his legs, and made them swell extremely; ever since that time, we have been held in most special contempt; your whores, that would have hanged themselves before to please us, now call us *civil villains**, our law, the bawdy courts, and they, that have preserved our bills, now shew them us, and expect restoration; nay the *ultimum refugium* fails us now : that is, to bring a boy with fifty or threescore pounds, and, within a year or two, turn him away, but keep his money; this is a black tune for us; ten groats given in a license now make me as jocund as a gratuity of ten pounds would before. Cannot you devise what course is to be taken?

Busy-body. Now, if I could draw a prohibition, I would leave my sheepskinhood, and convert it into a buckram bag; a Westminster attorney lives a king's life now; however, I am (if the oath, &c. shot out of our new cannons does not strike us quite dead) get acquaintance with parish clerks, and keep a horse that can smell out a testament; if my brother Copper-nose would die once, I would be made free of the girdlers, and beg the probation of citizens and aldermens wills; if all fail me, I will fly after Doctor Roan into France, and then we will eat capons, and revive our living.

* By way of ridicule, instead of Civilians.

VOX BOREALIS:

OR,

THE NORTHERN DISCOVERIE:

BY WAY OF DIALOGUE,

BETWEEN IAMIE AND WILLIE.

AMIDST THE BABYLONIANS.

Printed by Margery Mar-Prelat, in Thwackcoat-Lane, at the signe of the Crab-
tree Cudgell, without any priviledge of the Cater-Caps, the yeare coming on,
1641. Quarto, containing twenty-eight pages.

This is one of the earliest, and, I think, the most humorous and odd of all the
Pamphlets written against King Charles the First, and his party ; and, though
it is a severe invective against prelacy, carries with it so much merry conceit,
that it cannot be read without affording a pretty deal of mirth and entertainment ; especially in the poetical will of a dying soldier, which may be accounted
one of the best pieces of its kind, that ever was published.

THE EPISTLE.

MOST kind and courteous country-men: Being at Berwicke, it was
my chance to meet with two of my country-men there, the one of
them being lately come from London, and the other had been in the
camp ; where, after salutations past amongst us, they desired me to
write down their severall collections of passages, which, I confesse, are
not such as they would have been, if mischances had not happened:
For, it seems, the one was forced to burn his noates at London, and
the others were spoyled with water at Berwicke ; and, therefore, they
are but fragments, not whole relations: yet, such as they are, accept
of them, in regard of the good will of the giver, who may one day
make amends for what is here omitted: Which (as he is truely bound)
so he will duely indeavour to performe ; and will not cease to informe
you of any thing which may tend to the advancement of the cause,
and good of the countrey, whose peace and prosperity is dayly wished of

Yonr truely affected Friend.

———

THE PRINTER TO THE READER.

MARTIN Mar-Prelat was a bonny lad,
His brave adventures made the prelats mad:
Though he be dead, yet he hath left behind
A generation of the Martin kind.
Yea, there's a certain aged bonny lasse,
As well as he, that brings exploits to passe;
Tell not the bishops, and you s' know her name,
Margery Mar-Prelat, of renowned fame.
  But now, alas, what will the prelats doe ?
Her tippit's loose, and Boreas 'gins to blow ;
Shee'l scould in print, whole volumes till they roare,
And laugh to see them strangled in their goare;
While Boreas blows, shee'll put his wind in print,
And venture life to strike their fatall dint :
Shee'll doe as much for south, for east, or west,
If they'll but venture to blow at the beast :
For 'tis high time the winds should joyne as one,
To bluster vengeance on that cursed throne ;
Margery will joy, to see that happy day,
The winds conjoyn'd to blow the beast away :
How e're the north sends forth a lusty gale ;
A board ye prelats, and goe hoyst up sayle :
This wind will drive you to the Romish coast,
Fear not to goe, the Pope will be your host:
To speed your voyage, if you want some wind,
Margery will helpe you, though she break behind.
If this verse (reader) doe offend thy nose,
Vox Borealis brings perfumed prose,
  Which is so pleasant, that you cannot chuse
  But laugh to read this merry Northerne News.

———

Willie.

BROTHER Iamie, welcome to Berwicke : What hath drove you
hither so soon ?

Iamie.

O Billie Willie, thee does little kenn the cause, but ile tell ye :
When our brother Scouter came to Scotland, he left me to supply
his place; but I have had a hard task of it; for the search at London
was hotter then the presse at Paris, and the new invented oathes exceeded the Spanish inquisition : For all Scots men should have been sworn

to fight against the cause of God, his conscience, and his countrey. And I will tell thee truly, they were three such enemies, as I durst not venture against them, and therefore took my heels and ranne away.

Willie. Now well away fall them was the cause of that; on't! there's London news, indeed; have you no better?

Iamie. I had once good store of news in my pocket-book, but was betyde them made me burn it.

Willie. Burn it, brother, how came that to passe?

Iamie. Marie, I was forced to doe it, or els the hangman had done it for me, and, perhaps, burnt me with it; for all Scots men are counted Heretiques by the popes publication; and there's some of Bishop Bonners * brood alive at London, that faine would make marie-bonefiers of us.

Willie. Oh, this moves me much, and the more, because my noates had almost as bad luck as yours; for one day, being riding to water my horse, he stumbled, and I fell over head and luggs in the river, where I was like to be drowned; and all my papers (being in my pocket) were quite spoyled, insomuch as I cannot read them: But now, seeing our brother is here, let us rubbe up our memories, and recollect our collections, and he shall put it down in the best order we can deliver it; and you shall begin first, quoth Willie. Content, quoth Iamie; and thereupon he began as followeth :

> *My Fellow Scouters,*

I mean not to trouble you with any forraigne news, as of the conveening of the conclave of cardinalls at Rome, and of their consultations about the Scots businesse; nor how they have had a solemne procession, with prayers, for the good successe of the cartholique cause; nor how they have agreed to give a cardinalls cappe to † such as shall have the fortune to bring home the lost sheep againe to the Romish pitfold.

Nor will I trouble you with the mighty Spanish fleet now preparing (that in eighty-eight being but like a few fisherboats unto it) which, for a while, meanes only to hover up and down the seas; or, perhaps, to dance the Canaries a turn or two, and, when they see who is like to carry away the most knocks, then they mean to shuffle in for a share.

Nor how Banier is gone to Bohemia, plundred Pragge; and, if Generall Leslye were once come to him with 10000 Scots, he then would give the emperour a visit at Vienna.

Nor how the French embassadour hath importuned the hyring of some Venetian gallies for Marcellus, which is conceived had been imployed for the recoverie of the ilands of Gernsey and Gersey, to which his master layes a little, and is out of hope ever to have them, unlesse now, when the King was busie in this expedition for Scotland.

---

* Who, with Queen Mary's commission, burnt, and otherwise persecuted, all that opposed Popery.   † Archbishop Laud.

Nor of the King of Denmarks dealing at the Sound, and els where, in detayning all Scots commanders and provision from them that came there.

Neither will I insist how little the Hollanders observe either confederacie or conspiracie in these troubles, they selling powder and shot to the one, to kill the other; and armour to the English, for defence against the Scots, shewing themselves right juglers, that can play with both the hands, so they may have profit. But I leave all these things to the news-mongers at London, and onely tell you what I heard concerning our own troubles.

They say at London, that the cause of this combustion proceedeth from a quarrell for superiority, between black-capps and blew-capps; the one affirming that cater-caps keep square dealing; and the other tells them that cater-capps are like cater-pillars, which devoure all where they may be suffered; and the round cappe tells the other, that their cappe is never out of order, turn it which way you will; and they stand stiffly to it, that blewcapps are true capps, and better then black ones.

That they are, quoth Willie, and, if it comes once to the hurling of capps, we shall have ten to their one, let all the cater-capps in Christendome take their parts.

Others tell us, quoth Iamie, that there arose such a heat of hierarchie at Lambeth, as melted all the monopoly money * in the Exchequor: And it is thought, if the river had not been between, it would have quite consumed the power of the parliaments. But, however, it hath cast such a myst among the courtiers, as they cannot discerne what the quarrell is, but are led on hoodwincked, like so many blind buzzards, they not knowing whether, nor for what, nor to what end.

When a warre was concluded upon, then they began to differ about the generall, some alledging that it required one that had been in service; and others conceived, greatnesse of persons might asmuch availe, as goodnesse of commanders: But the papists, fearing that their patron should be jusled out by another, hung their lippe, and vowed they would not contribute, unlesse a papist were preferred; which was yielded unto, for fear the expedition should have miscarryed.

We heard from Scotland, haw the covenantters hoped that the King would get none but Papists and Atheists to fight agaist them, unlesse the King of Moroco sent him some of his Barbarians; and that they have chosen, for their chief ensigne, the silver bible, and flaming sword, which they will never put up, untill they have whipt the whore of Babylon out of their kingdome; and then, if they fight for any thing after, it will be to cast all their casheered mytres in a crown.

But the English tell us another tale, how the Kings army cares neither for their ensigne, nor them, but will teach them such cannonicall doctrine, ere they have done with them, as they never heard in Scotland before.

That the citizens of London refused to lend money, untill all monopolies were put down; whereupon, to please the people, thirty-

* Money raised by patents granted for the establishment of monopolies.

three patents were called in at a clappe : But, indeed, they were onely such as the proctors could make no benefit by.   But such as yeelded any profit (though with the greatest grievance) were never medled withall.   So as the proctors are grown now worse than before, whose cankered conditions can never be cured, untill a parliament cause their necks to be noynted with the oyle of a hempseed halter.

That the papists and prelats, and all deanes and doctors, gave very liberally towards those warres ; and, to say the truth, good reasons had they to bear the greatest burthen, who were the chiefest causers of it, and are the greatest burthen to the land, and will reape the greatest benefit by it, if their designe did not deceive them.

That the prelats had a project to make all the lawyers likewise to contribute to it, which caused great contention between them : whereupon, the bishops would have turned the common-law in cannon-law, and courts of equity, into simplicity : But a great lawyer opposed it, and told them plainly, that albeit it was spoken abroad, that the judges had overthrown the common-law, and the bishops the gospell, so as we may be said to be of no religion, that live neither under law nor gospell, yet he hoped to see a parliament, and then it would appear, who were parliament proofe, and who not.

Now Gods blessiug be upon his heart, quoth Willie, and, if a parliament come, I hope to see some of those bigg-bellied bishops, like so many false fellows, for all their knacks and knaveries, to shake their shanks upon a gallowes: For, if Gregory once get them under his hands, all their tricks and trumperies will not serve their turne, but he will make them and their corner-capps, look awry on their businesse.

Oh, quoth Iamie, they are too much maintained into it to come to that, for they suffer no other doctrine to be taught, either in court or countrey, but for the maintaining of ecclesiasticall authority ; and they have so prevailed, as every man stands in doubt which side to turn to.   Let us fight for episcopacie. says one : Let's stand for the truth, says another : but then comes the Kings proclamation, and that stoppes the mouth of all questions.   In the mean time, the clergy cannot but laugh heartily at the peoples simplicity, who are so forward to fight for them that are their enemies.

This businesse hath been carryed with such power and potencie, as there are many men which find armes to this expedition, that would be loath their sword should be drawn in the quarrell ; and many ministers purses appeared to this contribution, whose prayers went the clean contrary way : Yet, to please the prelats, and for feare of suspension, they were content to allow to this collection.

That all the doctors, about London, have long laboured for eight groats in the pound, of house-rent, for parsons duties, which, in some parishes, amounts to eight thousand pound per annum, and in some to five thousand pound, in others to three thousand pound, and the least about five hundred pound per annum ; which was like to have been effected the sooner, because they would have given the first two yeares increase towards the Scots Expedition.

Oh, quoth Willie, there had been brave places for our Scots Bishops.

Give them a rope and butter, quoth Iamie. But now you would laugh to see how lown-like our lord bishops walk up and down London, with halfe a score of casheered Scots ministers after them, like so many mourning pilgrims, all of them, as in a procession, waiting upon the old archbishop; but ye ken there is an old saying, ' There can be no holy procession where the divel carryes the crosse. Such alterations and innovations have been in the English churches, as he, that had been but three yeare absent out of the kingdome, could not have told at his return how to have behaved himselfe in the churche, when to have sit, nor when to have stood; when to have prayed, nor when to have read: but, as a dumb Diego, must crouch and kneel as the rest did, yet know not for what.

But God be thanked, since the Scots businesse begun, the church hath had a pretty quiet nappe of rest, and ceremonies stand at a stay.

That, in the heat of altering altars, much contention was amongst themselves. Some would have candlesticks placed, and all other implements; and others would have an altar made ready first, to receive the sacrifice when it should be sent them; insomuch, as the great doctor of all church-ceremonies protested, ' He was more troubled with the too much conformablenesse of some, nor with the non-conformablenesse of the others:' and the reason was, because the one runnes too fast on before, for the other to follow after. This is no small grace for conformers: why, herein they were like Mr. Michael Scot, who found the devil, his master, more worke than he was able to doe.

That Paul Tune-man, of the Temple, having spent a yeares preaching, to prepare his auditorie to admit of an altar, at the last prevailed; whereupon, that it might be the more perspicuous, he would not suffer any thing to stand neare it. But he brake his backe with the removing of the pulpit, which stood before it. And when he heard that the king and the Scots were agreed, and that the altars were like to down againe, away he went into the countrey, where, for very grief, he gave up the ghost, and shut out his feet and died: at whose buriall, a good old doctor brought this for his text at his funerall sermon, ' He which was killed betwixt the temple and the altar;' and his application proved true. He consumed his estate in suits with the Templers •, and spent his spirits in labouring to maintain the lawfullnesse of the altar: so he was killed between the one and the other.

That a madde cappe, and (I believe it was a blew one) coming in one day to a new altered church, and looking upon their implements, told his friend that was with him, ' That their altar betokened alteration of their religion; their plate, pride; their clasped booke, obscurity from the communality; the cushion, lazinesse in their calling; and their two darke tapers, blindnesse and ignorance: for, if their light shine no better than their blind tapers, it will never be able to light any man to heaven.'

There hath been such a number of ballad-makers, and pamphlet-writers, imployed this yeare, as it is a wonder every thing being printed, that hath any thing in it against the Scots, as the Loyalties speech, that

---

• Viz. The lawyers at the Temple.

there was any roome for that (which was made in Queen Elizabeths time, upon the Northerne rebellion) and now reprinted; but the author was ashamed of his name: after that dropt the Irish bishops booke, which cryed downe all the Covenanters, and called up some Iesuite to maintaine this Northerne combustion, worse then the Gunpowder-treason: and, if none come, it is thought he will act the Iesuites part himselfe, in something hereafter.

The first fruits of his grand service, was that hot prize which he played in the Starre-chamber of Dublin, at the conventing of Mr. Henry Stewart, his wife and two daughters, with one Iames Gray, for not taking the oath: his virulent revilements against the cause, and the maintainers thereof, made his face pale as ashes, and his ioynts to quiver, which argued an ill cause, and a worse conscience: but the saying proves true, *corruptio boni pessima*, the better man, the worse bishop.

After this, one blurts out a book, wherein (as if he had been a messenger from warres) he undertakes the ungirding of the Scots armour, but, God be thanked, his arme was too short to reach them; and I hope Gregory Brandon will one day gird him up in a hempen halter, or St. Iohnnestone ribband.

Pox upon those priests, quoth Willie, let us heare somewhat els, for the's no goodnesse in them.

Then, quoth Iamie, I will tell you somthing of poets and players, and ye ken they are merry fellows.

There was a poore man (and ye ken 'povertie is the badge of poetrie)' who, to get a little money, made a song of all the capps in the kingdome, and, at every verse end, concludes thus,

> Of all the capps that ever I see,
> Either great or small, blew capps for me.

But his mirth was quickly turned to mourning, for he was clapt up in the Clinke*, for his boldnesse, to meddle with any such matters. One Parker, the prelats poet, who made many base ballads against the Scots, sped but little better, for he and his Antipodes were like to have tasted of Justice Longs liberalitie: and hardly he escaped his powdering-tubb, which the vulgar people calls a prison.

But now he sweares he will never put pen to paper for the prelats againe, but betake himselfe to his pitcht kanne, and tobacco-pipe; and learne to sell his frothie pots againe, and give over poetrie.

But ile tell thee, I met with a good fellow of that quality, that gave me a few fine verses; and, when I have done, I will sing them.

In the meane time, let me tell ye a lamentable tragedie, acted by the prelacie, against the poore players of the Fortune play-house, which made them sing,

> Fortune my foe, why dost thou frown on me? &c.

Or they having gotten a new old play, called, 'The Cardinalls Con-

---

* The Bishop of Winchester's prison in Southwark.

spiracie, whom they brought upon the stage in as great state as they could, with altars, images, crosses, crucifixes, and the like, to set forth his pomp and pride. But woefull was the sight, to see how, in the middest of all their mirth, the pursevants came and seized upon the poore cardinall, and all his consorts, and carryed them away. And when they were questioned for it, in the high commission court, they pleaded ignorance, and told the archbishop, that they tooke those examples of their altars, images, and the like, from heathen authors. This did somewhat asswage his anger, that they did not bring him on the stage: but yet they were fined for it, and, after a little imprisonment, gat their libertie. And, having left them but a few old swords and bucklers, they fell to act the Valiant Scot, which they played five dayes with great applause, which vext the bishops worse then the other, insomuch as they were forbidden playing it any more; and some of them prohibited ever playing againe.

Well, quoth Willie, let the bishops be as angry as they will, we have acted the Valiant Scot bravely at Berwicke; and, if ever I live to come to London, Ile make one my selfe to make up the number, that it may be acted there to, and that with a new addition; for I can tell thee, here's matter enough, and ye ken that I can fence bravely, and flish flash with the best of them.

Nay, quoth Iamie, I believe you may save that labour, for every ladde at London learnes to exercise his armes: there has been brave branding amongst the boyes there upon this businesse, and they have divided themselves into three companies, the Princes, the Queens, and the Duke of Yorks: the first were called the English, the second the French, and the Duke of York were called the Scots Company, who, like brave blades, were like to beat both the other two. And I can tell thee, that there has been such hot service amongst them, that some of their youngest souldiers have been faine to be carryed heame out of the field: whereupon it was blabbed abroad, that boyes had done more then men durst doe here at Berwicke.

But all this sport was little to the court-ladyes, who begun to be very melancholy for lacke of company, till at last some young gentlemen revised an old game, called,

Have at thy coat, old woman.

But, let the old woman alone, she will be too hard for the best of them.

With these, and the like passages, the time was spent, untill news came of the peace, which did not please the prelats, yet they could not tell how to helpe it: faine would they have pickt a quarrell, but knew not how, untill ill-lucke at last did helpe him. For it seems that the Scots commissioners had made some noates of remembrance of such speeches as had been past between the king and them upon the pacification, which they gave unto the English nobilitie, who being (after the kings return) to give in accompt of their proceedings to the rest of the councell, they were questioned for having the said noates; and every one made some excuse, and, like simple honest men, confest their sillynesse; and were content to have it proclaymed, that they never heard such words spoken: Now, forsooth, because they could not hang a few papers, therfore they commanded they should be burnt by the common hangman, who, at the time appointed, came in as great state, as if he had been to bishop, or brand, Bastwick and Burton againe, to the Pallace-yard (alias, the prelats purgatory) with a halter in each hand, with two trumpets touting before him, and two men with a few loose papers following him; where, after reading of the proclamation, Gregory, very ceremoniously, put fire to the faggots, and so the poore innocent papers payd for it: when he had done, he cryed, 'God save the king,' and flourished his roapes, ' If any man conceale any such papers, he shall be hanged in these halters;' with which words, I was so afraid, that I runne home, and burnt all my papers, and so saved him a labour.

Now I wish the wagge in a widdie, quoth Willie, that so abuses king and counsell, as we may not keep a few papers for them; what a mischiefe meane they; are they ashamed of their doings, that the people must not know how things goe?

So it seems, quoth Iamie; but, if any thing were worth the hearing, it should be proclaimed with sound of trumpet; as ye kenne, the last Lent, the troupers used to ryde up and down streets from city to court, and from court to countrey, with their trumpets before them, which made the people run out to see them, as fast as if it had been the bagge-pipes playing along before the beares: but, at their returne, all that was layd aside; and, as if they had been ashamed of themselves, they stole into the town alwayes in the duske of the evening, where somtimes two, somtimes three, would come home together, driving their horses before, and a poke-mantle lying on the saddle, with their boots and sword tyed on the toppe of it: these lodged in Smithfield, and fed as long on their horses, as their hoast durst let them.

Others came home on foot, with their saddles on their backs, for they had sold their horse skinnes, and shoes, where they fell lame by the way, and these men landed at Pye Corner, where, after they had sold their saddles, like rusty rascalls, they eat out their swords.

Now I have told you all I can remember, for I came away assoone as the papers were burnt: but, if I had not been apparelled like a poore parson, all in blacke, with a cannonicall coat, I had been robbed many times by the way; for the souldiers returned home by hundreds, and all was fish that came in the net, where they could catch any thing. But, upon Newmarket heath, I mist my way, and met with a shep-heard, who told me, ' It was no wonder to see me so, for most of the ministerie had been out of the way for a long time together, and had misled the king to an unthriftie iourney, wherein he had spent more money than all the clergie of the kingdome were worth.' Well, quoth I, to the shepheard, every one to their calling, thou to thy hooke, and I to my booke; and so away I went, and never met with any thing worth noating by the way: so as I will onely sing my song, and con-clude.

SIR Iohn got on a bonny browne beast
  To Scotland for to ride a,
A brave buffe coat upon his back,
  A short sword by his side a.
Alas, young man, we Sucklings can
  Pull down the Scottish pride a.

He danc'd and pranc'd, and prankt about,
  'Till people him espide a;
With pye-ball'd apparrell, he did so quarrell,
  As none durst come him nye a.
But soft, Sir Iohn*, ere you come home,
  You will not look so high a.

Both wife and maid, and widow prayd,
  To the Scots he would be kind a;
He storm'd the more, and deeply swore
  They should no favour find a.
But, if you had been at Berwicke and seen,
  He was in another ruffe a.

His men and he, in theiri ollitie
  Did drinke, quarrell, and quaffe a,
'Till away he went like a Jack of Lent:
  But it would have made you to laugh a,
How away they did creep, like so many sheep,
  And he like an Essex calfe a.

When he came to the camp, he was in a damp
  To see the Scots in sight a,
And all his brave troops, like so many droops,
  To fight they had no heart a.
And, when the allarme cal'd all to arme,
  Sir Iohn he went to shite a.

They prayd him to mount, and ryde in the front
  To try his courage good a.
He told them the Scots had dangerous plots,
  As he well anderstood a.
Which they denyed, but he replyed
  It's shame for to shed blood a.

He did repent the money he spent,
  Got by unlawfull game a;
His curled locks could endure no knocks.
  Then let none goe againe a:
Such a carpet knight as durst not fight,
  For feare he should be slaine a.

    * Suckling, governor of Berwick.

Well (quoth Willie) as I remember there was some song here also at the camp of him. And I will sing so much of it as I can, because I will begin as you have ended; but mine is a more sinister verse then yours, for it hath two foot more, and it is to be sung, to the tune of Iohn Dorie, as followeth :

> Sir John got on an ambling naggc,
>   To Scotland for to goe,
> With a hundred horse, without remorse
>   To keep ye from the foe.
> No carpet knight ever went to fight
>   With halfe so much braveado ;
> Had you seen but his look, you would swear on a book
>   Hee'd conquered a whole armado.

But the valour of the knight, and the veyn of the poetrie, are both of so course a thred, that I had rather tell you the rest of it in plain prose.

Willie (being to make his relation) after a little pause said, ' It's not my meaning, Sirs, to mention any thing which happened in our way towards Berwicke ; neither what spoyles and pillagings the souldiers exercised ; nor how the troupers robbed and rifled every one they met with, and forceablie took away whatsoevir they could lay hands on, without respect of conscience.' And it seems the countrey had as little spirit, as they had conscience ; for could ever a free state, especially in time of peace, iudure such insolencies against persons, states, and families, and that from the scum of men, voyd both of fortitude and righteousnesse ; but such as had lost all tincture of their progenitors spirit, and subjected themselves to perfect slavery. An uncle of mine, well verst in military discipline, told me, ' That if Gretians, Romans, yea or Turks, were here to see a sort of whitelivered raggamuffins, under the name of souldierly overrunning, a warlike famous people from their very originall, witnesse the Romans testimony of them, they would say it, either they were not the same people, or, by way of transmigration, they had sent their soules to the Hollander :' but the Duke of Buckingham, alias, of our destruction, by the plot of his pragmatick bandeleer, Sir Dudley Larbetom, first bridled them, and sadled them, for the rutters to mount on ; which though they mist, yet they never cast the bridle and saddle, so that who will may ride them. But Ile leave such things to those that, if they durst, would faine complaine, and have cause to sing, The lamentation of their losses.

But I cannot omit to tell you of the great threatnings which were thundered out against the covenanters, all the way as they went along, and every molehill was made a mountaine, to aggrivate their rebellion ; and every man vowed to be revenged, though he neither knew of whom, nor for what : But, by that time that we had been there encamped three nights, we found (besides the Scots armie) two strong enemies more then we expected (hunger and cold) which so sharply assayled us, that, if our foes had not proved our friends, in relieving us, we had suffered much misery.

That, within a week after our first coming, sundry of our souldiers surfetted with eating of fresh salmon, insomuch, as they were ready to mutinie for want of meat; whereupon, by advise of councell, it was fit they should have libertie to take what they could get beyond Tweed.   But the honest souldiers knowing, that sweet meat must have sowre sauce, would not venture for it.

Then it seems, quoth Iamie, that they are bnt fresh water souldiers, not yet seasoned with the souldiers life; how would they be able to hold out a winter leager, if they cannot shift out a summer with good fresh salmon ?

A winter league, quoth Willlie, would burne all their bones in the north, for the best of them is no body, without a feather-bed at his back ; and either a dish of beef and brewesse, or bacon, and bagge-pudding in hfs belly; but, if he have that and his double beere, and his drabbe, he will stand to it stiffly.

Marie, now I remember, quoth Iamie, that they call a bagge-pudding Londons Joy; and I beleeve its that which makes many of them so bigge-bellied; but, if they cannot byte of a bannock, and bibbe of the brooke, they are not fit comerages for me; for I can fare hard, lye hard, and fight hard; and, if my tobacco-box afford me but two pipes a day, I shift out well enough for any thing else.

It must be better tobacco, quoth Willie, then that which the common souldiers had in the camp, which the sutlers made of cabbedge-leaves, and dock-leaves steeped in pisse, and dryed, with the blossomes of green broom.   This they sold for four pipes a penny; but it did so smoake and stinke, as if they had burnt their huts.

At our first coming, there was a great quarrell between the mus-queteers and the archers in the armie, about precedencie: The one saith, ' Hee's the onely man now in use; and the other blurts out his bolt, and tells them, ' That bows and arrowes won Bolloyne.' But a tall strippling, standing by, told them, ' That a minced pye was more acceptable then either;' and offered, ' If any man durst gainsay it, and would meet him at Berwicke bounds, with a minced pye, and two pew-ter spoons; if he did not beat him at his own weapons, he would be content to fast two dayes after.'

That it was feared, so soon as the army went home, there would have been civill warres between the men and the women, in the Northern Countreys, for superiority; partly because the men had done no feats of arms worthy of so brave an appointed army, and the ancient fame of their countrey; telling them, ' If they had been in their place, they would either, by valour, have won the breeches, or left their mothers daughters.   Others of some quality stormed, that their husbands were not knighted, and they ladyfied ; and told them, in some heat, ' That, if they could not be knighted under the banner, they would go nye to knight them under the curtin.'   But a witty blade, somwhat better experienced in the laws of Venus, than the rest, and having learned in the Low-Countreys to shelter himselfe behind a cannon basket, derided the matter very daintily, and gave the women good satisfaction: It's true, quoth he, that that old propheticall adage proves now too true:

> Waters shall waxe, and woods shall waine,
> And unman shall be man, and man shall be naine.

Where can this rather be verified, than in womens imperious thoughts, irrationall commands, usurped government, and metamorphorised apparell? Wherin women, against the laws of God, nature, nations, they act man, and play the very viragons. Man, by the contrary, being too vigorious, looseth God, his image, in his priviledge; in sitting in the saddle, and giving her the reines, he unmans himselfe; and, being woman in all, save wherin his wife would not have him; so he sitteth down in effect with Sardanapalus to the distaffe: But, to meddle no more with this hornet nest, and come to the particulars: You are to know, ladies, the huglesh spirit is not all lost; but our great plenty, much ease, and long peace, all ill used, have shortened our spirit, and made us to seek, except it be to roare, pipe, and pot in tavernes, and ale-houses, to make children gaze at buffe calfe and feather; with damnable oaths and villanous deeds to terrifie and torment the people; and, as many of them, in practise, know not the right hand from the left, so many of their commanders are ignoramusses in the very vocables of art: But, as the constable said to the captain, ' We must be dissembled in a trance; our commanders must learn to command, and we to doe; we must learne to creep before we goe; to stand before we dance; and how to handle armes, and to endure some hardship, before we fight.'

Againe, noble Amazons, take notice, that we had no commission to fight with the Scots; which if we had had, we would have gone nigh to have frighted them as ill, as the cowes of Barwick frighted us; but we were onely by flourishes to scare them; witnesse our going to Kelso market, to see how meat rated.

But, in the third place, a greater block then both these lay in the way, and that which hindered a shop-broken taylor, turned steward in a ship, to fight, namely, Want of a good cause. It is enough, thinke I, to venture bodies, though we venture no soules; and what shall a man have, but a vanishing vapour of report, when he hath sacrificed himselfe?

Lastly, If we had killed the Scots, the Papists would have cut our throats for our paines; and, as for knighting, I assure you, gentlewomen, a great many more have it, then can tell how to use it: And so the women were well pacified.

That there came divers carpet knights to the camp, onely for fashion, not for fighting, whose chiefest attendants are either poets, or players; at whose returne you shall either have the second part of Hobia Moko, or els Polydamna, acted, with a new addition. But, if it had once come to knocks, then you must have expected a tragedie instead of a commedie; as, The Losse of a Loyall Subject, The Prodigals Repentance, The Sucklings Succour, The Lost Lover, or some such pretty peece,

That, all the time the camp lay here, we had most lamentable wet wether, as if the heavens had mourned with continuall rayne, which our camp scarse called Scottish Teares; but I am sure it made good the old saying, A Scottish mist will wet an English-man to the skinne: And well it might be, for there was neither care taken for huts, nor tents; but, assoone as it was faire againe, in the sun-shine, they went all in hunting the lousie lare, where they made good that riddle, which put Homer to a stand: What they found they left behind them, and what they could not find they tooke with them. But, having done execution upon those grudge-pikes, at their returnes, they would bragge how many covenanted enemies they had killed, since they went out.

Why (quoth Iamie) were any covenanters killed? We heare no such news at London.

It is but onely a beare (quoth Willie) to call their lyce and back-byters their covenanted enemies.

Let them jeare on (quoth Iamie) if they dare kill nothing els but lyce, then I am content they should never have other imployment; for, indeed, it was told at London, That there was nothing among the souldiers in the Kings camp, but lyce, and long nayles, which, it seems, was all the imployment they had, or blood, which was shed there.

No (quoth Willie) they durst not doe so much as goe into Scotland to kill either man or beast there; and this they gave out for their excuse, That all the ground was undermined betwixt Berwicke and the Scottish camp, so as they durst not march on, for feare of blowing up. But they needed never feare that; for, unlesse the English Matchevilians undermined the Scots covenanters, and, by a long tayld traine from London to Edenburgh, blew up the parliament there (least they blew up the bishops) there is nothing els to be blown up.

That here, in the north, the kings coyne, which had been for so many yeares rackt out of the countrey into the kings coffers, hath been now most prodigally spent; and the monopoly-money, which hath lyen so many yeares mould in the exchequor, is now so well sunshined, and so often turned over from hand to hand, as it will not come there to be rusty againe this seaven yeares.

It is thought this climate hath an extraordinary operation in altering of mens constitutions and conditions; for our gallants have both changed their voices, and their words, since they came from London; for there they used to speake as bigge as bulbeggers, that fight in barnes, and at every word, Sirra, Rogue, Rascall, and the like. But it is otherwayes now; for their words are as if they whispered, for feare the Scots should heare them, and their words are turned to, Honest Iacke, Courage Souldiers, and the like; so as, if we had stayed but a little while longer, we should have been all fellows at football.

That a great many old souldiers lived by their shifts; some counterfeited fortune-tellers, some iuglers, and some moric-dancers; and, indeed, they sped best of all; for, whilst the wives without conveighs (which lay lurking about the house) would either get a duck or a henne, or others, perhaps, a lamb, or a pigge; and home they came to the camp, oftentimes with halfe a dozen of women at their heels, crying, Stoppe thiefe, stoppe; but never an honest man was in the way, and it is not the fashion for one thiefe to stay another. But, when they came to their huts, then there was all the sport to see them quarrell for dividing of it, untill the marshall or provost came, who, to stint the strife, kept it to himselfe: So, oftentimes, he that set it never eat it.

Oh (quoth Iamie) what belly-gods are these, that will robbe the poore people? If they had played such pranks in Scotland, they had been well banged, both backe and side.

I warrant (quoth Willie) that the northerne people dreamed of these broyles, many yeares agoe; for they have been so provident to prevent them, as they never planted any orchards: For, if there had been either fruit above ground, or roots in the ground, nothing had been left them; for they marcht by pares up and down, looking for a prey; but, as I tell, the countrey cozened them for that.

That one day, in a misty morning, about a dozen of camp royane ruffins had a desire to plunder a countrey village in Scotland. I will ranke them in order as they went out, least their disorderly returne home prevent me: First, there rode two carrubins, who in their rusty armor, and starved stalliones, lookt like a couple of brewers servants in leather jerkings, made of old boots, ryding for old caske. After them followed two light horse-men, with great saddles and petreonels, like a couple of fidlers with their musicall instruments in cases.

Next to these marcht foure footmen, with sow-skinne knapsaks, and halfe-pikes, like foure Banbury tinkers, with their buggets at their backs. And after them some musketeers with their rests in their hands, and their bandeleers about their neks, like so many sow-gelders. When they came to the village, the men were gone to the market, and the women were at milking. The horsemen stood behind the barnyard to receive what the others should bring them. The musketeers marcht into the milke-house, and the pikemen to the henroost, where the foules began to flutter, the geese to kekcle, and the dogs to barke, and all the village was presently in an uproare. Out came a wench crying, Come out, come out, for here are theeves come to robbe us: With that an allarum was beat on the bottome of an old kettle; and out came all the wives very well weaponed, some with rockes, some with forks, and some with flailes, crying, Where are these false swearing theeves? But, assoone as they found them, they so belaboured the poore pikemen, as happy was he could get first free from them; yet at last they got loose, and followed their horsemen, who fled away assoone as ever they heard the fray begin. In the meane time the musketeers had so panged their panches with butter-milke and whay, that they could scarce get out of the wives gripes, to come to their horsemen. But what with feare, and their strugling with the women for the victorie, most of them made bold with their breeches. But at last, when they see that the wives stood so stiffly to it, they ranne as fast away as they could; but there was such a wild goose chace, between the wives and them, as hes beene seldome seen, insomuch as, the poore pikemen having over-heat themselves, the butter-milke and whay had such an opperation, as they had got such a squirt, that the women could trace them wheresoever they fled; and still, as they overtooke them, they did so beswaddle them, that they cried for quarter. 'What is this,' quoth a woman, 'that the lowns calls quarter? If thy quarters have not enough, they shall have enough. Alas, Cummer, quoth another, he cryes for mercie: Then, quoth she, false thiefe, cry God this mercie, and Ile let thee alone. The poore man learned the language, and so that fray ended: But, withall, they promised never to come into that kingdome any more. When they had their libertie, it was bootlesse to bid them runne; for away they went with asmuch speed as their legges could carrie them. But a man might have found them by the sent all the way. All the spoyle, that this fray afforded, was onely their bandaleers for the boyes to play withall, and their rests for rockes for the wives to spinne withall.

Now Gods blessing and mine, quoth Iamie, light upon the good wives, for they have played their parts bravely. And I hope the English army never troubled them for it.

No, quoth Willie, but they lay upon the lurch a good while after for a revenge, and one day, early in the morning, stole into Scotland, thinking to have taken them tarde: But, when they came there, albeit they had shuffled all the coat cards in their own hands, and so thought it had been a won game; yet, when they saw clubbes turne up trump, they gave it over as a lost game, and never after offered them any injurie; but some of the souldiers were so trampled and trod upon, in their suddain retreat, that divers of them dyed presently after their returne; amongst whom, one, more godly then the rest, desired to have his will written; but there was none to doe it but a poet, and he made it in verse, which was as followeth:

BEING sore sicke, and ready for to dye,
Yet thanks be to God, in perfect memorie,
My will I make. And, first, I do bequeath
My soule to Christ, my body to the grave:
My braines unto my countrey, that they may
Not brainsick runne in such bad deeds as they.
My eares unto the King, that he may heare
His subjects suits in peace, and not in wearre.
My eyes unto the state, that they may see
All false seducers of his Majestie.
My tongue to such as dare not the truth tell.
My mind to those that thinke all is not well.
My nose to those that have not perfect sent,
To smell out those as hinder parliament.
My hand to him that meanes to shed no blood.
My heart to those that for the gospell stood.
My broad backe to the Protestants, that they
With patience suffer, and in love obey.
My legges I leave to lame men, to assist them:
If Scots come on, there's many that will misse them.
My feet to Franck who hath no heart to stay,
That better he may scape, and runne away.

I know no fit executor for this will:
But, if that any please it to fulfill,
I leave them power; and doe begge with teares,
England and Scotland to be overseers:
That each may have their own due legacie.
Soe farewell friends: Death calls away for me.

Within two or three days after this retreat, there was an agreement made between the two armies, and both of them were to dissolve their forces. Whereupon order was given in the Kings camp, that every man should have a monethes pay to carrie him home to his countrey: But the captaines and commanders did so shuffle and shirke the poore souldiers, that some of them had nothing, and the most had but foure or five shillings a piece, to travell three hundred miles: Yet, to give the devill his due, they did them a court-courtesie, in giving them a passe home to their countrey, with a licence to begge by the way, and a tiquet to all maiors, iustices, constables, and the like, not to trouble the stocks, nor whipping-posts, with any such souldiers as came from the Kings camp.

Now good gibbie get them, quoth Iamie, and ye kenn, that, if he once shake hands with any, they had need say their prayers, for they are not long lived after it. But what silly souldiers were those that would be put off so? Marie, it is no mervell then they begged and robbed all the way home. And so deeply swore, They would rather be hanged at home, then ever goe abroad in the Kings camp againe.

They could not helpe it, quoth Willie, for they might tell their tale one to another, for no-body els would heare them. And besides, they were so glad to be gone, as they never stayed for any conduct or company; for they were not so farre in love with the businesse, as to play Loath to depart: But every man shifted for himselfe, as soon as he could, for feare he should have been called backe againe, and put upon some new imployment there.

We could never, quoth Iamie, understand the truth of the agreement at the camp, some told one thing, some told another.

The effect of the agreement, quoth Willie, was thus, in brief, That both the armies should be dissolved. That the Kings castles should be surrendered. That the Kings shippes should depart the Firth. That a set assembly should be called, and have libertie to settle the government of the church. That a parliament should immediately follow, which should ratifie the assembly, and redresse the grievances of the kingdome.

Their demands, as I was informed, were these; that, besides the holding and confirmation of the assembly, to be holden by the succeeding parliament, they desired these particulars, namely, That the Scottish delinquents should be sent home to their tryall; Restoration of the states dammages, and, lastly, Security from further danger from the fireworks ingeneers of this combustion: And, whether these were granted or not, not to meddle with hand or seale, I referre myselfe to the martyred papers, and the consciences of some of the English lords.

Good agreements, brother, but badly performed : For assoone as the armies were dissolved, and the King possessed of the castles of Edinburgh, Dumbarton, &c. new cavells were raysed against the covenanters. And it was reported, That, under the colour of a parle with the lords at Berwicke, they should all have been detayned, and sent prisoners to London. But, as good happe was, they went not, but excused themselves to the king, because the appointed assemblies was then to begin, which hath since quite abolished bishops.

The King seemed displeased, and thereupon placed Generall Rothwen governour of the castle of Edenburgh. And now he, having gotten that by a tricke, which they never could have gotten by strength, keeps a couple of false knaves to laugh at the lords, a foole and a fidler ; and, when he and they are almost drunke, then they goe to singing of Scots iigges, in a jearing manner, at the covenanters, for surrendering up their castles.

The fidler he flings out his keels, and dances and sings :

> Put up thy dagger, Iamie,
> And all things shall be mended,
> Bishops shall fall, no not at all,
> When the parliament is ended.

Then the fool, he flirts out his folly, and, whilst the fidler plays, he sings :

> Which never was intended,
> But onely for to flam thee :
> We have gotten the game,
> Wee'll keep the same,
> Put up thy dagger, Iamie.

The devill a dagger, quoth Iamie, shalbe put up by me, nor, I beleeve, by any man in the kingdome, untill the parliament be ended, and have confirmed the putting down of bishops ; wee'll be no longer flim-flamb'd by any of them. And, for this trick, we will have that false papisticall traitor Rothwen, and all his knaveries, out of the castle ; or else we will make it too hot for him to hold it. I am in such a rage at these rascalls, as, if I had them here, I would beat them both black and blew, and teach them to sing another song, called, ' The Lowns Lamentation ;' yea, and make them dance after my pipe, ere I had done with them.

Peace, quoth Willie, patience will bring all to perfection, and time will discover the truth. But if this pacification was onely pretended, that they might get the castles into their custodie, and the parliament but onely promised, and never intended to confirm the abolishing of bishops, then we have just cause to doe that which was never dreamed on.

Dreamed on, quoth Iamie, if dreames prove true, I shalbe master of a mytre ere it be long ; for every night I am so troubled with finding of mytres, crucifixes, rich copes, and the like, that I thinke, to my comfort, it wilbe my fortune to fall upon the rifling of some of those belly-god bishops houses, before this warre be ended; and then let me alone to expone my dreame. And I hope, if I take pains, to pull down popery in such a manner, as it will not trouble my conscience hereafter.

I would it were come to that, quoth Willie, if it must needs come to it; but it were better the businesse ended in a peaceable way.

That will never be, quoth Iamie, for there is a time when Babylon must down, and the bishops, who are but whelps of that whores litter, must down before her; and why may not the time be now? For the pope had never such a blow as Scotland now hath given him; and, if England give him but such another, it will make him stagger.

Ha, Iamie, there thou hitst the marke, for all the pollicie that I have can never possesse me any possibility of bringing peace and safety, except the bloudy and undermining locusts be sent to the bottomlesse pit, from whence they came; and the whole litter of the whores whelps, as thou callest them, the bishops, with all their appendices, be rooted out: yea, except some carpenters arise, and saw off these strong hornes of the beast, which, by stickling, make so many leakes in the English church, she and all in her are like to perish; and then those hellish pirats, worse than Tunnees and Algeir, will have a bout with the bordering of the Scots: but I hope they shall be hanged first. The Scots have set the English a faire coppy, and, if they cannot write for these also, the Scots will lend their hand, if they be willing to learne. Yet not to write a letter, much lesse a line of rebellion; for, as they may compare with any nation in the world for their loyalty, so to terme the saving of the church, king, and state rebellion, is of the devill, the father of lyes.

I am confident, that the English will not be so forgetfull of their honour and profession, as to make such use of the Scots, as the monkey made of the spannell, in pulling the chestnut out of the fire with the spannells foot: but, as mutual necessity craves mutuall ayd, so I hope the Scots and English will, in a brotherly conjunction, like Ioab and Abijhai, help one another against the Syrians and Ammonites; that is, forraigne and domesticke enemies. ' If the Syrians be too strong for me,' saith Joab, ' then thou shalt helpe me; but, if Ammon be too strong for thee, then I will come and helpe thee,' 2 Sam. x. 11. The application is easie. But whither am I gone, certainly beyond both packe and packe pin, yea, and the warehouse too.

O Billie Willie, that some good engine had the hammering of this, and it might prove a bonny piece. But I meane well. Now to close up all, as I wish, with the spirit, and happinesse to attend those that dash Babels brats against the walls: so let both nations take heed of that curse denounced against those ' that doe the worke of the Lord negligently,' Psal. cxxxvii. 11. Jer. xlviii. 10.

By this time we were called to supper, and thereupon gave over discourse: and the next day after departed all three for Edenburgh, where agreed over againe to owne the hazard of a new journy to London, to see how things were carryed there. But the manner of the carriage, and how we shall dispose of our selves there, cannot be resolved till we

see the successe of this parliament. Till when, and ever, we remaine
ready to do our utmost indeavours in any thing that may tend to the
good of this kirk and kingdome.

POSTSCRIPT.

THROUGH fire and water we have past,
 To bring you Northerne news:
And, since as scouts we travelled last,
 We now that name refuse.

But, if henceforth new broyles appeare,
 And warre begin to rise,
Castiliano like, wee'll cloth our selves,
 And live like Spanish spyes.

THE

ATHEISTICAL POLITICIAN;

OR,

A BRIEF DISCOURSE

CONCERNING

NICHOLAS MACHIAVELL.*

The intention of this discourse appears to be levelled against the government and
ministry of K. Charles I. and by way of apology for Machiavell, which, I
think, is very artfully composed, endeavours to depreciate Archbishop Laud and
the Earl of Strafford, by alledging them to be more dishonest than Nicholas
Machiavell.

NICHOLAS Machiavell is cried down for a villain, neither do I
 think he deserves a better title; yet, when I consider he was not
only an Italian, but a courtier, I cannot chuse but commiserate his fortune, that he, in particular, should bear the marks, which belong to the
wisest statesmen in general.
 He, that intends to express a dishonest man, calls him a Machiavil-

* Published about the year 1641. Quarto, containing seven pages.

lian, when he might as justly say, a Straffordian *, or a Cantibirian † : we embrace the first apparition of virtue or vice, and let the substance pass by untouched.

For, if we examine the life of Lewis the Eleventh of France, we shall find he acted more ill, than Machiavell writ, or, for aught we know, ever thought, yet he hath wisdom inscribed on his tomb ; and, had he not kissed his crucifix ever after the doing a dishonest thing, pronouncing a sentence or two, that discovered the complexion of his heart, he might have past for as honest a man as all wise ancestors or any prince living in his time, who now lie quiet in their graves ; a favour this man is denied by ignorant and ungrateful posterity.

He was secretary to the State of Florence, of which he hath written an excellent and impartial history ; he had lived in the days of Pope Alexander the Sixth, been familiar with his son Cæsar, and what these princes were is sufficiently known.

No time was fuller of action, nor more shewed the instability of worldly honours, than the occurrences that happened in Italy at this time. Now, from a man wholly employed in court affairs, where it was thought madness to look beyond second causes, worse things might have been with better reason expected, than these so bitterly condemned ; which are, indeed, but the history of wise impieties, long before imprinted in the hearts of ambitious pretenders, and by him made legible to the meanest understanding ; yet he is more blamed for this fair expression, than they are that daily commit far greater impiety, than his, or any pen else, is able to express.

It was his profession to imitate the behaviour of princes, were it never so unseemly : nay, religion cannot condemn the speculation of ill in ministers of state, without laying herself and professors open to all injury.

For, upon how great disadvantage should a good prince treat with a bad neighbour, if he were not only familiar with the paths of wickedness, but knew other ways to shun them, and how to countermine their treacherous practices ?

Do any blame Albertus for writing obscenely ? Nay, do not they rather call him the Great, because he hath so plainly set open the closet of nature ? Indeed, if any man can pretend a just quarrel to Machiavell, they are kings ; for, as it is the ordinary course of light women to find fault with the broad discourse of that they maintain their power by, so statesmen may best blame the publication of these maxims, that they may put them in practice with more profit and security.

The unjust steward is commended for his worldly wisdom, and, what doth he say more of Cæsar Borgia, than that he was a politick tyrant ? An dif. without leave of the text, he propose him for an example, yet it is of ill : and who is more fit to be a pattern to a villain, than one of the same coat ?

Most of the estates in Italy did then voluntarily, or were compelled to change their masters ; neither could that school teach him any thing

---

* Alluding to the Earl of Stafford, beheaded in K. Charles I's reign.   † Alluding to Archbishop Laud.   N. B. These two were looked upon by the Author, and many others, his cotemporaries, to be evil counsellors to K. Charles I. and, as such, were Machiavells in England.

more perfectly than the way to greatness, nor he write a more acceptable treatise than aphorisms of state.

He saw the kingdom of Naples torn out of the house of Angieu by Ferdinand, and the people kept in tyranny both by the father and son ; he saw the no less mad than disloyal ambition of Lodowick, Duke of Milan, who took the government upon him out of the hands of young Galeas, with as much treachery and cunning as Francis Sforca, father to Galeas, had done from the Dukes of Orleans; he beheld Charles the Eighth, King of France, brought into Italy by the said Duke of Milan, to keep the people at gaze, whilst he poisoned his nephew, who was to expect the dukedom when he came of age ; he saw the descent of Charles winked at by Pope Alexander the Sixth, in hope to raise a house for his son Cæsar out of the ruins of some of the princes, in which he was deceived; for the French King made himself master of all Italy, entered Rome twice, put the holy father to take sanctuary in the castle St. Angelo, and there to subscribe to such conditions as the victorious king was pleased to prescribe him ; upon which his holiness came out : and, though Charles, in shew of reverence, did kiss his foot, yet he took his son Cæsar for hostage, to secure the performance of his promise, though he covered it with the name of ambassage, ever to reside with the king, in token of amity; and, after Cæsar had made an escape, the holy father, contrary to his oath, made a league against the French King.

He was an eye-witness of an amity contracted between the vicar of Christ and his known enemy the Turk ; with whom he * agreed for money to poison his † brother, who was fled into Christendom, for fear of Bajazet, then reigning, and was under the pope's protection at Rome; and might have been of excellent use to any prince that would have invaded the Turk, had not his holiness observed his promise to this monster, which he seldom kept with the best of men.

After all this, he saw the French King lose all Italy, with the same dexterity he had gained it; and Pope Alexander and his son both overthrown by one draught of poison, prepared by themselves for others; of which the father died presently, but the son, by reason of youth and antidote, had leisure to see, what he had formerly gotten, torn out of his hands, and he forced to flee to his father-in-law, the King of Navarre, in which service he was murthered.

To these ambitious practices of princes may be added the domesticall impiety of the pope, who was a corrival with his two sons in the love of his own daughter, the lady Lucretia, whom they all three enjoyed ; which bred such a hatred between the brothers, that Cæsar, being jealous that the other had a greater share in her affection, killed him one night, and threw him into the Tiber : nay, it could not be discerned when the head of the church spake truth or falshood, but by the extraordinary execrations he used, when he meant to deceive.

Neither are these only the commodities of Italy, but the usual traffick of all the courts in the world ; for the mark that God hath set upon Jeroboam, who, according to our dialect, may be stiled the Ma-

* The Pope.   † The Grand Seignor.

chiavell of the Jews, cannot scare most princes out of his path; and
how many kings have failed to set up altars, both at Bethel and Dan,
when they think their power may be weakened by the people going to
Jerusalem? Saul, being a private man, went to the prophet to ask after
his father's asses; but, being a king, went to the devil to know the success of a battle.

Christ himself saith, ' Not many great, not many mighty are called :' men in soft raiment may be found at court, but their consciences
are commonly seared and hard.

This makes me think, the wise men, that came from far to see our
Saviour, thought him an earthly prince, and not the King of Heaven,
else they would never have sought him in the court of Herod, from
whence nothing could come but cruelty and oppression.

The church of Rome, that did anciently deserve honour of all the
world, after it came to be a court, grew fruitful only in impiety; and,
though we do acknowledge her still to be a church, because she hath
all the lineaments of religion in her, yet they are so blended in superstition, pomp, and cruelty, that it is no easy task to find the truth amongst
them. For as a good fruit-tree leaves not to be the same as it was before, though covered and embraced with ivy and ill-weeds, the natural
daughters of time, which neither spare things sacred nor prophane; so
Rome may be called a church still, though covered with trash and idle
ceremonies; in which the pope and the cardinals shroud themselves, so
as, if knowledge, occasioned by the illumination of God, had not
houted them out of some corners of the world, they had not only
made good, by an unquestioned prescription, those errors in being, but
brought in more; and, being themselves masters of all temporal estates,
and were there nothing else against them, but greatnesss and impiety,
it were enough to convince them of falshood and novelty: pride is acknowledged by all to be the root of ill; now where doth it prosper so
well, or grow so strong as in princes, and such as do attend on their affairs? The effects of which sin can be contained in no narrower compass,
than the whole mass of impiety that is apt to commit; for it made
Phocas to kill his master, Cæsar to overthrow the liberty of the bravest
common-wealth that ever the world did, or is likely to behold; it
prompts the hands of children to pull unseasonably the pillows from
under the heads of their dying fathers; it is this that fills heaven and
hell with souls, the earth with blood; this pride made Charles the
Fifth to arm himself against his own pope, that very year in which
God had done him the honour to take one of the greatest monarchs in
Christendom prisoner; it caused his son Philip to mingle the blood of
his own child with the infinite quantity he spilt upon the face of Europe; yet his thirst could not be quenched, though he set a new world
a-broach in America, which he let run till it was as void of people,
as he was of pity.

Is a prince named in any chronicle, but in red letters? Nay, what
are chronicles: registers of blood, and projects to procure it, yet none
blames them that write them. I do not intend to make an apology for
him, being so well acquainted with the miseries of those, that are so un-

happy as to fall under the government of such principles ; all I aim at is, to prove that, if he were justly arraigned, he could not be condemn-ed by men in like place, who ever were his peers, if not worse, because advice without execution hurts only the giver.

Yet Machiavell saith, what prince had not rather be Titus than Nero ? But, if he will needs be a tyrant, he shews him the way that is least hurtful to his temporal estate, as if he should say, thou hast made thyself already an enemy to God and thy people, and hast no-thing to hope for, beyond the honour of this world, therefore, to keep thee from the fury of men, be sure thou art perfectly wicked, a task not hitherto performed, it being yet beyond example, that any tyrant should perform all the mischief that was requisite for his safety, no more than the best kings did ever all the good ; and of this he makes Cæsar Borgia, Alexander the Sixth's son, a pattern, who removed all the impediments that stood between him and his desires, and provided against all cross accidents but his own ; being sick at the time of his father's death, which hindered him so, as he had no leisure to attend his business, which was to make one succeed in his father's place, that might, at least, have favoured his projects : but I verily believe, as I see by daily experience, that those which go on in the same track, though they have brought their purposes to as happy a conclusion, yet they shall not want impediments, or discontents, that shall out-talk the pleasure of their ambition ; but, since it is oftentimes the will of God to give success to ill means wisely contrived, who can advise better than this Florentine ? A member of the Roman church, and is, in that regard, to be less blamed, because he had as much religion as the pope then in being ; with whom all impieties were as familiar as the air he breathed in.

Neither are these rules he speaks of omitted in the best kings, if they be wise ; for which of them doth not dispatch his ungrateful ac-tions by deputies ; and those that are popular with his own hands? Do any observe their promise so exactly, as not to fail when they see the profit greater than can be expected at another time ? And all this he saith only to a prince. For, had he given those documents to a son, or any other that had filled any narrower room than a kingdom, he might, with juster reason, have undergone all censure ; but, being to make a grammar for the understanding of tyrannical government, is he to be blamed for setting down the general rules of such princes? Now, if falshood and deceit be not their true dialect, let any judge that reads their stories : nay, cosenage is reduced into so necessary an art amongst them, that he, that knows not how to deceive, knows not how to live. That breach of faith, in private men, is damnable, and dishonourable, he cannot deny; but kings seem to have larger charters, by reason of their universal commerce ; and, as ambassadors may be excused, if they lye abroad for the good of their country, because they represent their masters persons : with far greater reason may they do it, than they that employ them, provided they turn not the edge of these qualities towards their own people, to whom they are tied in a more natural and honest obli-gation.

For a common-wealth is like a natural body, and, when it is all together, shews a comely structure; but search into the intrails, from whence the true nourishment proceeds, and you shall find nothing but blood, filth and stench : the truth is, this man hath raked too far in this, which makes him smell as he doth in the nostrils of ignorant people; whereas the better experienced know, it is the wholesome savour of the court, especially where the prince is of the first head.

A

DESCRIPTION OF THE SECT

CALLED

THE FAMILY OF LOVE:

With their common Place of Residence.

Being discovered by one Mrs. Susanna Snow, of Pirford near Chertsey, in the County of Surrey, who was vainly led away for a Time, through their base allurements, and at length fell mad, till by a great Miracle shewn from God, she was delivered.

O Israel, trust in the Lord, for in the Lord there is mercy, and with him is plenteous Redemption. Psal. cxxx.

London printed, 1641. Quarto, containing six pages.

IT was in the county of Surrey, at a village called Pirford, three miles from Chertsey, there dwelt a gentleman by name Snow, who had to his daughter a very beautiful and religious gentlewoman, who was not only a joy to the father, but also an exceeding joy to the mother ; she had not long gladded the hearts of her parents, with a virtuous and dutiful behaviour, when the devil, arch enemy to mankind, sought to subvert and eradicate this well planted virtue, and thus it happened :

This gentlewoman, Mrs. Susanna Snow, for so was she called, holding prattle with one of her father's men, one day began to question with him about the new sects of religion which now were so much talked of, enquiring what news he heard of any of them.

He answered, that it was his chance to be at a little village called Bagshot, not six miles from thence, where he heard of a company that got residence there, and every day had a meeting in a private place, which was mistrusted to be about the sign of the Buck, and they called themselves, The Family of Love; and most have a great suspicion that they came from London, and their number is about an hundred; but he told her it was the talk of the whole country. This Mrs. Susanna heard with patience, and marked with diligence every particular; she gave the servant but little answer, but she vowed in her heart to see the fashions of this sect.. Well, night grew on, and to bed they went; but she prevented the early sun in being up before her, so great a desire had this poor gentlewoman to thrust herself into danger. After she had broke her fast, and caused her man to set a side-saddle on a gelding, alone she took her journey, vowing not to return, till she had seen some of their behaviours which were of the family of love.

Thus she rode along undisturbed by meeting any passengers, till she came within half a mile of the village of Bagshot; but then she saw at the least an hundred persons, men and women, crossing over the heath, bending their course towards a wood called Birch-wood; to themwards she rides, and overtaking a sister which lagged behind the rest, she cried, well overtaken, sister; the sister of the family bid her welcome. Sister, quoth Mrs. Susanna, is your habitation here about Bagshot? The sister answered, That she sojourned in Bawwago. Then quoth she, sure you can resolve me one question, which is this, Do you know of any that came from London lately; there were about the number of an hundred, I was of the company, but they came away unknown unto me; and I heard that they sojourn here about this coast. The silly sister was not aware of her guile which she spoke, but answered her, that this was the company she meant sure. Mrs. Susanna asked again, Are these of the family? she answered, yes. Then Mrs. Susanna rode after, and overtook them, where this woman revealed the conference she had with Mrs. Susanna, and how that she thought her to be very zealously affected to the family; on these words, although she were unknown, yet she was entertained into their society, and went along with them.

Now you must understand that they have certain days, which are dedicated unto saints as they call them, as to Ovid, who wrote the art of loving; to Priapus, the first bawdy butcher that ever did stick pricks in flesh, and make it swell, and to many others, which they used to spend in poetising in the woods; thither they come, and after many pastimes there enacted, the poet desired them to sit down on the green, and then he began to speak most strong language, as this or the like, Let not us persuade ourselves, although that many would have us to believe it, that our great god Cupid is obeccated, for he penetrateth the intrails of the most magnanimous; after these or the like words, he recited part of a verse from Virgil's epigrams:

——*Non stat bene mentula crassa.*

Which to English I forbear, because it is obscene; on this he built his whole discourse, venting very strange obscene passages; after this was done, they go to dinner, where they had exceeding delicates, and after this repast they provided to return. Now here you must note, that the poet, viewing this new sister of the family, was so mightily inflamed with her, that either he must enjoy or perish; when they were walking home, therefore, he singled her out from the rest of the company, and spoke to her as follows:

' Fair sister, hard is that task, where I must die in silence, or else present unto you an unseemly suit; but so irksome is death, and so pleasant the enjoyment of my wishes, that I rather desire to be counted unmannerly than not amorous to your beauteous self.'

With these and such like words he courted her, till at length time and opportunity both favoured him so much, that she plaid a maids part indeed; she said, nay, and yet took it. This novice, having had his desire, conducted her to the company, and there left her among the rest of the sisters, where she staid for the space of a whole week, viewing their fashions, as the manner of their prayers, of their preaching, of their christening and burying, with many more things which will be too long for this little pamphlet to bear.

Now when she had seen as she thought enough, she stole away from them, not ceasing to think of the wrong she had sustained, by her consenting to the lust of the poetical brother; well, discontented she passed the way till she came in the presence of her father; he asked with very mild and loving terms, where she had been; she answered him, at her aunt's at Oakingham; with which answer her father was satisfied, but her mother was not, because she had sent thither before, to see if she had been there; yet her mother could get no other answer from her, than that she had been there; but seeing that she was come home again, they questioned the matter no more where she had been. But she had not been at home long, when she began to delight to be by herself, and to make much of melancholy, taknig delight in nothing, wherein she did heretofore; this her loving parents took notice of, but would not speak of it, and thus she continued for the space of ten or fourteen days; at last, she began to be very untowardly, and they could not rule her, for she would break glasses and earthen ware, and throw any thing at the heads of the servants, and incontinent she fell stark mad. I cannot express her father's grief, when he saw his only beloved daughter in this plight; but I will leave you to judge of it who have children of your own, how it would grieve you to see your children in such a plight. Her father, although he were almost distracted with grief to see his child thus lie on the wreck of misfortune, summons up his senses together, and at length he thought upon one Mr. Ybder, a very honest man, and a most reverend divine, living in Oxford; to him he sent, requesting him of all loves that he would come, and visit him in this his great distress; he presently dispatched horse and man, for Oxford they were bound. The man coming to Mr. Ybder's chamber, which is in Magdalen Hall, he found him within, to whom he delivered his message. Master Ybder came along with him; he was no sooner arrived at Master Snow's house, but the poor gentleman almost frantick for his daughter's distemperature, with tears in his eyes, began and related, what you have here before read, to Master Ybder, who presently desired that he might but see her. This good old man, with all diligence, being still in hope of her recovery, conducted him into the chamber where his daughter was; she had no sooner fixed her eyes upon them entering, but she shreeked out, and cried, the devil, the devil; I am damned, I am damned, I am damned, with many such like horrid horrible exclamations; then stepped forwards Mr. Ybder, and told her that she was deceived, God surely would not leave her soul so, if she would but endeavour as she had done heretofore, for said he, " Christ came not into the world to call the righteous, but sinners to repentance;" and again, " Seek and ye shall find, knock and it shall be opened unto thee; and although thou hast played the harlot with many lovers, yet return again unto me, saith the Lord," at the third chapter of Jeremy, and the first verse.

She hearkened unto Master Ybder very patiently, for the space of half an hour, but then she began to be very troublesome, and sometimes outrageous; at last, she called for some wine, for she was very thirsty, she said. Wine was brought unto her in a Venice-glass; her father, good old man, spoke to her to drink to Mr. Ybder, for he had taken great pains with her; she looked very wildly on him, and threw the glass to the ground, with these words, ' That it was as impossible for her to be saved, as for that glass to rebound into her hand unbroken, which, contrary to the expectation of all, this glass did;' Well, said this gentlewoman, I will yet trust in the Lord my Redeemer, for he is merciful and long-suffering; with these words she praised God, and began, as from the beginning, to relate the case of her distemperature, desiring Mr. Ybder, that he would pray with her, and for her; and thus by the mercy of God was this gentle-woman delivered.

ROME FOR CANTERBURY;

OR,

A true Relation of the Birth and Life of

WILLIAM LAUD, ARCHBISHOP OF CANTERBURY.

Together with the whole Manner of his Proceeding, both in the Star-Chamber, High-commission Court, in his own House; and some Observations of him in the Tower. Dedicated to all the Arminian Tribe, or Canterburian Faction, in the Year of Grace 1641. Whereunto is annexed a Postscript in Verse.

Printed in the Year 1641.   Quarto, containing eight pages.

GREATNESS and goodness are two several blessed attributes conferred upon man; but seldom meet in one person; greatness may be stiled a gift inferred by fortune: but goodness, a grace infused by God. The first labours in mistrust, and is born the bond-slave of chance, seldom attended without envy; and, though to many persons it appears exceeding pleasant, yet the higher we are seated, although by virtue, the greater is our fall, if corrupted by vice. By honour and office men become great; yet it is not the place that maketh the person, but the person that maketh the place honourable: And that preferment and power, which is both well acquired, and worthily conferred. *Non est invitamentum ad tempus, sed perpetuæ virtutis præmium;* is no temporary invitation, but a perpetual inheritance.

Goodness is of a contrary condition; men are not to be accounted good, either for their authority or age, but for their sincerity and actions: He, that is good, is better than the good he doth; and he, that is evil, is worse than the bad deed done by him. All great men are not considerately good; but all good men are consequently great. Greatness and goodness, with grace added, to cement them together, make unquestionably a perfect and compleat man. Here was grace, which, had it been celestially inspired, as it was but temporally disposed, might to that greatness have so combined goodness, as, from thence, could have grown no such tribulation.

Howsoever, let no man grieve at his present afflictions; for they are the rods, by which God chastiseth his children: There is nothing that the world can take away from us, because it can give nothing unto us. Fame fadeth, potency perisheth, wealth wasteth; true riches consist in our constancy in casualty, and, though perturbation and punishment be the prison of the body, yet courage and comfort are the liberty of the soul, to which I only add patience, which is so allied to fortitude, that she seemeth to be either her sister or her daughter. Things, that compulsively come upon us, should be borne with patience and courage, of which we have had a late precedent; and more generous it is for a man to offer himself to death in triumph, than to be drawn unto it with terror: *Gaudet patientia duris.* I come now to the person.

He was born at Reading, of honest parents; his father was a clothier in that town, of a competent estate, and careful to see his children to be well educated and instructed. This his son William, being of an excellent wit, and pregnant capacity, was sent from the grammar school to Oxford, where he was admitted into St. John's College, where shortly he proved an ingenious disputant; and before he took his first degree of batchelor, was well versed in logick, philosophy, and the liberal arts; after he devoted himself to the study of theology, in which he proceeded doctor, with no common applause, attaining to the dignities belonging to so famous an academy; and, being of an active spirit, was called from thence to the court, where he grew so gracious, that, after some private preferments, he was first made Bishop of St. Davids, and thence, removed to London; and, after the decease of the right Reverend George Abbot, Archbishop of Canterbury, was inaugurated into that prime see, and was metropolitan of all England; steps that his predecessor, who was a clothier's son in Guilford, had trod before him, who in less than two years was Bishop of Coventry and Litchfield, London, and Canterbury.

What this prelate's deportment (now in agitation) in so high a dignity was, is sufficiently noised amongst all; made apparent by his Draconical censures in the Star-chamber, the high commission court, &c. And it was a great aspersion justly cast upon such high authority, that he so much affected *summum jus,* justice without mercy, as sparing neither person nor profession; and, to leave all others, witness, how he did persecute the good Bishop of Lincoln, Dr. Williams, being of his own degree and function: His (more than) severity in his rigorous censure and sentence upon Master Burton the divine, Master Prynne the lawyer, and Doctor Bastwick the physician, and even that poor fellow Thomas Bensted, whom he caused to be hanged, drawn, and quartered; he could make that a matter of treason, though he was but a subject: His threatening of honest judges, his menacing other officers and ministers of the King, his sternness and surly answers even to gentlemen of worth, and now parliament-men, who have but pleaded for poor men, in just causes: It was a good wish, that either he might have more grace, or no grace at all, which is now come to pass.

It is observed by some, that, in all the time of his pontifical prelacy, he never promoted any to church preferment, that savoured not of the Arminian sect; and still, when benefices fell, that were either in his gift, or where his power was to have them bestowed, he hath caused such men to be instituted, and inducted, as either were dunces in learning, or debauched in their lives: Such men being most apt, for their temporising or ignorance, to embrace any innovation that should be brought into the church: Nay, when places have not been void, but supplied by pious pastors, and devout ministers, that were constant professors of the protestant faith, yet, by spies and intelligencers, such cavils have been made at their doctrines and disciplines, that, notwithstanding their charge of wife and children, and that their utter undoings impended upon the taking away of their means, yet they have been supplanted, that the other might subsist in their places; the first turned out, the latter taken in; but that which far transcends the former, that he hath laboured to suppress the French and Dutch protestant churches here in London, who, for their conscience and religion's sake, have abandoned their countries to avoid persecution, and have made this famous city their asylum and sanctuary for themselves and families.

It hath been observed also, that he never gave censure upon a jesuit, or seminary, or any Popish priest, though brought before him by his own warrant, and the pursuivant employed by himself. For, though apprehended, yet they were never punished; but, if to-night imprisoned, to-morrow infranchised and set at liberty; or else he so cautelously and cunningly dealt by his agents, Secretary Windibank, Sir John Lambe, and others, that they were sent abroad, and he seen to have no hand in the business; when, in the interim, all the rigorous sentences that passed him, were against the zealous professors of our protestant religion.

A poor curate, having long waited to speak with this great archbishop, and being, after much attendance, admitted to his presence, in their discourse, the great metropolitan told him, he was an idle fellow; to whom the other replied, it is most true, for, had I not been so, I could not have spared so many idle hours to attend upon your grace, to such small purpose. At which he being much moved, said, Why, what fellow dost thou think of us bishops? Who replied, I will, in plain terms, tell your grace what I think of you: I can no better compare you, than unto the huge brass andirons, that stand in great men's chimnies, and us poor ministers to the low creepers: You are they that carry it out in a vain glorious shew, but we the poor curates undergo, and bear the burthen. Another told him, when he used to play upon other men's miseries, that his lordship must needs be witty (he being a very little man) that his head and his heart were so near together.

Some have observed, that, as he was a prelate, and primate, so he greatly favoured the letter P. (by which may be conjectured) the Pope, whose emblasons, amongst other of his pontifical escutcheons, are three bishops, viz. (I take it three bibles); and, to shew he much affected that episcopal letter, his three benevolent and well beneficed chaplains were Browne, Bray, and Baker. And, for the letter P, he was also a great patron and protector to Dr. Pocklington, who, for publishing one book, called, Sunday is no Sabbath, wherein he vilified all the observance due to *Dies Domini*, the Lord's Day; and another, intituled, The Christian's Altar, wherein he would have first produced, and after propagated popish superstition, he did confer upon him three or four benefices, worth some two or three hundred per annum, and a prebendary in Windsor, valued at three hundred more by the year.

Many are the probabilities that he purposed to bring popery into the kingdom; as the Scotch Service-book, differing from our English liturgy, especially in words concerning receiving the eucharist, or Lord's supper, which was the first incendiary of all these late troubles between the two kingdoms of England and Scotland, in which some blood hath been drawn, but infinite treasure exhausted. Apparency needeth no proof; but that we leave to the censure of the higher powers, being an argument, as it hath been long, so now at this present in agitation: Yet the better to define that which before was disputable, when he came first into the Tower, and not being acquainted with the place, he desired, that by no means he should be lodged where the Bishop of Lincoln had before lain; and, being demanded the reason, because they were sweet and good, he made answer, O, but I fear they smell so of puritanism, that the very air will half stifle or choak me. These, sympathising with the rest, may give the world room to suspect his religion.

Upon Monday, being the tenth of May, when it was known that the lieutenant should prepare himself to die, tidings was brought to the archbishop of the setting up of the scaffold upon Tower-hill, whereon the deputy of Ireland was to suffer death; he immediately spoke to his men, saying, It is no matter when or where we die, so we first have time to make our peace and reconciliation with God; we are all of us born to die, though there be many several ways to death; for death must at last conquer, and have victory over the bodies of all flesh whatsoever. Be of good comfort, do not ye be discouraged for me: I am a man of sorrow, and born to this sorrow: Lord, give me strength to bear thy chastisements patiently, and endure them constantly, even to the end and period of my life: I am indeed a man born of a woman, of a short continuance, and full of trouble and heaviness; a man indeed, made like to vanity, and compared to the flowers of the field, here this day, it may be, gone to-morrow; nay, I am worse, a child of wrath, a vessel of dishonour, begotten in uncleanness, living in care and wretchedness, and dying in distress. O Lord, I will cry unto thee night and day, before I pass through this vale of misery; I will sum up all my offences, I will confess my vileness before thee, and will not be ashamed; for true confession is the very way whereby I may come unto thee, who art the way, and the only true way, that leads unto life eternal.

O the most happy life which the angels enjoy, in the right blessed kingdom, void of death everlasting; where no times succeed by ages, where the continual day without night hath no end, where the conquering soldier, joined to that joyful choir of angels, and crowned with the crown of everlasting glory, doth sing to his God a song amongst the songs of Sion.

I meddle not with any state business whatsoever; but it seems he bore no great affections to the Scots, which is probable, by the little love they bare unto him: But most sure we are, that he was arrested of high and capital treason, first committed to the knight of the black rod, and thence conveyed to the Tower, where, ever since, he hath been in custody of the lieutenant, of whose demeanor, during his abode there, I shall next speak, by the true information of some credible persons that have observed his deportment. He was not only frequent and fervent in, and at his orisons in his own chamber, where he spent the greatest part of the morning at his private meditations, but very careful and observant at the week day's service, at the chapel; but especially on the Lord's Day he came duly, and prostrated himself devoutly on his knees, giving great attention both to the service and sermon; and taking special notice of some particular psalms that were sung before the parson went up into the pulpit, especially the second part of the three and thirtieth psalm, the second part of the forty-ninth, and the first part of the hundred and fortieth, which are worthy any man's reading, being so aptly picked out for that purpose, he called the clerk unto him, and courteously demanded of him, Whether he happened on them by accident, or had called them out by his own conceit? The plain old man ingenuously confessed unto him, That he chose them out purposely to put him in mind of his present estate; at the which he modestly smiling, made him no further answer, but departed towards his lodging. Further, he was heard to say, that, if ever God delivered him from that present durance, and that the King would restore him to his pristine dignities, he would much improve that place, meaning the church, in remembrance that he had been there a prisoner. It is also reported, that a gentleman of quality coming to the Tower to give him a visit, and, asking his grace how it fared with him at that present; he made him answer, I thank God I am well, for it hath pleased his sacred Majesty, my Sovereign, to provide for me an honourable and convenient lodging, where I have good and wholesome fare, and where, notwithstanding all my troubles and tribulations, I never yet broke an hour of my usual and contented sleep. And the morning when the late Earl of Strafford passed by his lodging, as he was led to the place of execution, and moved his hat unto him, then standing, and looking out of his window, he held up his hands and eyes towards heaven, without speaking any thing audible to the observers, as if he prayed earnestly, and inwardly, for the salvation of his soul, &c. He was observed also sometimes to speak those words of the psalmist, Psalm lxxxii. ver. 6, 7. I have said, ye are gods, and children of the Most High, but ye shall die as men, and ye princes fall like others, &c.

POSTSCRIPT.

All, bishops! Where's your power you brag'd of late
Was unremoveable? Where's that glorious state
You pray'd in? Are your pompous mitres, copes,
Thus quickly chang'd for halberts, if not ropes?
What! has the blue-head Scot thus turn'd the game,
That what before was glory, now's your shame?

Can Lesley's regiment thus wheel about,
The brigade of our clergy ? Put to rout
Our bishops, deans, and doctors ; not a man,
Amongst so vast a multitude, that can,
With all their titles, dignities, withstand
The Switzish-Scottish elderships command ?
Has Calvin's doctrine puzzled all your choir,
Silenc'd your organs, and yourselves with fear ?
Can neither Laud's, nor Wren's, strong canons make
Stiff Henderson subscribe ; nor yet to quake
At the report ? What ! Were they not of strength ?
Or naught'ly cast ? Or did they fail in length ?
Invent some stratagem, employ your brains,
And answer the pure challenger with strains
Of primitive doctrine ; that the world may see
The apostolick warrant for the prelacy.
Employ your chaplains pens, and muster all
The stalls of prebends ; for the time doth call,
And waits an answer : Give some living to
Some scholar, that this venturous task shall do.
The cause concerns you nearly : Will ye not
Now vindicate the quarrel with the Scot ?
Why did ye enter in the lists, and mould
Your canons to dismount Geneva's hold ?
Ye did begin the counter-march, and would
Ye thus fly off again, if that ye could ?
The Exonian prelate hath twice given a charge,
One jesuit hath given fire unto 't at large :
Both miss'd the mark, march on, and quickly mine
Yourselves, and prove your prelacy divine.
Where are your chaplains, all so far renown'd,
Who for your cause, the like could not be found ?
They have great skill in cringing, bowing, writing,
Let's see their weapons, and their skill in fighting :
Produce their arg'ments for such store of wealth,
Gotton by simony, base usury, and stealth.
Let's know your tenure, by what right ye hold
Such store of livings ? And yet starve the fold.
Do not delude us longer with such toys,
More fit for mimick apes, or slaves, or boys :
Now speak, or never, else you will be thought
To be Rome's calves, far better fed than taught,

SIR THOMAS ROE'S SPEECH *

IN PARLIAMENT.

WHEREIN HE SHEWETH

The Cause of the Decay of Coin and Trade in this Land,

ESPECIALLY

OF MERCHANTS TRADE.

And also propoundeth a way to the House, how they may be increased.

Printed in the year, 1641.   Quarto, containing twelve pages.

———

IT is a general opinion, that the trade of England was never greater, and it may be true, that if it be so, yet it will not absolutely conclude, that the kingdom doth increase in riches, for the trade may be very abundant, and yet, by consumption and importance of more than is expected, the stock may waste.

The balance would be a true solution of the question, if it could be rightly had; but, by reason it must be made up by a medium of the books of rates, it will be very uncertain.

Therefore we must seek another rule, that is more sensible, upon which we may all judge, and that may be by the plenty or scarcity of money; for it is a true rule, if money increase, the kingdom doth gain by trade; if it be scarce, it loseth.

Let us therefore consider; first, whether our gold and silver be not decreased, and then by what means it is drained; and lastly, how it may be prevented, and what remedies are applicable to effect it.

It is out of doubt our gold is gone to travel without license, that is visible beyond seas, and every receiver of sums of money must find it privately; and I fear the same of silver, for observing the species of late coining many half crowns were stamped, which are no more to be seen, and by this measure, I conclude the kingdom grows poor.

The causes of this decay of money may be many, it may be stolen out for profit, going much higher beyond seas, especially in France and Holland.

Much hath been drawn away by the stranger upon fears of our

* This is the 156th number in the Catalogue of Pamphlets in the Harleian Library.

troubles, of which I have experience by exchanges, and exchanges are the great mystery, especially such as are used as a trade, and governed by bankers who make many returns in a year, and gain by every one, more than the interest of a year; and the greatest danger to a state is, when money is made merchandise, which should be but the measure thereof.

And here I will propose a problem, whether it were profitable to a kingdom or not, that the stranger for many years had a great stock, here at interest, and still hath some; I confess it hath supplied the necessities of merchants, and helped to drive trade. But my quere is this, suppose the first principal were truly brought in by the stranger, yet doubling every ten years, what becomes of the increase? have they not lived by our trade, and the merchant-adventurers, and soaked the kingdom of as many times principal, as they have practised this usury many times ten years, and in the end drawn or carried all away? This is a point to a state very considerable.

Much coin hath been drawn away, without doubt, by the French, who have brought in wares of little bulk, perhaps without custom, but of dear price, and, having turned it into gold, have returned without investing any part thereof; and such petty merchants cannot be reached by the statute of employments.

Another cause of scarcity of coin, may be the over-strict rule of the uncurrentness of any good coin, and that it must be sold here, as bullion; in that case, what stranger will bring in money? Whereas, if every good species be current, according to this allay, and weight in proportion to our coin, or rather a little higher, it will draw, namely, money by degrees into England; as lower grounds do water from higher, though they see not the channels: And we see France, Holland, and Germany admit all good coins, though foreign, for and above their intrinsick value.

But I will end this search, by proposing some general remedies; for I do now but make essays, and give occasion to more subtle and particular disquisitions:

1. To the first leak of stealing away coin, I would make it felony by an act; for, if a man may justly suffer death for robbing of a private man, I see no injustice nor cruelty to inflict the same punishment upon him that robs a kingdom.

2. That the neighbour princes and states do cry up our money, and so entice it from us. This, in my judgment, ought to be provided for by our treaties, which was the old way, especially of commerce, by agreeing and publishing of placarts, according to a true par: For that prince, that will make a treaty of commerce, doth it for the use of the commodity; which, certainly, I would deny any prince, that would not consent to keep monies even, by their true values; at least, that would set a higher price upon our money, than the King hath done; and if our coin did either keep beyond the seas, the English value, or were bullion and uncurrent, the stronger should have as little of our money, as we have of theirs.

F f 3

How to recover the stranger's money drawn away, since our troubles, is a hard endeavour, and can no ways be brought to pass, but by peace and trade; and the resolution of this will fall into the general remedy, which I shall propose.

The pedling French trade must be met with, by diligent search, at the landing of these creamers, what they bring in, and by suffering none of them to pass any goods by private warrants; but that, according as they shall be valued, they give bond to invest it in English commodities, natural or naturalised, and that with surety: Nay, in this case, not to allow them exchange by bills; for it will not hurt the commonwealth, if, by any rigour, they were beaten out of their private toyish traffick.

I shall not doubt to offend any but the mint, which may be recompensed to his Majesty, in his customs, if money be plentiful; for all goods will follow money. If I did propose the currentness of all goods, and great species of foreign coins, for their true intrinsick value, according to the pay with ours; and if I say a little higher, according to occasions, keeping our own coin pure and constant to be cried down, as much under, according to occasions, I think it will be a policy both reasonable and profitable, by experience tried in other states.

But, leaving these empirical practices, I come now to the great and infallible rule and remedy, which is, in plain English, to settle and assure the ground of trade upon staple-commodities; which, like the lady of Whitsontide to her pipe money, will dance after that; for, as merchandise doth follow money, so doth money, commodity.

I said at first, it was a general opinion, that trade never flourished more than now, and it may be so; but we must consider this be not accidental and changeable, and depending more upon the iniquity or misery of the times, than upon our own foundation and industry; and, if that be so, then it is no sure ground for a state to rely upon; for if the causes change, the effects will follow.

Now it is true, that our great trade depends upon the troubles of our neighbours, and we enjoy almost the trade of christendom; but, if a peace happen betwixt France, Spain, and the United Provinces, all these will share what we now possess alone; and therefore we must provide for that day, for nothing stands secure but upon its own foundation.

To make, then, our own trade secure, we must consider our own staple commodities, whereof wool is the chiefest, and seek the way to both, to keep up the price at home, and the estimation of all commodities made of that, and to be vented abroad.

Some other helps we have, as tin, lead, and such like; but I dare confidently affirm, that nothing exported, of our own growth, hath balanced our riotous consumption at home, but those foreign commodities, which I call naturalised, that is, that surplus of our East-India trade, which being brought home in greater quantities, than are spent within the kingdom, are exported again, and become in value and use as natural commodities; and therefore, by the way, I hold it absolutely necessary to maintain that trade, by a regulation with the Dutch, of which more reason shall be given, when that particular shall be taken into consideration.

We have yet another great help which is our own, and wants only our industry, to gather the harvest; which is our fishing and erecting of busses, both for the inriching of our kingdom, and the breeding of mariners; and this by private industry, though to private loss, is beaten out already, and shall be offered to the commonwealth, if they please to accept of it; and to give you one only encouragement, I do avow, that, before the Dutch were lately interrupted by the Dunkirkers, by their industry, and our fish, they made as great returns between Dantzick and Naples, as the value of all our cloth, which is one million yearly; and this, in a due place, I desire should have its due weight and consideration.

We have one help more, if we knew how to use it, that is, by the new drained lands in the fens, most fit for flax and hemp, to make all sorts of linnen for the body, for the house, and sails for ships; that is a Dutch and French trade: But, in Holland, one acre of ground is rented at three pounds, which if the Hollanders may have in the fens for ten or twelve shillings, it will be easy to draw the manufacture into England, which will set infinite people at work, and we may be able to serve other nations with that, which we buy dear from them; and then the state and kingdom will be happy and rich, when the King's customs shall depend upon commodities exported, and those able to return all things which we want, and then our money must stay within our kingdom, and all the trade return in money. To encourage you to this, I give you one example:

That if the several sorts of callicoes made of cotton wools, in the Mogul's and Dan's dominions, doth cloath, from head to foot, all Asia, a part of Europe, Egypt, much of Africa, and the Eastern islands, as far as Sumatra; which makes that prince, without mines, the richest prince in the world; and, by his Majesty's grace and privileges granted to the Dutch, I am confident we may make and undersel, in all linnen cloth, all the nations in Europe.

But I have now wandered far from my theme, which was the decay of trade, and of the woollen commodity.

I must first, therefore, present to your consideration the causes thereof, in my observations, whereof some are internal, and some external.

The internal have proceeded from our own false making, and stretching, and such like practices, whereby, indeed our cloth is discredited; I speak by experience, from Dantzick and Holland, northward to Constantinople, as I will instance in due time.

This false lucre of our own, and the interruption in the dying and dressing projected, and not overcome, gave the first wound, though, could it have been compassed, it had doubled the value of our commodity.

This hath caused the Dutch, Silesians, and Venetians to attempt the making of cloth, and now, by experience, as I am informed, the half is not vented, that was in the latter age.

Another internal cause hath risen from such impositions, as have made our cloth too dear abroad, and, consequently, taught others to provide for themselves.

Another internal cause hath sprung from pressures upon tender consciences, in that many of our clothiers, and others, have forsaken the kingdom, and carried their arts with them, to the inexpressible detriment of the commonwealth.

The external causes have been the want of perfection, and countenance to our merchants, established abroad in factories, by the state, and by the treaties; whereby the capitulations have not been kept, nor assured to them, neither in Prussia, nor in the Sound, nor Hamburgh, nor Holland, nor in the East; and this I dare say, that Laban never changed Jacob's wages so often, as the Hollanders have forced our merchants to change their residences, and the very course of this trade, by laws and tricks, for their own advantage, of which the merchant-adventurers will more fully inform you.

Another external cause is lamentable, a report of the increase of pirates, and the insecurity of the Mediterranean seas: whereby Bristol, and the western ports, that cannot have so great shipping as London, are beaten out of trade and fishing; and, if once those thieves shall find the way to Bank, and Newfoundland, they will undo the west parts of England.

I will trouble you with a consideration, very considerable in our government, whether, indeed, London doth not monopolise all trade: In my opinion, it is no good state of a body, to have a fat head, thin guts, and lean members.

But, to bring something before you of remedy, I say thus, for my first ground, that, if our cloth be not vented, as in former years, let us embrace some other way, to spend and vent our wools. Cloth is a heavy and hot wearing, and serves but one cold corner of the world: But if we embrace the new draperies, and encourage the Walloons, and others, by privileges, and naturalisations, we shall employ all the wool we have, set more people to work, than by cloth, and a pound of wool, in those stuffs, true made, will outsel two pounds in cloth; and thus we may supply France, Italy, Spain, Barbary, and some parts of Asia, by such light and fine stuffs, as will fit those warmer regions, and yot have sufficient for the cold climates, to be spent and adventured in true made cloth, by the reputation both of our nation and commodity.

But, in this course, I must observe, that these strangers, so fit to be nourished, and being protestants, may have privileges to use their own rights in religion, so as they be not scandalous, as the Dutch and French had granted to them by Queen Elisabeth; and certainly, the settling of religion secure in England, the fear whereof made many weak minds to waver, and abandon this country, is, and will be a great means to resettle both the great and lesser manufactures of woollen commodities.

For the external causes, we must fly to the sanctuary of his Majesty's gracious goodness and protection; who, I am confident, when the whole business shall be prepared for him, and that we have shewed him our duty and love, and settled his customs, in such a bountiful way, as he may reap his part of the fruit of trade; I am confident, I say, that he will vouchsafe you all favour, fit to be conferred upon good subjects; and not only to protect you abroad, by his forces and authority, and by treaties with his neighbours, but by increasing the privileges of merchants at home, and confirming all their charters; the breach whereof hath been a great discouragement unto them; and, without which duly observed, they cannot regulate their trade.

There are some particulars, in the Spanish trade, perhaps worthy of animadversion, as underselling a good commodity to make money, or barter for tobacco, to the imbasement of our own staple for smoke, which, in a due place, ought to be taken into regulation.

Another consideration, for a ground of trade, ought to be the nature of it, with whom, and for what we trade, and which trade is most principally to be nourished; which, out of doubt, are the Northern trades, which are the root of all others, because the materials, brought from those parts, as from Sweden, Muscovy, Norway, Prussia, and Livonia, are fundamental, and of absolute necessity; for, from these trades, get we the materials of shipping, as pitch, tar, cordage, masts, and such like, which inables us to make all the southern trades, themselves, of less use, being only wine, fruit, oranges, and curiosities for sauces, or effeminacy; but, by these, we sail to the East-Indies, and may erect a company of the West-Indies, for the golden fleece which shall be prepared for you, whensoever you are ready for so great a consultation.

The right way to nourish these northern trades, is, by his Majesty's favour, to press the King of Denmark to justice, not to insist on his intolerable taxes, newly imposed upon trade, in the passage of the Sound; in example whereof, the elector of Brandenburgh, joined with the King of Poland, hath likewise more than trebled the ancient and capitulated duties; which, if that they shall continue, I pronounce all the commerce of the Baltick sea so overburthened, that the eastland company cannot subsist, nor, without them, and the Muscovy company, the navigation; but that the materials for shipping will be doubled, which will eat out all trades. I have given you but essays, and struck little sparks of fire before you; my intention is but to provoke the wit and abilities of others; I have drawn you a map, wherein you cannot see things clearly and distinctly; only I introduce matter before you, and now I have done, when I have shewed you the way how to enlarge and bring every particular thing into debate.

To which end, my motion and desire is this, that we may send to every several company of merchants, trading in companies, and under government and privileges; and to ask of them, what are their grievances in their general trade (not to take in private complaints:) what are the causes of decay, or abuses in their trades, and of the want of money, which is visible; and of the great losses, both to the kingdom, and to every particular, by the late high exchanges: And to desire every one of these companies, to set down their judgment, in writing to the committee, by a day appointed. And having, from them, all the general state of the complaints, severally, we shall make some judgments of these relations one to another: this done, I desire to require all the same several companies, upon their own papers, to propose to us, in writing, the remedies applicable in their judgment: which materials having all together, and comparing one with another, we shall discover that truth which we seek ; that is, whether trade and money decay or not? And how to remedy it.

But I have one request more, and so I will ease you of my loss of your time. That when, from all these merchants, we shall have before us so much matter, and without such variety, and, perhaps, not without private and particular ends, that then you will give me leave to represent to you the names of some general, and others disinterested and well experienced in many particulars, who may assist our judgments in all the premises, particularly in money and exchanges, and give us great light to prepare our result and resolution, to be, by the whole house of commons, represented to his Majesty; and, for expedition, that a sub-committee may be named, to direct this information from the merchants.

A

TRUE DESCRIPTION,

OR

RATHER A PARALLEL BETWEEN

CARDINAL WOLSEY, ARCHBISHOP OF YORK,

AND

WILLIAM LAUD, ARCHBISHOP OF CANTERBURY,

Printed in the year 1641. Quarto, containing eight pages.

THERE be two primates, or archbishops, throughout England and Wales, Canterbury and York, both Metropolitans, York of England, Canterbury of all England ; for so their titles run. To the primate of Canterbury are subordinate thirteen bishops in England, and four in Wales; but the primate of York hath at this time but two suffragans in England, namely, the bishops of Carlisle and Durham? though he had in King Lucius's days, who was the First Christian king of this our nation, all the prelacy of Scotland within his jurisdiction; Canterbury commanding all from this side the river Trent to the furthest limits of Wales, and York commanding all from beyond the

Trent to the utmost bounds of Scotland: and hitherto their prime archiepiscopal prerogatives may, not improperly, be paralleled.

In the time of Henry the First, were potent two famous prelates, Anselm of Canterbury, who durst contest against the king ; and Girald, of York, who denied to give place, or any precedence at all to Anselm. Thomas Becket, who was first chancellor, and afterwards Archbishop of Canterbury, in the reign of Henry the Second, bore himself so insolently against the king his sovereign, that it cost him his life, being slain in the church, as he was going to the altar. But, above all, the pride, tyranny, and oppression of the Bishop of Ely, in the reign of Richard the First, wants example ; who was at once Chancellor of England and regent of the land, and held in his hand at once the two Archbishopricks of York and Canterbury; who never rode abroad without a thousand horse for his guard to attend him, whom we may well parallel with the now great Cardinal of France ; and need he had of such a train to keep himself from being pulled to pieces by the oppressed prelates and people, equally extorting from the clergy and laity ; yet he, in the end, disguising himself in the shape of an old woman, thinking to pass the sea at Dover, where he waited on the strand, a pinnace being hired for that purpose, he was discovered by a sailor, and brought back to abide a most severe sentence. Stephen Lancthon, Archbishop of Canterbury, in the time of King John, would not absolve the land, being for six years together indicted by the pope, till the king had paid unto him, and the rest of the bishops, eighteen thousand marks in gold. And thus I could continue the pride of the prelacy, and their great tyranny, through all the kings reigns ; but I now fall upon the promised parallel betwixt Thomas Wolsey, Archbishop of York and Cardinal, and William Laud, doctor in divinity, and Archbishop of Canterbury.

They were both the sons of mean and mechanick men, Wolsey of a butcher, Laud of a clothworker ; the one born in Ipswich, threescore miles, the other in Reading, thirty miles distant from the city of London ; both of them very toward, forward, and pregnant grammar-scholars, and of singular apprehensions, as suddenly rising to the first form in the school. From thence, being young, they were removed to the University of Oxford, Wolsey admitted into Maudlin college, Laud into St. John's ; and, as they were of different times, so they were of different statures, yet either of them well shaped, according to their proportions : Wolsey was of a competent tallness, Laud of a less size, but might be called a pretty man, as the other a proper man ; both of ingenious and acute aspects, as may appear by this man's face, the other's picture. In their particular colleges they were alike proficients, both as active of body as brain, serious at their private studies, and equally frequent in the schools ; eloquent orators, either to write, speak, or dictate ; dainty disputants ; well versed in philosophy, both moral, physical, and metaphysical, as also in the mathematicks, and neither of them strangers to the muses, both taking their degrees according to their time ; and, through the whole academy, Sir Wolsey was called the Boy-batchelor, and Sir Laud, the Little Batchelor.

The main study, that either of them fixed upon, was theology; for, though they were conversant in all the other arts and sciences, yet that they solely professed, and by that came their future preferment. Wolsey, being batchelor, was made schoolmaster of Maudlin school, in Oxford, but Laud came in time to be master of St. John's college, in Oxford, therein transcending the other, as also in his degrees of master of arts, batchelor of divinity, and doctor of divinity; when the other, being suddenly called from the rectorship of his school, to be resident upon a country benefice, took no more academical degrees, than the first of batchelor; and, taking a strange affront by one Sir Amius Paulet, a knight in the country, who set him in the stocks, he endured likewise divers other disasters; but that disgrace he made the knight pay dearly for, after he came to be invested in his dignity. Briefly, they came both to stand in the prince's eye. But, before I proceed any further, let me give the courteous reader this modest caveat, that he is to expect from me only a parallel of their acts and fortune, but no legend of their lives; it therefore briefly thus followeth.

Both these from academicks coming to turn courtiers; Wolsey, by his diligent waiting, came to insinuate himself into the breasts of the privy-counsellors. His first employment was in an ambassy to the emperor, which was done by such fortunate, and almost incredible expedition, that by that only he grew into first grace with King Henry the Seventh, father to King Henry the Eighth. Laud, by the mediation and means, wrought by friends, grew first into favour with King James, of sacred memory, father to our now Royal Sovereign King Charles. They were both at first the king's chaplains; Wolsey's first preferment was to be Dean of Lincoln, of which he was after bishop. Laud's first ecclesiastical dignity was to be Dean of St. David's, of which he was after bishop also. And both these prelatical courtiers came also to be privy-counsellors. Wolsey, in the beginning of Henry the Eighth's reign, was made bishop of Tournay, in France, soon after bishop of Lincoln, and before his full consecration, by the death of the incumbent, was ended, translated to the Archbishoprick of York, and all this within the compass of a year; Laud, though not so suddenly, yet very speedily, was from St. David's removed to London, and from London to Canterbury, and this in the beginning of the reign of King Charles. Thus, you see, they were both archbishops; and, as Laud was never cardinal, so Wolsey was never Canterbury.

But, in some things, the Cardinal much exceeded Canterbury, as in holding all these bishopricks at once, when the other was never possessed but of one at one time. The Cardinal also held the Bishoprick of Winchester, of Worcester, Bath and Wells, with a fourth, and two abbotships in Commendam: he had besides an hat sent him from Rome, and made himself cardinal, that, being before but York, he might overtop Canterbury. But our William, howsoever he might have the will, yet never attained to that power, and, howsoever he could not compass a hat from Rome, yet made the means to have a consecrated mitre sent from Rome; which was so narrowly watched, that it came not to his wearing. Moreover, the Cardinal extorted the chancellorship from Canterbury; but we find not that Canterbury ever either intrenched upon the jurisdiction, or took any thing away from the Archbishoprick of York.

Wolsey likewise far outwent him in his numerous train, and the nobleness thereof, being waited on not only by the prime gentry, but even of earls, and earls sons, who were listed in his family, and attended him at his table; as also in his hospitality, his open house being made free for all comers, with the rare and extraordinary state of his palace, in which there were daily up-rising and down-lying a thousand persons, who were his domestick servants. Moreover, in his many entertainments of the kings with masks, and mighty sumptuous banquets, his sumptuous buildings, the prince-like state he carried in his foreign ambassages, into France, to the emperor, &c. in which he spent more coin in the service of his king, for the honour of his country, and to uphold the credit of his cardinal's cap, than would, for the time, have paid an army royal. But I answer in behalf of our Canterbury, that he had never that means or employment, by which he might make so vain-glorious a shew of his pontificality, or archiepiscopal dignity: for unbounded minds may be restrained within narrow limits, and, therefore, the parallel may something hold in this too.

They were also in their judicial courts equally tyrannous; the one in the chancery, the other in the high commission; both of them at the council-board, and in the star-chamber, alike draconically supercilious. Blood drawn from Dr. Bonner's head, by the fall of his cross, presaged the Cardinal's downfall. Blood drawn from the ears of Burton, Prynne, and Bastwick, was a prediction of Canterbury's ruin; the first accidental, the last premeditate and of purpose. The Cardinal would have expelled all the Lutherans and Protestants out of the realm, this our Canterbury would have exiled both our Dutch and French church out of the kingdom. The Cardinal took main delight in his fool Patch, and Canterbury took much delight in his party-coloured cats. The Cardinal used, for his agents, Bonner, and others; Canterbury for his ministers, Duck, Lamb, and others. They both favoured the see of Rome, and respected his holiness in it. The Cardinal did profess it publickly, the Archbishop did reverence it privately. The Cardinal's ambition was to be pope, the Archbishop strove to be patriarch; they both bid fairly for it, yet lost their aim; and far easier it is for men to descend, than to ascend.

The Cardinal, as I have said, was very ambitious; the Archbishop was likewise of the same mind, though better moulded, and of a more politick brain, having a close and more reserved judgment in all his observations, and more fluent in his delivery. The Cardinal was very curious in his attire, and ornament of his body, and took great delight in his train, and other his servants, for their rich apparel: the Archbishop's attire was neat and rich, but not so gaudy as the Cardinal's was; yet he took as much felicity in his gentlemen's rich apparel, especially those that waited on his person, as ever the Cardinal did, tho' other men paid for them; and if all men had their own, and every bird her feather, some of them would be as bare as those that profess themselves to be of the sect of the Adamites. To speak truth, the Archbishop's men were all given to covetousness and wantonness, that I never heard of were in the Cardinal's men.

As the Cardinal was sumptuous in his buildings, as that of White-hall, Hampton-court, &c. as also in laying the foundation of two famous colleges, the one at Ipswich, where he was born, the other at Oxford, where he had his breeding; so Christ-church, which he left unfinished, Canterbury hath since repaired; and wherein he hath come short of him in building, though he hath bestowed much on St. John's College, yet he hath outgone him in his bounty of brave voluminous books, being fourscore in number, late sent to the Bodleian or University Library. Farther, as the Cardinal was chancellor of Oxford, and as the Cardinal, by plucking down of small abbies, to prepare stone for his greater structures, opened a gap for the King, by which he took the advantage utterly to raze and demolish the rest; so Canterbury, by giving way for one bishop to have a temporal trial, and to be convicted, not by the clergy, but the laity, left the same path open both for himself, and the rest of the episcopacy; of whch, there before scarce remained a precedent.

I have paralleled them in their dignities; I will conclude with a word or two concerning their downfalls. The Cardinal fell into the displeasure of his king, Canterbury into an extreme hatred of the commons : both were arrested of high treason, the Cardinal by process, Canterbury by Parliament. The Cardinal at Keywood castle, near York, Canterbury at Westminster, near London; both their falls were speedy and sudden: the Cardinal sat as this day in the high court of chancery, and within two days after was confined to his house; Canterbury as this day sat at the council-board, and in the upper-house of parliament, and the same day was committed to the black rod, and from thence to the Tower. The Cardinal died at Leicester, some say of a flux; Canterbury remains still in the Tower, only sick of a fever. *Vanitas vanitatum omnia vanitas.*

THE

BILL OF ATTAINDER

That passed against

THOMAS EARL OF STRAFFORD.

Printed for J. A. 1641. Quarto, containing six pages.

WHEREAS the knights, citizens, and burgesses of the house of commons in this present parliament assembled, have, in the name of themselves, and all the commons of England, impeached Thomas Earl of Strafford, of high treason, for endeavouring to subvert the

ancient and fundamental laws and government of his Majesty's realms
of England and Ireland, and to introduce an arbitrary and tyrannical
government against law in the said kingdoms; and for exercising a
tyrannous and exorbitant power over, and against the laws of the said
kingdoms, over the liberties, estates, and lives of his Majesty's subjects;
and likewise for having, by his own authority, commanded the laying
and assessing of soldiers upon his Majesty's subjects in Ireland, against
their consents, to compel them to obey his unlawful commands and
orders, made upon paper petitions, in causes between party and party,
which accordingly was executed upon divers of his Majesty's subjects,
in a warlike manner, within the said realm of Ireland ; and, in so doing,
did levy war against the King's Majesty, and his liege people in that
kingdom : and also, for that he, upon the unhappy dissolution of the
last parliament, did slander the house of commons to his Majesty, and
did counsel and advise his Majesty, that he was loose and absolved
from rules of government, and that he had an army in Ireland, which
he might employ to reduce this kingdom ; for which he deserves to undergo the pains and forfeitures of high treason.

And the said Earl hath been also an incendiary of the wars between
the two kingdoms of England and Scotland : all which offences have
been sufficiently proved against the said Earl upon his impeachment.

Be it therefore enacted by the King's most Excellent Majesty, and
by the lords and commons in this present parliament assembled, and
by authority of the same, that the said Earl of Strafford, for the heinous crimes and offences aforesaid, stand and be adjudged and attainted of high treason, and shall suffer the pain of death, and incur
the forfeitures of his goods and chattels, lands, tenements, and hereditaments, of any estate of freehold or inheritance, in the said kingdoms
of England and Ireland, which the said Earl, or any other to his use,
or in trust for him, have or had, the day of the first sitting of this present parliament, or at any time since.

Provided, that no judge or judges, justice or justices whatsoever,
shall adjudge or interpret any act or thing to be treason, nor hear or
determine any treason, nor in any other manner than he or they should
or ought to have done before the making of this act, and as if this act
had never been had or made. Saving always unto all and singular persons and bodies politick and corporal, their heirs and successors, others
than the said Earl and his heirs, and such as claim by, from, or under
him, all such right, title, and interest, of, in, and to all and singular
such of the said lands, tenements, and hereditaments, as he, they, or
any of them, had before the first day of this present parliament, any
thing herein contained to the contrary notwithstanding.

Provided, that the passing of this present act, and his Majesty's assent thereunto, shall not be any determination of this present sessions of
parliament, but that this present sessions of parliament, and all bills
and matters whatsoever, depending in parliament, and not fully enacted
and determined, and all statutes and acts of parliament, which have their
continuance until the end of this present session of parliament, shall
remain, continue, and be in full force, as if this act had not been.

THE

ACCUSATION AND IMPEACHMENT

OF

WILLIAM LAUD, ARCHBISHOP OF CANTERBURY,

BY THE HOUSE OF COMMONS,

In Maintenance of the Accusations, whereby he standeth charged with
High-Treason.

Printed anno dom. 1641. Quarto, containing eight pages.

I.

IMPRIMIS, That he, the said Archbishop of Canterbury, hath endeavoured to subvert the fundamental laws of this kingdom, by giving his Majesty advice, both private and publick, at the council table, and high commission, and other places, and so would have them governed by the civil law; and said, he would make the proudest subject in the kingdom give way to him; and, being told it was against law, he replied he would make it law, and that the King might, at his pleasure, take away without law, and make it warrantable by God's law.

II.

Item, His countenancing of books for the maintenance of his unlimited power, wherein the power of the parliament is denied, and the bishop's power set up.

III.

Item, That he traiterously went about to interrupt the judges, by his threatenings, and other means, to constrain them to give false judgment in the case of ship-money; as will appear by writings under his own hand, and by the testimonies of divers persons of good worth and quality.

IV.

Item, That he hath taken bribes, and sold justice in the high commission court, as archbishop, and hath not only corrupted the judges there, but hath also sold judicial places to be corrupted.

V.

Item, That he hath traiterously endeavoured the incroachment of jurisdiction, institution of canons, and they are not only against law, but prejudicial, and against the liberties of the subjects; that he hath enlarged his jurisdictions by making these canons; and that he hath exercised his authority very cruelly, both as counsellor, as a commissioner, annd as a judge; and this authority is derived from his own order, and not from the King.

VI.

Item, That he hath traiterously assumed to himself a capital power over his Majesty's subjects, denying his power of prelacy from the King.

VII.

Item, That, by false erroneous doctrines, and other sinister ways and means, he went about to subvert religion, established in this kingdom, and to set up popery and superstition in the church.

VIII.

Item, That, by divers undue means and practices, he hath gotten into his hands the power and nominating of ministers to spiritual promotions, and hath presented none but slanderous men thereunto; and that he hath presented corrupt chaplains to his Majesty.

IX.

Item, That his own ministers, as Heywood, Layfield, and others, are notoriously disaffected to religion; and he hath given power of licensing of books to them.

X.

Item, That he hath traiterously endeavoured to reconcile us to the church of Rome; and to that end hath employed a jesuit, a papist, and hath wrought with the pope's agents in several points.

XI.

Item, That to suppress preaching, he hath suspended divers good and honest ministers, and hath used unlawful means, by letters, and otherwise, to set all bishops to suppress them.

XII.

Item, That, he hath traiterously endeavoured to suppress the French religion here with us, being the same religion we are of, and also the Dutch church, and to set division between them and us.

XIII.

Item, That he hath traiterously endeavoured to set a division between the King and his subjects, and hath gone about to bring in innovations into the church, as by the remonstrances may appear, and hath induced the king to this war with the Scots; and many men, upon their death-beds, to give money towards the maintenance of this war, and hath caused the clergy to give freely towards the same, and hath brought in many superstitions and innovations into the church of Scotland, and that he procured the King to break the pacification, and thereby to bring in a bloody war between the two kingdoms.

XIV.

Item, That, to save and preserve himself from being questioned and sentenced from these and other his traiterous designs, from the first year of his now Majesty's reign, until now, he hath laboured to subvert the rights of parliamentary proceedings, and to incense his Majesty against parliaments, and so that, at Oxford, he gave forth many such words against it, and so hath continued ever since.

By all which words, counsels, and actions, he hath traiterously laboured to alienate the hearts of the King's liege people from his Majesty, and hath set a division between them, and to ruin and destroy his Majesty's kingdoms; for which they impeach him of high-treason, against our Sovereign Lord the King, his crown and dignity.

And the said commons by protestation, saving to themselves the liberty of exhibiting, at any time hereafter, any other accusation or impeachment against the said William Laud, Archbishop of Canterbury, and also to the replying to the answers, that he the said Archbishop shall make unto the said articles, or to any of them; and of offering proof also of the premisses, or any part of them, or any other impeachment or accusation that shall be exhibited by them, as the case shall, according to the course of parliament, required; do pray, that he the said William Laud, Archbishop of Canterbury, be put speedily to answer for all and every the premisses, that such proceedings, examinations, tryals, and judgments may be, upon every of them, had and used, as is agreeable to law and justice.

LEICESTE'R'S COMMONWEALTH

Fully epitomised, conceived, spoken, and published, with most earnest Protestation of all dutiful good will, and affection towards this Realm, for whose good only it is made common to many. Contracted in a most brief, exact, and compendious way, with the full Sense and whole Meaning of the former Book, every Fragment of Sense being interposed. With a pleasant Description of the first Original of the Controversies betwixt the two Houses of York and Lancaster.

Printed in the year 1641. Quarto, containing sixteen pages.

A Scholar, lawyer, and gentleman, being convened together in Christmas time, retired themselves after dinner, into a large gallery, for their recreation: the lawyer having in his hand a little book, then newly put forth, containing, 'A defence of the publick justice done, of late, in England, upon divers priests, and other papists, for treason.' Which book the Lawyer having read before, the Gentleman asked his judgment thereon.

Lawyer. It is not evil penned, in my opinion, to shew the guiltiness of some persons therein named in particular; yet not so far forth, I believe, and in so deep a degree of treason, as, in this book generally is inforced without indifferency.

Gent. For my part, I protest that I bear the honest papist (if there be any) no malice for his deceived conscience; but since you grant the papist, both in general, abroad and at home, and, in particular, such as are condemned, executed, and named in this book, to be guilty, how can you insinuate, as you do, that there is more inforced upon them, by this book, than there is just cause so to do?

Lawyer. Good Sir, I stand not here to examine the doings of superiors, or to defend the guilty, but wish heartily rather their punishment, that deserve the same. But not only those, whom you call busy papists, in England, but also those, whom we call hot puritans, among you, may be as well called traytors, in my opinion; for that every one of these, indeed, doth labour indirectly, if not more, against the state, seeing each one endeavoureth to increase his party, or faction, that desireth a governor of his own religion. And, in this case, are the protestants in France and Flanders, under catholick princes; the Calvinists under the Duke of Saxony, the Lutherans under Casinere, the Grecians, and other Christians, under the Emperor of Constantinople, under the Sophy and Cham of Tartary, and under other princes, that are not with them in religion. All which subjects do wish, no doubt, in their hearts, that they had a prince and state of their own religion, instead of that which now governeth them; and, consequently, in this sense they may be called traytors: and so, to apply this to my purpose, I think, Sir, in good sooth, that, in the first kind of treason, as well the zealous papist, as also the puritan in England, may well be called, and proved traytors.

Gent. I grant your distinction of treasons to be true; but your application thereof to the papists and puritans, as you call them, be rather divers degrees, than divers kinds; and the one is but a step to the other, not differing in nature, but in time, ability, or opportunity. For if the Grecians, under the Turk, and other Christians, under other princes of a different religion; as also the papists and puritans in England, have such alienation of mind from the present regiment, and do covet so much a governor and state of their own religion; then, no doubt, but they are also resolved to employ their forces, for accomplishing and bringing to pass their desires, if they had opportunity; and so being now in the first degree, or kind of treason, do want but occasion or ability to break into the second.

Lawyer. True, Sir, if there be no other cause or circumstance that may withhold them.

Gent. And what cause or circumstance may stay them, when they shall have ability, or opportunity, to do a thing which they so much desire?

Lawyer. Divers causes, but especially the fear of servitude under foreign nations, may restrain them from such attempts; as, in Germany, both catholicks and protestants joined together against strangers, that offered danger to their liberties. So that, by this example, you see, that fear of external subjection may stay men in all states, and, consequently, both papists and puritans in the state of England, from passing to the second degree of treason, although they were never so deep in the first, and had both ability, time, will, and opportunity for the other.

Schol. It seems to be most clear, and now I understand what the lawyer meant before, when he affirmed, that, although the most part of papists, in general, might be said to deal against England, in regard of their religion, and so incur some kind of treason, yet not so far forth as in this book is inforced; though, for my part, I do not see that the book inforceth all papists in general to be properly traytors, but such as only in particular are therein named, or that are by law attainted, or condemned, or executed. And what will you say to those in particular?

Lawyer. That some, here named in this book, are openly known to have been in the second degree of treason, as Westmoreland, Norton, Sanders, &c. but divers others (namely the priests and seminaries) I conceive, that to the wise of our state, who had the doing of this business, the first degree of treason was sufficient to dispatch them, especially in such suspicious times as these are, to the end that, being hanged for the first, they should never be in danger to fall into the second, nor yet to draw other men to the same, which, perhaps, was most of all misdoubted.

Gent. It appertaineth not to us to judge what the state pleaseth to do, for it must as well prevent inconveniences, as remedy the same, when they are happened. But, my good friends, I must tell you plain, that I could wish, with all my heart, that either these differences were not amongst us at all, or else that they were so temperately, on all parts, pursued; as the common state of our country, the blessed reign of her Majesty, and the common cause of true religion, were not endangered thereby.

Lawyer. But many participate the black Moors humour that dwell in Guiney, whose exercise, at home, is, as some write, the one to hunt, catch, and sell the other, and always the stronger to make money of the weaker. But now, if in England, we should live in peace and unity, as they do in Germany, and one should not prey upon the other; then should the great falcons for the field, I mean the favourites of the time, fail of their great prey.

Gent. Truly, Sir, I think you rove nearer the mark than you think; for, if I be not deceived, the very ground of these broils are but a very prey, in the greedy imaginations of him who tyranniseth the state; and, being himself of no religion, feedeth not yet upon our differences in religion, to the fatting of himself, and ruin of the realm; for whereas, by the common distinction, there are three notable differences of religion in this land; the two extreams whereof are the papist and puritan, and the religious protestant obtaining the mean: This fellow, being of neither, maketh his gain of all, and as he seeketh a kingdom by the one extream, and spoil by the other; and so he useth the authority of the third, to compass the first two, and to countermine each one, to the overthrow of all three.

Schol. In good sooth, I see now, Sir, where you are; you are fallen into the common place of all our ordinary talk and conference in the university; for I know you mean my Lord of Leicester, who is the subject of all pleasant discourse, at this day, throughout this realm.

Gent. Not so pleasant, as pitiful, if all matters and circumstances were well considered, except any man take pleasure to jest at our own miseries; which are like to be the greater by his iniquity (if God avert it not) than by all the wickedness of England besides; he being the man, by all probability, that is like to be the bane, and fatal destiny of our state, with the eversion of true religion, whereof, by indirect means, he is the greatest enemy that the land doth nourish: A man of so base a spirit as is known to be, of so extreme ambition, pride, falsehood, and treachery; so born, so bred up, so nursed in treason from his infancy, descended of a tribe of traytors, and fleshed in conspiracy against the royal blood of King Henry's children in his tender years, and exercised in drifts ever since against the same, by the blood and ruin of divers others; and finally, a man so well known to bear secret malice against her Majesty, for causes irreconcileable. Wherefore, I do assure myself, it would be most pleasant to the realm, and profitable to her Majesty, to wit, that this man's actions might be called publickly to tryal, and liberty given to good subjects, to say what they know against the same, as it was permitted in the first year of King Henry the Eighth against his grandfather, and in the first of Queen Mary against his father; and then I would not doubt, but, if these two, his ancestors, were found worthy to lose their heads for treason, this man would not be found unworthy to make the third in kindred, whose treacheries do far surpass them both.

Lawyer. My masters, have you not heard of the proviso made in the last parliament for punishment of all those, who speak so broad of such men as my Lord of Leicester is?

Gent. Yes, I have heard, that my Lord of Leicester, being ashamed of his actions, desired a restraint, that he might lie the more securely in harbour from the tempest of men's tongues, which tattled busily at that time, of divers of his lordship's deeds, which he would not have divulged; as of his preparation to rebellion upon Monsieur's commission into the land, of his disgrace and checks received at court, of the fresh death of the noble Earl of Essex, and of his hasty snatching up of his widow, whom he sent up and down the country by privy ways, thereby to avoid the sight and knowledge of the Queen's Majesty; and although he had not only satisfied his own lust on her, but also married and remarried her contentation of her friends; yet denied he the same by solemn oaths to her Majesty, and received the communion thereupon, so good a conscience he hath. No marvel, therefore, if he, not desiring to have these and other actions known publickly, was so diligent a procurer of that law for silence.

Schol. It is very probable, that his lordship was in great distress about that time, when Monsieur's matters were in hand, whereof he desired less speech among the people. But, when my Lord of Warwick said openly, at his table in Greenwich, That the marriage was not to be suffered, he caused an insurrection against the Queen's own Majesty; and when her Royal Majesty should have married to the brother and heir apparent of France, being judged by the best, wisest, and faithfullest protestants of the realm, to be both convenient, profitable, and honourable; this tyrant, for his own private lucre, endeavoured to alienate for ever, and make this great prince our mortal enemy, who sought the love of her Majesty with so much honour and confidence, as never prince did.

Gent. For the present I must advertise you in this case, that you may not take hold so exactly of my lord's doings, for they are too many to be recited, especially in women's affairs, in touching their marriages, and their husbands; for, first, his lordship hath a special fortune, that, when he desireth any woman's favour, then what person soever standeth in his way, hath the luck to die quickly, for the finishing of his desires. As for example, when his lordship was in full hope to marry her Majesty, and his own wife stood in his way, as he supposed, she was slain to make way for him.

Long after this he fell in love with the Lady Sheffield, and then had he also the same fortune to have her husband to die quickly by an artificial catarrh, that stopped his breath. The like good chance had he in the death of my Lord of Essex, and that at a time most fortunate for his purpose.

He poisoned also one Mrs. Alice Draykot, a goodly gentlewoman, whom he affected much himself; and, hearing that she was dead, lamented her case greatly, and said, in the presence of his servants, Ah, poor Alice, the cup was not prepared for thee, although it was thy hard destiny to taste of it.

Also Sir Nicholas Throgmorton, whom my Lord of Leicester invited to a supper, at his house in London, was there poisoned with a sallad, by an incurable vomit.

The late Lady Lenox also, who came of the royal blood by Scotland, who never could affect her, took the pains to visit her with extraordinary kindness; but, after some private discourse with her, at his departure, she fell into an extraordinary flux, which many did avouch to come by his means.

But this is not all, touching his marriage and contracts with women, changing wives and minions, by killing the one, denying the other, using the third for a time, and fawning on the fourth. Wherefore he had terms and pretences of contracts, precontracts, post contracts, protracts, and retracts; as for example, after he had killed his wife, and so broken that contract, then forsooth would he needs make himself husband to the Queen's Majesty, and so defeat all other princes by vertue of his precontract. And, after this, his lust compelling him to another place, he would needs make a post contract with the Lady Sheffield; but yet, after his concupiscence, changing again, he resolved to make a retract of this protract, and to make a certain new protract, which is a continuation for using her for a time, with the widow of Essex.

Schol. I have read much in my time of the carnality and licenciousness of many outrageous persons in this kind; but I never read, nor heard the like of him in my life, whose concupiscence and violence run jointly together; neither holdeth he any rule in his lust, besides only the motion and suggestion of his own sensuality: For there are not, by report, two noble gentlemen about her Majesty (I speak upon some account of them that know much) whom he hath not sollicited by potent ways. And, seeking pasture among the waiting-gentlewomen of her Majesty's chamber, he hath offered three hundred pounds for a night; and, if that would not make up the sum, he would otherwise; having reported himself, so little shame he hath, that he offered to another of higher place a hundred pound lands a year, with many more jewels to do the act.

Gent. Nay he is so libidinous, that he hath given to procure love in others, by conjuring sorcery, and other such means. But I am ashamed to make any more mention of his filthiness.

Schol. To draw you from the further stirring of this unsavoury puddle, and foul dunghill, I will recount a pretty story concerning his daughter born of the Lady Sheffield in Dudley Castle: I was acquainted three months past, with a certain minister, that now is dead, living at Dudley Castle, for compliment of some sacred ceremonies, at the birth of my Lord of Leicester's daughter in that place; and the matter was so ordered by the wily wit of him that had sowed the seed, that, for the better covering of the harvest, and secret delivery of the lady Sheffield, the good wife of the castle also, whereby Leicester's appointed gossips might, without suspicion, have access to the place, should feign herself to be with child, and, after long and sore travel, God knows, to be delivered of a cushion, as she was indeed, and a little after a fair coffin was buried with a bundle of clouts in shew of a child; and the minister caused to use all accustomed prayers and ceremonies, for the solemnizing thereof: For which thing afterward the minister, before his death, had great grief and remorse of conscience, with no small detestation of the most irreligious device of my Lord of Leicester, in such a case.

Gent. This was a most atheistical designment, and withal so unworthy, that it did, alone, deserve a correspondent punishment; and no doubt but that God, who hath an impartial eye in viewing such voluntary iniquities, will one day render unto him, according to his demerits; to whose supreme justice, I leave him; yet, gentlemen, if you please, I will relate most apparently unto you his intended murder against the Earl of Ormond: Leicester did offer five hundred pounds, to have him privately murthered: But, when that device took no effect, he appointed the field with him, but, secretly suborning his servant William Killegre to lie in the way, where Ormond should pass, and so massacre him with a caliver, before he came to the place appointed. Which matter, though it took no effect, for that the matter was taken up, before the day of meeting, yet was Killegre placed afterwards in her Majesty's privy chamber by Leicester, for shewing his ready mind to do for his master so faithful a service.

Schol. So faithful a service indeed; in my opinion, it was but an unfit preferment, for so facinorous a fact. Yet, I hear withal, that he is a man of great impatience, fury, rage, and ire, and whatsoever thing it be that he conceives, either justly, or unjustly, he prosecuteth the same, with such implacable cruelty, that there is no abiding his fury.

His treacheries towards the noble Earl of Sussex, in their many breaches, is notorious to all England, as also the bloody practices against divers others.

But, among many, none were more odious, and misliked of all men, than those against monsieur Simiers, a stranger, and ambassador; whom first he practised to have poisoned, but, when that device took no place, then he would have slain him at the Black-friars, at Greenwich, as he went forth at the garden gate; but, missing of that purpose too, he dealt with certain Flushiners, and other pirates, to sink him at sea, with the English Gentlemen his favourers, that accompanied him, at his return into France.

Lawyer. Now verily, Sir, you paint unto me a strange pattern of a perfect potentate, in the court; for the common speech of many wanteth not reason I perceive, which call him the heart, and life of the court.

Gent. They, which call him the heart, upon a little occasion more would call him the head; and then I marvel, what would be left for her Majesty, when they take from her both life, heart, and headship in her own realm.

Lawyer. Yet durst no subject presume to contradict his hellish opinions, but rather gave their assertion unto, for fear of the damage of their lives.

Schol. But he hath ammunition, to what intent I know not, for in Killingworth Castle, he hath ready armour to furnish ten thousand soldiers, of all things necessary, both for horse and man; besides the great abundance of ready coin there laid up sufficient, for any great exploit to be done within the realm.

Gent. He hath many lands, possessions, seigniories, and rich offices of his own: favour and authority with his prince; the part and portion in all suits, that pass by grace, or are ended by law: He doth chop and change what lands he listeth with her Majesty; possesseth many licenses to himself, as of wine, oils, currants, cloth, velvets with his new office of alienation, which might inrich towns, corporations, countries, and commonwealths: He disposeth at his will ecclesiastical livings of the realm, in making bishops, &c. of whom he pleaseth; he sweepeth away the glebe from many benefices throughout this land; he scoureth the university, and colleges, where he is chancellor, and selleth both head-ships, and scholar-places, and all other offices, and dignities, that, by art and violence, may yield money. He driveth the parties out of their possessions, and maketh title to what land he pleaseth: He taketh in whole forests, commons, woods, and pastures to himself; these, and in all these he doth insult, notwithstanding his former impiety.

He released Calais to the French, most traiterouly, as his father before him sold Bulloign to the French, by like treachery.

What should I speak of his other actions, whereof there would be no end? As of his dealing with Master Robinson of Staffordshire, with false arraignment; with Master Richard Lee, for his mannor of Hockenorton; with Master Ludwick Grivell, by seeking to bereave him of all his living at once, if the drift had taken place; with George Witney, in the behalf of Sir Henry Leigh, for enforcing him, to forego the comptrollership of Woodstock, which he held by patent from King Henry the Seventh; with my Lord Barkeley, whom he inforced to yield up his lands to his brother Warwick, which his ancestors had held quietly before two hundred years. What shall I speak of his intolerable tyranny upon Sir John Throgmorton, whom he brought to his grave, by perpetual vexations; and upon all the line of King Henry against this man's father, in King Edward and Queen Mary's days? Upon divers of the Lanes, for one man's sake of that name before-mentioned, that offered to take Killingworth Castle: Upon some of the Giffords, and others, for Throgmorton's sake; in his endless persecuting Sir Drew Drewry, and many other courtiers both men, and women; but especially Leicester was supposed to use this practice, for bringing the scepter finally to his own head; and that he would not only employ himself to defeat Scotland, and Arbeda to defeat Huntingdon; but also would use the marriage of the Queen imprisoned, to defeat them both if he could. Which marriage he being frustrated of, was not ashamed to threaten a treacherous vindication against her Majesty's royal person. But I hope her Majesty will set out a fair proclamation, with a bundle of halters for all such traitors.

Lawyer. I applaud your well wishings to the state; yet I do observe much by reading over our country's affairs; and, among other things, I do abhor the memory of that time, and do dread all occasion, that may lead us to the like in time to come; seeing that, in my judgment, neither the civil wars of Marius and Sylla, or of Pompey and Cæsar among the Romans, nor yet the Guelphians and Gibbelines among the Italians, did ever work so much woe, as this did to our poor country: wherein, by the contention of York and Lancaster, were fought fifteen or sixteen pitched fields, in less than an hundred years. That is, from the eleventh or twelfth year of King Richard the Second's reign, unto the thirteenth year of King Henry the Seventh. At what time, by cutting off the chief titler of Huntingdon's house, to wit, young Edward Plantagenet, Earl of Warwick, son and heir to George, Duke of Clarence, the contention was most happily quenched and ended, wherein so many fields were fought between brethren and inhabitants of our own nation. And therein about the same quarrel were slain, murthered, and made away about nine or ten kings, and kings sons, besides above forty earls, marquisses, and dukes of name; but many more lords, knights, great gentlemen, and captains, and of the common people without number, and by particular conjecture very near two hundred thousand. For that, in one battle fought by King Edward the Fourth, there are recorded to be slain, on both parts, five and thirty thousand seven hundred and eleven persons, besides other wounded persons, to be put to death afterwards, at the pleasure of the conqueror; at divers battles after, ten thousand slain at a battle: As in those of Barnet and Tewksbury fought in one year.

Schol. I pray, Sir, open unto me the ground of these controversies between York and Lancaster; I have heard a large relation thereof, but no original.

Lawyer. The controversy between the houses of York and Lancaster took its actual beginning in the issue of King Edward the Third, and Edmond Earl of Lancaster, whose inheritance fell upon a daughter named Blanch, who was married to the fourth son of King Edward the Third, named John of Gaunt, born in the city of Gaunt, in Flanders, and so by his wife became Duke of Lancaster, and heir of that house. And for that his son Henry of Bullingbrook pretended, among other things, that Edward Crookback was the elder son of King Henry the

Third, and unjustly put by the inheritance of the crown, for that he was crook-backed and deformed: He took by force the kingdom from Richard the Second, nephew to King Edward the Third, by his first son, and placed the same in the house of Lancaster, where it remained for three whole descents, until afterwards Edward Duke of York, descended of John of Gaunt's younger brother, making claim to the crown by title of his grandmother, that was heir to Lionel Duke of Clarence, John of Gaunt's elder brother, took the same from Henry the Sixth by force, out of the house of Lancaster, and brought it back again to the house of York. This, therefore, was the original of all those discords between them.

Gent. But let us not digress from our former discourse concerning Leicester's treacherous actions. I have a friend yet living that was toward the old Earl of Arundel in good credit, and by that means had occasion to deal with the late Duke of Norfolk in his chiefest affairs before his troubles; who did often report strange things from the duke's own mouth, of my Lord of Leicester's most treacherous dealing towards him, for gaining of his blood, as after appeared true. This Leicester hath also deceived her Majesty divers times, in forging of letters as if they came from some prince, when they were his own forgery: he had likewise a hellish device to entrap his well deserving friend Sir Christopher Hatton, in matter of Hall his priest, whom he would have had Sir Christopher to hide, and send away; being touched and detected in the case of Ardent, thereby to have drawn in Sir Christopher himself, and made him accessary to this plot. What mean all these pernicious late dealings against the Earl of Shrewsbury, a man of the most ancient and worthiest nobility of our realm? It is only Leicester's ambitious mind, that causes all this.

But it is very strange to see, what a contemner of the prerogatives of England he is, and how little account he makes of all the ancient nobility of our realm, how he contemneth, derideth, and debaseth them: Which is the fashion of all such, as mean to usurp; to the end, that they may have none, who shall not acknowledge their first beginning and advancement from themselves.

His base and abject behaviour, in his last disgrace about his marriage, well declared what he would do, in a matter of more importance, by deceiving of Sir Christopher Hatton; and by abusing my lord treasurer in a letter, for which her highness did much rebuke him.

It was affirmed by many that all the broils, troubles, dangers, and disturbances, in Scotland, did proceed from his complot, and conspiracy.

His unworthy scandal, which he cast on the Earl of Shrewsbury, was perfidious: wherefore in regard of these innumerable treacheries, for preventing of succeeding calamities, to tell you plainly my opinion, and therewith to draw to an end of this our conference, I should think it the most necessary point of all; for her Majesty to call his lordship to an account among others, and to see what other men could say against him, at length, after so many years of his sole accusing and pursuing of others. I know and am very well assured, that no act, which her Majesty hath done, since the coming to the crown, nor any that lightly her Majesty may do hereafter, can be of more utility to herself, and to the realm, or more grateful unto her faithful and zealous subjects, than this noble act of justice will be, for trial of this man's deserts towards his country.

And so likewise now to speak in our particular case, if there be any grudge or grief at this day, any mislike, repining, complaint, or murmur against her Majesty's government, in the hearts of her true and faithful subjects, who wish amendment of that which is amiss, and not the overthrow of that which is well, I dare avouch upon conscience that either all, or the greatest part thereof, proceedeth from this man. And, if her highness do permit, and command the laws, daily to pass upon thieves, and murderers, without exception, and that for one fact only, as by experience we see; how then can it be denied in this man, who in both kinds hath committed more enormous acts, than may be well recounted?

As in the first of theft, not only by spoiling, and oppressing almost infinite private men; but also whole towns, villages, corporations, and countries, by robbing the realm with inordinate licenses, by deceiving the crown, with racking, changing, and imbezzling the lands, by abusing his prince, and sovereign, in selling his favour, both at home and abroad, with taking bribes for matter of justice, grace, request, supplication, or whatsoever suit else may depend upon the court, or on the prince's authority.

In which sort of traffick, he committeth more theft oftentimes in one day, than all the way-keepers, cut-pursers, cozeners, pirates, burglares, or others of art that in a whole year within this realm.

As for the second, which is murder, you have heard before, somewhat said and proved; but yet nothing to that, which is thought to have been in secret committed upon divers occasions, at divers times; in sundry persons, of different calling in both sexes, by most variable means of killing, poisoning, charming, inchanting, conjuring, and the like; according to the diversity of men, places, opportunities, and instruments for the same. By all which means, I think, he hath more blood lying upon his head at this day, crying vengeance against him at God's hands and her Majesty, than ever had private man in our country before, were he never so wicked.

Whereto if we add all his intollerable licentiousness, in all filthy kind and manner of carnality, with all his sorts of wives, friends, and kinswomen. If we add his injuries, and dishonours done, hereby to infinite; if we add his treasons, treacheries, and conspiracies about the crown, his disloyal hatred against her Majesty, his perjury, his rapes, and most violent extortions upon the poor, his abusing of the parliament, and other places of justice, with the nobility, and whole commonalty besides; if we add also his open injuries, which he offered daily to religion, and the ministers thereof, by turning all to his own gain; if I say, we should lay together all those enormities before her Majesty, and thousand more in particular, which might and would be gathered, if his day of trial were but in hope to be granted: I do not see in equity and reason, how her highness sitting on the throne, and at the royal stern, as she doth, could deny her subjects this most lawful request; considering that every one of these crimes, a-part, requireth justice of its own nature; and much more altogether ought to obtain the same, at the hand of any good and goodly magistrate in the world.

Before this discourse was fully ended, the night came on a-pace, and it being supper-time, the mistris came to call them to supper, wherefore their further speech was intercepted.

AN HONOURABLE SPEECH

MADE IN

THE PARLIAMENT OF SCOTLAND,

BY THE EARL OF ARGYLE

(Being now Competitor with Earl Morton for the Chancellorship)

The thirtieth of September, 1641, touching the Prevention of National Dissension, and Perpetuating the happy Peace and Union betwixt the two Kingdoms, by the frequent Holding of Parliaments.

London, Printed by A. N. for J. M. at the George in Fleetstreet, Anno 1641. Quarto, containing six pages.

My Lords.

WHAT was more to be wished on earth, than the great happiness this day we enjoy? viz. To see his Royal Majesty our native Sovereign, and his loyal subjects of both his kingdoms, so really united, that his Majesty is piously pleased to grant unto us, his subjects, our lawful demands, concerning religion and liberties, and we his subjects of both nations, chearfully rendering to his Majesty that duty, affection, and assistance, which he hath just cause to expect from good people, and each nation concurring in brotherly amity, unity, and concord, one towards the other.

Oh, what tongue is able to express the honour and praise due to that great and good God, who in these late commotions suffered not the counsels of either kingdom to despair of the safety of either commonwealth, but through his blessing to their painful and prudent endeavours hath wrought such an happiness for us; that now, after the great toil and trouble which we have on both sides so long endured, we may each man with his wife, children, and friends, under his own vine and fig-tree, and all under his Majesty's protection, refresh himself, with the sweet fruits of peace? Which I beseech the lord of peace to make perpetual to both nations.

And, to that end, my earnest desires are, that all our best studies and endeavours may be employed, for some time, in contriving and establishing such wholesomelaws in both kingdoms, whereby, as much as in us lies, the opportunity and occasion of producing the like calamities, as lately threatened both nations, may, for the future, be prevented, if in any age hereafter such miscreants shall go again to attempt it.

It is, my lords, notorious, that the late incendiaries, that occasioned the great differences betwixt his Majesty and his subjects, took much advantage and courage by the too long intermission of the happy constitution of parliaments, in the vacancy of which they, by false informations, incensed his Majesty against his loyal subjects, and by their wily insinuations extorted from his Highness proclamations for to yield obedience to their innovations in the kirk, and patents for projects, whereby the poor subject was both polled and oppressed in his estate, and enthralled in his conscience; and thus, by their wicked practices, his Majesty was distasted, and his subjects generally discontented, insomuch that, had not the great mercy of God prevented them, they had made an obstruction betwixt his Majesty, and his liege people, and had broken those mutual and indissoluble bonds of protection and allegiance, whereby, I hope, his Royal Majesty, and his loyal and dutiful subjects of all his three kingdoms, will be ever bound together. To which let all good subjects say, *Amen.*

My Lords, the distaste of his Majesty, nor discontents of his subjects, could never have come to that height they did, nor consequently have produced such effects, had not there been such an interposition, by these innovators, and projectors, betwixt his Majesty our glorious sun, and us his loyal subjects, that his goodness appeared not, for the time, to us, nor our loyalty and obedience to him. For no sooner was that happy constellation, the parliament in England, raised, and thereby those vaporous clouds dissipated, but his Majesty's goodness, his good subjects loyalty, and their treachery evidently appeared.

Our brethren of England, my lords, finding the intermission of parliaments to be prejudicial and dangerous to the state, have taken care, and made provision for the frequent holding of them; whose prudent example my motion is may be our pattern forthwith to obtain his Majesty's royal assent, for doing the like here in this kingdom. By which means his Majesty may in due time hear, and redress the grievances of his subjects, and his subjects, as need shall require, chearfully aid and assist his Majesty; and not only the domestick peace and quiet of each kingdom be preserved, but likewise all national differences, if any happen, may be, by the wisdom of the assemblies of both kingdoms, from time to time composed and reconciled, to the perpetuating of the happy peace and union betwixt both nations.

THE EARL OF STRAFFORD
CHARACTERISED,

IN A LETTER SENT TO A FRIEND IN THE COUNTRY.

Printed in 1641. Octavo, containing eight pages.

Noble Sir,

I AM inforced to complain of your impetuous commands, and the tax you impose upon me, above all the rest of your vassals, but especially of this of my Lord of Strafford's; as though I alone were inspired with an illumination, beyond the wisdom of the parliament, which on so long consultation hath not yet determined the articulate point of your question; yet thus much I shall positively deliver as a part of my belief: That, howsoever my Lord of Strafford be cried up for a most incomparable and accomplished instrument of state, yet he is human, and subject to such infirmities as were incident to our first progenitors; and this is a particular of my faith, not of my opinion.

But, if it may satisfy your curiosity to be informed of the general conceptions, I shall then present you with as various a collection of votes and censures, as there are fancies in the several factions daily raised by the work of art and time, which qualifieth poison, mollifieth flints, and changeth the face of all things from their first beings and appearances, which have much befriended my Lord of Strafford.

But, whether his lordship be guilty of high treason, I cannot determine.

Sure it is, many foul things stick upon him by manifest proofs, which neither his fineness of wit, nor all the fig-leaves in paradise can cover.

True it is, the house of commons stand stiff to make good their first charges, which are now inforced and prosecuted to the last article, this very day, which, should it not prove treason, on joint rehearsal of the house, and so adjudged by the lords, it would then seem to me to be a strain of popular fury, rather than the legitimate issue of a court of parliament.

True it is, that before the quarter-part of the accusations were charged upon him, he was by way of prejudication acquitted by many of both sexes, and favoured not of a few of both houses, and some of his Majesty's council, and the papistical party, his friends, and followers, and generally by ladies.

The first reasons are best known unto themselves.

By the second, for respects due to their patron.

By the third, for interests and obligations of dependency.

By the fourth, if well considered, for many feminine and affected considerations. As the natural pity and consideration of women sympathising with his afflictions, with the sadness of his aspect, their facility with his complacences, their lenity with his pathetical oratory.

On the other side, there is a rigid, strong, and inflexible party, that say, if he be not found a traytor, the parliament must make him so for the interest of the publick.

And so I shall present you with the inclinations of another party, and of no despicable number of account, which pretend to have more solidity of judgment than fo be carried away with private interest, partial respects, which seem to be touched with the King's, and the commons safety, and to be sensible of the commons sufferance.

And these commonly rip up his life and conversation together, with the progress of his estate and fortunes, and all concluding for his descent and family to be of the noblest and highest rank of gentry, under the degree of baronage; his patrimony so plentiful, as that it equalises most of the barons of the land; his education noble, and to these of his own acquisition of strong and able natural parts.

And, if the adage be true, that, *Multa ex vultu dignoscuntur;* and though they mark him for a wise and promising face, yet they unhappily observe in him a dark and promiscuous countenance, clouded, unlovely, and presaging an envious and cruel disposition. And this general query is made of him:

What was that, which he would have had, who, suspicion excepted, might have been a king at home, had not restless ambition, habituated in his nature, interrupted the course of his repose, and disordered the many helps he had to have lived in plenty, and died in felicity?

But disquieted, as all ambition is turbulent, in his cogitations, and in his first exposition, agitated by the blasts of his own aspirings, it is said of him that in his own country he was transported by the violence of his will to carry all before him, and, come what would of it, to overthrow all that withstood him.

Of such predominant a pitch he was in his own constellation, and propension, which could not rest there, but must break out into a wider extent, for his thoughts soared so high, as men who knew him well affirmed, that he held himself injured by the state, that he came no sooner to the helm.

Whither to come, he journied through a wilderness of popular acclamations, and affected the dangerous name of fame, of being sovereign protector of the commonwealth.

For which he so much pretended, that in all parliaments he became another Jacques de Ortinel. And they aver it for truth, that, in those times, his intimate friends and associates thought it wisdom to shun his conversation, so forward he was in taxing the motions of the King and state.

And, as it is said, not without a malignant humour, and a repugnant spirit, always withstood the King's profit, and stinted the parliamentary contributions, at his own will and pleasure, crossing the designs of state, and infusing, by his stubborn example, a spirit of contradiction in the assemblies of these times; which how fatal they have been to ours, I leave to your judgment, and which hath ever since bred an aversion in his Majesty towards his people and his parliaments.

An office wherein they say he did far more mischief, than in this for which he stands now arraigned for his life.

And this is the description or abstract of the first part of his life, as he was the minion of the people, which, they say, he esteems as the folly of his youth.

May you now be pleased to receive something of his second act, as he was a minister of the King's, into whose service, as they say, and I think not untruly, he was purchased and bought from the affections of the people, at a higher price than all the privadoes of Edward the Second, and Richard the Second. For that this only man hath cost, and lost the King, and kingdom, more treasure and loyalty than Pierce, Gaveston, and the two Spencers, and the Marquis of Dublin, did ever cost, their being all put together.

And sure I am, it is the common opinion of the kingdoms, that should he be taken out of the hands of justice, and the revenge of the publick made frustrate, and the expectations of the three kingdoms disappointed, who hath invaded the whole, by the power of his counsels, and the parties, by the grievous oppressions of his Majesty's good people, wheresoever he had to do, they say, that his Majesty's dominions stand in greater danger and hazard, than ever; and, as it may fall out, to be of a more lamentable consequence than is fit to be expressed.

How fatal may one man's ambition be, and his exorbitant humour, work towards the distraction of a state, which they do thus demonstrate by way of suspicion:

First, admitting the King's affections may be disposed, together with the great party, which he hath in the upper house, to acquit him and others.

And that, thereby the house of commons should hold themselves bound by the interest committed unto them by their countries, to make protestations against the lords.

What then may become of a divided body? Secondly, it is questioned, Whether any future subsidies will be granted, customs and impositions be paid the king, without any insurrection?

Thirdly, Whether the Scots will depart the kingdom; and, if they should, whether on good cause, they may not return, when they shall see a division tend to a fatal confusion, both in the heart of the state, and in the body of the kingdom, rather than they will give opportunity to the papists and libertines to come in for a share?

Wherefore, it is generally concluded by the best and most impartial judgments, That there is no proportion between the riddance of a few monstrous and exorbitant members, and the general safety of the King and his kingdoms.

That there is a necessitated policy, that my Lord of Strafford, the bishop, and some others, should be given up as a just sacrifice, to appease the people, and to make a compensation for the injury done to them and the publick.

And thus have you the second act of the great vice-roy's progress, with the opinion of all and the best judgments here about the town, which I find to be suitable to yours in the country.

A DISCOURSE

SHEWING

In what State the three Kingdoms are in at this present.

Printed in the Year 1641.   Quarto, containing eight pages.

SIR,

A S the faces of all Britain shew their hearts and inclinations, so if their hearts were glazed with a chrystal, they would appear fearful of the future; were not the representative body of the state careful to cure the present malady, purge the distempered humours, and save the much gangrened body, by cutting some rotten and putrified members off, which infect, infest, and invade the republick; this makes me chearful to discover the conceptions of the wise, and not as an orator, but relate their opinion as their auditor: I hope it will take away from me ostentation, and trouble from the reader, even to give ease of discourse.

Their profound sighs, and earnest prayers, might quicken my ingeny, better than the sound of excellent instruments can revive the spirit; to present this with all obedience to my sovereign, and faith to the country, and declare what is convenient to be done at this time, submitting myself modestly to head and body.

Now if those streams of tears, and sweet perfumes, make not my pen fruitful and odoferous, pardon my rudeness, and consider the state we are now in.

When our miserable condition perceived, before the access of the universal body, by the wrinkles put on the brow of ruined affairs, counsel weakened, and reputation of state blasted, that the people cry out against such instruments; What miserable condition are we brought to ? Oh God! suffer not ill counsellors to be as a bad spleen, to swell so big as to make lean the commonwealth, that our empty purses be not filled with blood, though with tears; wherefore, I humbly beseech the head to produce such effect, as the sun on moist and cold grounds; to reduce the general capacity, to such an influence of justice, peace, religion, and liberty; and that, in lieu thereof, the people may make a rich and potent king.

As all rivers return to the ocean, so shall the laybrinth, we are in, be by the help of wise Ariadne's escaped, and the golden fleece, continuance of gospel, justice, peace, and downy tranquillity, with the help of those godly Medea's, be preserved and procured : Therefore, not as a lawyer, give me leave as a well-wisher to the state, to put the case by way of supposition.

If the fundamental laws be quite overthrown, religion altered, the nobility taken away by councils of war, as the Lord Mount-Norris should have been; the meaner sort used as Prynne, Burton, and Bastwick; the propriety of goods taken away from the subject ; an army force an arbitrary way of government, and justice, bought and sold; what misery will follow, when the judges shall affirm it legal, the clergy wrongfully in their pulpits teach it, and the cabinet-council authorise the conveniency, for matter of state ? Therefore, to have our laws established, religion maintained, the pride of prelates abased, justice administered, liberty settled, and peace continued for after times : It is necessary, the King, lords, and commons join in a most severe punishment, that none, in the Postea, dare to enterprise, the surprise and ruin of the common good; for it is an infallible maxim, The King is richer in the hearts, than in the treasures of his subjects.

Surely there was never a fitter time, nor a more convenient occasion then now, when three kingdoms unite for their own safety ; when the Scot hath an army on foot for this purpose, and the King hath promised they shall not be interrupted in their counsels, and God requires it for his glory.

Especially when ministers of state have begun to act this fatal tragedy, the guiltiness by so many lively testimonies proved, and the treason by precedents and weighty authority assured, by law maintained, and by all the commons-house adjudged; who have power by the 25th of Edward the Third; and when it is brought to so good a pass by the lords, who both have legislative power; why should not lords and commons bring it to perfection, that the King sign, that who shall dare to alter religion, innovate law, or take away liberty of the subject, be condignly punished, and, for the future, cause an express law to be made on purpose, to attaint blood, forfeit life, lands, and goods, if any shall essay such crying exorbitances ?

If by the law it be high treason to kill a commissioner of Oyer and Terminer, in time of justice; à majori, to confound the whole body, when a commissioner, is but one poor member of the body politick.

2. To make a law, that none be capable of any place of government, that hath, or shall give such counsel, and leave the rest to the triennial parliament, and not grasp too much, lest all the harpies fly away.

Likewise, it is necessary to make a remonstrance of the necessity of giving 300,000 pounds, to the Scots, to give satisfaction to future ages, that it was no pusillanimity, but upon mature deliberation ; because the evident necessity, and inevitable dangers cast upon us by ill counsel, justly caused it.

To the purpose, the house of commons hath done wisely, to endeavour to clip the wings of the clergy, that they may fly into no temporal place, whose pens and tongues have uttered such poison against the common good, and in their pride, would willingly adhere to Rome; as by many superstitions it plainly appears, they have introduced some Babylonian ceremonies, and made a bridge unto the church, by the Arminian opinion, to pass over to popery.

The state of Venice, jealous of any their members confederating with enemies, cause them to be strangled, and hanged up between columns, confiscate their goods and estates, banish their children, and make them incapable of government; if for jealousy, much more, for so foul acts committed, ought they to die, by the law of God and man

Among the Athenians, Lacedemonians, and Romans; whosoever should go about to alter the form of government, or laws, without publick consent, hath been ever accounted the highest traitor; witness their ostracism, and many such exemplary punishments, used to such wretches.

If destroying the head be high treason, then ruining the state of the body must be; for if it be suffocated with gross spirits, the head will not only ach, but be apoplectical or lethargical, such a sympathy or rather relation is betwixt head and members, that no rhetorick or eloquence can take it away: In this case it is no pity, but convenient to destroy the brood of such vipers, and by our law the intention makes it treason. But how many ways the Lord of Strafford hath perpetrated this intention, hath been often proved.

In 18, and 21, Jacobi, the whole house adjudged it treason, to alien the hearts of the subjects from the sovereign, which hath been done by his counsellors. His imprisoning without law, was high treason, in Sir Haukin Hanby, 25. E. 3. Art. 61, who was drawn, hanged, and quartered.

Judge Thorpe's giving such an oath, contrary to law, was high treason; and is not his?

The reason Richard the Second was deposed, plainly manifested, was, because he suffered divers malefactors to escape, condemned by parliament, which caused the oppression of the subject and ruin of the kingdom.

In all ages, a lethargy in Kings hath caused their ruin; witness Edward the Second, Richard the Second, and Henry the Sixth. I humbly desire God to bless his Majesty. But consider we, that the three kingdoms will not be satisfied, unless the wrong received be expiated with the oblation of some, who hath caused a heretick condition.

The Lord of Strafford hath had counsel, in case of treason, when none hath had the like since the conquest.

So the whole world may see with what temper, gravity, and patience they proceed.

Edward Earl of Northumberland, in the 8th of Richard II, because his deputy let the Scots take Berwick Castle, was condemned of high treason, and yet he never consented thereunto, for it was done without his privity; but the Lord of Strafford writ to the mayor of Newcastle, to let in the Scots, and caused the arms to be taken away from the four adjacent counties, making them incapable of defence.

Wherefore it is visible as the sun, he is guilty, besides his other crimes; now this delay of punishment hath kindled such a fire, as all the subjects of the three kingdoms are in a flame, and will not be satisfied:

Ex parvis magna crescunt.

I pray God divert the evil, and give us true repentance.

THE

NEGOTIATIONS OF THOMAS WOLSEY,

THE

GREAT CARDINAL OF ENGLAND.

CONTAINING HIS LIFE AND DEATH, viz.

I.   The Original of his Promotion.

II.   The Continuance in his Magnificence.

III.   His Fall, Death, and Burial.

Composed by Mr. Cavendish, one of his own Servants, being his Gentleman-Usher.

London, printed by William Sheers, 1641. Quarto, containing one-hundred twenty-six pages.

IT seemeth no wisdom to credit every light tale, blazed abroad in the mouths of vulgars, for we daily hear, how, with their blasphemous trump, they spread abroad innumerable lyes, without either shame or honesty, which, *prima facie*, shew forth a visage of truth, as though it were an absolute verity, though indeed nothing less; and, amongst the better sort, those babblings are of no validity.
I have read the allegations of divers worthy authors against such false rumours and opinions of the common people, who delight in nothing more, than to hear strange things, and to see new alterations of authority, rejoicing sometimes in such novelties, which afterwards

do produce repentance. Thus, may all men of understanding conceive the madness of the rude multitude, and not give too much credence to every sudden rumour, until the truth be perfectly known, by the report of some approved and credible persons, that commonly have the best intelligence.

I have heard, and also seen set forth in divers printed books, some untrue imaginations, after the death of divers persons, who, in their lives, were in great estimation, invented rather to bring their honest names in question than otherwise.

Now, forasmuch as I intend to write here some special proceedings of Cardinal Wolsey, the great archbishop, his ascending unto honour and great promotion, his continuance in it, and sudden falling from the same : A great part thereof shall be of mine own knowledge, and some part from credible persons informations.

This Cardinal was my lord and master, whom, in his life-time, I served, and so remained with him in his fall continually, during the time of all his troubles, both in the south and north parts, until he died. In all which time, I punctually observed all his demeanors, as also in his great triumph and glorious estate.

And, since his departure, I have heard divers surmised and imagined tales concerning his proceedings and dealings, which I myself have certainly known to be most untrue, unto which I could have sufficiently answered according to truth : But conceiving it to be much better to be silent, than to reply against their untruths, whereby I might, perhaps, have rather kindled a great flame of displeasure, than have quenched one spark of their untrue reports ; therefore I did refer the truth thereof to the Almighty, who knows the truth of all things.

Nevertheless, whatsoever any man hath conceived of him in his life, or since his death ; thus much, I dare say, without offence to any, that, in my judgment, I never saw this realm in better obedience, and quiet, than it was in the time of his authority, nor justice better administered, with partiality, as I could justly prove, if I should not be taxed with too much affection.

I will therefore here desist to speak any further, by the way of apology, and proceed now to speak of his original, and ascending through fortune's favour to high dignity, and abundance of wealth.

An Advertisement to the Reader.

WHO pleaseth to read this history advisedly, may well perceive the mutability of honour, the tottering state of earthly dignity, the deceit of flattering friends, and the instability of princes favours.

This great cardinal having experience of all this, witness his fleeting from honour, the loss of friends, riches, and dignities, being forgotten of his prince, whilst fortune smiled, having satiety of all these : and she, bending her brow, deprived him of all terrestrial joys, who, by twenty years study and pains, had obtained so great wealth and dignity, and, in less than one year, lost all.

And thus was his honour laid in the dust.

CHAP. I.

Of the Cardinal, his Original, and who he was.

TRUTH it is, Cardinal Wolsey was an honest poor man's son in the town of Ipswich, in the county of Suffolk, and there born, who being but a child was very apt to learn; wherefore, by means of his parents, and other his good friends, he was maintained at the university of Oxford, where, in a short time, he prospered so well, that, in a small time, as he told me with his own mouth, he was made batchelor of arts, when he was but fifteen years of age, and was most commonly called the boy batchelor. Thus, prospering in learning, he was made fellow of Magdalen college in Oxford; after that, he was made master of Magdalen School, at which time were the Lord Marquis of Dorset's sons there at school, committing unto him as well their education as their instructions and learning.

It pleased this Lord Marquis, against Christmas, to send as well for the schoolmaster as for the scholars home to his house, for their recreation in that pleasant and honourable forest. They being a while there, the Lord Marquis their father perceiving them to be well improved in learning for the time: He was so well contented, that he, having a benefice in his gift, being at that present void, gave the schoolmaster the same, in regard of his diligence. After Christmas, at his departure to the university, he having the presentation thereof, repaired to the ordinary for his institution; and, being then furnished with all his instruments, at the ordinary's hands, for his preferment, made haste, without any further delay, to his benefice, to take possession thereof. Now you shall understand, that the schoolmaster had not been long there, but one Sir James Pawlet, Knt. dwelling in the country thereabouts, took an occasion of displeasure against him, but upon what ground I know not: Insomuch, that Sir James was so bold as to set the schoolmaster by the heels during his displeasure, which affront was afterwards neither forgotten, nor forgiven: For, when the schoolmaster mounted so high as to be lord chancellor of England, he was not forgetful of his old displeasure most cruelly ministered unto him by Sir James, but sent for him, and after a very sharp reproof enjoined him not to depart out of London, without license first obtained; so that he continued in the Middle Temple the space of five or six years, and afterwards lay in the Gatehouse next the stairs, which he re-edified, and sumptuously beautified the same all over on the outside, with the cardinal's arms, his hat, his cognisance and badges, with other devices, in so glorious a manner, as he thought thereby to have appeased his old displeasure.

This may be a good precedent for men in authority, which work their own wills without wit, to remember that greatness may decay. And those, whom they do punish more of humour than justice, may afterwards be advanced to great honour, as this Cardinal was, and they abased as low as this Sir James was, which seek revenge. Who would have thought, when Sir James Paulet punished this poor school-master, that ever he should have mounted to so great dignity as to be chancellor of England, considering his mean parentage and friends? These be the wonderful works of God's Providence. And I would wish, that all men in authority would fear God, in all ages, in the time of their triumph and greatness, considering that advancement and authority are not permanent, but many times slide and vanish suddenly away; as princes pleasures alter and change, or, as all living creatures must, of necessity, pay the debt due to nature, which no earthly creature can resist.

Shortly after, it chanced the said Lord Marquis died, after whose decease, the schoolmaster thinking himself but a weak beneficed man, and that he had left his fellowship in the college; for, as I understand, if a fellow of that house be once promoted to a benefice, he shall, by the rules of the same house, be dismissed of his fellowship; and now, being also destitute of his singular good lord, as well as of his fellowship, which was most of his relief, thought long to be provided of some other help, to defend him from all such storms as he might meet with. In his travel thereabouts, he grew acquainted with a very great and ancient knight, who had a great place in Calais, under King Henry the Seventh. This knight he served, and behaved himself so discreetly, that he obtained the special favour of his said master; insomuch that, for his wit and gravity, he committed all the care and charge of his said office to his said chaplain. And, as I understand, his office was the treasurership of Calais, who, in regard of his great age, shortly after was discharged of his said office, and so returned into England, intending to live a more private life; but, through his instant labour and good favour, his chaplain was preferred to be the King's chaplain. And, when he had once cast anchor in the port of promotion, how he then bestirred himself, I shall now declare.

He having, then, just occasion to be daily in sight of the King in his closet, not spending the rest of the day in idleness, would attend those men, whom he thought to bear most rule in the council, and were most in favour with the King; which, at that time, was Dr. Fox, Bishop of Winchester, and lord privy-seal; and also Sir Thomas Lovell, Knight, a very sage and wise counsellor, being master of the wards and constable of the Tower.

These ancient and grave counsellors, in process of time, perceiving this chaplain to be a man of a very acute wit, thought him a meet instrument to be employed in greater affairs.

Not long after, it happened that the King had an urgent occasion, to send an ambassador to Maximilian the Emperor, who lay, at that present, in the Low Countries, at Flanders, and not far from Calais.

Now the bishop of Winchester and Sir Thomas Lovell, whom the King most esteemed, as the chiefest of his council, one day, advising

and debating with themselves upon this ambassage; and, by this time,
they saw they had a convenient occasion to prefer the King's chaplain,
whose excellent eloquence, and learning, they highly commended unto
the King's Highness; who giving ear unto them, and being a prince of
an excellent judgment and modesty, he commanded them to bring his
chaplain, whom they so commended, before his Grace; and being come,
his Majesty, to prove his ability, entered into discourse with him, concerning matters of state, whereby, the King had so well informed himself, that he fonnd him to be a man of a sharp wit, and of such excellent parts, that he thought him worthy to be put in trust with matters
of greater consequence.

———

CHAP. II.

Of the Cardinal's speedy Dispatch in his first Ambassage to the Emperor Maximilian.

THE King, being now resolved to employ him in this ambassage,
commanded him, thereupon, to prepare himself for his journey; and,
for his dispatch, wished him to repair to his Grace, and his council, of
whom he should receive his commission and instruction. By means
whereof, he had then a fit occasion to repair, from time to time, into
the King's presence, who had, thereby, daily experience of his singular
wisdom, and sound judgment. Thus having his dispatch, he took his
leave of the King at Richmond, about four o'clock in the afternoon,
where he launched forth in a Gravesend barge, with a prosperous wind
and tide; and his happy speed was such, that he arrived at Gravesend
in little more than three hours, where he tarried no longer, than the
post-horses were provided; and he travelled so speedily, that he came
to Dover the next morning, where the passengers were under sail to
pass to Calais; so that, long before noon, he arrived there, and having
post-horses prepared, departed from thence, without tarrying, making
such hasty speed, that he was, that night, with the Emperor; who, understanding of the arrival of the King of England's ambassador, would,
in no wise, delay time, but sent for him incontinently; for his affection
to the King of England was such, that he was glad of any opportunity to do him a courtesy.

The ambassador declares the sum of his ambassy unto the Emperor,
of whom he craved speedy expedition, which was granted him; so that,
the next day, he was clearly dispatched, and all the King's requests
fully accomplished and granted. At which time, he made no further
stay, but took post-horses that night, and rode, without intermission,
to Calais, being conducted thither by divers nobles, appointed by the
Emperor; and, at the opening of the gates of Calais, he came thither,
where the passengers were ready to return for England, insomuch that
he arrived at Dover, between ten and eleven o'clock in the forenoon.

And, having post-horses in readiness, he came to the court at Richmond that same night; where, taking his repose until morning, he pre-

sented himself unto his Majessy, at his first coming out of his bedchamber to his closet, to mass, whom, when he saw, he checked, for that he was not on his journey.

Sir, quoth he, if it may please your Highness, I have already been with the Emperor, and dispatched your affairs, I trust, to your Grace's contentation; and, thereupon, presented the King with his letters of credence from the Emperor. The King, wondering at his speedy return, he being so well furnished with all his proceedings, for the present, dissembled his admiration and imagination in that matter, and demanding of him, whether he encountered with his pursuivant, which he sent unto him with letters, imagining him to be scarce out of London, which concerned very material passages, which were omitted in their consultation, which the King earnestly desired should have been dispatched in his ambassage.

Yes, forsooth, quoth he, I met with him yesterday, by the way; and, though I had no knowledge thereof, yet, notwithstanding, I have been so bold, upon my own discretion, perceiving the matter to be very necessary in that behalf, that I dispatched the same : and, forasmuch as I have been so bold to exceed my commission, I most humbly crave your royal remission and pardon.

The King, inwardly rejoicing, replied, we do not only pardon you, but give you our princely thanks, both for your good exploit, and happy expedition; and dismissed him for that present, and bade him return to him again after dinner, for a further relation of his ambassage, and so the King went to mass.

It is not to be doubted, but this ambassador had, all this while, visited his great friends, the bishop of Winchester, and Sir Thomas Lovell, to whom he had declared the effect of his ambassage ; and, also, his Majesty's commendations of him did not a little rejoice the worthy counsellors, forasmuch as he was of their preferment; and, shortly after, the King gave him, for his diligent service, the deanery of Lincoln, which was, in those days, one of the greatest promotions, that he gave, under the degree of a bishop; and he grew more and more in estimation and authority, and was, afterwards, promoted to be almoner.

Now, not long after, when death, that favoureth no estates, nor King, nor Emperor, had taken away the wise King Henry the Seventh out of this present life, it was a wonder to see, what practices and devices were then used about the young Prince, Henry the Eighth ; the great provision that was then made, for the funeral of the one, and for the coronation of the other, by the now Queen Catharine, and mother, after the Queen's Highness that now is, whose virtuous life Jesu long preserve.

After the solemnizations, and costly triumphs, our natural, young, courageous, lusty Prince, and Sovereign, Lord King Henry the Eighth, entering into his flower, and lusty youth, took upon him the royal scepter, and imperial diadem of this fertile nation, the twenty-second of April, *anno dom.* 1509, which, at that time, flourished with all abundance of riches, wherewith the King was most inestimably furnished, called then the Golden World.

Now, shortly after, the almoner, seeing he had a plain path-way to promotion, behaved himself so politickly, that he was made one of the King's Privy-council, and increased in favour daily; to whom he gave a house, at Bridewell, near Fleet-street, where he kept his house for his family, and so he daily attended upon the King, being in special favour.

His sentences in the Star-chamber were ever so pithy and witty, that, upon all occasions, they assigned him, for the fluent eloquence of his tongue, to be the expositor to the King in all their proceedings; in whom the King received so great content, that he called him still nearer to his person; and the rather, because he was most ready to advance the King's own will and pleasure, having no respect to the case.

Now the King being young, and much given to his pleasure, his old counsellors advised him to have recourse, sometimes, to the council, about his weighty affairs; but the almoner, on the contrary, persuaded him to mind his pleasure, and he would take his care and charge upon himself, if his Majesty would countenance him with his authority, which the King liked well; and thus none was, like to the almoner, in favour with the King.

CHAP. III.

Of King Henry's Invading France, in his own Person, with the Cardinal's Assistance.

THUS the almoner continuing in high favour, till, at last, many presents, gifts, and rewards, came in so plentifully, that, I dare say, he wanted nothing, for he had all things in abundance, that might either please his fancy, or inrich his coffers, for the times so favourably smiled upon him, but, to what end, you shall hereafter hear. Therefore, let all men, to whom fortune extendeth her favour and grace, take heed, they trust not her subtle and fair promises, for, under colour thereof, she carrieth an envious gall : for, when she seeth her servant in highest authority, she turneth her favour, and pleasant countenance, into frowns.

This almoner climbed up fortune's wheel, so that no man was in estimation with the King, but only he, for his witty qualities and wisdom.

He had an especial gift of natural eloquence, and a filed tongue to pronounce the same; so that he was able, therewith, to persuade and allure all men to his purposes, in the time of his continuance in fortune's favour.

In the fifth year of the reign of King Henry the Eighth, it chanced, that the realms of England and France were at variance, but upon what ground, or occasion, I know not; insomuch that the King was fully resolved, in his own person, to invade France with a puissant army: it was, therefore, thought very necessary, that his royal enterprises should be speedily provided, and furnished, in every degree, in things apt and convenient for the same: for expedition thereof, the King thought no man's wit so meet for policy, and painful travel, as the almoner, to whom he committed his whole affiance and trust therein; and he being nothing scrupulous, in any thing that the King would command, although it seemed very difficult, took upon him the whole charge of the business, and proceeded so therein, that he brought all things to good effect, in direct order, for all manner of victuals and provisions, convenient for so noble a voyage and army.

All things being thus prepared, by him, in order, the King, not intending to neglect or delay any time, but, with noble and valiant courage, to advance his royal enterprise, passed the seas between Dover and Calais, where he prosperously arrived: and, after he had there made his arrival, and landed all his provision, and ammunition, and sat in consultation about his weighty affairs, marched forth, in good order of battle, till he came to the strong town of Turwine, to the which he laid strong siege, and made a sharp assault, so that, in short space, it was yielded unto him; unto which place, the Emperor Maximilian resorted to him with a great army, like a mighty prince, taking of the King's wages.

Thus, after the King had taken this strong town, and taken possession thereof, and set all things in good order, for the defence and preservation thereof, to his Majesty's use, then he retired from thence, and marched towards Tournay, and there laid siege in like manner; to which he gave so fierce assault, that the enemies were constrained to render the town to his Majesty. At which time, the King gave unto the almoner the bishoprick of the same see, towards his pains and diligence sustained in that journey. And when he had established all things, according to his princely mind and pleasure, and furnished the same with men, and captains of war, for the safeguard of the town, he prepared for his return to England.

But now you shall understand, by the way, that, whilst the King was absent with a great power in France, the Scotish King invaded England, against whom the Queen sent a great army, the Earl of Surrey being general, where he overthrew the Scots at Blamston, called Hoddenfield, where the King of Scots was slain, with divers of his nobility, and eighteen thousand men, and they took all his ammunition for war.

By this time, the King returned into England, and took with him divers noble personages of France, being prisoners; as the Duke of Longuido, Viscount Clermont, with divers others, that were taken in a skirmish.

And, thus, God gave him victory at home, and victory abroad, being in the fifth year of his reign, anno dom. 1513.

<hr />

CHAP. IV.

The King's Promoting his Almoner, being made Cardinal, and Lord Chancellor of England.

THE King being returned into England, the see of Lincoln became void by the death of Dr. Smith, late bishop there; which bishoprick the King gave to the almoner elect of Tournay, who was not negligent to take possession thereof, but made all speed for his consecration, the solemnisation thereof being ended, he found a way to get into his hands all his predecessor's goods, whereof I have seen divers parts that furnished his house.

It was not long after, but Dr. Bambrige, Archbishop of York, died at Rohan, in France, being there the King's ambassador; unto which see the King presented the last new Bishop of Lincoln, so that he had three bishopricks in his hands at one time, all in one year given him. Then prepared he again for his translation from the see of Lincoln to that of York, as he did before to his installation.

After which solemnisation done and being then archbishop, and *Primas Angliæ*, thought himself sufficient to compare with that of Canterbury, and did thereupon advance his crosses in the courts, and every other place, as well in the precinct and jurisdiction of Canterbury, as any other place; and, forasmuch as Canterbury claimeth a superiority over York, as well as over any other bishoprick within England, and, for that cause, claimeth an acknowledgment, as in ancient obedience of York, to abate advancement of his crosses, to the crosses of Canterbury.

Notwithstanding, York not desisting to bear the same, although Canterbury gave York a check for the same, and told him, it was presumption, by reason whereof, there ingendered some grudge between them: but, shortly after, he obtained to be made cardinal and *Legatus de Latere*, unto whom the Pope sent the Cardinal's cap, and certain bulls, for his authority in that behalf, whereupon, he was installed at Westminster in great triumph, which was executed by all bishops with their mitres, caps, and other ornaments; and, after all this, he was made Chancellor of England, and Canterbury, who was the chancellor, was dismissed.

Now, he being in the chancellorship, and endowed with the promotions of archbishop and cardinal *de latere*, thought himself so fully furnished, that he was now able to surmount Canterbury in all jurisdictions; and, in all ecclesiastical powers, to convocate Canterbury, and all other bishops, and spiritual persons, to assemble at his convocations, where he would assign to take upon him the convention of all ministers, and others within their jurisdictions, and visited all the spiritual houses in their diocess, and all manner of spiritual ministers, as commissioners, scribes, apparitors, and all other necessary officers to furnish his courts; and did convene, by convention, whom he pleased through this realm and dominion, and all other persons, to the glory of his dignity.   Then he had two great crosses of silver, whereof one was of his archbishoprick, and the other of his legateship, borne before him wheresoever he rode, or went, by two of the tallest priests that he could get in this realm.

And, to the increase of his gain, he had in his hand the bishoprick of Durham, and St. Albans, in commendam; also, when Dr. Fox, bishop of Winchester, died, he did surrender Durham to the King, and took himself to Winchester.   He had also, as it were in farm, the bishopricks of Bath, Worcester, and Hereford, for the incumbents of them were strangers.   He had also, attending upon him, men of great possessions, and the tallest yeomen, for his guard, in the realm.

CHAP. V.

Of the Orders and Offices of his House and Chapel.

AND first, for his house, you shall understand, that he had in his hall three boards, kept with three several officers, that is to say, a steward, that was always a priest; a treasurer, that was ever a knight; and a comptroller, that was an esquire; also a confessor, a doctor, three marshals, three ushers in the hall, besides two almoners and grooms.

Then had he in the hall-kitchen two clerks, a clerk-comptroller, and a surveyor over the dresser, with a clerk in the spicery, which kept continually a mess together in the hall; also he had in the kitchen two cooks, labourers, and children, twelve persons; four men of the scullery, two yeomen of the pastry, with two other paste-layers under the yeomen.

Then had he in his kitchen a master-cook, who went daily in velvet or sattin, with a gold chain; besides two other cooks, and six labourers in the same room.

In the larder, one yeoman and a groom; in the scullery, one yeoman and two grooms; in the buttery, two yeomen and two grooms; in the ewry, so many; in the cellar, three yeomen and three pages; in the chandery, two yeomen; in the wayfary, two yeomen; in the wardrobe of beds, the master of the wardrobe, and twenty persons besides; in the laundry, a yeoman, groom, and thirteen pages, two yeomen-purveyors, and a groom-purveyor; in the bakehouse, two yeomen and grooms; in the wood-yard, one yeoman and a groom; in the barn, one yeoman; porters at the gate, two yeomen and two grooms; a yeoman in his barge, and a master of his horse; a clerk of the stables, and a yeoman of the same; a farrier, and a yeoman of the stirrup; a mult-lour and sixteen grooms, every one of them keeping four geldings.

Now will I declare unto you the officers of his chapel, and singing-men of the same.   First, he had there a dean, a great divine, and a man of excellent learning; and a sub-dean, a repeater of the choir, a gospeller, an epistler of the singing priests, and a master of the children:

in the vestry, a yeoman, and two grooms, besides other retainers that came thither at principal feasts.

And, for the furniture of his chapel, it passeth my weak capacity to declare the number of the costly ornaments, and rich jewels that were occupied in the same; for I have seen, in procession about the hall, forty-four rich copes of one settle worn, besides the rich candlesticks, and other necessary ornaments to the furniture of the same.

Now you shall understand, that he had two cross-bearers, and two pillar-bearers in his great chamber; and in his privy chamber, all these persons, the chief chamberlain, a vice-chamberlain, a gentleman-usher, besides one of his privy-chamber; he had also twelve waiters, and six gentlemen waiters; also he had nine or ten lords, who had each of them two or three men to wait upon him, except the Earl of Derby, who had five men.

Then he had gentlemen cup-bearers, and carvers; and of the sewers, both of the great chamber, and of the privy chamber, forty persons; six yeomen ushers, eight grooms of his chamber; also he had of alms, who were daily waiters of his board at dinner; twelve doctors and chaplains, besides them of his, which I never rehearsed; a clerk of his closet, and two secretaries, and two clerks of his signet: four counsellors learned in the law.

And, for that he was chancellor of England, it was necessary to have officers of the chancery to attend him for the better furniture of the same.

First, he had a riding clerk, a clerk of the crown, a clerk of the hamper, and a chafer; then he had a clerk of the check, as well upon the chaplains, as upon the yeomen of the chamber; he had also four footmen, garnished with rich running coats, whensoever he had any journey. Then he had a herald of arms, a serjeant of arms, a physician, an apothecary, four minstrels, a keeper of his tents, an armourer, and instructor of his wards, an instructor of his wardrobe of robes, a keeper of his chamber continually; he had also in his house a surveyor of York, a clerk of the green cloth. All these were daily attending, downlying and uprising: and at meat, he had eight continual boards for the chamberlains, and gentlemen officers, having a mess of young lords, and another of gentlemen; besides this, there was never a gentleman, or officer, or other worthy person, but he kept some two, some three persons to wait upon them; and all others, at the least, had one, which did amount to a great number of persons.

Now, having declared the order according to the chain roll, use of his house, and what officers he had daily attending to furnish the same, besides retainers, and other persons, being suitors, dined in the hall: and, when shall we see any more such subjects that shall keep such a noble house? Therefore here is an end of his houshold; the number of persons in the chain were eight hundred persons.

===

CHAP. VI.

Of his second Ambassage to the Emperor Charles the Fifth.

AFTER he was thus furnished, in manner as I have before rehearsed unto you, he was sent twice on ambassage to the Emperor Charles the Fifth, that now reigneth, and father to King Philip, now our Lord and Sovereign: forasmuch as the old Emperor Maximilian was dead, and, for divers other urgent occasions, touching his Majesty, it was thought fit that about such weighty matters, and to so noble a prince, the Cardinal was most meet to be sent on this ambassage; and he, being one ready to take the charge thereof upon him, was furnished, in every respect, most like a great prince, which was much to the honour of his Majesty, and of this realm: for, first, he proceeded forth like a cardinal, having all things correspondent; his gentlemen, being very many in number, were clothed in livery coats of crimson velvet of the best, and chains of gold about their necks; and his yeomen, and all his mean officers, were clad in fine scarlet, guarded with black velvet one handbreadth. Thus furnished, he was twice sent in this manner to the Emperor in Flanders, then lying at Bruges, whom he did most nobly entertain, discharging all his own charges, and his men's. There was no house in the town of Bruges, wherein any of my Lord's gentlemen were lodged or had recourse, but that the owners of the houses were commanded by the Emperor's officers, upon the pain of their lives, to take no money for any thing that the Cardinal's men did take of any kind of victuals; no, although they were disposed to make costly banquets, further commanding their said hosts than they should want nothing which they honestly required, or desired to have.

Also the Emperor's officers every night went through the town from house to house, where any Englishmen had recourse, or lodged, and served their livery for all night, which was done on this manner: first, the officers brought into the house a casteel of fine manchet, then two silver pots of wine, and a pound of sugar, white lights, and yellow lights, a bowl of silver, and a goblet to drink in, and every night a staff torch. This was the order of their livery every night; and then, in the morning, when the officers came to fetch away their stuff, they would account for the gentlemen's costs the day before.

Thus the Emperor entertained the Cardinal, and his train, during the time of his ambassy. And, that done, he returned into England with great triumph, being no less in estimation with the King than he was before, but rather much more; for he increased daily in the King's favour, by reason of his wit and readiness to do the King pleasure in all things.

In the one-and-twentieth year of King Henry the Eighth's reign, *anno dom.* 1529, this Emperor Charles the Fifth came into England, who was nobly entertained.

CHAP. VII.

Of the Manner of his going to Westminster-Hall.

NOW must I declare the manner of his going to Westminster-hall in the term time: First, when he came out of his privy-chamber, he most commonly heard two masses in his chapel or chamber. And I heard one of his chaplains say since, that was a man of credit, and excellent learning, that, what business soever the Cardinal had in the day-time, he never went to bed with any part of his service unsaid, no, not so much as one collect, in which, I think, he deceived many a man: then, going into his chamber again, he demanded of some of his servants if they were in readiness, and had furnished his chamber of presence, and waiting chamber: he, being then advertised, came out of his privy-chamber about eight of the clock, ready apparelled, and in red, like a cardinal; his upper vesture was all of scarlet, or else of fine crimson taffata, or crimson sattin ingrained, his pillion scarlet, with a black velvet tippet of sables about his neck, holding in his hand an orange, the meat or substance thereof being taken out and filled again with a part of sponge, with vinegar, and other confections against pestilent airs, the which he most commonly held to his nose, when he came to the presses, or when he was pestered with many suitors: and before him was borne the broad seal of England, and the cardinal's hat, by some lord, or some gentleman of worship, right solemnly: and, as soon as he was entered into his chamber of presence, where there were daily attending on him as well noblemen of this realm, as other worthy gentlemen of his own family, his two great crosses were there attending upon him; then cry the gentlemen-ushers that go before him bare-headed: On masters before, and make room for my lord. Thus, when he went down into the hall with a serjeant of arms before him, bearing a great mace of silver, and two gentlemen carrying two great plates of silver; and, when he came to the hall-door, there his mule stood trapped all in crimson velvet, with a saddle of the same.

Then were attending him, when he was mounted, his two cross-bearers, and his two pillar-bearers, all upon great horses, and in fine scarlet; then he marched on with a train of gentry, having four footmen about him, bearing every one of them a pole-ax in his hand: and thus passed he forth till he came to Westminster, and there alighted and went in this manner up to the Chancery, and staid a while at a bar, made for him beneath the Chancery; and there he communed sometimes with the judges, and sometimes with other persons, and then went up to the Chancery, and sat there till eleven of the clock to hear suits, and to determine causes; and from thence he would go into the Star-chamber, as occasion served him; he neither spared high nor low, but did judge every one according to right.

Every Sunday he would resort to the court, being then at Greenwich, with his former rehearsed train and triumph, taking his barge at his own stairs, furnished with yeomen standing upon the sails, and his gentlemen within and about, and landed at the Three Cranes in the Vine-tree; and from thence he rode upon his mule with his crosses, his pillars, his hat, and his broad seal carried before him on horseback along Thames-street until he came to Billingsgate; and there he took his barge, and so went to Greenwich, where he was nobly entertained by the lords in the King's house, being there with staves in their hands, as the treasurer, comptroller, with many others, and conveyed into the King's chamber, and so went home again in the like triumph.

CHAP. VIII.

Of the Cardinal's Magnificence in his Houses.

HE lived a long season ruling all things in this realm appertaining to the King by his wisdom, and all other matters of foreign regions, with whom the King had any occasion to meddle. All ambassadors of foreign potentates were ever disposed by the cardinal's wisdom, to whom they had continual access for their dispatch.

His house was always resorted unto like a King's house, with noblemen and gentlemen; and when it pleased the King's Majesty, as many times it did, he would, for his recreation, resort unto the Cardinal's house, against whose coming there wanted no preparations or goodly furnitures, with victuals of the finest sort that could be had for money or friendship.

Such pleasures were here devised for the King's delight, as could be invented or imagined; banquets set with masquers and mummers, in such a costly manner, that it was glorious to behold; there wanted no damsels meet to dance with the masquers, or to garnish the place, for the time, with variety of other pastimes. Then were there divers kinds of musick, and many choice men and women singers appointed to sing, who had excellent voices. I have seen the King come suddenly thither in a masque, with a dozen masquers all in garments like shepherds, made of fine cloth of gold and silver wire, and six torch-bearers, besides their drummers, and others attending on them with vizards, and clothed all in sattin. And, before his entering into the hall, you shall understand that he came by water to the water-gate without any noise, where were laid divers chambers and guns charged with shot, and at his landing they were discharged, which made such a rattling noise in the air, that it was like thunder: It made all the noblemen, gentlemen, and ladies, to muse what it should mean coming so suddenly, they sitting quietly at a banquet. In this sort you shall understand, that the tables were set in the chamber of presence covered, and my lord cardinal sitting under his cloth of state, and there having all his service alone; and then were there set a lady and a nobleman, a gentleman and a gentlewoman, thoughout all the tables in the chambers on the one side, which were made all joining, as it were, but

one table.   All which order was done by my Lord Sands, then lord
chamberlain to the King, and by Sir Henry Guildford, then comptroller
of the King's house.

Then, immediately after this great shot of guns, the cardinal desired
the lord chamberlain to see what it did mean, as though he knew
nothing of the matter; they then looked out of the window into the
Thames, and, returning again, told him, that they thought they were
noblemen and strangers arrived at the bridge, and coming as ambassadors from some foreign prince: With that, said the cardinal, I desire
you, because you can speak French, to take the pains to go into the
hall, there to receive them into the chamber, where they shall see us,
and all those noble personages, being merry at our banquet, desiring
them to sit down with us, and take part of our fare.

Then went they incontinently into the hall, where they were received
with twenty torches, and conveyed up into the chamber with such a
number of drums and flutes, as I have seldom seen together at one time
and place.

Then, at their arrival into the chamber, they went two and two
together directly before the cardinal where he sat, and saluted them
very reverently: To whom the lord chamberlain, for them, said; ' Sir,
forasmuch as they are strangers, and cannot speak English, they have
desired me to declare unto you, that they, having understanding, at
this your triumphant banquet, were assembled such a number of fair
dames, they could do no less, under the supportation of your grace,
than to view as well their incomparable beauties, as to accompany them
at mumchance, and after that to dance with them, so to beget their
better acquaintance.'

And, furthermore, they require of your grace license, to accomplish this cause of their coming.

When the cardinal said he was willing, and very well content they
should do so.

Then went the masquers, and first saluted all the dames, and then
returned to the most worthy, and there opened the great cup of gold,
filled with crowns, and other pieces, to cast at.

Thus perusing all the gentlewomen, of some they won, and to some
they lost.   And, having viewed all the ladies, they returned to the
cardinal with great reverence, pouring down all their gold, which was
above two hundred crowns.   At all, quoth the cardinal, and casting the
dye he won it, whereat was made great joy.

Then, quoth the cardinal to my lord chamberlain, I pray you go
tell them, that to me it seemeth that there should be a nobleman
amongst them, that better deserves to sit in this place than I, to whom
I should gladly surrender the same, according to my duty, if I
knew him.

Then spoke my lord chamberlain to them in French, declaring my
lord cardinal's words; and, they rounding him again in the ear, the lord
chamberlain said unto my lord cardinal:

Sir, quoth he, they confess that among them is such a noble personage, whom, if your grace can point out from the rest, he is contented
to disclose himself, and to accept of your place most willingly.

With that the cardinal, taking good advice, went amongst them; and at the last, quoth he, it seemeth to me, that the gentleman with the black beard should be he; and with that he rose out of his chair, and offered the same to the gentleman with the black beard, with the cup in his hand: But the cardinal was mistaken, for the person to whom he then offered his chair was Sir Edward Nevill, a comely knight, and of a goodly personage, who did more resemble his Majesty's person than any other in that masque.

The King, seeing the cardinal so deceived in his choice, could not forbear laughing, but pulled down his vizard, and Sir Edward Nevill's also, with such a pleasant countenance and chear, that all the noble estates desired his Highness to take his place: To whom the King made answer, that he would first go and shift him: And thereupon he went into the cardinal's bed-chamber, where was a great fire prepared for him, and there he newly apparelled himself with rich and princely garments ; and, in the King's absence, the dishes of the banquet were clean taken away, and the tables covered again with new and perfumed cloaths, every man sitting still until the King's Majesty, with his masquers, came in among them, every man new apparelled.

Then the King took his seat under the cloth of estate, commanding every person to sit still as they did before; and then came in a new banquet before his Majesty of two hundred dishes, and so they passed the night in banqueting and dancing until morning, which much rejoiced the cardinal, to see his sovereign lord so pleasant at his house.

CHAP. IX.

Of the original Instrument of the Cardinal's Fall, Mistress Anne Bullen.

NOW you shall understand, that the young lord of Northumberland attended upon my lord cardinal, who, when the cardinal went to court, would ever have conference with Mistress Anne Bullen, who then was one of the maids of honour to Queen Catharine, insomuch that at last they were contracted together, which, when the King heard, he was much moved thereat, for he had a private affection to her himself, which was not yet discovered to any, and then advised the cardinal to send for the Earl of Northumberland, his father, and take order to dissolve the contract made between the said parties; which the lord cardinal did, after a sharp reprehension, in regard he was contracted without the King and his father's knowledge: He sent for his father, who came to London very speedily, and came first to my lord cardinal, as all great personages did, that in such sort were sent for, of whom they were advertised of the cause of their sending for: And, when the earl was come, he was presently brought to the cardinal into the gallery. After whose meeting, my lord cardinal and he were in secret communication a long space ; after their long discourse, and drinking a cup of wine, the earl departed, and, at his going away, he sat down at the gallery end in the hall, upon a form, and, being set, called his son unto him, and said:

Son, quoth he, even as thou art, and ever hast been a proud, disdainful, and very unthrifty master, so thou hast now declared thyself: Wherefore what joy, what pleasure, what comfort, or what solace can I conceive in thee? That thus, without discretion, hast abused thyself, having neither regard to me thy natural father, nor unto thy natural sovereign lord, to whom all honest and loyal subjects bear faithful obedience, nor yet to the prosperity of thy own estate; but hast so unadvisedly ensnared thyself to her for whom thou hast purchased the King's high displeasure, intolerable for any subject to sustain. And, but that the King doth consider the lightness of thy head, and wilful qualities of thy person, his displeasure and indignation were sufficient to cast me, and all my posterity, into utter ruin and destruction. But he, being my singular good lord, and favourable prince, and my lord cardinal my very good friend, have, and do clearly excuse me in thy lewdness, and do rather lament thy folly, than malign thee, and have advised an order to be taken for thee, to whom both I and you are more bound, than we conceive of. I pray to God that this may be a sufficient admonition unto thee, to use thyself more wisely hereafter; for, assure thyself, that, if thou dost not amend thy prodigality, thou wilt be the last earl of our house: For thy natural inclination, thou art masterful and prodigal, to consume all that thy progenitors have, with great travel, gathered and kept together with honour: But, having the King's Majesty my singular good lord, I trust, I assure thee, so to order my succession, that thou shall consume thereof but a little.

For I do not intend, I tell thee truly, to make thee heir; for, thanks be to God, I have more boys, that, I trust, will use themselves much better, and prove more like to wise and honest men; of whom I will chuse the most likely to succeed me.

Now, good masters and gentlemen, quoth he unto us, it may be your chances hereafter, when I am dead, to see those things, that I have spoken to my son, prove as true as I now speak them; yet, in the mean time, I desire you all to be his friends, and tell him his faults in what he doth amiss; wherein you shall shew yourselves friendly to him; and so I take my leave of you. And, son, go your ways unto my lord your master, and serve him diligently; and so parted, and went down into the hall, and took his barge.

Then, after long and large debating the matter about the Lord Piercy's assurance to Mrs. Anne Bullen, it was devised, that the contract should be infringed and dissolved, and that the Lord Piercy should marry one of the Earl of Shrewsbury's daughters. And so, indeed, not long after he did; whereby the former contract was broken and dissolved, wherewith Mrs. Anne was greatly displeased; promising, That, if ever it lay in her power, she would do the cardinal some displeasure; which indeed she afterwards did. But yet he was not altogether to be blamed, for he did nothing, but what the King commanded; whereby the Lord Piercy was charged to avoid her company. And so was she, for a time, dicharged the court, and sent home to her father; whereat she was much troubled and perplexed; for all this time she knew nothing of the King's intended purpose. But we may see, when fortune doth begin to frown, how she can compass a matter of displeasure, through a far fetched mark : Now, therefore, of the grudge, how it began, that in process of time wrought the cardinal's utter destruction.

CHAP. X.

Of Mrs. Anne Bullen's Favour with the King.

OH Lord, what a great God art thou! that workest thy wonders so secretly, that they are not perceived, until they be brought to pass and finished.

Attend now, good reader, to this story following, and note every circumstance, and thou shalt, at the end, perceive a wonderful work of God against such as forget him and his benefits.

Therefore, I say, consider; after this my Lord Piercy's troublesome business was over, and all things brought to an end, then Mrs. Anne Bullen was again admitted to the court; where she flourished in great estimation and honour, having always a prime grudge against my lord cardinal, for breaking the contract between the Lord Piercy and herself, supposing it had been his own device and no other's; and she, at last, knowing the King's pleasure, and the depth of his secrets, then began to look very haughtily and stout, lacking no manner of rich apparel, or jewels, that money could purchase.

It was, therefore, imagined by many through the court, that she, being in such favour, might do much with the King, and obtain any suit of him for her friends. All this while, she being in this estimation in all places, there was no doubt, but good Queen Catharine, having this gentlewoman daily attending upon her, both heard by report, and saw with her eyes, how all things tended against her good ladyship; although she seemed neither to Mrs. Anne Bullen, nor the King, to carry any spark of discontent, or displeasure; but accepted all things in good part, and with great wisdom, and much patience dissembled the same, having Mrs. Anne Bullen in more estimation for the King's sake, than when she was with her before, declaring herself indeed to be a very patient Grissel, as, by her long patience in all her troubles, shall hereafter most plainly appear.

For the King was now so enamoured of this young gentlewoman, that he knew not how sufficiently to advance her.

This being perceived by all the great lords of the court, who bore a secret grudge against my lord cardinal, for that they could not rule in the kingdom as they would for him, because he was *Dominus fac totum* with the King, and ruled as well the great lords, as the mean subjects; whereat they took an occasion to work him out of the King's favour, and consequently themselves into more estimation,

And, after long and secret consultation with themselves, how to
bring this matter to pass, they knew very well, that it was somewhat
difficult for them to do absolutely of themselves; wherefore they
perceiving the great affection and love, the King bore to Mrs. Anne
Bullen, supposing in their judgments, that she would be a fit instrument
to bring their earnest intentions to pass, therefore they often consulted
with her to that purpose; and she, having both a very good wit, and
also an inward grudge and displeasure against my lord Cardinal, was
ever as ready to accomplish their desires, as they were themselves;
wherefore there was no more to do, but only to imagine an occasion to
work their malice by some pretended circumstances.   Then did they
daily invent divers devices how to effect their purpose; but the
enterprise thereof was so dangerous, that, though they would fain have
attempted the matter with the King, yet durst they not, for they knew
the great zeal the King did bear unto the cardinal; and this they knew
very well, That, if the matter they should propound against him, was
not grounded upon a just and urgent cause, the King's love was such
towards him, and his wit such withal, that he could with his policy
vanquish all their enterprises, and then, after that, requite them in the
like nature, to their utter ruin.

. Therefore they were compelled to forbear their plots, till they might
have some better ground to work upon.   And now the cardinal,
perceiving the great zeal, the King bore to this gentlewoman, framed
himself to please her, as well as the King: To that end, therefore, he
prepares great banquets and feasts, to entertain the King and her,
at his own house, she all this while dissembling the secret grudge in her
breast.   Now the cardinal began to grow into wonderful inventions
not heard of before in England; and the love between this glorious
lady and the King grew to such perfection, that divers things
were imagined, whereof I forbear here to speak, until I come to the
proper place.

CHAP. XI.

*Of the Variance between the French King and the Duke of Bourbon,
who fled to the City of Pavia, where the King besieged him.*

THEN began a certain grudge between the French King and the
Duke of Bourbon to break out, insomuch that the Duke, being now at
variance with the house of France, was compelled, for safeguard of his
life, to fly and forsake his country, fearing the King's malice and
indignation.

The cardinal, having intelligence hereof, contrived, that the King
our Sovereign Lord should obtain the duke to be his general in his
wars against the French King, with whom our king had then an occasion
of war; and the rather, because the Duke of Bourbon was fled to the
emperor to invite him to the like purpose, where he moved the King
in this matter.   And, after the King was advised thereof, and conceiv-

ed the cardinal's invention, he mused more and more of this matter, until it came into a consultation amongst the council; so that it was concluded, that an ambassador should be sent to the emperor about this matter. And it was further concluded, that the King and the emperor should join in those wars against the French King; and that the Duke of Bourbon should be the King of England's champion, and general in the field, who had a number of good soldiers, over and besides the emperor's army, which was not small; and that the King should pay the duke monthly wages for himself and his retinue.

For which purpose John Russel, who was afterwards created Earl of Bedford, lay continually beyond the seas in a secret place, both to receive money from the King, and to pay the same monthly to the duke; so that the duke began the wars with the French King in his own territories and dukedom, which the King had gotten into his own hands, being not perfectly known to the duke's enemies, that he had any aid from our Sovereign Lord; and thus he wrought the French King much displeasure, insomuch that the French King was constrained to prepare a present army, and, in his own person, to resist the duke's power. And, battle being joined, the King drove him to take Pavia, a strong town in Italy, with his host of men, for his security; where the King incamped himself wonderfully strong, intending to close the duke within the town, lest he should issue out, and skirmish with him.

The French King in his camp sent secretly into England a private person (being a very witty man) to treat of a peace between his master and our Sovereign Lord; his name was John Jokin, who was kept as secretly as might be, no man having intelligence of his arrival; for he was no Frenchman born, but an Italian, a man of no great estimation in France, nor known to be much in his master's favour, but taken to be a merchant; and, for his subtle wit, was elected to treat of such an ambassage, as the French King had given him in commission.

This Jokin was secretly conveyed to Richmond, and there staid, until such time as the cardinal resorted thither to him, where, after Easter term was ended, he kept his feast of Whitsontide very solemnly; in which season, my lord cardinal caused this Jokin divers times to dine with him, who seemed to be both witty, and of good behaviour. He continued long in England after this, till, at the last, as it should seem, he had brought the matter, which he had in commission, to pass. Whereupon, the King sent out immediately a restraint unto Sir John Russel, that he should retain that month's pay still in his hands, until the King's pleasure should be further made known, which should have been paid to the duke, being then incamped within the town of Pavia. For want of which money, the duke and his men were much dismayed, when they saw no money come, as it was wont to do; and, being in this dangerous case, where victuals began to grow scanty and very dear, they imagined many ways what should be the reason that the King's money came not; some said this, and some said that, mistrusting nothing less than the true cause thereof.

CHAP. XII.

Of the Duke of Bourbon's Stratagem, and Victory, wherein the French
King was taken Prisoner.

NOW the duke and his soldiers were in great misery, for want of
victuals, and other necessaries, which they could, by no means, get
within the town: Hereupon, the captains and soldiers began to grudge
and murmur, being, for want of victuals, all like to perish; and, being
in this extremity, came before the duke, and said, ' Sir, we must,
of force and necessity, yield to our enemies; and better were it for
us so to do, than to starve like dogs.' But, when the duke heard this,
he replied, with weeping tears, ' Sirs, you have proved yourselves
valiant men, and of noble hearts, in this service; and, for your
necessity, whereof I myself do participate, I do not a little lament;
but I shall desire you, as you are noble in heart and courage, so to
take patience, for two or three days, and, if succour come not then
from the King of England, as I doubt nothing less, I will then consent
to you all, to put ourselves and lives unto the mercy of our enemies;'
whereunto they all agreed, and tarried till two days were passed,
expecting relief from the King: Then, the duke, seeing no remedy,
called his noble captains and soldiers before him, and, weeping, said,
' You noble-men, and captains, we must yield ourselves unto our
enemies, or else famish; and, to yield the town and ourselves, I know
well the cruelty of our enemies; as for my part, I pass not for their
cruelties, for I shall suffer death, I know very well, most cruelly, if I
come once into their hands: It is not, therefore, for myself that I do
lament, it is for your sakes, it is for your lives, and for the safeguard
of your persons, for, so that you might escape your enemies hands,
I would willingly suffer death. Good companions, and noble soldiers,
I do require you all, considering the miserable calamities and dangers
we are in, at this present, to sell our lives most dearly, rather than to
be murdered like beasts; therefore, if you all consent with me, we
will take upon us, this night, to give our enemies assault, and, by that
means, we may either escape, or else give them an overthrow; for it
were better to die in the field, like men, then to live, prisoners, miserably
in captivity; to which they all agreed.

' Then, (quoth the duke) you all perceive the enemies camp is
strong, and there is no way to enter upon them, but one, and that
entry is planted with great ordnance, and strength of men, so that it is
impossible to attain to our enemies, that way, to fight with them in
their camp; and also, now of late, you perceive, they have had
but small doubt of us, in regard they have kept but slender watch.

' Therefore, my advice is, there shall issue out of the town, in the
dead time of the night, from us, a certain number of you, that be the
most likely to assault the camp, and they shall give the assault,
secretly, against the place of the entry, which is most strong and
invincible; which force, and valiant assault, shall be to them, of the

camp, so doubtful, that they will turn the strength of the entry, that lieth over-against your assault, to beat you from your purpose; then will I enter out, at the postern gate, and come to the place of their strength newly turned, and there, before they be aware, will I enter, and fight with them in the camp, and win their ordnance, which they have newly turned, and beat them with their own pieces, and then may you come, and join with me in the field.'

This device pleased them all wonderful well, who did then prepare themselves, all that day, for that device, and kept themselves secret and close, without any noise, or shot of pieces, in the town, which gave the enemy the less fear of the assault; for, at night, they went all to their tents, and couched quietly, nothing mistrusting what after happened; so, in the dead of the night, when they were all at rest, the assailants issued out of the town, and there, according to the duke's appointment, they gave so cruel and fierce an assault, that they, in the camp, had much ado to withstand them; and then, as the duke before declared, they, within, were compelled to turn the shot, that lay at the entry, against the assault; then issued out the duke, and, with him, about fifteen or sixteen-hundred men, or more, secretly in the night. The enemy being ignorant of his coming, until he entered the field, and, at his entry, he took all the ordnance that lay there, and slew the gunners; then charged the pieces against the enemies, and slew them wonderfully, and cut down their tents and pavilions, and murdered many therein, before they were aware of his coming, suspecting nothing less than his entry; so that he won the field, before the King could arise, and the King was taken in his lodging, before he was harnessed. And, when the duke had won the field, the French King taken, and his men slain; his tents robbed and spoiled, and the King's coffers searched; the Duke of Bourbon found the league, under the great seal of England, newly made, between the King of England and the French King, whereby he perceived the impediment of his money, which should have come to him from the King, having, upon due search of this matter, further intelligence, that all this business was devised by the cardinal of England: Whereupon, the duke conceived such indignation against the cardinal, that he went immediately to Rome, and there intended to sack the town, and to have taken the Pope; but, at the first assault of the town, the duke was the first man that was there slain; notwithstanding, the captains continued their assaults, and, at last, many of the town fled, with the Pope, to the Castle of Angelo, where he continued in great calamity.

I have written this history more at large, because it was thought the cause of all this mischief; wherefore, you may see, whatsoever a man doth purpose, be he prince or prelate, yet God dispatcheth all things at his pleasure and will, it being a folly for any wise man to take upon him any weighty enterprise of his own will, without calling upon God, for his grace and assistance in all his proceedings.

I have seen princes, either when they would call a parliament, or any other great assembly, that they would first call to God, most reverently, for his grace therein; and now I see the contrary, as it seems, they trust more to their own minds and wills, than to God's good grace, and, even thereafter, oftentimes do their matters take effect; wherefore, not only in this history, but divers others, may be perceived most evident examples. Yet I see no man, almost, in authority, or high estate, regard the same; which is the greater pity, and the more to be lamented. Now here I desist to speak any further of this matter, and to proceed to others.

CHAP. XIII.

Of the French King's Redemption out of Captivity, and the Cardinal's Ambassage into France.

UPON the taking of the French King, there were divers consultations, and various opinions amongst the council; some held, that our Sovereign Lord the King could invade the realm of France, and might easily conquer the same; forasmuch as the King, with the most part of the noblemen of France, were in captivity; some said again, that the King, our master, ought to have had the French King prisoner, forasmuch as he was taken by our King's champion, and captain-general, the Duke of Bourbon, and the Emperor; insomuch that the King was advised, thereby, to occasion of war against the Emperor, because he kept the King of France out of our King's possession, with divers imaginations and devices, as their fancies served, which were too long here to relate.

Thus were they in long consideration, whereof every man in the court talked as his fancy served him, until, at the last, divers ambassadors, from the realm of France, came to the King our Lord, desiring him to take order with the Emperor for the French King's delivery, as his Highness's wisdom should think best, wherein my Lord Cardinal bore great rule; so that, after great deliberation and advice taken, it was thought good, by the Cardinal, that the Emperor should deliver the French King out of his ward, upon sufficient pledges.

And, afterwards, it was thought meet, that the King's two sons, that is to say, the Dauphin and the Duke of Orleans, should be delivered, in hostage, for security of the Emperor, and the King our Sovereign Lord, upon all such demands and requests, as should be demanded of the French King, as well by the Emperor, as by our sovereign Lord.

The Cardinal lamenting the French King's captivity, and the Pope's great adversity, who yet remained in the castle of Angelo, either as prisoner, or else for defence against his enemies, endeavoured, and laboured all that he could, with the King and his council, to take some order, for the quietness of them both.

At the last, as you heard before, divers of the great states, and lords of the council, with my Lady Anne, lay in continual wait, to espy a convenient occasion, to take the Cardinal in a snare.

Therefore, they consulted with the Cardinal, and informed him, that they thought it a necessary time for him, to take upon him the King's commission, to travel beyond the seas, and, by his wisdom, to compass a present peace amongst these great princes and potentates, encouraging him thereto, and alledging, that it was more meet for his wisdom, discretion, and authority, to bring so weighty a matter to pass, than any other within this realm: their intent was no other, but to get him from the King, that they might adventure, by the help of their chief mistress, to deprave him unto the King, and so, in his absence, bring him into his disgrace, or, at the least, to be in less estimation.

Well, the matter was so handled, that the Cardinal was commanded to prepare himself for the journey, which he took upon him, but, whether willingly or not, I cannot say; but this I know, that he made so short abode, after the perfect resolution thereof, that he caused all things to be prepared speedily for his journey, and every one of his servants were appointed, that should attend him in the same.

When all things were concluded, and provided for this noble journey, he advanced forwards, in the name of God. My Lord had with him such of the lords and bishops, as were not of the conspiracy.

Then marched he forward from his new house at Westminster, through all London, over London-bridge, having a great many gentlemen, in a rank, before him, in velvet coats, and, the most part of them, with chains of gold about their necks. And all his yeomen followed him, with noblemen, and great men's servants, all in orange-tawny coats, and the cardinal's hat, with T. and C. for Thomas Cardinal, embroidered upon them, as well upon his own servants coats, as all the rest of the gentlemen, and his sumpter mules, which were twenty, and more, in number: and when all his carriages and carts, and other his train, were passed before, he rode very sumptuously, like a cardinal, with the rest of his train, on his mule, with his spare mule, and his spare horse, covered with crimson velvet, and gilded stirrups, following him. And, before him, he had his two great silver crosses, his two pillars of silver, the King's broad-seal of England, and his cardinal's hat, and a gentleman carrying his balance, otherwise called his cloke-bag, which was made of fine scarlet, all embroidered, very richly, with gold. Thus he passed through London, as I said before; and, all the way in his said journey, he was thus furnished, having his harbingers, in every place, before, which prepared lodgings for him, and his said train.

The first journey he made was two miles beyond Deptford in Kent, to Sir Richard Wiltshire's house; the rest of his train were lodged in Deptford, and in the country thereabouts.

The next day he marched to Rochester, where he lay in the bishop's palace, and the rest were lodged in the city.

The third day he rode from thence to Feversham, and there lodged in the abbey, and his train in the town, and some about in the country.

The fourth day, he rode to Canterbury, where he was kindly entertained by the bishop of the city, and there he continued four or five days. In which season was the jubilee, and a great fair in the town, by reason it was the feast of St. Thomas, their patron; upon which day there was a solemn procession, wherein my Lord Cardinal was in his legantine ornaments, with his hat upon his head, who commanded the monks and the quire, to sing the Latin after this sort, '*Sancta Maria ora pro Papa Nostro Clemente.*' and, in this manner, perused the Latin through; my Lord Cardinal kneeling at a stool before the quire-door, prepared for him, with carpets and cushions: all the monks, and the quire, stood in the body, singing the Litany; at which time I saw my Lord Cardinal weep tenderly, which James I, and others, conceived to be for grief, that the Pope was in such calamity and danger of the lance-knights.

The next day, I was sent with letters from my Lord to a Cardinal in Calais, in post, so that I was, the same night, in Calais. At my arrival, I found, standing upon the pier, without the Lanthorn-gate, all the council of the town, to whom I delivered up my message, and my letters, before I entered the town; where I lay until my Lord came thither, who arrived two days after my coming thither, before eight o'clock in the morning, and was received of all the noble officers and council of the town, and the mayor of the staple, with procession, the clerks being in rich copes, having many rich crosses.

In the Lanthorn-gate, a stool, with cushions and carpets, was set for him, where he kneeled, and made his prayers: at which time, they fenced him in with seizures of silver, and sprinkled water; that done, they passed on before him, in procession, until he came unto St. Mary's church, where, at the high altar, turning him to the people, he gave them his benediction and pardon, and then he repaired, with a great number of noblemen and gentlemen, to a place in the town, called the Chequer, where he kept his house, so long as he abode in the town, going immediately into his naked bed, because he was somewhat troubled with sickness, by reason of his passage by sea.

That night he called unto him Monsieur de Bees, Captain of Bulloigne, with divers others gallants and gentlemen, who had dined with him that day, and, having some further consultation with my Lord Cardinal, he, and the rest of the gentlemen, departed again to Bulloigne.

Thus my Lord was daily visited with one or other of the French nobility.

When all his train and carriage were landed, and all things prepared for his journey, his Grace called all his noblemen and gentlemen into the privy chamber, where, being assembled before him, he said: I have called you hither to declare unto you, that I would have you both consider the duty you owe to me, and the good-will I semblably bear to you for the same. Your intendment of service is to further the authority I have, by commission from the King, which diligent observance of yours I will hereafter recommend to his Majesty; as also to shew you the nature of the Frenchmen, and withal to instruct you with the reverence you shall use me for the high honour of the King's Majesty, and to inform you, how you shall entertain and accompany the Frenchmen, when you meet at any time.

Concerning the first point, you shall understand for divers weighty affairs of his Grace's, and for mere advancement of his royal dignity, he hath assigned me in this journey to be his lieutenant; what reverence, therefore, belongeth to me, for the same, I will shew you.

By vertue therefore of my commission and lieutenantship, I assume and take upon me to be esteemed in all honour and degrees of service, as unto his highness is meet and due, and that by me nothing be neglected that to his state is due and appertinent; for my part, you shall see that I will not omit one jot thereof: Therefore, one of the chief causes of your assembly, at this time, is to inform you, that you be not ignorant of your duty in this; I wish you therefore, as you would have my favour, and also charge you all in the King's name, that you do not forget the same in time and place, but that every of you do observe his duty to me, according as you will, at your return, avoid the King's indignation, or deserve his highness's thanks; the which I will set forth at our return, as each of you shall deserve.

Now to the second point, the nature of the Frenchmen is such, that at their first meeting, they will be as familiar with you, as if they had known you by long acquaintance, and will commune with you in their French tongue, as if you knew every word; therefore, use them in a kind manner, and be as familiar with them, as they are with you; if they speak to you in their natural tongue, speak to them in English, for if you understand not them, no more shall they you. Then speaking merrily to one of the gentlemen, being a Welchman, Rice, quoth he, speak thou Welch to them, and doubt not, but thy speech will be more difficult to them, than their French shall be to thee. Moreover, he said unto them all, let your entertainment and behaviour be according to all gentlemen's in humility, that it may be reported, after our departure from thence, that you were gentlemen of very good behaviour and humility; that all men may know, you understand your duties to your King, and to your master. Thus shall you not only obtain to yourselves great commendations and praises, but also greatly advance your prince and country.

Now being admonished of these things, prepare yourselves against to-morrow, for then we purpose to set forward. Therefore, we his servants, being thus instructed, and all things being in a readiness, proceeded forward; the next day being Mary Magdalen's day, my lord cardinal advanced out of Calais, with such a number of black coats, as hath been seldom seen; with the ambassador, went all the peers of Calais, and Groynes. All other gentlemen, besides those of his train, were garnished with black velvet coats, and chains of gold. Thus passed he forward, with his troop before, three in a rank, which compass extended three quarters of a mile in length, having his crosses, and all other his accustomed glorious furniture carried before him, as I have formerly related, except the broad seal, the which he left with Doctor Taylor, then master of the rolls, until his return.

Thus passing on his way, we had scarce gone a mile, but it began to rain so vehemently, that I have not seen the like for the time; which endured until we came to Bulloigne, and before we came to Standingfield, the cardinal of Lorrain, a goodly young gentleman, gave my lord a meeting, and received him with much joy and reverence, and so passed forth with my lord in communication, until we came near the said Standingfield, which is a religious place, standing between the English, French, and Imperial dominions, being a neuter, holding of neither of them. Then there we waited for my Lord Le Count Brian, captain of Picardy, with a great number of stradigats or arboncies standing in array, in a great piece of green oats, all in harness upon light horses, passing on with my lord in a wing into Bulloigne, and so after into Picardy, for my lord doubted, that the emperor would lay some ambushment to betray him; for which cause, he commanded them to attend my lord for the safety of his own person, to conduct him from the danger of his enemies.

Thus rode he accompanied, until he came nigh to Bullogine, within an English mile, where all the worshipful citizens of Bulloigne came and met him, having a learned man that made an oration in Latin to him, unto the which my lord made answer; and that done, Monsieur de Bees, captain of Bulloigne, with his retinue, met him on horseback, with all his assembly. Thus he marched into the town, lighted at the abbey gate, from whence he was conveighed into the abbey with procession, and there they presented him with the image of our lady, commonly called, Our Lady of Bulloigne, where were always great offerings; that done, he gave his blessing to the people, with certain days of pardon: Then went he into the abbey to his lodging, but all his train were lodged in the high base town.

The next day, after he had heard mass, he rode to Muterel, where he was in like manner saluted by the worshipful of the town, all in livery alike, where also a learned oration was made to him in Latin, which his grace answered again in Latin. And as he entered in at the gate, there was a canopy of silk, embroidered with like letters, as his men had on their coats: And when he was alighted, his footmen had it, as due to their office. There were also made pageants for joy of his coming, who was called in the French tongue, whither he rode or came, *Le Cardinal de Patifagus*, and in Latin, *Cardinalus Patifagus*, and was accompanied all that night, with the gentlemen of the country thereabouts.

The next day he took his journey towards Abovile, where he was in like manner entertained, and conveighed into the town, and most honourably welcomed with divers kinds of pageants, both costly, and wittily contrived to every turning of the streets; as he rode through the town, having a canopy borne over him, richer than at Muterel; and so conveighed him to his lodging, which was a fair house, newly built with brick, at which house, the French King, Lewis, was married to the King's sister, which was married after to the Duke of Suffolk. In this town of Abovile he remained eight or nine days, where resorted unto him divers of the French King's council, every day continually feasting, and entertaining him, and the other lords.

At the time of his departing out of the town, he rode to a castle beyond the water, called by some, Le Channel Percequeine, standing and adjoining to the said water, upon a great hill and rock, within the which, there was a college of priests: The situation whereof was like to the castle of Windsor in England, and there he was received with a solemn procession, conveighing him first to the church, and then to the castle upon the bridge, over the water of Some, where King Edward the Fourth met with the French King, as you may read at large in the chronicles of England.

My lord was no sooner seated in his lodging, but I heard, that the French King would come that day to the city of Amience, which was not above six English miles from thence. And being desirous to see his coming thither, I took with me two of my lord's gentlemen, and rode presently thither : And being but strangers, we took up our lodging, at the sign of the Angel, directly over against the west door of the cathedral church, De Nostre Dame, where we staid in expectation of the King's coming : And about four of the clock, came Madam Regent the King's mother, riding in a very rich chariot, and with her within was the Queen of Navarre, her daughter, attended with a hundred or more of ladies and gentlewomen following, every one riding upon a white palfrey, also her guard which was no small number. And within two days after the King came in, with a great shot of guns, and there were divers pageants made only for joy of his coming, having about his person, and before him, a great number of noblemen and gentlemen, in three companies : The first were Switzers and Burgonians with guns ; the second were Frenchmen with bows ; the third were Le Carpe-fall Scotchmen, who were more comely persons than all the rest. The French guard and Scotch had all one livery, being apparelled with rich coats of white cloath, with a guard of silver bullion of a handful broad : The King came riding on a rich jennet, and did alight at the said great church, and was conveighed with procession to the bishop's palace, where he was lodged. The next morning I rode again to Picegueny, to attend upon my lord, and when I came, my lord was ready to go on horseback, to ride towards Amience, and passing on his way, he was saluted by divers noble personages, making him orations in Latin, to whom my lord made answer, ex tempore.

Then was word brought him, that the King was ready to meet him, wherefore he had no other shift, but to light at an old chapel, that stood hard by the high-way, and there he newly apparelled himself in rich array ; and so mounted again upon another mule, very richly trapped with a foot-cloath of crimson velvet, purled with gold, and fringed about the edges with a fringe of gold very costly, his stirrups of silver gilt, bosses of the same, and the cheeks of his mule's bit were all gilt with fine gold ; and by that time he was mounted again in this gorgeous manner, the King was come very near, within less than an English quarter of a mile, his guard standing in array upon the top of an high hill, expecting my lord's coming ; to whom my lord made as much haste, as conveniently he could, until he came within a pair of butts length, and there he staid. The King, perceiving that, caused Monsieur Van de Mount to issue from him, and to ride to my lord cardinal, to know the cause of his tarrying ; and so Monsieur Van de Mount, being mounted upon a very fair jennet, took his race with his horse, till he came even to my lord, and then he caused his horse to come aloft twice or thrice so near my lord's mule, that he was in doubt of his horse, and so alighted; and in humble reverence, did his message to my lord; that done, he repaired to the King.

And then the King advanced forward, seeing my lord do the like, and in the mid way they met, embracing each other with amiable countenances. Then came into the place all noblemen and gentlemen, on both parts, who made a mighty press.

Then the King's officers cried, *Penant de la vant*, i. e. March, March: So the King, with the lord cardinal on his right hand, rode towards Amience, every English gentleman being accompanied with another of France. The train of these two great princes was two miles in length, that is to say, from the place of their meeting, unto Amience, where they were nobly received with guns, and pageants, until the King had brought my lord to his lodging, and then departed for that night. The King being lodged in the bishop's palace; And the next day, after dinner, my lord rode with a great train of English noblemen and gentlemen, unto the court to the King, at which time, the King kept his bed; yet, nevertheless, my lord came into his bed-chamber, where on the one side of the bed sat the King's mother, and on the other side, the Cardinal of Lorrain, accompanied with divers other gentlemen of France, and, after some communication, and drinking of wine, with the King's mother, my lord departed, and returned to his own lodging, accompanied with divers other lords and gentlemen.

Thus continued my lord at Amience, and also the King, fourteen days feasting each other divers times, and there, one day at mass, the King and my lord received the holy sacrament, as also the Queen Regent, and the Queen of Navarre; after that it was determined, that the King and my lord should remove, and so they rode to a city, called Champaigne, which was more than twenty miles from Amience, unto which town I was sent to provide lodging for my lord; and in my travel, I having occasion to stay by the way, at a little village, to shoe my horse, there came to me a servant from the castle, there perceiving me to be an Englishman, and of my Lord Legate's servants, as they then called my lord; and desired me to go into the castle, to the lord his master, who he thought would be very glad to see me: To whom I consented, because I desired acquaintance with strangers, especially with men of authority, and honourable rank; so I went with him, who conducted me to the castle, and, at my first entrance, I was among the watchmen, who kept the first ward, being very tall men, and comely persons, who saluted me very kindly; and, knowing the cause of my coming, they advertised their lord and master; and forthwith the lord of the castle came out unto me, whose name was Monsieur Crooksley, a nobleman born; and, at his coming, he embraced me, saying, that I was heartily welcome, and thanked me, that I was so gentle as to visit him, and his castle, saying, that he was preparing to meet the King, and my lord cardinal, and to invite them to his castle; and when he had shewed me the strength of his castle, and the walls, which were fourteen feet broad, and I had seen all the houses, he brought me down into a fair inner court, where his jennet stood ready for him, with twelve other of the fairest jennets, that ever I saw, especially his own, which was a mare; which jennet, he told me, he had four hundred crowns offered for her; upon these twelve jennets were mounted twelve goodly gentlemen, called Pages of Honour; they rode all bare-headed, in coats of cloth of gold, guarded with black velvet, and they had all of them boots, of red Spanish leather.

Then took he his leave of me, commanding his steward, and other of his gentlemen, to conduct me to his lady to dinner; so they led me up to the gate-house, where then their lady and mistress lay, for the time that the King and the cardinal should tarry there. And after a short time the Lady Crooksley came out of her chamber into her dining-room, where I attended her coming, who did receive me very nobly, like herself, she having a train of twelve gentlemen, that did attend on her. Forasmuch, quoth she, as you are an English gentleman, whose custom is to kiss all ladies and gentlewomen in your country without offence, yet it is not so in this realm; notwithstanding, I will be so bold as to kiss you, and so shall you salute all my maids. After this we went to dinner, being as nobly served, as ever I saw any in England, passing all dinner-time in pleasing discourses.

And shortly after dinner I took my leave, and was constrained, that night, to lie short of Champaigne, at a great walled town, called Moundrodrey, the suburbs whereof my Lord of Suffolk had lately burned; and early in the morning I came to Champaigne, being Saturday, and market-day, where at my first coming I took up my inn, over-against the market-place, and being set at dinner in a fair chamber, that looked out into the street, I heard a great noise, and clattering of bills; and looking out I saw the officers of the town, bringing a prisoner to execution, and with a sword, cut off his head. I demanded what was the offence, they answered me, for killing of red deer in the forest near adjoining. And incontinently they held the poor man's head upon a pole in the market place, between the stag's horns, and his four quarters set up in four places of the forest.

Having prepared my cardinal's lodging in the great castle of the town, and seen it furnished, my lord had the one half assigned, and the King the other half, and in like manner they divided the gallery between them; and in the midst thereof, there was made a strong wall, with a window and a door, where the King and my lord did often meet and talk, and divers times go one to the other, through the same door. Also there was lodged in the same castle Madam Regent, the King's mother, and all the ladies and gentlewomen that did attend on her.

Not long after came the lord chancellor of France, a very witty man, with all the King's grave counsellors, where they took great pains daily in consultation. At which time, I heard my lord cardinal fall out with the chancellor of France, laying to his charge, that he went about to hinder the league which was before his coming concluded upon, by the King our sovereign lord, and the French King their master. Insomuch that my lord stomached him stoutly, and told him, it was not he that should infringe the amiable friendship. And if the French King his master, being there present, would follow his, the chancellor's, counsel, he should not fail, shortly after his return, to feel the smart, what it was to maintain war against the King of England, and thereof he should be well assured; insomuch that his angry speech and bold countenance made them all doubt how to quiet him to the council, who was then departed in a great fury.

Now here was sending, here was coming, here was intreating, and here was great submission and intercession made unto him to reduce him to his former communication, who would in no ways relent, until Madam Regent came to him herself, who handled the matter so well, that she brought him to his former communication, and by that means, he brought all things to pass, that before he could not compass, which was more out of fear than affection, the French King had to the matter in hand; for now he had got the heads of all the council under his girdle.

The next morning, early after this conflict, the cardinal arose, about four of the clock, and sat him down to write letters into England, unto the King, commanding one of his chaplains to prepare him ready; insomuch that the chaplain stood ready in his vestures until four of the clock in the afternoon. All which season, my lord never rose to eat any meat, but continually writ letters with his own hand; and about four of the clock in the afternoon, he made an end of writing, commanding one Christopher Gunner, the King's serjeant, to prepare himself, without delay, to ride post into England with his letters, whom he dispatched away before ever he drank. That done, he went to mass and mattins, and other devotions with his chaplains, as he was accustomed to do; and then went to walk in a garden, the space of an hour and more, and then said evening song, and so went to dinner and supper, making no long stay, and so went to bed.

The next night following, my lord caused a great supper to be made, or rather a banquet, for Madam Regent, and the Queen of Navarre, and other noble personages, lords and ladies. At which supper was Madam Lewis, one of the daughters of Lewis, the last King, whose sister lately died; these two sisters were by their mother inheritors of the duchy of Bretagne. And, forasmuch as King Francis had married one of the sisters, by which he had one moiety of the said duchy, he kept the said Madam Lewis, the other sister, without marriage to the intent the whole duchy might descend to him, or his successors after his death, for lack of issue of her.

But now let us return to the supper or banquet, where all those noble personages were highly feasted. And in the midst of the said banquet, the French King, and the King of Navarre, came suddenly in, who took their places in the lowest part thereof: There was not only plenty of fine meats, but also much mirth and solace, as well in merry communion, as also the noise of my lord's musick, who played there all that night so cunningly, that the two kings took great delight therein, insomuch that the French King desired my lord to lend them unto him for the next night. And after the supper or banquet ended, the lords fell to dancing, amongst whom one Madam Fountaine had the praise. And thus passed they most part of the night before they parted.

The next day the King took my lord's musick, and rode to a nobleman's house, where was some living image, to whom he had vowed a night's pilgrimage; and to perform his devotion when he came there, which was in the night, he danced and caused others to do the same, and the next morning he returned to Champaigne.

The King being at Champaigne, gave order that a wild boar should be lodged for him in the forest, whither my lord cardinal went with him to see him hunt the wild boar, where the Lady Regent, with a number of ladies and damsels, were standing in chariots, looking upon the toil; amongst these ladies stood my lord cardinal to regard the hunting, in the Lady Regent's chariot.   And within the toil was the King, with divers ladies of France ready furnished for the high and dangerous enterprize of hunting of this perilous wild swine.

The King, being in his doublet and hose all of sheep's colour cloth, richly trimmed, in his slip, a brace of very great grey-hounds, who were armed as their manner there is, to defend them from the violence of the beasts tusks.   And the rest of the King's gentlemen, that were appointed to hunt, were likewise in their doublets and hose, holding each of them a very sharp boar's spear.   Then the King commanded the keepers to uncouch the boar; and that every person within the toil should go to a standing, among whom were divers gentlemen of England.

The boar presently issued out of his den, and being pursued by a hound, came into the plain, where he staid a while, gazing upon the people, and the hound drawing near him, he espied a bush upon a bank; under the bush lay two Frenchmen, who fled thither, thinking there to be safe; but the boar smelling them, and thrusting his head into the bush, these two men came away from thence, as men use to fly from the danger of death.

Then was the boar, by violence of the hunters, driven from thence, who run straight to one of my lord's footmen, being a very tall man, who had in his hand an English javelin, with which he defended himself a great while.   But the boar continued foaming at him with his great tusks; at the last, the boar broke in sunder his javelin, so that he was glad to draw his sword, and therewith stood upon his guard, until the hunters came and rescued him, and put the boar once again to flight to another gentleman of England, one Mr. Ratcliff, who was son and heir to the Lord Fitzwalter, now Earl of Sussex, who, by his boar's spear, rescued himself.   There were many other passages, but I forbear prolixity, and return to the matter in hand.

Many days were spent in consultation, and expectation of Christopher Gunner's return, who was formerly sent post into England, with letters, as I said before: At last he returned with letters, upon receipt whereof, my lord prepared, with all expedition, to return to England.

The morning that my lord intended to remove, being at mass in his closet, he consecrated the chancellor of France a cardinal, and put his hat on his head, and his cap of scarlet, and then took his journey, and returned into England with all the expedition he could, and came to Sayne, and was there nobly entertained of my Lord Staines, who was captain of that place; and from thence went to Calais, where he staid a while for shipping of his goods, and, in the mean time, he established a work to be there kept for all nations: But how long, or in what sort, it continued, I know not; for I never heard of any great good it did, or of any assembly of merchants, or traffick of merchandise, that were brought thither for so great and mighty a matter, as was intended for the good of the town. This being established, he took shipping, for Dover, and from thence rode post to court.

The King being then in his progress at Sir Henry Wyat's house in Kent, of whom I and others of his servants thought he should have been nobly entertained, as well of the King himself, as of the nobles: But we were all deceived in our expectation. Notwithstanding, he went immediately to the King after his return, with whom he had long talk, and continued two or three days after in the court, and then retired to his house at Westminster, where he remained till Michaelmas-term, which was within a fortnight after, and there he exercised his place of chancellorship, as he had done before.

And, immediately after the beginning of the term, he caused to be assembled in the Star-chamber all the noblemen, judges, and justices of the peace of every shire throughout England, that were at Westminster-hall then present. And there he made a long oration, declaring the cause of his ambassage into France, and of his proceedings therein; saying, That he had concluded such an amity and peace, as was never heard of in this realm, between our Sovereign Lord the King's Majesty, the Emperor, and the French King, for a perpetual peace, which shall be confirmed in writing, under the seals of both realms, engraven in gold: Offering further, that our King should receive yearly, by that name, out of the duchy of Normandy, all the charges and losses he had sustained in the wars.

And also, forasmuch as there was a restraint made of the French Queen's dowry (whom the Duke of Suffolk had married) for many years together during the wars, it was concluded, That she should not only receive the same, according to her just right, but also the arrearages, being unpaid during the said restraint, should be perfected shortly after. The resort of ambassadors out of France should be such a great number of noblemen and gentlemen, to confirm the same, as hath not been seen, heretofore, repair hither out of one realm.

This peace thus concluded, there shall be such an amity between them of each realm, and intercourse of merchandise, that it shall be seen to all men to be but one monarchy. Gentlemen and others may travel from one country to another, for their recreations and pleasure; and merchants of either country may traffick safely, without fear of danger; so that this realm shall ever after flourish.

Therefore may all Englishmen well rejoice, and set forth the truth of this ambassy in the country. Now, my masters, I beseech you, and require you, in the King's behalf, that you shew yourselves as loving and obedient subjects, in whom the King may much rejoice, &c. And so he ended his oration, and broke up the court, for that time.

CHAP. XIV.

Of the French Ambassadors Entertainment and Dispatch.

NOW the great long-looked-for ambassadors are arrived, being in number eight persons, of the noblest and most worthy gentlemen in all France; who were nobly received from place to place, and so conveyed, through London, to the Bishop's palace in Paul's Church-yard, where they were lodged; to whom divers noblemen resorted, and gave them noble presents (especially the mayor of the city of London) as, wines, sugars, beeves, muttons, capons, wild fowl, wax, and other necessary things in abundance, for the expences of his house.

They resorted to the court, being then at Greenwich, on Sunday, and were received of the King's Majesty, of whom they were entertained highly.

They had a commission to establish our King's highness in the order of France; to whom they brought, for that intent, a collar of fine gold, with a Michael hanging thereat, and robes appertaining to the said order; which were of blue velvet, and richly embroidered; wherein I saw the King pass to the closet, and afterwards in the same to mass.

And, to gratify the French King for his great honour, he sent incontinently noblemen here in England, of the order of the Garter; which garter the herald carried into France unto the French King, to establish him in the order of the garter, with a rich collar and garter, and robes according to the same; the French ambassadors still remaining here until the return of the English.

All things being then determined and concluded concerning the perpetual peace, upon solemn ceremonies and oaths, contained in certain instruments concerning the same, it was concluded there should be a solemn mass sung in the cathedral church of Paul in London, by the cardinal, the King being present at the same in his traverse to perform all things determined.

And, for the preparation thereof, there was a gallery from the west-door of Paul's church, through the body of the same, up to the choir, and so to the high altar into the traverse. My lord cardinal prepared himself to sing the mass, associated with twenty-four mitres of bishops and abbots, who attended him with such ceremonies, as to him were then due, by reason of his legative prerogative.

And, after the last Agnus, the King rose out of the traverse, and kneeled upon a carpet and cushions before the high altar; and the like did the great master of France, chief ambassador, that here represented the King's person of France; between whom the lord cardinal divided the blessed sacrament, as a perfect oath and bond for security of the said covenants of the said perpetual peace.

That done, the King went again into the traverse, this mass being ended, which was solemnly sung both by the choir of the same church, and all the King's chapel.

Then my lord took and read the articles of peace openly before the King and all others, both English and French; and there, in sight of all the people, the King put his hand to the gold seal, and subscribed with his own hand, and delivered the same to the grand master of France, as his deed, who semblably did the like. That done, they departed, and rode home with the cardinal, and dined with him, passing all the day after in consultation of weighty affairs touching the articles and conclusion of the said peace.

Then the King departed to Greenwich by water; at whose departure it was concluded, by the King's device, that all the Frenchmen should remove to Richmond, and hunt there; and from thence to Hampton-court, and there to hunt likewise; and the lord cardinal there to make a banquet, or supper, or both: and from thence they should ride to Windsor, and there hunt; and afterwards return to the King at Greenwich, and there to banquet with him before their departure.

This determined, they all repaired to their lodgings; then was there no more to do, but to make preparation in all things for the entertainment of this great assembly at Hampton-court, at the time appointed by my lord cardinal, who called before him all his chief officers, as stewards, treasurers, clerks, and comptrollers of his kitchen; to whom he declared his whole mind touching the entertainment of the Frenchmen at Hampton-court; to whom he also gave command neither to spare for any cost, or expence, nor pains to make them such a triumphant banquet, that they might not only wonder at it here, but also make a glorious report, to the great honour of our King and this realm.

Thus, having made known his pleasure, to accomplish his commandment, they sent out all the carriers, purveyors, and other persons to my lord's friends to prepare: Also they sent to all expert cooks, and cunning persons in the art of cookery in London, or elsewhere, that might be gotten, to beautify the noble feast.

Then the purveyors provided, and my lord's friends sent in such provision, that it was a wonder to see it.

The cooks wrought both day and night in many curious devices, where was no lack of gold, silver, or any other costly thing; the yeomen and grooms of his wardrobe were busied in hanging the chambers with costly hangings, and furnishing the same with beds of silk, and other furniture for the same in every degree.

Then my lord sent me, being his gentleman-usher, and two others of my fellows, to foresee all things touching our rooms to be richly garnished; wherein our pains was not small; but daily we travelled up and down, from chamber to chamber, to see things fitted.

Then wrought joiners, carpenters, painters, and all other artificers needful, that there was nothing wanting to adorn this noble feast. There was carriage and re-carriage of plate, stuff, and other rich implements, so that there was nothing lacking, that could be devised or imagined for that purpose. There were also provided two-hundred and eighty beds, with all manner of furniture to them, too long here to be related.

The day assigned to the French being come, they were ready assembled before the hour of their appointment; wherefore the officers caused them to ride to Hanworth, a park of the King's within three miles of Hampton-court, there to spend the time in hunting till night; which they did, and then returned, and every of them were conveyed to their several chambers, having in them good fires, and store of wine, where they remained till supper was ready.

The chambers, where they supped and banqueted, were adorned thus:

First, the great waiting-chamber was hung with very rich cloth of arras; and so all the rest, some better than others; and furnished with tall yeomen to serve. There were set tables round about the chambers, banquet-wise, covered; also a cupboard, garnished with white plate, having also in the same chamber four great plates, to give the more light, set with great lights; and a great fire of wood and coals.

The next chamber was the chamber of presence, richly hanged, also, with cloth of arras, and a sumptuous cloth of state, furnished with many goodly gentlemen to serve. The tables were ordered, in manner as the others were, save only the high table was removed beneath the cloth of state, towards the midst of the chamber, with six desks of plate, garnished all over with fine gold, saving one pair of candlesticks of silver, and gilded, with lights in the same; the cupboard was barred about, that no man could come very near it, for there were divers pieces of great store of plate to use; besides, the plates that hung on the walls, to give light, were silver, and gilt, with wax lights.

Now were all things in readiness, and supper fit; the principal officers caused the trumpets to blow, to warn them to supper: Then the officers conducted the noblemen where they were to sup, and, they being set, the service came up, in such abundance, both costly, and full of devices, with such a pleasant noise of musick, that the Frenchmen, as it seemed, were wrapped up in a heavenly paradise. You must understand, that my lord cardinal was not there all this while; but the French monsieurs were very merry with their rich fare, and curious cates and knacks; but, before the second course, my lord cardinal came in, booted and spurred, suddenly amongst them; at whose coming, there was great joy, every man rising from his place, whom my lord cardinal caused to sit still, and keep their places, and, being in his riding apparel, called for his chair, and sat him down in the midst of the high table, and was there as merry and pleasant, as ever I saw him in my life.

Presently after, came up the second course, which was above one-hundred several devices, which were so goodly and costly, that, I think, the Frenchmen never saw the like.

But the rarest curiosity of all the rest, they all wondered at, which, indeed, was worthy of wonder, were castles, with images in the same, like St. Paul's church, for the model of it; there were beasts, birds, fowls, personages, most excellently made, some fighting with swords, some with guns, others with cross-bows, some dancing with ladies, some on horseback, with compleat armour, justling with long and sharp spears, with many more strange devices, which I cannot describe; amongst all, I noted, there was a chess-board made of spice plate, with men of the same, and of good proportion.

And, because the Frenchmen are very expert at that sport, my lord cardinal gave the same to a French gentleman, commanding, that there should be made a good case, to convey the same into his country.

Then called my lord for a great bowl of gold, filled with hippocras, and, putting off his cap, said, ' I drink a health to the King my sovereign lord, and next unto the King your master:' And, when he had drunk a hearty draught, he desired the grand master to pledge him a cup, which cup was worth five hundred marks; and so all the lords, in order, pledged these great princes. Then went the cup merrily about, so that many of the Frenchmen were led to their beds; then went my lord into his privy-chamber, making a short supper, or rather a short repast, and then returned again into the presence-chamber; amongst the Frenchmen, behaving himself in such a loving sort, and, so familiarly towards them, that they could not sufficiently commend him.

And, while they were in communication and pastime, all their livery were served to their chambers; every chamber had a bason and ewer of silver, and a great livery-pot, with plenty of wine, and sufficient of every thing.

Thus furnished was every room about the house; when all was done, then were they conducted to their lodgings.

In the morning, after they had heard mass, they staid and dined with my lord, and so departed towards Windsor; and, as soon as they were gone, my lord returned to London, because it was in the midst of the term.

You must conceive, the King was privy to this magnificent feast, who then intended far to exceed the same, which I refer to the Frenchmen's return. Now the King had given command to his officers, to provide a far more sumptuous banquet for the strangers, than they had at the cardinal's, which was not neglected. After the return of these strangers from Windsor, which place they much commended for the situation thereof, the King invited them to the court, where they dined, and, after dinner, they danced, and had their pastime till supper-time.

Then was the banquet-chamber, in the little yard at Greenwich, furnished for the entertainment of these strangers, to which place they were conducted by the greatest personages, then being in the court, where they did both sup and banquet; but to describe to you the order hereof, the variety of costly dishes, and the curious devices, my weak ability, and shallow capacity, would much eclipse the magnificence thereof: But thus much take notice of, that, although that banquet at Hampton-court was marvellous sumptuous, yet this banquet excelled the same, as much as gold doth silver in value ; and, for my part, I never saw the like.

In the midst of the banquet, there were turning at the barriers lusty gentlemen in compleat armour, very gorgeous, on foot, and the like on horseback ; and, after all this, there was such an excellent interlude, made in Latin, that I never saw or heard the like, the actors apparel being so gorgeous, and of such strange devices, that it passeth my poor capacity to relate them.

This being ended, there came a great company of ladies and gentlewomen, the chiefest beauties in the realm of England, being as richly attired, as cost could make, or art devise, to set forth their gestures, proportions, or beauties, that they seemed, to the beholders, rather like celestial angels, than terrestrial creatures, and, in my judgment, worthy of admiration; with whom the gentlemen of France danced and masked, every man choosing his lady, as his fancy served: that done, and the maskers departed, came in another mask of ladies and gentlewomen, so richly attired, as I cannot express; these ladies maskers took each of them one of the Frenchmen to dance, and here note, that these noble women spoke all of them good French, which delighted them much to hear the ladies speak to them in their own language.

Thus, triumphantly, did they spend the whole night, from five o'clock in the night, until two or three o'clock in the morning, at which time the gallants drew all to their lodgings, to take their rest.

As neither health, wealth, nor pleasure, can always last, so ended this triumphant banquet, which, being passed, seemed, in the morning, to the beholders, as a phantastick dream.

Now, after all this solemn banqueting, they prepared, with bag and baggage, to return; and, thereupon, repaired to the King, and, in order, every man took his leave of his Majesty, and the nobles, by whom the King sent his princely pleasure and commendations to the King their master, thanking them for their pains; and, after great communication had with the great master of that ambassage, he bade them adieu.

Then they came to Westminster to my lord cardinal, to do the like, of whom he received the King's reward, which I shall hereafter relate.

First, every man, of honour and estimation, had plate, some to the value of two or three hundred pounds, and some of four hundred pounds, besides the great gifts before received of his Majesty, as gowns of velvet, with rich furs, great chains of gold, and some had goodly horses of great value, with divers other gifts of great value, which I cannot call to remembrance; but the worst of them had the sum of twenty crowns; and thus, being nobly rewarded, my lord, after humble commendations to the French King, bade them farewel, and so they departed.

The next day they were conveyed to Dover, to the sea-side, with all their furniture, being accompanied with many English young gallants; and what report of their royal entertainment they made in their own country, I never heard.

CHAP. XV.

Of the King's Discovery of his Love to Mrs. Anne Bullen to the Cardinal, with the Cardinal's Dislike, and also the Opinions of all the learned Bishops in England, and foreign Universities.

AFTER this began new matters, which troubled the heads and imaginations of all the court, wherewith all their stomachs were full, but little digestion, viz. the long concealed affection of the King to Mrs. Anne Bullen now broke out, which his Majesty disclosed to the cardinal, whose often persuasions, on his knees, took no effect.

My lord, thereupon, being compelled to declare to his Majesty his opinion and wisdom, in the advancement of the King's desires, thought it not safe for him to wade too far alone, or to give rash judgment in so weighty a matter, but desired leave of the King to ask counsel of men of ancient and famous learning, both in the divine and civil laws.

Now this being obtained, he, by his legantine authority, sent out his commissions for the bishops of this realm, who, not long after, assembled all at Westminster, before my lord cardinal; and not only these prelates, but also the most learned men of both universities, and some from divers cathedral colleges in this realm, who were thought sufficiently able to resolve this doubtful question.

At this learned assembly was the King's case consulted of, debated, argued, and judged, from day to day: But, in conclusion, when these ancient fathers of law and divinity parted, they were all of one judgment, and that contrary to the expectation of most men. And I heard some of the most famous and learned amongst them say, The King's case was too obscure for any man, and the points therein were doubtful, to have any resolution therein, and so, at that time, with a general consent, departed, without any resolution or judgment.

In this assembly of bishops, and divers other learned men, it was thought very expedient, that the king should send out his commissioners into all universities in Christendom, as well here in England, as foreign regions, there to have this case argued substantially, and to bring with them, from thence, every definition of their opinions of the same, under the seal of every university; and thus much, for this time, were their determinations.

And, thereupon, divers commissioners were presently appointed for this design; so some were sent to Cambridge, some to Oxford, some to Lorrain, others to Paris, some to Orleans, others to Padua, all at the proper costs and charges of the king, which, in the whole, amounted to a great sum of money; and all went out of this realm, besides the charge of the ambassage, to those famous and notable persons of all the universities, especially such as bore the rule, or had the custody of the university seals, who were fed by the commissioners with such great sums of money, that they did easily condescend to their requests, and grant their desires.

By reason whereof, all the commissioners returned with their purpose, furnished, according to their commissions, under the seal of every several university, whereat there was no small joy conceived of the principal parties; insomuch that ever after the commissioners were had in great estimation, and highly advanced, and liberally rewarded, far beyond their worthy deserts. Noswithstanding, they prospered, and the matter went still forward, having now, as they thought, a sure staff to lean upon.

These proceedings being declared unto my lord cardinal, he sent again for the bishops, to whom he declared the effect of these commissioners pains, and, for assurance thereof, shewed them the instruments of each university, under their several seals; and, the business being thus handled, they went again to consultation, how things should be ordered.

At last it was concluded, that it was very meet the king should send unto the pope's holiness the opinions of both universities of England, and also foreign universities, which were manifestly authorised by their common seals: and it was also thought fit, the opinions of the worthy prelates of England should be sent to the pope, comprised in an instrument, which was not long time in finishing.

Nor was it long after, that the ambassadors were assigned for this design, who took their journey accordingly, having certain instruments, that, if the pope would not, thereupon, consent to give judgment, definitively in the king's case, then to require another commission from his holiness, to be granted to his legate, to establish a court here in England, for that purpose only, to be directed to my lord cardinal, legate of England, and to cardinal Campaine, bishop of Bath, which the king gave him at a certain time, when he was sent ambassador hither from the pope's holiness, to determine, and rightly judge according to their consciences. To the which, after long suit made, and for the good-will of the said cardinal, the pope granted their suit.

Then they returned into England, relating unto the king, that his grace's pleasure should be now brought to pass substantially, being never more likely, considering the state of the judges.

Long was the expectation, on both sides, for the coming over of the legate from Rome, who, at last, arrived in England, with his commission, and, being much troubled with the gout, his journey was long and tedious, before he could get to London, who should have been most solemnly received at Blackheath; but he desired not to be so entertained with pomp and vain glory, and, therefore, he came, very privately, on his own horse, without Temple-Bar, called Bath-Place, where he lay; the house being furnished with all manner of provision of my lord's. So, after some deliberation and consultation, in the ordering of the king's business, now in hand, by his commission, and articles of his ambassage, which being read, it was determined, that the king, and the good queen, his lawful wife, should be judged at Bridewell, and in Black-friars, and, some place thereabouts, the court to be kept, for the disputation and determination of the causes and differences, between the king and the queen, where they were to repair before these two legates, who sat as judges; before whom the king and queen were cited, and summoned to appear, which was a strange sight, and the newest device that ever was heard or read of in any story or chronicle: a king and a queen to be compelled to appear in a court, as common persons, within their own realm and dominions, and to abide the judgments and decrees of their subjects, being a prerogative belonging to the royal diadem.

CHAP. XVI.

A new Court erected to determine the King's Case, two Cardinals being Judges, having Power to convene the King and Queen, and the Issue thereof.

IT it a wonderful thing to consider the strength of princes' wills, when they are bent to have their pleasure fulfilled, wherein no reasonable persuasions will serve the turn; how little do they regard the dangerous sequels that may ensue as well to themselves as to their subjects.   And, amongst all things, there is nothing that makes them more wilful than carnal love, and various affecting of voluptuous desires, wherein nothing could be of greater experience than to see what inventions were furnished, what laws were enacted, what costly edifices of noble and ancient monasteries were there overthrown, what diversities of opinions then arose, what extortions were then committed, how many learned and good men were then put to death, and what alterations of good ancient laws, customs, and charitable foundations, were turned from the relief of the poor, to the utter destruction and desolation, almost to the subversion, of this noble realm.

It is a thousand pities to understand the things that since have happened to this land, the proof whereof hath taught all us Englishmen lamentable experience.   If men's eyes be not blind, they may see, and, if their ears be not stopped, they may hear; and if pity be not exiled, their hearts may relent and lament at the sequel of this inordinate love, altho' it lasted but a while.   'O Lord God, withhold thine indignation from us.'

You shall understand, as I said before, that there was a court erected at Black-friars, London, where these two cardinals sat as judges: Now will I describe unto you the order of the court.

First, there were many tables and benches set in manner of a consistory, one seat being higher than another for the judges aloft; above them three degrees high was a cloth of estate hanged, and a chair royal under the same, wherein sat the king, and some distance off sat the queen; and at the judges' feet sat the scribes and officers for the execution of the process; the chief scribe was doctor Stevens, after bishop of Winchester, and the apparitor, who was called doctor of the court, was one Cooke of Westminster.   Then before the king and the judges sat the archbishop of Canterbury, doctor Warham, and all other bishops; there stood, at both ends within, counsellors learned in the spiritual laws, as well on the king's side, as the queen's side, Dr. Sampson, afterwards bishop of Chichester, and Dr. Hall, after bishop of Worcester, with divers others; and proctors in the same law were Dr. Peter, who was afterwards chief secretary, and doctor Tregunmill, with divers others.

Now, on the other side, there were council for the queen, Dr. Fisher bishop of Rochester, and Dr. Standish bishop of St. Asaph in Wales, two brave noble divines, especially the bishop of Rochester, a very godly man, whose death many noblemen and many worthy divines much lamented, who lost his head about this cause, before it was ended, upon Tower-hill; as also another ancient doctor called doctor Ridley, a little man but a great divine. The court being thus ordered, as is before expressed, the judges commanded the cryer to proclaim silence, whilst the commission was both read to the court and to the people there assembled: That done, and silence being again proclaimed, the scribes commanded the cryer to call King Henry of England; whereunto the king answered and said, Here: then called he again the queen of England, by the name of Catharine, queen of England, Come into the court, &c. Who made no answer thereunto, but rose immediately out of her chair where she sat; and, because she could not come to the king directly, by reason of the distance, therefore she came round about the court to the king, and kneeled down at his feet, saying these words in broken English, as followeth:

Sir, quoth she, I beseech you do me justice and right, and take some pity upon me, for I am a poor woman and a stranger, born out of your dominions, having here no indifferent council, and less assurance of friendship. Alas! sir, how have I offended you? What offence have I given you, intending to abridge me of life in this sort? I take God to witness, I have been to you a true and loyal wife, ever conformable to your will and pleasure; never did I contrary or gainsay your mind, but always submitted myself in all things, wherein you had any delight or dalliance, whether it were little or much, without grudging or any sign of discontent: I have loved for your sake all men whom you have loved, whether I had cause or not, were they friends or foes; I have been your wife this twenty years, by whom you had many children: And, when I first came to your bed, I take God to witness, I was a virgin; whether it were true or no, I put it to your conscience. If there be any cause that you can alledge, either of dishonesty, or of any other matter, lawful to put me from you, I am willing to depart with shame and rebuke; but, if there be none, then I pray you let me have justice at your hands.

' The king your father was a man of such an excellent wit in his time, that he was accounted a second Solomon; and the king of Spain, my father Ferdinand, was taken for one of the wisest kings that reigned in Spain these many years. So they were both wise men and noble princes; and it is no question but they had wise counsellors of either realm, as be now at this day, who thought not, at the marriage of you and me, to hear what new devices are now invented against me, to cause me to stand to the order of this court. And I conceive you do me much wrong, nay you condemn me for not answering, having no council but such as you have assigned me: You must consider that they cannot be indifferent on my part, being your own subjects, and such as you have made choice of out of your own council, whereunto they are privy, and dare not disclose your pleasure.

' Therefore, I must humbly beseech you, to spare me, until I know how my friends in Spain will advise me: But, if you will not, then let your pleasure be done.'

And with that she rose, making a courtesy to the king, and departed from thence, all the people thinking she would have returned again to her former seat; but she went presently out of the court, leaning upon the arm of one of her servants, who was her general receiver, one Mr. Griffith.

The king, seeing that she was ready to go out of the court, commanded the cryer to call her again by these words, Catharine, queen of England, come into court. Lo, quoth Mr. Griffith, you are called again. Go on, quoth she, it is no matter: It is no indifferent court for me, therefore I will not tarry; go on your way; and so they departed, without any further answer at that time, or any appearance in any other court after that.

The king, seeing she was departed thus, and considering her words, said to the audience these few words in effect :

Forasmuch, quoth he, as the queen is gone, I will in her absence declare unto you all : She hath been to me a true obedient wife, and as comfortable as I could wish or desire; she hath all the virtues and good qualities that belong to a woman of her dignity, or in any of meaner estate; her conditions will well declare the same.

Then, quoth the cardinal, I humbly beseech your highness, to declare unto this audience, whether I have been the first and chief mover of this matter unto your highness, or no, for I am much suspected of all men.

My lord cardinal, quoth the king, you have rather advised me to the contrary, than been any mover of the same. The special cause that moved me in this matter, is a certain scruple that pricked my conscience, upon certain words spoken by the bishop of Bayonne, the French ambassador, who came hither to consult of a marriage between the princess our daughter, the lady Mary, and the duke of Orleans, second son to the king of France; and, upon resolution and determination, he desired respite to advertise the king his master thereof, whether our daughter Mary should be legitimate, in respect of my marriage with this woman, being sometime my brother's wife : which words, I pondering, begot such a scruple in my conscience, that I was much troubled at it, whereby I thought myself in danger of God's heavy displeasure and indignation; and the rather, because he sent us no issue male, for all the issue male that I have had by my wife died incontinently after they came into the world, which caused me to fear God's displeasure in that particular. Thus, my conscience being tossed in that wave of troublesome doubts, and partly in despair to have any other issue, than I had already by this lady, my now wife; it behoved me to consider the estate of this realm, and the danger it stands in for lack of a prince to succeed me. I thought it therefore good, in release of this mighty burthen on my conscience, as also for the quiet estate of this realm, to attempt a trial in the law herein: whether I might lawfully take another wife, without stain of carnal concupiscence, by which God may send more issue, in case this my first copulation was not good? I not having any displeasure in the person, or age of the queen, with whom I could be well contented to continue, if our marriage may stand with the law of God, as with any woman alive; in which point consisteth all the doubt that we go about, now to know by the learned wisdom of you our prelates and pastors, of this realm and dominion, now here assembled for that purpose, to whole consciences and learning I have committed the care and judgment, according to which I will, God willing, be well contented to submit myself, and obey the same. And, when my conscience was so troubled, I moved it to you, my lord of Lincoln, in confession, then being my ghostly father: and, forasmuch as you were then in some doubt, you moved me to ask counsel of the rest of the bishops; whereupon I moved it to you, my lord cardinal, to have your license, forasmuch as you are metropolitan, to put this matter in question; and so I did to all you, my lords, to which you all granted under your seals, which is here to shew. That is truth, quoth the bishop of Canterbury, and, I doubt not, but my brothers will acknowledge the same. No, sir, not so, under correction, quoth the bishop of Rochester, for you have not my hand and seal. No, quoth the king, Is not not this your hand and seal, and shewed it to him in the instrument with seals? No, forsooth, quoth the bishop: How say you to that, quoth the king, to the bishop of Canterbury? Sir, It is his hand and seal, quoth the bishop of Canterbury. No, my lord, quoth the bishop of Rochester, indeed you were in hand with me to have both my hand and seal, as other of the lords had done; but I answered, that I would never consent to any such act, for it was much against my conscience. And therefore my hand and seal shall never be set to such an instrument, God willing, with many other words to that purpose. You say truth, quoth the bishop of Canterbury, such words you used; but you fully resolved at the last, that I should subscribe your name, and put to your seal, and you would allow of the same; all which, quoth the bishop of Rochester, under correction, my lord, is untrue. Well, quoth the king, we will not stand in argument with you, you are but one. And so the king arose up, and the court was adjourned until the next day, at which time the cardinals sat again, and the council on both sides were there present to answer.

The king's council alledged the matrimony not good, nor lawful at the beginning, because of the carnal copulation that Prince Arthur had with the queen: this matter was very narrowly scanned on that side, and, to prove the carnal copulation, they had many reasons and similitudes of truth; and being answered negatively again, on the other side, it seemed that all their former allegations were doubtful to be tried, and that no man knew. ' Yes, quoth the bishop of Rochester, I know the truth. How can you know the truth, quoth the cardinal, more than any other person? Yes, forsooth, my lord, quoth he, I know that God is the truth itself, and never saith but truth, 'and he saith thus: *Quos Deus conjunxit, homo non separet.* And, forasmuch as this marriage was joined, and made by God to a good intent, therefore, I said, I knew the truth, and that man cannot break upon any wilful action, which God hath made and constituted. So much do all faithful men know, quoth my lord cardinal, as well as you, therefore, this reason is not sufficient in this case; for the king's council do alledge many presumptions, to prove that it was not lawful at the beginning, *Ergo*, it was not ordained by God, for God doth nothing without a good end; therefore, it is not to be doubted, but, if the presumptions be true, which they alledge to be most true, then the conjunction neither was, nor could be of God; therefore I say unto you, my lord of Rochester, you know not the truth, unless you can avoid their presumptions upon just reasons.'

'Then,' quoth Dr. Ridley, 'it is a great shame and dishonour to this honourable presence, that any such presumptions should be alledged in this open Court.' 'What,' quoth my lord cardinal, '*Domine Doctor Reverende*.' 'No, my lord, there belongs on reverence to this matter, for an unreverent matter may be unreverently answered;' and so left off, and then they proceeded to other matters.

Thus passed this court from session to session, and day to day, till a certain day the king sent for the cardinal to Bridewell, who went into the privy-chamber to him where he was, about an hour, and then departed from the king, and went to Westminster in his barge; the Bishop of Carlisle, being with him, said, 'It is a hot day to-day.' 'Yes,' quoth the cardinal, 'if you had been as well chafed as I have been within this hour, you would say you were very hot.' My lord no sooner came home, but he went to bed, where he had not laid above two hours, but my Lord of Wiltshire, Mrs. Anne Bullen's father, came to speak with him from the king; my lord commanded he should be brought to his bed's-side, who told him, it was the king's mind he should forthwith go with the cardinal to the queen, being then at Bridewell, in her chamber, and to persuade her, through their wisdoms, to put the whole matter into the king's own hands, by her consent; which should be much better for her honour, than stand to the trial at law, and thereby be condemned, which would tend much to her dishonour and discredit.

To perform the king's pleasure, my lord said he was ready, and so prepared to go: 'But,' quoth befurther to my Lord of Wiltshire, 'you, and others of the lords of the council, have put fancies into the head of the king, whereby you trouble all the realm, but, at the length, you will get but small thanks, both of God and the world;' with many other earnest words and reasons, which did cause my Lord of Wiltshire to be silent, kneeling by my lord's bed's-side, and, in conclusion, departed.

And then my lord rose, and took his barge, and went to Bath-house, to Cardinal Campaine's, and so went together to Bridewell, to the queen's lodgings, she being then in her chamber of presence; they told the gentleman-usher, that they came to speak with the queen's grace, who told the queen, the cardinals were come to speak with her; then she rose up, having a skain of red silk about her neck, being at work with her maids, and came to the cardinals, where they staid, attending her coming, at whose approach, quoth she: ' Alack, my lords, I am sorry that you have attended on me so long; what is your pleasures with me? ' If it please your grace,' quoth the cardinal, ' to go to your privy-chamber, we will shew you the cause of our coming.'

' My lord,' said she, ' if you have any thing to say to me, speak it openly before all these folk, for I fear nothing that you can say to me, or against me, but that I am willing all the world should both see and hear it, and, therefore, speak your minds openly.'

Then began my lord to speak to her in latin: ' Nay, good my lord, speak to me in English,' quoth she, ' although I do understand some latin.' ' Forsooth,' quoth my lord, ' good madam, if it please your grace, we come both to know your mind, what you are disposed to do in this matter, and also to declare to you, secretly, our counsels and opinions, which we do for very zeal and obedience to your grace.'

' My lords,' quoth she, ' I thank you for your good-wills, but to make answer to your requests I cannot so suddenly; for I was set amongst my maids at work, little thinking of any such matter, wherein is requisite some deliberation, and a better head than mine to make answer; for I need counsel in this case, which concerns me so near, and friends here I have none, they are in Spain, in my own country: also, my lords, I am a poor woman, of too weak a capacity to answer such noble persons of wisdom as you are, in so weighty a matter. And, therefore, I pray you, be good to me, a woman destitute of friendship here in a foreign region, and your counsel I also shall be glad to hear;' and therewith she took my lord by the hand, and led him into her privy-chamber, with the other cardinal, where they staid a while, and I heard her voice loud, but what she said, I know not.

This done, they went to the king, and made a relation unto him of the passages, between the queen and them, and so they departed.

This strange case proceeded, and went forward from court-day to court-day, until it came to that, that every man expected to hear judgment given, at which time, all their proceedings were openly read in latin; that done, the king's council, at the bar, moved for judgment; quoth Cardinal Campaine, ' I will not give judgment until I have related the whole proceedings to the pope, whose counsel and commandment, I will, in this case, observe: The matter is too high for us to give hasty judgment, considering the persons, and the doubtful occasions alledged, and also whose commissioners we are, by whose authority we sit.

' It is good reason, therefore, that we make our chief Lord of Counsel acquainted with the same, before we proceed to judgment definitive: I came not to please for any favour, reward, or fear, of any person alive, be he king, or otherwise; I have no such respect to the person, that I should offend my conscience. And the party-defendant will make no answer here, but rather doth appeal from us; I am an old man, both weak and sickly, and look every day for death: what shall it avail me, to put my soul in danger of God's displeasure, to my utter damnation, for the favour of any prince in this world? My being here is only to see justice administered, according to my conscience.

' The defendant supposeth that we be not indifferent judges, considering the king's high dignity and authority within this realm. And, we being both his subjects, she thinks we will not do her justice; and, therefore, to avoid all these ambiguities, I adjourn to the court of Rome, from whence our jurisdiction is arrived; for, if we should go further than our commission doth warrant us, it were but a folly, and blameworthy, because then we shall be breakers of the orders, from whom we have, as I said, our authority derived;' and so the court was dissolved, and no more done.

Thereupon, by the king's commandment, stepped up the Duke of Suffolk, and, with a haughty countenance, uttered these words:

' It was never thus in England, until we had cardinals amongst us.'

Which words were set forth with such vehemency, that all men marvelled what he intended, the duke futher expressing some opprobrious words.

My Lord Cardinal, perceiving his vehemency, soberly said, ' Sir, of all men in this realm, you have least cause to dispraise cardinals; for, if I poor cardinal had not been, you should not, at this present, have had a head on your shoulders, wherewith to make such a brag in despight of us, who wish you no harm, neither have given you such cause to be offended with us. I would have you think, my lord, I, and my brother, wish the king as much happiness, and the realm as much honour, wealth, and peace, as you, or any other subject, of what degree soever be be, within this realm, and would as gladly accomplish his lawful desires.

' And now, my lord, I pray you, shew me what you would do in such a case as this, if you were one of the king's commissioners, in a foreign region, about some weighty matter, the consultation whereof was very doubtful to be decided: Would you not advertise the king's majesty, before you went through with the same? I doubt not but you would, and, therefore, abate your malice and spight, and consider that we are commissioners for a time, and cannot, by vertue of a commission, proceed to judgment, without the knowledge and consent of the head of the authority, and license obtaind from him, who is the pope.

' Therefore do we neither more nor less, than our commission allows us; and, if any man will be offended with us, he is an unwise man; therefore pacify yourself, my lord, and speak like a man of honour and wisdom, or hold your peace; speak not reproachfully of your friends, you best know what friendship I have shewn you: I never did reveal to any person, till now, either to my own praise or your dishonour.' Whereupon the duke went away, and said no more, being much discontented.

This matter continued thus a long season, and the king was in displeasure against my Lord Cardinal, because his suit had no better success to his purpose.

Notwithstanding, the cardinal excused himself, by his commission, which gave him no authority to proceed to judgment, without the knowledge of the pope, who reserved the same to himself. At last they were advertised, by a post, that they should take deliberation in the matter, until his council were opened, which should not be till Bartholomew-tide next.

The king, thinking it would be too long before it would be determined, sent an ambassador to the pope, to persuade him to shew so much favour to his majesty, as that it might be sooner determined.

On this ambassage went Dr. Stephen Gardener, then called by the name of Dr. Steven, secretary to the king, afterwards Bishop of Winchester. This ambassador staid there till the latter end of summer, of whose return you shall hereafter hear.

CHAP. XVII.

Of certain Passages conducing to the Cardinal's Fall.

NOW the king commanded the queen to be removed from the court, and sent to another place; and presently after the king rode on progress, and had in his company Mistress Anne Bullen; in which time Cardinal Campaine made suit to be discharged, and sent home to Rome; and, in the interim, returned Mr. Secretary; and it was concluded, that my lord should come to the king to Grafton in Northamptonshire; as also Cardinal Campaine, being a stranger, should be conducted thither by my Lord Cardinal. And so, the next Sunday, there were divers opinions that the king would not speak with my lord; whereupon there were many great wagers laid.

These two prelates being come to the court, and alighting, expected to be received of the great officers, as the manner was, but they found the contrary: nevertheless, because the Cardinal Campaine was a stranger, the officers met him with staves in their hands in the outward court, and so conveyed him to his lodging prepared for him; and, after my lord had brought him to his lodging, he departed, thinking to have gone to his chamber, as he was wont to do. But it was told him, he had no lodging or chamber appointed for him in the court; which news did much astonish him.

Sir Henry Norris, who was then groom of the stool, came unto him, and desired him to take his chamber for a while, until another was provided for him; for, I assure you, here is but little room in this house for the king, and therefore, I humbly beseech your grace, accept of mine for a season. My lord, thanking him for his courtesy, went to his chamber, where he shifted his riding apparel.

In the mean time came divers noblemen of his friends to welcome him to the court, by whom my lord was advertised of all things touching the king's favour or displeasure ; and, being thus informed of the cause thereof, he was more able to excuse himself.

So my lord made him ready, and went to the chamber of presence with the other cardinal, where the lords of the council stood all of a row in order in the chamber, and saluted them both : And there were present many gentlemen, which came on purpose to observe the meeting and countenance of the king to my Lord Cardinal. Then, immediately after, the king came into the chamber of presence, standing under the cloth of state.

Then my Lord Cardinal took Cardinal Campaine by the hand, and kneeled down before the king, but what he said unto him, I know not, but his countenance was amiable, and his majesty stooped down, and with both his hands took him up, and then took him by the hand, and went to the window with him, and there talked with him a good while.

Then, to have beheld the countenance of the lords and noblemen that had laid wagers, it would have made you smile, especially those that had laid their money that the king would not speak with him.

Thus they were deceived, for the king was in earnest discourse with him, insomuch that I could hear the king say, How can this be, is not this your hand? and pulled a letter out of his own bosom, and shewed the same to my lord. And, as I perceived, my lord so answered the same, that the king had no more to say ; but said to my lord, Go to your dinner, and take my Lord Cardinal to keep you company, and after dinner I will speak further with you, and so they departed. And the king that day dined with Mistress Anne Bullen in her chamber.

Then was there set up in the presence chamber a table for my lord, and other lords of the council, where they dined together ; and sitting at dinner telling of divers matters, The king should do well, quoth my Lord Cardinal, to send his bishops and chaplains home to their cures and benefices. Yea, marry, quoth my Lord of Norfolk, and so it were meet for you to do also. I would be very well contented therewith, if it were the king's pleasure to license me, with his grace's leave, to go to my cure at Winchester. Nay, quoth my Lord of Norfolk, to your benefice at York, where your greatest honour and charge is. Even as it shall please the king, quoth my Lord Cardinal ; and so they fell upon other discourses. For, indeed, the nobility were loth he should be so near the king, as to continue at Winchester. Immediately after dinner they fell to council till the waiters had also dined.

I heard it reported by those that waited on the king at dinner, that Mistress Anne Bullen was offended as much as she durst, that the king did so graciously entertain my Lord Cardinal : Saying, sir, is it not a marvellous thing to see into what great debt and danger he hath brought you, with all your subjects? How so, quoth the king? forsooth, quoth she, there is not a man in all your whole realm of England, worth a hundred pounds, but he hath indebted you to him, meaning of loan, which the king had of his subjects. Well, well, quoth the king, for that matter there was no blame in him, for I know that matter better than you, or any else.

Nay, quoth she, besides that, what exploits hath he wrought in several parts and places of this realm, to your great slander and disgrace? There is never a nobleman, but, if he had done half so much as he hath done, were well worthy to lose his head. Yea, if my Lord of Norfolk, my Lord of Suffolk, my father, or any other man, had done much less than he hath done, they should have lost their heads before this.

Then I perceive, quoth the king, you are none of my Lord Cardinal's friends. Why, sir, quoth she, I have no cause, nor any that love you. No more hath your grace, if you did well consider his indirect and unlawful doings.

By that time the waiters had dined, and took up the table, and so for that time ended their communication.

You may perceive by this, how the old malice was not forgotten; but begins to kindle and be set on fire, which was stirred by his ancient enemies, whom I have formerly named in this treatise.

The king, for that time, departed from Mistress Anne Bullen, and came to the chamber of presence, and called for my lord, and, in the great window, had a long discourse with him, but of what, I know not: Afterwards the king took him by the hand, and led him into the privy-chamber, and sat in consultation with him all alone, without any other of the lords, till it was dark night; which blanked all his enemies very sore, who had no other way but by Mistress Anne Bullen, in whom was all their trust and affiance for the accomplishment of their enterprises; for, without her, they feared all their purposes would be frustrated.

Now at night was warning given me, that there was no room for my lord to lodge in the court; so that I was forced to provide my lord a lodging in the country, about Easton, at one Mr. Empston's house, where my lord came to supper by torch-light, being late before my lord parted from the king, who willed him to resort to him in the morning, for that he would talk farther with him about the same matter; and in the morning my lord came again, at whose coming the king's majesty was ready to ride, willing my lord to consult with the lords in his absence, and said he would not talk with him, commanding my lord to depart with Cardinal Campaine, who had already taken his leave of the king.

This sudden departure of the king's was the especial labour of Mistress Anne Bullen, who rode with him purposely to draw him away, because he should not return till the departure of the cardinals. The king rode that morning to view a piece of ground to make a park of, which was afterwards, and is at this time called Harewell Park, where Mistress Anne had provided him a place to dine in, fearing his return before my lord cardinal's departure.

So my lord rode away after dinner with Cardinal Campaine, who took his journey towards Rome, with the king's reward, but what it was I am not certain.

After their departure, it was told the king, that Cardinal Campaine was departed, and had great treasure with him of my lord cardinal's of England, to be conveyed in great sums to Rome, whither they surmised he would secretly repair out of this realm. Insomuch, that they caused a post to ride after the cardinal to search him, who overtook him at Calais, and staid him until search was made; but there was found no more than was received of the king for a reward.

Now, after Cardinal Campaine was gone, Michaelmas term drew on, against which time my lord cardinal repaired to his house at Westminster; and, when the term began, he went into the hall in such manner as he was accustomed to do, and sat in the chancery, being then lord chancellor of England, after which day he never sat more; the next day he staid at home for the coming of my Lords of Norfolk and Suffolk, who came not that day, but the next: And did declare unto my lord, that it was the king's pleasure he should surrender up the great seal of England into their hands, and that he should depart unto Ashur, which is a house near unto Hampton-Court, belonging unto the bishoprick of Winchester.

The cardinal demanded of them to see their commission that gave them such authority; who answered again, they were sufficient commissioners, and had authority to do no less from the king's own mouth. Notwithstanding, he would in no wise agree to their demand in that behalf, without further knowledge of their authority, telling them, that the great seal was delivered to him by the king's own person, to enjoy the ministration thereof, together with the chancellorship, during the term of his life, whereof, for surety, he had the king's letters patents to shew; which matter was much debated between him and the dukes, with many great words, which he took patiently, insomuch that the Dukes were fain to depart without their purpose at that time, and returned to Windsor to the king; and, the next day, they returned to my lord with the king's letters; whereupon, in obedience to the king's command, my lord delivered to them the broad seal, which they brought to Windsor to the king.

Then my lord called his officers before him, and took account of all things they had in their charge; and, in his gallery, were set divers tables, upon which were laid divers and great store of rich stuffs, as whole pieces of silk of all colours, velvets, sattins, musks, taffaties, grograms, scarlets, and divers rich commodities. Also, there were one thousand pieces of fine holland, and the hangings of the gallery with cloth of gold, and cloth of silver, and rich cloth of bodkin of divers colours, which were hanged in expectation of the king's coming.

Also, of one side of the gallery, were hanged the rich suits of copes of his own providing, which were made for colleges at Oxford and Ipswich; they were the richest that ever I saw in all my life: Then had he two chambers adjoining to the gallery, the one most commonly called the Gilt-Chamber, the other the Council-Chamber, wherein were set two broad and long tables, whereupon were set such abundance of plate of all sorts, as was almost incredible to be believed, a great part being all of clean gold; and, upon every table and cupboard where the plate was set, were books, importing every kind of plate, with the contents, and the weight thereof.

Thus were all things furnished and prepared, giving the charge of the said stuff, with other things remaining in every office, to be delivered to the king, as he gave charge; all things being ordered as is before rehearsed, my lord prepared to depart, and resolved to go by water; but, before his going, Sir William Gascoigne, being his treasurer, came unto him, and said, Sir, quoth he, I am sorry for your grace, for I hear you are straight to go to the Tower: Is this the best comfort, quoth my lord, you can give to your master in adversity? It hath always been your inclination to be light of credit, and much lighter in reporting of lyes; I would you should know, Sir William, and all those reporters too, that it is untrue, for I never deserved to come there; although it hath pleased the King to take my house ready furnished for his pleasure, at this time, I would all the world should know, I have nothing, but it is of right for him, and of him I received all that I have; it is therefore convenient and reasonable to tender the same to him again.

Then my lord, with his train of gentlemen and yeomen, which was no small company, took his barge at his privy stairs, and went by water to Putney, at which time, upon the water, were abundance of boats filled with people, expecting to have seen my lord cardinal go to the Tower, which they longed to see. Oh! wondering and new-fangled world! Is it not a time to consider the mutability of this uncertain world? For the common people ever desire things for novelty's sake, which after turn to their small profit or advantage. For, if you mark the sequel, they had small cause to rejoice at his fall; I cannot see, but all men in favour are envied by the common people, though they do minister justice truly.

Thus continued my lord at Ashur three or four weeks, without either beds, sheets, table-cloths, or dishes to eat their meat in, or wherewith to buy any. But there were good store of all kind of victuals, and of beer, and wine plenty; but afterwards my lord borrowed some plate and dishes of the Bishop of Carlisle.

Thus continued my lord in this strange state till after Allhallowstide; and being one day at dinner, Mr. Cromwell told him, That he ought in conscience to consider the true and good service that he and other of his servants had done him, who never forsook him in weal nor woe: Then, quoth my lord, Alas! Tom, you know I have nothing to give you nor them, which makes me both ashamed and sorry that I have nothing to requite your faithful services: Whereupon Mr. Cromwell told my lord, That he had abundance of chaplains, that were preferred by his grace to benefices of some one thousand pounds, and others five hundred pounds, some more and some less; and we your poor servants, who take more pains in one day's service, than all your idle chaplains have done in a year; and, therefore, if they will not impart liberally to you in your great indigence, it is pity they should live, and all the world will have them in indignation for their great ingratitude to their master.

Afterwards, my lord commanded me to call all his gentlemen and yeomen up in the great chamber, commanding all the gentlemen to stand on the right hand, and the yeomen on the left side; at last, my lord came out in his rochet, upon a violet gown, like a bishop, who went with his chaplains to the upper end of the chamber, where was a great window, beholding his goodly number of servants, who could not speak to them until the tears ran down his cheeks; which, being perceived of his servants, caused fountains of tears to gush out of their sorrowful eyes in such sort, as would cause any heart to relent.

At last my lord spoke to them to this effect and purpose, saying, Most faithful gentlemen, and true-hearted yeomen, I much lament that in my prosperity I did not so much for you as I might have done, and was in my power to do; I consider that, if in my prosperity I should have preferred you to the king, then should I have incurred the king's servants displeasure; who would not spare to report behind my back, that there could no office in the court escape the cardinal and his servants, and by that means I should have run into open slander of all the world; but now it is come to pass, that it hath pleased the king to take all that I have into his hands, so that I have now nothing to give you, for I have nothing left me but the bare cloaths on my back; with many other words in their praise: And so he, giving them all hearty thanks, went away; and afterwards many of his servants departed from him, some to their wives, some to their friends, and Mr. Cromwell to London, it being then the beginning of the parliament.

CHAP. XVIII.

The Cardinal is accused of High Treason in the Parliament-House, against which Accusation, Mr. Cromwell (late Servant to him,) being a Burgess in the Parliament, made Defence.

THE aforesaid Mr. Cromwell, after his departure from my lord, devised with himself to be one of the burgesses of the parliament: And, being at London, he chanced to meet one Sir Thomas Russel, knight, a special friend of his, whose son was one of the burgesses of the parliament, of whom, by means, he obtained his room, and so put his feet into the parliament-house; and, three days after his departure from my lord, he came again to Ashur, and, I being there with my lord, he said unto me, with a pleasant countenance: I have adventured my feet, where I will be better regarded before the parliament be dissolved. And, after he had some talk with my lord, he made haste to London, because he would not be absent from the parliament, to the intent he might acquaint my lord what was there objected against him, thereby the better to make his defence, insomuch, that there was nothing at any time objected against my lord, but he was ready to make answer thereunto; by means whereof, he, being earnest in his master's behalf, was reputed the most faithful servant to his master of all others, and was generally, of all men, highly commended.

Then was there brought a bill of articles into the parliament-house, to have my lord condemned of high-treason, against which bill, Mr. Cromwell did inveigh so discreetly, and with such witty persuasions, that the same would take no effect. Then were his enemies constrained to indict him of a *premunire*, and all was to entitle the king to all his goods and possessions, which he had obtained and purchased for the maintenance of his colleges of Oxford and Ipswich, which were both most sumptuous buildings. To the judges, that were sent to take my answer herein, he thus answered :

' My lords judges, quoth he, the king knoweth, whether I have offended or no in using my prerogative for the which I am indicted : I have the king's license in my coffer, to shew under his hand and broadseal, for the executing and using thereof in a most large manner, the which now are in the hands of mine enemies ; but, because I will not here stand to contend with his Majesty in his own case, I will here presently before you confess the indictment, and put myself wholly to the mercy and grace of the king, trusting that he hath a conscience and reason to consider the truth, and my humble submission and obedience, wherein I might well stand to my trial with justice. Thus much may you say to his highness, That I wholly submit myself under his obedience in all things, to his princely will and pleasure, whom I never disobeyed or repugned, but was always contented and glad to please him before God, whom I ought most chiefly to have believed and obeyed, which I now repent : I most heartily desire you to have me commended to him, for whom I shall, during my life, pray to God to send him much prosperity, honour, and victory over his enemies.' And so they left him.

After which, Mr. Shelley, the judge, was sent to speak with my lord, who, understanding he was come, issued out of his privy-chamber, and came to him to know his business ; who, after due salutation, did declare unto him, That the king's pleasure was, to demand my lord's house, called York Place, near Westminster, belonging to the bishoprick of York ; and that you do pass the same according to the laws of this realm : His highness hath sent for all his judges and learned council, to know their opinions for your assurance thereof, who be fully resolved, that your grace must make a recognisance, and, before a judge, acknowledge and confess the right thereof to belong to the king and his successors, and so his highness shall be assured thereof.

Wherefore, it hath pleased the king to send me hither to take of you the recognisance, having in your grace such affiance, that you will not refuse to do so ; therefore I do desire to know your grace's pleasure therein.

Master Shelley, quoth my lord, I know the king of his own nature is of a royal spirit, not requiring more than reason shall lead him to by the law ; and therefore I counsel you, and all other judges and learned men of his council, to put no more into his head, than law, that may stand with conscience ; for, when you tell him, that, although this be law, yet it is not conscience ; for law without conscience is not fit to be ministered by a king, nor his council, nor by any of his ministers ; for every council to a king out to have respect to conscience before the rigour of the law : *Laus est facere quod decet, non quod licet.* The king ought, for his royal dignity and prerogative, to mitigate the rigour of the law ; and therefore, in his princely place, he hath constituted a chancellor to order for him the same ; and therefore the Court of

Chancery hath been commonly called the Court of Conscience, for that it hath jurisdiction to command the law, in every case, to desist from the rigour of the execution. And now I say to you, Master Shelley, Have I a power, or may I with conscience give that away, which is now mine, for me and my successors? If this be law and conscience, I pray you, shew me your opinion.

Forsooth, quoth he, there is no great conscience in it; but, having regard to the king's great power, it may the better stand with conscience, who is sufficient to recompence the church of York with the double value.

That I know well, quoth my lord; but there is no such condition, but only a bare and simple departure of others rights: If every bishop should do so, then might every prelate give away the patrimony of the church, and so, in process of time, leave nothing for their successors to maintain their dignities; which would be but little to the king's honour.

Well, quoth my lord, let me see your commission; which was shewed to him; then quoth my lord, Tell his highness, that I am his most faithful subject, and obedient beadsman, whose command I will in no wise disobey, but will in all things fulfil his pleasure, as you the fathers of the law say I may. Therefore I charge your conscience to discharge me; and shew his highness, from me, that I must desire his Majesty to remember there is both heaven and hell: And, thereupon, the clerk took and wrote the recognisance, and, after some secret talk, they departed.

Thus continued my lord at Ashur, receiving daily messages from the court, some good and some bad, but more ill than good; for his enemies, perceiving the good affection the king bore always to him, devised a means to disquiet his patience, thinking thereby to give him occasion to fret and chase, that death should rather ensue, than otherwise; which they most desired; for they feared him more after his fall, than they did in his prosperity; fearing, if he should, by reason of the king's favour, rise again, and be again in favour, and great at the court, they his enemies might be in danger of their lives, for their cruelty wrongfully ministered unto him, and, by their malicious surmises, invented and brought to pass against him: and did continually find new matters against him, to make him vex and fret; but he was a wise man, and did arm himself with much patience.

At Christmas he fell very sore sick, most likely to die: The king, hearing thereof, was very sorry, and sent Dr. Butts, his physician, unto him; who found him very dangerously sick in bed, and returned to the king: the king demanded, saying, Have you seen yonder man? Yes, sir, quoth he. How do you like him? quoth the king. Sir, quoth he, if you will have him dead, I will warrant you, he will be dead within these four days, if he receive no comfort from you shortly.

Marry! God forbid, quoth the king, that he should die, for I would not lose him for twenty thousand pounds; I pray you, go to him, and do your care to him.

Then must your grace, quoth Dr. Butts, send him some comfortable message. So I will, quoth the king, by you; therefore make speed to him again, and you shall deliver him this ring from me, for a token. [In the which ring was the king's image engraven, with a ruby, as like the king as might be devised.] This ring he knoweth well, for he gave me the same; and tell him, that I am not offended with him in my heart for any thing; and that shall be known shortly; therefore bid him pluck up his heart, and be of good comfort: and I charge you, come not from him, till you have brought him out of the danger of death, if it be possible.

Then spoke the king to Mrs. Anne Bullen: good sweetheart, as you love me, send the cardinal a token at my request, and, in so doing, you shall deserve our thanks. She, being disposed not to offend the king, would not disobey his loving request, but took incontinently her tablet of gold, that hung at her side, and delivered it to Dr. Butts, with very gentle and loving words; and so he departed to Ashur with speed. And after him the king sent Dr. Cromer, Dr. Clement, and Dr. Wotton, to consult and advise with Dr. Butts for my lord's recovery.

Now, after Dr. Butts had been with him, and delivered him the tokens from the king and Mrs. Anne Bullen, with the most comfortable words he could devise, on the king's and Mrs. Anne's behalf, he advanced himself in his bed, and received the tokens very joyfully, giving him many thanks for his pains and good comfort. He told him further, that the king's pleasure was, that he should minister unto him for his health. And, for the better and more assured ways, he hath also sent Dr. Cromer, Dr. Clement, and Dr. Wotton, all to join for his recovery: therefore, my lord, quoth Dr. Butts, it were well they were called to visit you, and to consult with me for your disease.

At which motion my lord was contented, and sent for them to hear their judgments; but he trusted more to Dr. Cromer, than all the rest, because he was the very means to bring him from Paris to England, and gave him, partly, his exhibition in Paris. To be short, in four days they set him again upon his feet, and he had gotten him a good stomach to meat. All this done, and my lord in a right good way of amendment, they took their leaves, and departed: to whom my lord offered his reward; but they refused, saying, the king had given a special commandment, that they should take nothing of him, for, at their return, he would reward them of his own cost.

After this, my lord continued at Ashur till Candlemas; before, and against which feast, the king caused to be sent to my lord three or four loads of stuff; and most thereof, except beds and kitchen-stuff, was loaded in standers, wherein were both plate, and rich hangings, and chapel-stuff, which was done without the knowledge of the lords of the council; for all which he rendered the king most humble and hearty thanks, and afterwards made suit to the king to be removed from Ashur to Richmond; which request was granted.

The house of Richmond, a little before, was repaired by my lord, to his great cost; for the king had made an exchange with him for Hampton-court. Had the lords of the council known of these favours from the king to the cardinal, they would have persuaded the king to the contrary; for they feared, lest his now abode near the king might move the king at some season to resort unto him, and to call him home again, considering the great and daily affection the king bore unto him. Therefore they moved the king, that my lord might go down to the north, to his benefice there, where he might be a good stay, as they alledged, to the country. To which the king condescended, thinking no less, but that all had been true, according to their relation, being with such colour of deep consideration, that the king was straightway persuaded to their conclusion: Whereupon, my lord of Norfolk ordered Mr. Cromwell, who daily did resort to my lord, that he should say to him, That he must go home to his benefice. Well, then, Thomas, quoth my lord, we will go to Winchester. I will, then, quoth Mr. Cromwell, tell my lord of Norfolk what you say. And so he did, at his next meeting of him. What should he do there? quoth the duke. Let him go to the rich bishoprick of York, where his greatest honour and charge lie; and so shew to him. The lords, who were not his friends, perceiving that my lord was disposed to plant himself so nigh the king, thought then to withdraw his appetite from Winchester; moved the king to give my lord a pension of four thousand marks out of Winchester, and all the rest to be distributed amongst the nobility and his servants; and so, likewise, to divide the revenues of St. Albans; whereof some had two hundred pounds; and all the revenues of his lands, belonging to his colleges at Oxford and Ipswich, the king took into his own hands; whereof Mr. Cromwell had the receipt and government before, by my lord's assignment. Wherefore it was thought very necessary, that he should have the same still, who executed all things so well and exactly, that he was had in great estimation for his behaviour therein.

Now it came to pass, that those, to whom the king had given any annuities, or fees for term of life, or by patent, could not be good, but only for and during my lord's life; forasmuch as the king had no longer estate therein, but what he had by my lord's attainder in the *Præmunire;* and, to make their estate good and sufficient, there was no other way, but to obtain my lord's confirmation of their patents; and, to bring this about, there was no other means, but by Mr. Cromwell, who was thought to be the fittest instrument for this purpose; and, for his pains therein, he was worthily rewarded; and his demeanour, his honesty, and wisdom were such, that the king took great notice of him, as you shall hereafter hear.

Still the lords thought long, till my lord was removed further off the king's way; wherefore, among others of the lords, my lord of Norfolk said: 'Mr. Cromwell, methinks, the cardinal, thy master, makes no haste to go northwards; tell him, if he go not away, I will tear him with my teeth; therefore I would advise him to prepare away with speed, or else I will set him forward.' These words reported Mr. Cromwell to my lord at his next repair, which was then at Richmond, having obtained license of the king to remove from Ashur to Richmond. And, in the evening, my lord being accustomed to walk in the garden, and I being with him standing in an alley, I espied certain images of beasts, counterfeited in timber; which I went nearer, to take the better view of them; among whom I there saw stand a dun cow, whereat I most mused of all those beasts: my lord then suddenly came upon me unawares, and, speaking to me, said: What have you espied there, whereat you look so earnestly?

Forsooth, quoth I, if it please your grace, I here behold these images, which, I suppose, were ordained to be set up in the king's palace; but amongst them all I have most considered this cow, which seems to me the artificer's master-piece. Yea, marry, quoth my lord; upon this cow hangs a certain prophecy, which perhaps you never heard of; I will shew you, there is a saying,

> When the cow doth ride the bull,
> Then, priest, beware of thy scull.

Which saying, neither my lord that declared it, nor I that heard it, understood the effect, although the compass thereof was working, and then like to be brought to pass; this cow the king gave by reason of the earldom of Richmond, which was his inheritance. This prophecy was afterwards expounded in this manner: the dun cow, because it is the king's beast, betokens the king, and the bull betokens Mrs. Anne Bullen, who after was queen; her father gave the black bull's head in his cognisance, which was his breast; so that, when the king had married queen Anne, it was thought of all men to be fulfilled, for what a number of priests, religious and secular, lost their heads for offending of those laws made, to bring this matter to pass, is not unknown to all the world; therefore it may well be judged that this prophecy is fulfilled.

You have heard what words the duke of Norfolk spoke to master Cromwell touching my lord's going into the north; then said my lord, Tom, it is time to be going: therefore I pray you, go to the king, and tell him I would go to my benefice at York, but for lack of money, desiring his grace to help me to some; and you may say, that the last money I had from his grace was too little to pay my debts, and to compel me to pay the rest of my debts were too much extremity, seeing all my goods are taken from me: also shew my lord of Norfolk, and the rest of the council, that I would depart, if I had money: Sir, quoth Mr. Cromwell, I shall do my best, and so, after other communication, departed, and came to London; then, in the beginning of Lent, my lord removed his lodging into the Charter-house at Richmond, where he lay in a lodging that Dr. Collet made for himself; and every afternoon, for the time of his residence, there would he sit in contemplation, with some one of the most ancient fathers there, who converted him to dispose the vain glory of this world, and they gave unto him shirts of hair to wear next his body, which he wore divers times after.

The lords assigned that my lord should have a thousand marks pension out of Winchester, for his going down into the north; which when the king heard of, he commanded that it should be forthwith paid unto Mr. Cromwell. And the king commanded Mr. Cromwell to repair to him again, when he had received the said sum, which he accordingly did: to whom his majesty said, Shaw your lord that I have sent him ten thousand pounds of my benevolence, tell him he shall not lack, and bid him be of good comfort. Mr. Cromwell, on my lord's behalf, thanked the king for his royal liberality, towards my lord, and with that departed to Richmond, to whom he delivered the money, and the joyful tidings, wherein my lord did not a little rejoice; forthwith there was a preparation made for his going. He had with him, in his train, one hundred and sixty persons, having with him twelve carts to carry his goods, which he sent from his college at Oxford, besides other carts of his daily carriage, of his necessaries for his buildings; he kept his solemn feast of Easter, at Peterborough, and, upon Palm-Sunday, he bore his palm, and went in procession with the Monks, and upon Thursday he made his Maunday, having fifty-nine poor people whose feet he washed and kissed, and after he had dried them, he gave every one of then twelve pence, and three ells of good canvass, to make them shirts, and each of them a pair of new shoes, and a cask of red-herrings; on Easter-day, he rose to the resurrection, and that day he went in procession in his cardinal's vestments, having his hat on his head, and sung the high mass there himself solemnly; after his mass, be gave his benediction to all the hearers, with clean remission. From Peterborough he took his journey into the north, but made some stay by the way, and many passages happened in his journey too tedious here to relate. At the last he came to Stoby, where he continued till after Michaelmas, exercising many deeds of charity; most commonly every Sunday, if the weather served, would he go to some poor parish church thereabouts, and there would say the divine service, and either said or heard mass, and then caused one of his chaplains to preach the word of God to the people, and afterwards he would dine in some honest house in the town, where should be distributed to the poor alms, as well of meat and drink, as money to supply the want of meat and drink, if their number did exceed; thus with other good deeds, practising himself, during the time of his abode there, between party and party, being at variance. About Michaelmas, after he removed from thence to Cawood castle, within seven miles of the city of York, where he had much honour and love from all men, high and low, and kept a plentiful house for all comers; also he built and repaired the castle, which was much decayed, having at the least three hundred persons daily at work, to whom he paid wages lying there: where all the doctors and prebends of the church of York did repair to my lord, according to their duties, as unto the chief head, patron, and father of their spiritual dignities, who did most joyfully welcome him into those parts, saying: It was no small comfort unto them, to see their head among them, who had been so long absent from them, being like unto fatherless and comfortless children for want of his presence; and that they trusted shortly to see him amongst them in his own church. To whom he made answer, That it was the most special cause of his coming, to be amongst them as a father, and a natural brother.

Sir, quoth they, you must understand the ordinances and rules of our church, whereof, although you be the head and sole governor, yet you are not so well acquainted as we be therein: therefore, if it please your grace, we shall, under favour, open unto you some part of our ancient laws and customs of our church, that our head, prelate, and pastor, as you now are, might not come above our choir door, until by due order he be installed. And if you should happen to die before your installation, you should not be buried above in the choir, but below in the nether part of the body of the church. Therefore we humbly desire and beseech you, in the name of all our brethren, that you would vouchsafe to do therein, as our ancient fathers, your predecessors, have done, and that you will not break the laudable customs of our church; to the which we are obliged by oath at our first admittance to observe that, and divers others, which in our chapter do remain upon record.

These records, quoth my lord, would I fain see, and then shall you know further of my advice and mind in this business.

A day was signed to bring their records to my lord, at which time they resorted to my lord with their register and books of records, wherein were fairly written their institutions and rules, which every minister of their church was most principally and chiefly bound to observe, and infallibly keep and maintain.

When my lord had read the records, he did intend to be at the cathedral church of York, the next Monday, after Allhallows-day, against which time due preparation was made for the same; but not in so sumptuous a wise, as were his predecessors before him: Nor yet in such sort, as the fame and common report was afterwards made of him, to his great slander. And to the false reporters no small dishonesty, to become divulgers of such notorious lyes, as I am sure they were: For I myself was sent by my lord to York, to see that all things there should be ordered and provided for that solemnity, in a very decent form, to the honour of that ancient and worthy monastery of York.

It came to pass, that upon Allhallows-day, one of the head and principal officers of the said cathedral church, which should have had my doing at my lord's installation, was with my lord at Cawood, and sitting at dinner, they fell into communication of this matter, and the order and ceremony thereof: He saying that my lord cardinal should go a foot from a chapel, which stands without the gates of the city, called St. James's chapel, unto the minister upon cloth, which should be distributed to the poor, after his said passage to the church. Which most lord hearing, replied and said, Although, perhaps, our predecessors have gone upon cloth, yet we intend to go on foot without any such pomp, or glory, in the vamps of our hose. And, therefore, he gave order to his servants, to go as humbly thither, as might be, without any sumptuous apparel; for I intend, on Sunday, to come to you to be installed, and to make but one dinner for you at the close, and the next day to dine with the mayor, and so return again hither.

The day being not unknown to all the country, the gentlemen, abbots, and priors had such provision sent in, that was almost incredible for store and variety.

The common people held my lord in great estimation for his purity and liberality, and also for his familiar gesture, and good behaviour amongst them. By means whereof, he gained much love of all the people in the north parts of England.

CHAP. XIX.

*Of the Cardinal's Fall, and how he was arrested of High
Treason.*

WHAT chanced before his last troubles at Cawood, as a sign or
token from God of that which should follow, I will now, God willing,
declare. My lord's enemies being then at court about the king, in good
estimation, and honourable dignities; seeing now my lord in great
favour, and fearing the king would now call him home again, they
therefore did plot amongst themselves to dispatch him by means of some
sinister treason, or to bring him into the king's great indignation, by
some other means.

This was their daily study and consultation, having, for their special
help and furtherance, as many vigilant attendants upon him, as the
poets feign Argus had eyes.

The king, with these their continual complaints, was moved to much
indignation, and thought it good that the cardinal should come up, and
to stand to his trial in his own person; which his enemies did not like.
Notwithstanding, he was sent for, and after this sort:

First, they devised that Sir Walter Welch, knight, one of the king's
privy-chamber, should be sent down with a commission into the north;
and the earl of Northumberland, who was sometime brought up in the
house of my lord, being joined in commission with him, should arrest
my lord of high treason. This being resolved upon, Sir Walter Welch
prepared for his journey, with his commission and certain instruments
annexed to the same, and took horse at the court gate upon Allhallows-
day, towards my lord of Northumberland's.

Now will I declare what I promised before of a certain sign or token
of my lord's troubles ensuing.

Upon Alhallows-day, my lord sitting at dinner, having, at his board's
end, divers of his chaplains to bear him company for want of other
guests; you shall now understand, that my lord's great cross, which
stood by, fell, and in the fall broke Doctor Bonner's head, inasmuch
that some blood ran down. My lord, perceiving the fall thereof, demanded of those that stood by him, what was the matter that they
stood so amazed; I shewed him, of the fall of his great cross upon
Dr. Bonner's head: Quoth my lord, Hath it drawn any blood? Yea,
quoth I. With that he cast his head aside, and soberly said, *Malum
omen*, and thereupon suddenly said grace, and rose from table, and
went to his bed chamber, but what he did there I cannot tell. Now
mark how my lord expounded the meaning thereof, in his fancy, to me
at Pontefract, after his fall: First, that the great cross that he bore
as Archbishop of York betokened himself, and Doctor Austin the
physician, who overthew the cross, was he that accused my lord,
whereby his enemies caught an occasion to overthow him; it fell on
Dr. Bonner's head, who was then master of my lord's faculties, and
spiritual jurisdiction, who was then damnified by the fall thereof;

and moreover the drawing of blood betokeneth death, which did suddenly after follow.

Now the appointed time drew near for the installation and sitting at dinner; the Friday before the Monday, that he should have been installed at York, the Earl of Northumberland, and Mr. Welch, with a great company of gentlemen of the earl's house, and of the country whom they had gathered in the king's name, to accompany them, yet not knowing to what end, came to the hall of Cawood (the officers being at dinner) and my lord not fully dined, not knowing any thing of the earl's being come.

The first thing that the earl did, after he had set the hall in order, he commanded the porter to deliver the keys of the gates to him; which he would in no wise do, although he was threatened and commanded in the king's name, to make deliverance thereof to one of the earl's servants; which he still refused, saying to the earl, that the keys were delivered to him by his lord and master, both by oath and other command.

Now some of the gentlemen that stood by the earl, hearing the porter speak so stoutly, said, ' He is a good fellow, and a faithful servant to his master, and speaks like an honest man; therefore give him your charge, and let him keep the keys still;' then said my lord, You shall well and truly keep the keys to the use of our Sovereign Lord the King, and you shall let none pass in nor out of the gates, but such as from time to time you shall be commanded by us, being the king's commissioners during our stay here; and with that oath he received the keys of the earl and Mr. Welch's hands; but of all these doings knew my lord nothing, for they had stopped the stairs that none should go to my lord's chamber, and they that came down could not go up again. At the length, one escaped up, and shewed my lord, that the Earl of Northumberland was in the hall; whereat, my lord wondered, and, at the first, believed him not, till he heard it confirmed by another: Then saith my lord, I am sorry, we have dined; for I fear, our officers have not provided fish enough for the entertainment of him, with some honourable chear fitting his estate and dignity: And with that my lord arose from the table, and commanded to let the cloth lie, that the earl might see how far forth they were at their dinners; and, as he was going down stairs, he encountered with my Lord of Northumberland; to whom my lord said, You are heartily welcome, my lord, and so they embraced each other: Then saith my Lord Cardinal, If you had loved me, you would have sent me word before of your coming, that I might have entertained you, according to your honour. Notwithstanding, you shall have such chear, as I can make you for the present, with a right good-will; trusting you will accept thereof in good part, and hoping hereafter to see you oftener, when I shall be more able to entertain you; this said, my lord took him by the hand, and led him to his chamber, whom followed all the earl's servants; and, they being there all alone, saving I, which kept the door, as my office required, being gentleman-usher, and these two lords standing at a window, the earl trembling said: I arrest you of high-treason; with which words, my lord was well nigh astonished, standing still a good while, without speaking one word.

But, at the last, saith my lord, What authority have you to arrest me? The earl saith, I have a commission so to do. Shew it me, saith my lord, that I may see the contents thereof. Nay, sir, that you may not, saith the earl. Then saith my lord, hold you contented, for I will not obey your arrest, for there have been between your ancestors, and my predecessors, great contentions and debates, and therefore, unless I see your authority, I will not obey you.

Even as they were debating the matter in the chamber, so likewise was Master Welch busy in arresting Dr. Austin, at the door, saying, Go in, you traytor, or I shall make thee: With that I opened the portal door, and did thrust in Dr. Austin before him, with violence. The matter on both sides astonished me very much, marvelling what all this should mean, until, at the last, Master Welch, being entered my lord's chamber, began to pluck off his hood, being of the same cloth his cloke was, which hood he wore, to the intent he should not be known, who kneeled down to my lord; to whom my lord said, Come hither, gentleman, and let me speak with you, commanding him to stand up, and said thus: My Lord of Northumberland hath arrested me, but by what authority I know not; if you be privy thereunto, joined with him therein, I pray you shew me. Indeed, my lord, if it please your grace, says Master Welch, I pray have me excused; there are annexed to our commission certain instructions, as you may not see nor be privy to. Why, saith my lord, be your instructions such as I may not see nor be privy thereunto? yet peradventure, if I be privy unto them, I may help you the better to perform them, for it is not unknown to you, that I have been of counsel, in as weighty matters as these are; and I doubt not, but I shall do well enough, for my part, and prove myself a true man against the expectations of my cruel enemies; I see the matter, whereupon it groweth. Well, there is no more to do, I trow, thou art of the privy-chamber, your name is Mr. Welch; I am contented to yield to you, but not to the earl, unless I see his commission, and also you are a sufficient commissioner in this behalf, being one of the privy-chamber: Therefore, put your commission in execution, spare me not, I will obey you and the king, for I fear not the cruelty of mine enemies, no more than I do the truth of my allegiance, wherein, I take God to witness, I never offended his majesty in word or deed, and therein I dare stand face to face with any, having a difference without partiality.

Then came my Lord of Northumberland, and commanded me to avoid the chamber: And, being loth to depart from my master, I stood still, and would not remove; to whom he spoke again and said, There is no remedy, you must depart; with that I looked upon my master, as who would have said, Shall I go? and, perceiving by his countenance, that it was not for me to stay, I departed and went into another chamber, where were many gentlemen and others to hear news; to whom I made a report of what I heard and saw, which was great heaviness to them all.

Then the earl called into his chamber divers of his own servants, and, after he and Master Welch had taken the keys from my lord, he committed the keeping of my lord unto five gentlemen, and then they went about the house, and put all things in order, intending to depart the next day, and to certify the king, and the rest of the lords, what they had done.

Then went they busy about to convey Dr. Austin away to London with as much speed and privacy, as they could possibly, sending with him divers persons to conduct him, who was bound to his horse like a traytor.

And this being done, when it was near night, the commissioners sending two grooms of my lords to attend him in his chamber, where he lay all night, the rest of the earl's men watched in the chamber, and all the house was watched, and the gates safe kept, that no man could pass or repass until next morning.

About eight of the clock next morning, the earl sent for me into his chamber, and commanded me to go to my lord; and, as I was going, I met with Master Welch, who called me unto him, and shewed me how the king's [majesty bore unto me his principal favour for my love and diligent service, that I had performed to my lord : Wherefore, saith he, the king's pleasure is, that you shall be about him as chief, in whom his highness putteth great confidence and trust; and thereupon gave me in writing the articles: Which when I had read, I said I was content to obey his majesty's pleasure, and would be sworn to the performance thereof; whereupon he gave me my oath.

That done, I resorted to my lord, whom I found sitting in a chair, the table being ready spread for him. But, so soon as he perceived me to come in, he fell into such a woful lamentation, that would have forced a flinty heart to mourn.

I then comforted him as well as I could, but he would not : ' For, quoth he, I am much grieved that I have nothing to reward you, and the rest of my true and faithful servants, for all the good service that they and you have done me, for which I do much lament.'

Upon Sunday following, the earl and Mr. Welch appointed to set forward ; for my lord's horse and ours were brought ready into the inner court, where we mounted, and coming towards the gate, ready to ride out, the porter had no sooner opened the same, but we saw without, ready attending, a great number of gentlemen, and their servants, such as the earl had appointed for that service, to attend and conduct my lord to Pontefract that night.

But, to tell you the truth, there were also many of the people of the country assembled at the gate, lamenting his departure, in number above three thousand, who, after the opening of the gate, that they had a sight of him, cried out, with a loud voice, ' God save your grace, God save your grace, the foul evil take them that have taken you from us ; we pray God, that vengeance may light upon them.' And thus they ran after him through the town of Cawood, for he was there very well beloved, both of rich and poor.

=====

CHAP. XX.

Of the Cardinal's Entertainment at the Earl of Shrewsbury's, and of his death and burial at Leicester.

AFTER our departure from Cawood, we came to Doncaster ; the third day we came to Sheffield-park, where my Lord of Shrewsbury lived, within the lodge, and the earl and his lady, and a great company of gentlewomen and servants, stood without the gate, to attend my lord's coming; at whose alighting, the earl received him with much honour, and embraced him, saying these words: ' My Lord, you are most heartily welcome to my poor lodge, and I am glad to see you.'

Here my lord staid a fortnight, and was most nobly entertained; he spent most of his time, and applied his mind to prayers continually, in great devotion. It came to pass, as he sat one day at dinner, I, being there, perceived his colour, divers times, to change; I asked him if he was not well; who answered me, with a loud voice, ' I am suddenly taken with a thing at my stomach as cold as a whet-stone, and am not well; therefore take up the table, and make a short dinner, and return to me again suddenly.' I made but a little stay, but came to him again, where I found him still sitting, very uneasy: He desired me to go to the apothecary, and ask him if he had any thing would break wind upwards; he told me, he had: Then I went and shewed the same to my lord, who did command me to give him some thereof, and so I did, and it made him break wind exceedingly: ' Lo,' quoth he, ' you may see it was but wind, for now, I thank God, I am well eased;' and so he arose from the table, and went to prayers, as he used, every day after dinner.

In the afternoon, my Lord of Shrewsbury sent for me to him, to whom he said, ' Forasmuch as I have always perceived you to be a man, in whom your lord putteth great affiance, and I myself, knowing you to be a man very honest;' with many words of commendations and praise, more than becometh me to rehearse, he said, ' Your lord and master hath often desired me to write to the king, that he might answer his accusations before his enemies: And, this day, I have received letters from his majesty, by Sir William Kingston, whereby I perceive, that the king hath him in good opinion, and, upon my request, hath sent for him, by the said Sir William Kingston.

' Therefore, now I would have you play your part wisely with him, in such sort, as he may take it quietly, and in good part, for he is always full of sorrow, and much heaviness, at my being with him, that I fear he would take it ill, if I bring him tidings thereof; and therein doth he not well, for I assure you, that the king is his very good lord, and hath given me most hearty thanks for his entertainment; and, therefore, go your way to him, and persuade him, that I may find him quiet at my coming, for I will not tarry long after you.'

' Sir,' quoth I, ' and, if it please your lordship, I shall endeavour, to the best of my power, to accomplish your lordship's command; but, sir, I doubt, when I name this Sir William Kingston, that he will mistrust some ill, because he is constable of the tower, and captain of the guard, having, in his company, twenty-four of the guard to accompany him.' ' That is nothing,' quoth the earl; ' what, if he be constable of the tower, and captain of the guard, he is the fittest man, for his wisdom and discretion, to be sent about such a business; and, for the guard, it is only to defend him from those that might intend him any ill: Besides that, the guard are, for the most part, such of his old servants, as the king hath took into his service, to attend him most justly.' ' Well, sir,' quoth I, ' I shall do what I can,' and so departed, and went to my lord and found him in the gallery, with his staff and his beads in his hands; and seeing me, he asked me what news; 'Forsooth,' quoth I, 'the best news that ever you heard, if you can take it well.' 'I pray God it be true, then,' quoth he. 'My Lord of Shrewsbury,' said I, 'your most assured friend, hath so provided, by his letters to the king, that his majesty hath sent for you, by Master Kingston, and twenty-four of the guard, to conduct you to his highness.' 'Master Kingston!' quoth he, and clapped his hand on his thigh, and gave a great sigh.

'May it please your grace,' quoth I, 'I wish you would take all things well, it would be much better for you; content yourself, for God's sake, and think, that God and your good friends have wrought for you, according to your own desires: And, as I conceive, you have much more cause to rejoice, than lament or mistrust the matter; for, I assure you, that your friends are more afraid of you, than you need be of them: And his majesty, to shew his love to you, hath sent Master Kingston to honour you, with as much honour as is your grace's due, and to convey you in such easy journies, as is fitting for you, and you shall command him to do, and that you shall have your request. And I humbly intreat you, to imprint this my persuasion in your highness's discretion, and to be of good chear; wherewith you shall comfort yourself, and give your friends, and poor servants, great comfort and content.'

'Well,' quoth he, 'I perceive more than you can imagine, or do know.' Presently after came my lord, to acquaint him with that I had so lately related; my lord cardinal thanked the earl for his great love, and called for Master Kingston, who came to him presently, and, kneeling down before him, saluted him in the king's behalf, whom my lord, bareheaded, offered to take up, but he would not: 'Then,' quoth my lord, 'Master Kingston, I pray you stand up, and leave your kneeling to me, for I am a wretch repleat with misery, not esteeming myself, but, as a meer abject, utterly cast away, but without desert, God knows; therefore, good Master Kingston, stand up.'

Then Master Kingston said, 'The king's majesty hath him commended unto you.' 'I thank his highness,' quoth my lord, 'I hope he is in good health.' 'Yes,' quoth Master Kingston, 'and he hath him commended unto you, and commanded me to bid you be of good chear, for he beareth you as much good-will as ever he did.

'And whereas report hath been made unto him, that you should commit, against his majesty, certain heinous crimes, which he thinketh to be; but yet, he, for administration of justice, in such cases requisite, could do no less than send for you, that you might have your trial, mistrusting nothing your truth and wisdom, but that you shall be able to acquit yourself of all complaints and accusations, extended against you; and you may take your journey to him at your pleasure, commanding me to attend you.'

'Master Kingston,' quoth my lord, 'I thank you for your good news; and, sir, hereof assure yourself, if I were as able and lusty, as ever I was, to ride, I would go with you post: but, alas! I am a diseased man, having a flux,' (at which time it was apparent that he had poisoned himself) ‘ it hath made me very weak ; but the comfortable news you bring is of purpose, I doubt, to bring me into a fool's paradise, for I know what is provided for me : Notwithstanding, I thank you for your good-will, and pains taken about me, and I shall, with speed, make ready to ride with you.’

After this, I was commanded to make all things ready for our departure the morrow after.

When my lord went to bed, he fell very sick of the flux, which caused him to go to stool, from time to time, all that night; insomuch that, from that time till morning, he had fifty stools ; and the matter, that he voided, was very black, which the physicians called Adust, whose opinions were, that he had not above four or five days to live.

Notwithstanding, he would have ridden with Mr. Kingston the next day, had not the Earl of Shrewsbury advised him to the contrary ; but, the next day, he took his journey with Master Kingston, and them of the guard, who, espying him, could not abtain from weeping, considering he was their old master, and now in such a miserable case ; whom my lord took by the hand, and would, as he rode by the way, sometimes talk with one, and sometimes with another, till he came to a house of my lord's, standing in the way, called Hardwick-hall, where he lay all that night, extremely ill. The next day, he came to Nottingham, and, the next day, to Leicester-abbey, and, the next day, he waxed very sick, that he had almost fallen from his horse, so that it was night, before he got to Leicester-abbey ; where, at his coming in at the gates, the abbot, with all their convent, met him with many lighted torches, whom they honourably received, and welcomed with great reverence.

To whom my lord said, ‘ Father Abbot, I am come to lay my bones amongst you :’ Riding still on his mule, till he came to the stairs of his chamber, where he alighted ; Master Kingston, holding him by the arm, led him up the stairs, who told me afterwards, that he never felt so heavy a burden in all his life ; and, as soon as he was in his chamber, he went straight to bed ; this was upon Saturday, and so he continued.

On Monday in the morning as I stood by his bed-side, about eight of the clock in the morning, the windows being close shut, and having wax lights burning upon the cupboard, I thought I perceived him drawing on towards death. He, perceiving my shadow upon the bed-side, asked who was there. Sir, quoth I, it is I : How do yon, quoth he, well? Ay, sir, quoth I, if I might see your grace well : What is it o'clock, quoth he ? I answered, it was about eight of the clock. Quoth he, that cannot be, rehearsing eight of the clock so many times. Nay, quoth he, that cannot be, for at eight of the clock you shall see your master's time draw near, that I must depart this world. With that, Dr. Palmer, a worthy gentleman, standing by, bid me ask him if he would be shriven, to make him ready for God, whatever chanced to fall out, which I did. But he was very angry with me, and asked, ‘ What I had to do to ask him such a question ? Till, at last, the doctor took my part, and talked with him in latin, and pacified him.

After dinner, Mr. Kingston sent for me, and said, sir, the king hath sent unto me letters, by Mr. Vincent, our old companion, who hath been in trouble in the tower, for money that my lord should have at his departure. A great part of this money cannot be found; wherefore the king, at Mr. Vincent's request, for the declaration of the truth, hath sent him hither with his grace's letters, that I should examine my lord, and have your counsel therein, that he may take it well and in good part. And this is the cause of my sending for you, therefore, I desire your counsel therein, for acquittal of this poor gentleman, Mr. Vincent.

Sir, quoth I, according to my duty you shall; and, by my advice, you shall resort unto him in your own person to visit him, and, in communication, break the matter unto him: and, if he will not tell you the truth, then you may certify the king thereof; but in any case, name not, nor speak of my fellow Vincent: also I would not have you to detract the time, for he is very sick, and I fear that he will not live past a day or two; and accordingly Mr. Kingston went to my lord, and demanded the money, saying, that my Lord of Northumberland found a book at Cawood house, that you had but lately borrowed ten-thousand pounds, and there is not so much as one penny to be found, who hath made the king privy to the same; wherefore, the king hath written to me, to know what is become thereof, for it were pity that it should be holden from you both. Therefore, I require you, in the king's name, to tell me the truth, that I may make a just report unto his majesty, of your answer.

With that, quoth my lord, Oh good Lord, how much doth it grieve me that the king should think any such thing in me, that I should deceive him of one penny, seeing I have nothing, nor ever had, God be my judge, that I ever esteemed so much mine own, as his majesty's, having but the bare use of it, during my life, and after my death, to leave it wholly to him; wherein his majesty hath prevented me. But for this money, you demand of me, I assure you, it is none of my own, for I borrowed it of divers of my friends to bury me, and to bestow amongst my servants, who have taken great pains about me; notwith-standing, if it be your pleasure to know, I must be content; yet I be-seech his majesty, to see it satisfied for the discharge of my conscience to them that I owe it to. Who be they, quoth Mr. Kingston? That shall I tell you, quoth my lord, I borrowed two-hundred pounds of John Allen of London, another two-hundred pounds of Sir Richard Gresham, and two-hundred pounds of the master of the Savoy; and also two-hundred of Dr. Higden, dean of my college, at Oxford; two-hundred pounds of the treasurer of the church; and two-hundred pounds of Mr. Ellis, my chaplain; and another two-hundred pounds of a priest. I hope the king will restore it again, forasmuch as it is none of mine.

Sir, quoth Mr. Kingston, there is no doubt in the king, whom you need not distrust; but Sir, I pray you, where is the money? Quoth he, I will not conceal it, I warrant you, but I will declare it unto you before I die, by the grace of God; have a little patience with me, I pray you, for the money is safe enough in an honest man's hands, who will not keep one penny thereof from the king.

So Mr. Kingston departed, for that time, my lord being very weak, and about four of the clock, the next morning, as I conceived, I asked him how he did. Well, quoth he, if I had any meat, I pray you give me some.

Sir, quoth I, there is none ready; then he said, you are much to blame, for you should have always meat for me in readiness, whensoever that my stomach serves me; I pray you get some ready for me; for I mean to make myself strong to-day, to the intent I may go confession, and make me ready for God; quoth I, I will call up the cooks to prepare some meat, and also I will call Mr. Palmer, that he may discourse with you, till your meat be ready. What a good-will, quoth my lord, and so I called Mr. Palmer, who rose and came to my lord.

Then I went and acquainted Mr. Kingston, that my lord was very sick, and not like to live. In good faith, quoth Mr. Kingston, you are much to blame, to make him believe he is sicker than he is. Well, Sir, quoth I, you cannot say, but I gave you warning, as I am bound to do; upon which words he arose, and came unto him, but before he came, my lord cardinal had eaten a spoonful or two of callis made of chickin, and after that he was in his confession, the space of an hour: And then Mr. Kingston came to him, and bade him good-morrow, and asked him how he did, Sir, quoth he, I watch but God's pleasure, to render up my poor soul to him. I pray you, have me heartily commended unto his Royal Majesty, and beseech him on my behalf to call to his princely remembrance all matters that have been between us from the beginning and the progress : And especially between good Queen Catherine, and him, and then shall his grace's conscience know whether I have offended him, or not.

He is a prince of a most royal carriage, and hath a princely heart, and, rather than he will miss or want any part of his will, he will endanger the one half of his kingdom.

I do assure you, I have often kneeled before him, sometimes three hours together, to persuade him from his will and appetite, but could not prevail: And, Master Kingston, if I had but served God, as diligently as I have served the King, he would not have given me over in my grey hairs. But this is the just reward that I must receive for my diligent pains and study, not regarding my service to God, but only to my prince. Therefore, let me advise you, if you be one of the privy-council, as by your wisdom you are fit, take heed what you put in the King's head, for you can never put it out again.

And I desire you further, to request his grace in God's name, that he have a vigilant eye to suppress the hellish Lutherans, that they increase not through his great negligence, in such a sort, as he be compelled to take up arms to subdue them, as the King of Bohemia was; whose commons being infected with Wickliff's heresies, the King was forced to take that course.

Let him consider the story of King Richard the Second, the second son of his progenitor; who lived in the time of Wickliff's seditions and heresies: did not the commons, I pray you, in his time, rise against the nobility and chief governors of this realm ; and, at the last, some of them were put to death, without justice or mercy, and, under pretence of having all things common, did they not fall to spoiling or robbing, and, at last, took the King's person, and carried him about the city, making him obedient to their proclamations?

Did not also the traiterous heretick, Sir John Oldcastle, Lord Cobham, pitch a field with hereticks against King Henry the Fourth, where the King was in person, and fought against them, to whom God gave the victory?

Alas! If these be not plain precedents and sufficient persuasions to admonish a prince: Then God will take away from us our prudent rulers, and leave us to the hands of our enemies. And then will ensue mischief upon mischief, inconveniencies, barrenness and scarcity, for want of good orders, in the common wealth, from which God of his tender mercy defend us.

Master Kingston, farewell; I wish all things may have good success, my time draws on; I may not tarry with you, I pray you remember my words.

Now began the time to draw near, for he drew his speech at length; his tongue began to fail him, his eyes perfectly set in his head, and his sight failed him. Then we began to put him in mind, of Christ's passion, and caused the yeoman of the guard, to stand by privately, to see him die, and bear witness of his words and departure, who heard all his communications.

And then presently the clock struck eight, at which time he gave up the ghost; and thus departed he this life, one of us looking upon another, supposing he prophesied of his departure.

We sent for the abbot of the house to anoint him, who speedily came as he was ending his life, who said certain prayers before that the life was out of his body.

Here is the end and fall of pride; for, I assure you, he was the proudest man alive, having more regard to the honour of his person, than to his spiritual function, wherein he should have expressed more meekness and humility: For pride and ambition are both linked together; and ambition is like choler, which is an humour that makes men active, earnest, and full of alacrity and stirring, if it be not stopped or hindered in its course; but, if it be stopped, and cannot have its way, it becometh dust, and thereby malign and venomous. So ambitious and proud men, if they find the way open for their rising and advancement, and still get forwards, they are rather busy than dangerous; but, if they be checked in their desires, they become secretly discontented, and look upon men and matters with an evil eye, and are best pleased when things go backwards: But I forbear to speak any further therein.

The cardinal being departed, Mr. Kingston sent post to London one of the guard; then were Mr. Kingston and the abbot in consultation about the funeral, which was solemnised the day after, for Mr. Kingston would not stay the return of the post.

They thought good, that the mayor of Leicester and his brethren should see him personally dead, to prevent false reports that he was alive. And, in the interim, whilst the mayor was sent for, his bones were laid in the coffin, and his shirt of hair, and his over-shirt of fine holland, were taken off, and put into the coffin, together with all such ornaments wherewith he was invested, when he was made arch-bishop, as mitre, cross, ring, and pall, with all other things due to his orders.

Thus he lay all that day with his coffin open and bare-faced, that all that desired might see him; and about three of the clock he was buried by the abbot with great solemnity. And being in the church, his corpse was set in the Lady's-Chapel with many tapers, and poor men about him, holding torches in their hands, who watched the corpse all that night, whilt the canons sung divers dirges, and other divine orisons.

And, at four of the clock the next morning, the cardinal's servants and Mr. Kingston came to the church to the execution of many ceremonies, in such manner as is usual at bishops burials; and so he went to mass, where the abbot did offer, and divers others; and then went to bury the corpse in the middle of the said chapel; by this time it was six of the clock, being St. Andrew's day.

Then we prepared for our journey to the court, where we attended his Majesty. The next day I was sent for to the King, conducted by Mr. Norris, where the King was in his night-gown of Rochet velvet, furred with sables, before whom I kneeled the space of an hour, during which time his Majesty examined me of divers particulars concerning my lord cardinal, wishing, rather than twenty-thousand pounds, that he had lived.

He asked me concerning the fifteen-hundred pounds, which Mr. Kingston moved to my lord. Quoth I, I think I can perfectly tell your grace where it is, and who hath it. Can you, quoth the King, I pray you tell me, and you shall not be unrewarded?

Sir, quoth I, after the departure of Mr. Vincent from my lord at Scrooby, who had the custody thereof, leaving it with my lord in divers bags, he delivered it to a certain priest, safely to be kept for his use. Is this true, quoth the King? Yea, quoth I, without doubt, the priest will not deny it before me, for I was at the delivery thereof, who hath gotten divers other rich ornaments, which are not registered in the book of my Lord's inventory, or other writings, whereby any man is able to charge him therewith, but myself.

Then said the King, let me alone for keeping this secret between me and you. Howbeit, three may keep counsel, if two be away; and, if I knew my cap was privy to my counsel, I would cast it into the fire and burn it; and, for your honesty and truth, you shall be our servant in our chamber, as you were with your master.

Therefore, go you your ways to Sir John Gage, our vice-chamberlain, to whom we have spoken already, to admit you our servant in our chamber, and then go to the Lord of Norfolk, and he shall pay you your whole year's wages, which is ten pounds: Is not it so, quoth the King? Yea, forsooth, and if it please your grace, quoth I: And withal, said the King, you shall receive a reward from the Duke of Norfolk.

So I received ten pounds of the duke for my wages, and twenty pounds for my reward; and his Majesty gave me a cart and six horses, the best that I could chuse out of my lord's horses, to carry my goods, and five marks for my charges homewards.

THE

ORDERS, PROCEEDINGS, PUNISHMENTS, AND PRIVILEGES

OF THE

COMMONS HOUSE OF PARLIAMENT

IN ENGLAND.

Printed Anno Dom. 1641.   Quarto, containing thirty pages.

CHAP. I.

What Persons may be Burgesses in Parliament, what not.

THE son and heir of an earl may be; and so was the Lord Russel, Elis. 6.

He that hath no voice in the higher house; so the son and heir apparent of a baron; and so was Mr. Henry Brooke.

A prebendary may not be; and therefore Alexander Nowel was refused, because he was prebendary of Westminster; whereupon a writ was issued to chuse another for Leo in Cornwall.

Sir Henry Piercy was chosen knight for two several counties; and thereupon it was adjudged by the house, that he should serve for that county which first chose him, 13 Elis.

If a burgess be incurably sick, another may be chosen in his place, by license of the house; but not if he be easily sick, or sent in his Majesty's service, unless the house will allow of a new election, 18 Martii, 23 Elis.

And it was then ordered, that, during the session, no writs should issue to chuse knights or burgesses, but by warrant of the house to the clerk of the crown, according to the ancient usage.

The burgesses of Sandwich were kept out of the house, until the perfect return was known. 13 Edw. VI.

One Cavell was returned for Travayny and Ludders-hall; he appeared for Ludders-hall; and therefore a writ issued to chuse another for Travayny, 11 Mar. 7. Edw. VI.

William Gregham and ———————— were returned knights for Norfolk; and the writ, returned by the lord chancellor, suppressed it by great motion, and directed another writ to chuse others.

A burgess, indicted of felony, shall not be removed before conviction, 8 Feb. 23. Elis.

Walter Vaughan was received, notwithstanding an outlawry, because it appeared that it was for debt, and that he had compounded for it.

A burgess outlawed was denied the privilege of the house; but, upon the question, and upon a division of the house, he was allowed the privilege against an arrest in London, 24 Feb. 5 Elis.

CHAP. II.

The Choice of the Speaker, his Presentment, Placing, and Speech.

HE that shall be speaker, must be a knight, or a burgess returned, and cometh to the house, and taketh the ordinary oath, as others.

The fittest seat for him is the lowest row, and the midst thereof; for so he may be best heard, when he shall speak.

One of his Majesty's council doth use to propound, That it is his Majesty's pleasure, that they shall freely chuse a speaker for them; and yet commendeth, in his opinion, some person by name.

Then he, which is so recommended, standeth up, and prayeth to be heard, before they proceed to the choice of him, and, withal, disableth himself (giving them thanks for their good opinion of him) as being not equally learned in the laws with others, that have had the place.

Not being eloquent by nature, or art; nor experienced in the affairs of the commonwealth, or in the orders of the house, being of mean countenance, wealth, or credit.

Being careful for their credit, more than his own, and therefore bound to shew and discover his wants, which otherwise might be covered by their good opinion.

If they press him, he is to yield, and so is brought to the chair; and then they usually give two or three days respite, before he be presented to the King.

Upon the day of his presentment to the King, he cometh to the bar of the higher house, or other appointed place, where his Majesty shall assign; and, after their solemn courtesies, sheweth how he is elected, reneweth the reasons of his disability, desireth to be discharged, and that they of the commons house may have license to proceed to a new election of another.

Then the lord chancellor, receiving his Majesty's pleasure, enableth him.

Hereupon, the speaker gives thanks for that opinion conceived of him; promiseth to do his dutiful endeavour; and desireth, that his ready good-will may be accepted in place of all.

And so, with a low courtesy, beginneth his oration, which commonly standeth upon these parts, viz.

1. Entrance aptly taken from the time or person.
2. The praise of his Majesty's government, or laws of his time.
3. Thanksgiving for summoning the parliament, whereby the sores of the commonwealth may be prevented and remedied.

4.   Promise of all diligence and fidelity in them of the lower house.

5.   Assurance of his own duty, as power will permit.

6.   The petitions that be ordinary, &c.

First, For injoining the privilege of the house; then for themselves, their goodness and servants.

CHAP. III.

The first Reading of any Bill.

UPON the first reading of a bill, the speaker, taking the bill in one hand, and his cap in the other hand, may say: ' you have heard the bill, the contents whereof are these, &c.' And, after the rehearsal thereof, may read another, without suffering any man, if he may stay him, to speak unto it, but rather to advise thereof until the next reading; which is a means not only to hear effectual speech, but also to save a great deal of time.

A bill may not be committed upon the first reading, and yet, 27 Jan. 23 Elis. the proviso for the clerk of the market was, upon the first reading thereof, committed with the bill.

See afterwards, that the subsidy of the clergy passeth at the first reading; and so the pardon.

CHAP. IV.

The second Reading of a Bill.

At the second reading of a bill, it ought to be either ingrossed, committed, or rejected; and if any shall offer to speak thereto, after that three have spoken all on one side, the speaker may say, that the bill is sufficiently spoken unto; What is your pleasure? Will you have it ingrossed, or committed?

And, if the more voices will have it ingrossed, it must be done accordingly.

And, if the more voices will have it committed, then the speaker intreats them to appoint the committees; and, that done, their names, and the time and place of meeting, and the day of their report shall be indorsed upon it.

If the more voices be not apparently discerned, then the speaker may put the question again still: ' As many, as will have this bill ingrossed, say, Ay.' ' And, after that voice, so many, so will not have it ingrossed, say, No.'

Again, if the sides seem equal, the speaker may pray all those that be on the affirmative, to go down with the bill, and the rest to sit in their places; and the sides shall be numbered by tellers to be appointed

by the speaker, and the greater number shall prevail, and the less
number shall go, and fetch them up, in token of consent; and the
speaker shall report the yea, or no, according to the stronger side.

One bill may be twice read in one day.

A bill may be committed after the ingrossing.

CHAP. V.

Orders to be observed by such as shall speak.

If two persons shall rise to speak, the speaker must appoint him to
speak first, that first arose, and offered to speak.

One man may not speak twice to one bill in one day, although he
will change his opinion, except it be only for the moving of some order.

Every man, that will speak, must direct his speech to the speaker,
and not to any other, but only by circumlocution, as by saying,
' He which spoke with the bill, or he which made this, or that
reason.'

If any touch another by nipping, or unreverent speech, the speaker
may admonish him.

If any shall speak dishonourably of the King, or his council, he is
not only to be interrupted, but may be also sent by the house unto the
Tower. As for example,

Withers, a burgess for London, Elisabeth, uttered certain speeches,
whereby it seemed, that he noted the Lord William Howard, then
lord-chamberlain and sometimes lord-admiral, with corruption, but
named him not; and therefore it was thought, he should not be
punished, nor put to answer for it.

If any speak too long, and speak within the matter, he may not
be cut off; but if he be long, and out of the matter, then may the
speaker gently admonish him of the shortness of the time, or the
business of the house, and pray him to make as short as he may.

But if he range in evil words, then to interrupt him, saying: ' I
pray you to spare these words, they become not this place of state and
council.

' It hath not been the order here so to do, I pray you take care of
us all, considering what danger the report hereof may breed unto us.'

No speech ought to be made but only in matter in bill, and therefore
all other motions ought to be represented, and the movers, if the
matter be good, to put their desire into a bill.

CHAP. VI.

License from the King, to proceed.

A BILL exhibited by clothiers of Devonshire, for remitting the act of relief, for making of cloths, redelivered unto them, with promise, that they should receive an answer thereof, at the return of the knights of the shire the sixth of November, 1 Edward the Sixth; and afterwards suit was made by the speaker, the privy-council, and twelve others, to know his Majesty pleasure, whether they might treat thereof.

And three days after it was answered, they might treat thereof, having in regard the cause of the granting of that relief.

The speaker shewed, that it was the Queen's pleasure, that the house should proceed no further with the bill, for the revenues of the Queen, because it extended to divers which had accounted 5 Mart. and 4 and 5 Phil. and Ma.

Three of the privy-council, whereof Sir Edward Rogers, then comptroller, was one, delivered to the house her majesty's express commandment, that they should proceed no further with their suit, which was in a sort moved to be reiterated by a speech of this writer, W. L. But that they should satisfy themselves with her promise.

And then Peter Wentworth, and James Dalton, moved, whether this did not restrain the liberty of the house; upon which, after many arguments, they resolved to cease till the next day, 9 Nov. 8 Elis. And afterwards 23.

Now the Queen revoked her said commandment, and gave them liberty to proceed; but, upon consultation, amongst themselves, they spared to proceed any further.

It was ordered, that Mr. Warner should receive, of the speaker, a bill, exhibited by Hubbart, and his wife, against Sir Nicholas Hare, and that certain of the house should hear, and, if they could, determine the cause; the protector's grace, to make an end thereof. 11 Feb. 1 Ed. VI.

CHAP. VII.

Calling of the House, and the Pain of their Absence.

IT is a common policy, to say upon the reading, that the house shall be called on Saturday; to say it shall be called on Wednesday; and so from day to day, by fear thereof, to keep the company together.

It was ordered, That no knight, or burgess, should depart without license of the house, or of the speaker, to be entered with the clerk of the crown, that he make no writ, to levy such fees or wages, 18 Mart. 23 Elis. and upon the first day of the parliament, there was moreover laid upon each knight, which had not appeared, twenty pounds; and upon every burgess, ten pounds.

See the statute Ed. V. Fol. 2. Statute Cap.

4. Whereupon this double punishment, for absence, is grounded.

After that the committees have made their report and opinion of any bill, referred to their consideration, it shall be thrice read, and it may be spoken unto at every reading.

It was ordered, that the committees of the lower house, upon a conference with the lords, might urge any reasons, tending to the maintenance of any thing that had passed the house; but, not of any new thing to be propounded, until the house were first made privy thereto.

———

CHAP. VIII.

The third Reading of a Bill.

WHEN a bill is ingrossed, and hath received the third reading, it must either pass, or be rejected by the more voices; if it pass, then it must be indorsed, *Soit baillé aux Seigneurs ;* and if it be rejected, it must not come any more in the house.

At one day, after a bill is passed, and not sent away, the speaker may discover any mistaking of words therein, which may be amended, and thrice read, and passed by. Question, 30 Januarii, 23 Elis.

If the lords agree to any bill sent unto them from the lower house, it must be indorsed, *Les Seigneurs ont assentis,* and then it shall be remanded to the lower house.

And, if the lords first pass a bill, and send it to the lower house, which also agree thereto, it must be indorsed, *Les Commons ont assentis.*

But, if there be any difference for alteration of a bill, between the lords and commons, then it is requisite that some special persons of each house meet, and confer, that the one house may understand the meaning of the other.

A bill signed by the king, and sent to the lower house, may not be altered in any part thereof, without his majesty's license.

But if a bill come from the lords, and not signed by him, it may be altered by noting what should be taken from it, or added unto it.

A bill that came from the lords was amended, and a scroll of addition in parchment, put unto it, and sent to the lords, without any indorsement, *soit baille aux seigneurs ;* and for want thereof they would not proceed, but remanded it to pass the bill, and withdraw that addition, or else to indorse it, and thereupon it was indorsed, 8 Mart. 23 Elis.

A bill from the lords is wont to be sent by some of the King's learned council, who are to make three courtesies upon the delivery thereof.

The speaker is to receive it with his cap in his hand, and to say the house will have consideration of it.

Then must he shew unto the house the intituling of them, and after two or three days, according to the exigency of the cause, he may read and pass them as before.

A bill, which passed from the lower house, was remanded by the lords with an addition, and Puckering the speaker, foreseeing the inclination of the house to overthrow the bill, demanded the question only, touching a small addition, which was denied, and so the bill indirectly dashed, but the body thereof saved and untouched.

If a bill pass by the question, yet any admission may be made, thrice read, and agreed, *Sedente Curia*, and so any addition to a bill itself.

The bill of navigation was but half read, and, by reason of a long argument, was respited the next day, but some doubted of that order.

The bill of counterfeiting instruments, or seals of office, was, at the third reading, long argued, and referred for further argument till the next day, and then also committed to the first committees, and others, 9 Feb. 29 Elis.

CHAP. IX.

Respite from Sitting.

IF the sitting be respited for a day, or more, by order, yet then the speaker, accompanied with some, ought in that respite, to read a bill *Pro forma, exceptis diebus non juridicis.*

CHAP. X.

Evidences given by the Lords in the Lower House.

UPON the attainder of Sir Thomas Seymour, Lord Admiral, it was ordered in the lower house, that the speaker and privy council should desire of the Queen, That the lords which gave evidence in the higher house, might also give the same in the lower house. 2 Mart. 1º E. vi.

CHAP. XI.

Fees for the Speaker and Serjeant.

THE speaker is wont to have one-hundred pounds of the prince for the parliament.

Of the subject, for every private Bill for assurance, five pounds before he deliver it out of his hand.

For every name in any bill for denisens, five pounds, unless he do agree for less.

The serjeant hath two shillings of every burgess, and four shillings of every knight, for each sessions of parliament.

CHAP. XII.

Punishment of Offences.

UPON complaint of Sir Robert Brandling, burgess of Newcastle, that Witherington, and others, had made an assault upon him :

It was ordered, That the lord chancellor should award an attachment, to the lord president in the north, against Witherington ; and the house desired the lords of the council to receive the bill of Sir Robert against Witherington, and to take order therein, according to their ancient custom.

And, when the bill was read to Witherington, he confessed the assault ; and after, one Ellaker, servant to the Duke of Suffolk, was, for the same cause, sent in by his master ; and it was ordered, That he should remain in the ward of the serjeant of the house, till he found surety to appear in the King's-Bench, when he should be appointed, and to be bound to the peace : And, after that he was bound to the peace, Sir Robert sued for his discharge, and four of the house were appointed to desire the duke's favour for him, 15 Feb. 6 Elis. and 5 April 7.

Monington was sent to the Tower for striking Johnson, a burgess ; and yet he excused himself, that he knew him not to be a burgess ; and, after two days, he was fetched by the serjeant, and discharged by the house ; and, for that Johnson prayed that he might go safe, that was committed to two of the house, 24 April, 1 Mar.

John Savage wounded Ceder Meniall, servant to Brooke, a knight of the parliament ; and it was established, that proclamation shall be where the fact was done, That Savage should render his body in the King's Bench within a quarter of a year.

Moreover, it is accorded, that likewise it be done in time to come, in like case. Statute 5 Fol. 2 Cap. 6. and the same is confirmed 11 Hen. vi. Cap. 11.

CHAP. XIII.

Punishment of Offences committed by them of the House.

THE chancellor of the duchy, Sir Ambrose Cane, complained of Sir Thomas White, alderman of London, for calling him to witness of misliking the book of Common-Prayer.

Sir Thomas answered, That he said, that Mr. Chancellor wished that the book might be well considered; and he asked the chancellor forgiveness, and had it, 6 Mart. 1 Elis.

Upon the bill of confirmation of letters patent, Thomas Copely said, That he feared that by this the Queen might give away the crown from the right inheritors, and therefore he was committed to the custody of the serjeant; but, forasmuch as he excused himself by his youth, the house moved the Queen to pardon him, who would not presently grant, but said, That she would not be unmindful of their request. 5 Martii 4 & 5 Phil. *et Mariæ*.

Thrower was committed, for saying, If a bill came in for women's wires, they would dispute it, and put it to the question, 7 April, 1 Elis.

Upon Story's submission, being in the tower, it was ordered, That the privy-council of the house should declare unto the house, That their resolution was, to have him discharged, and to pray the King to pardon his offences.

Sir Edward Warner, Lieutenant of the Tower, was sent out of his house to the Tower, for an offence done before the summons of the parliament; and Sir William Cecil, then secretary, said, That the Queen was then assured by her justices, that she might commit any of the house during the parliament, for any offence against her crown and dignity, and that they shewed divers precedents thereof.

The servants of Sir Henry Jones, a knight of the house, did hurt a servant of one Gardiner, a Burgess; the master was awarded to the Sheriff of London to bring them into the court, and their master gave sureties, that they should appear the next term, and answer both the Queen and the party, and so they were delivered by the privilege, to wait upon their masters; and so, by conference of this case with Sir Edward Warner's, it seemeth, a man shall not have the privilege of the house for a criminal offence, that immediately toucheth the Queen, but where it toucheth her indirectly, as by trespass against another.

Pearne was committed to the Marshalsea for pickery, without any notice given to the house.

If any of the house be to answer any contempt, or offence, he must go to the bar, and not keep his place.

Arthur Hall, burgess, for Grantham in Lincolnshire, submitted himself at the bar, for writing and imprinting a book, wherein he defaced the authority of the lower house, or their estate of Parliament ; and he was put out of the doors, and these points, touching him, were resolved, viz.

' That he be committed to the tower, which is the prison for this house, for a certain time, and pay a fine to the Queen, and be severed from being a member of the house; make a warrant to the clerk of the crown, to direct a brief to the sheriff of Lincolnshire, for the borough of Grantham, to chuse and return a new burgess ; that it be published by order of the house, that his book is false, and seditious ; and that himself be brought into the house, to have this judgment pronounced against him by the speaker, in the name of all the house; that the serjeant be commanded to convey him to the Tower, by warrant from the house, signed by the speaker, and that all the proceeding be written, read, and entered, as other causes of the house are.' 14 Feb. 23 Elis.

Dr. Story was reprehended, for being of the lower house ; he came of council with the Bishop of Winchester, before the lords in the higher house, touching a parliament cause, and acknowledged his offence.   23 Mart. 1 Elis.

The house had agreed, 23 Elis. to have a common fast, whereof the Queen misliked not for the matter, but for the innovation of order without her privity, and without ecclesiastical authority, for which the commons submitted themselves, and she gave them their pardon.

Amongst many questions resolved upon in that parliament, 21 Fol. 2, this was one : After the assembly of the parliament, and after the chief matters being propounded by the King, for which he called the parliament:

The lords and commons might treat of other matters first, and forbear to handle those, until the matters, propounded by them, were discussed, notwithstanding that they were also enjoined to the contrary by the King.

It was answered, That they might not so treat, and that, if they did, they were to be punished as traytors ; but 1 Hen. IV. this parliament and those resolutions of 21 Fol. 2 were repealed, and sundry of the judges that joined in that resolution were hanged ; so before.

Note, That the King, 15 and 10 of the parliament, may as well dissolve, as he did, summon it, if he like not their proceeding, and therefore this resolution was needless.

Mr. Cope, Lukenor, Hurleston, Braynbridge, and others, were committed to the Tower by the Queen, for that, before the parliament, they had sundry conventions for the preferring in parliament a book touching the rates of the church, and a form of an act for the establishing the same.

Which also they did print, prefer, and urge in parliament : But it seemed, that if they had treated thereof only in time of parliament, being burgesses, they should not have been impeached, Februarii 28 Elis.

That the Gate-house is sometimes used for a prison to this house.

CHAP. XIV.

Privileges for them of the House.

SEE the statute, 8 Hen. VI Cap. 1, where it is said, That the clergy, called to the convocation, shall enjoy such liberties, or defence, in coming, tarrying, and going, as the lords and commonalty of England called to the parliament.

It is the order, that, if any burgess require privilege for himself, and his servant, he shall have a warrant signed by the speaker, to obtain the writ of privilege; and, for that William Ward, burgess for Lanc, got such a writ, without such a warrant, it was commited to divers to be examined. 22 Februarii, 6 Ed. VI.

Certain of the house went, by order, to the Common-Pleas, to excuse the appearance of Mr. Palmer, a burgess, in attaint. 4 Nov. 5 Edw. VI. Hugh Lloyd.

It is ordered, That Hugh Lloyd, by *Procedendo*, should be put from the privilege, and be delived from the sheriff of London, in whose ward he was before; but he escaped, and was taken, and sent to the Gate-house for the time, and the next day sent to London, in such case as he was before the privilege granted; and to abide the order of the house, whilst it should sit, though he agreed with his creditor, called Gordon, or, after the session, to abide the order of the privy-council for his misdemeanour, 28 Mar. 6 Edw. VI. And, afterwards, 15 April, it was ordered, That, when he had satisfied his creditors, he should be delivered from the Compter to the serjeant of the house, and discharged of imprisonment there, notwithstanding any action laid upon him in London, after his first imprisonment.

There was also one Criktoft then committed to the Gate-house, and discharged, paying his fees.

Beaumount, of the lower house, served a Subpoena upon the Earl of Huntington, of the higher house; whereupon the lords sent complaint thereof to the house, which certified, That it was no breach of the privilege, 17 April. 1 Mar. because it requireth no appearance, as I think, and restraineth not the person.

William Allen, burgess for Caln in Wiltshire, had the privilege against an attachment upon a process out of the exchequer, 21 April. 1 Mar. to consider, whether the process were for the Queen, or for a common person.

Pledall, burgess, was bound by recognisance to appear in the Star-chamber within twelve days after the end of the parliament; and, upon complaint thereof, it was answered, by conference of the lords with the justices and learned council, That it was no breach of the privilege, 6 Decemb. 1 & 2 Phil. & Mar.

Stroode, burgess, intending to exhibit bills in parliament, for abuses in the court of Stannaries, was there, by means of one Turse, an under-steward, presented and taken, for certain sums that were laid upon him; and thereupon this act, 4 H. VIII. cap. 8, was made, viz.

' All suits, accusations, condemnations, executions, fines, amercements, punishments, corrections, charges, and impositions, put or had, or hereafter to be put or had unto, to, or upon the said Richard Stroode, and to every other of the persons, that now be of this present parliament, or that of any parliament hereafter shall be, for any bill, speaking, reasoning, or declaring of any matter or matters concerning the parliament to be commanded, or treated of, shall be utterly void, and of none effect.'

CHAP. XV.

The Bill of Subsidy.

THE manner is, when a subsidy is granted, to carry it alone, and the pardon to the King, leaving the rest of the bills in the chamber; and this is done to prepare the royal assent to the rest, and to present the subsidy.

The bill of subsidy is offered by the commons only; for the lords, besides the common usage for other bills, do send it to the house again, after that they have thrice read it, and there it remaineth to be carried by the speaker, when he shall present it, 18 Mar. 25. Elis.

After motion made for a subsidy, the device and dealing therein is committed to divers, who agree upon articles, which they do bring in to be ordered by the house: That Mr. attorney-general shall draw it into form of an act; which done, it hath three readings, and so passeth all other bills; only the considerations in the preamble are penned by some committees, whereof some are always of the privy-council.

CHAP. XVI.

Subsidies of the Clergy.

The confirmation of the subsidy, granted by the clergy, passed to the question upon the first reading thereof, 4 Mart. 29 Elisabeth.

CHAP. XVII.

The general Pardon.

It is sent to the house, signed with the King's hand, and being once read, it is demanded, if they be contented to accept it, and so passeth to the question, 18 Mart. 25 Elisabeth.

CHAP. XVIII.

The Presence of the King.

IF he come not the first day of the parliament, then must there be an adjournment until another day, by letters patents, for otherwise all is dissolved.

If he come in the end of the parliament, then it may be prorogued by his word only uttered by the lord keeper, or chancellor.

CHAP. XIX.

The Royal Assent to Bills passed both the Houses.

THE royal assent is commonly in person yielded by the words of the King uttered by the clerk of the crown, in French, thus, viz.

To all bills generally to be enacted *Le Roy le veut.*

To private bills, *Soit fait come c'est desire.*

To those that shall not pass, *Le Roy se advisera.*

To the grants of subsidy, *Le Roy renda grand mercies;* and according to the variety they are indorsed also.

But the royal assent may be by letters patents in his absence.

CHAP. XX.

The Attendance of the Warden of the Fleet.

IT was ordered, That the speaker, in the name of the house, should command the warden of the Fleet, which is a minister of this house, that two of his servants should attend at the stair-head, by the door of the lower house, to repress, and apprehend lacquies, and servants, and to bring them to the house, 2 Februarii, 23 Elis.

END OF VOL IV.

AN
ALPHABETICAL INDEX,
TO THE FOURTH VOLUME.

PAGE

PAGE

Im The Story

personalised classic books

JANE
IN
WONDERLAND

LEWIS
CARROLL

UNIQUE GIFT

FOR KIDS, PARTNERS
AND FRIENDS

Timeless books such as:

Kids

Alice in Wonderland · The Jungle Book · The Wonderful Wizard of Oz
Peter and Wendy · Robin Hood · The Prince and The Pauper
The Railway Children · Treasure Island · A Christmas Carol

Adults

Romeo and Juliet · Dracula

Highly
Customizable

Change
Books Title

Replace
Characters Names
with yours

Upload
Photo for
inside page

Add
Inscriptions

Visit
Im The Story .com
and order yours today!

CPSIA information can be obtained
at www.ICGtesting.com
Printed in the USA
BVHW071231200819
556319BV00014B/1406/P